Come, ride with me,

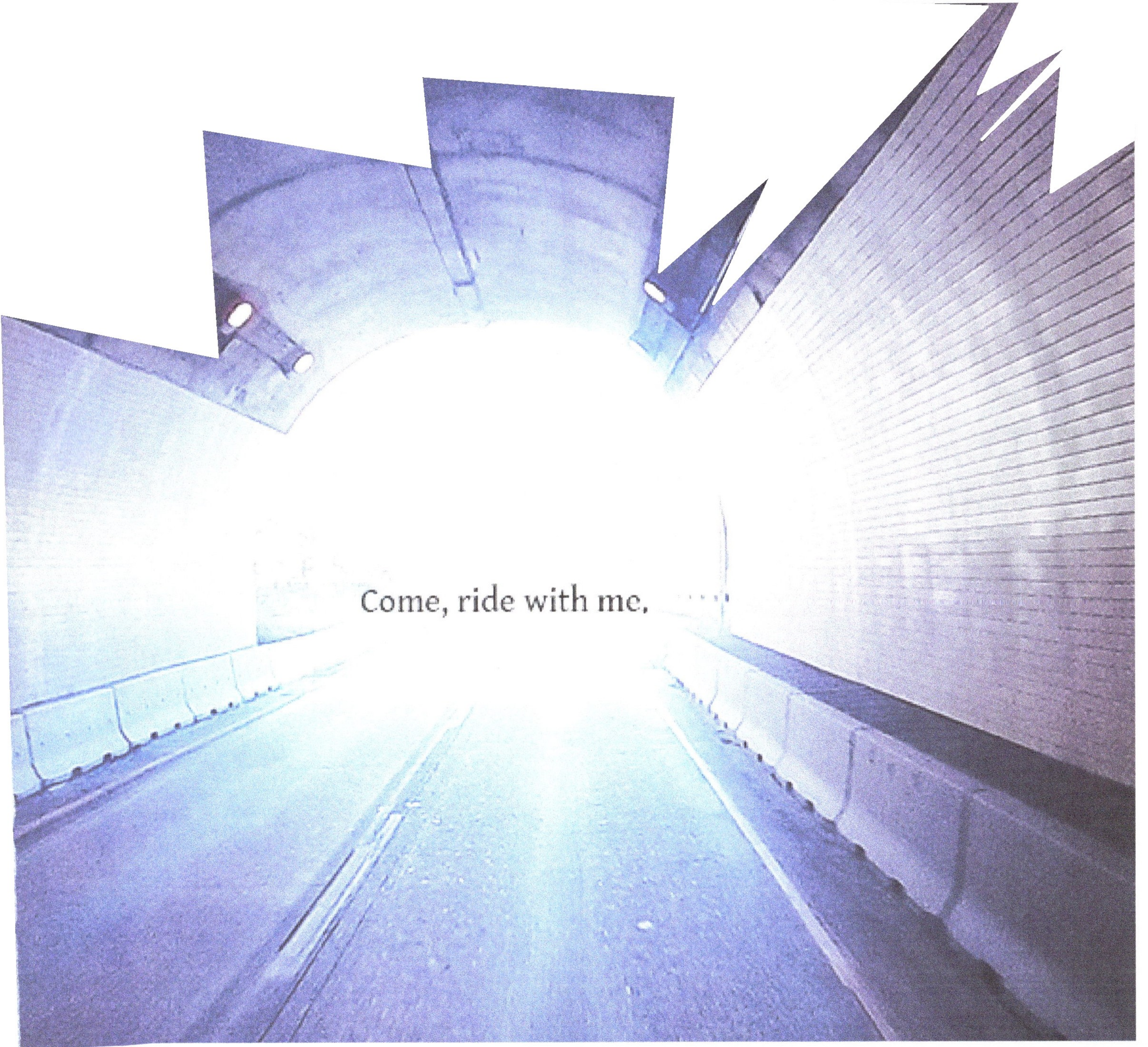

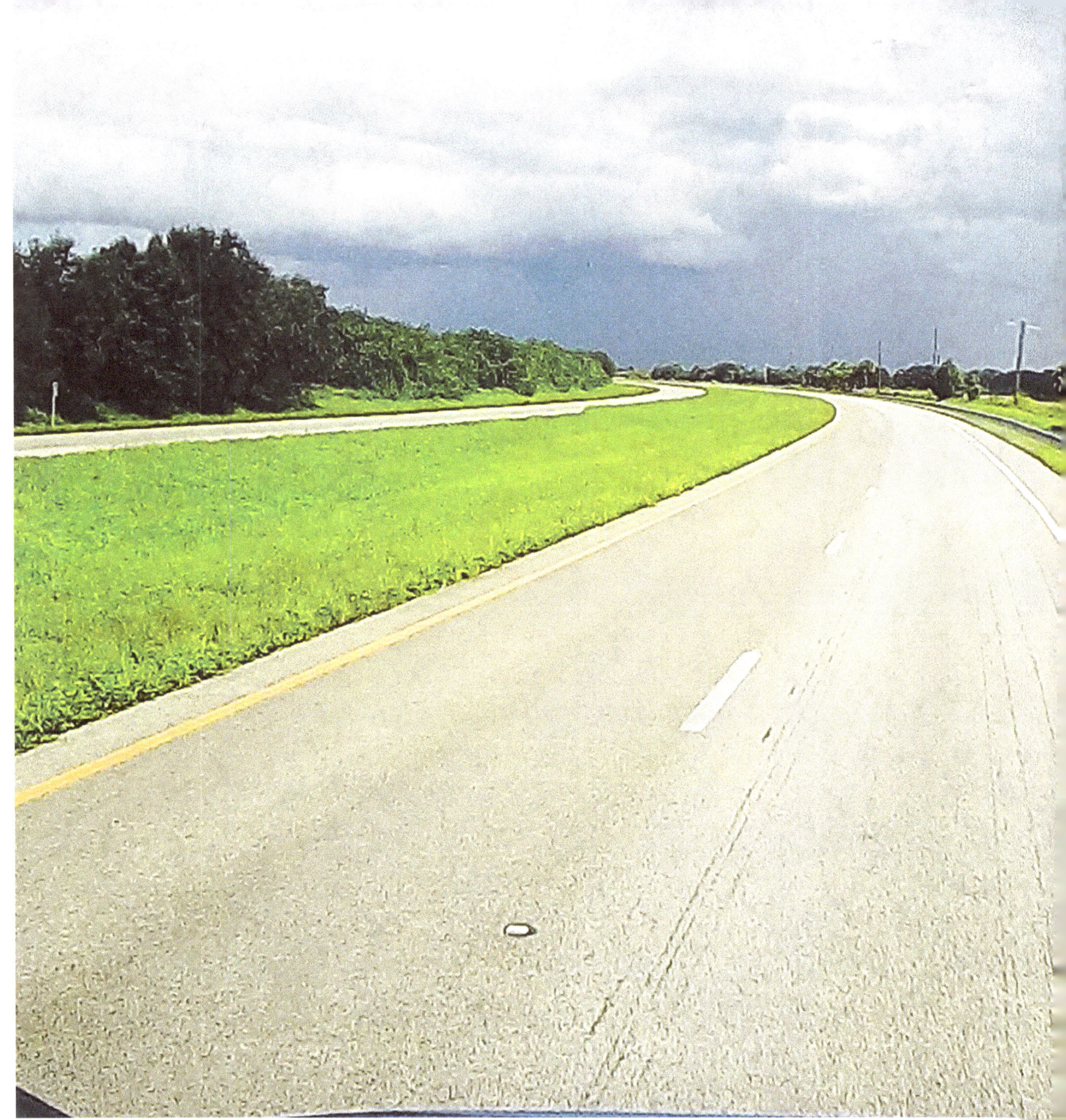

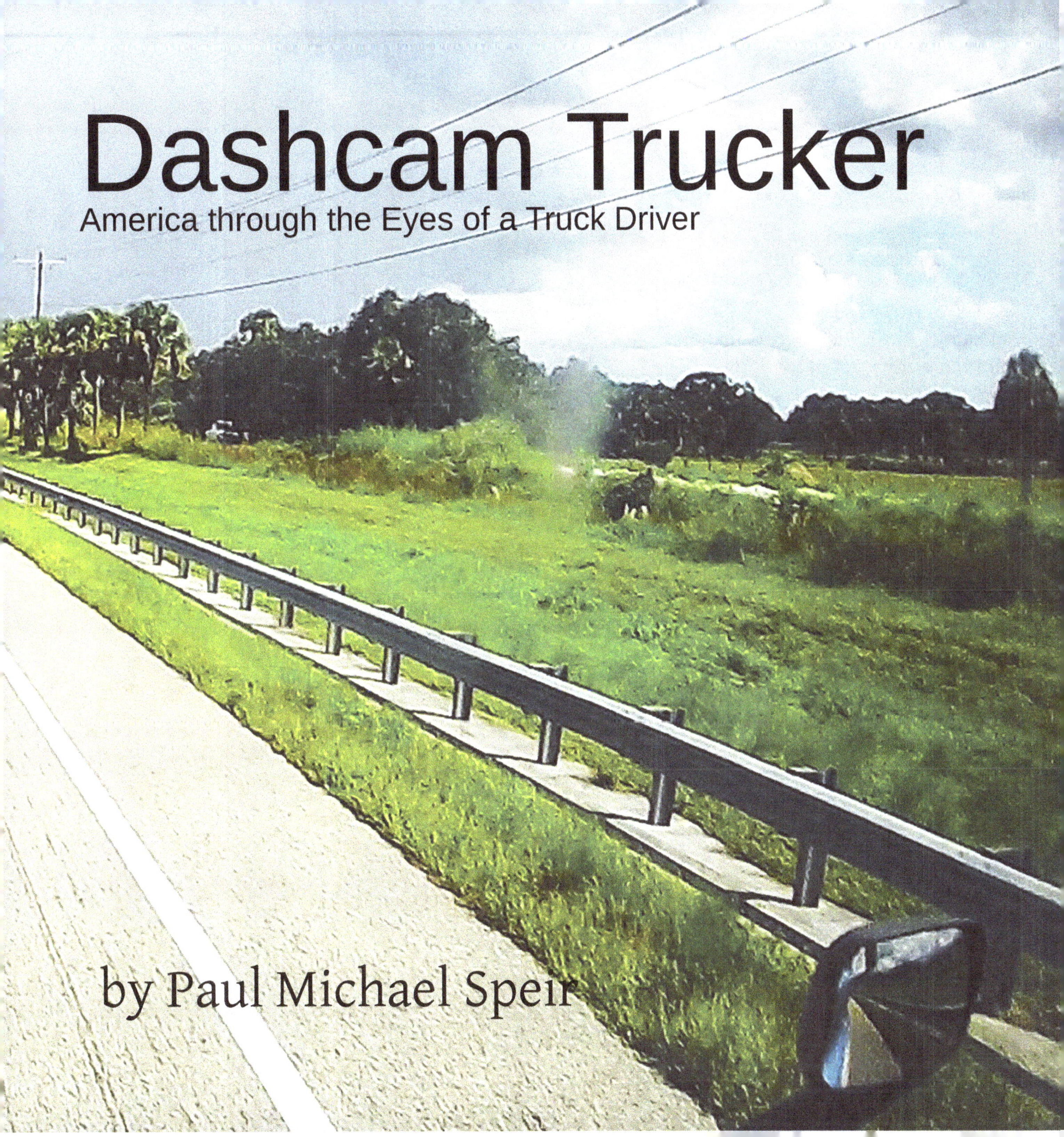

Dashcam Trucker
America through the Eyes of a Truck Driver
by Paul Michael Speir

First paperback edition, 2019

Published by Speir Publishing

Images on pages 80 & 81 captured by Mark Speir
All others captured by Paul Speir

All images captured with a Garmin Dashcam were captured safely, utilizing all necessary safety proto-cols. Capturing images while operating a moving vehicle is prohibited by all government agencies and in no way is this book promoting such practices. There are other ways to capture images while on the move, and the author of this book encourages you to utilize those practices.

Designed by Paul Speir & Stacy Speir

Manufactured in the United States

10 9 8 7 6 5 4 3 2 1

ISBN 13: 978-0-9826765-7-8
ISBN 10: 0-9826765-7-3

For Willow, River, Aria and Stacy.
While there is so much beauty in the world,
none of it compares to the four of you.

Introduction

Perhaps some find a path in life and devote themselves wholeheartedly to it. Perhaps they find fulfillment in it and do well. I have not been one of those people. I find *everything* to be fascinating and worth pursuing, and choosing just one has never been possible nor desirable. However, a sad truth in life is that pursuing every interest, to a man such as myself who has such a seemingly-unending list of interests, is a game played while young or while wealthy.

I am neither young nor wealthy, but I did have my fair share of enjoyment while I was young. From playing in rock and heavy metal bands to designing and publishing books to driving a taxi in two major cities, to directing a ministry, operating a thrift store and pastoring a church—my life has been full of dreams and passions that perhaps were not ever very successful, but were pursued with determination and abandon.

My greatest passion became my family, as my wife gave me one daughter after another after another. Soon caring for my wife and three girls became the one interest I found worth pursuing above all others. And so, one day after a satisfying drive with the family from Oklahoma City to San Diego and back, I found myself applying to a trucking company. I decided that it was time to settle down in a career that would be interesting and lucrative while satisfying the wanderlust I have always had hidden away, and once I set my mind to a thing I generally cannot be dissuaded.

I left home in August of 2017 and found myself in an intense training period. Driving a vehicle that is over seventy feet long and weighs upwards of eighty thousand pounds is a difficult chore, to say the least. My first week was studying for the Commercial Driver's License permit test, taking intense physicals, drug tests, and so on. Then a trainer contacted me and in the blink of an eye I was driving through Missouri, up through Kansas, Nebraska, Wyoming and into Utah. For a guy that loves to travel but in truth hasn't done very much of it in his life, this was amazing.

Soon I graduated and leased a 2019 Freightliner Cascadia, number 690066, and I was in love. If you have never had the chance to go inside a semi truck, I would recommend you do so. The first time I set foot in a truck was back in the early 2000's, when I was a stoner kid from San Antonio on a hitchhiking trip to try to get his life right. The driver of that truck was friendly, spoke not a word of English, and absolutely did not help me get off drugs—he asked me if I smoked, so I tried to hand him a cigarette and he said, "No, you smoke mota?" and proceeded to roll a joint.

His truck was amazing to me, having never been in one before, but compared to my Freightliner it was a piece of garbage. My truck had all the bells and whistles. I installed a 32 inch television, a refrigerator, microwave, sound bar to boost the volume if I so pleased, Darth Vader floor mats (thank you again for those, Stacy), and little rugs to tidy it all up. In short, it was comfortable, as it needed to be.

For almost a year that truck was my home away from home. I would go to work and work for three weeks straight, then come home for six days and spoil my wife and kids rotten. It was an unbalanced life, as every truck driver quickly finds out. My children were young and they often had dreams that I had died or had chosen to never come back home. I missed my family desperately and often fell into dark pits of depression. At times I hated my career choice and plotted to end it and find another way to support my family. Other times I loved it and plotted ways to keep going but find a better balance.

In the end, what I had to do was to find a project to keep me sane in the weeks I was gone. That project turned into what you hold now in your hands. There are some realities to this career. It is exhausting, exciting, fun, lonely, and most of all dangerous. A 2016 study ranked truck driving as the seventh most dangerous job in the country, with 24.7 fatal injuries per 100,000 workers. Ironically, I'm actually writing this while nursing a possibly broken toe and a banged up knee, from slipping off the top step of the cab while climbing down. If I hadn't been holding onto the hand-holds with both hands it undoubtedly would have been a much worse injury, so I count my blessings.

As real and dangerous as on the job injuries are, the bulk of the fatalities come from traffic accidents. Trucking companies do not like to litigate insurance claims, would far prefer to settle even when it is obvious the trucker was not at fault. People know this and that knowledge makes us a target for those with the inclination to abuse it. It is far too common to see a vehicle come up and keep pace with a semi truck, then suddenly cut the truck off and try to get it to collide. The result of such an accident could be losing our license, losing our job, certainly a significant loss of income, or even injury or death.

One easy way to protect ourselves is to purchase a good dash camera, and this is what I did the moment I had my own truck. Over time I began to see other uses for this camera. As a long haul trucker I drive in and around every one of the lower forty-eight states in the continental United States, and let me tell you—we have a beautiful country! Over time I began snapping pictures every time I saw something I found to be particularly beautiful. Throughout Colorado, Utah, Wyoming, California, New Mexico, Arizona, and on into the Heartland of America—Iowa corn fields, the plains of Kansas and Oklahoma, the Kudzu covering the trees in Tennessee and Georgia, the palm trees and traffic in southern Florida. All of it was exciting and worthy of being captured by my dash cam.

Soon I realized that I had more than a photo album here; I had a book. Perhaps a book only my kids would like, but a book nonetheless. The photos are raw and gritty, but this is America as most have never seen it before—raw, gritty, unedited, the way I see it every day. As you go through it, you may enjoy looking to the bottom of the photograph and noting the GPS coordinates. Go to Google Maps and type those in, then explore the world a bit. You will see the George Washington Bridge, the Missouri River, the Shenandoah Valley, the Battle of Little Big Horn, an artist's odd work on the side of a Montana highway, the beauty of Vail, and so much more. Don't stop with the photos inside the book—take this opportunity to dive in and learn and explore!

And so, here is the fruit of my labor, the project that helped me through the countless weeks and months spent apart from the loves of my life. As I write this I am still apart from them—parked at a truck stop in Wisconsin, actually—but I know this phase of my life is soon over, and perhaps by the time you read this, whoever you are, I will be in the arms of my wife and children once more—this time for good, with the memories of my travels burning bright in my mind, and me content to let them stay memories and nothing more.

Paul Speir

October, 2018

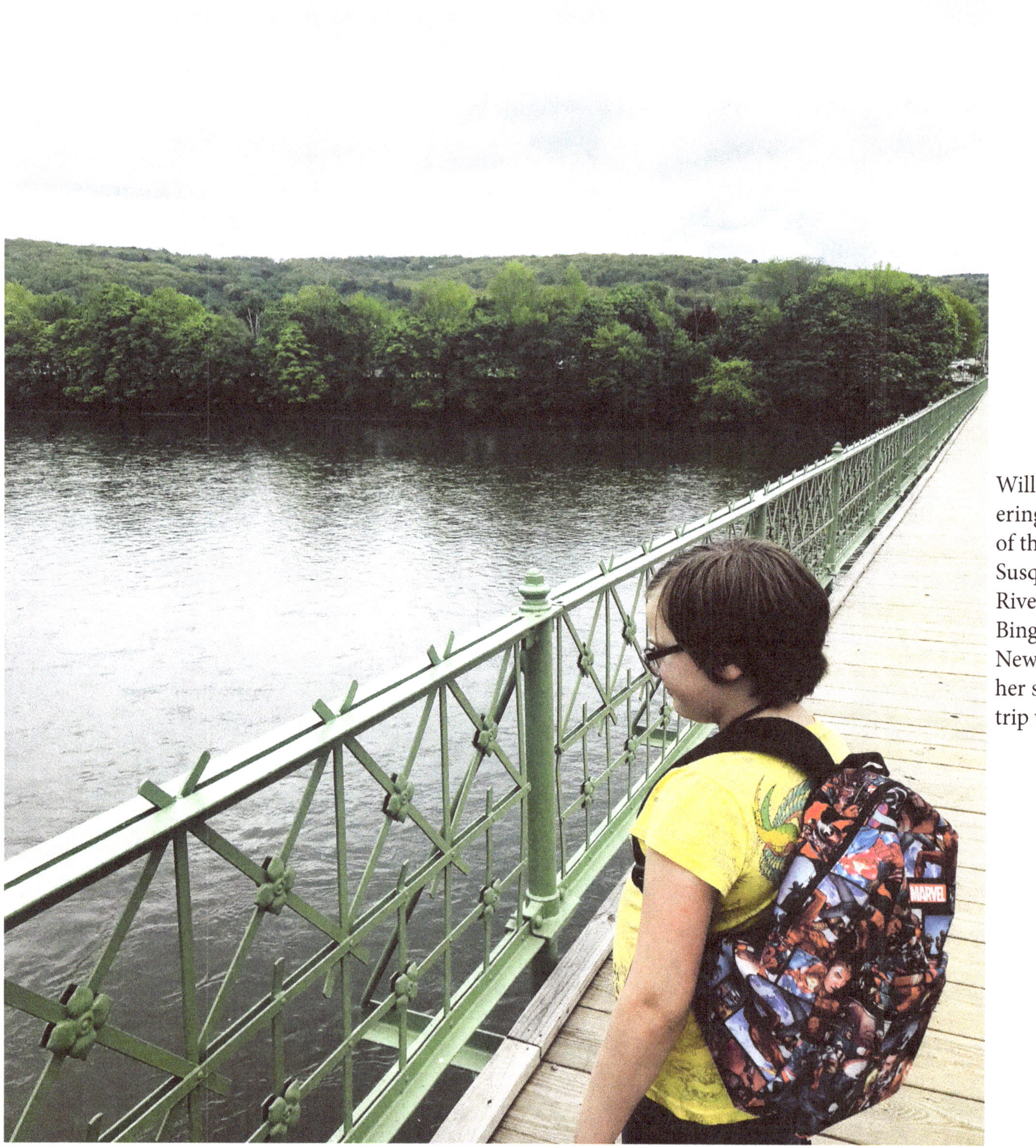

Willow, discovering the beauty of the Susquehanna River in Binghamton, New York, on her summer trip with me.

Part One
The Bridges & Tunnels of America

I have always loved tunnels and bridges and rivers—my second daughter's name is River, after all—but my experience with these was fairly limited until recently. Now, however, I have traveled over the Yellowstone River in Montana, the mighty Mississippi more times than I can count, the Ohio and Tennessee and Colorado and Vermilion and on and on, so many I couldn't begin to list them all here.

Rivers are beautiful and majestic at times, and the bridges that span them are amazing feats of engineering. Tunnels, however, are something else entirely. I wonder at times why I find them so fascinating. Yes, they too are amazing feats of engineering. Tunneling under a mountain or body of water is incredibly difficult, costly and time-consuming. More than that, on a primal level I always feel a thrill of danger when I pass through a tunnel. Whether we like to think about it or not, even the wisest among us is capable of making mistakes and the earth is constantly changing. I can't help imagining the mountain shifting and crumbling around me whenever I am driving into a hole we little humans punched into the earth. Perhaps I'm morbid, but the danger of it is always exciting.

I am sitting in a Flying J travel stop in Pennsylvania as I write this and a few hours ago I passed through the Lehigh tunnel in Lehighton. That tunnel is just a few pages away, in the midst of tunnels from Baltimore to West Virginia to Colorado, and bridges from New York City to Chattanooga. I hope you enjoy them as much as I did.

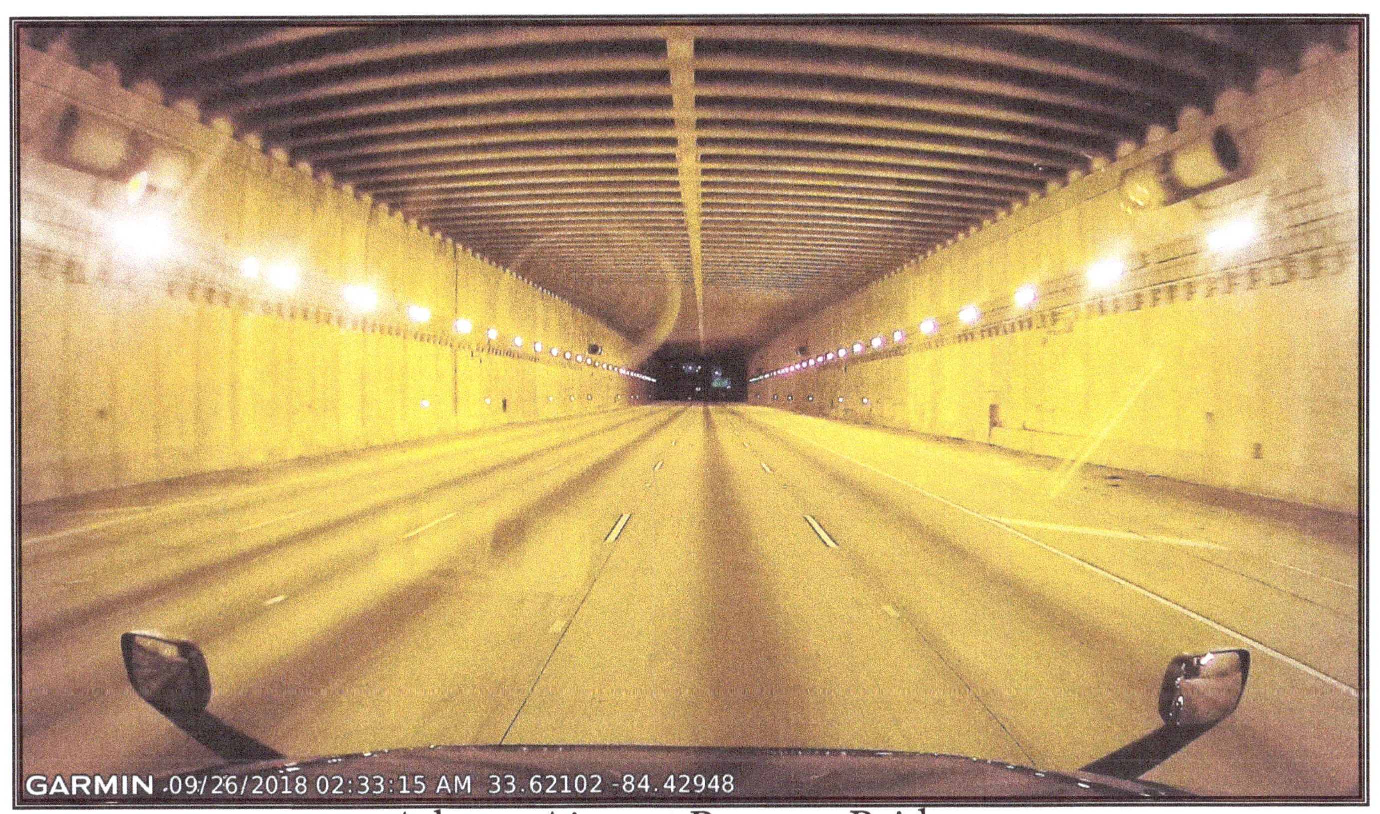

Atlanta Airport Runway Bridges,
The Perimeter (285), Atlanta, Georgia

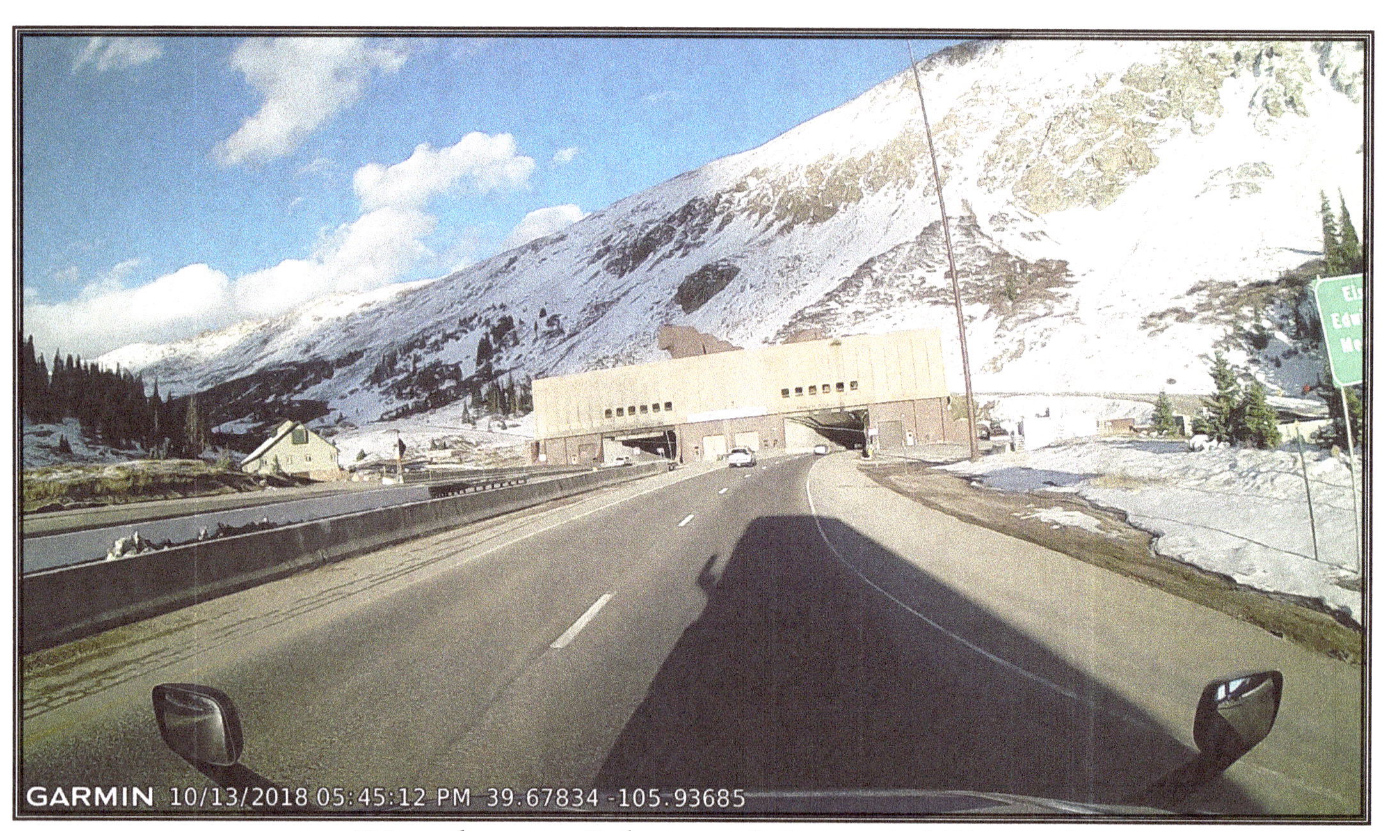

Eisenhower-Johnson Memorial Tunnel
I-70, Parshall, Colorado

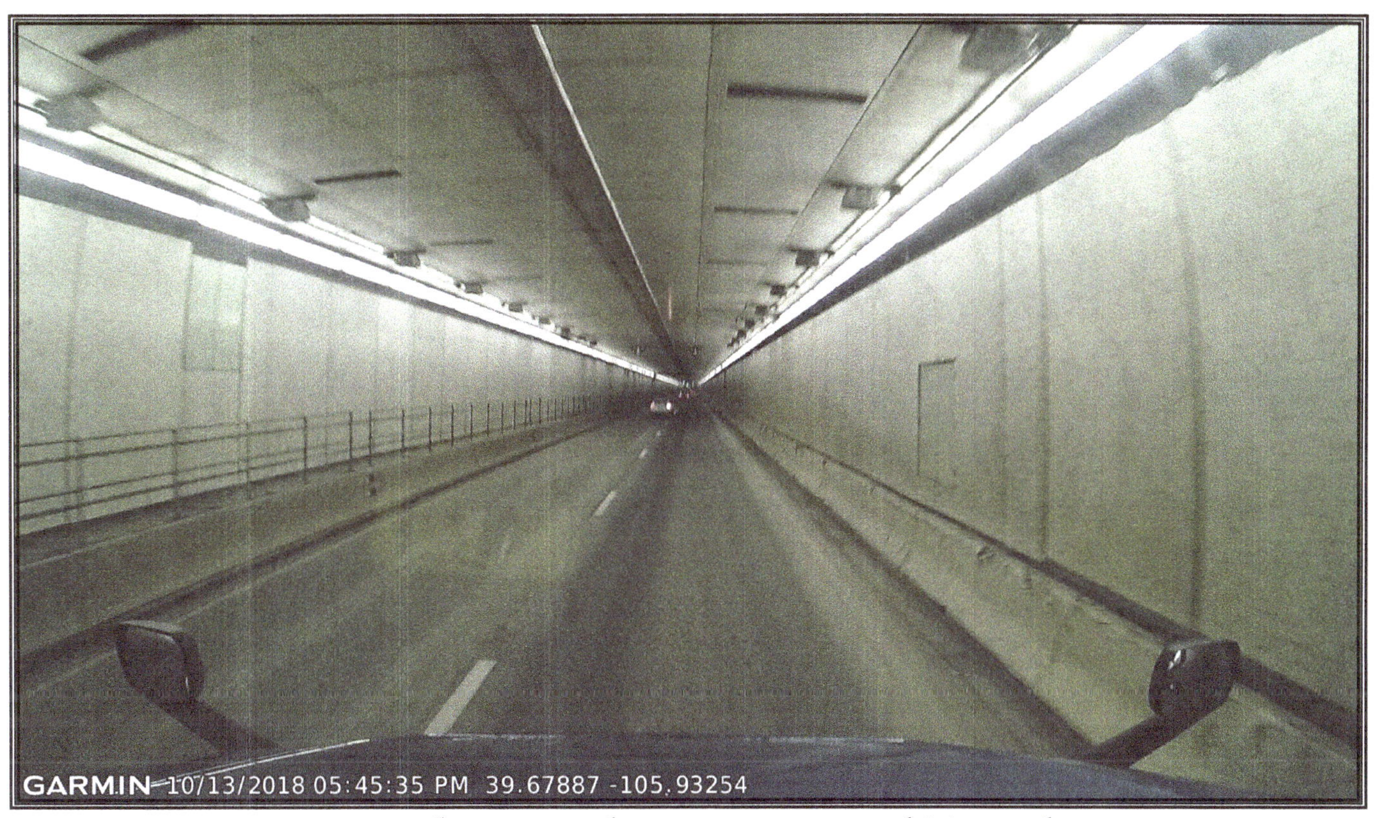

Eisenhower-Johnson Memorial Tunnel
I-70, Parshall, Colorado

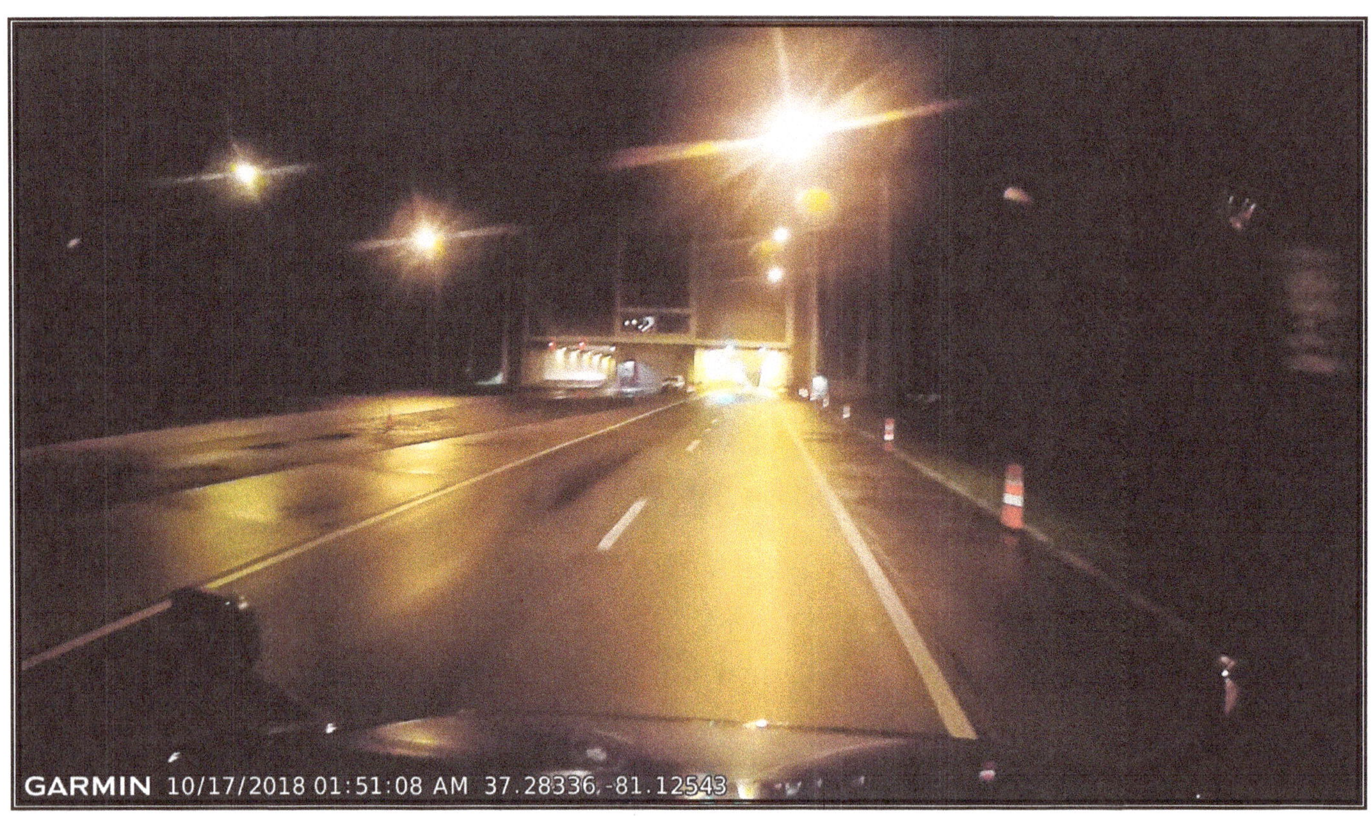

The East River Mountain Tunnel
I-77, Rocky Gap, Virginia

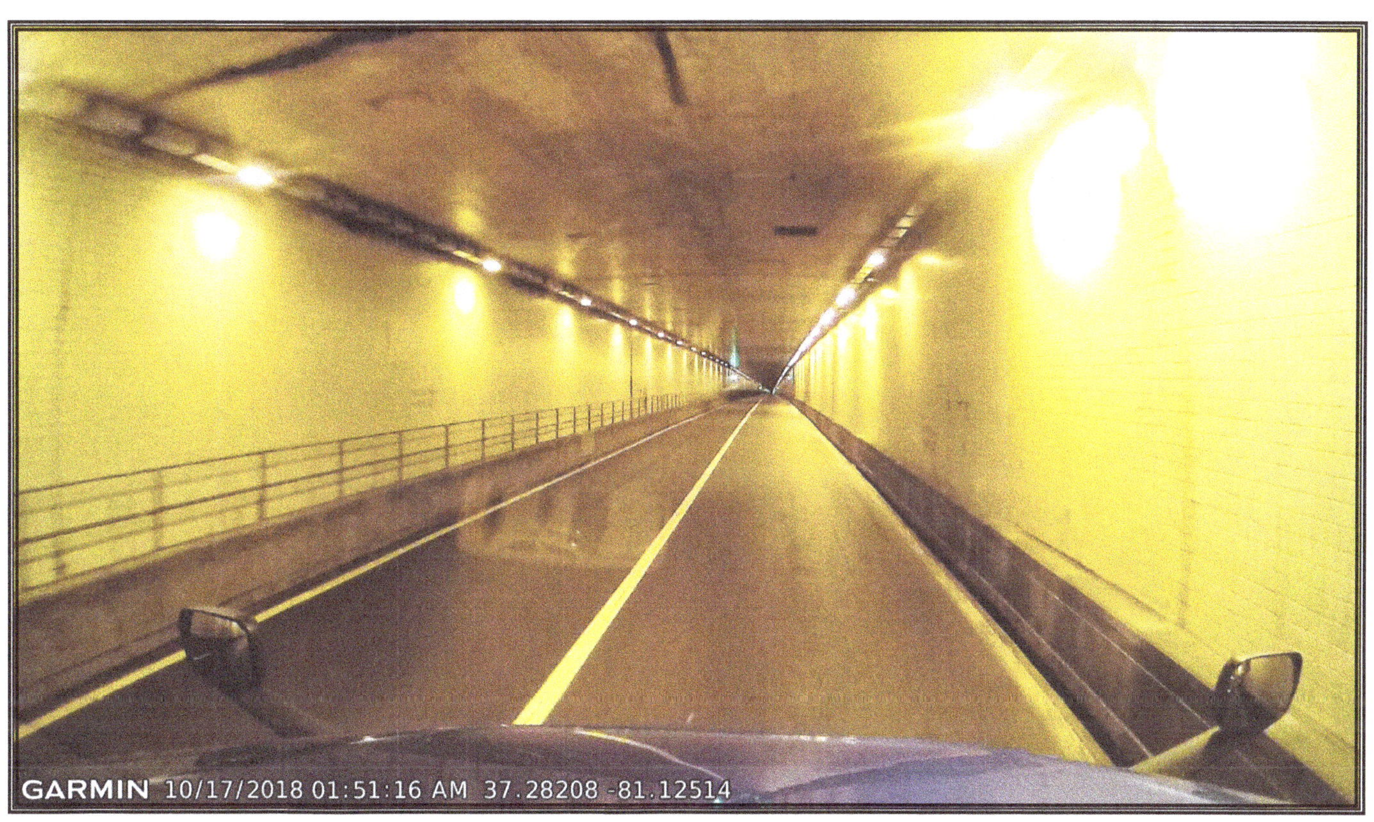

The East River Mountain Tunnel
I-77, Rocky Gap, Virginia

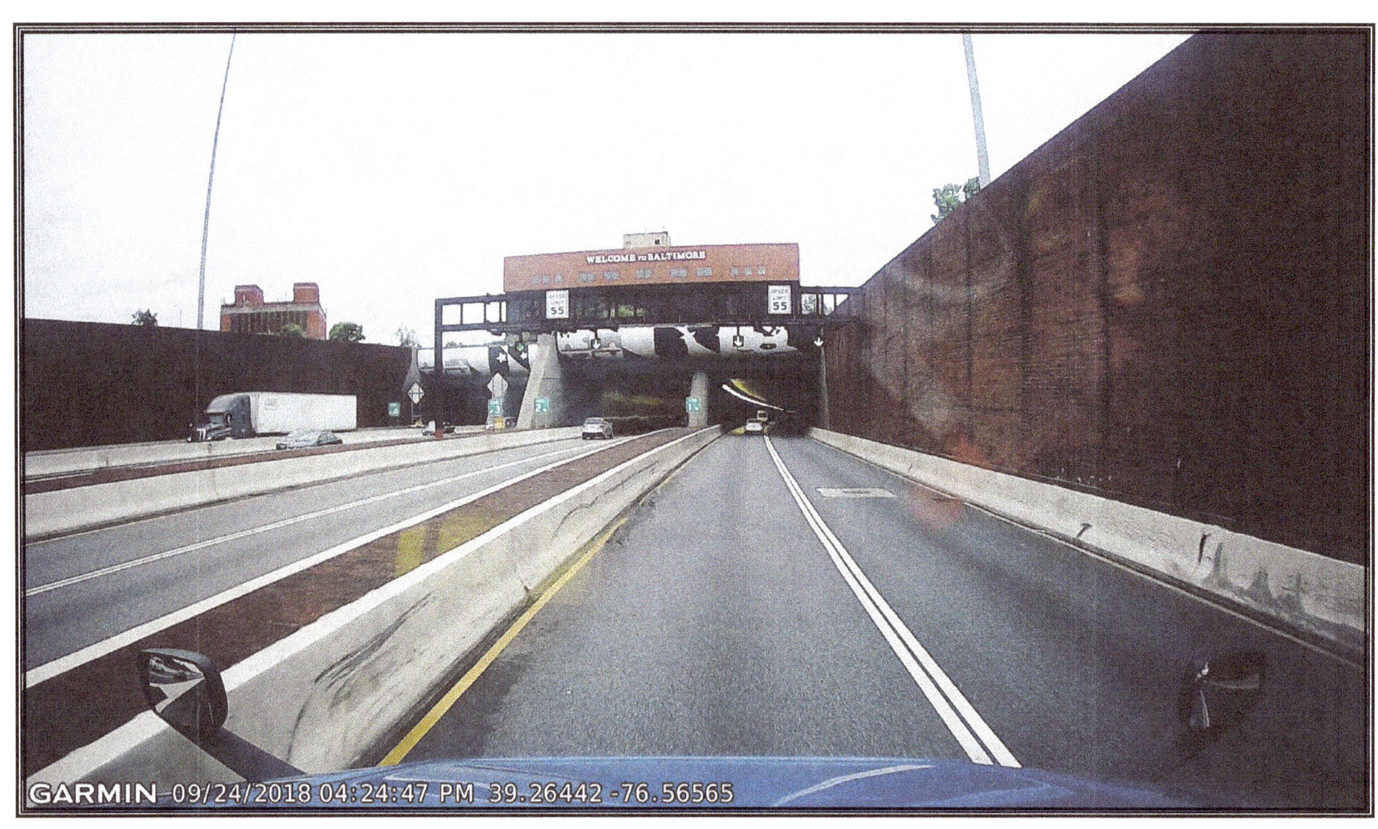

The Baltimore Harbor Tunnel
I-895, Baltimore, Maryland

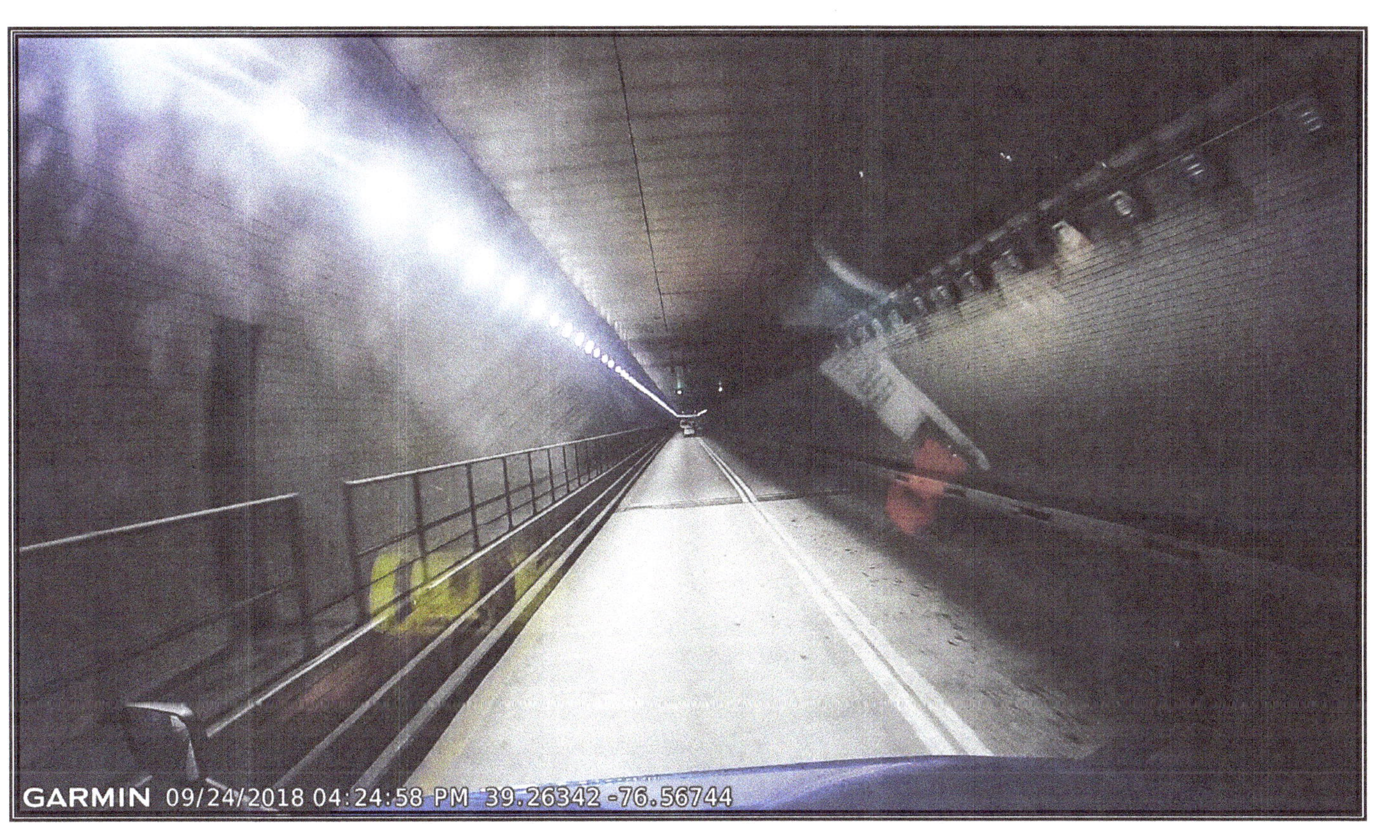

The Baltimore Harbor Tunnel
I-895, Baltimore, Maryland

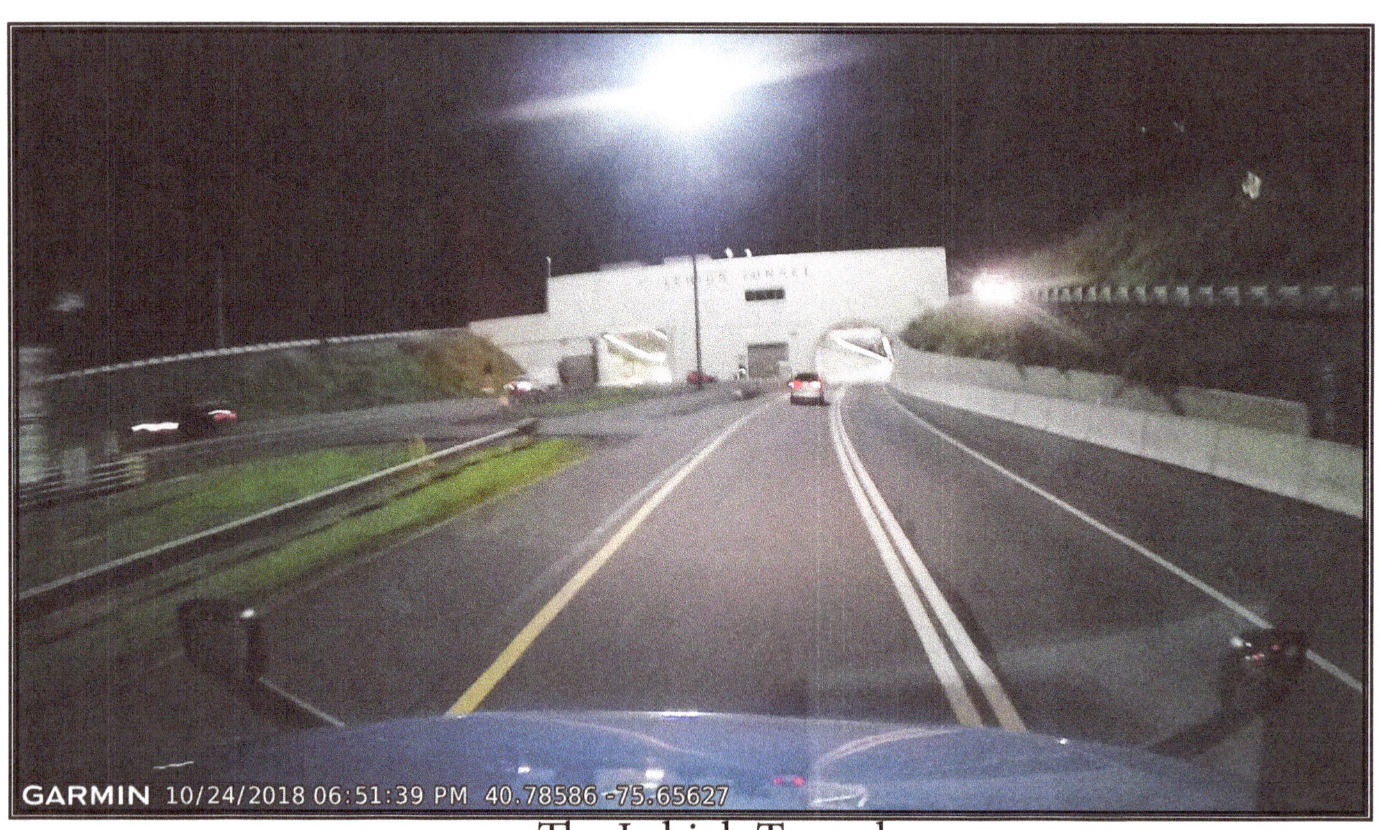

The Lehigh Tunnel
I-476, Lehighton, Pennsylvania

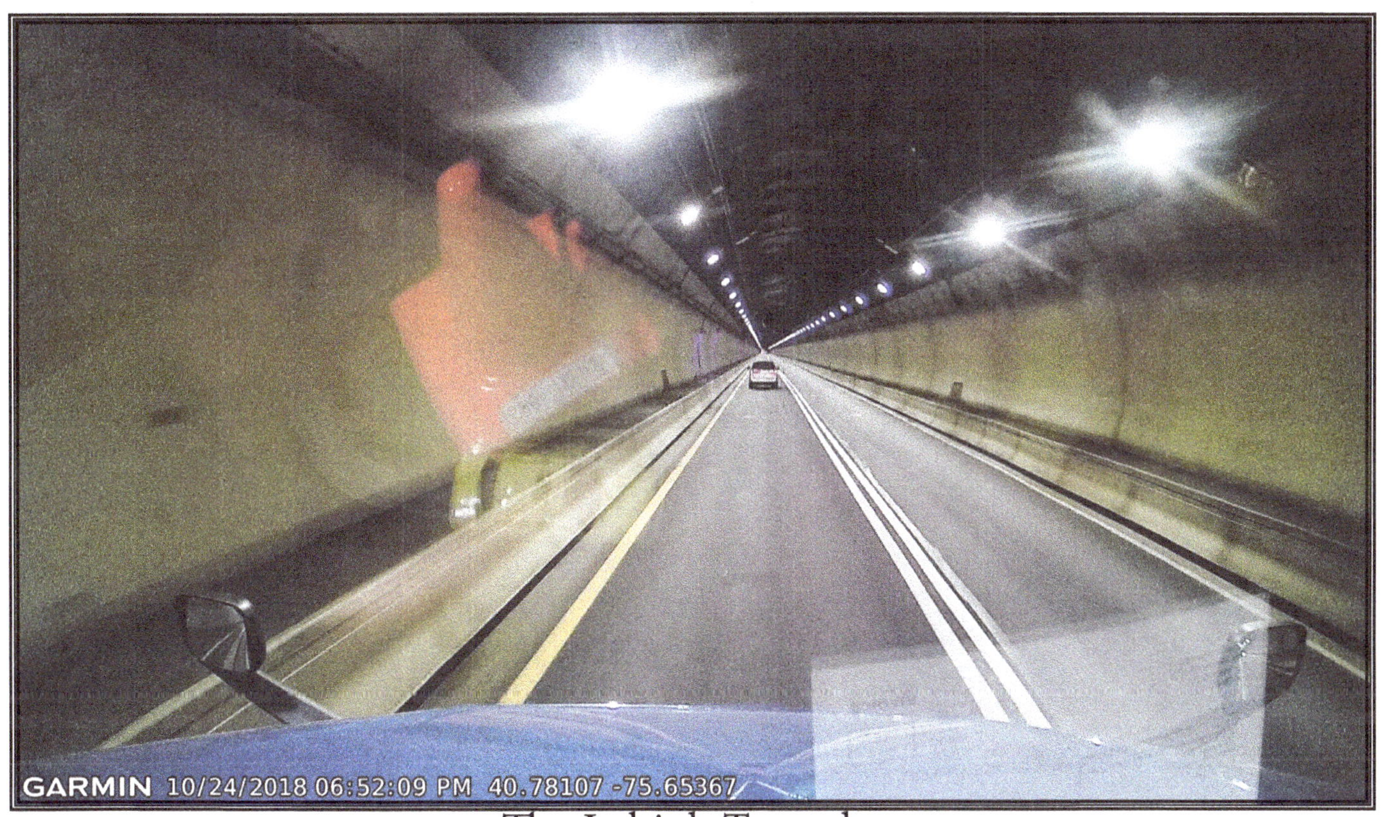

The Lehigh Tunnel
I-476, Lehighton, Pennsylvania

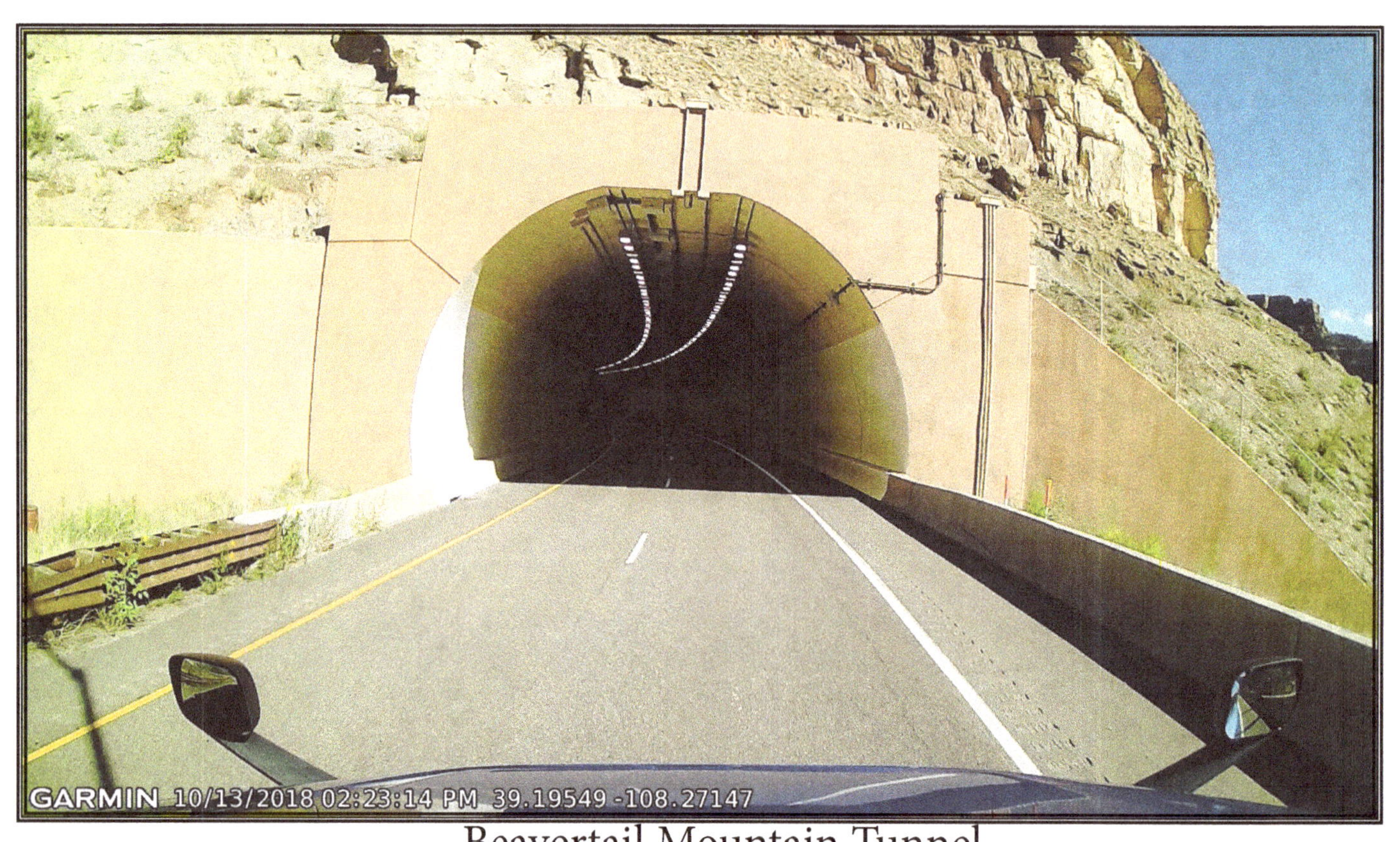

Beavertail Mountain Tunnel
I-70, De Beque, Colorado

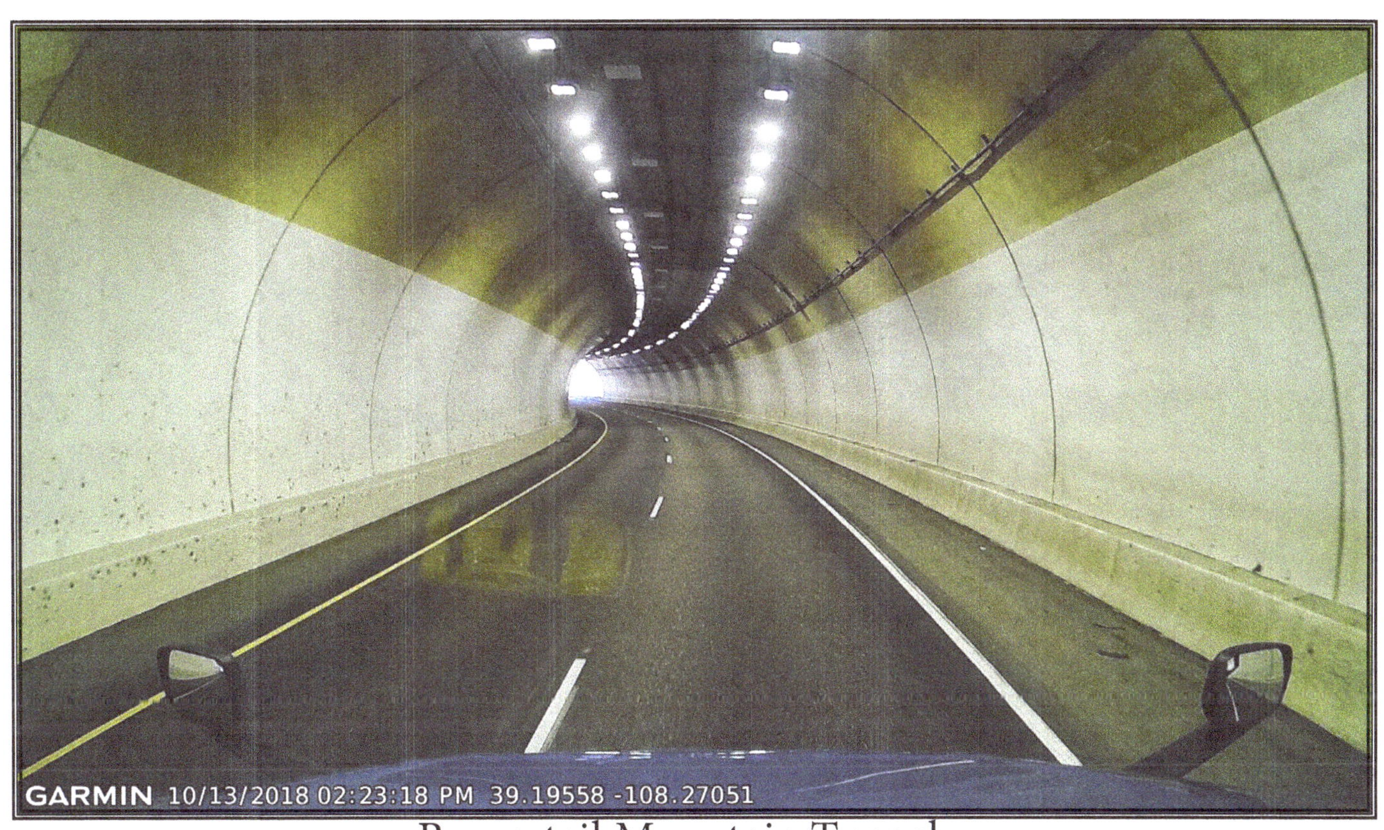

Beavertail Mountain Tunnel
I-70, De Beque, Colorado

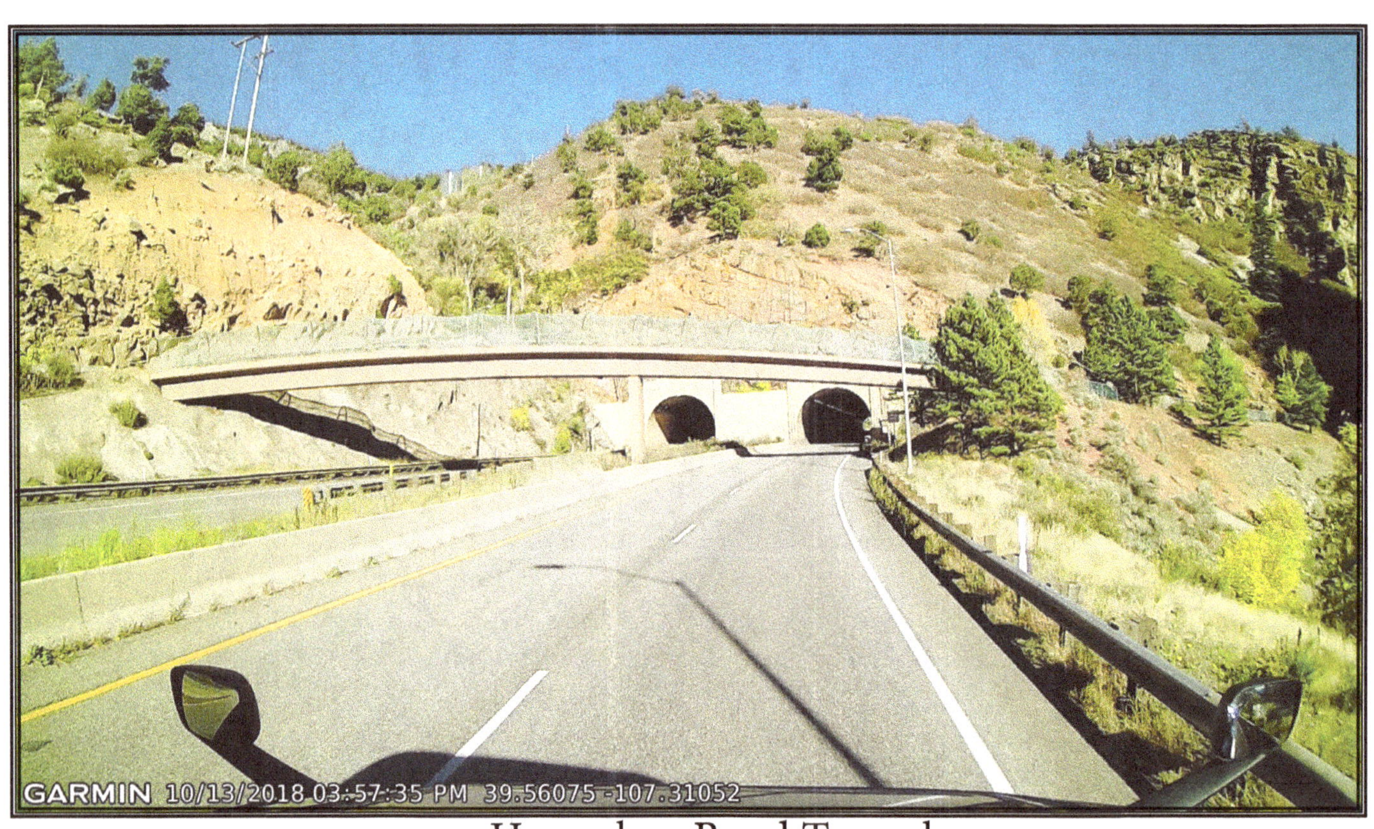

Horseshoe Bend Tunnel
I-70, Glenwood Springs, Colorado

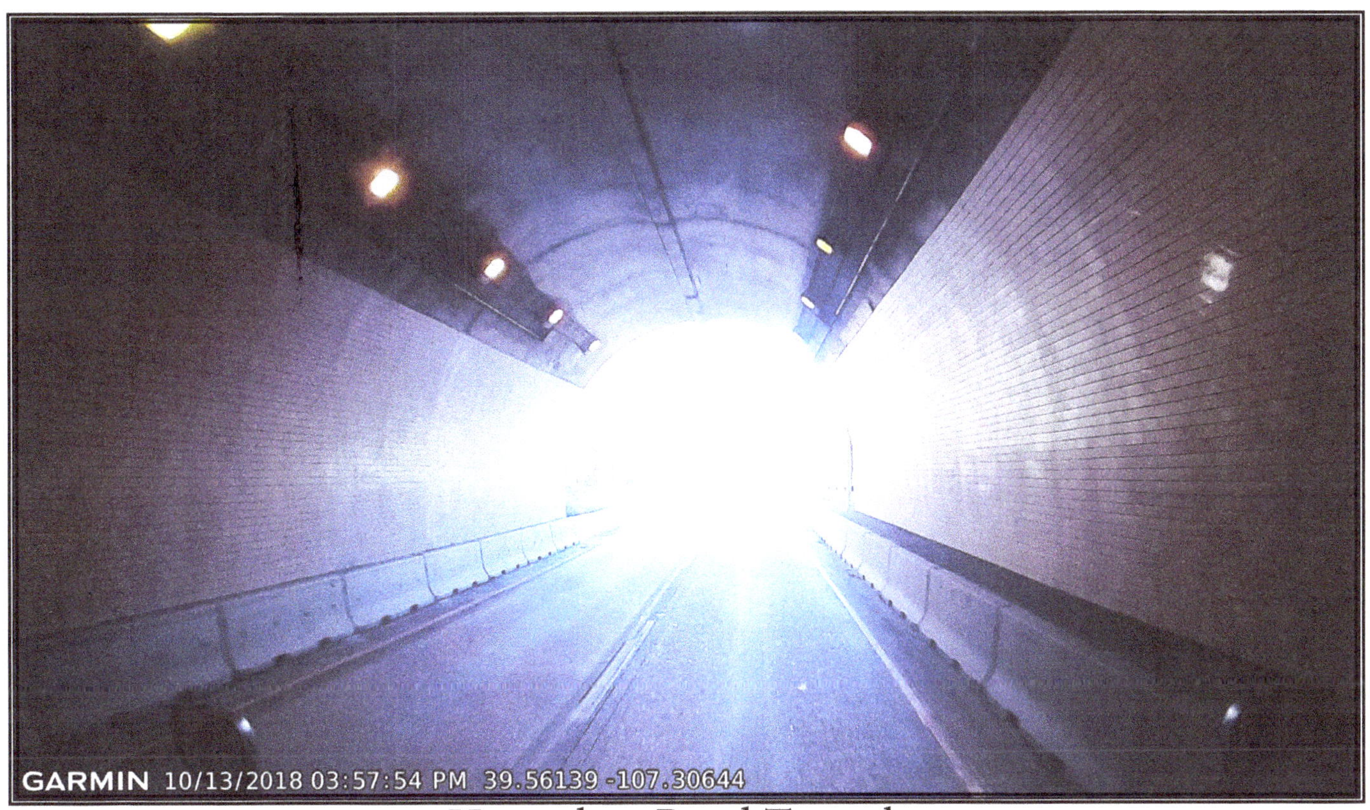

Horseshoe Bend Tunnel
I-70, Glenwood Springs, Colorado

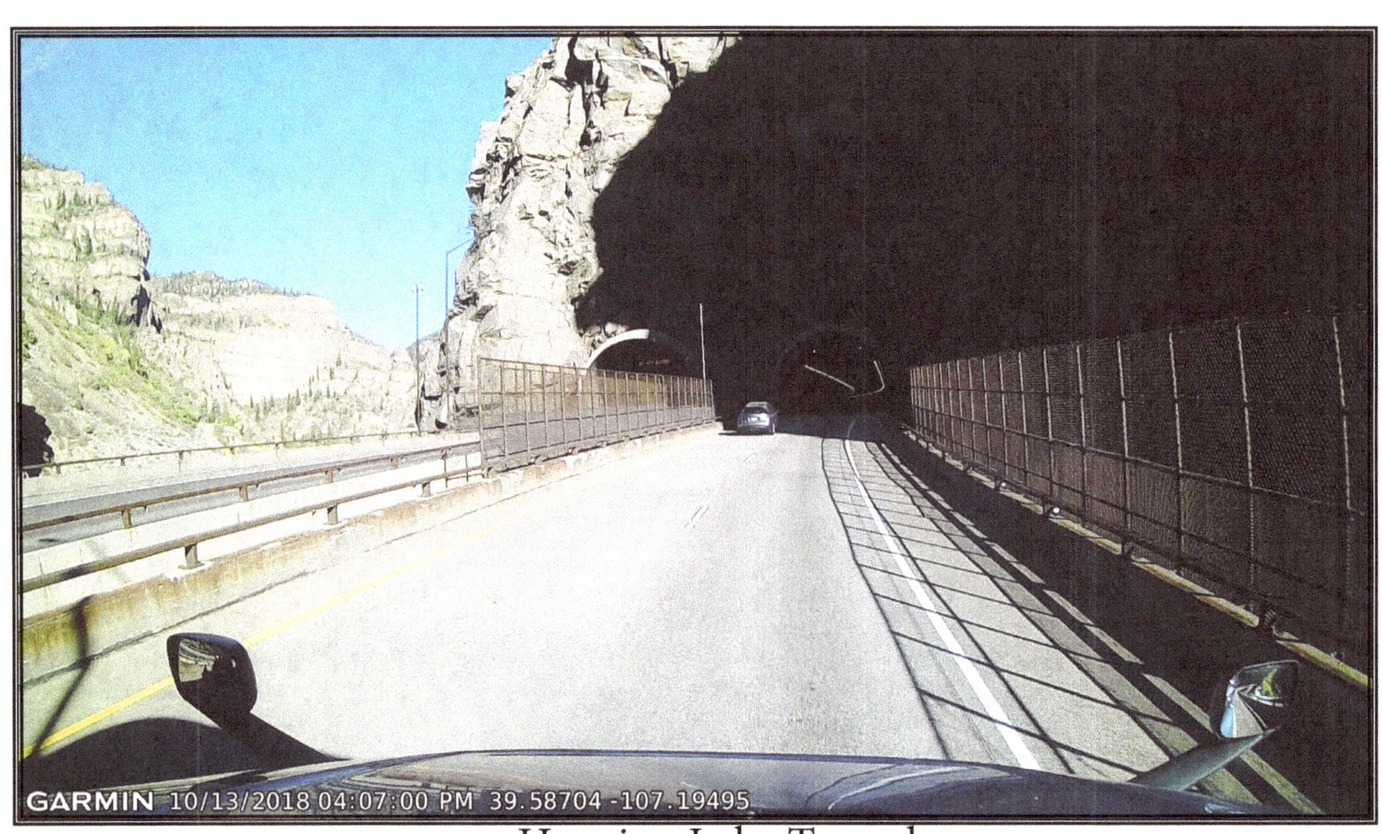

Hanging Lake Tunnel
I-70, Glenwood Springs, Colorado

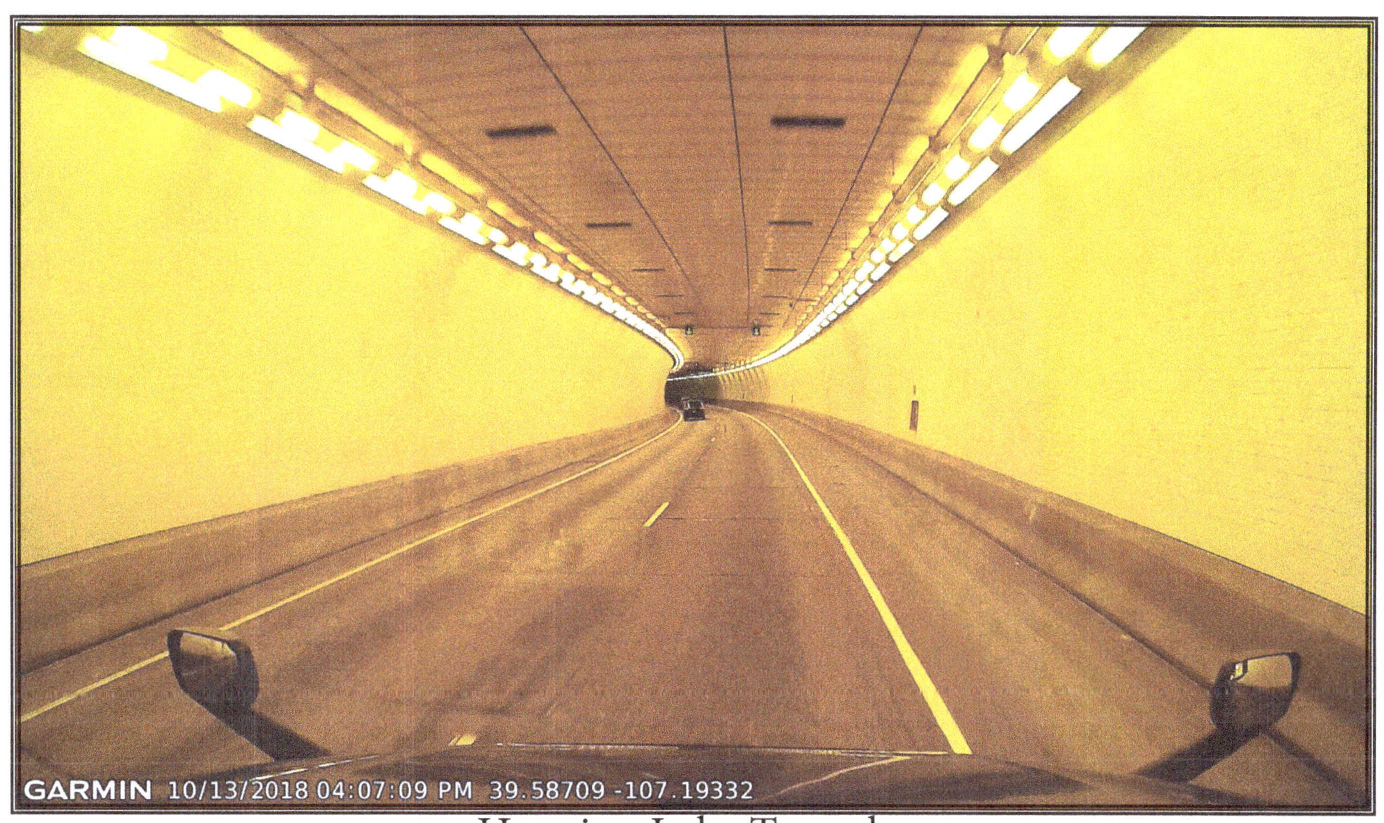

Hanging Lake Tunnel
I-70, Glenwood Springs, Colorado

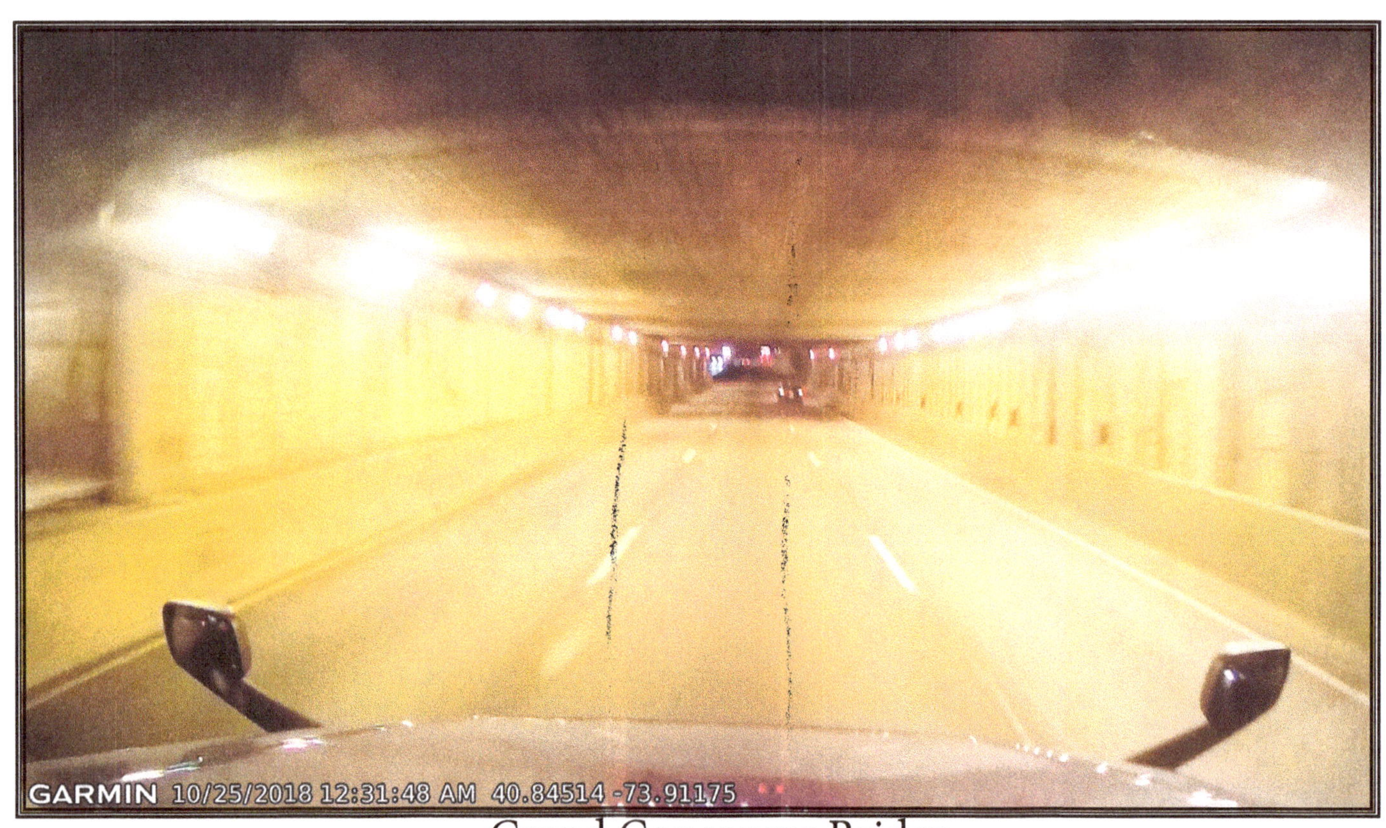

Grand Concourse Bridge
I-95, Bronx, New York

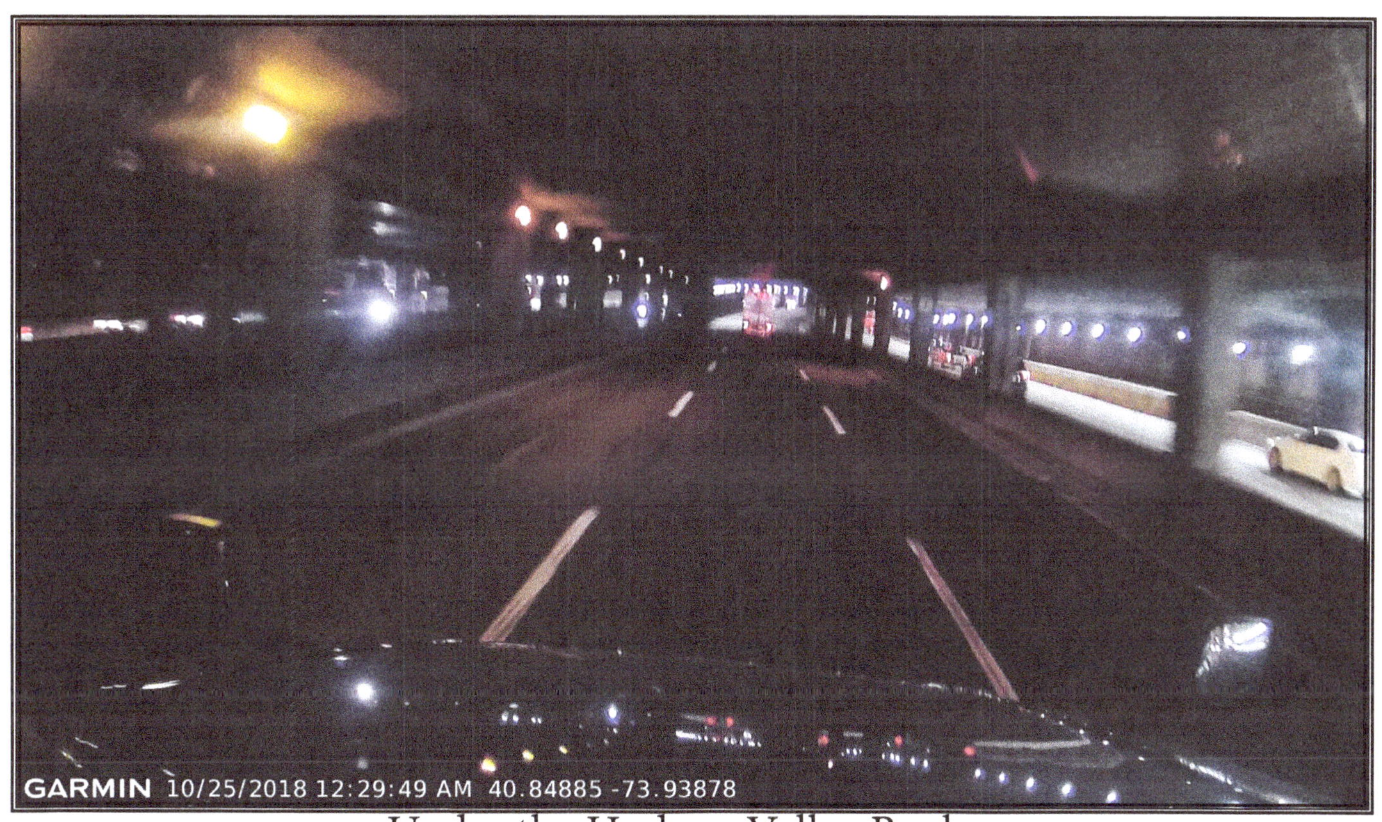

Under the Hudson Valley Bank
I-95, New York, New York

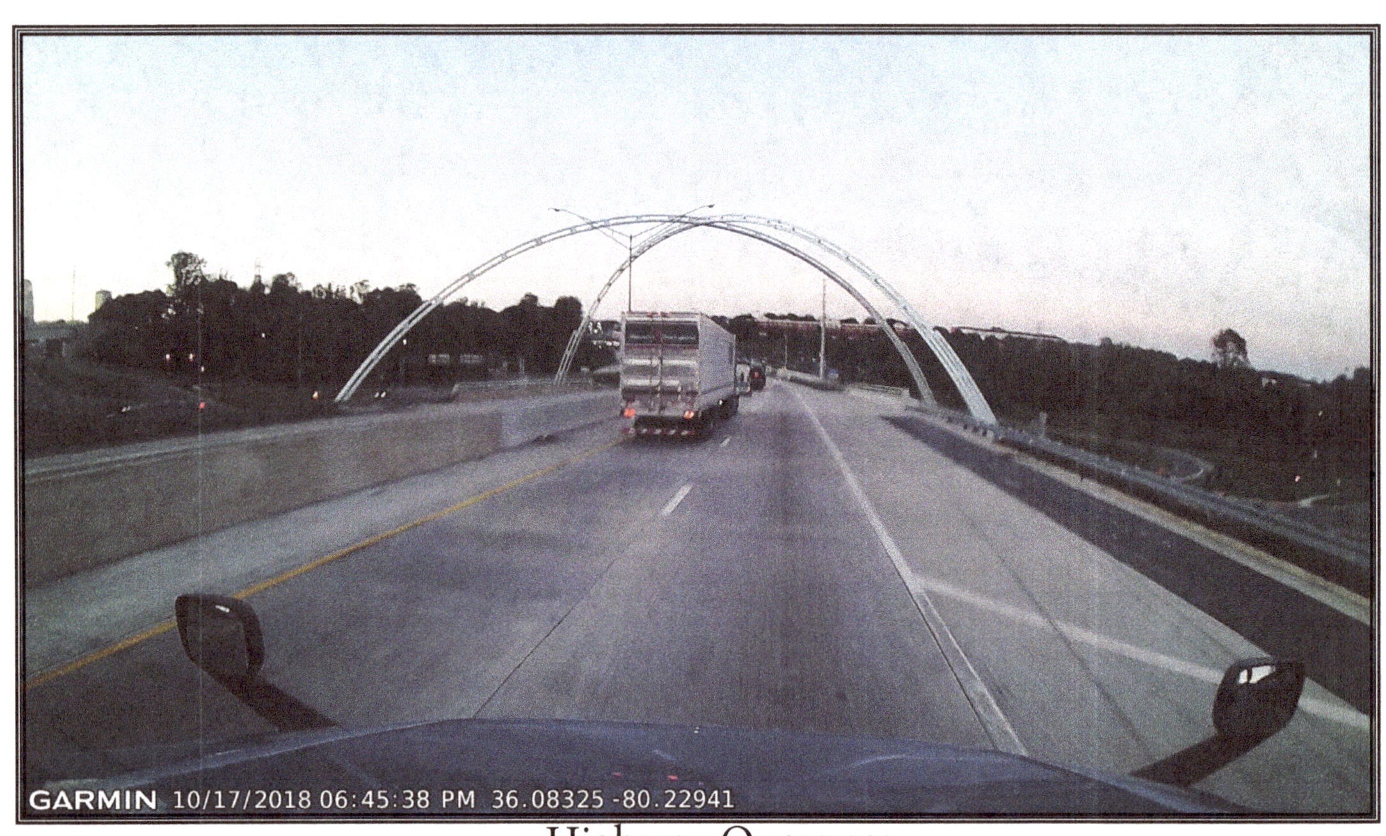

Highway Overpass
US-52, Winston-Salem, North Carolina

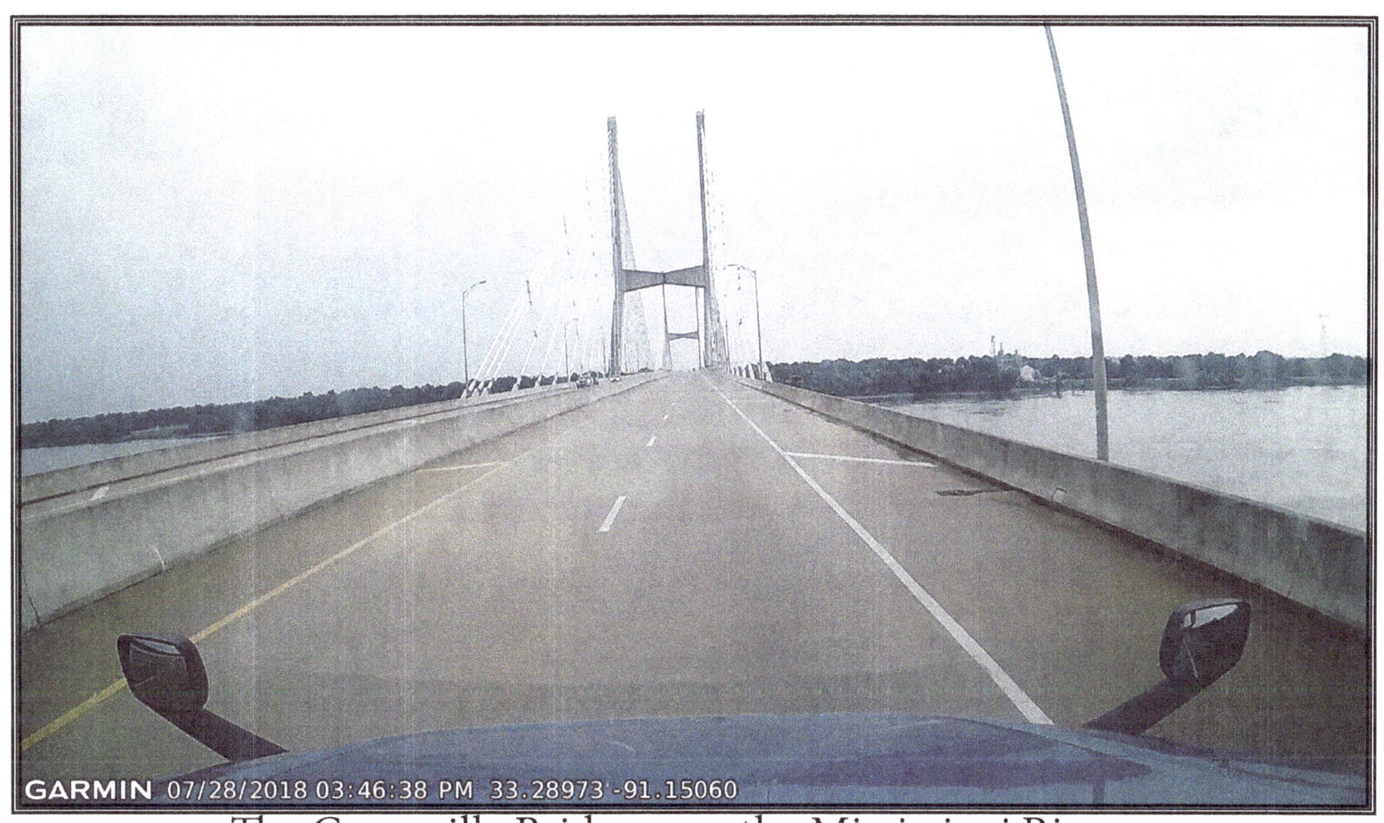

The Greenville Bridge over the Mississippi River
US-278, Lake Village, Arkansas

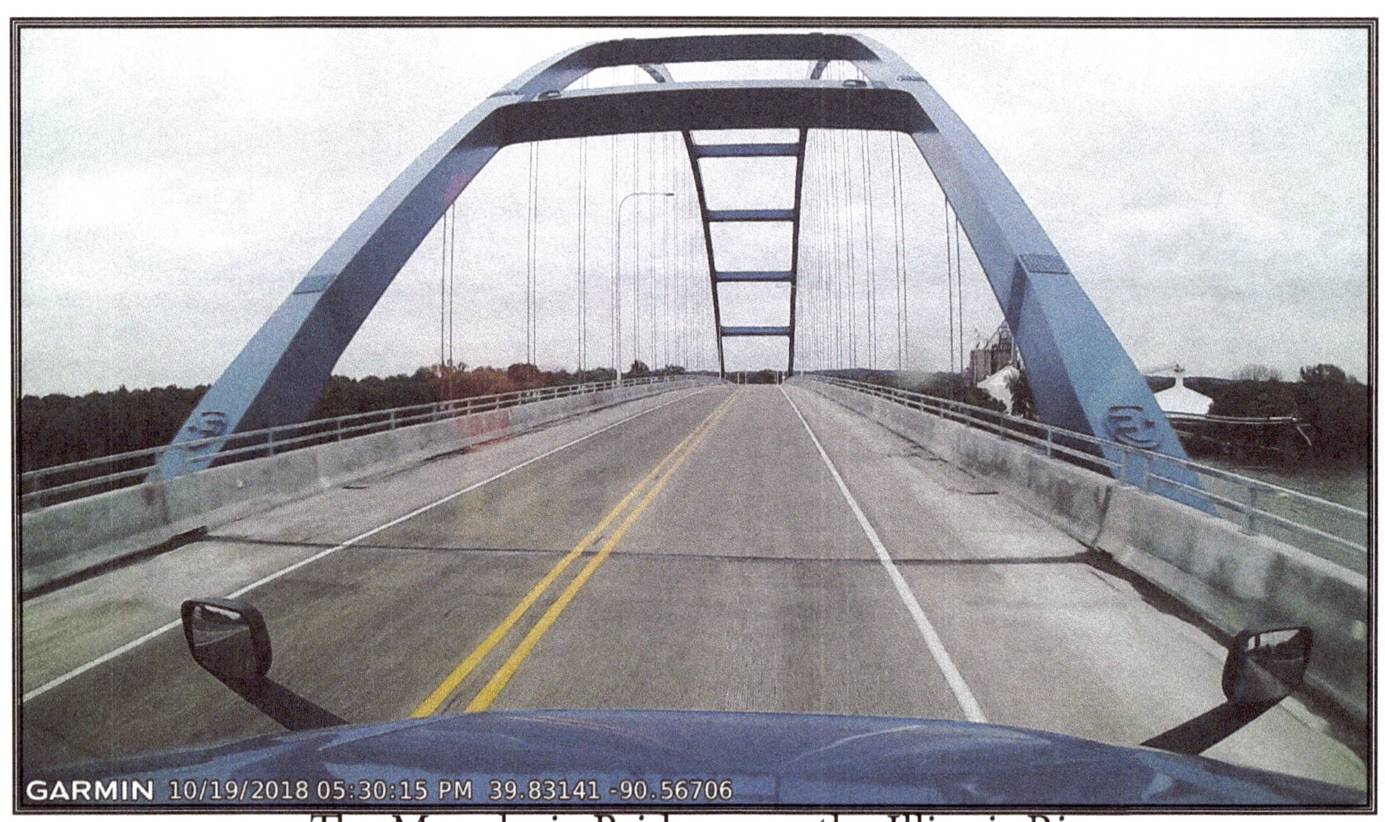

The Meredosia Bridge over the Illinois River
IL-104, Meredosia, Illinois

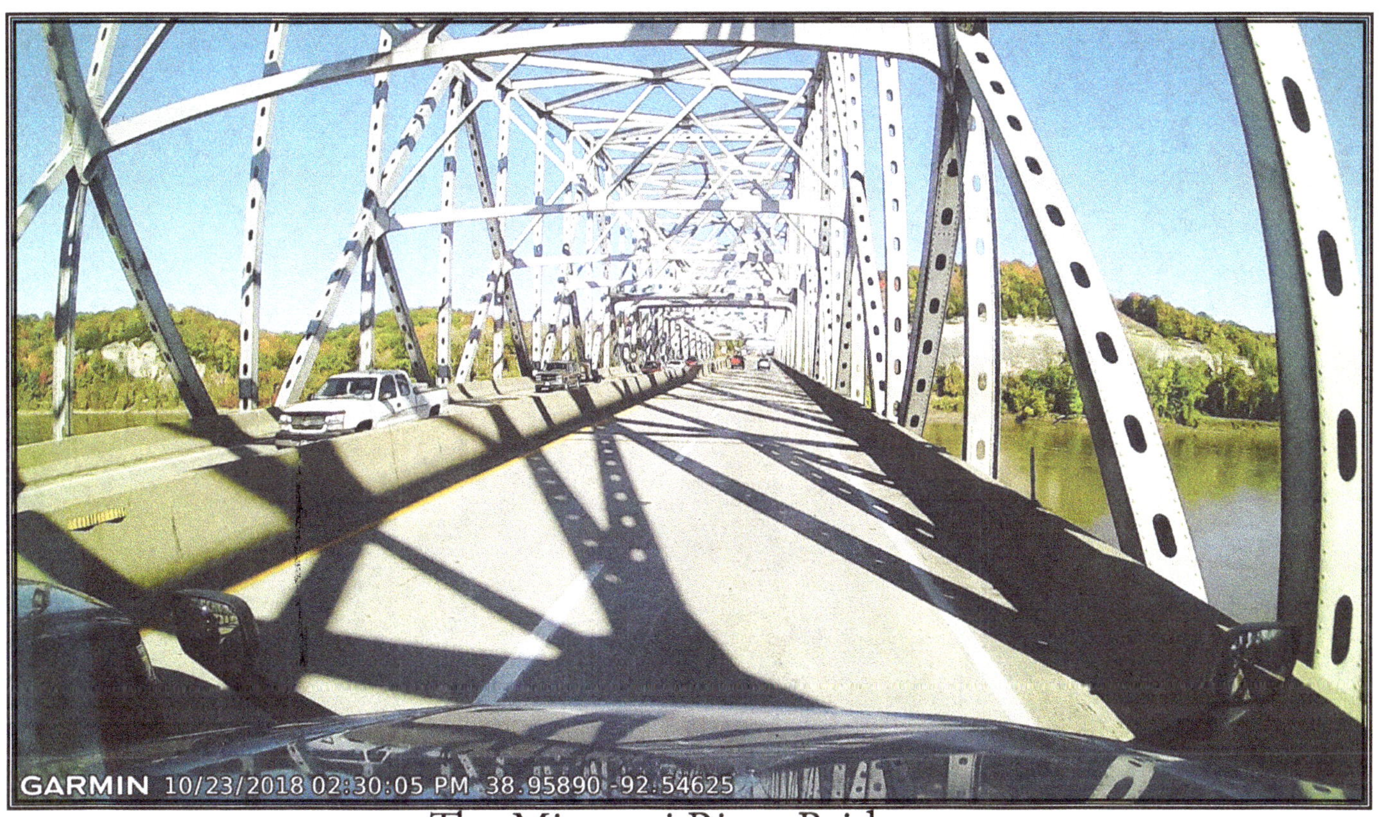

The Missouri River Bridge
I-70, Rocheport, Missouri

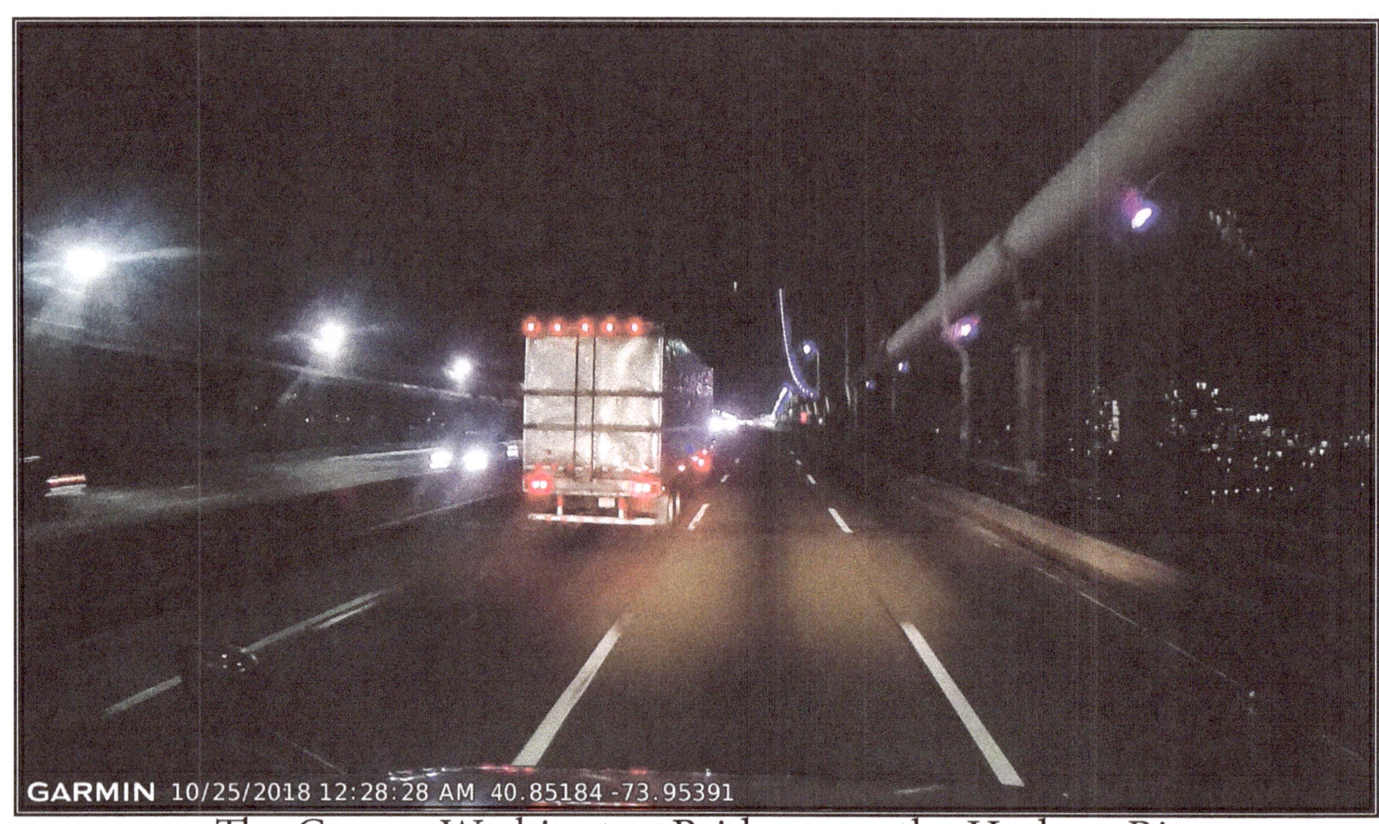

The George Washington Bridge over the Hudson River
I-95, Fort Lee, New Jersey

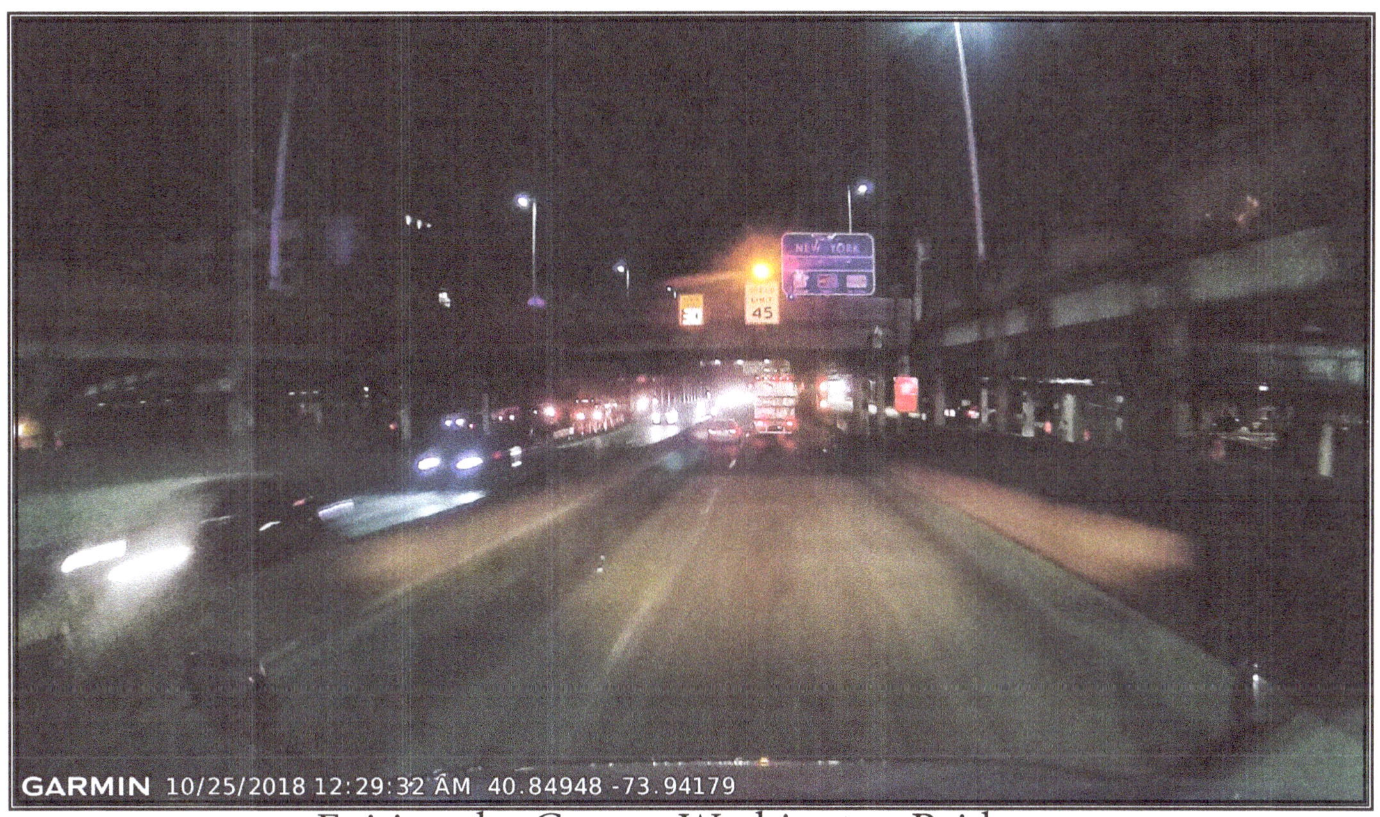

Exiting the George Washington Bridge
I-95, New York, New York

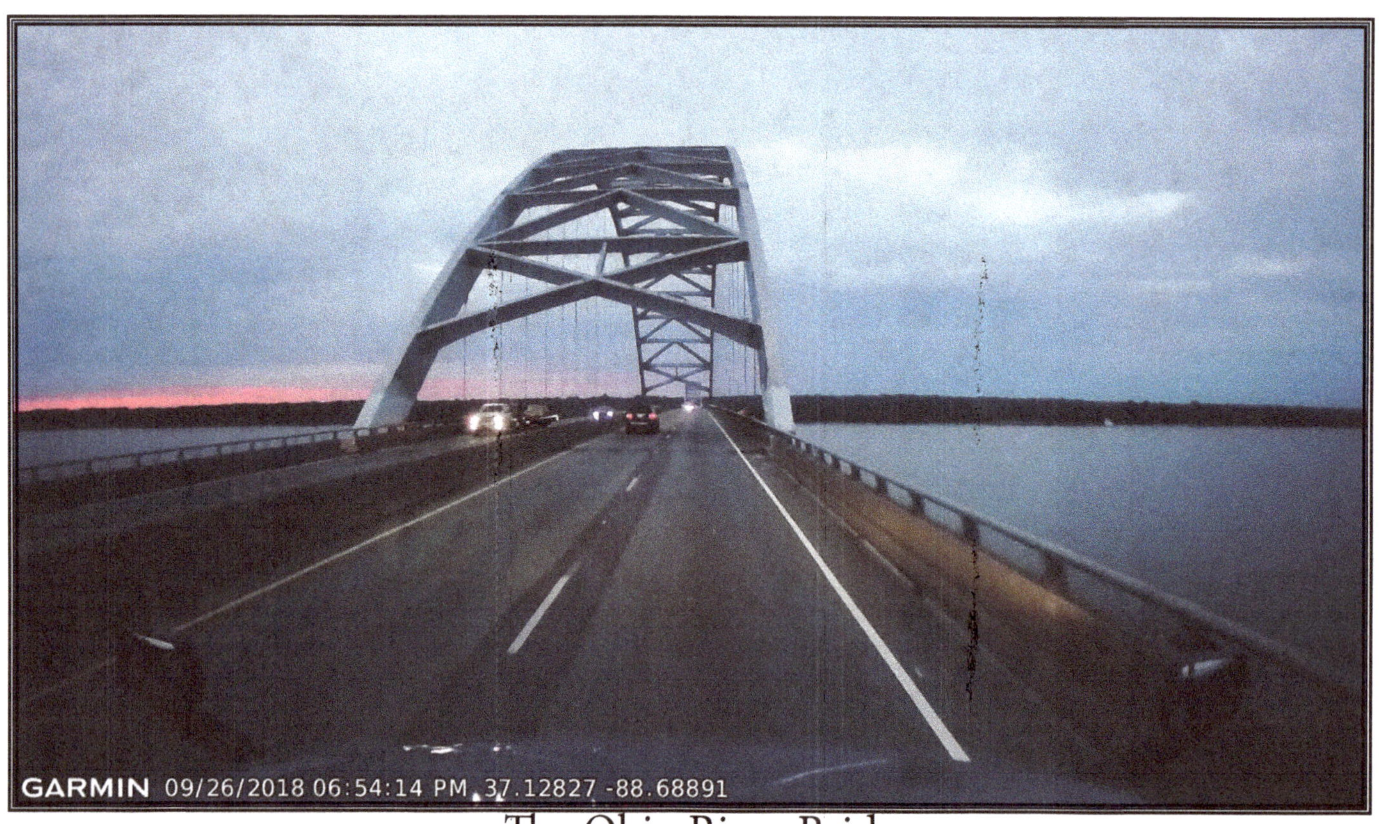

The Ohio River Bridge
I-24, Paducah, Kentucky

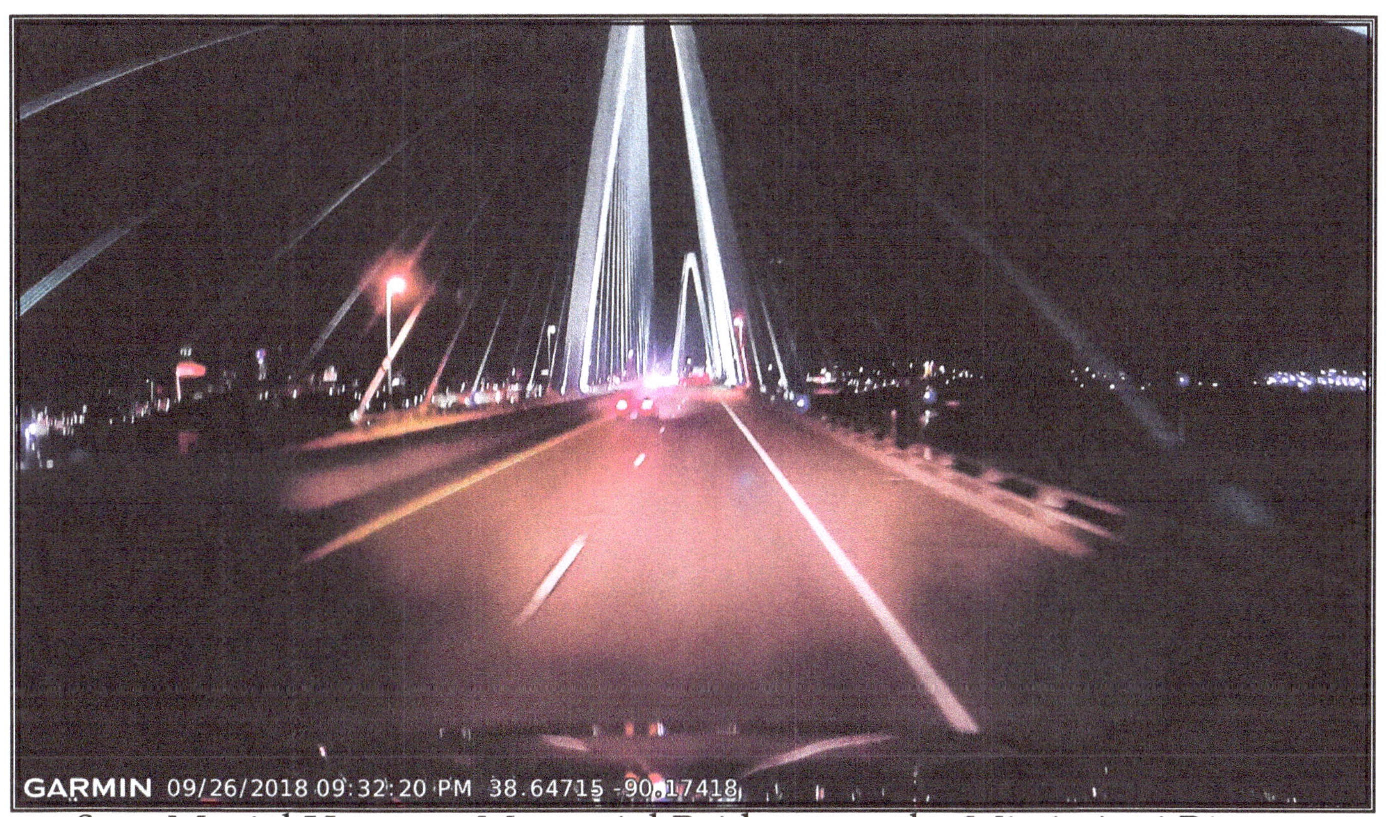

Stan Musial Veterans Memorial Bridge over the Mississippi River
I-70, St. Louis, Missouri

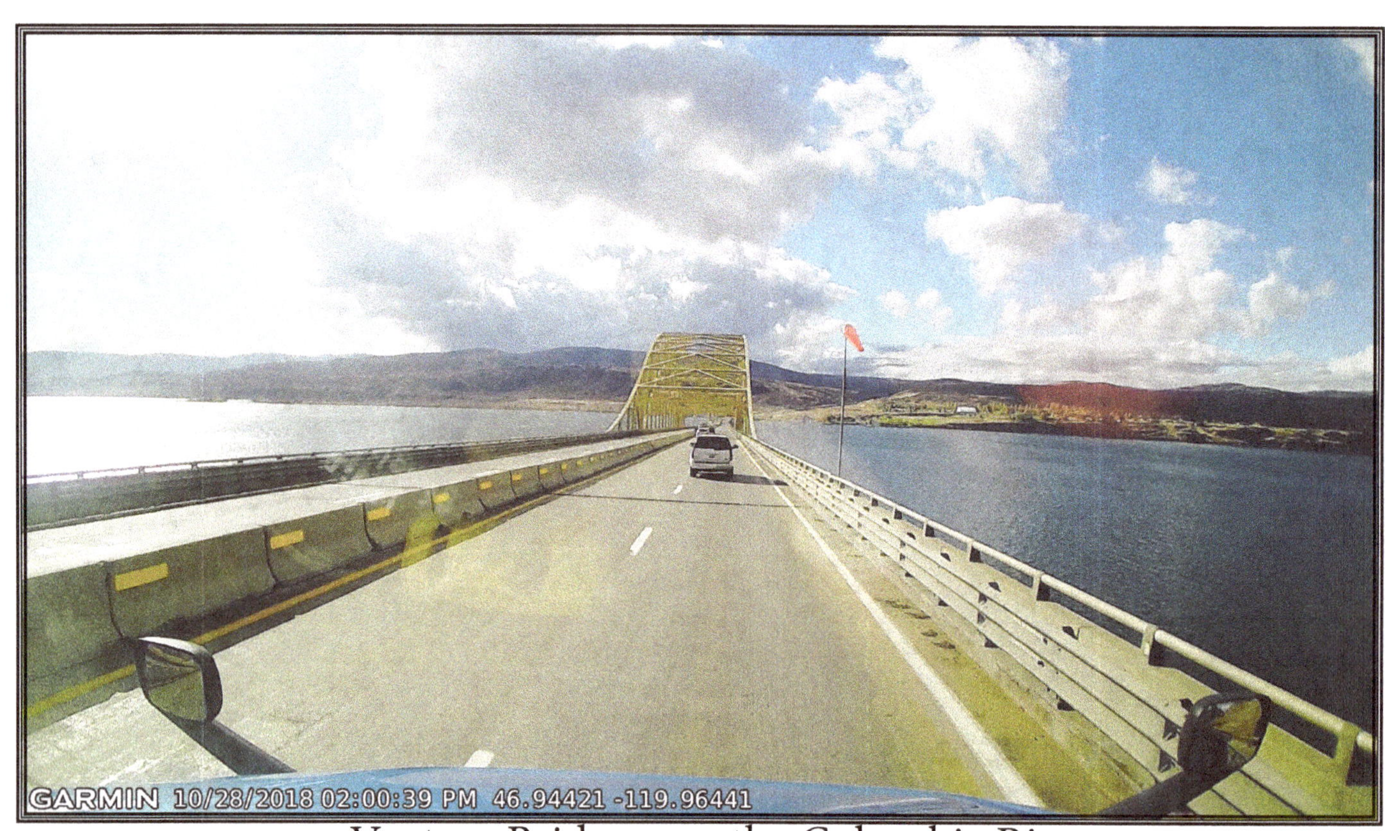

Vantage Bridge over the Columbia River
I-90, Vantage, Washington

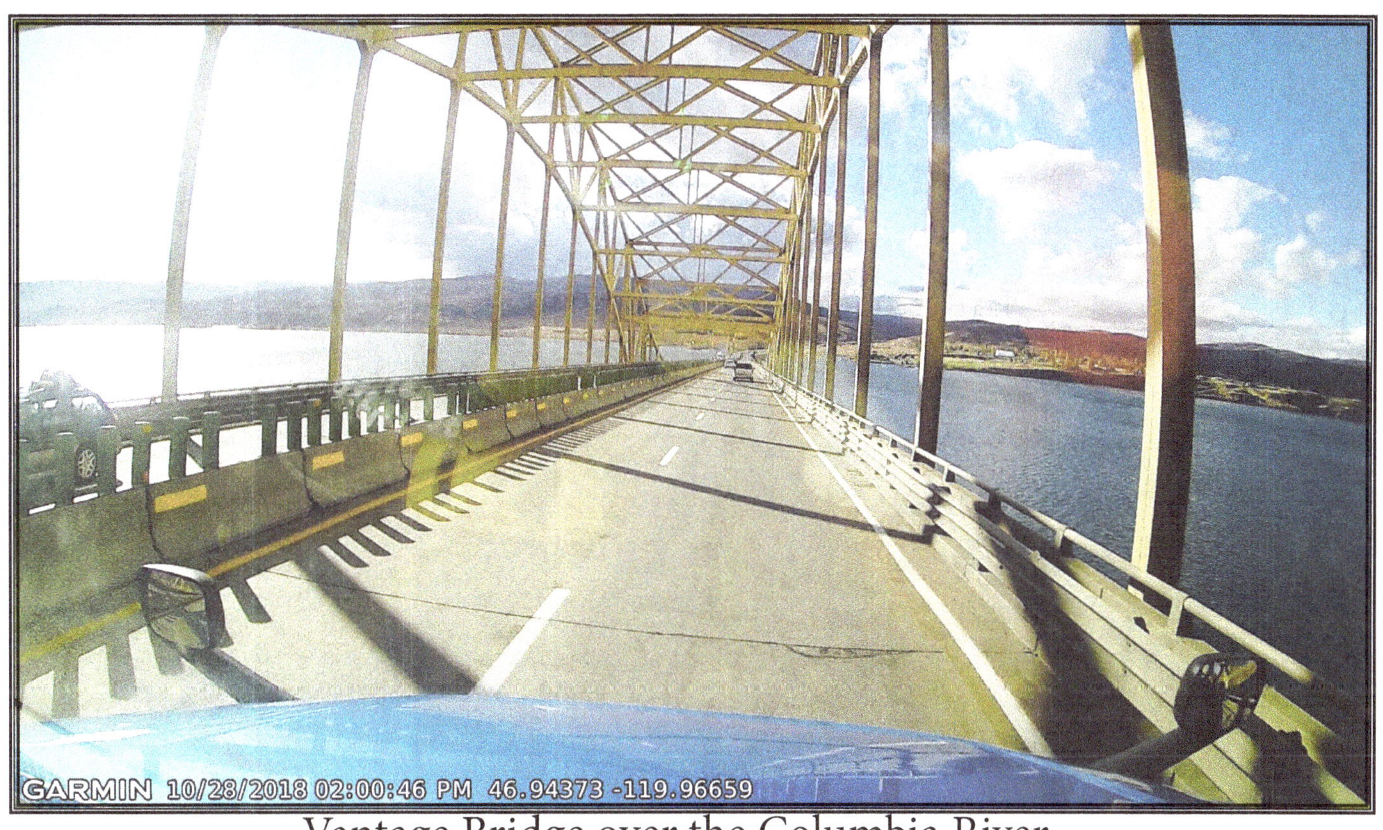

Vantage Bridge over the Columbia River
I-90, Vantage, Washington

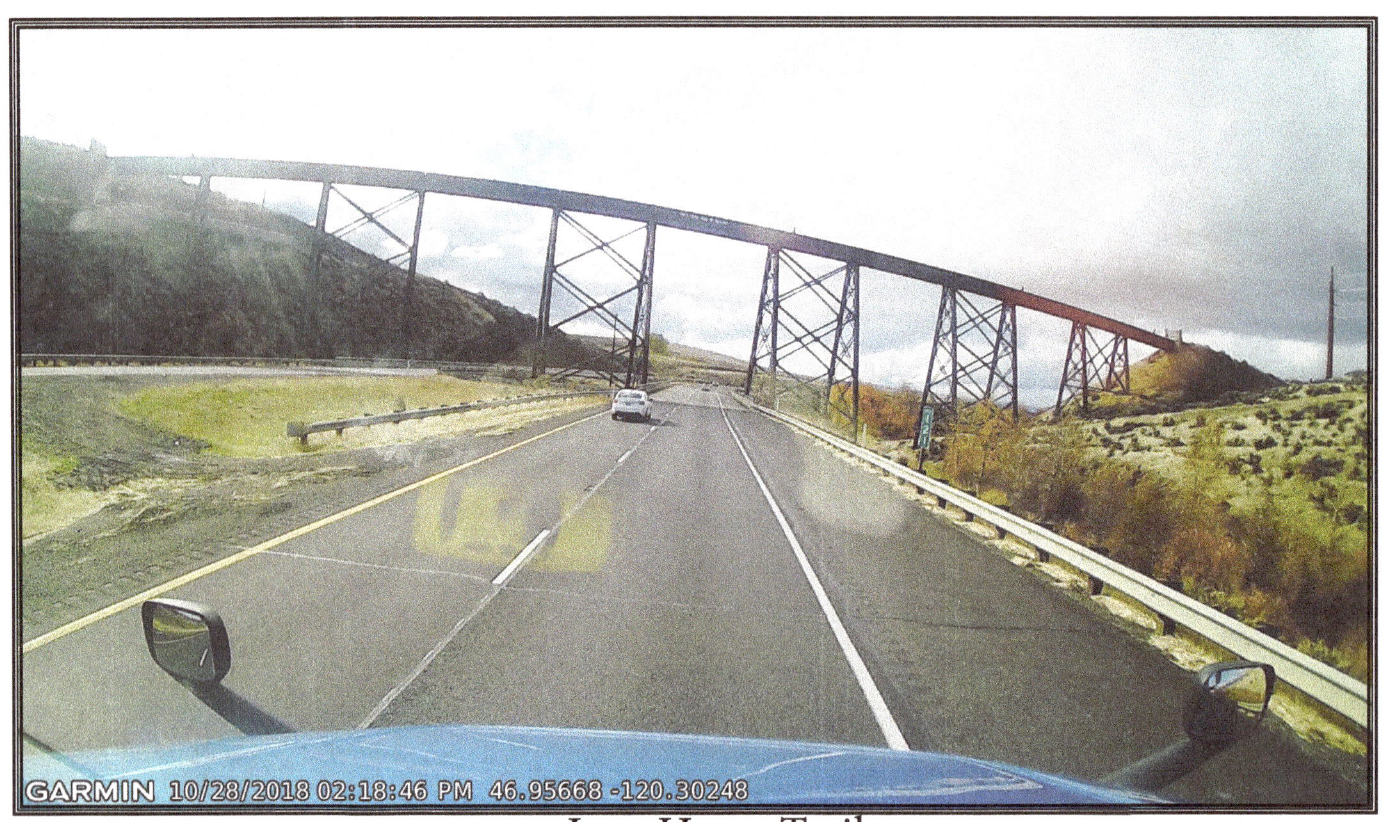

Iron Horse Trail
I-90, Ellensburg, Washington

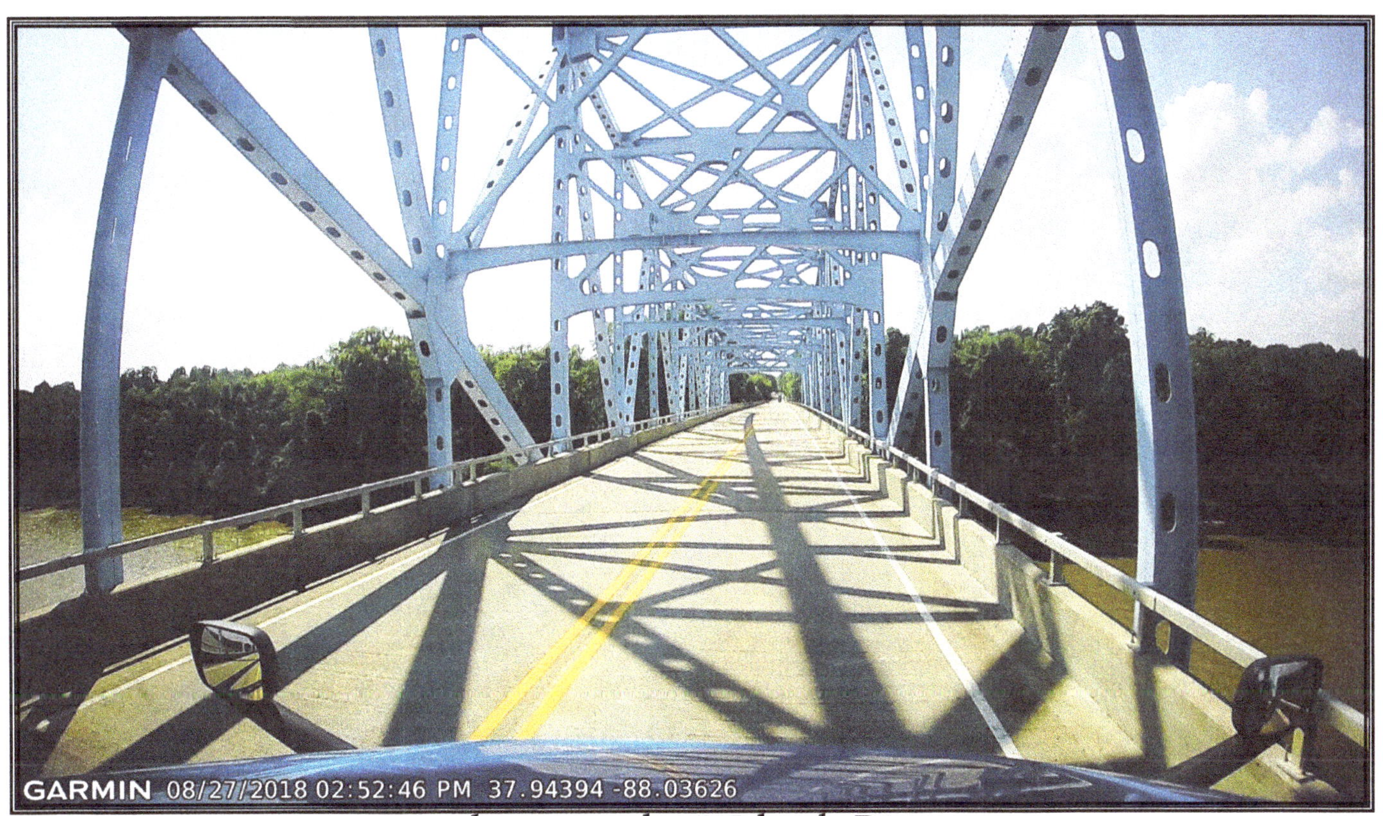

Bridge over the Wabash River
IL-141, Rising Sun, Illinois

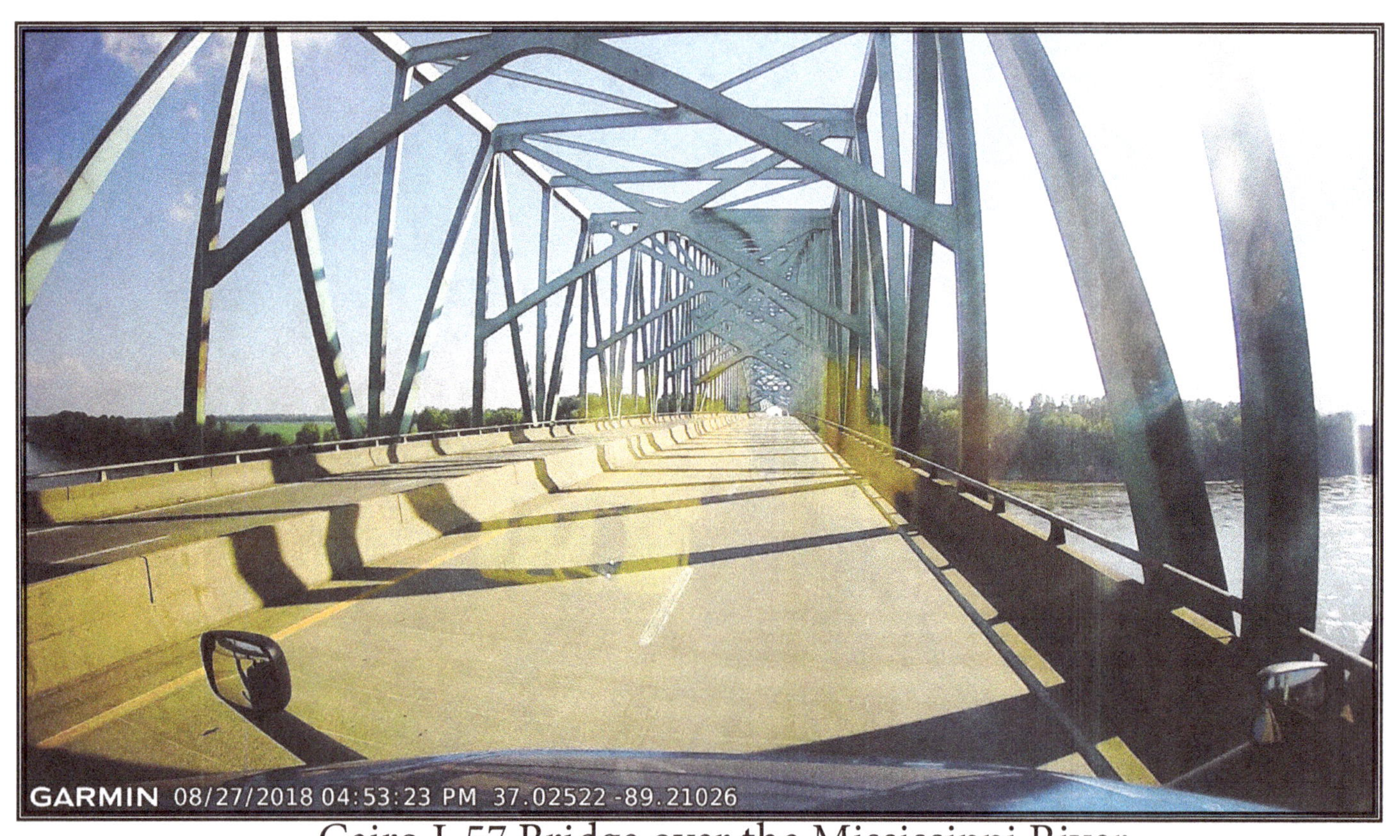

Cairo I-57 Bridge over the Mississippi River
I-57, Cairo, Illinois

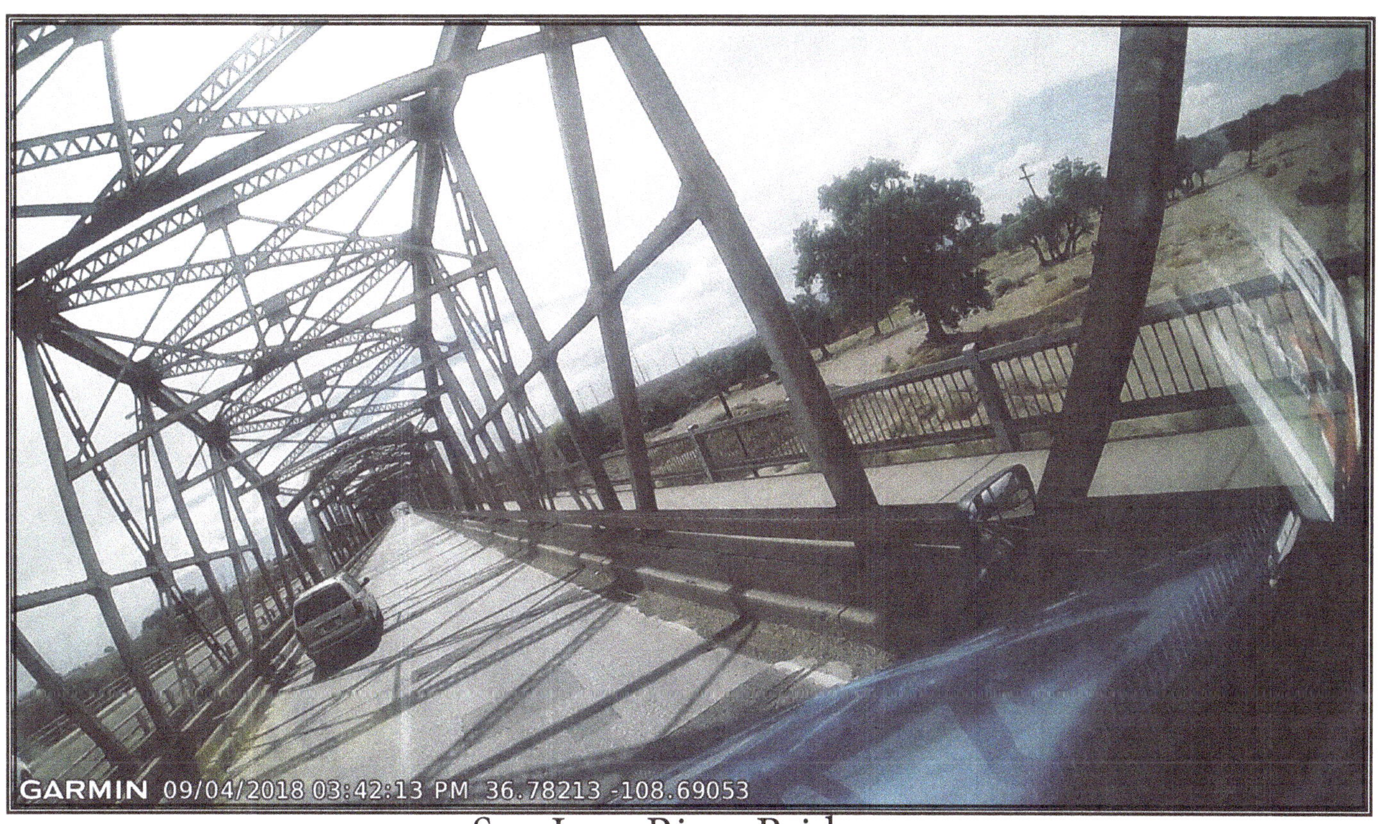

San Juan River Bridge
Old Highway 64, Shiprock, New Mexico

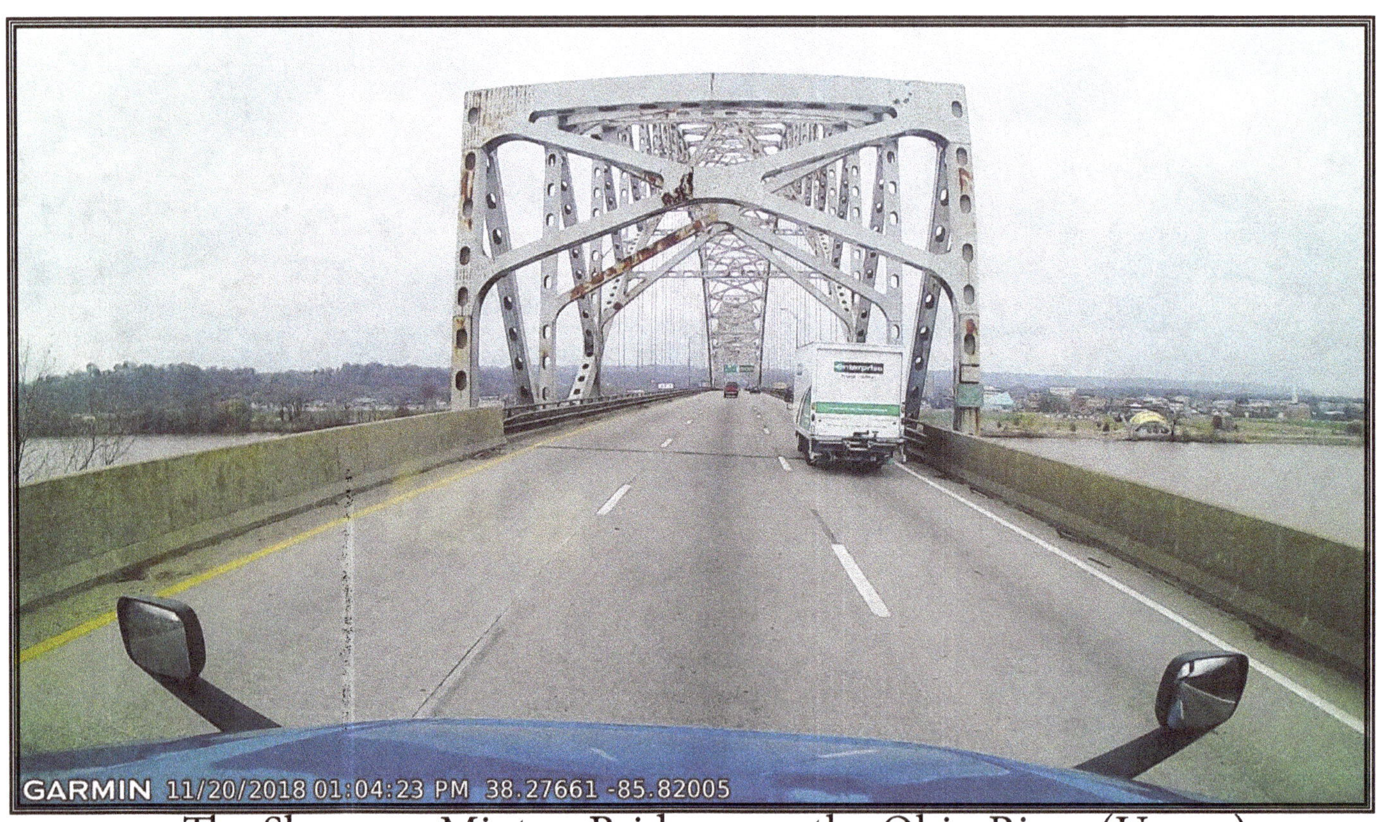

The Sherman Minton Bridge over the Ohio River (Upper)
I-64, Louisville, Kentucky

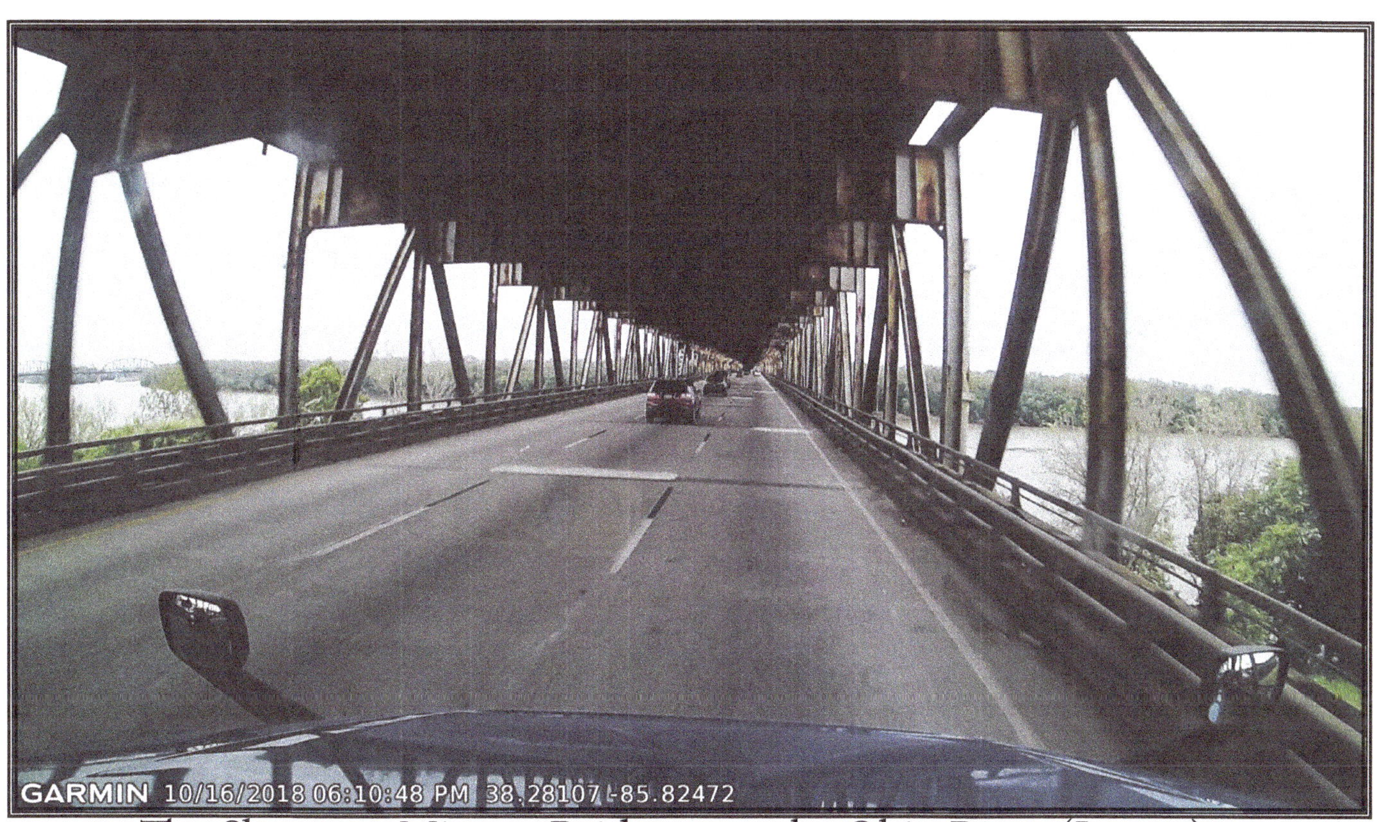

The Sherman Minton Bridge over the Ohio River (Lower)
I-64, Louisville, Kentucky

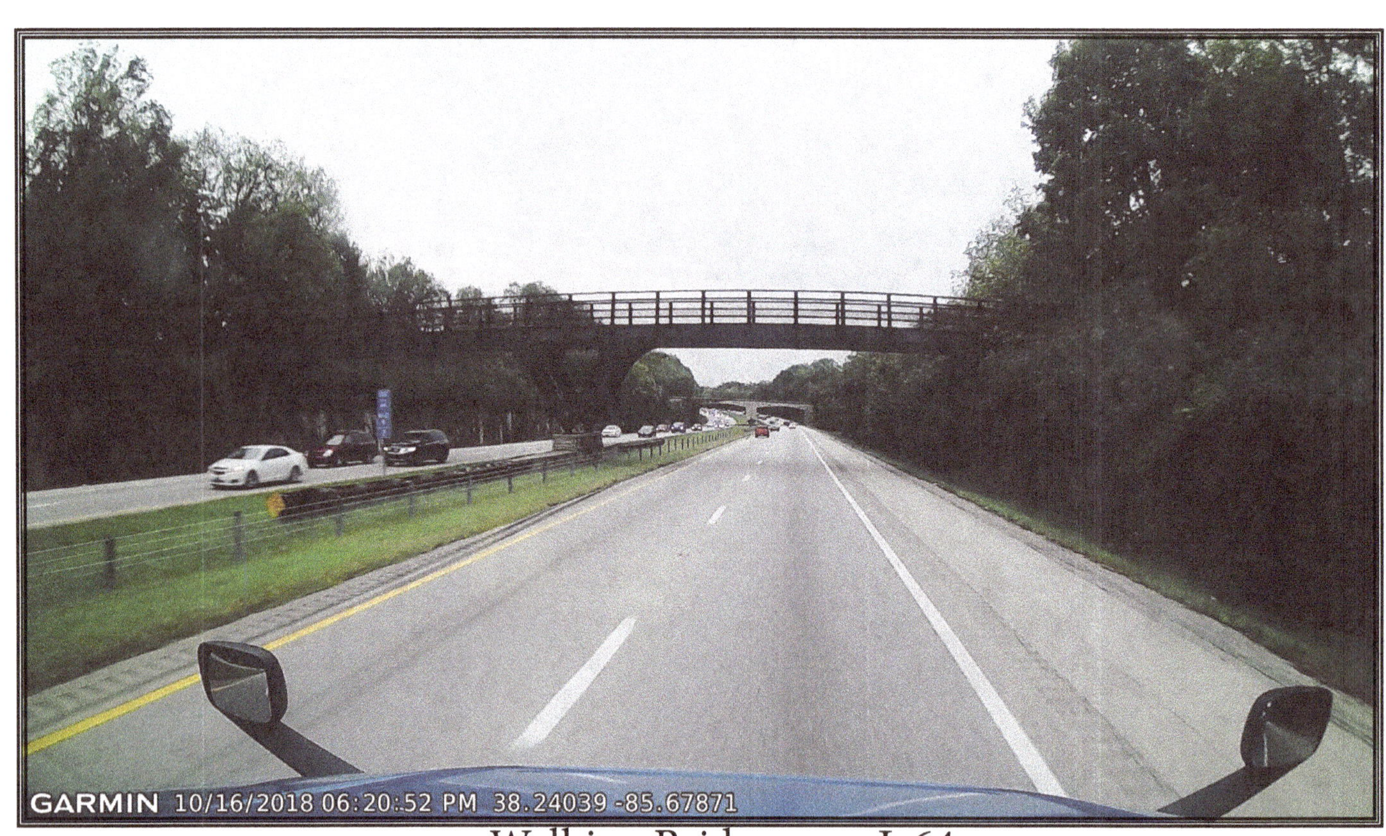

Walking Bridge over I-64
I-64, Louisville, Kentucky

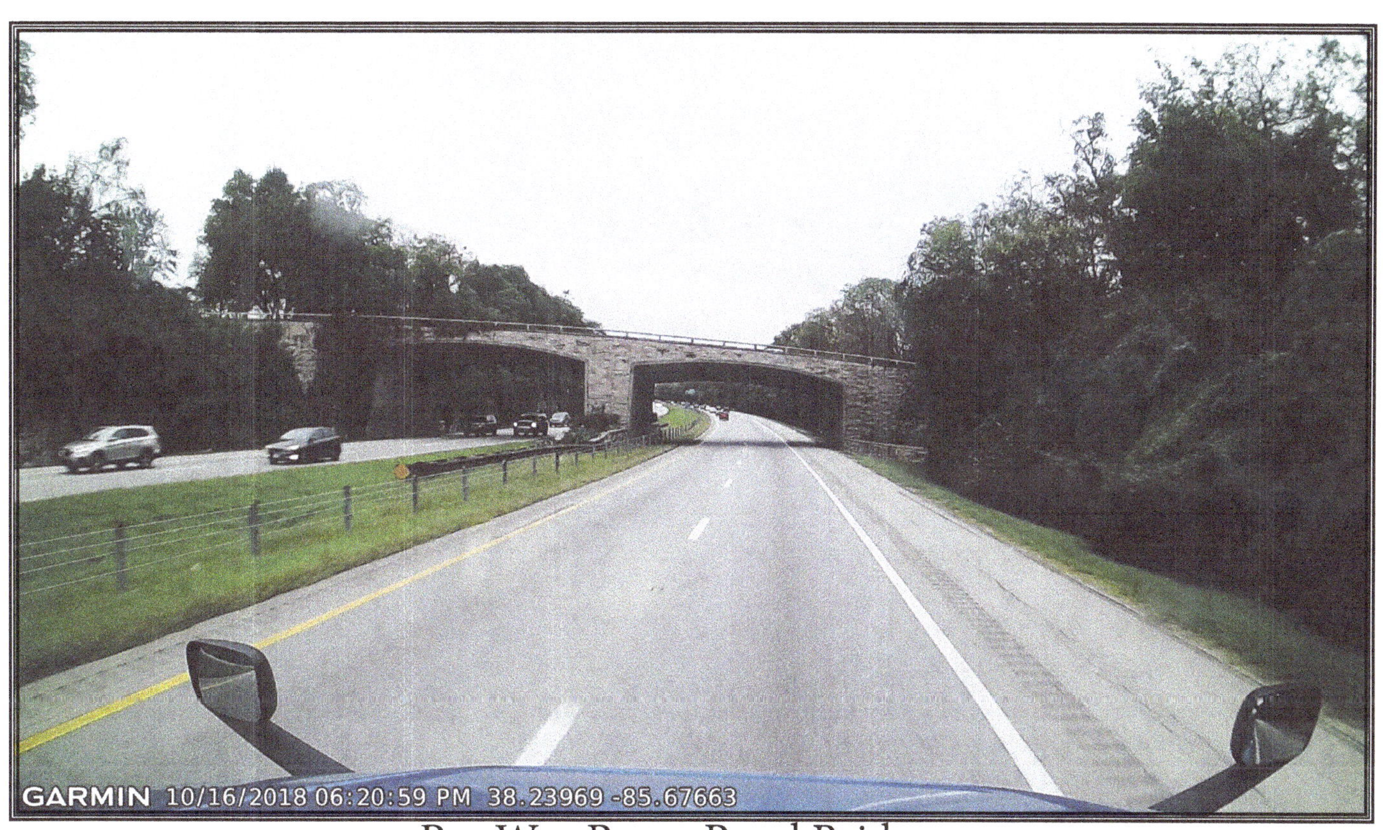

Pee Wee Reese Road Bridge
I-64, Louisville, Kentucky

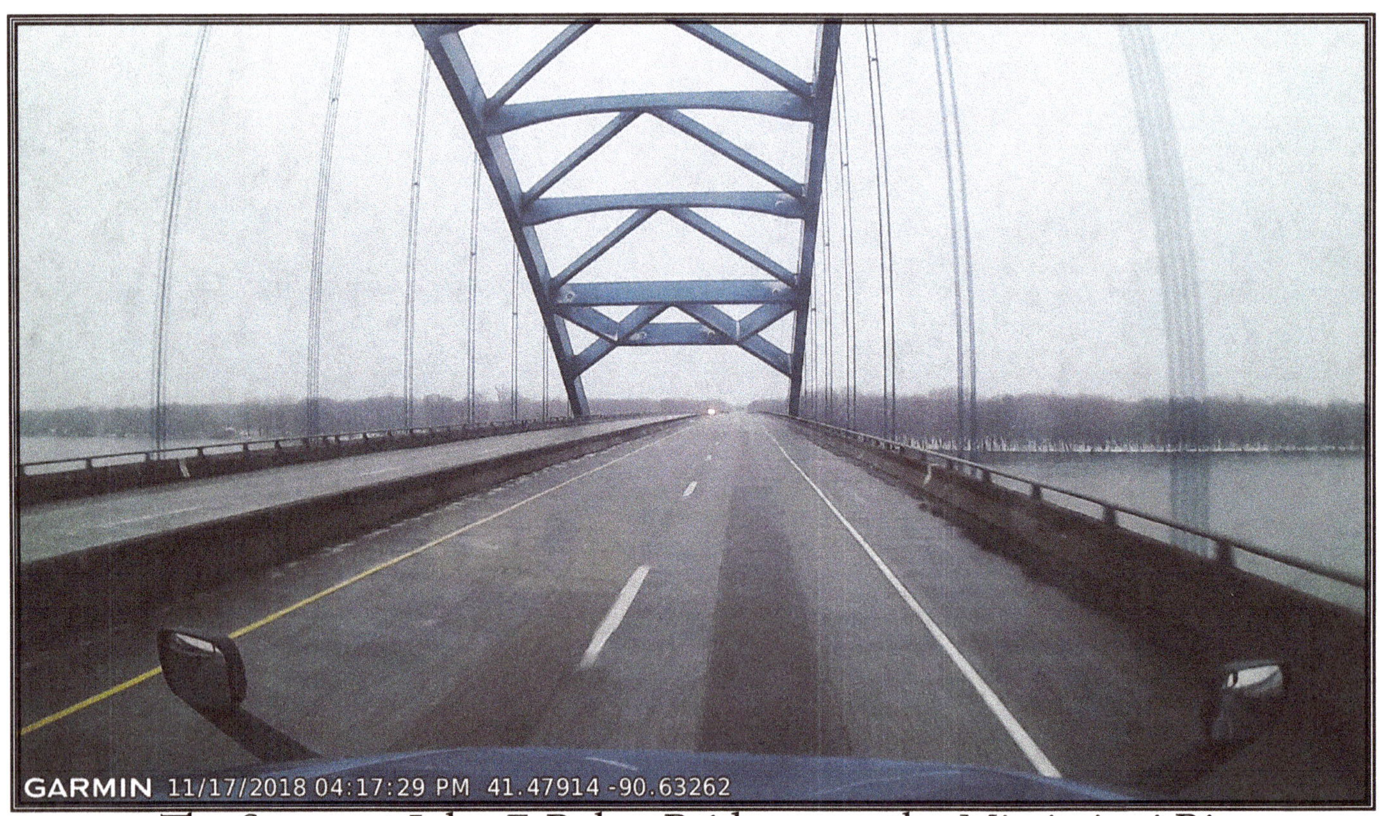

The Sergeant John F. Baker Bridge over the Mississippi River
I-280, Davenport, Iowa

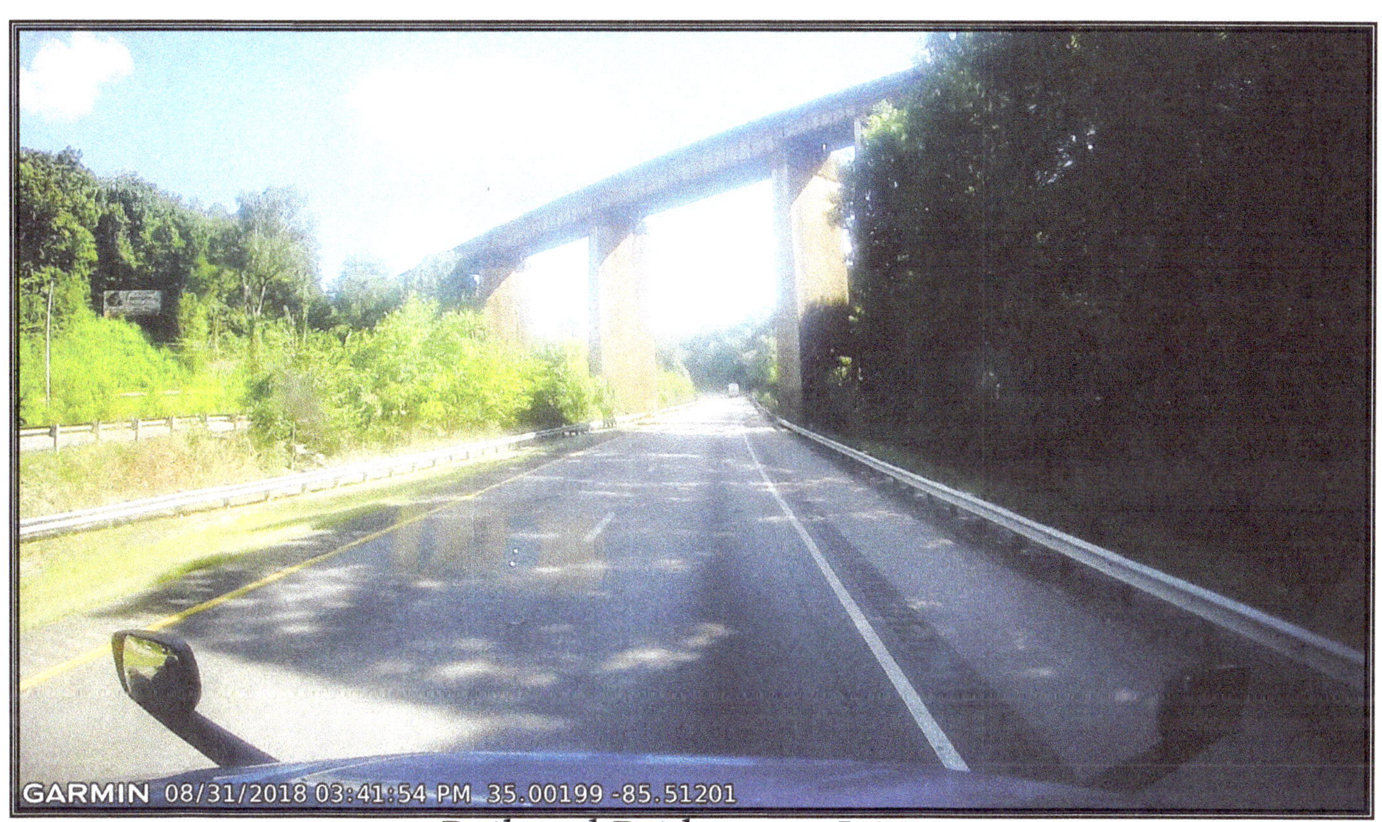

Railroad Bridge over I-24
I-24, Whiteside, Tennessee

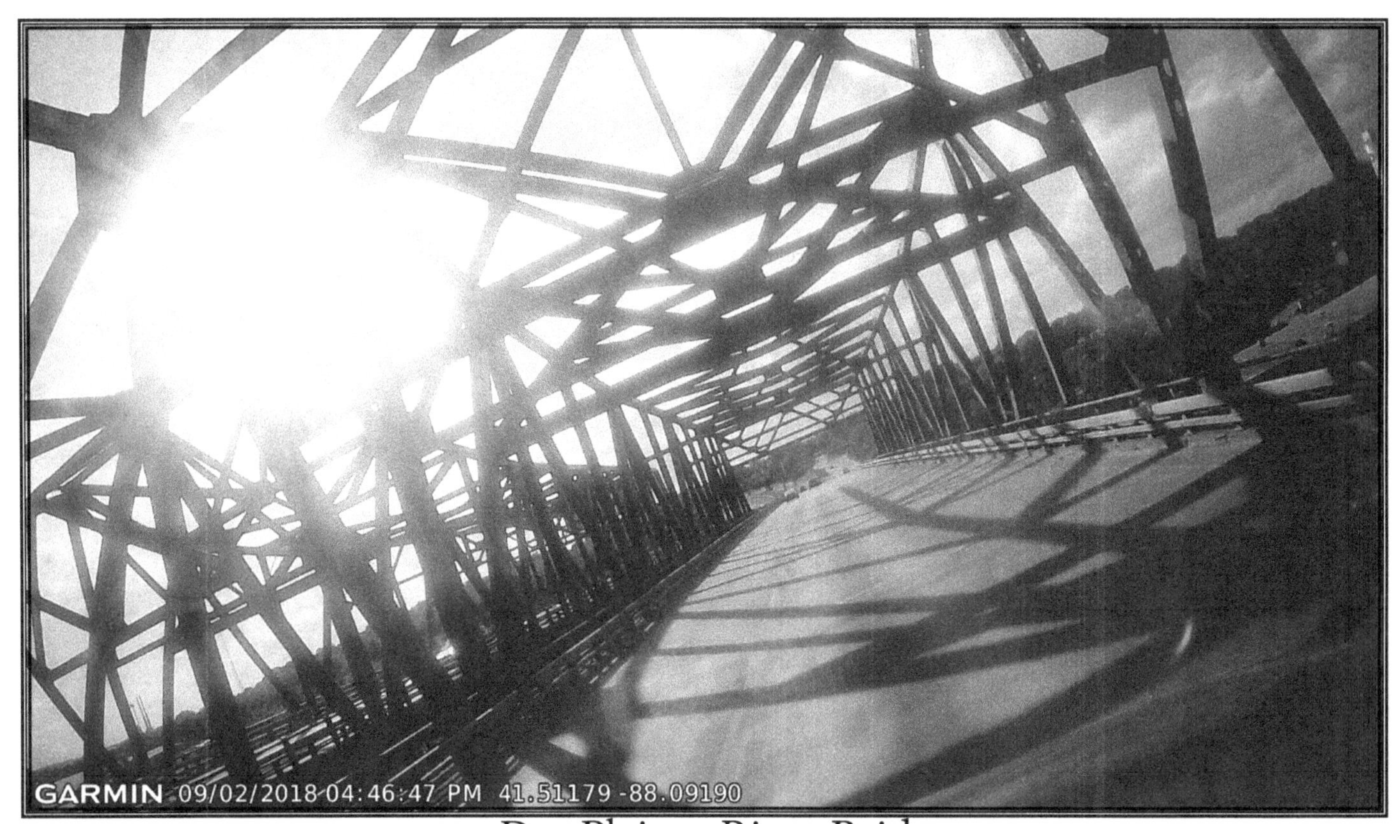

Des Plaines River Bridge
I-80, Joliet, Illinois

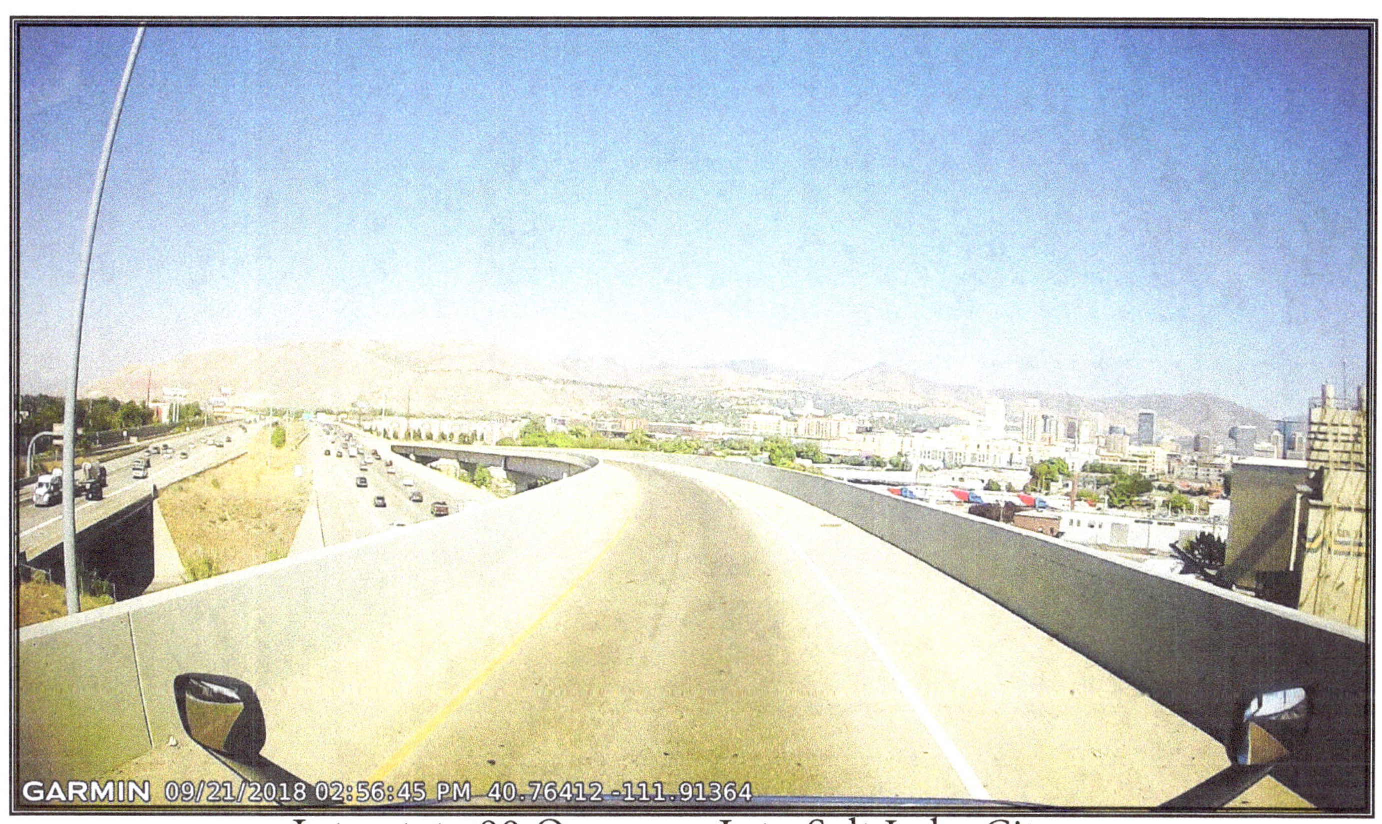

Interstate 80 Overpass Into Salt Lake City
I-80, Salt Lake City, Utah

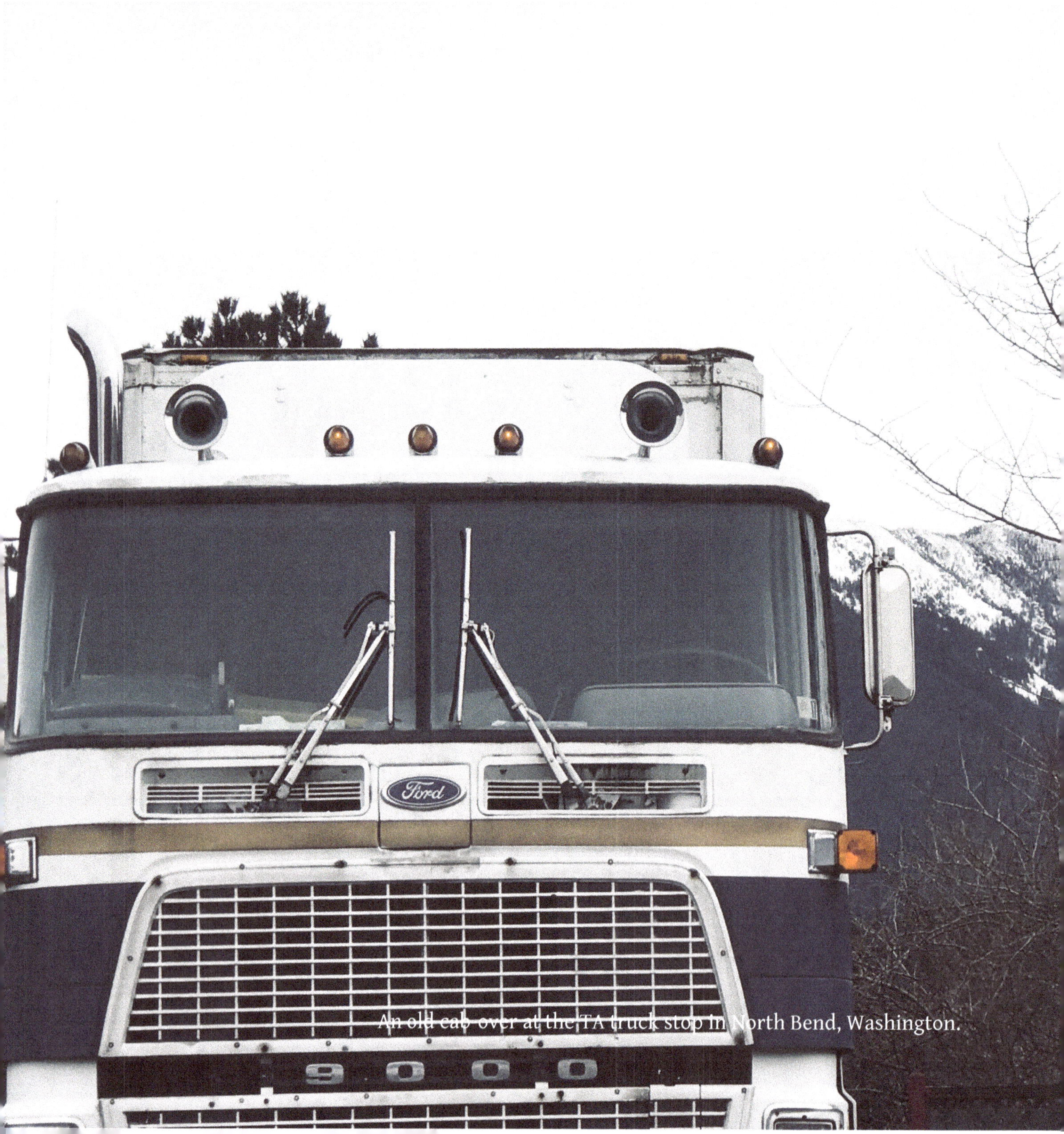

An old cab over at the TA truck stop in North Bend, Washington.

Part Two
Truck Stops, Rest Areas, Ports of Entry, Terminals
& Distribution Centers

The lifeblood of America begins in distribution centers across the country. Everything you have is loaded onto a trailer and picked up by somebody like myself and carried to a grocery store or distribution center to be distributed at a later date. On the surface this is just as vibrant and fast-paced as the blood flowing through your veins, except somewhere along the line every truck must come to a stop, every driver must rest.

The reality is, the trucking industry is one of the most heavily regulated industries in America, and of those regulations the Hours of Service regulations are the most strict and heavily enforced. The moment our trucks begin moving we have eleven hours of drive time, with three hours available to break within a fourteen hour day. The moment those eleven hours are up, our trucks absolutely must be parked and they cannot move again for ten hours under any circumstances. Drivers have ended up in prison for violating these regulations.

The regulations do serve a purpose, but one unfortunate side effect is the over-crowding of truck stops and rest areas. As a common traveler you have seen many of these—brand name stops, such as Loves, Petro, Flying J, Pilot, and so on. To you they are simply gas stations. Convenience stores. To truck drivers they are places of refuge, showers, laundromats—very often, home. Some are grand, with movie theaters and video games and luxurious tubs and showers. Others are dirty and grimy and altogether unpleasant. In the end, when our clock is nearing zero, we are always glad to drive in and find an open parking spot, regardless of the size and glamour of the stop.

Next time you're in a truck stop, take a look around. These guys and gals who are sitting around the lounge area or eating alone in the diner—they are there in a large part to help you out. For you they drive this country, to bring everything you could possibly want or need. Maybe you could give them a smile, a hug, or buy them a cup of coffee. It would bring a smile to the lips of a weary and lonely traveler, and that is a deed worth doing.

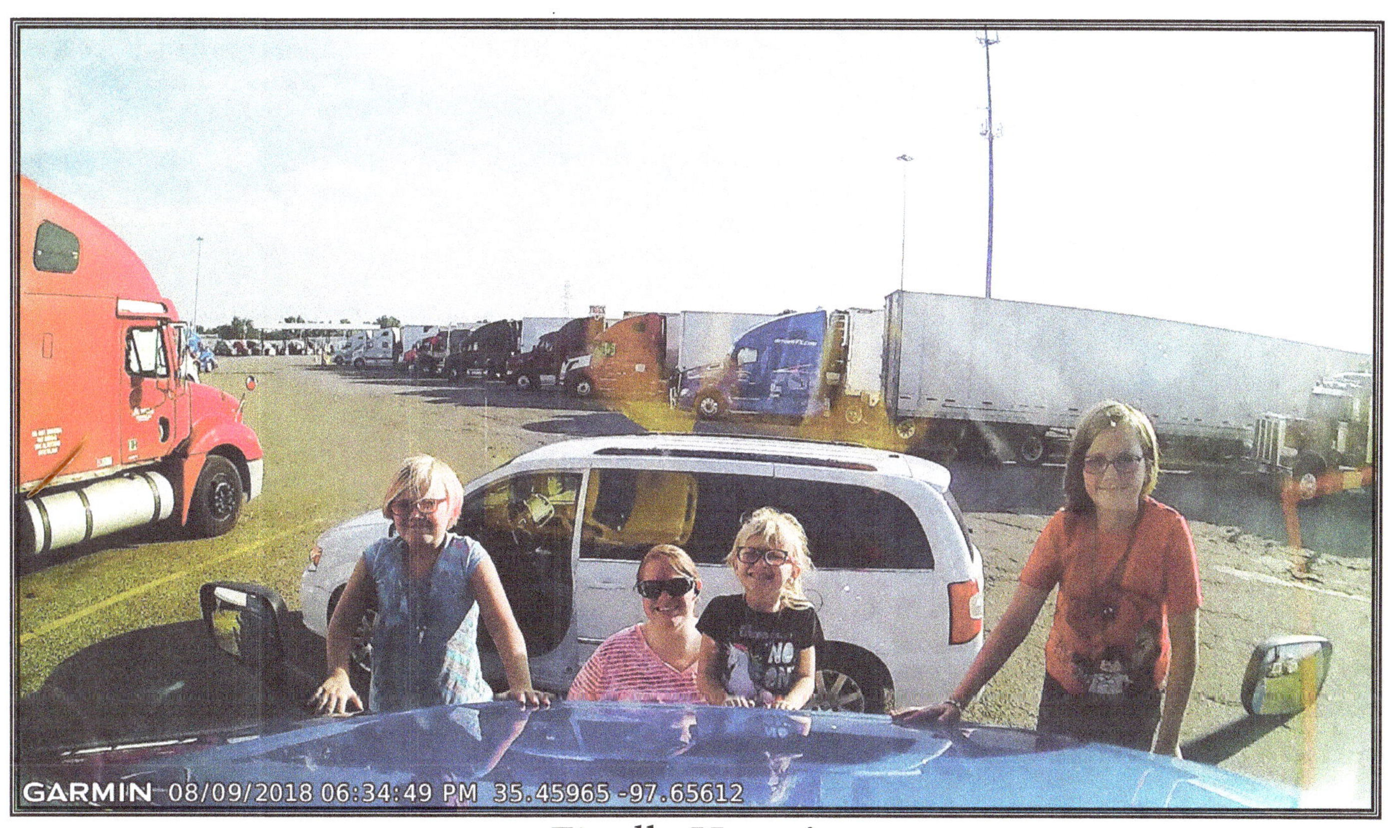

Finally Home!
From left: River, Stacy, Aria and Willow
TA, Oklahoma City, Oklahoma

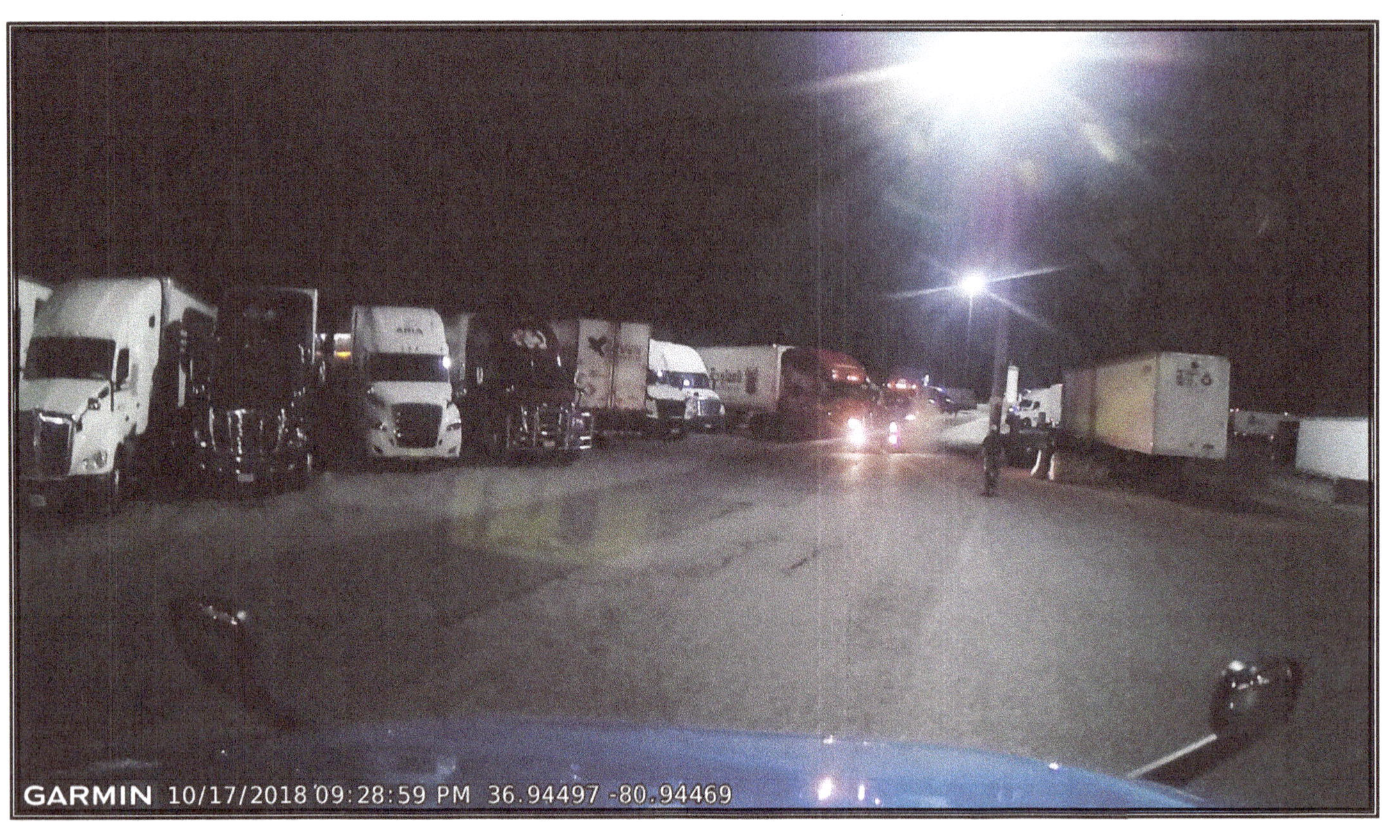

Flying J Travel Center
I-77, Fort Chiswell, Virginia

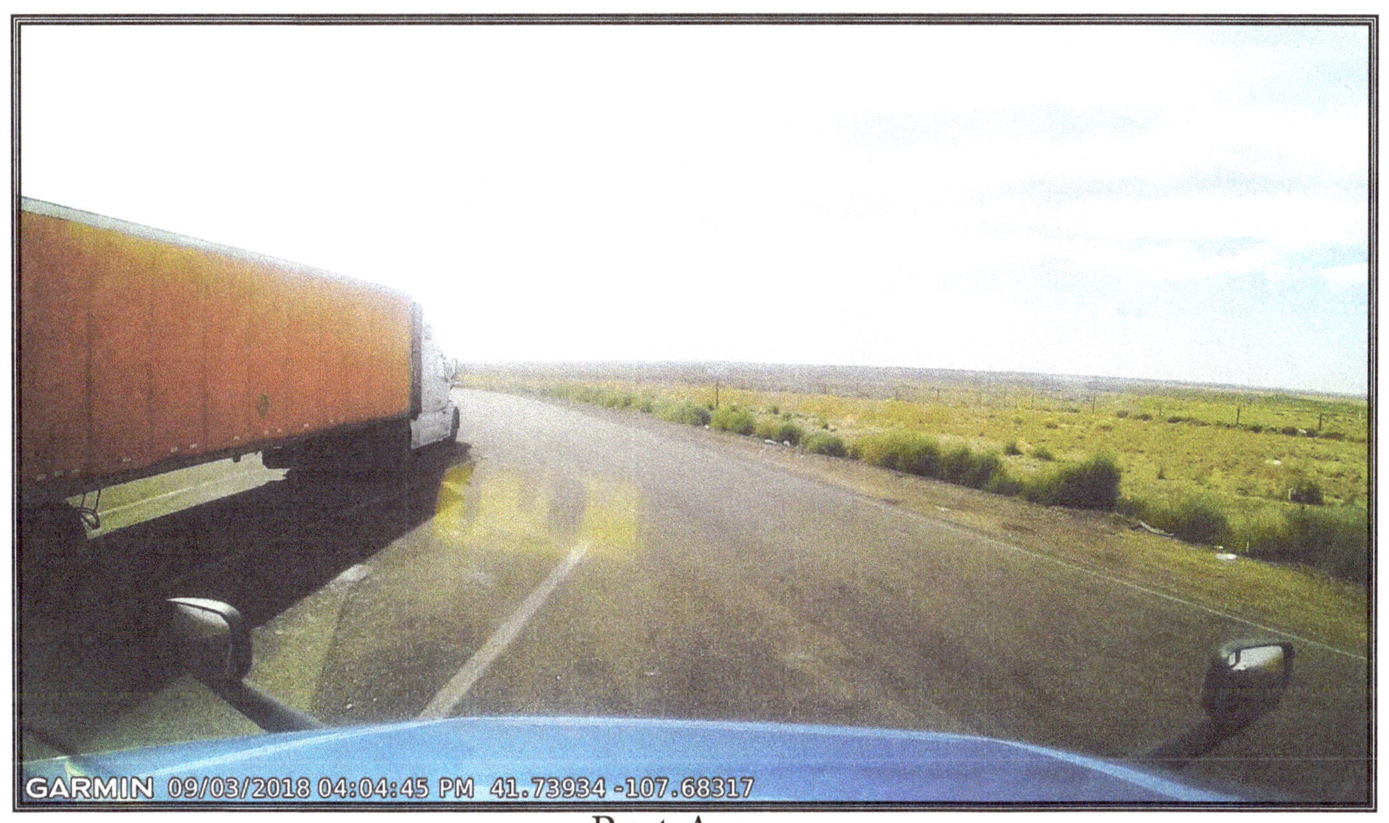

Rest Area
I-80, Creston, Wyoming

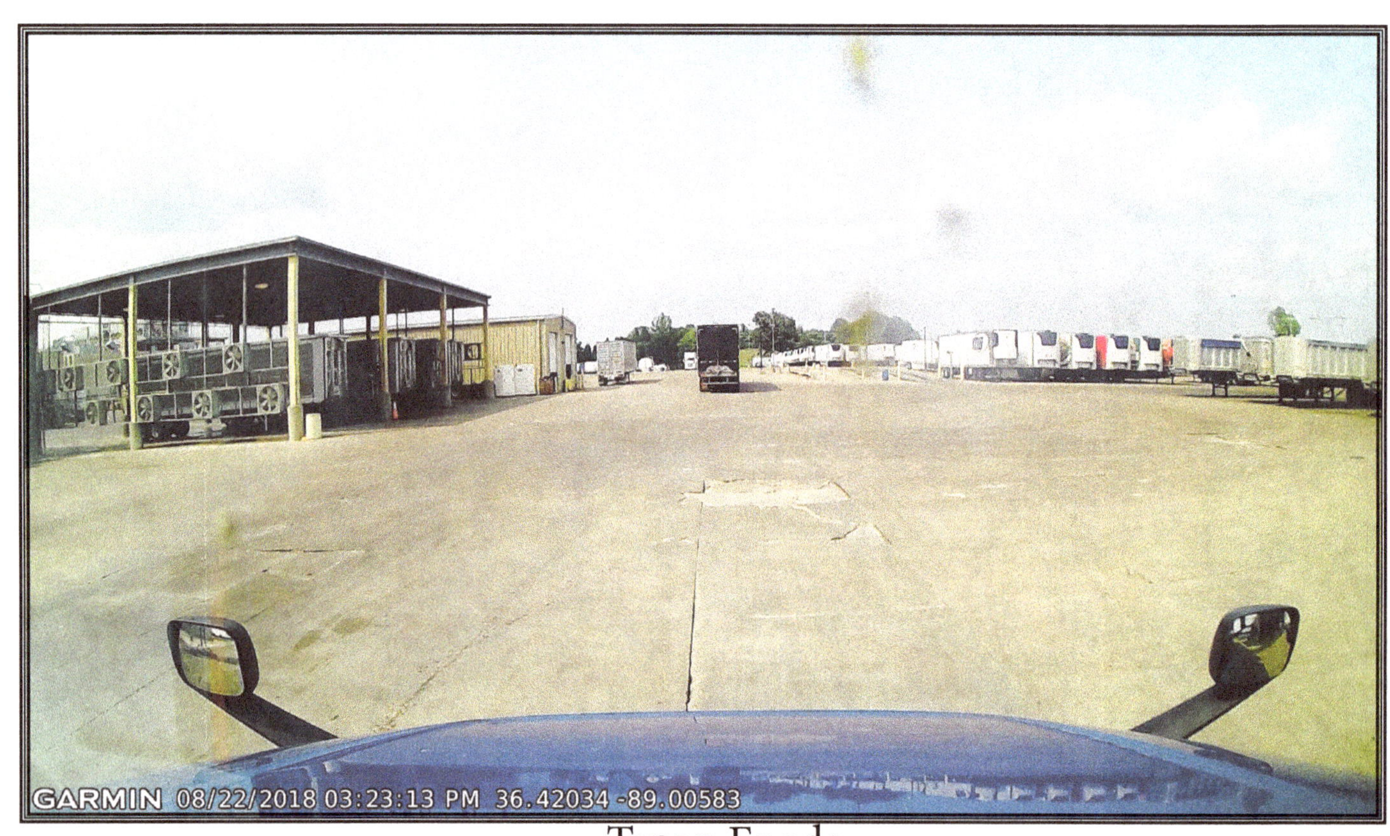

Tyson Foods
TN-22, Union City, Tennesee

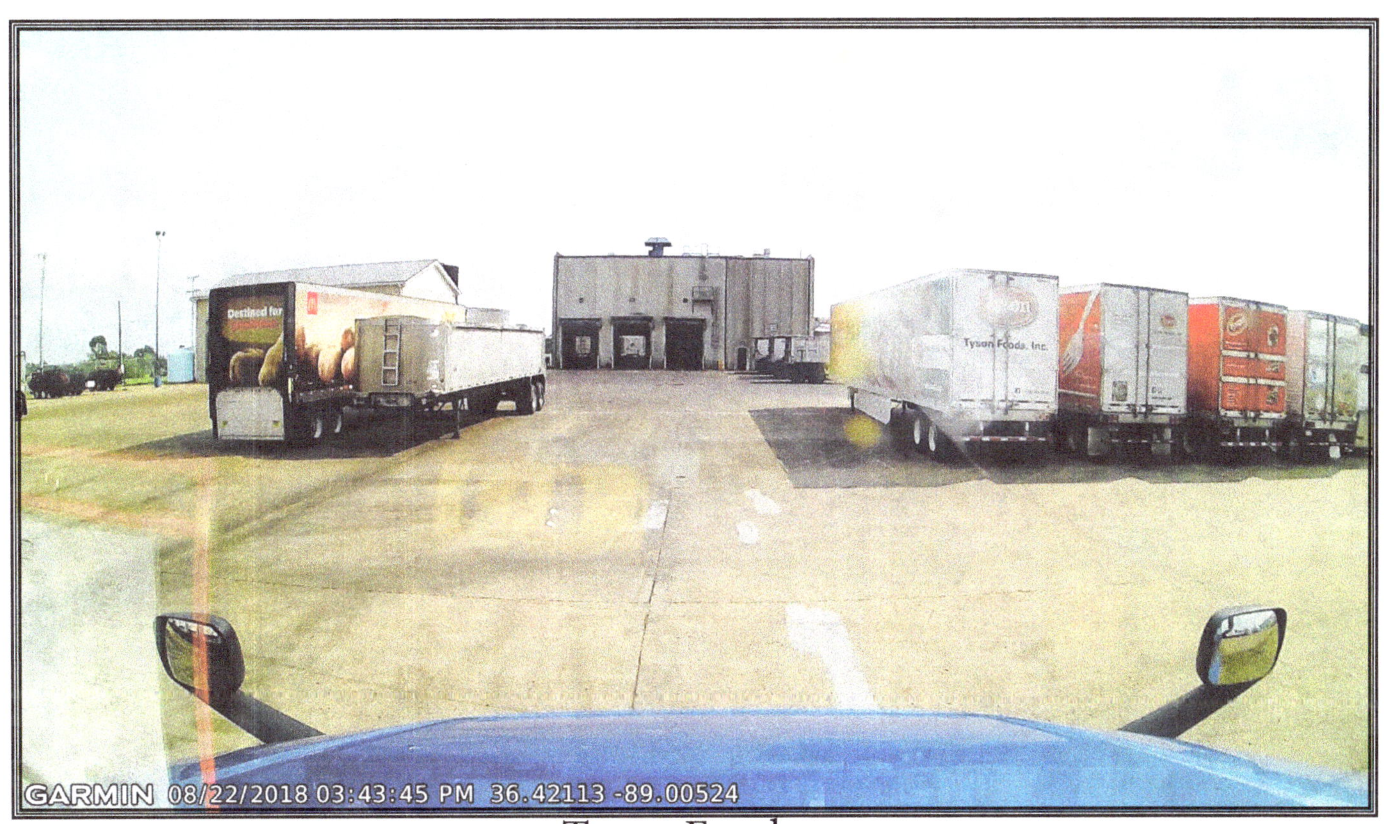

Tyson Foods
TN-22, Union City, Tennessee

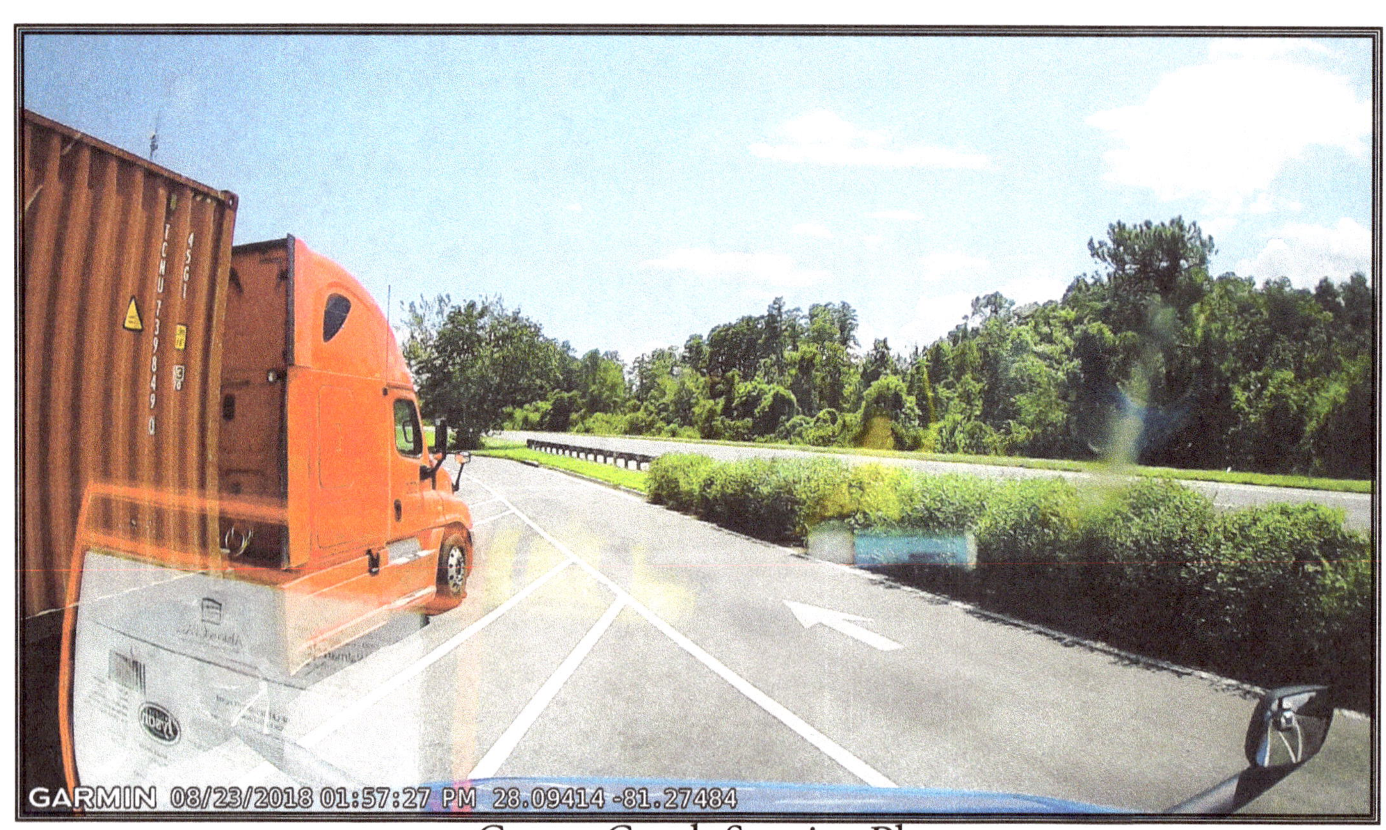

Canoe Creek Service Plaza
Florida Turnpike, Kenansville, Florida

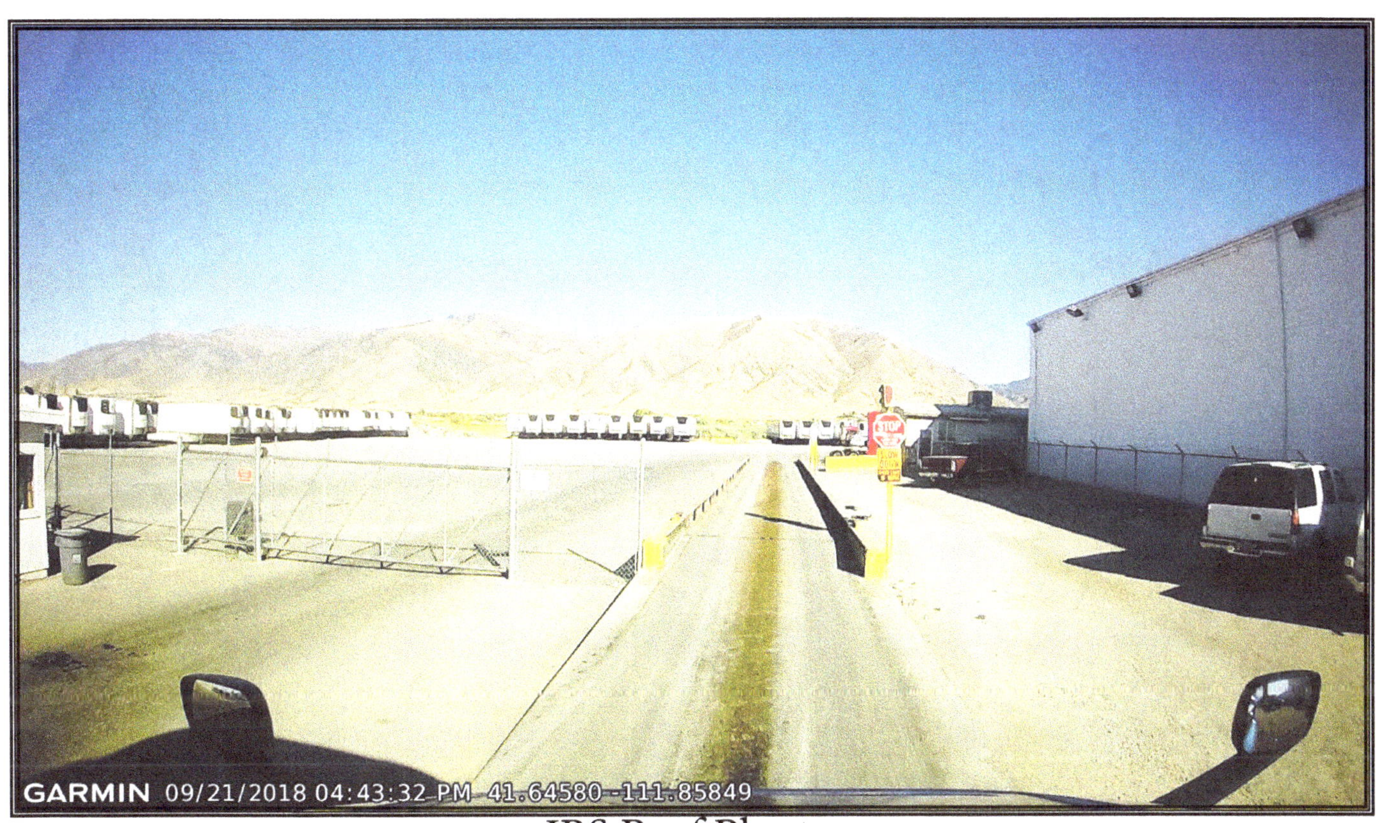

JBS Beef Plant
Hyrum, Utah

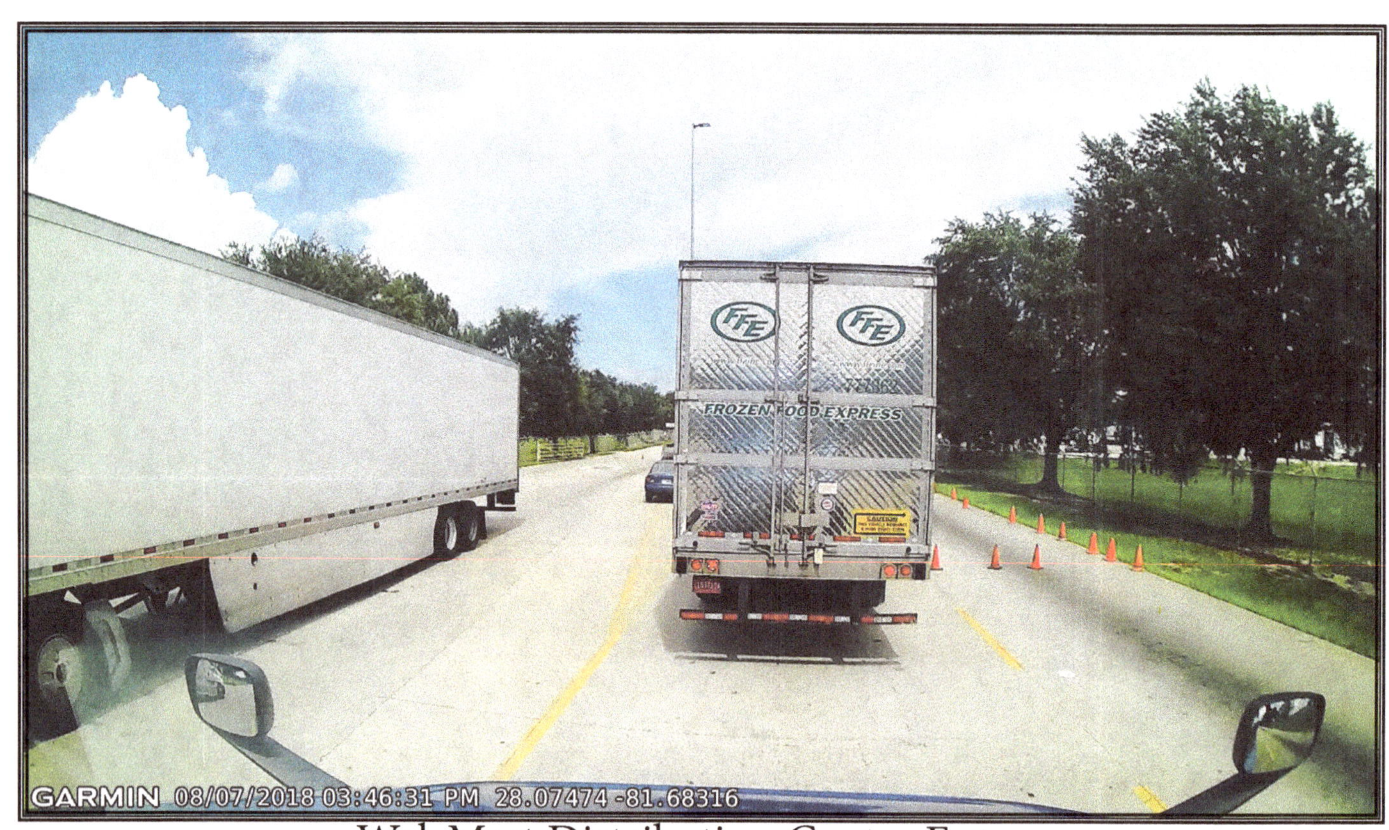

Wal-Mart Distribution Center Entrance
Winter Haven, Florida

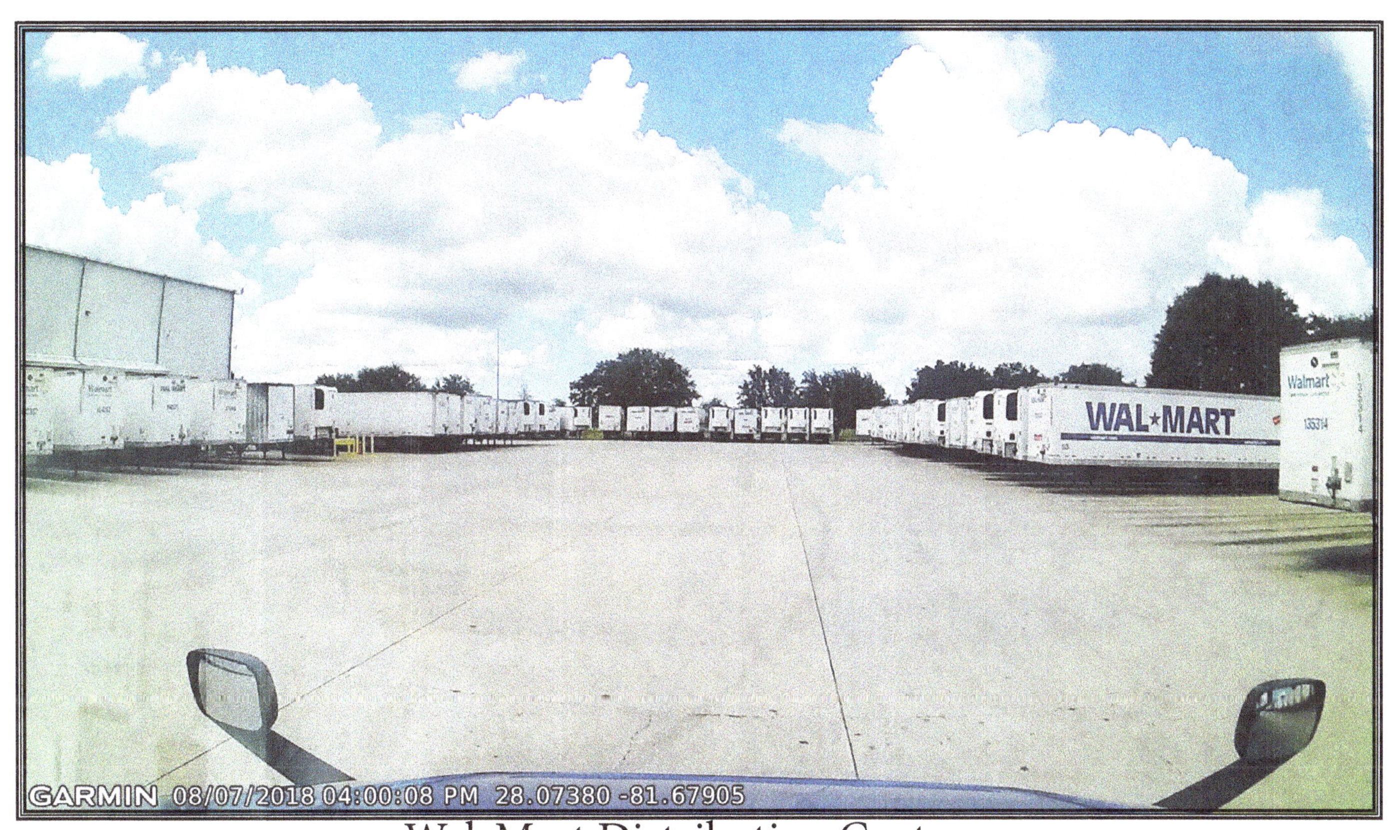

Wal-Mart Distribution Center
Winter Haven, Flori

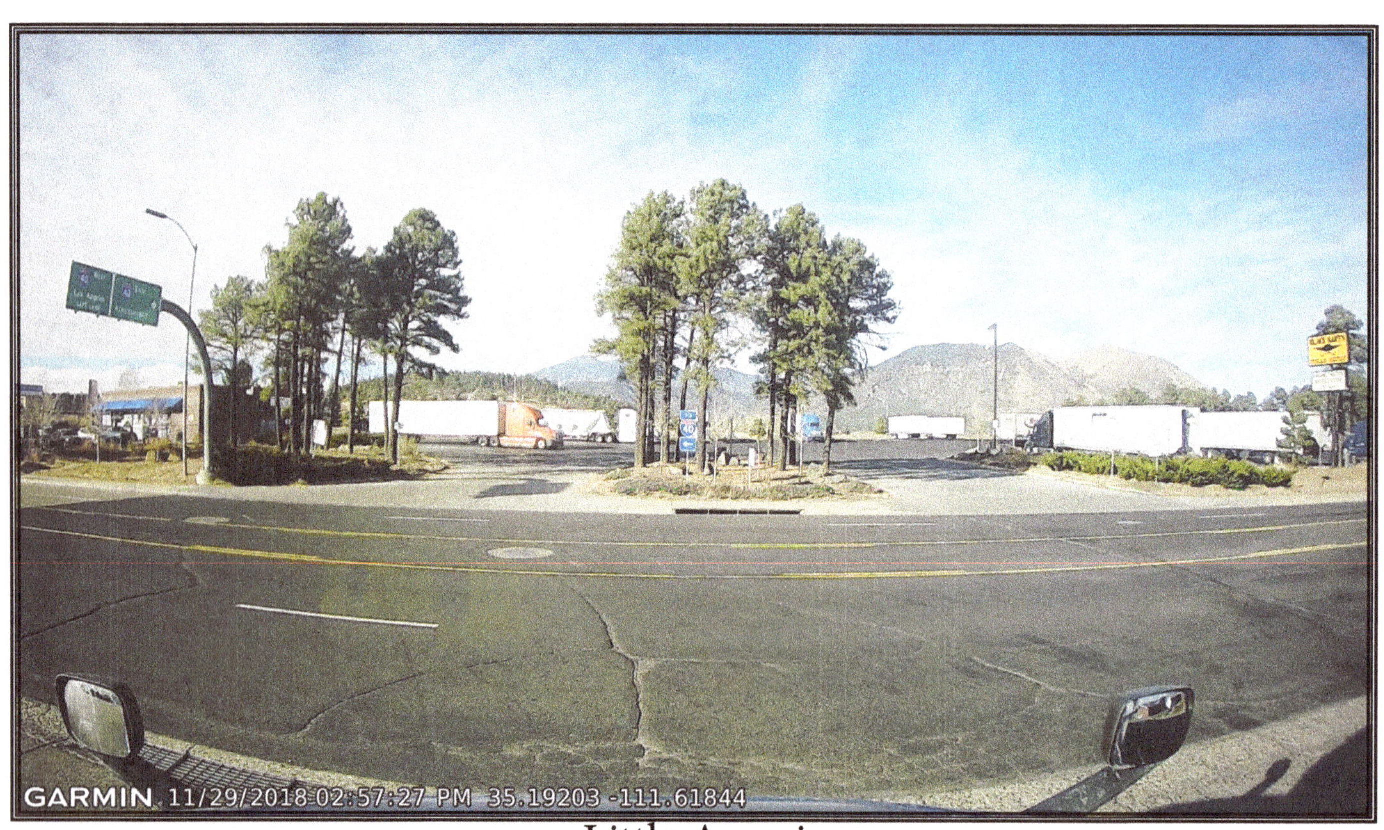

Little America
I-40, Flagstaff, Arizona

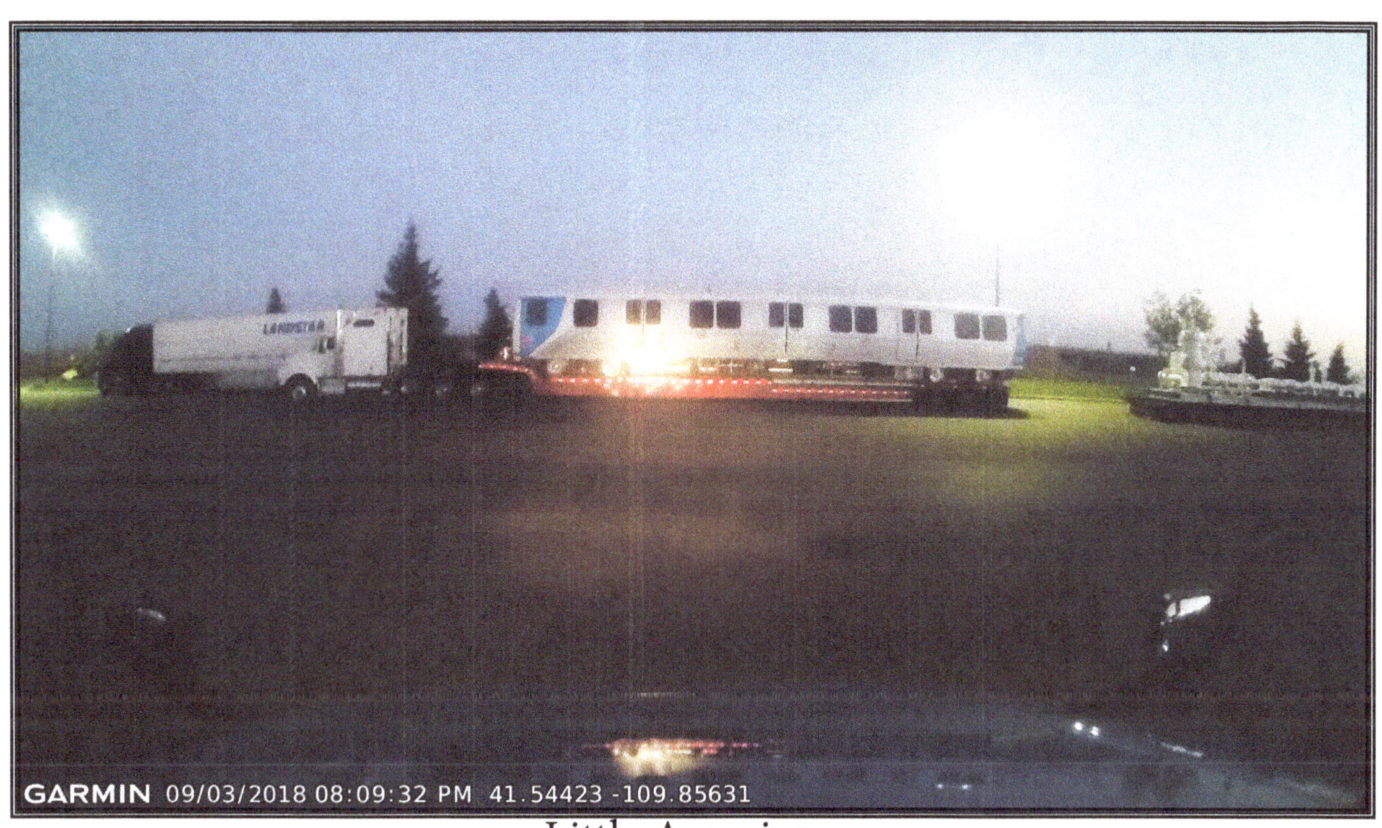

Little America
I-80, Little America, Wyoming

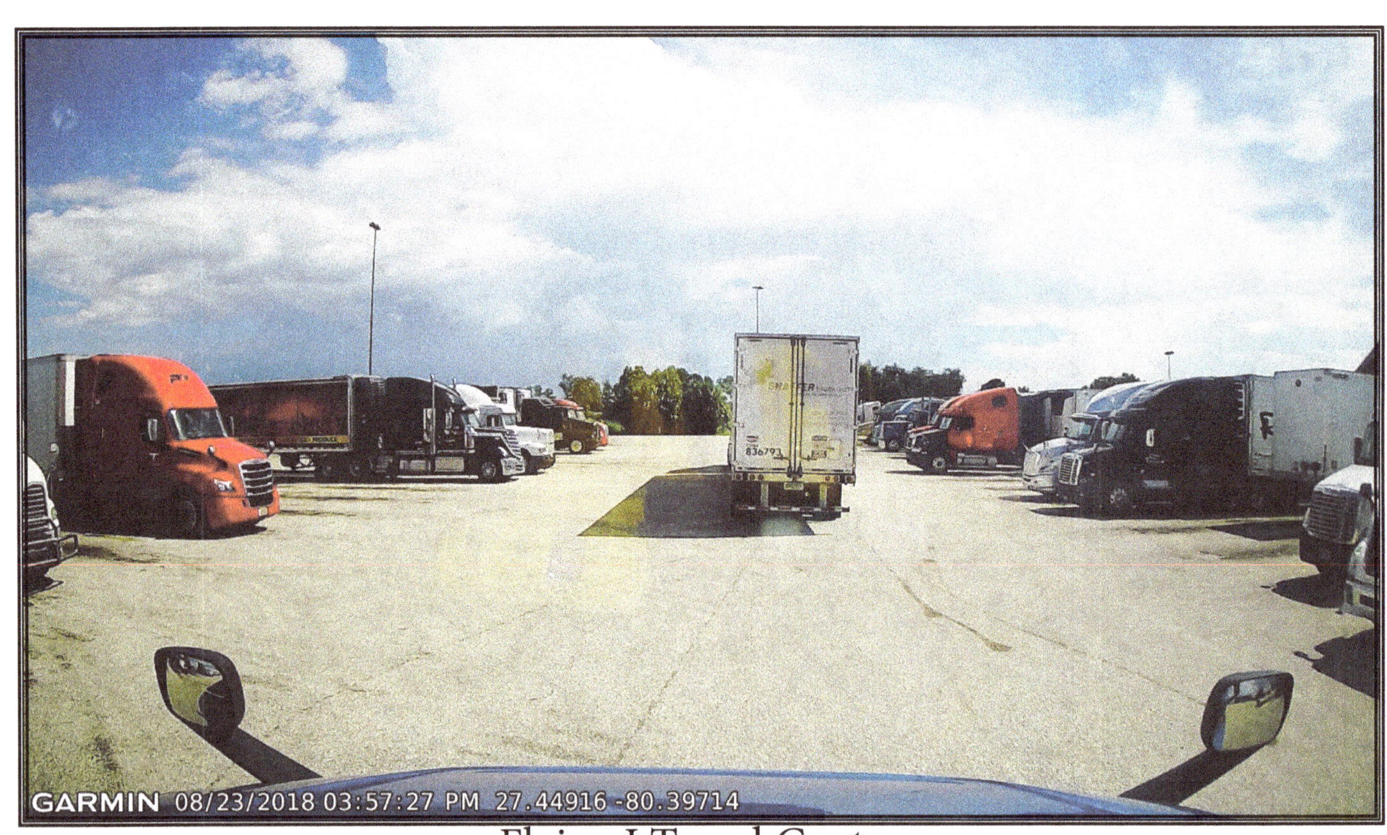

Flying J Travel Center
I-95, Fort Pierce, Florida

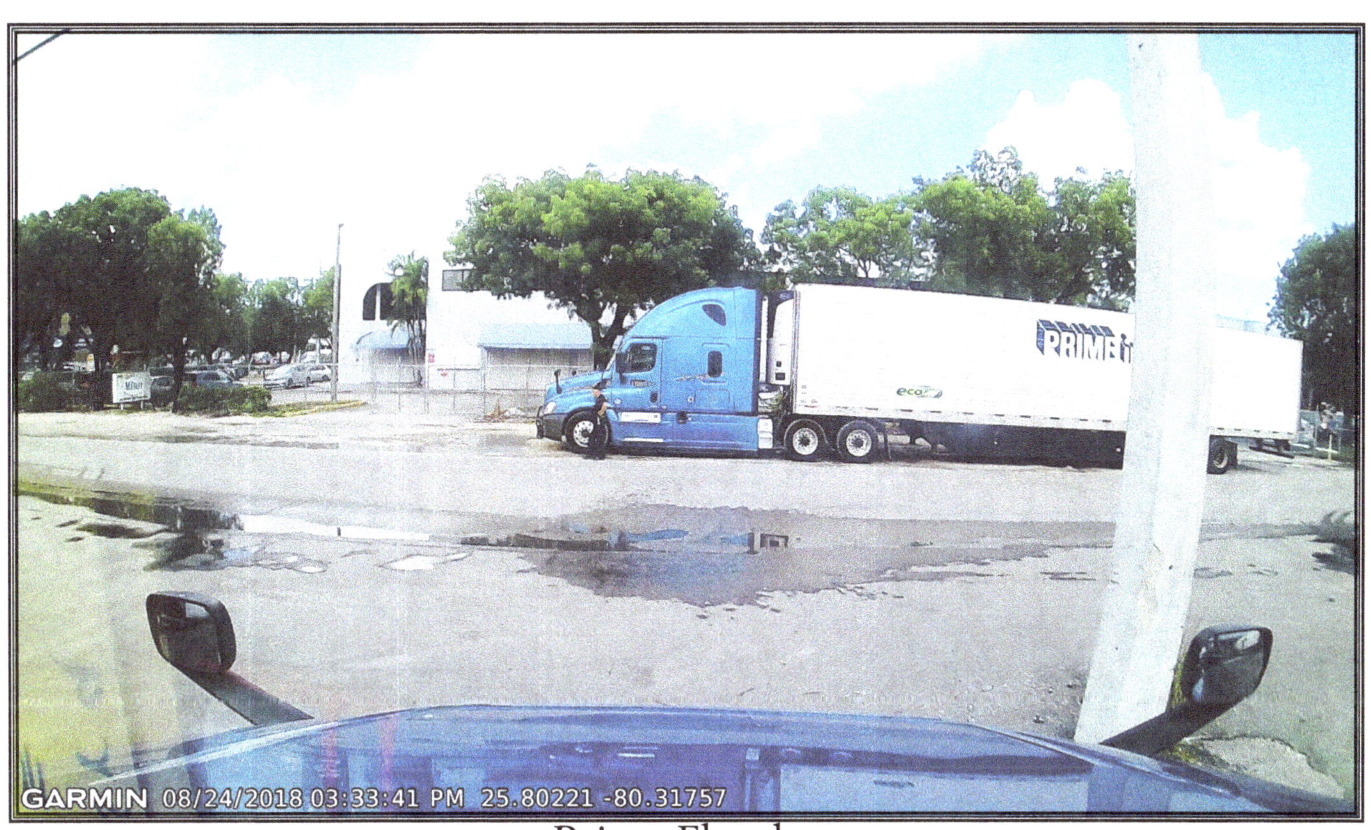

Prime Floral
Miami, Florida

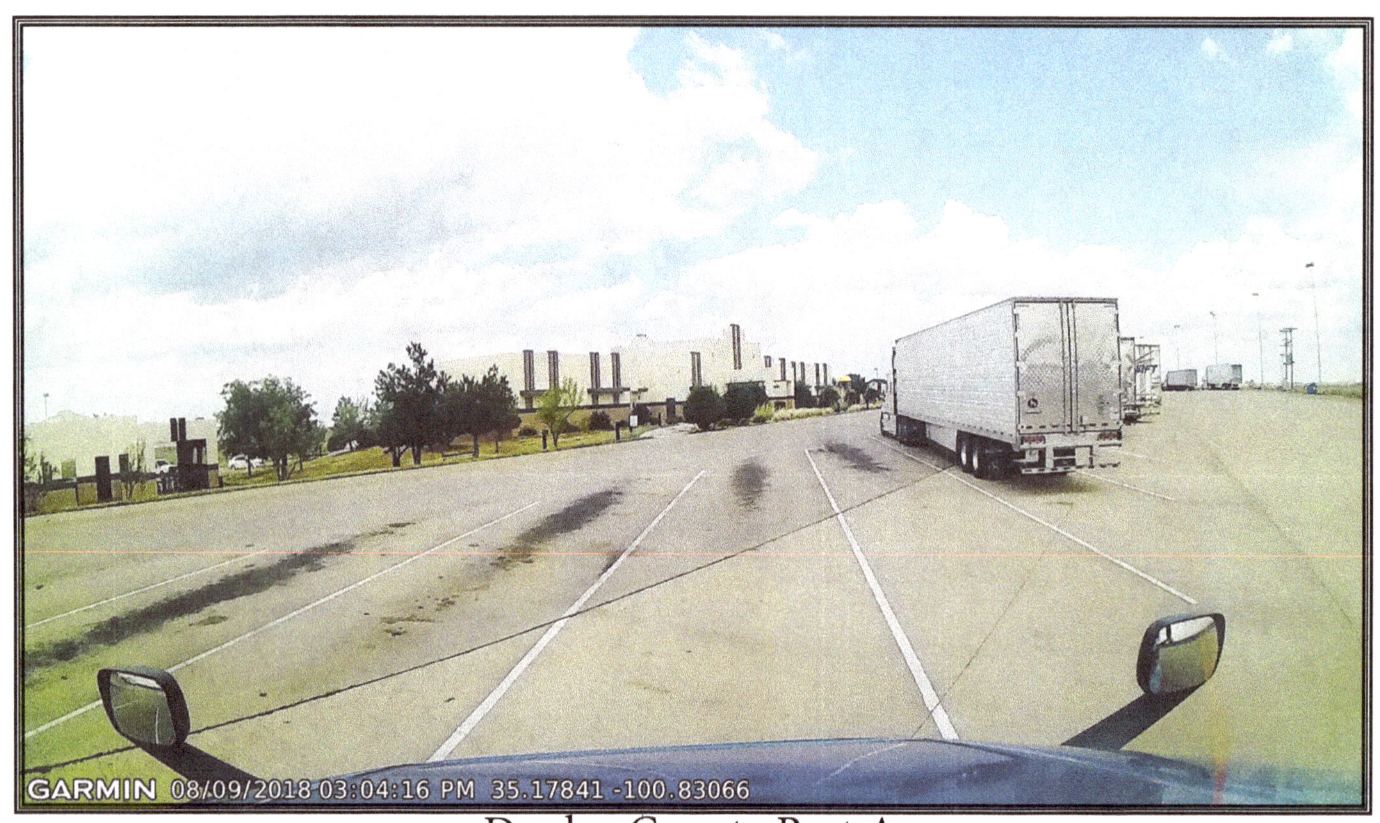

Donley County Rest Area
I-40, Clarendon, Texas

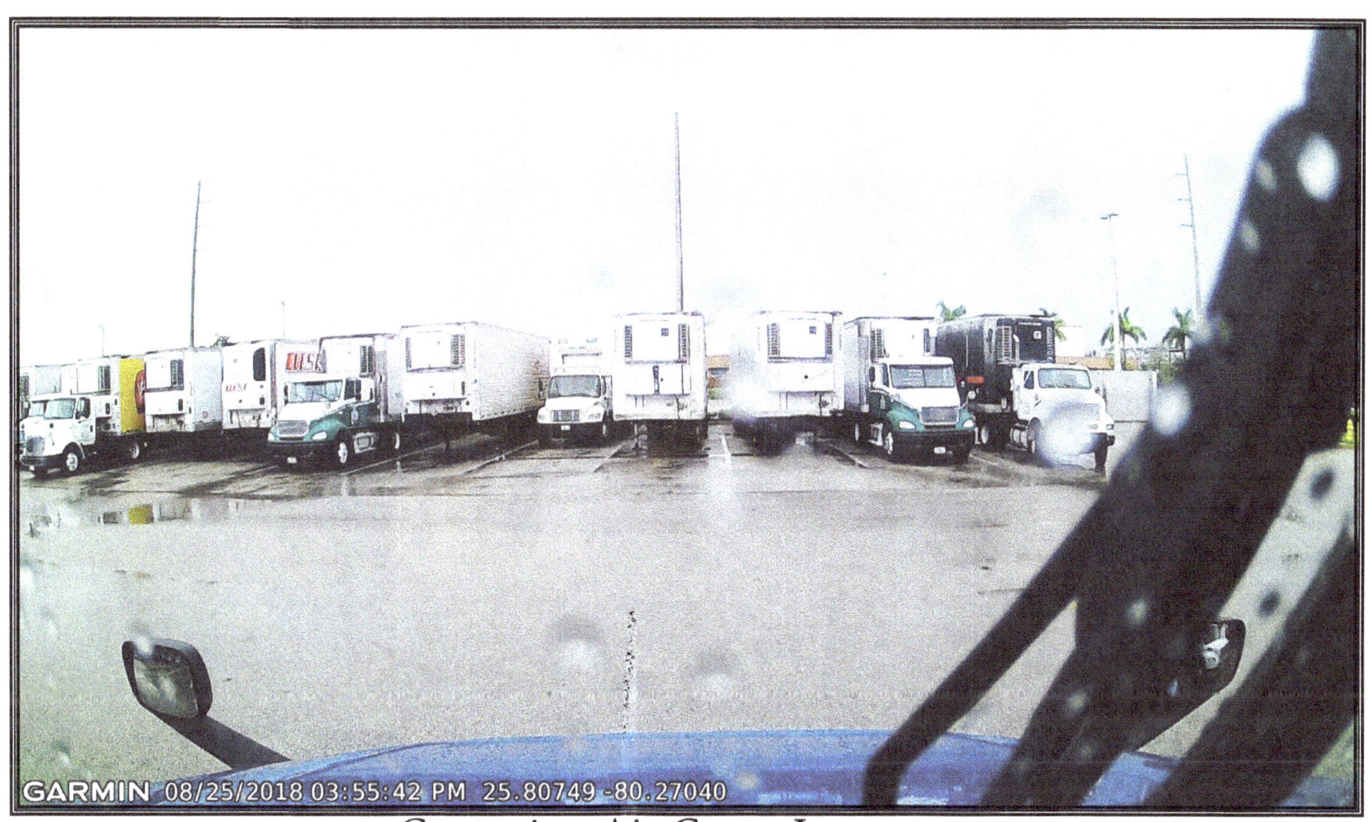

Centurion Air Cargo Imports
Miami, Florida

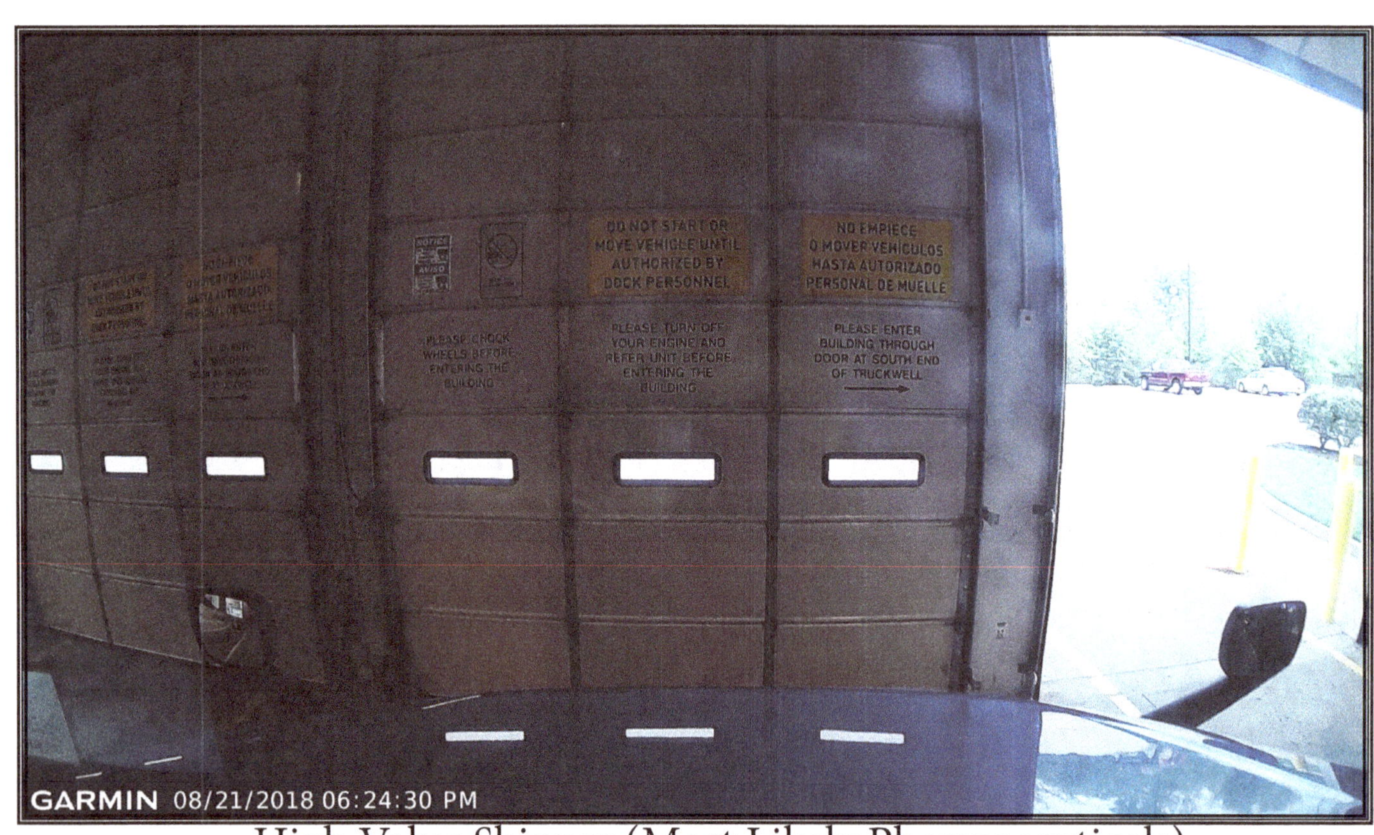

High Value Shipper (Most Likely Pharmaceuticals)
Somewhere, Indiana

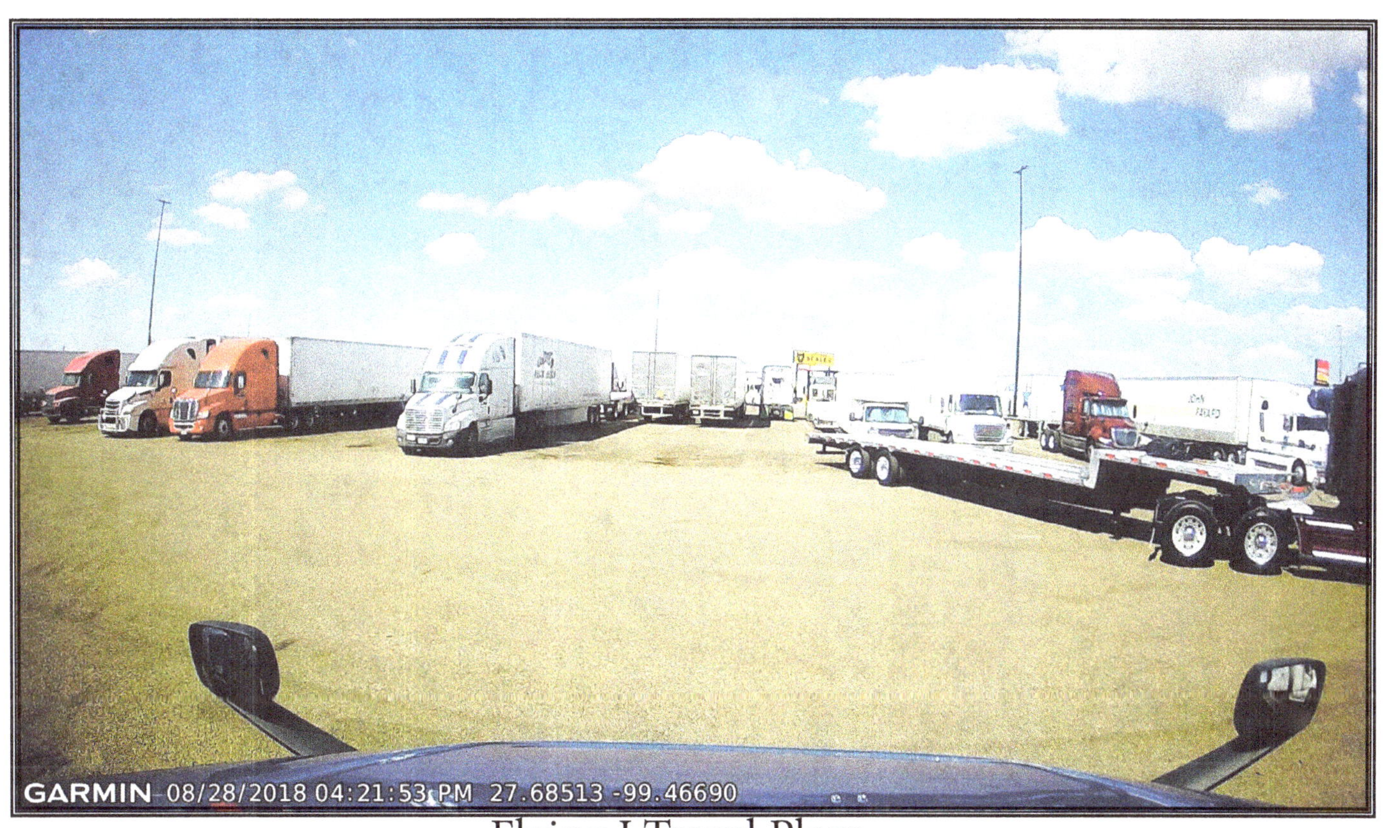

Flying J Travel Plaza
I-35, Laredo, Texas

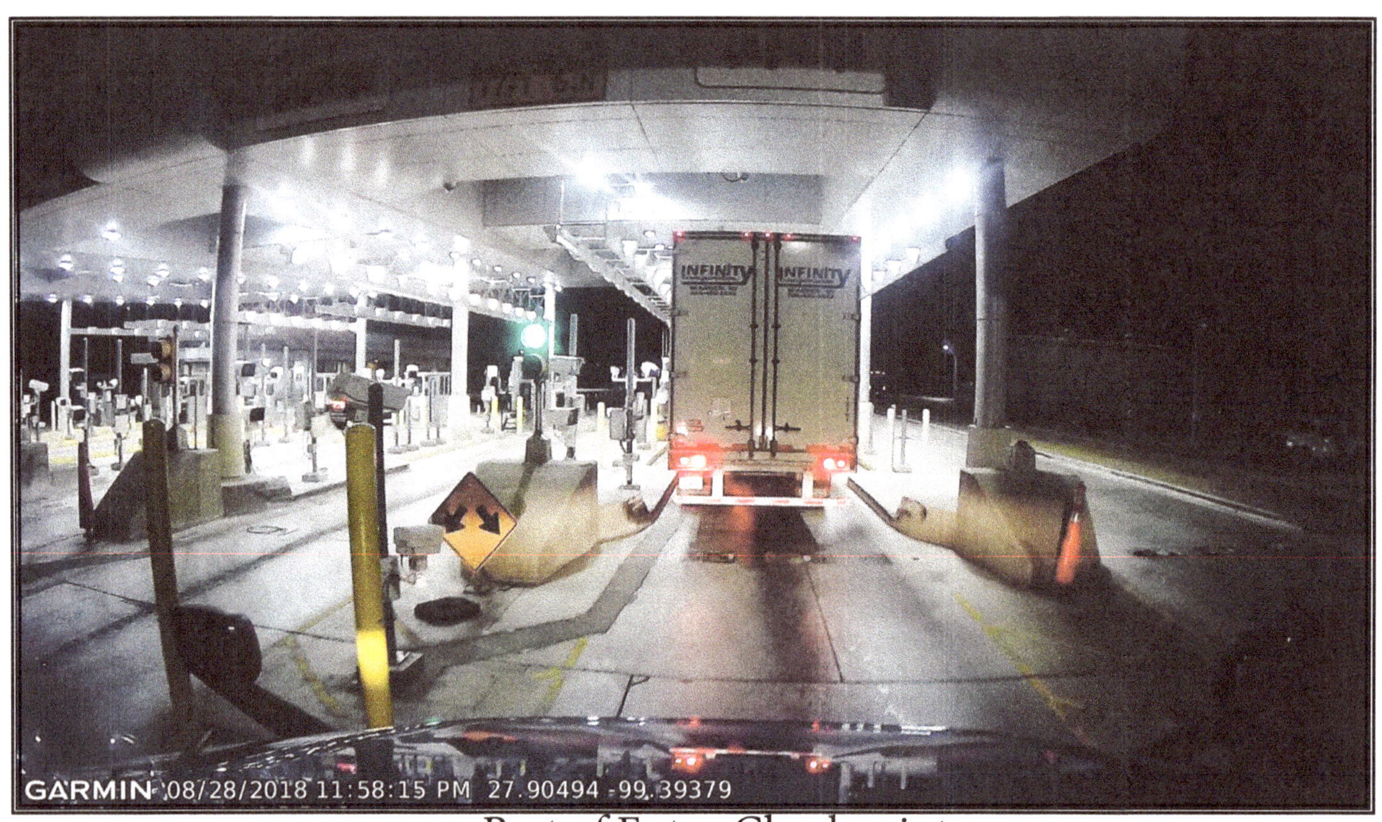

Port of Entry Checkpoint
I-35, Encinal, Texas

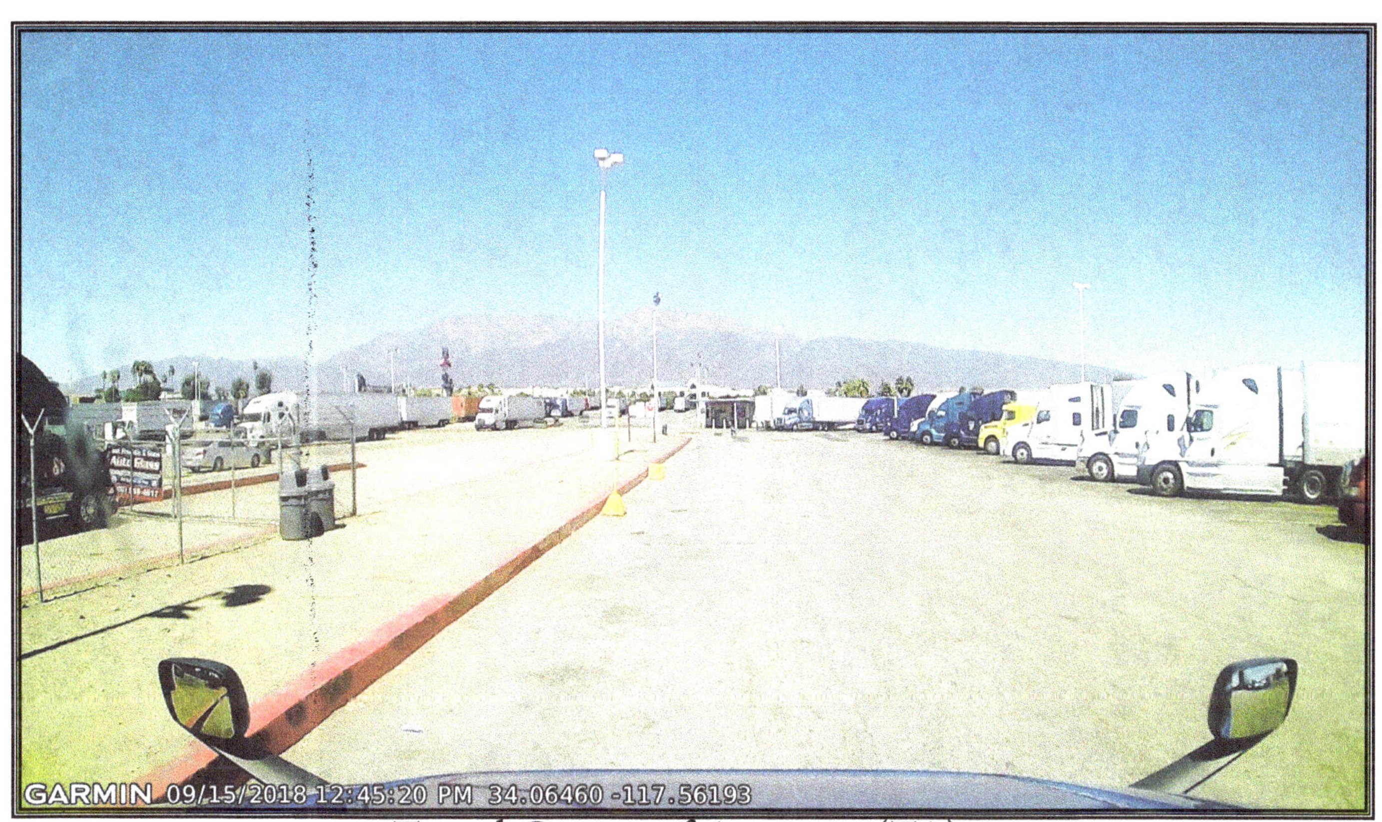

Travel Center of America (TA)
I-10, Ontario, California

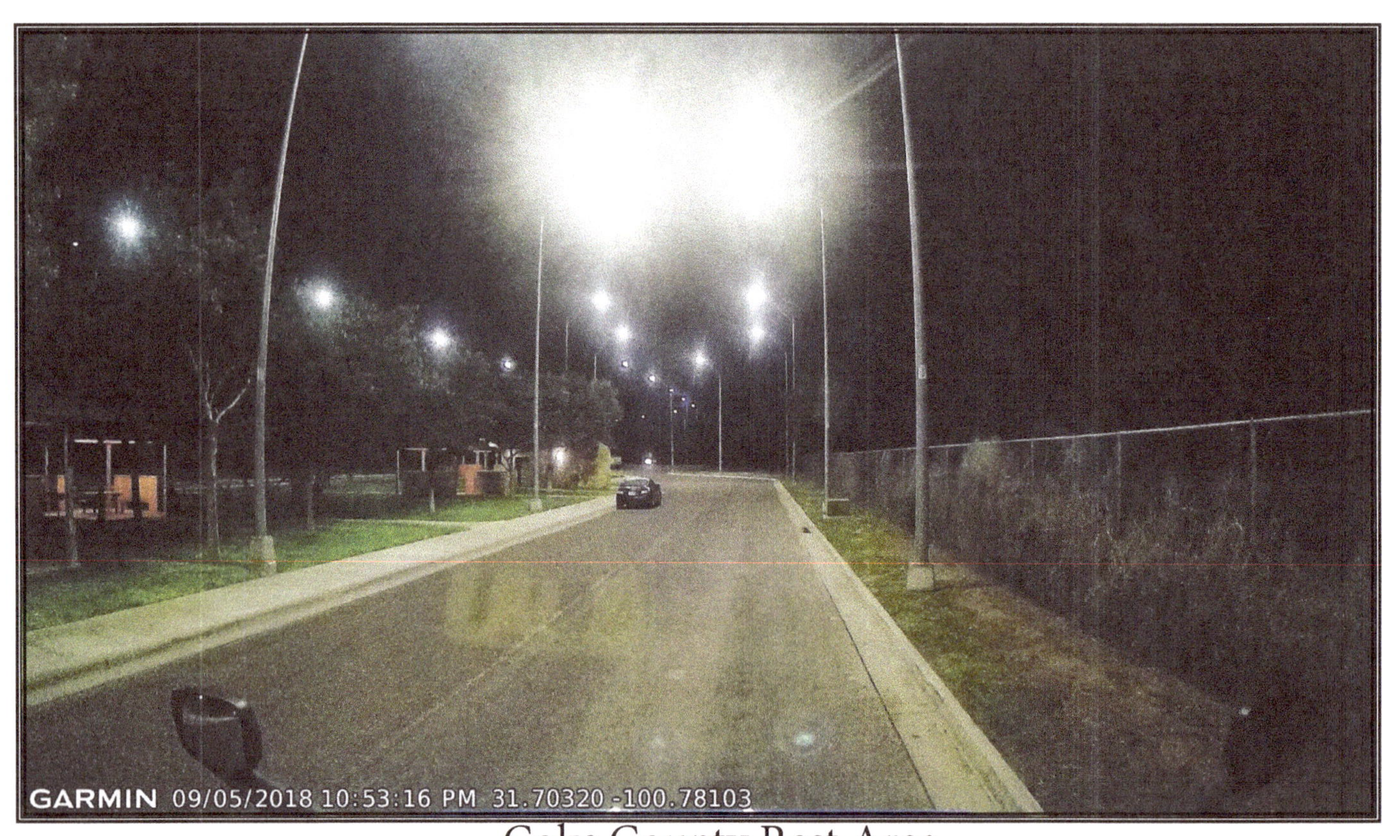

Coke County Rest Area
US-87, Robert Lee, Texas

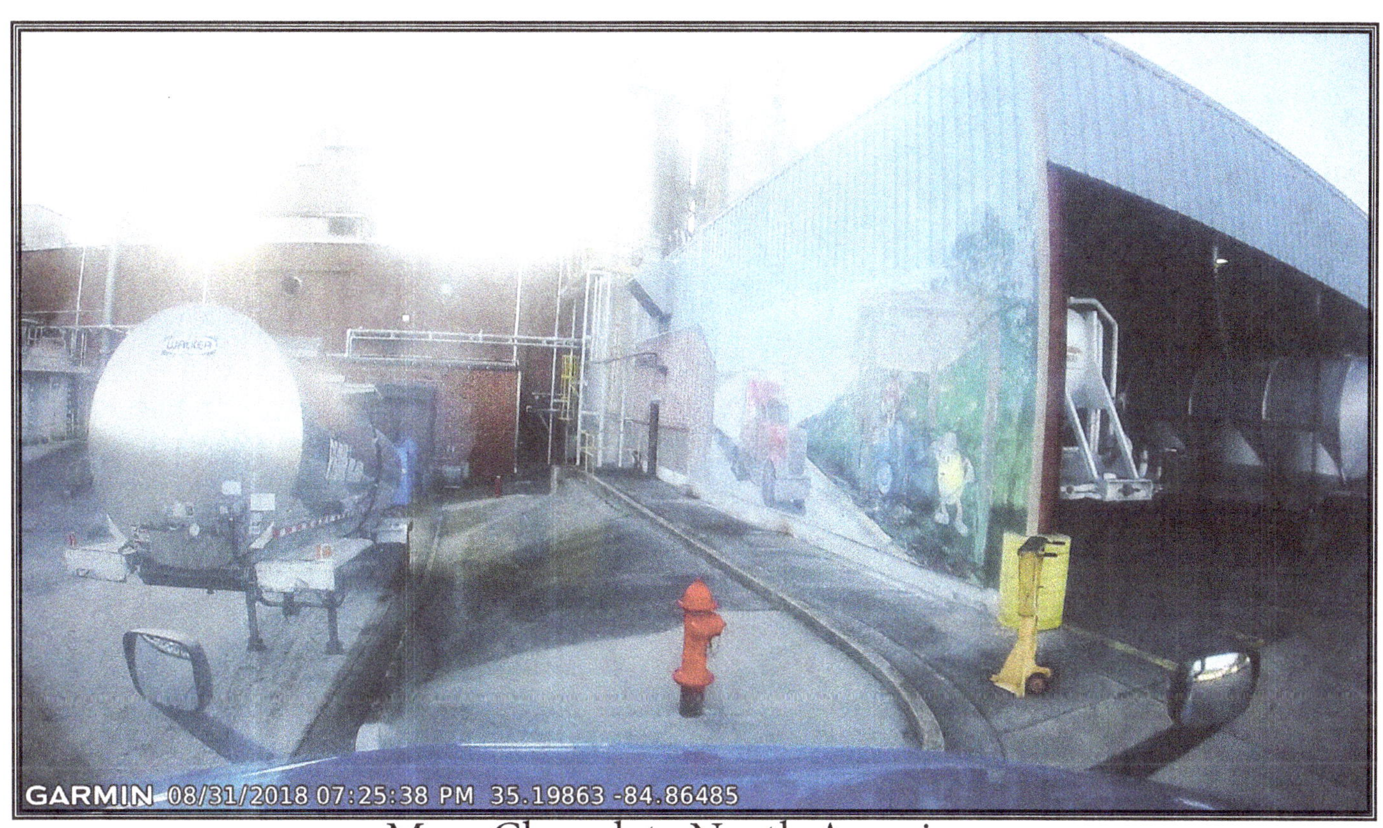

Mars Chocolate North America
Cleveland, Tennessee

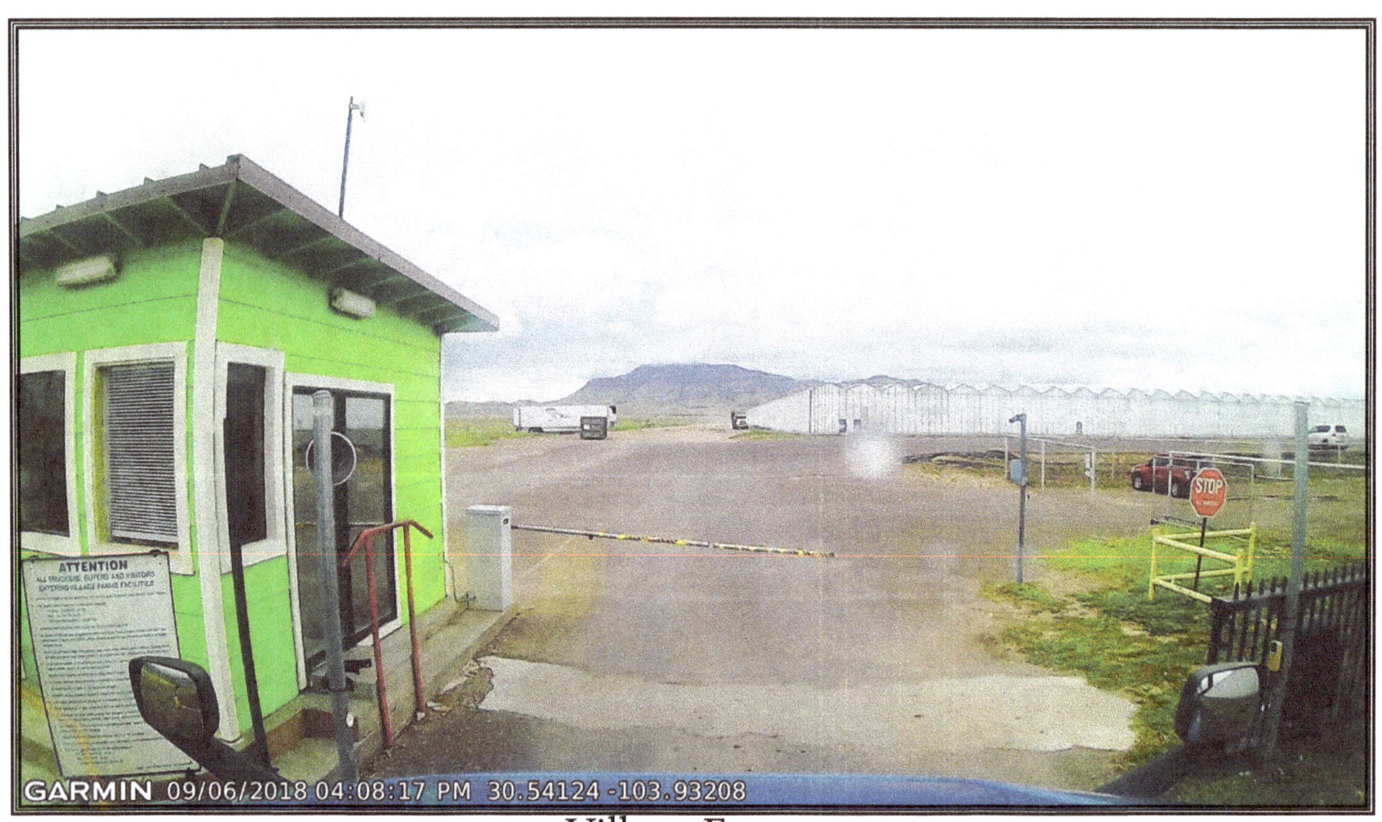

Village Farms
US-17, Fort Davis, Texas

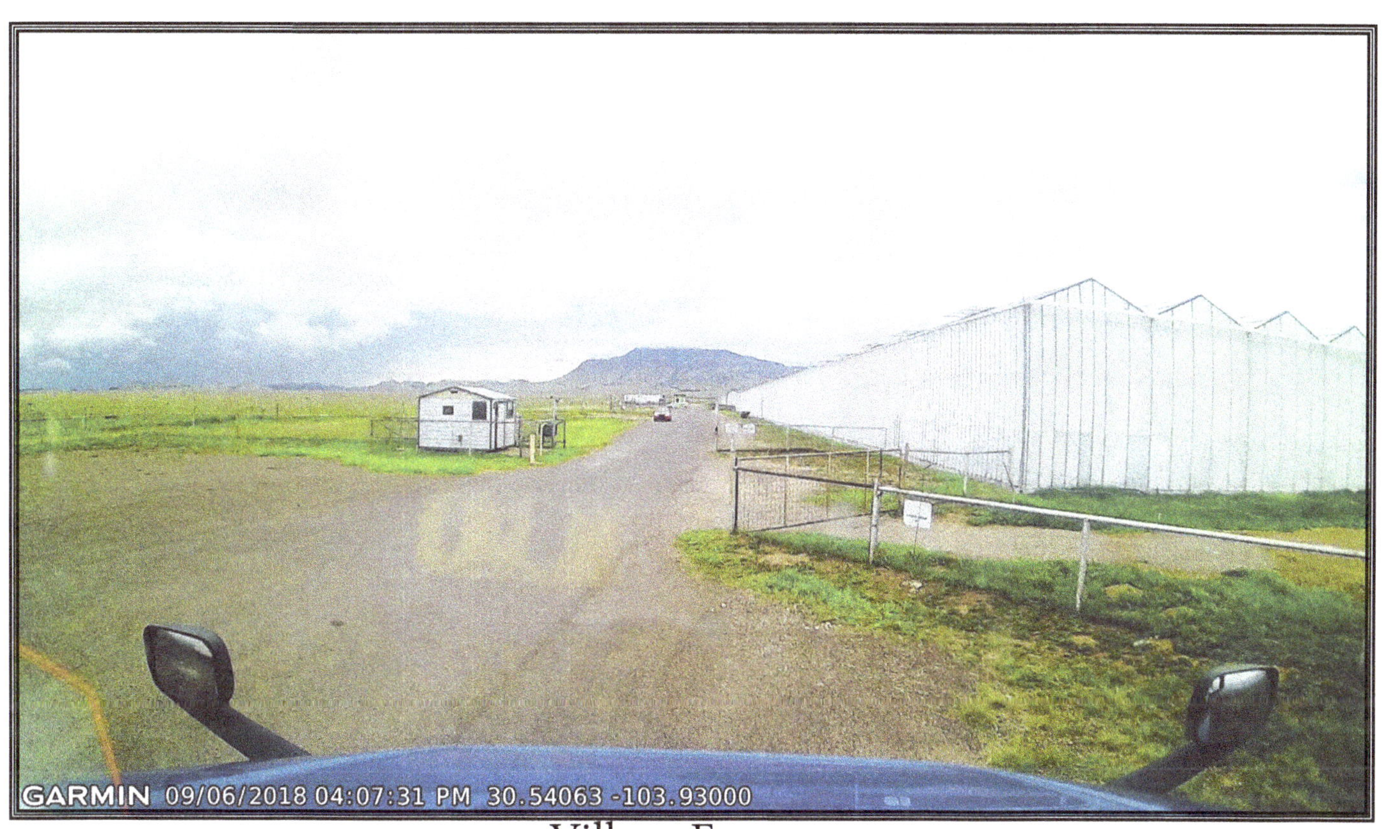

Village Farms
US-17, Fort Davis, Texas

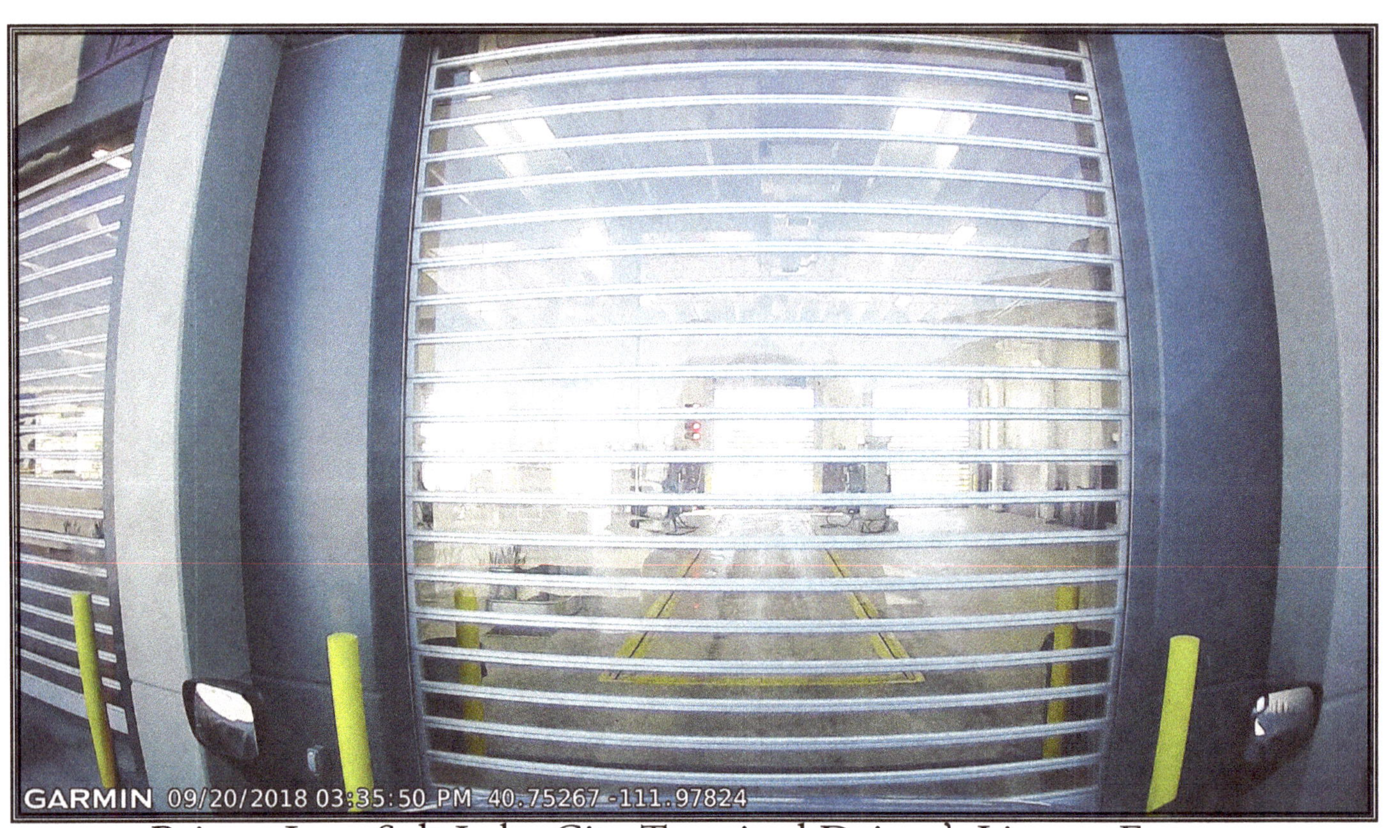

Prime, Inc., Salt Lake City Terminal Driver's Lineup Entrance
Salt Lake City, Utah

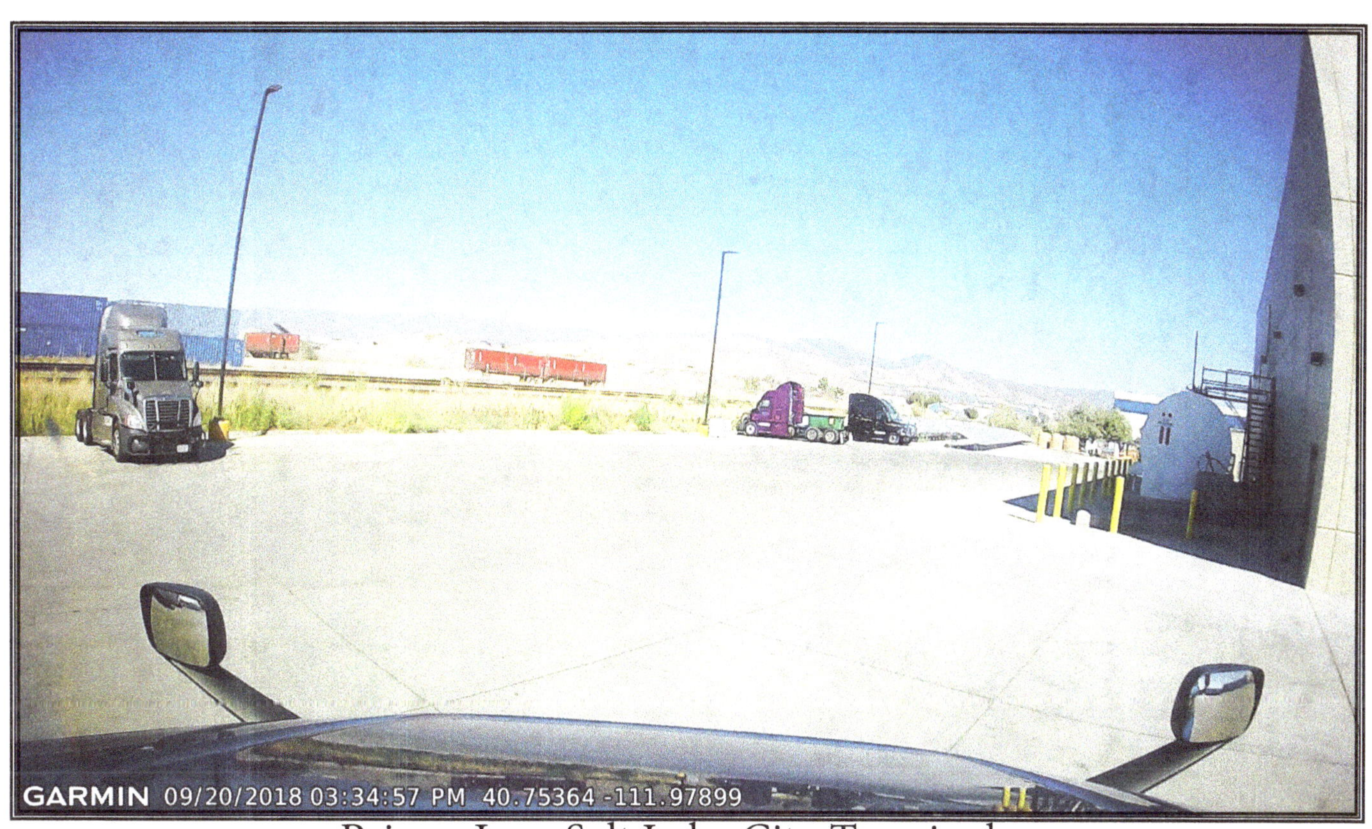

Prime, Inc., Salt Lake City Terminal
Salt Lake City, Utah

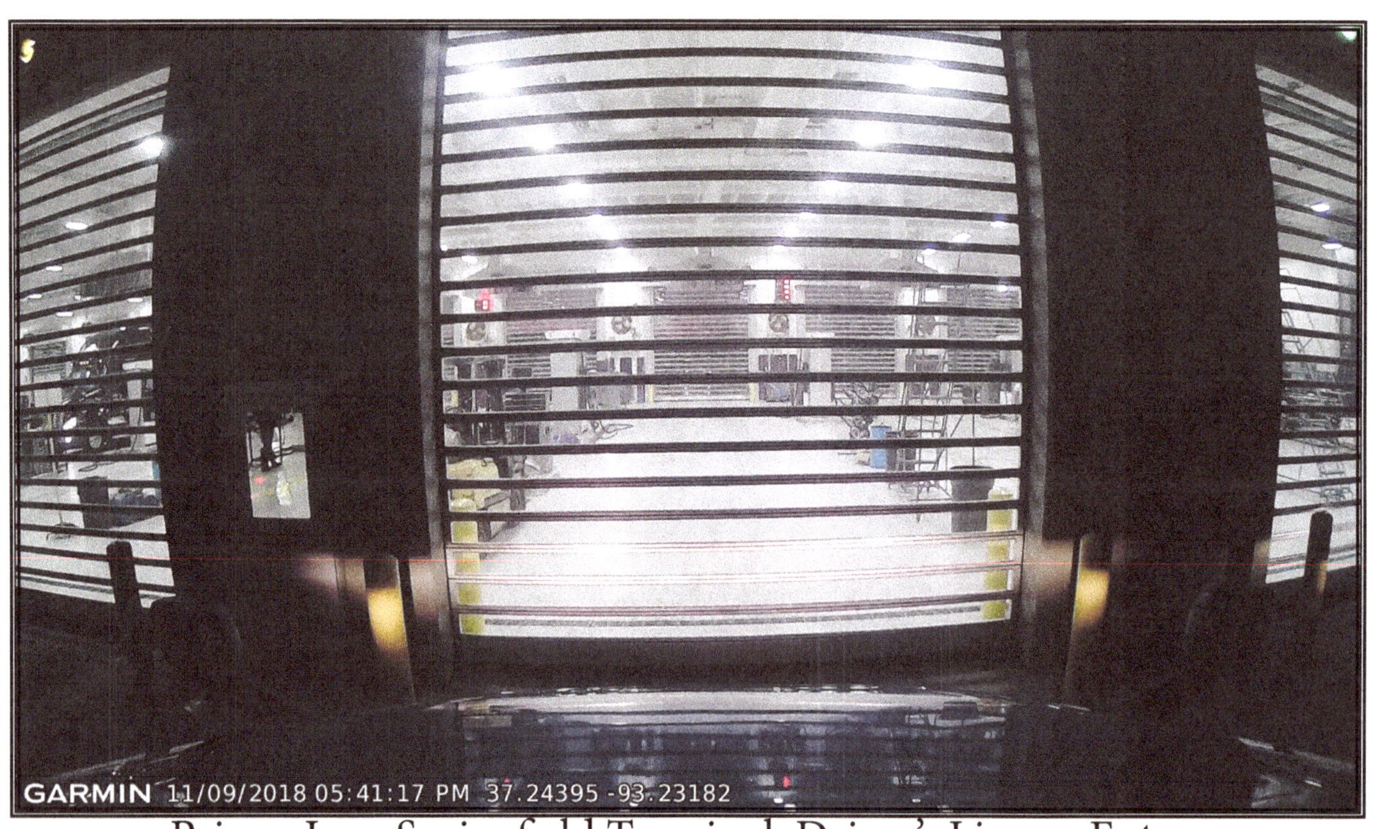

Prime, Inc., Springfield Terminal, Driver's Lineup Entrance
Springfield, Missouri

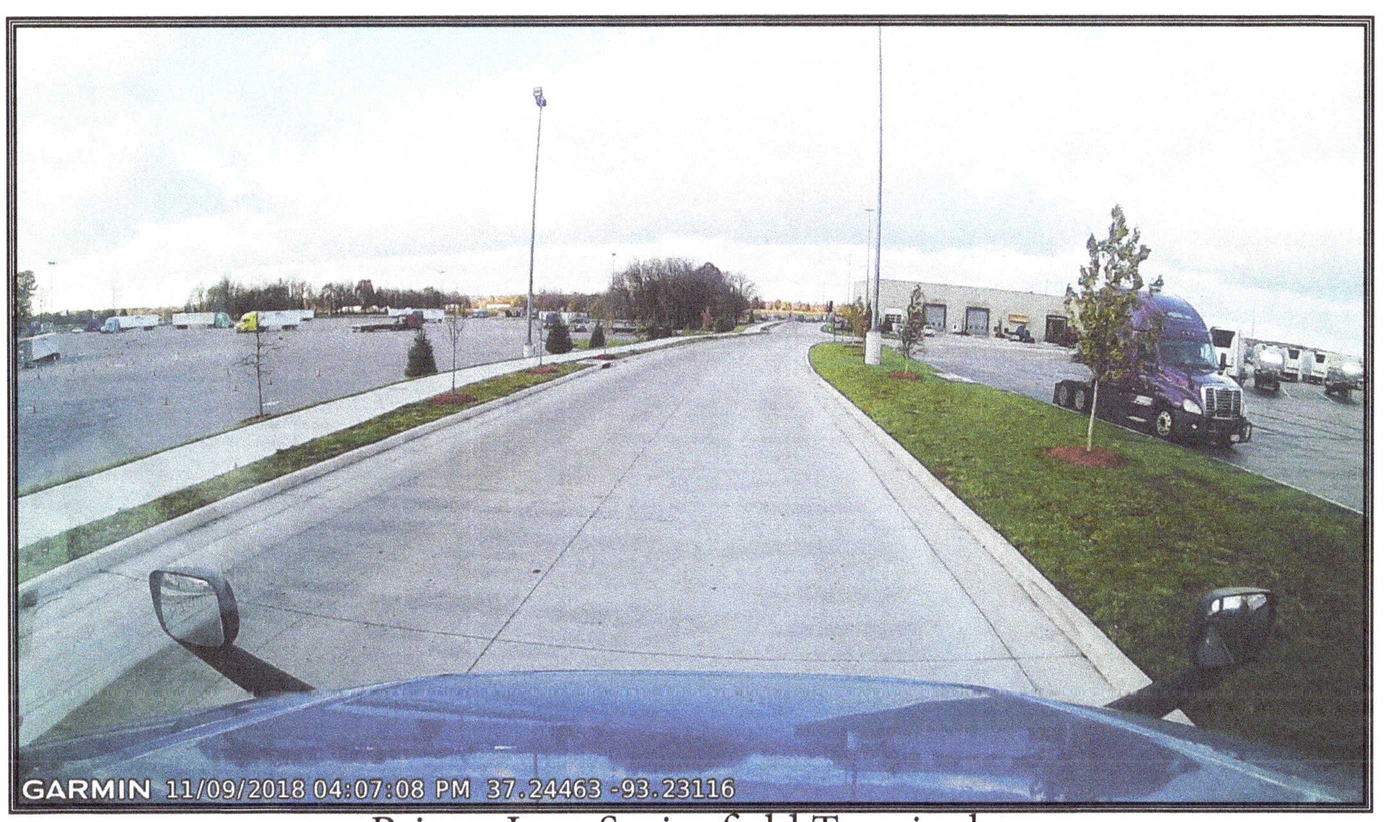

Prime, Inc., Springfield Terminal
Springfield, Missouri

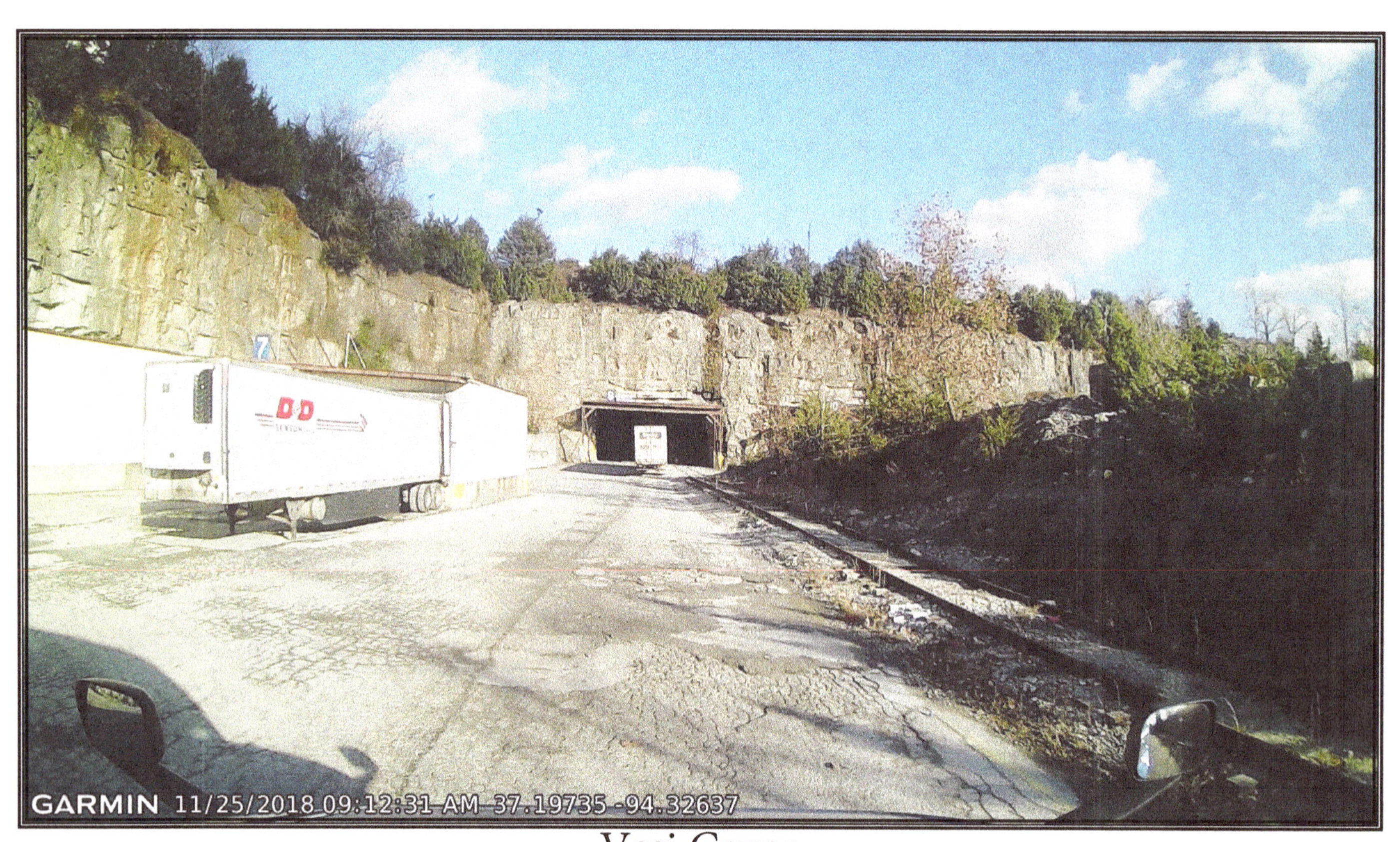

Vssi Caves
Civil War Road, Carthage, Missouri
Photo Credit: Mark Speir, my brother and co-driver

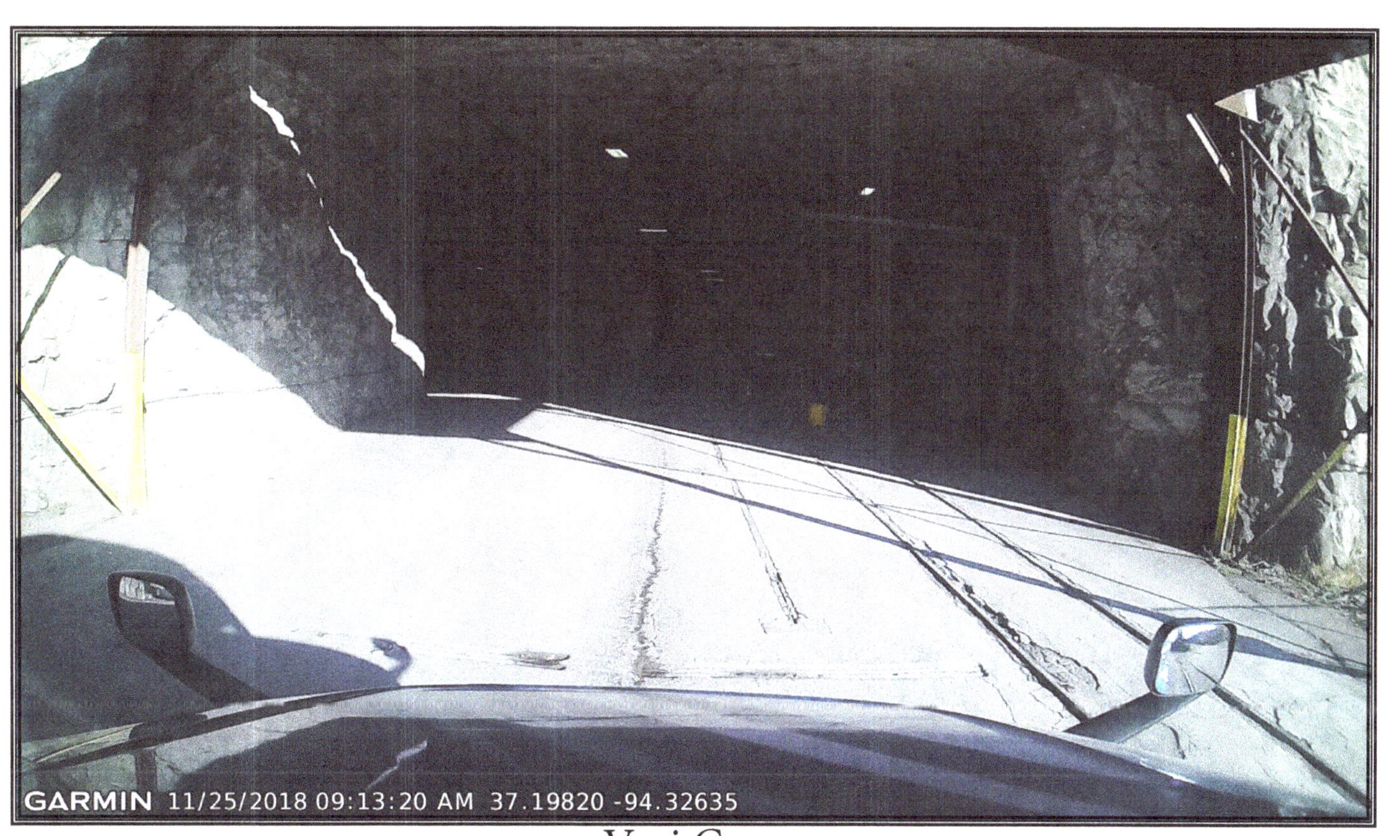

Vssi Caves
Civil War Road, Carthage, Missouri
Photo Credit: Mark Speir, my brother and co-driver

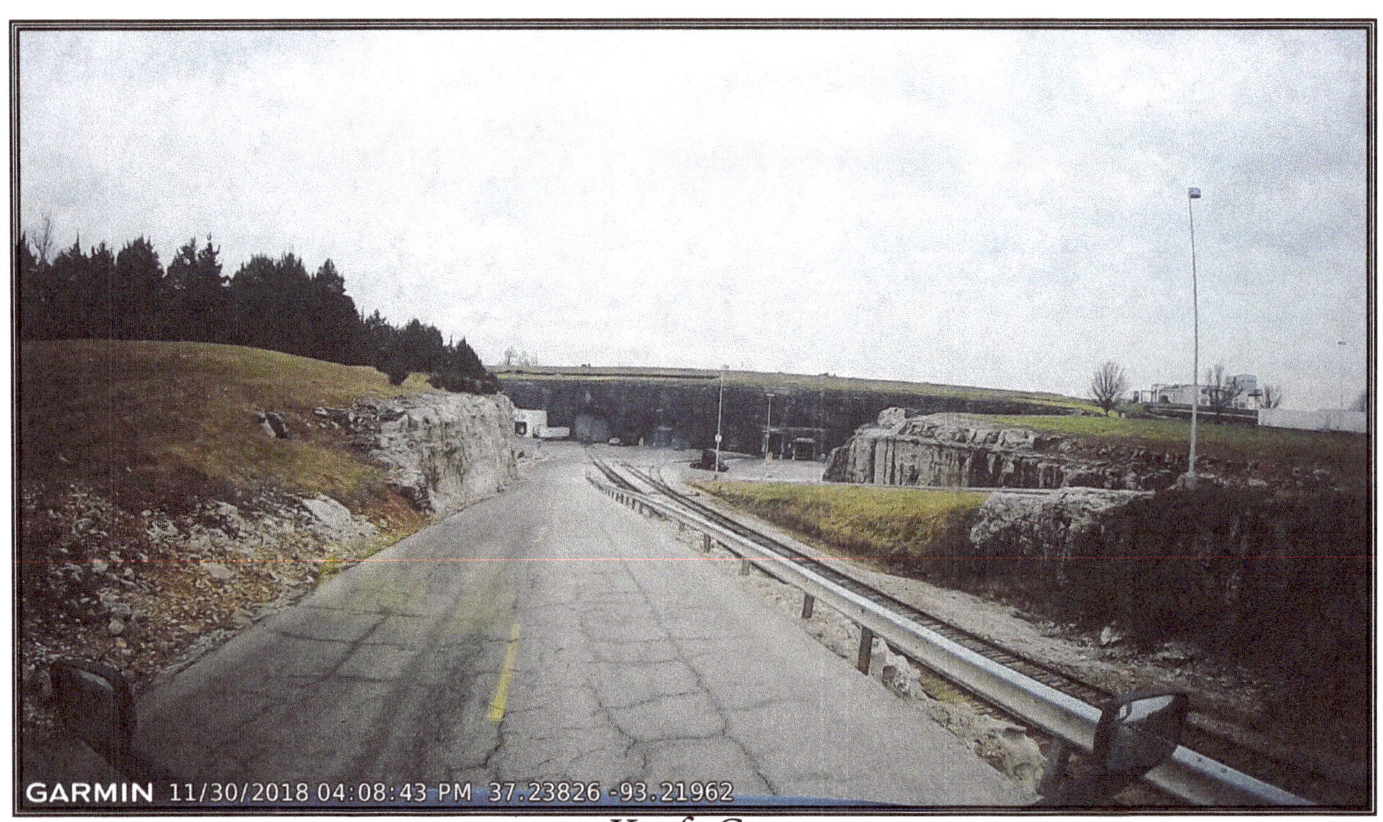

Kraft Caves
Springfield, Missouri

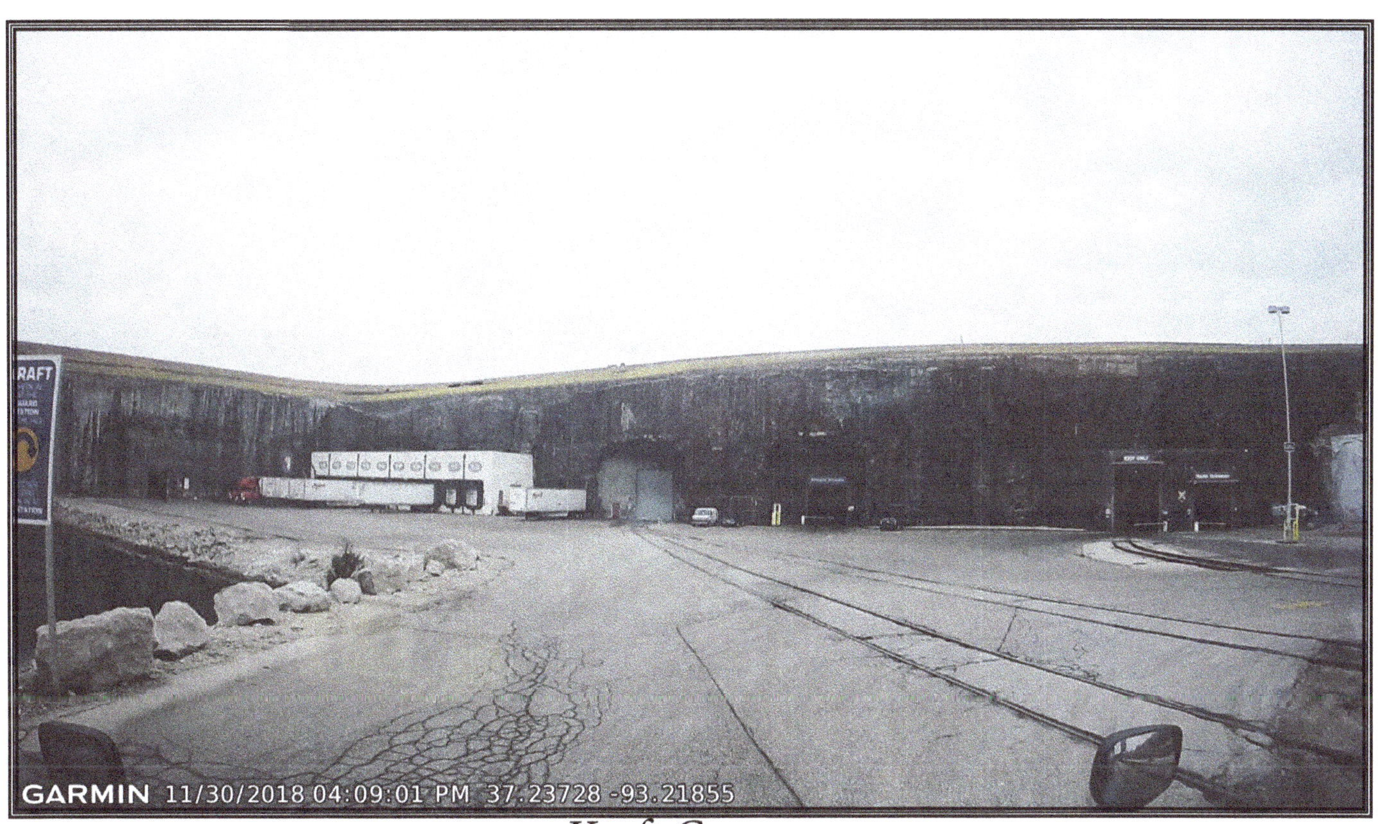

Kraft Caves
Springfield, Missouri

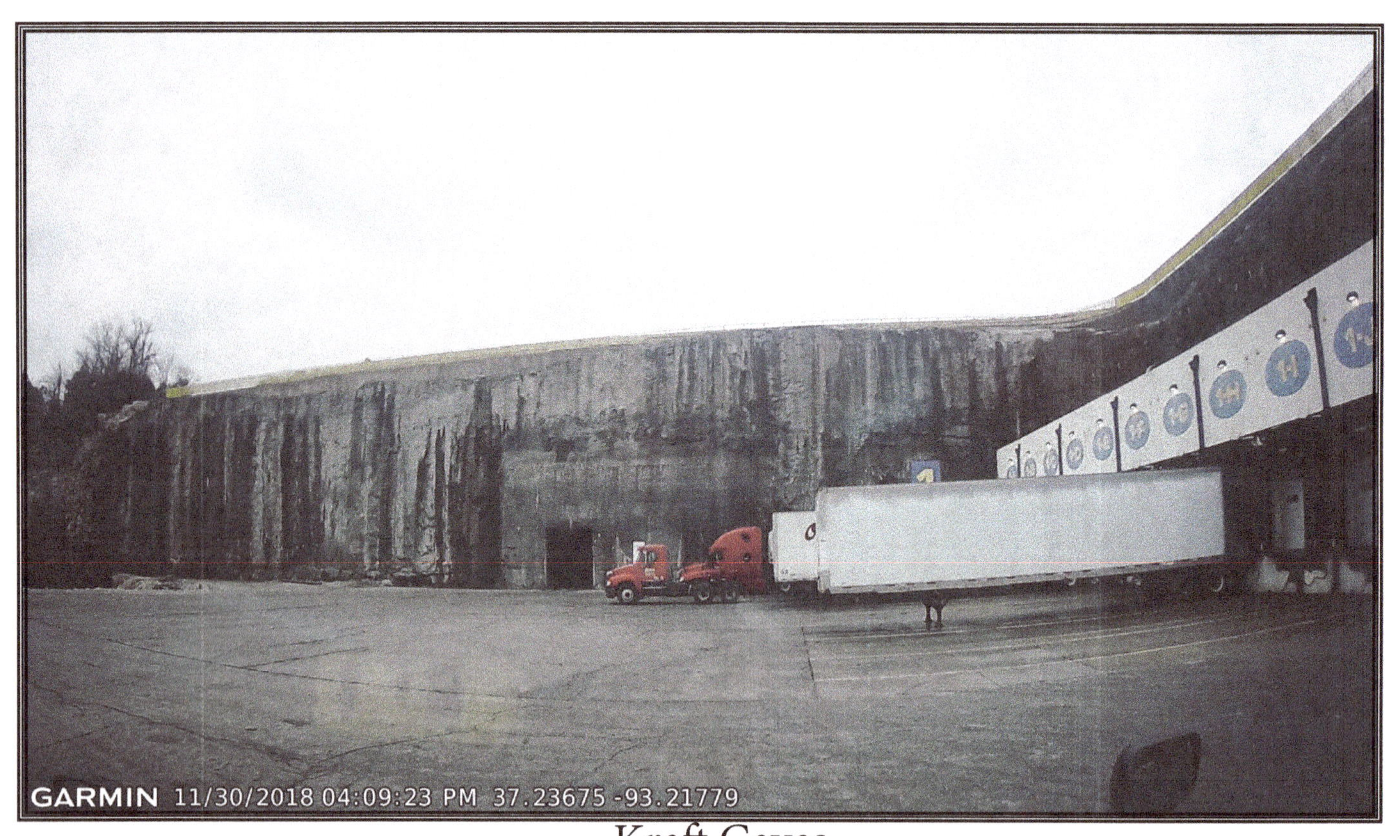

Kraft Caves
Springfield, Missouri

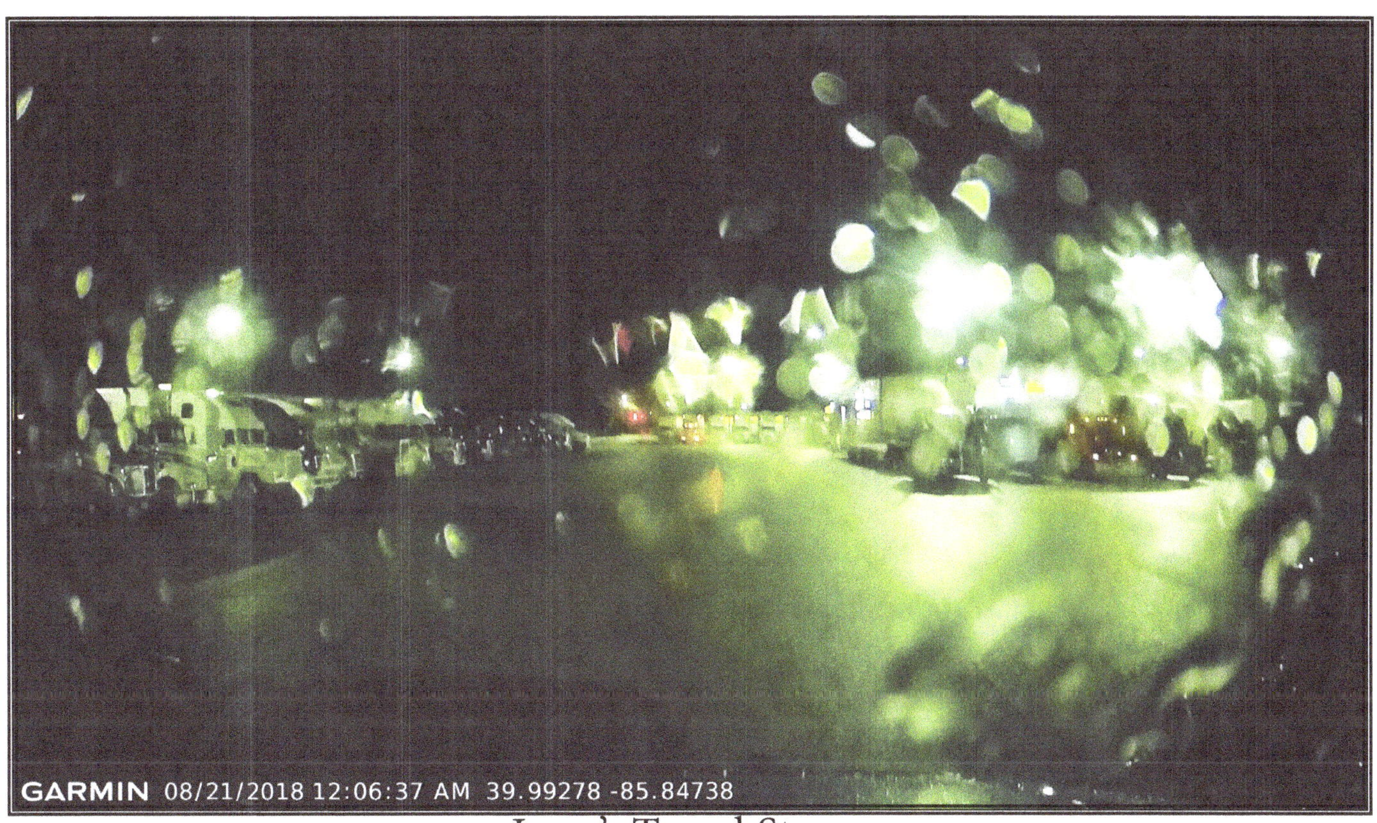

Love's Travel Stop
I-69, Green Township, Indiana

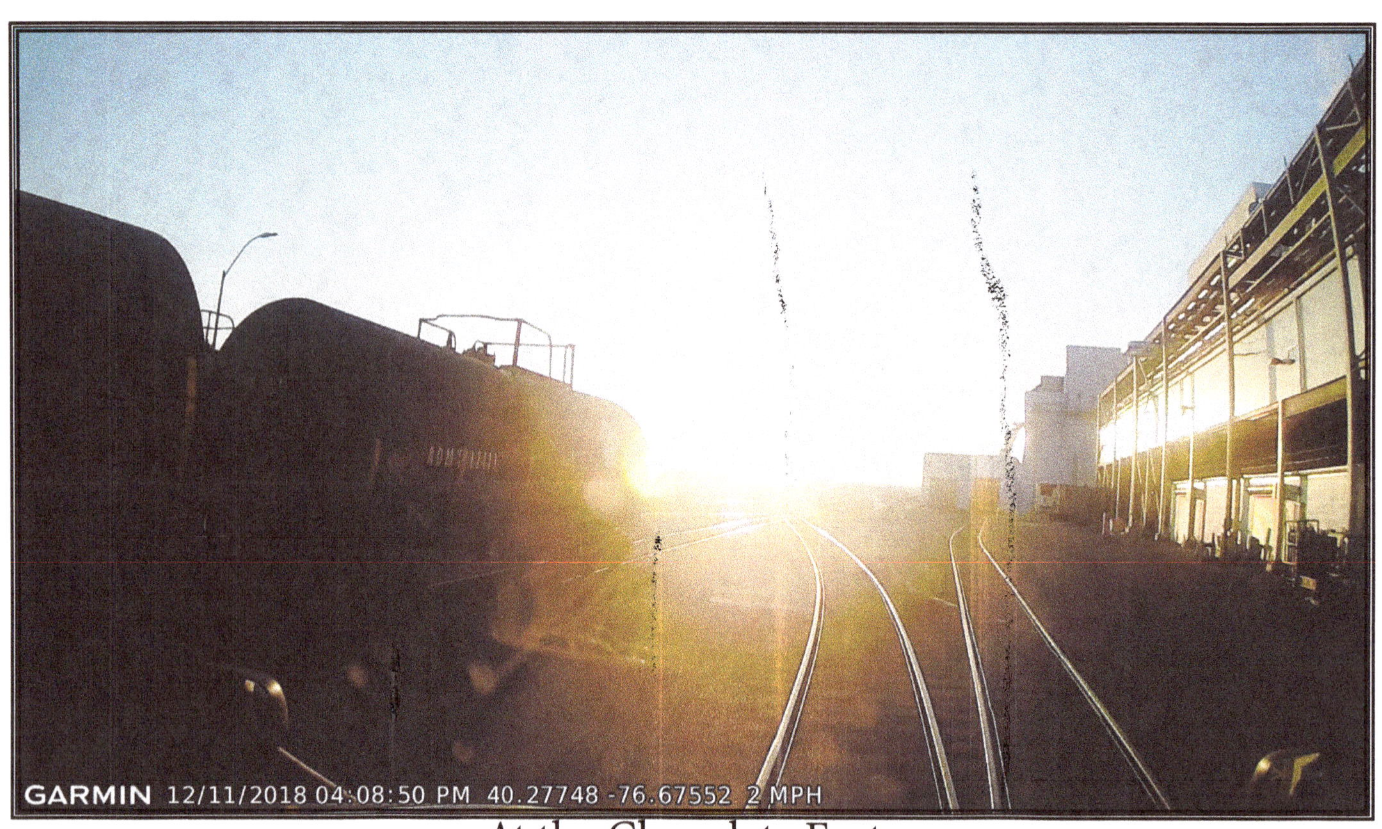

At the Chocolate Factory
Hershey, Pennsylvania

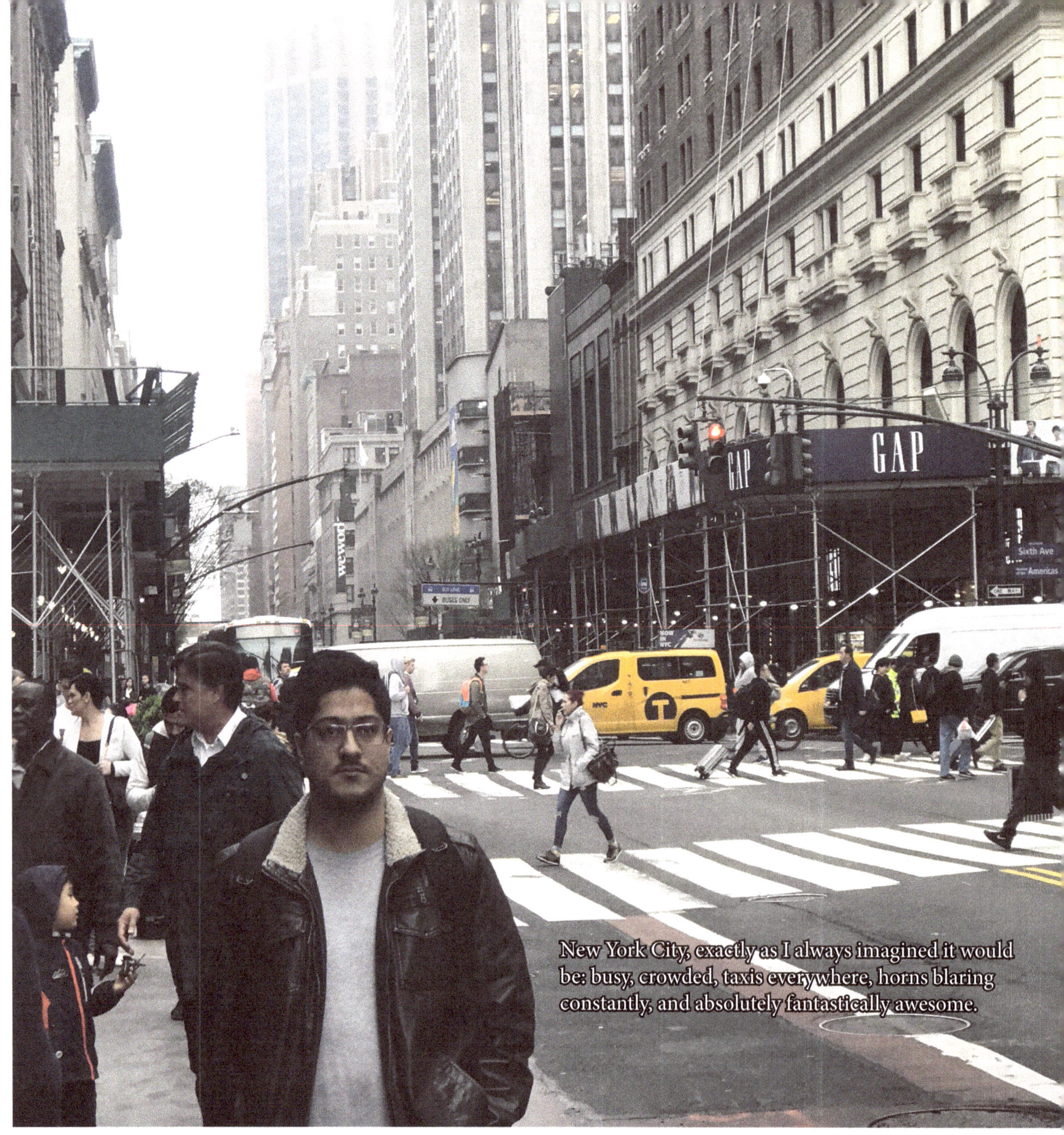

GAP
Sixth Ave
Americas
New York City, exactly as I always imagined it would
be: busy, crowded, taxis everywhere, horns blaring
constantly, and absolutely fantastically awesome.

Part Three
Cities, Towns & Everything in Between

In the past year I have traveled to most major cities and countless small towns and townships across this great country of ours. When possible I parked the truck and took Uber, taxis, or public transportation to go explore the local scene. I have explored Santa Maria, Ontario, Los Angeles, Allentown, St. Louis, Binghamton, and New York City, to name a few.

What have I learned in my travels? People are the same everywhere you go. Sure, in small-town Wisconsin they are perhaps friendlier than in New York City, when viewed in large groups. But if you get down to a more personal level, the subway attendant who helped me understand the intricacies of the New York City subway system was just as friendly as the clerk in the Wisconsin convenience store who offered to mail the letter to my wife rather than have me walk four blocks to the post office.

America is a beautiful country, and one of the things that makes it beautiful is its diversity. Everywhere you go in America you will find a sampling of humanity. You will find the greedy, the angry, the sad, the despairing, the vengeful, the lovely, the charismatic, the joyful, the poor. Often you will find all of these at once, and that is okay. This is what it means to be human, and we all experience the full gambit of emotions that make up the human condition. Everywhere you go in this country you will find somebody just like you, somebody just like me.

And that is what makes the cities, towns and everything in between so beautiful.

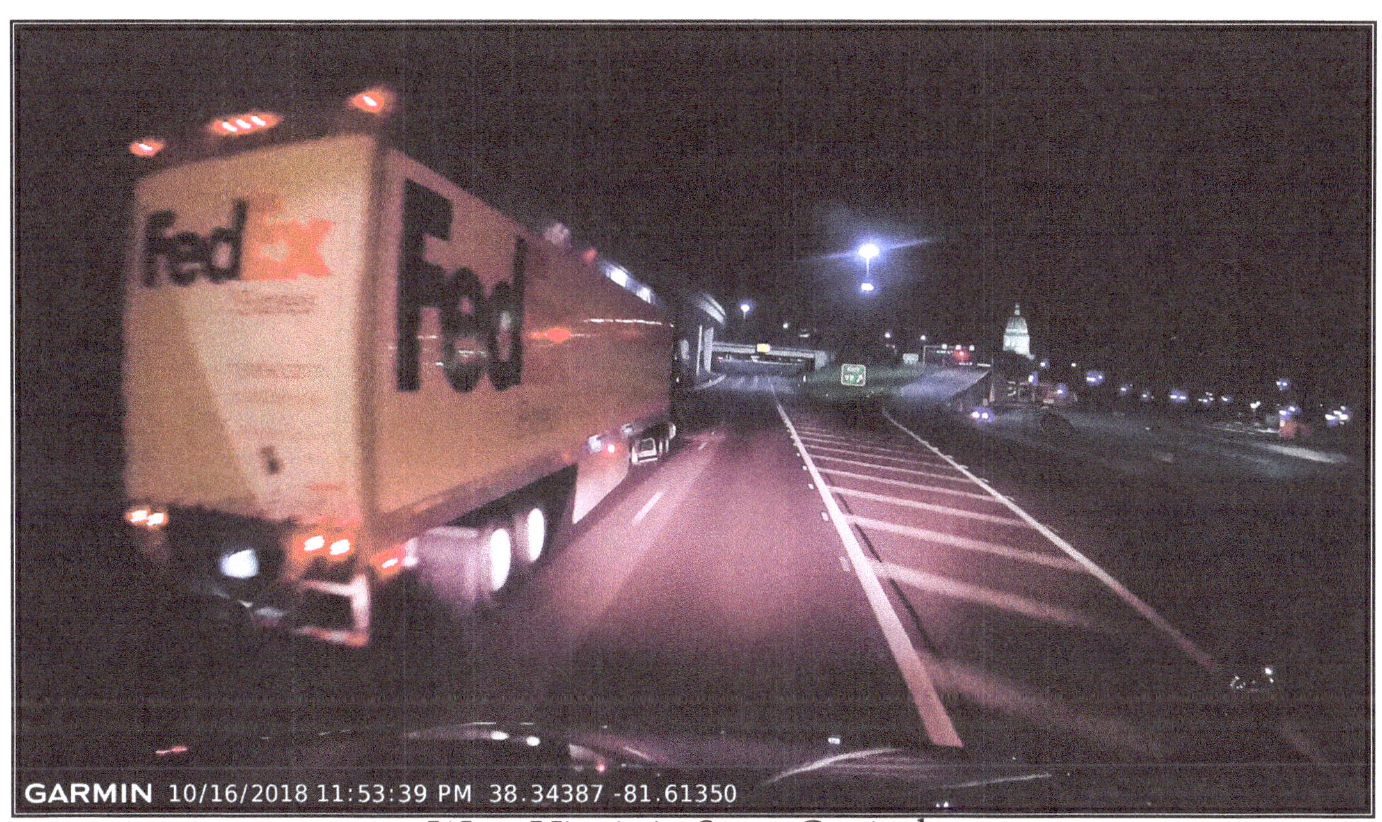

West Virginia State Capitol
I-77, Charleston, West Virginia

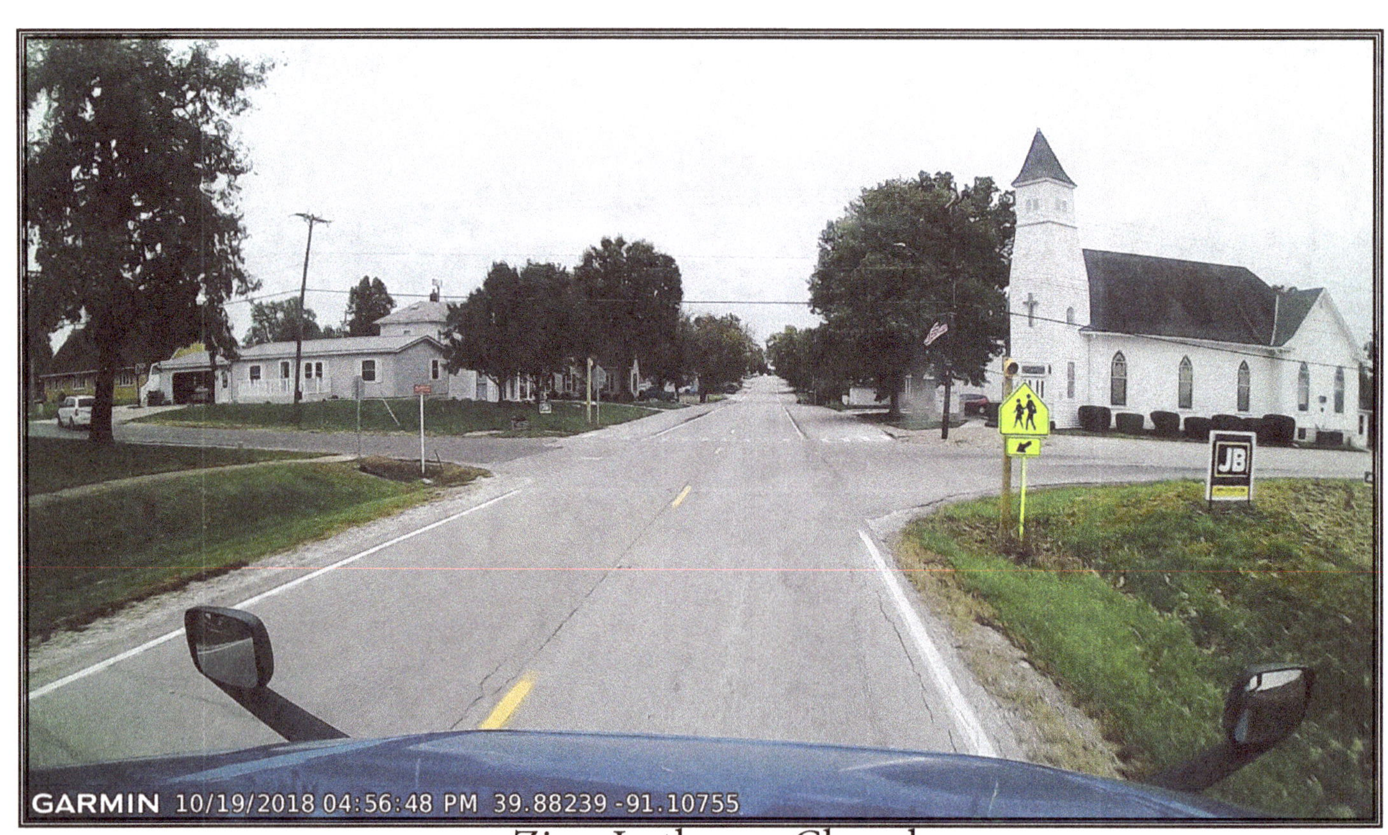

Zion Lutheran Church
Main St., Liberty Township, Illinois

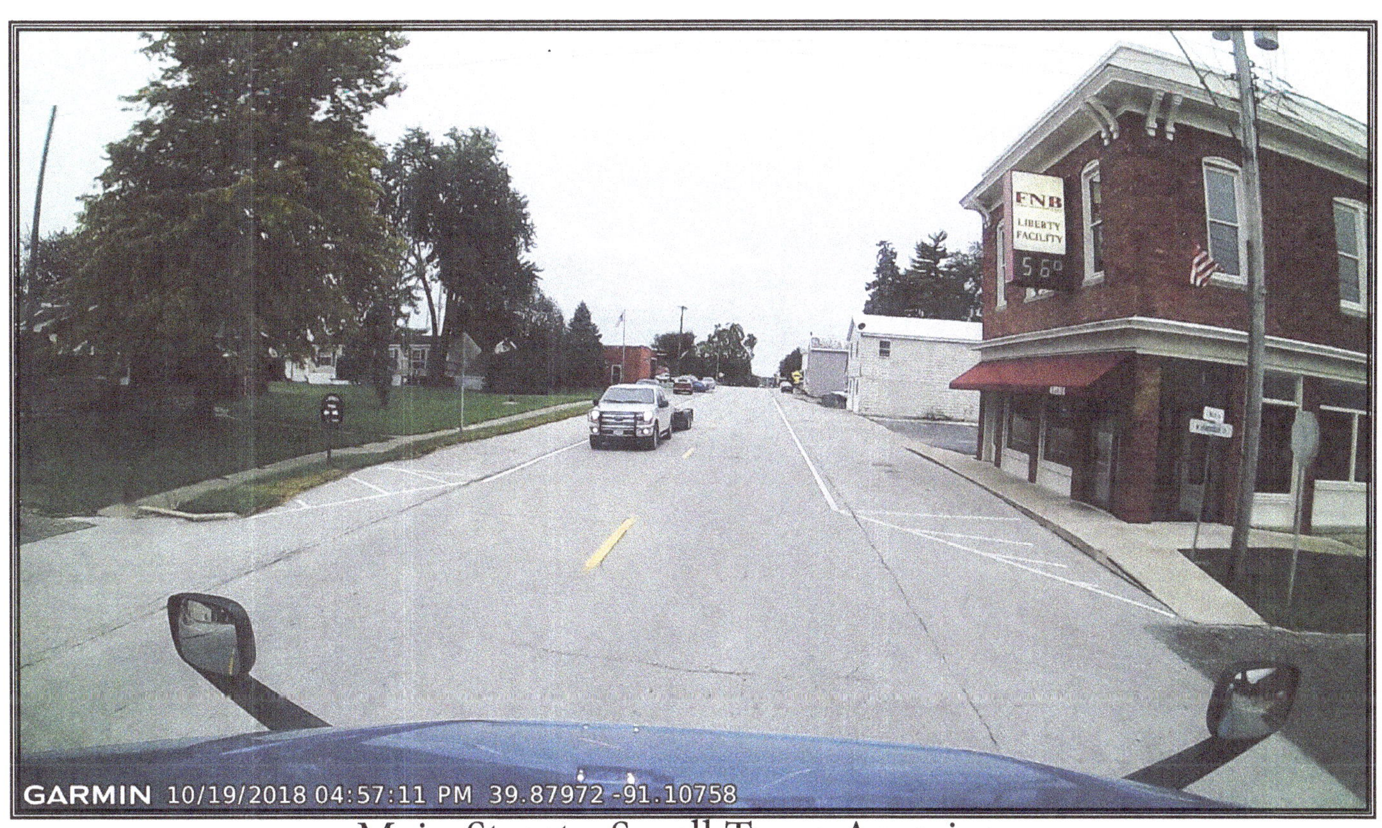

Main Street - Small Town America
Liberty Township, Illinois

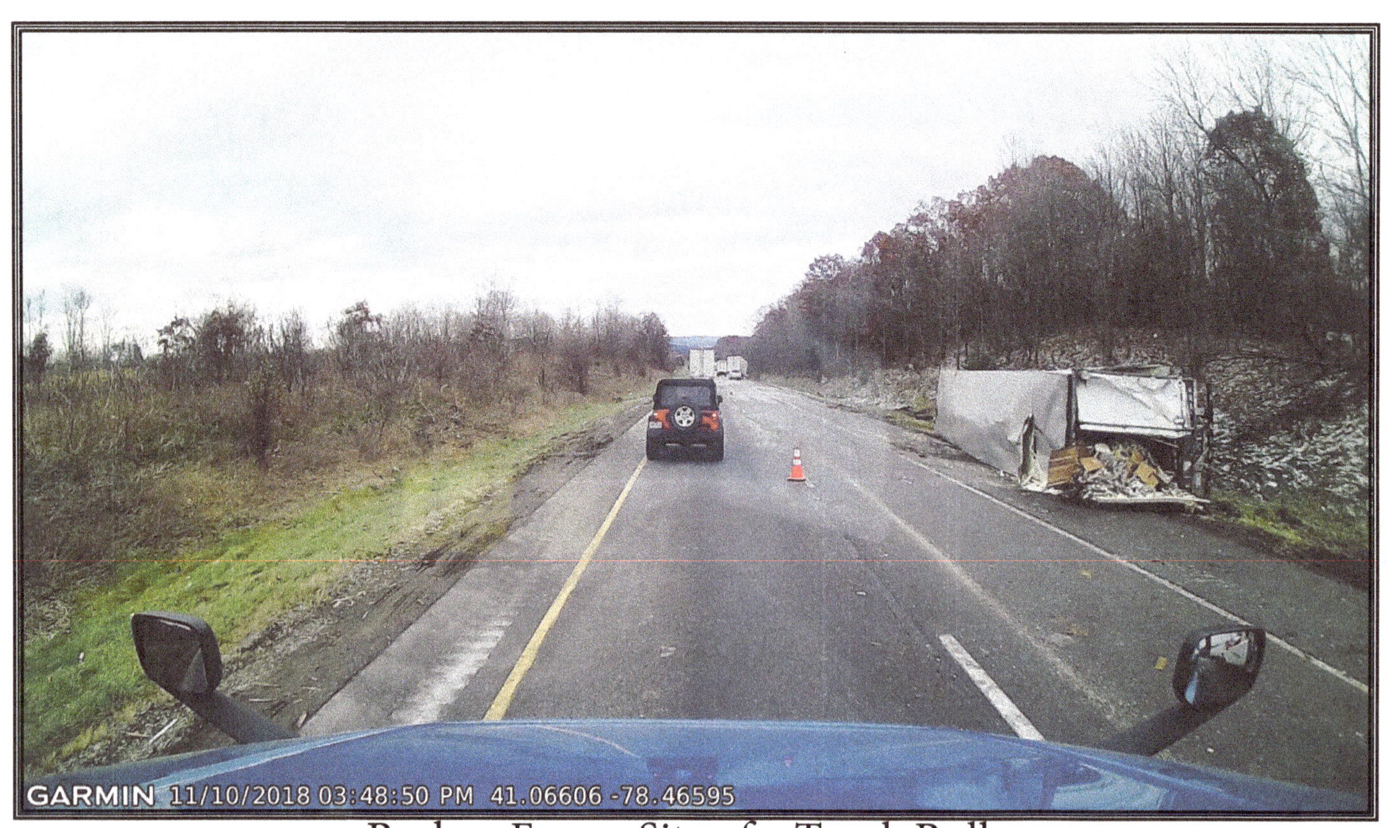

Broken Eggs—Site of a Truck Rollover
I-80, Clearfield, Pennsylvania

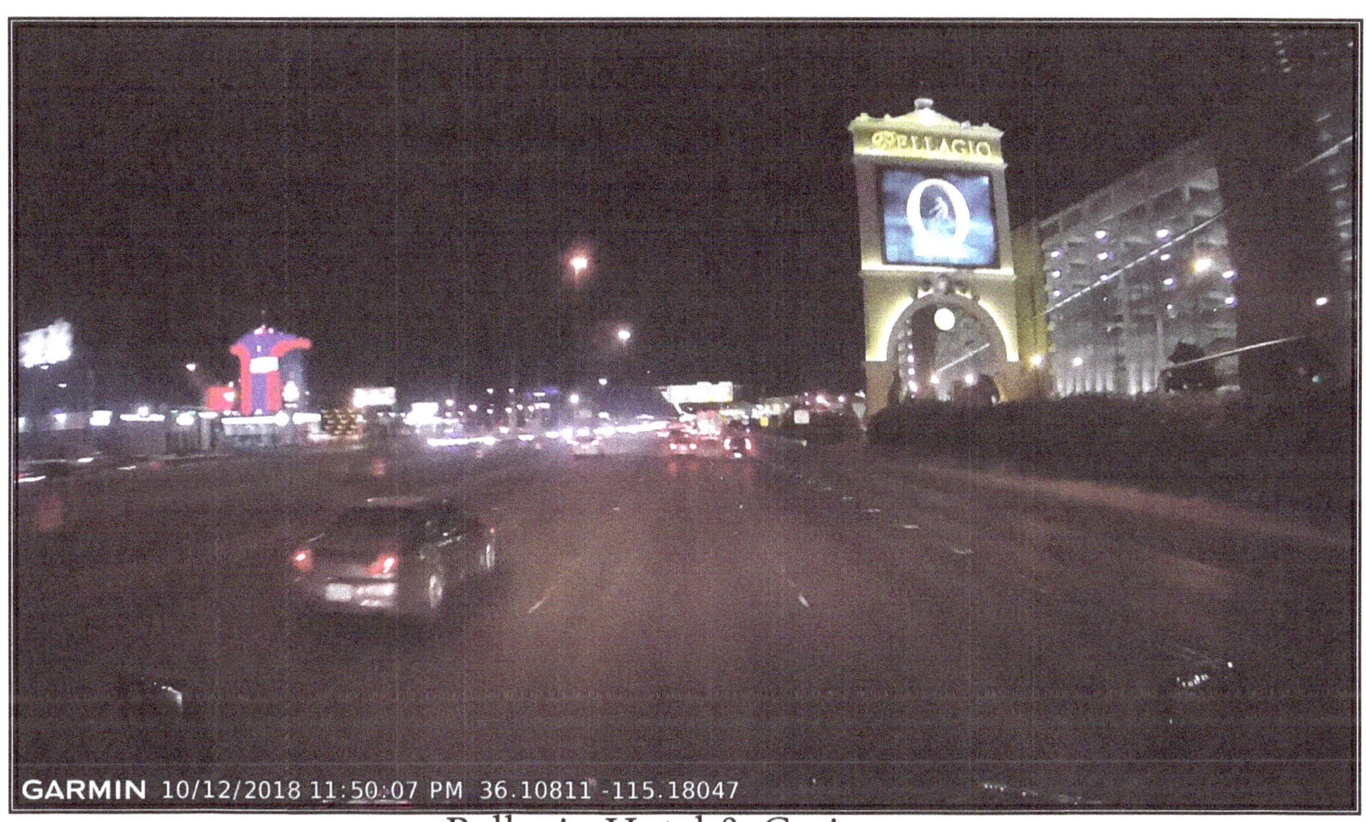

Bellagio Hotel & Casino
I-15, Las Vegas, Nevada

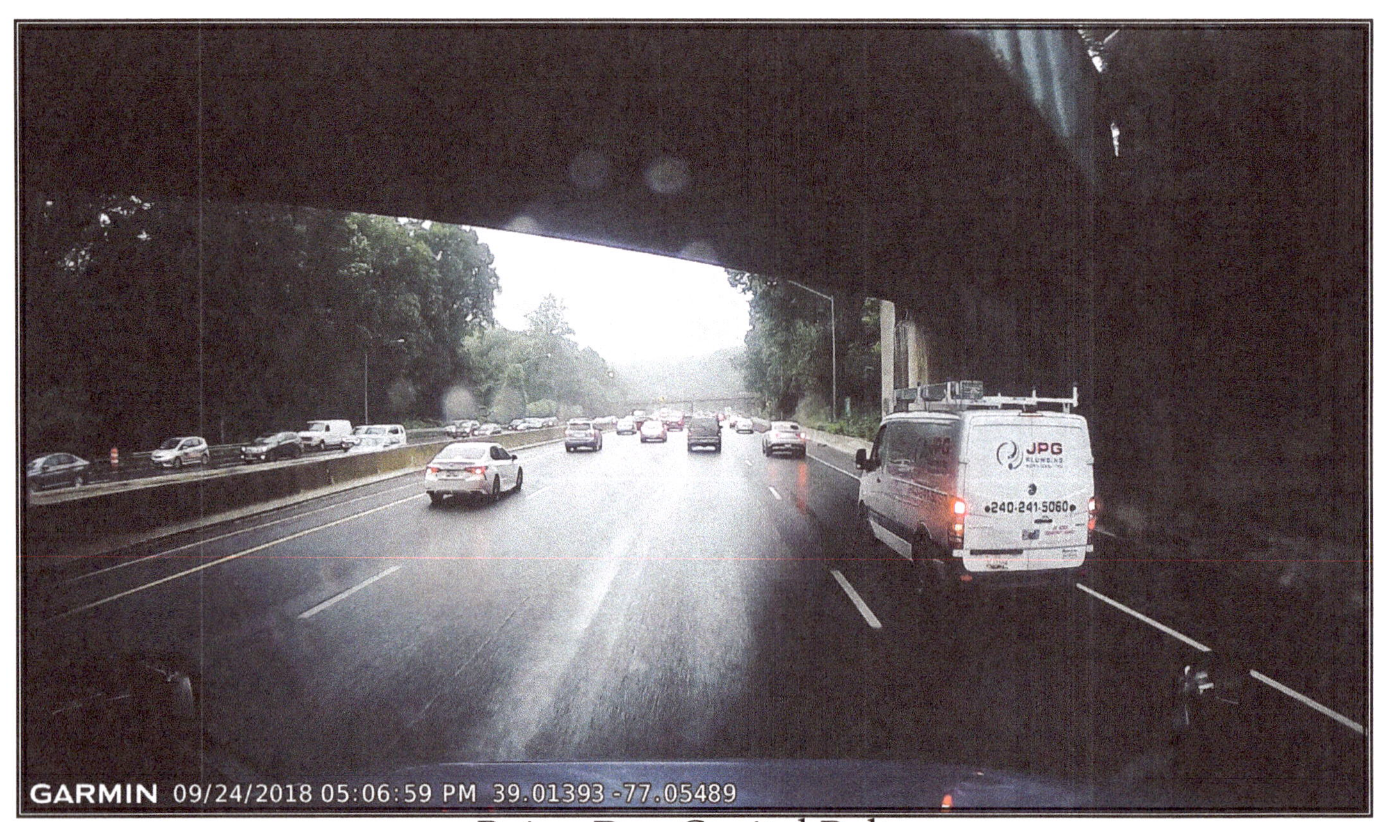

Rainy Day Capital Beltway
I-495, Silver Spring, Maryland

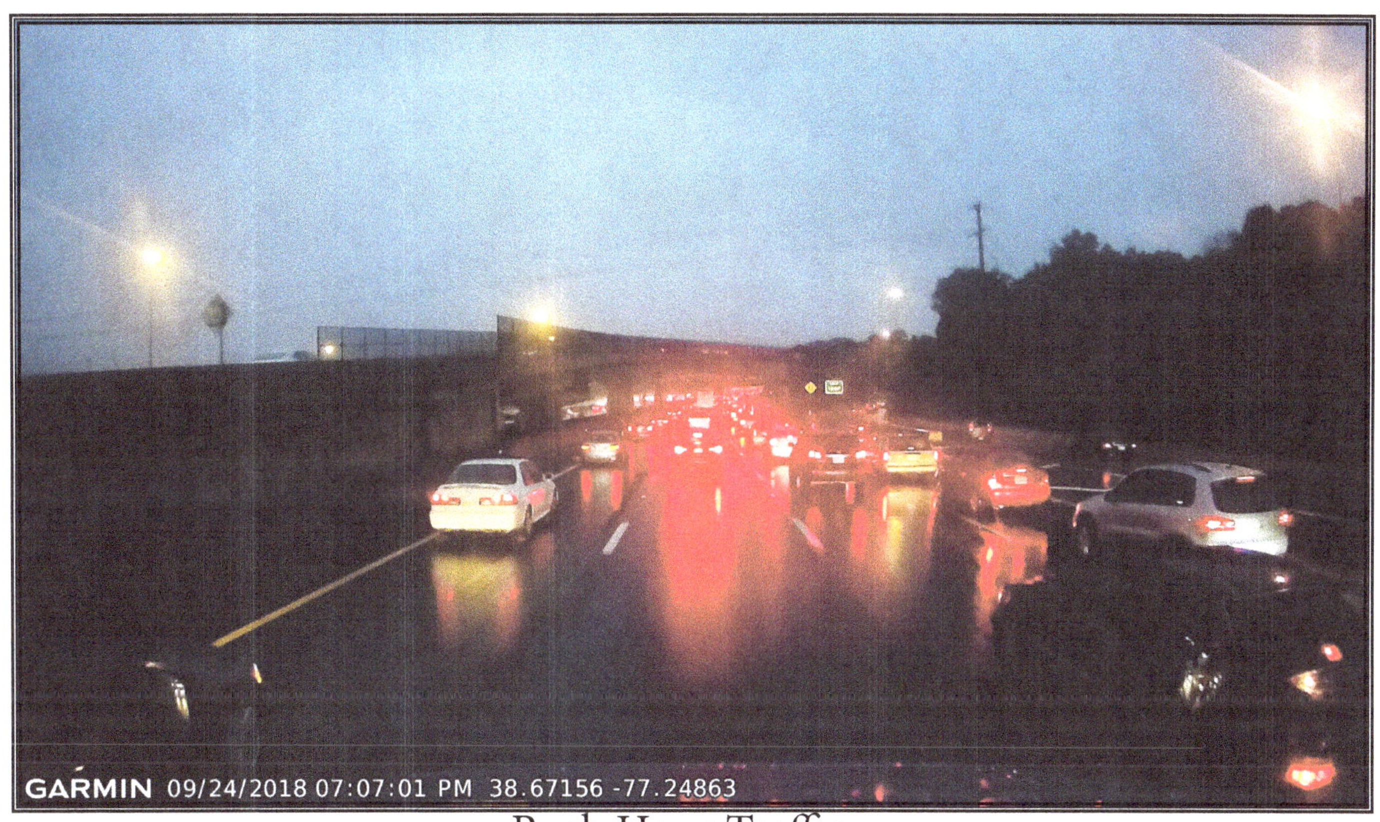

Rush Hour Traffic
I-95, Woodbridge, Virginia

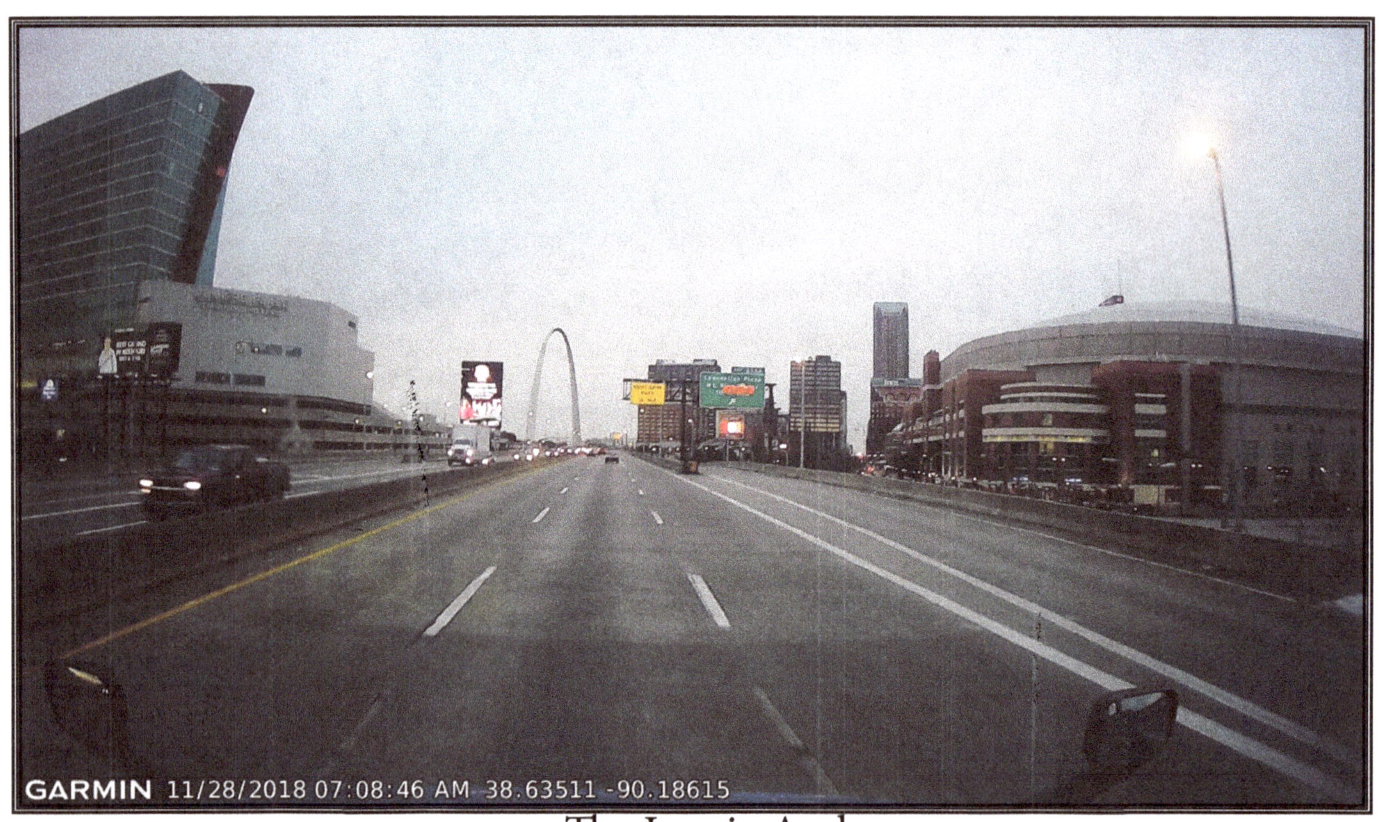

The Iconic Arch
I-44, St. Louis, Missouri

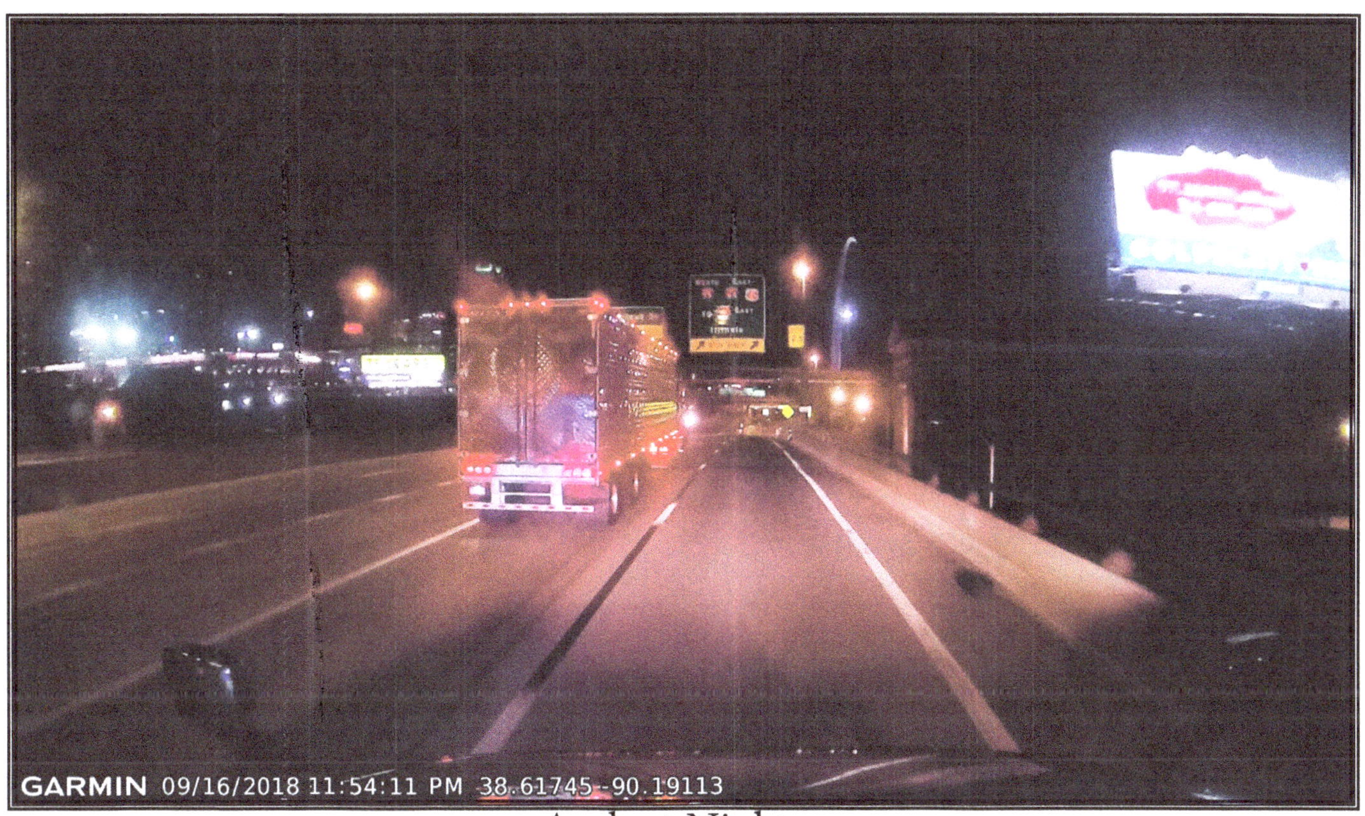

Arch at Night
I-44, St. Louis, Missouri

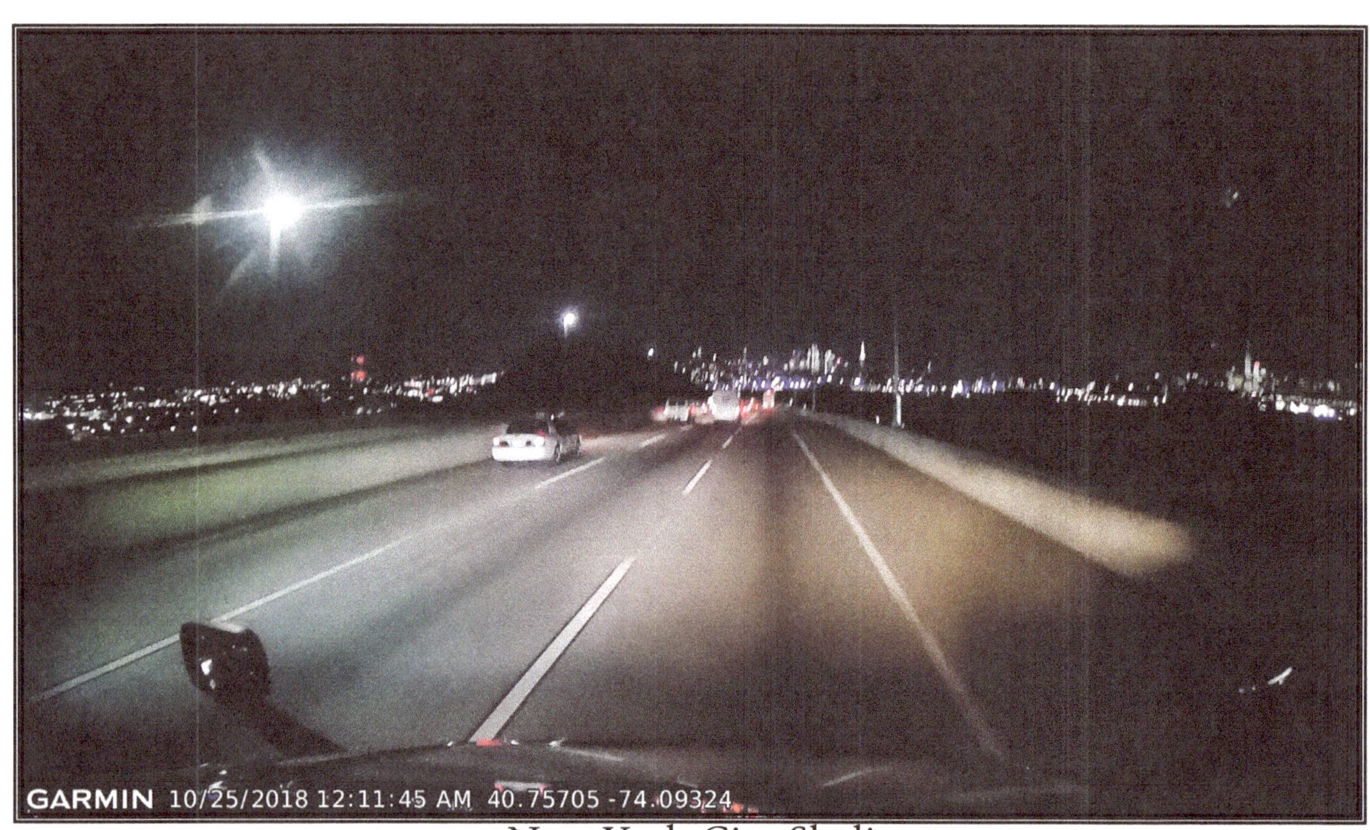

New York City Skyline
New Jersey Turnpike, Secaucus, New Jersey

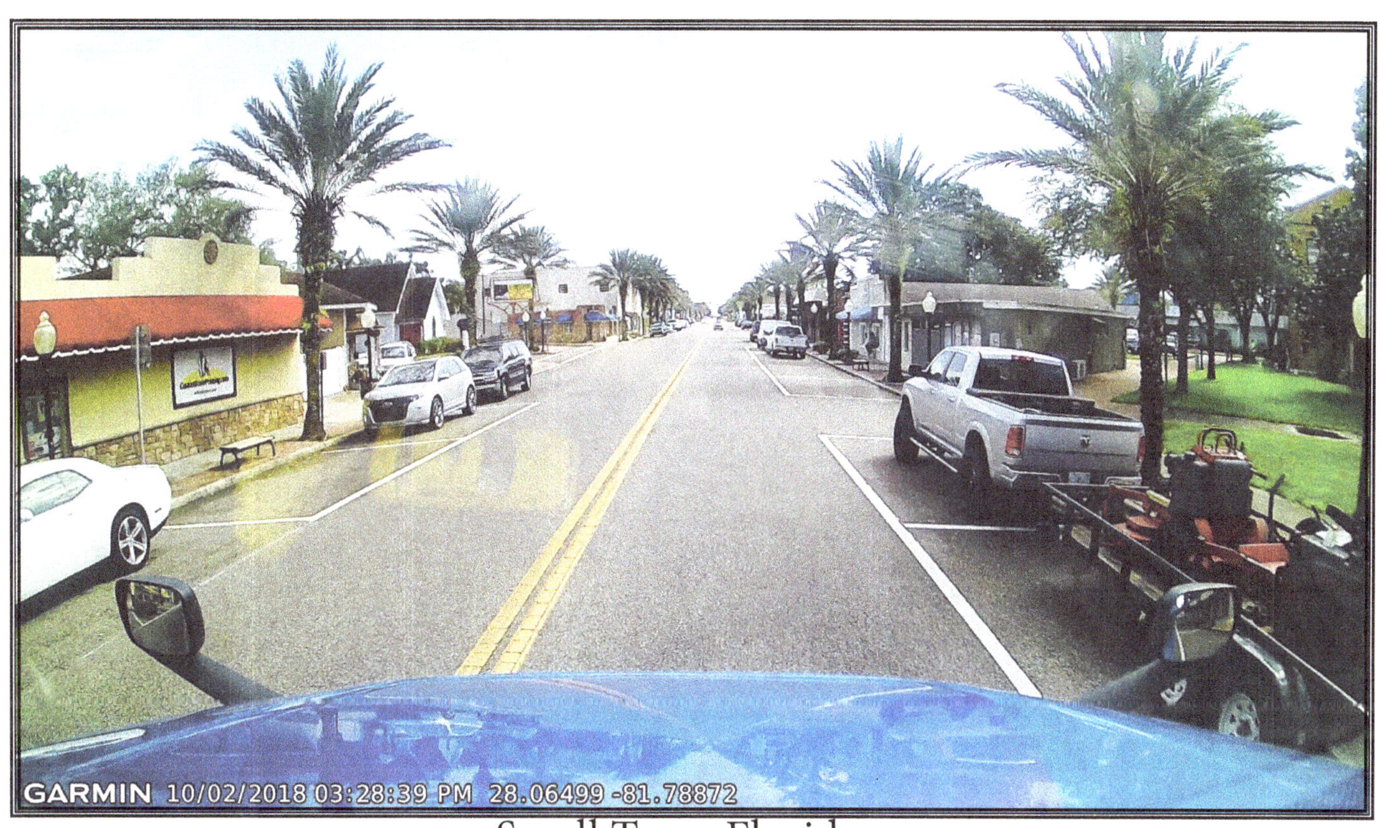

Small Town Florida
Auburndale, Florida

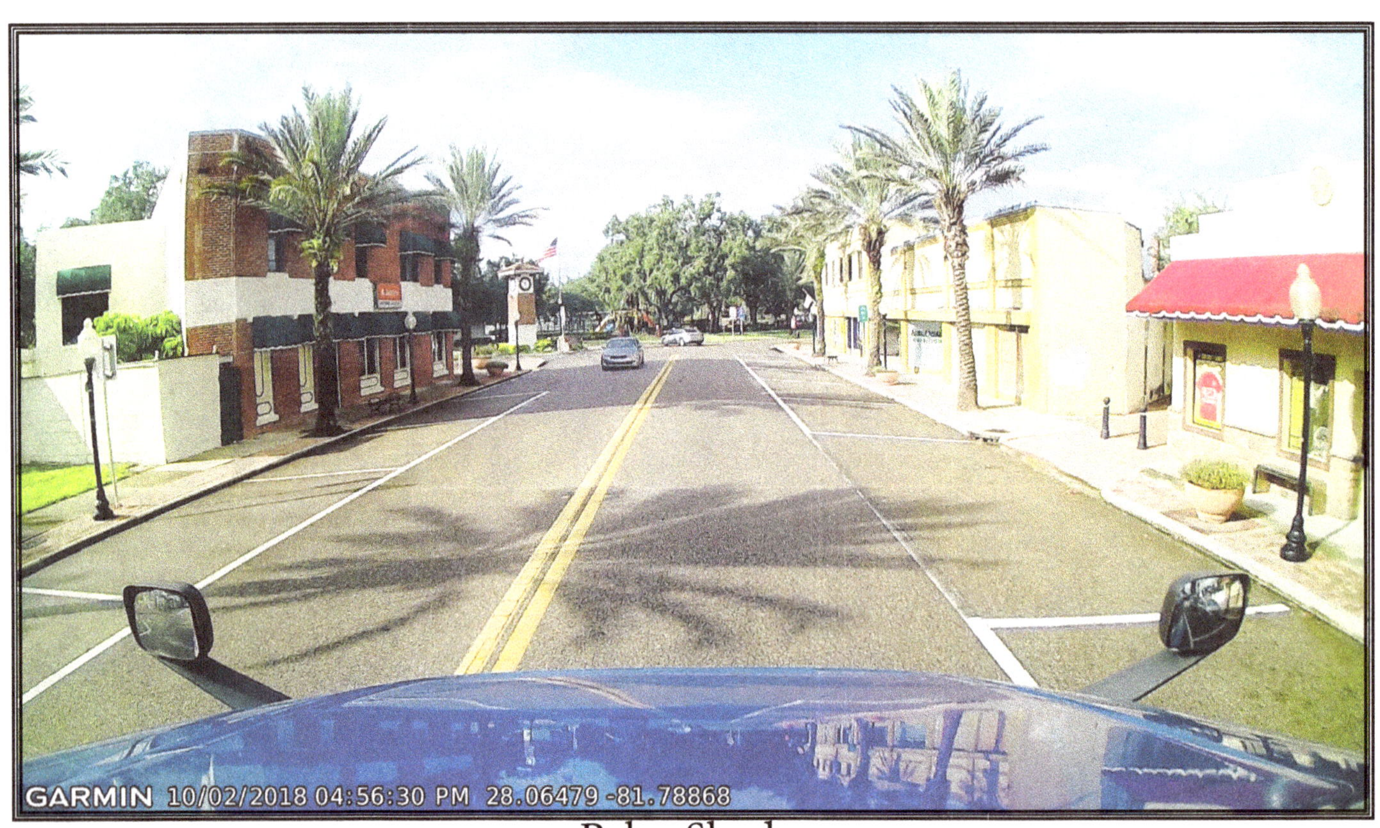

Palm Shadows
Auburndale, Florida

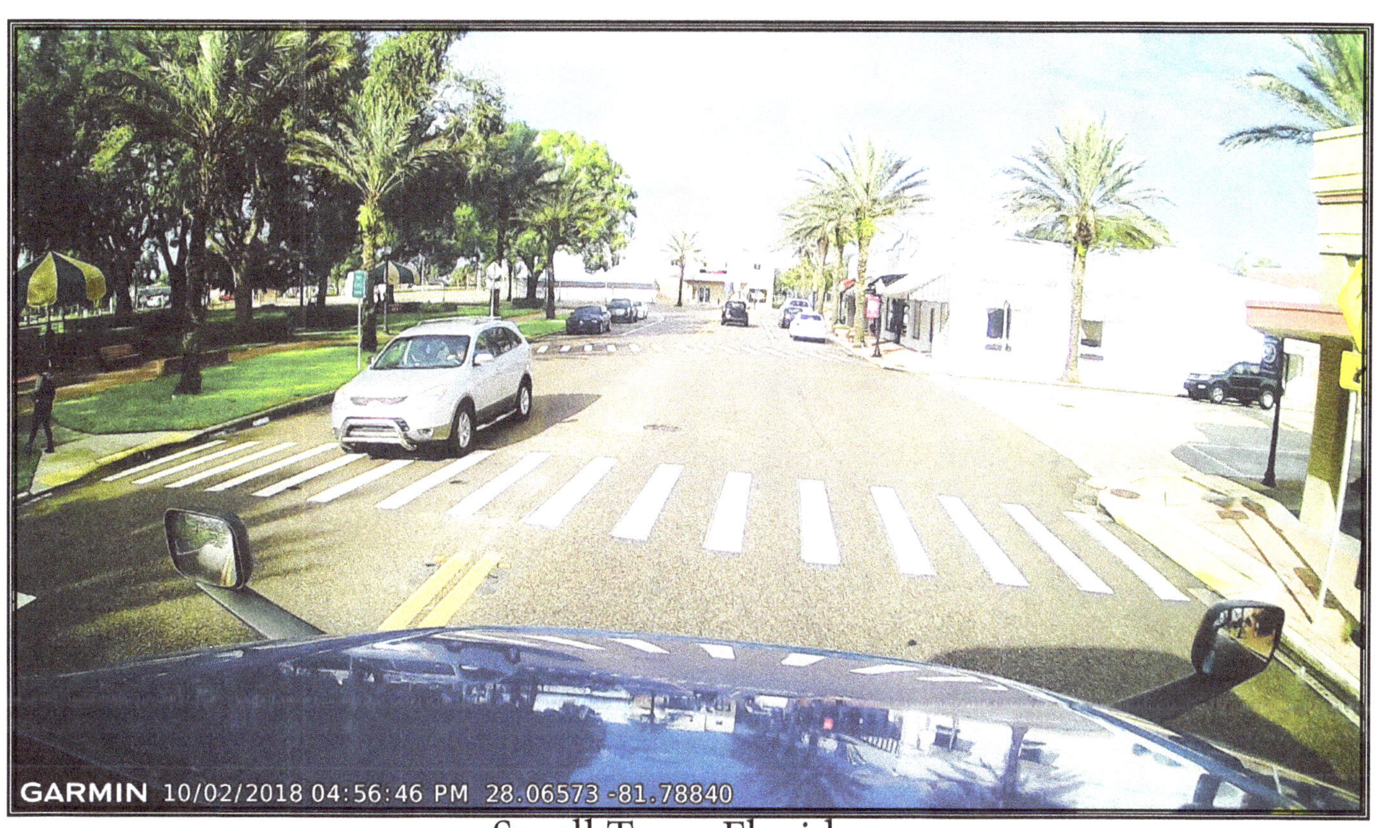

Small Town Florida
Auburndale, Florida

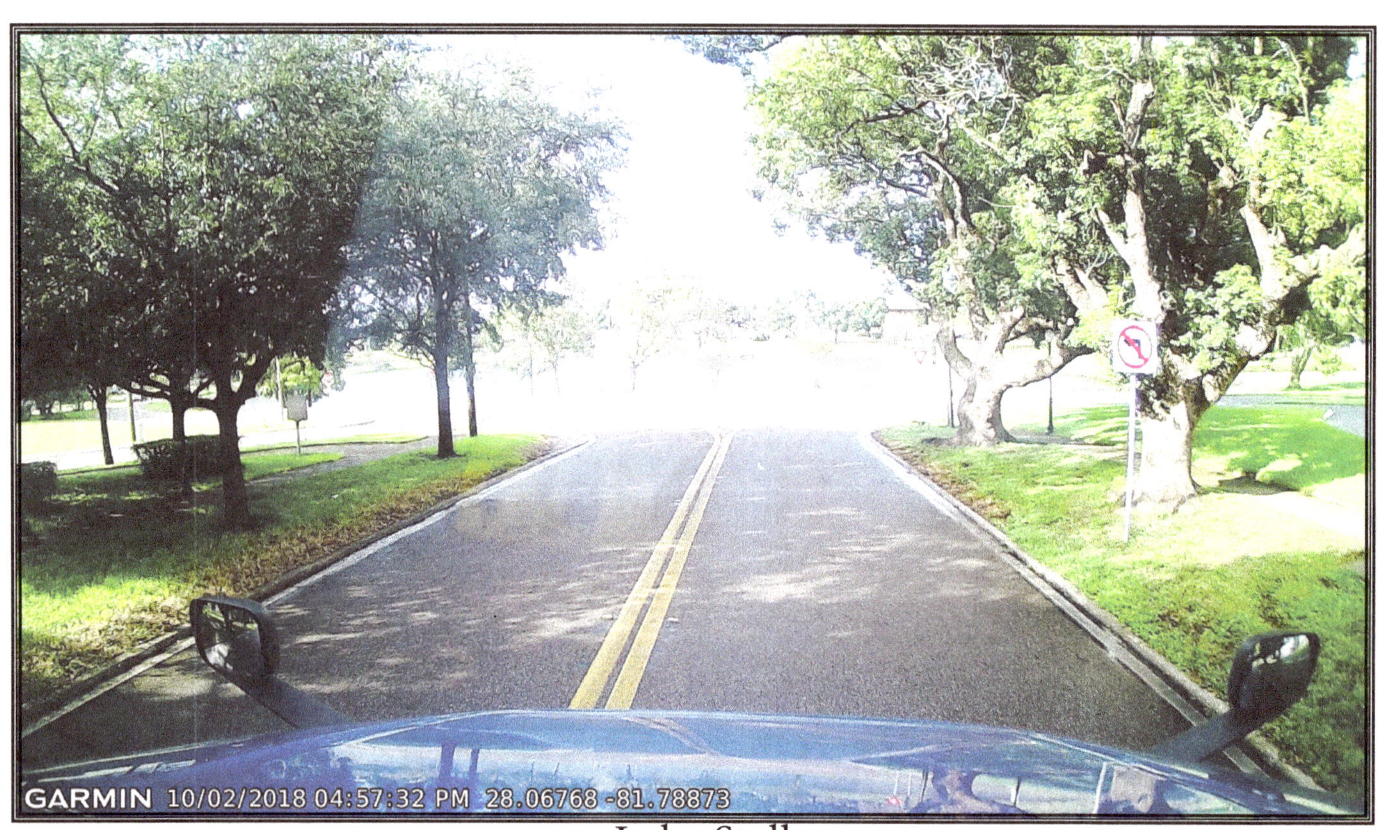

Lake Stella
Auburndale, Florida

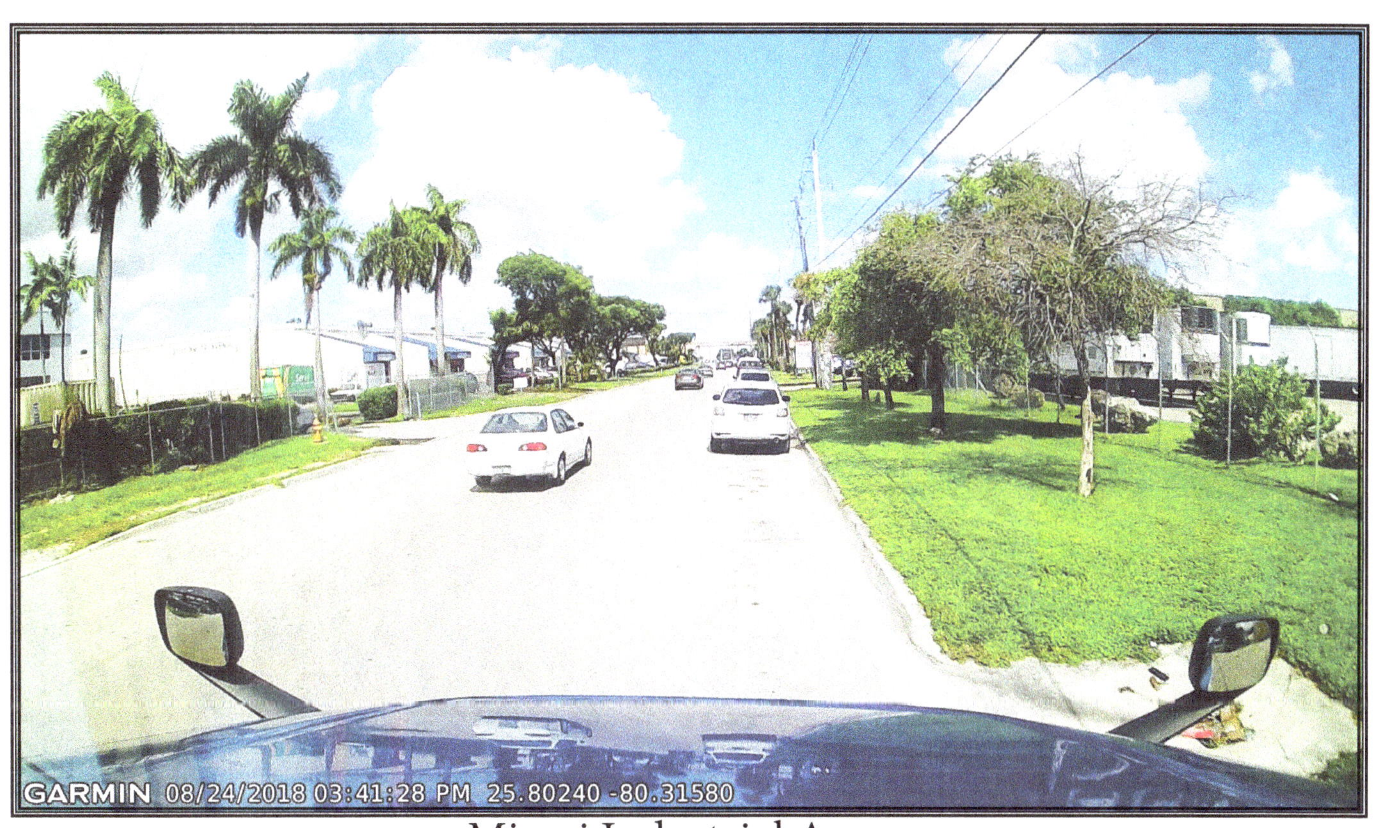

Miami Industrial Area
Miami, Florida

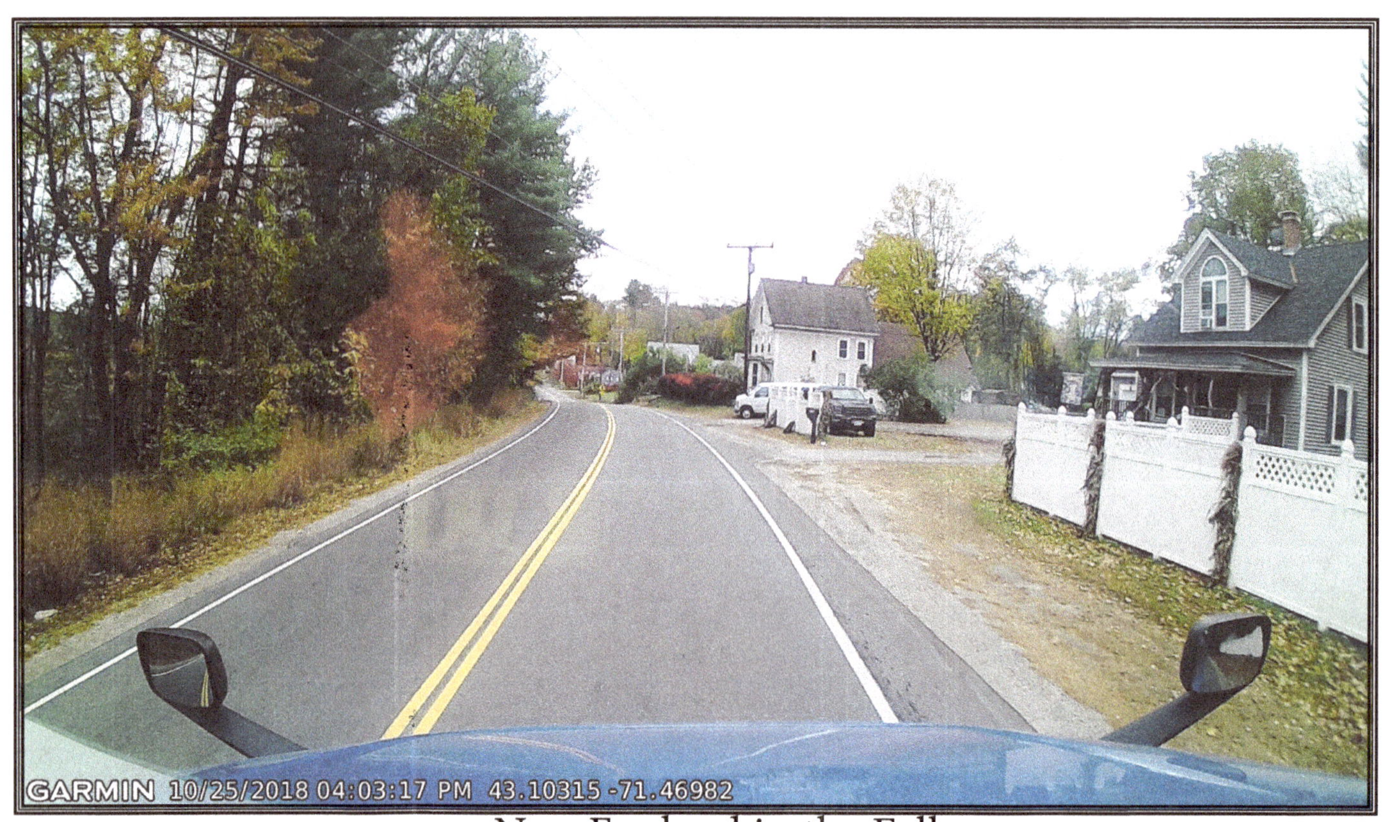

New England in the Fall
NH-3A, Hooksett, New Hampshire

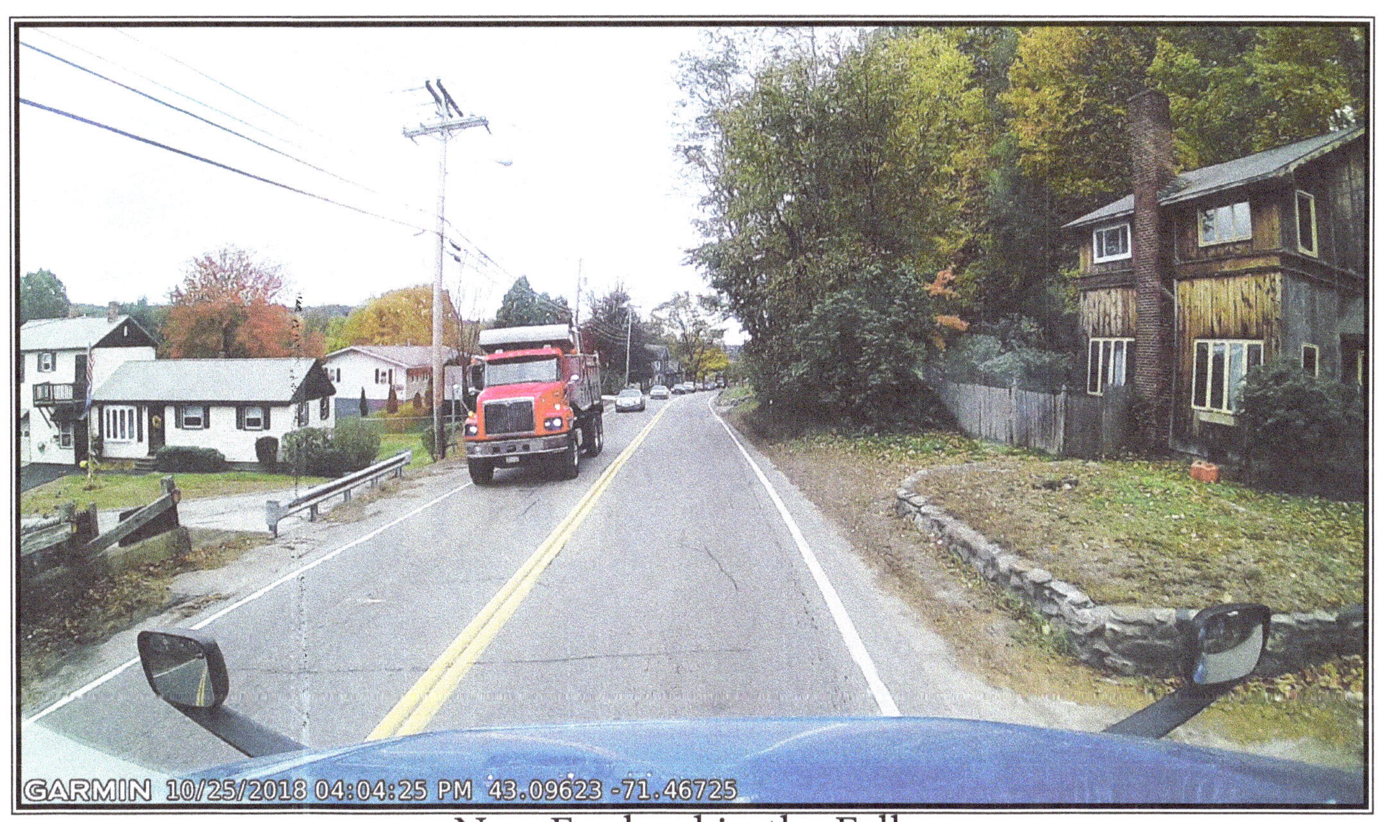

New England in the Fall
NH-3A, Hooksett, New Hampshire

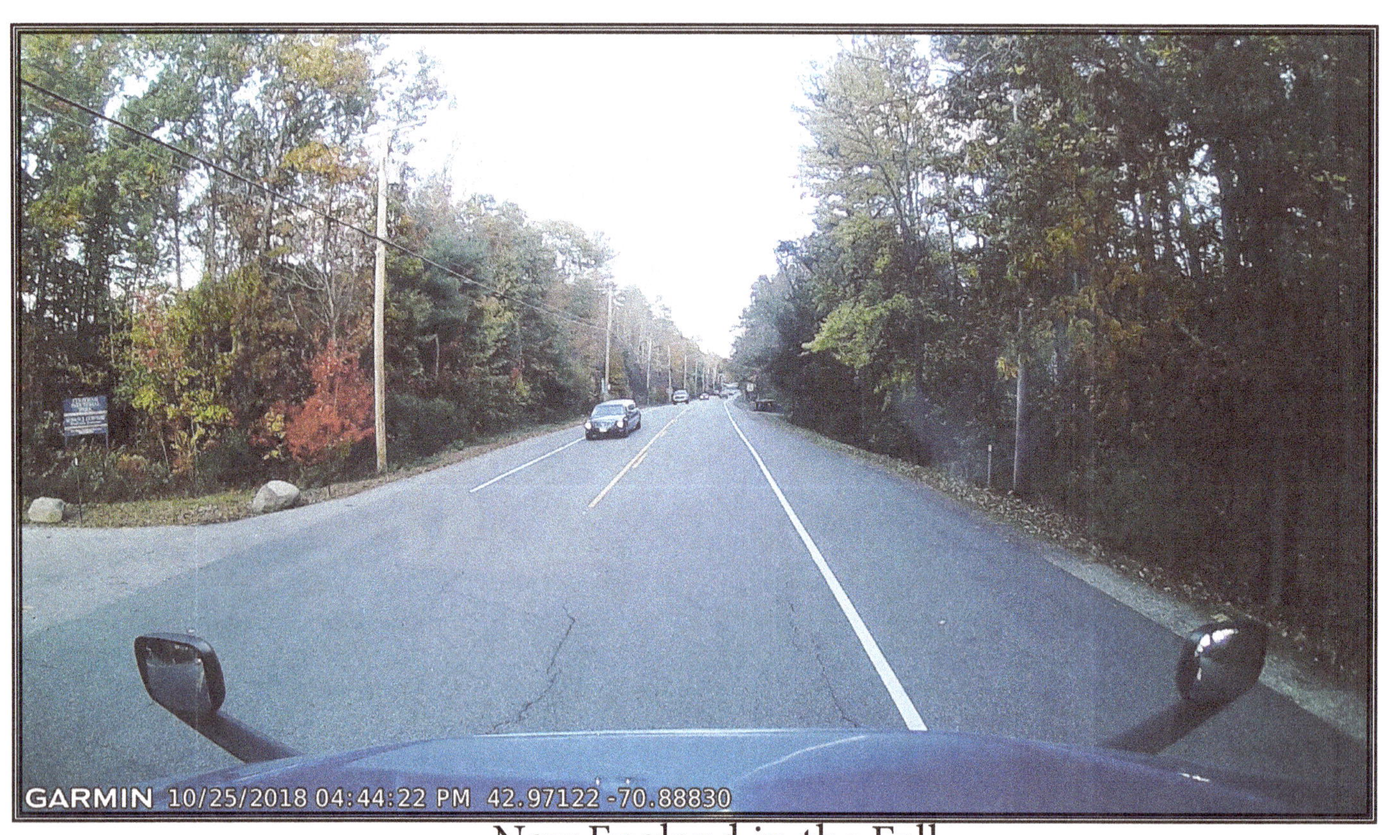

New England in the Fall
NH-111, Exeter, New Hampshire

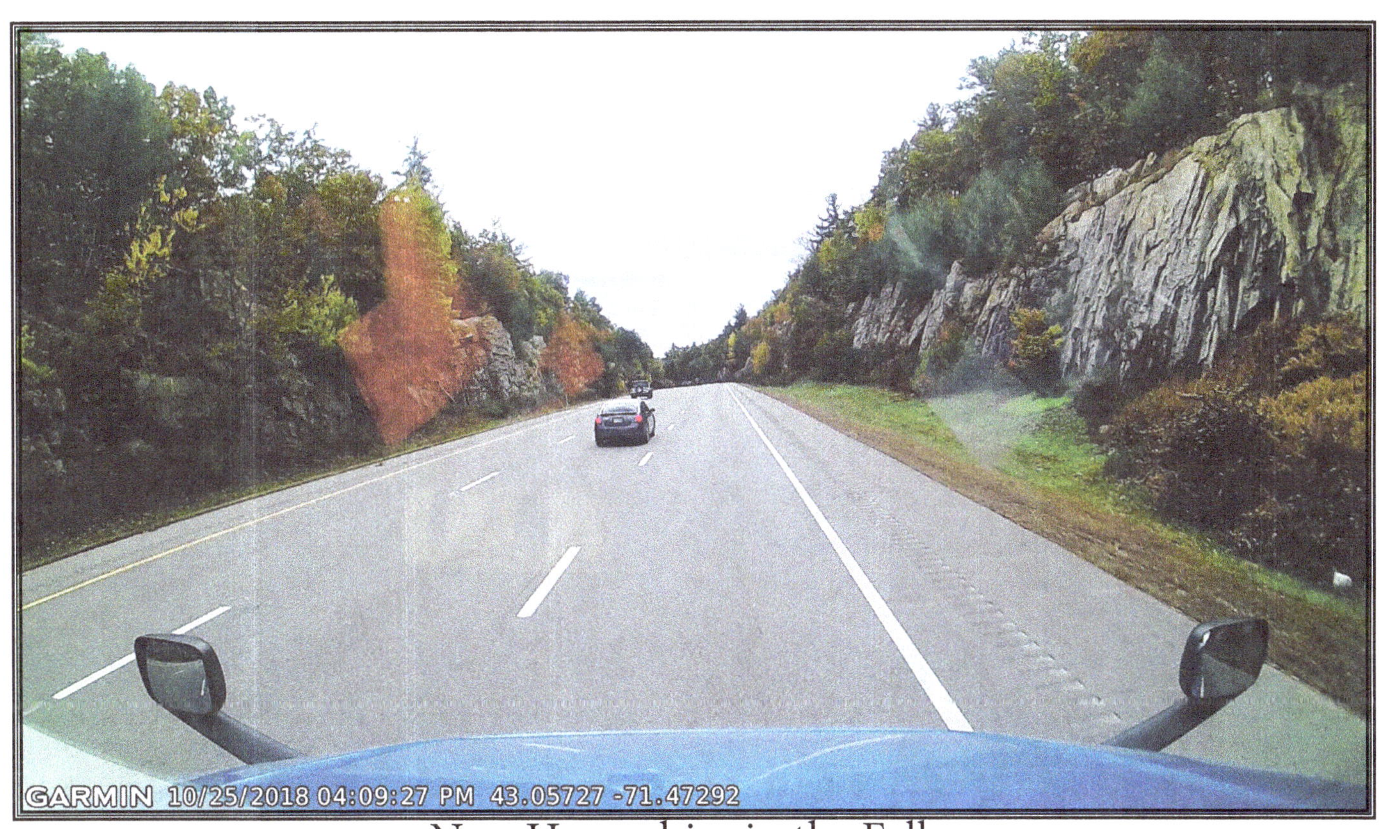

New Hampshire in the Fall
I-95, Hooksett, New Hampshire

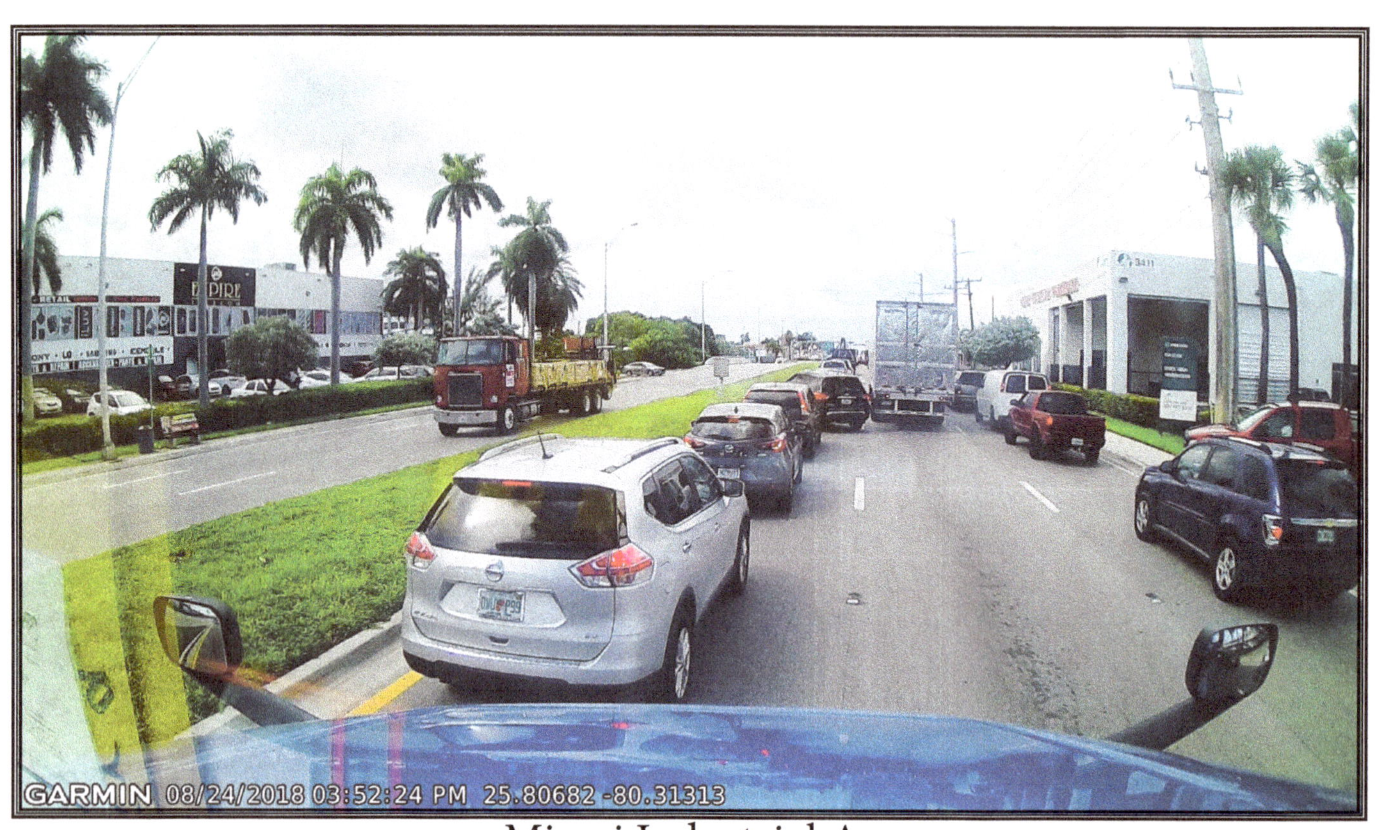

Miami Industrial Area
Miami, Florida

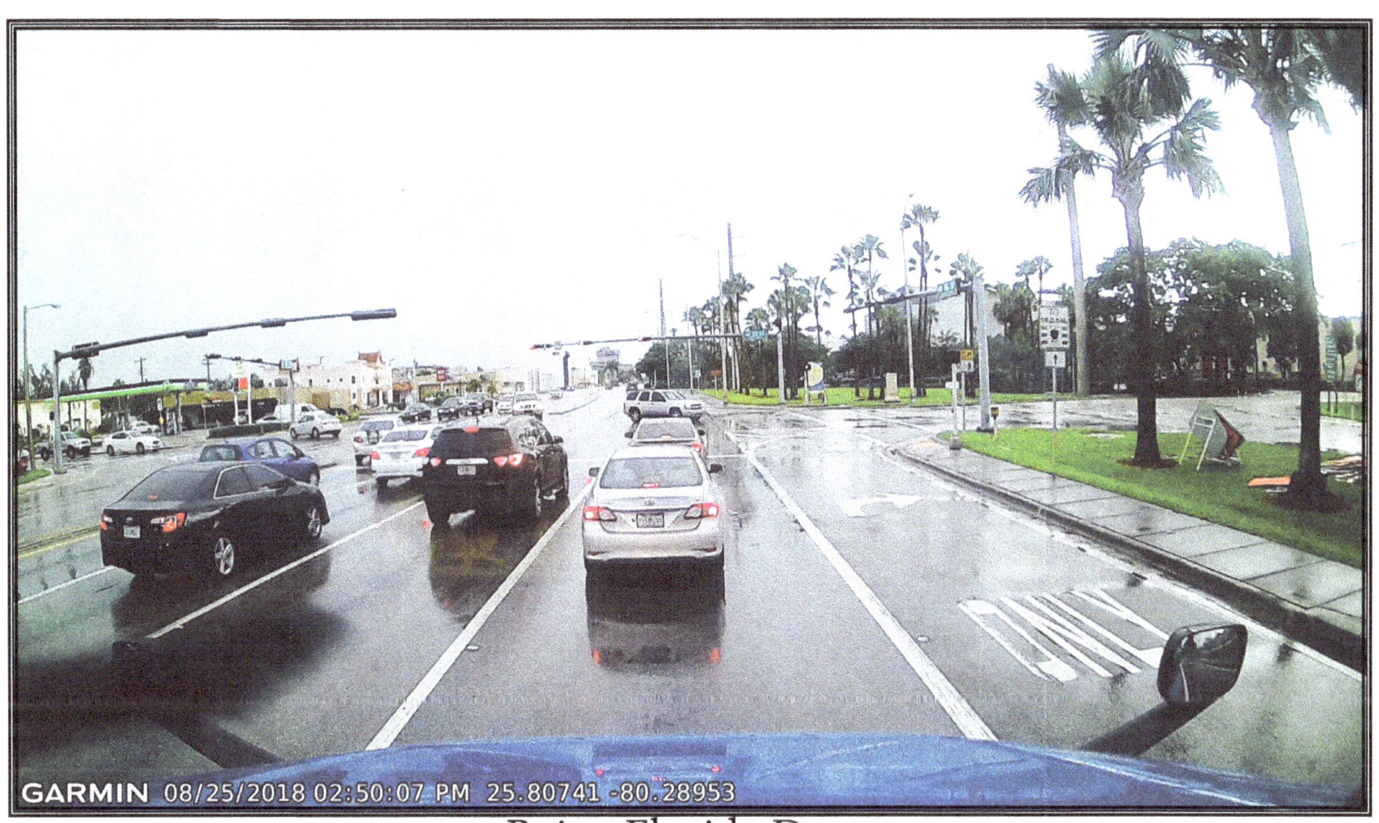

Rainy Florida Day
Miami, Florida

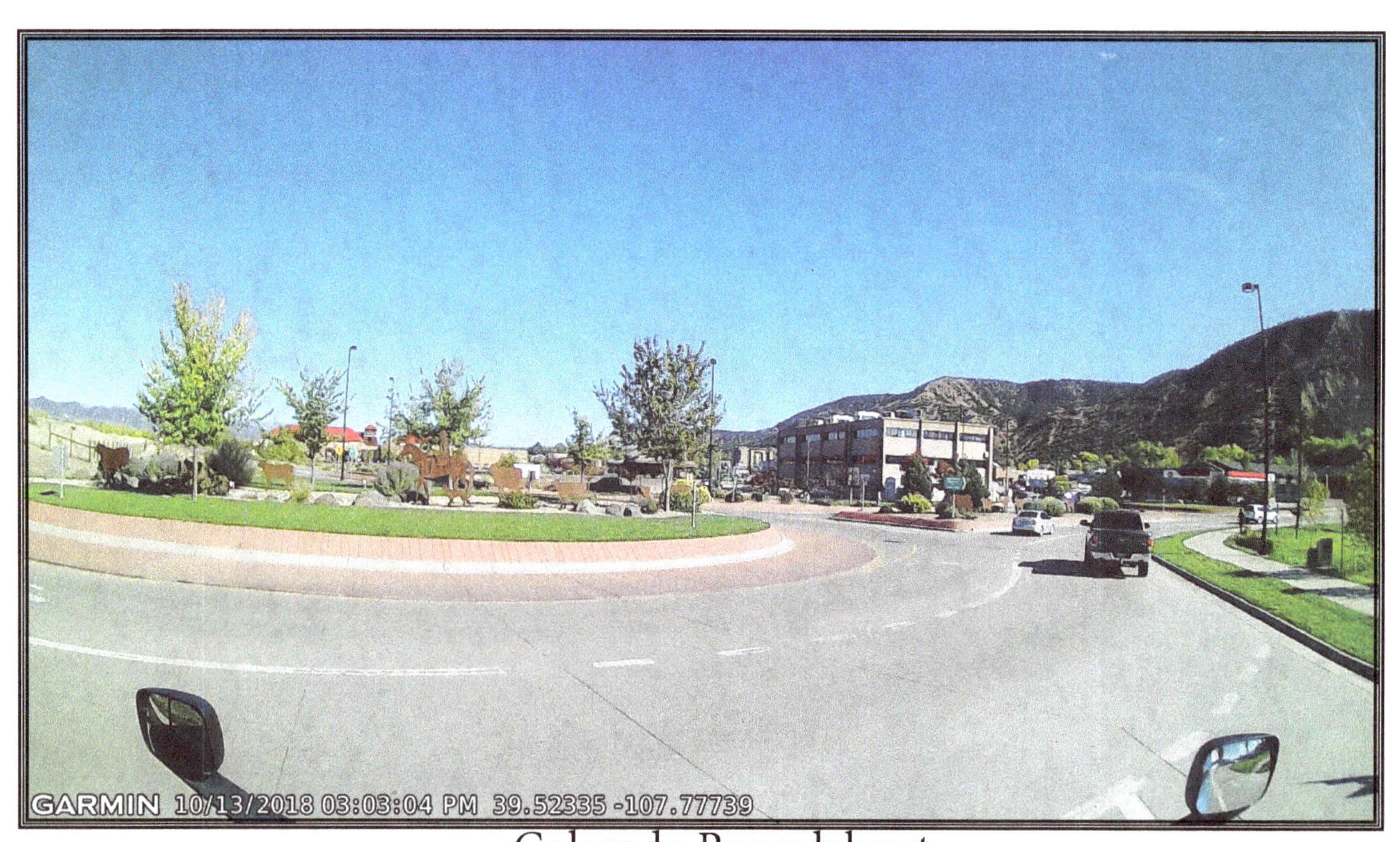

Colorado Roundabout
I-70, Rifle, Colorado

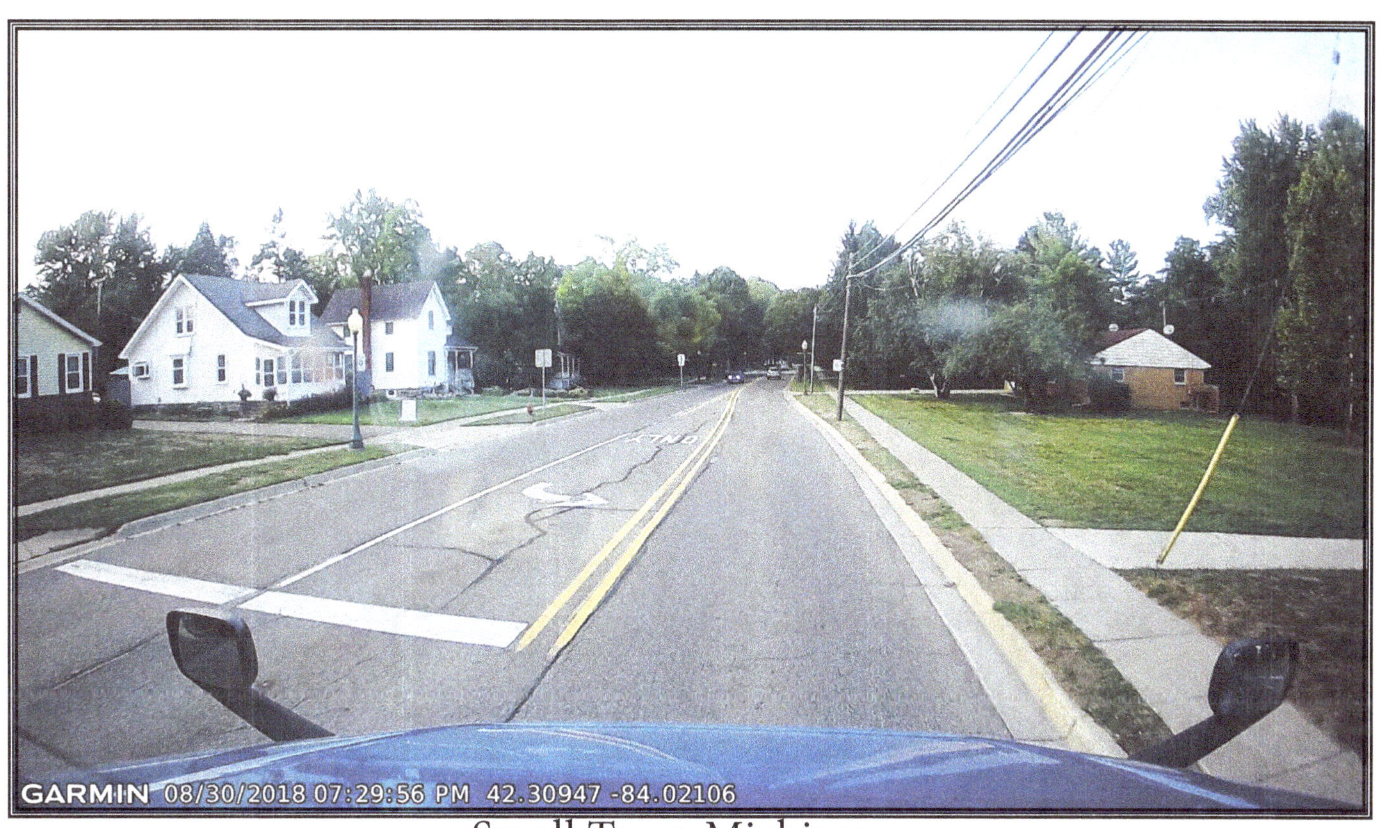

Small Town Michigan
Main Street, Chelsea, Michigan

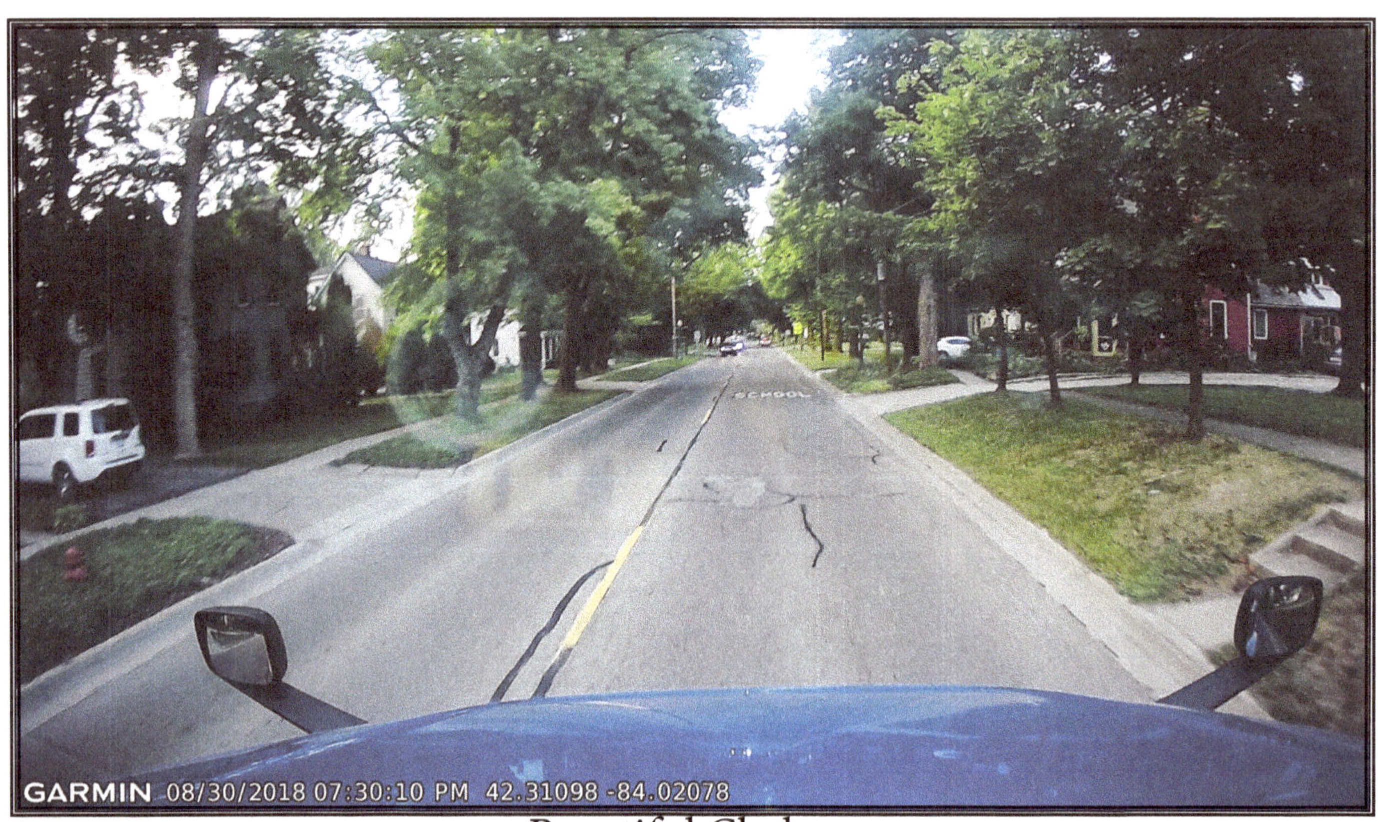

Beautiful Chelsea
Main Street, Chelsea, Michigan

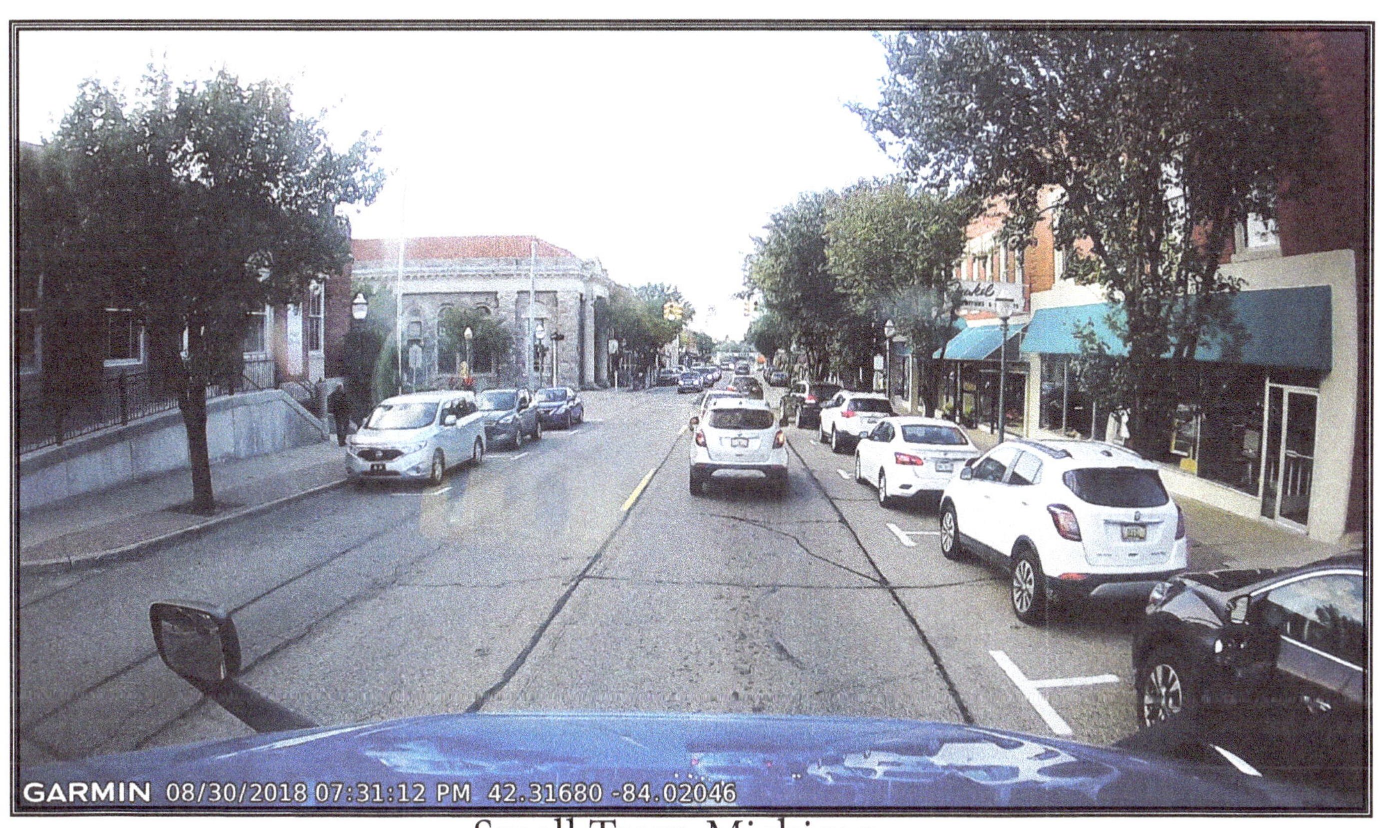

Small Town Michigan
Main Street, Chelsea, Michigan

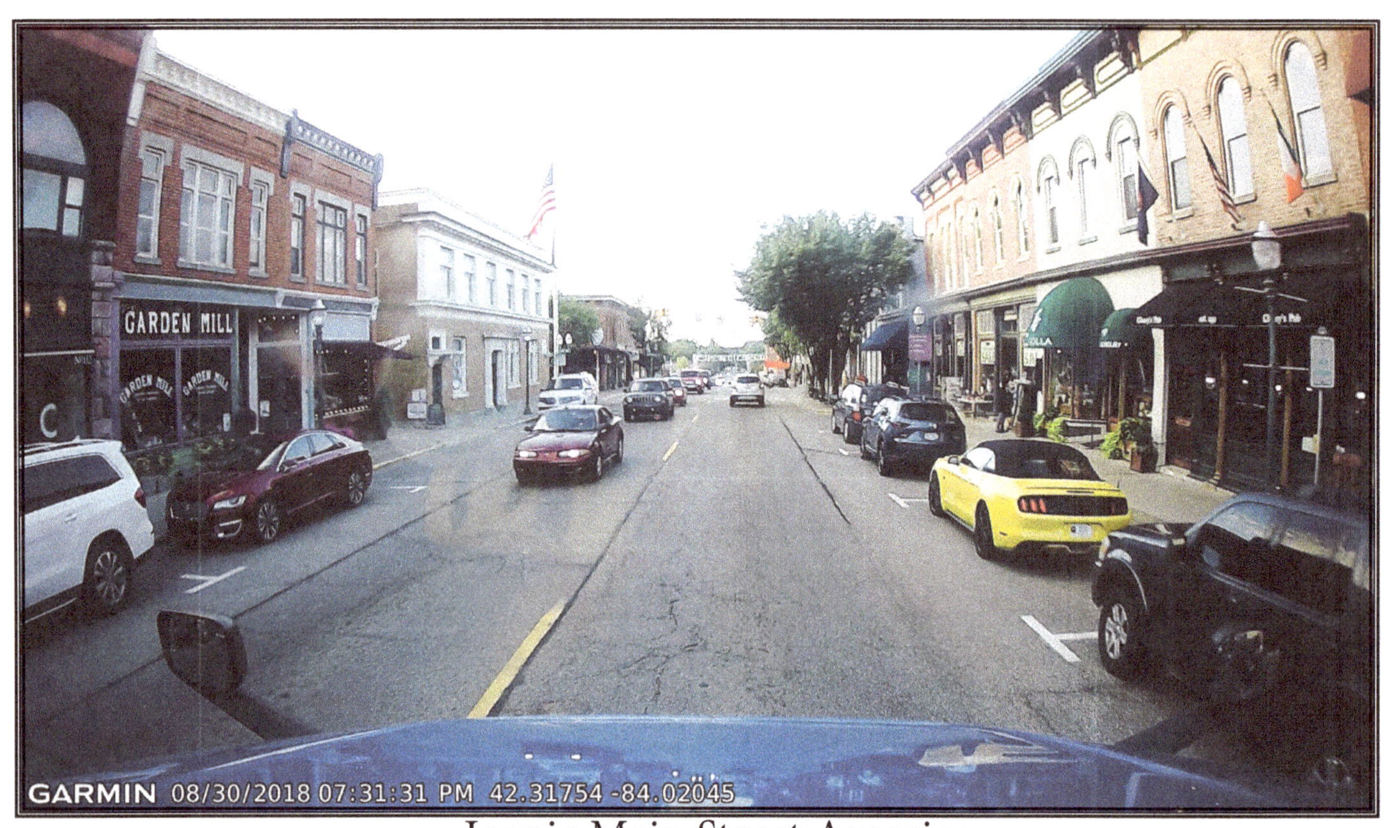

Iconic Main Street America
Main Street, Chelsea, Michigan

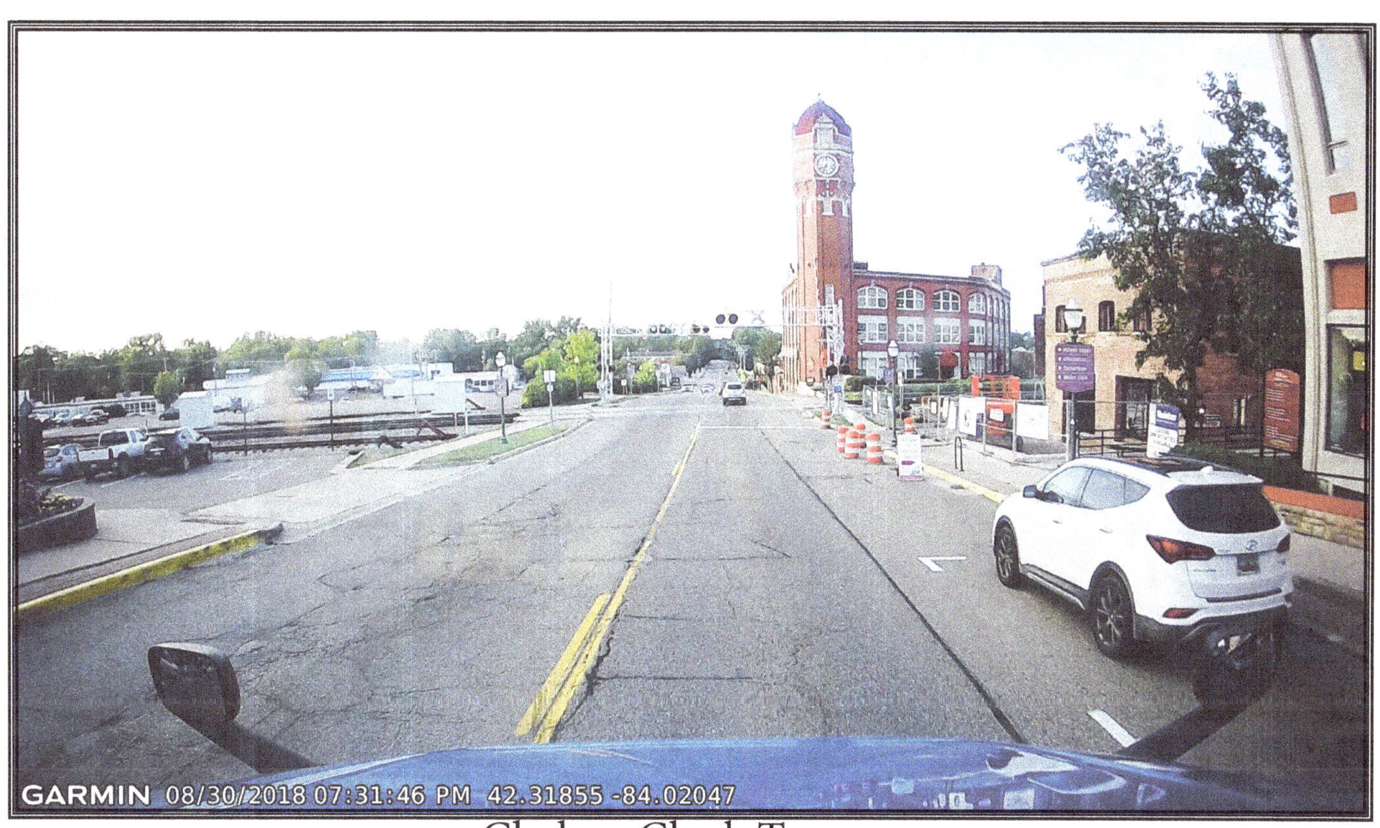

Chelsea Clock Tower
Main Street, Chelsea, Michigan

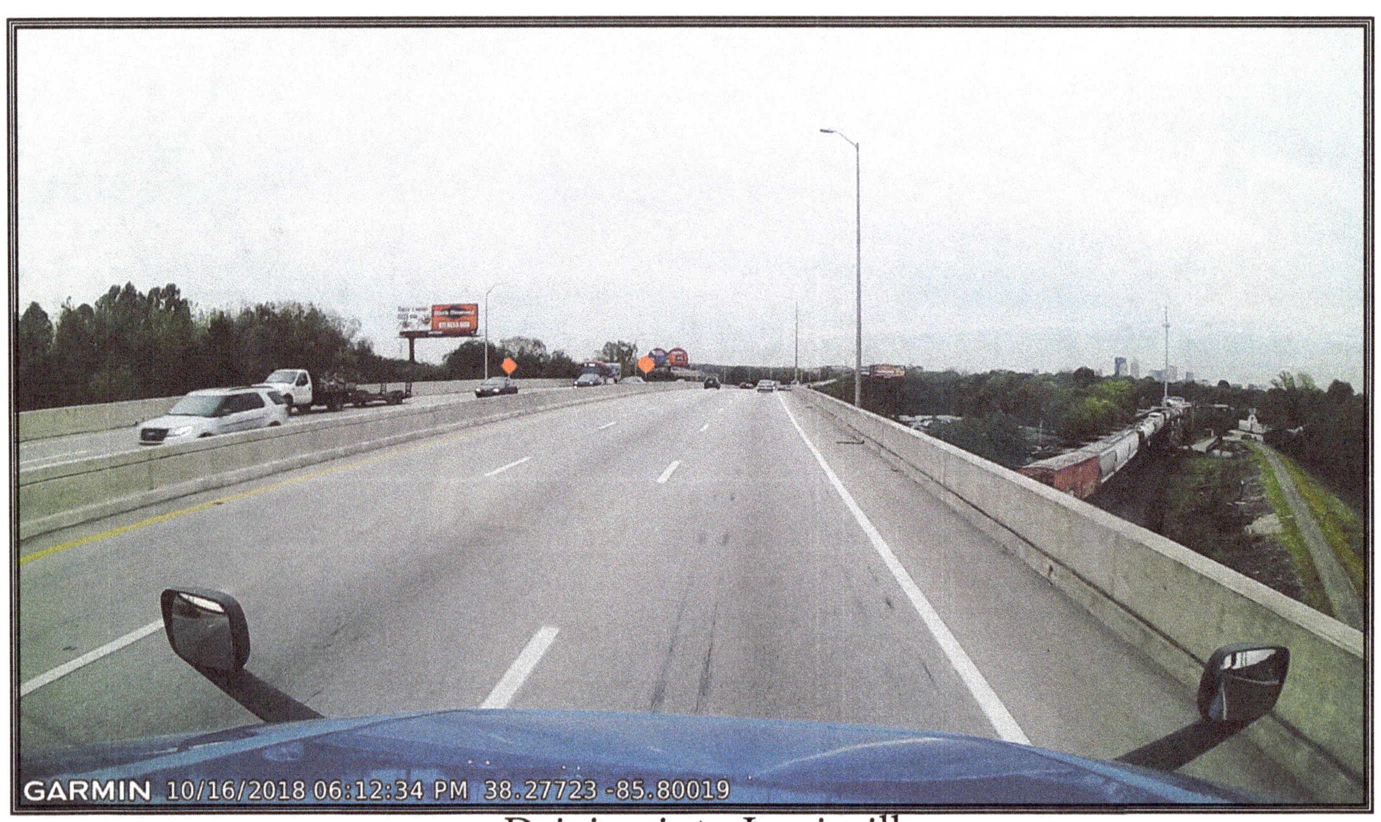

Driving into Louisville
I-64, Louisville, Kentucky

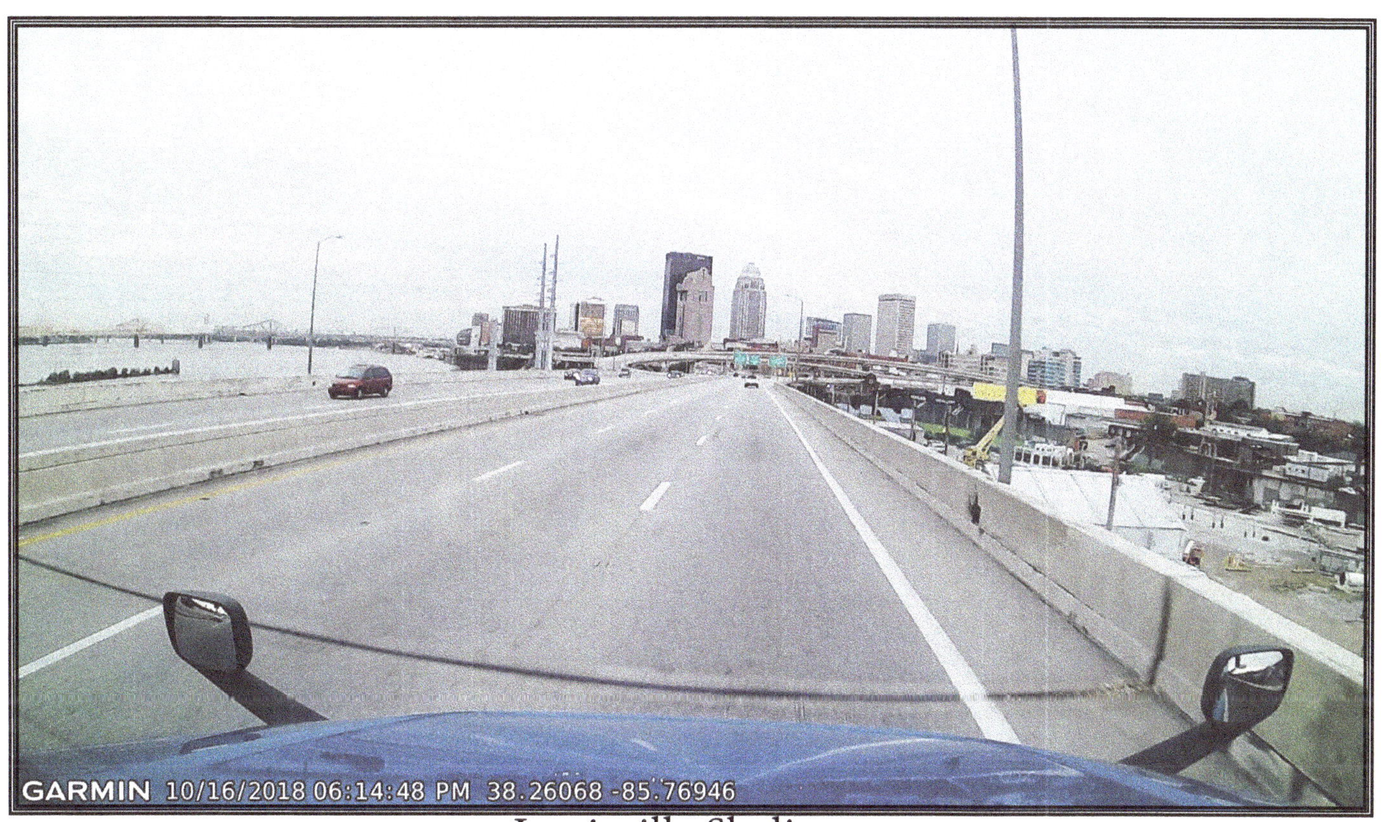

Louisville Skyline
I-64, Louisville, Kentucky

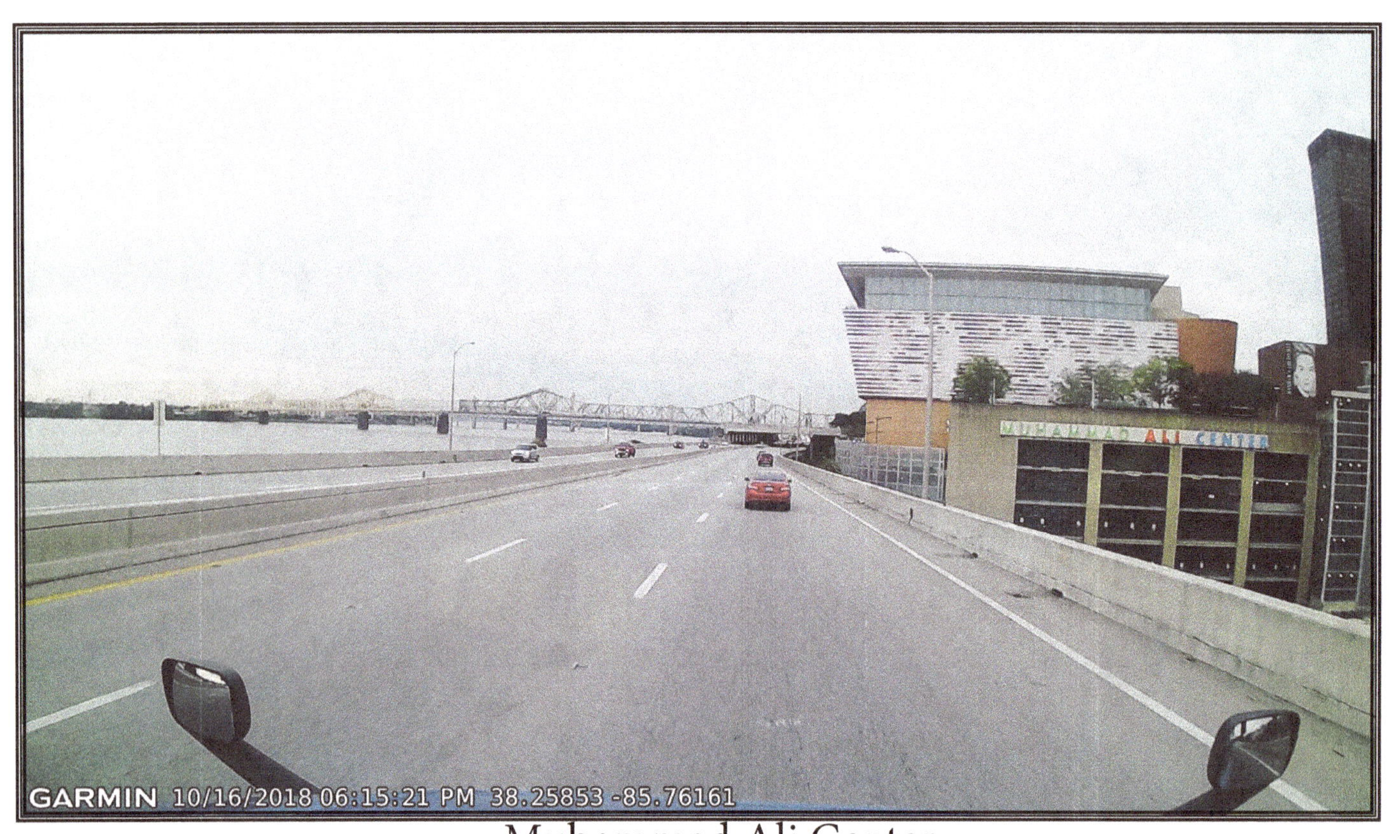

Muhammad Ali Center
I-64, Louisville, Kentucky

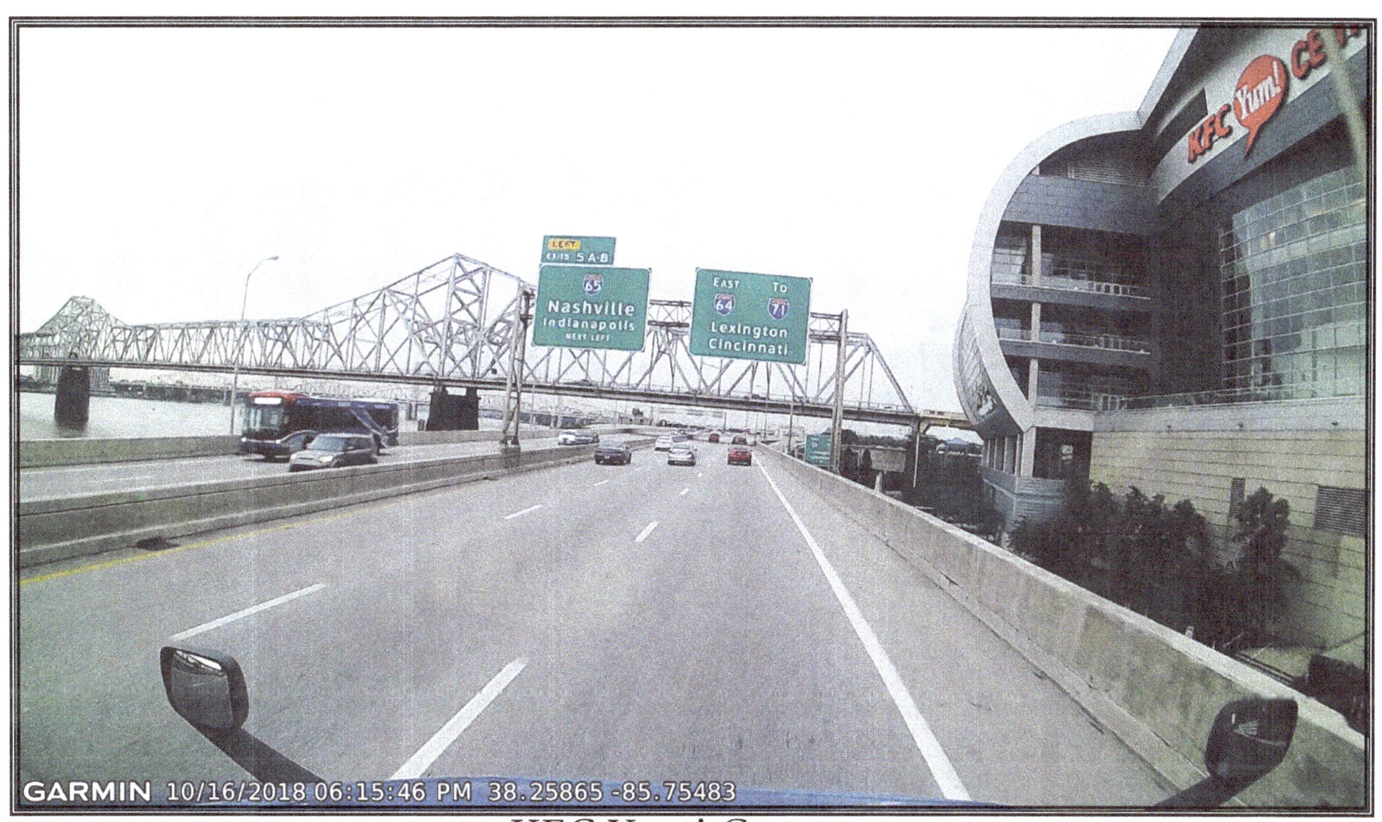

KFC Yum! Center
I-64, Louisville, Kentucky

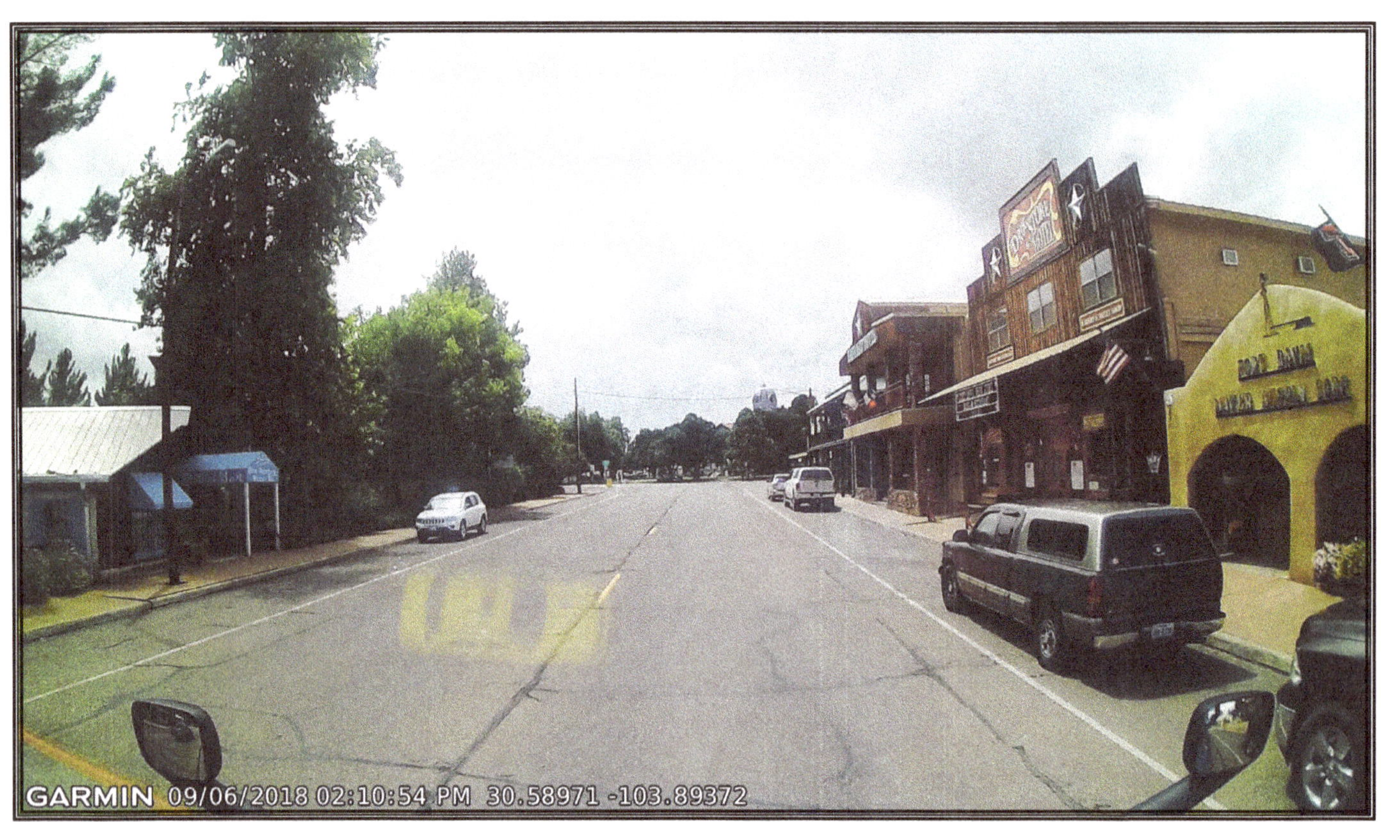

Historic Fort Davis
State Street, Fort Davis, Texas

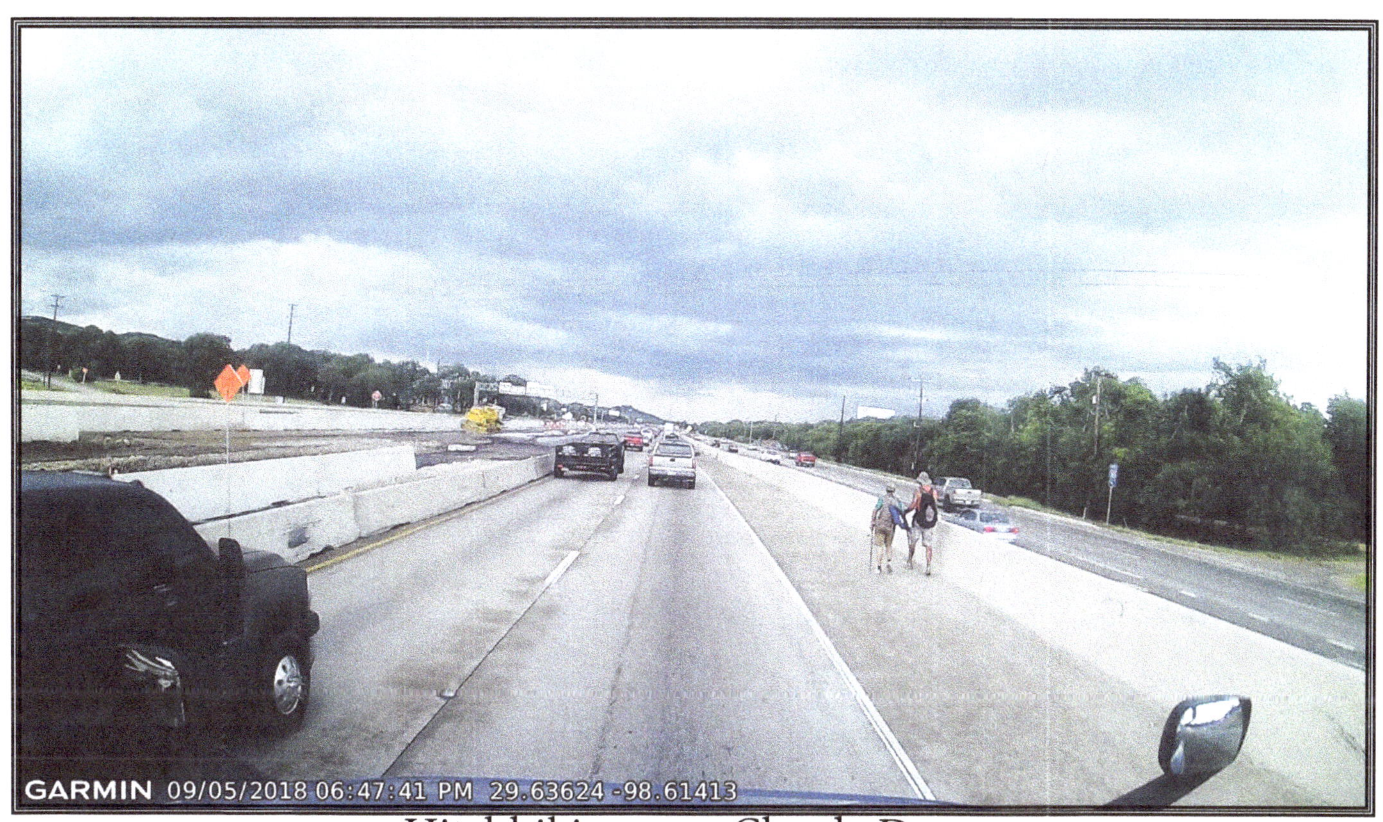

Hitchhiking on a Cloudy Day
I-10, San Antonio, Texas

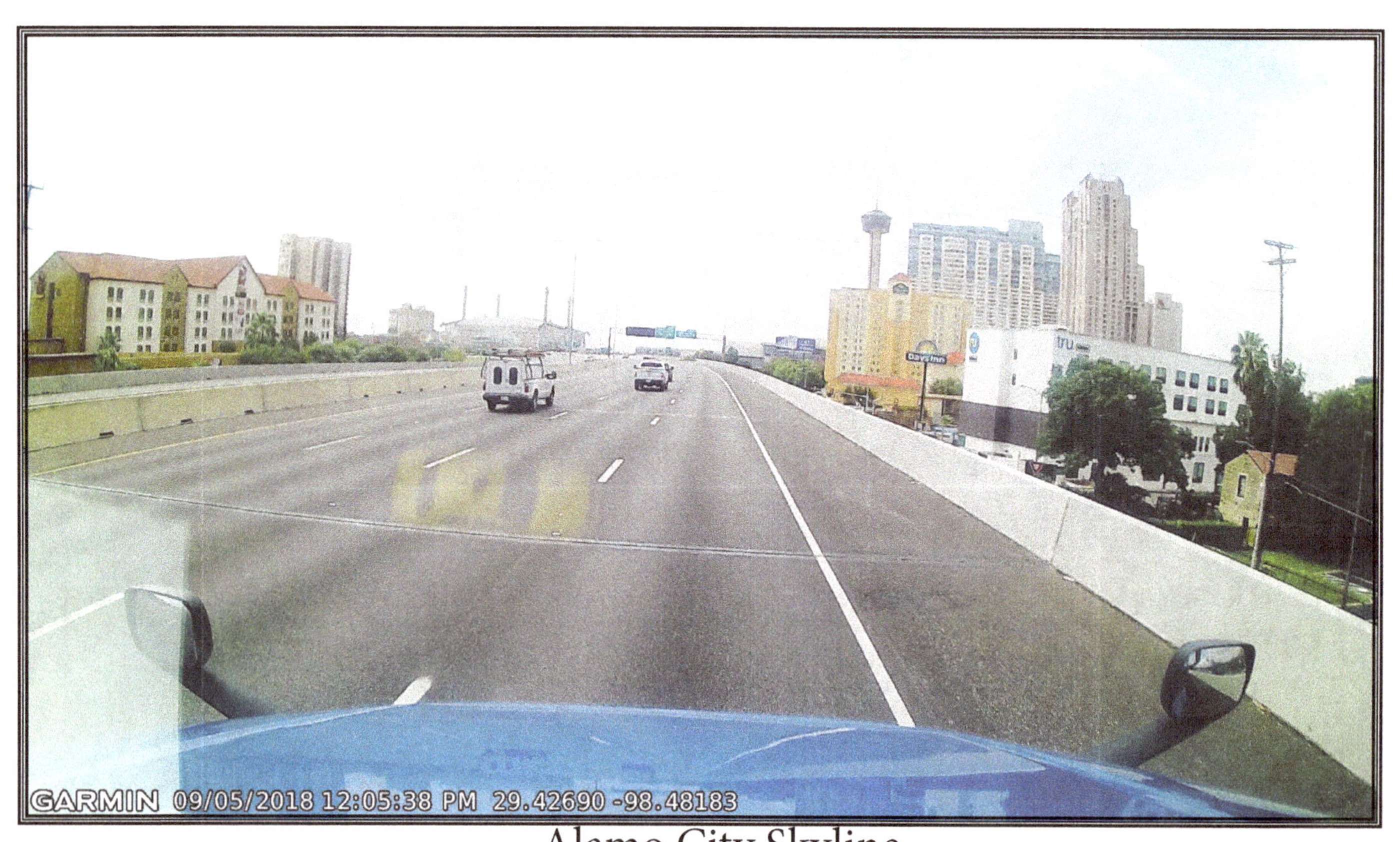

Alamo City Skyline
I-37, San Antonio, Texas

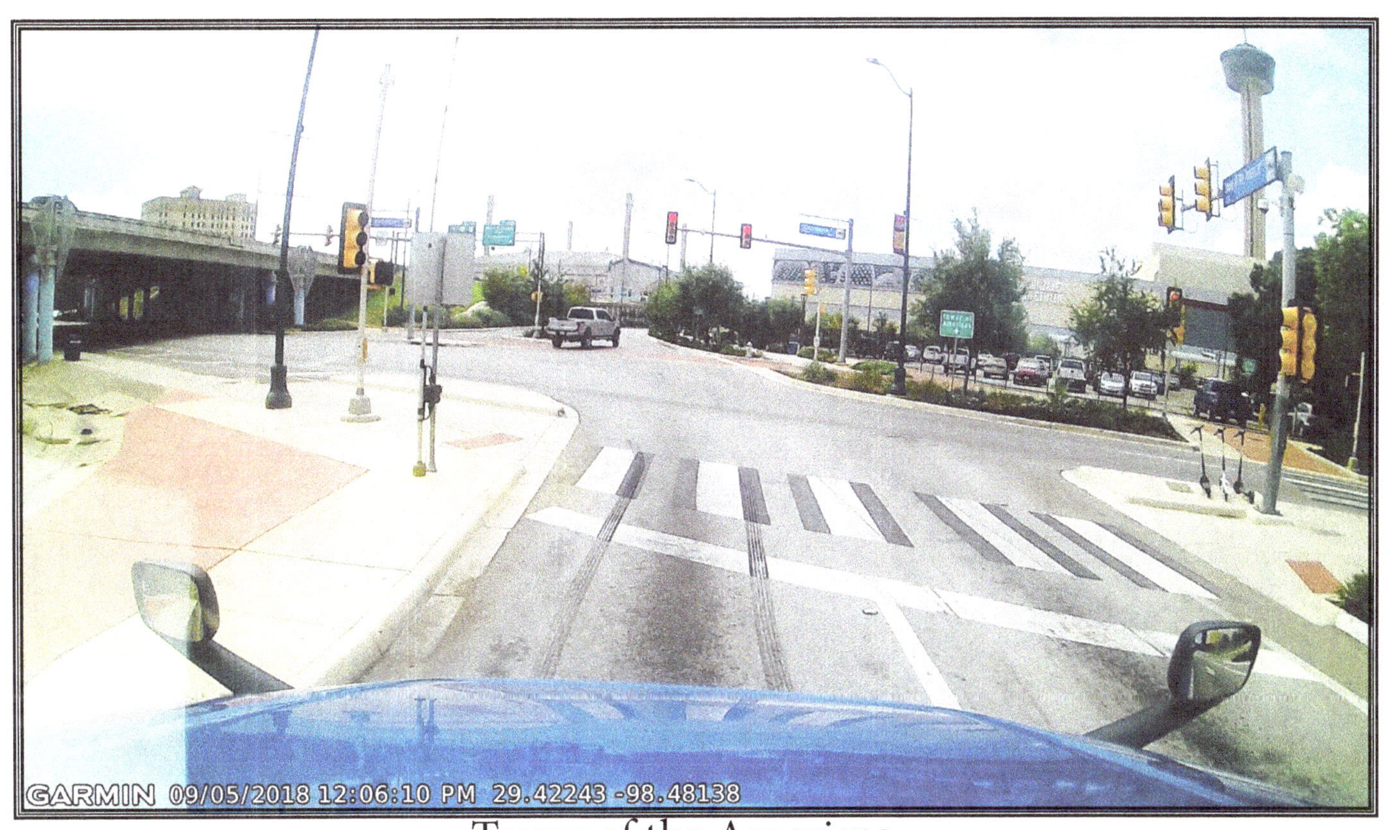

Tower of the Americas
I-37, San Antonio, Texas

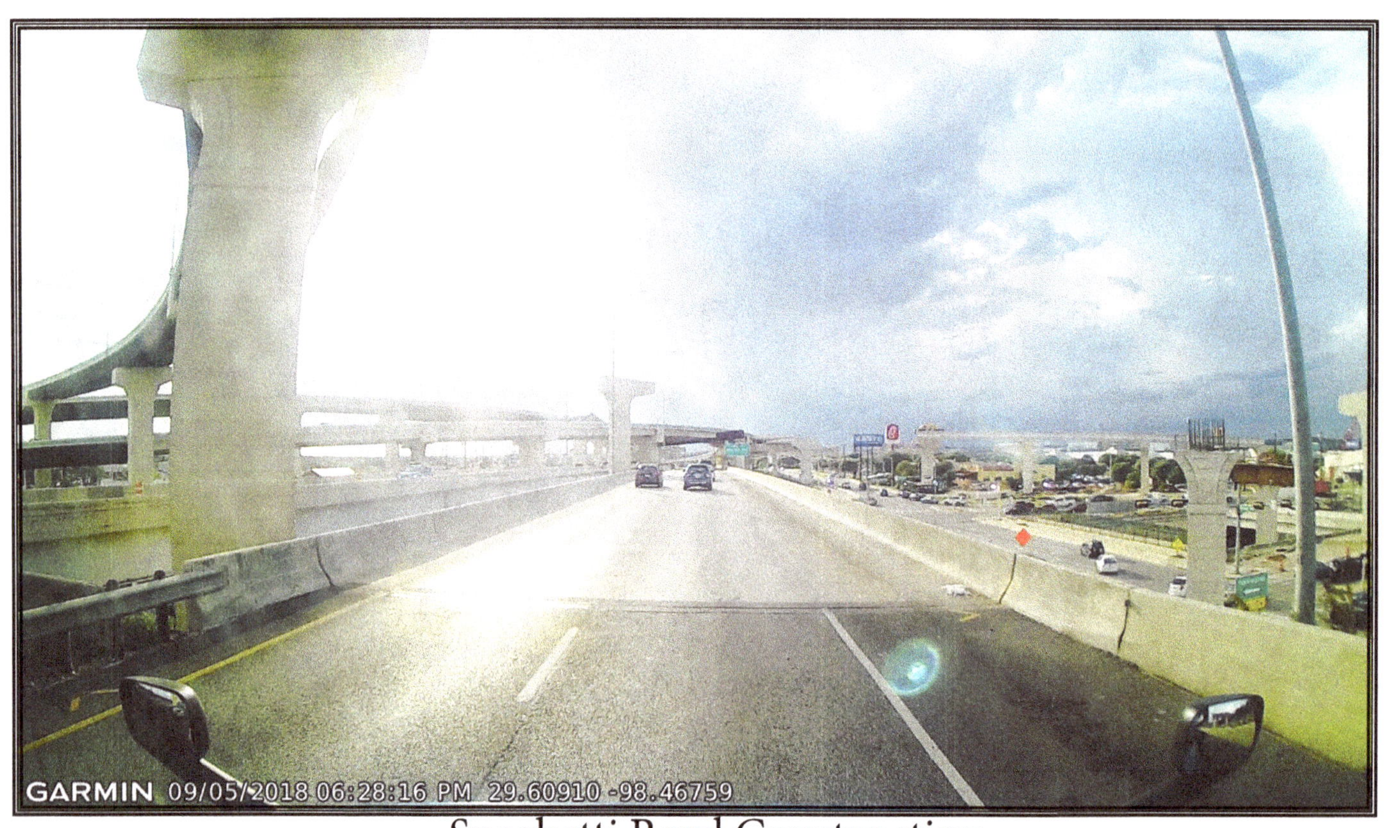

Spaghetti Bowl Construction
Loop 1604, San Antonio, Texas

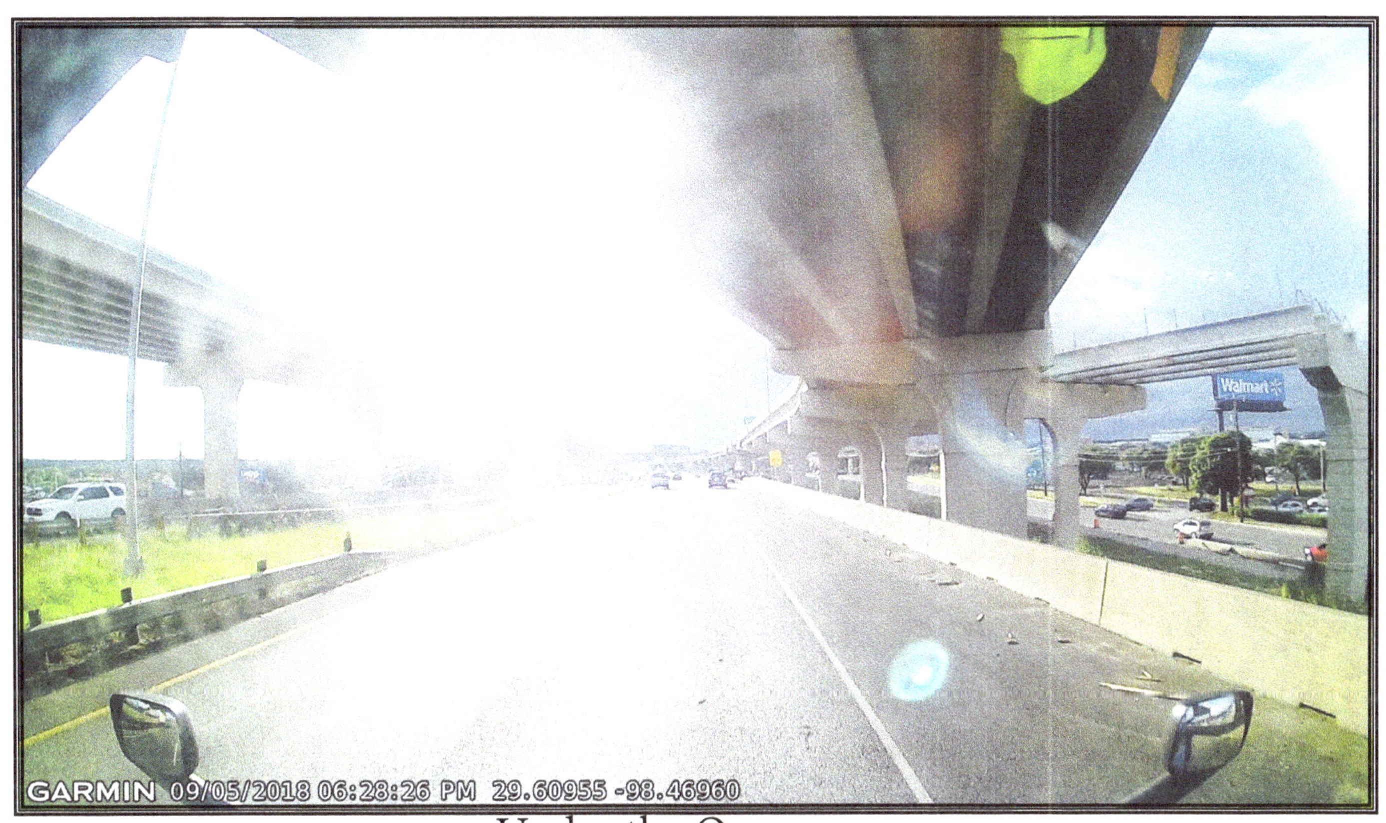

Under the Overpass
Loop 1604, San Antonio, Texas

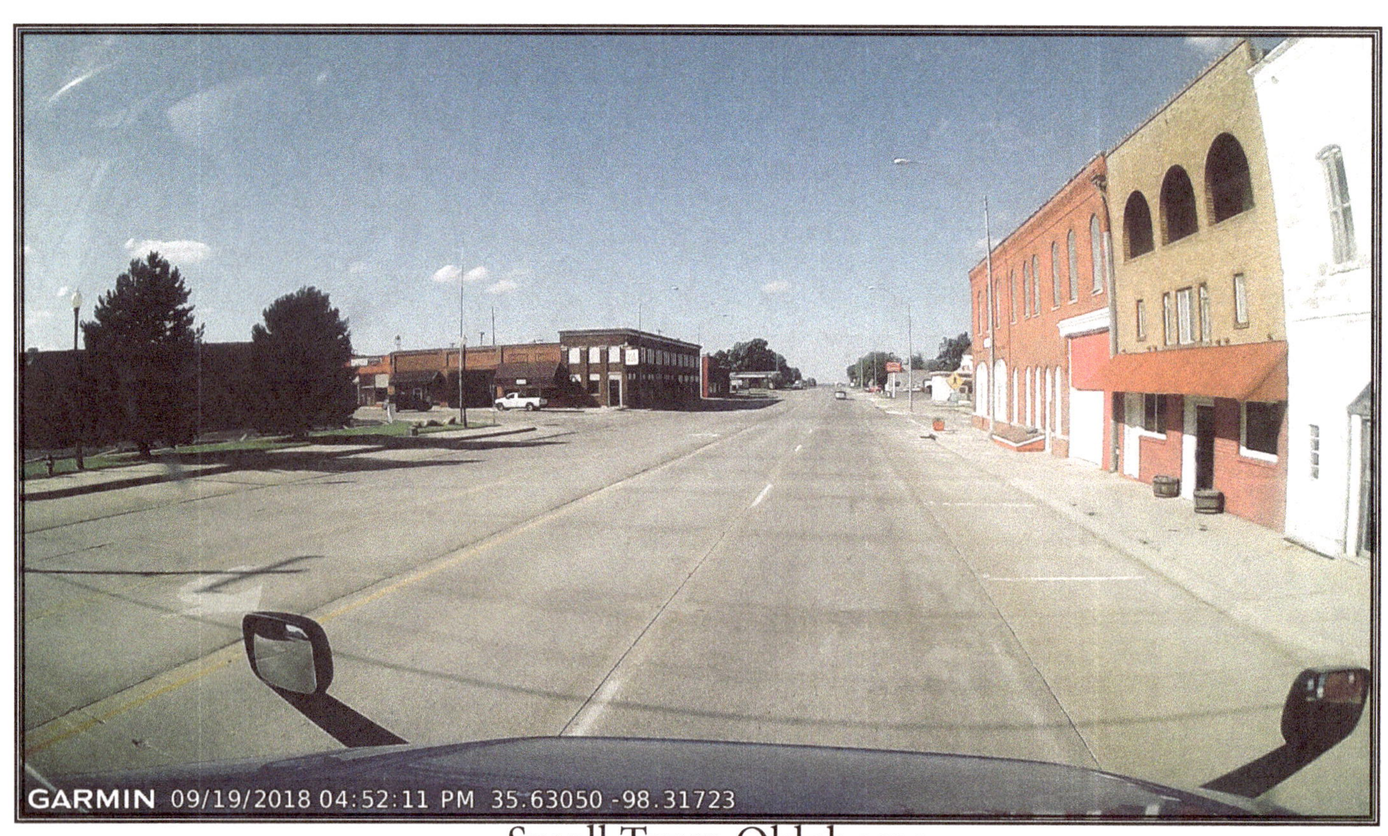

Small Town Oklahoma
Geary, Oklahoma

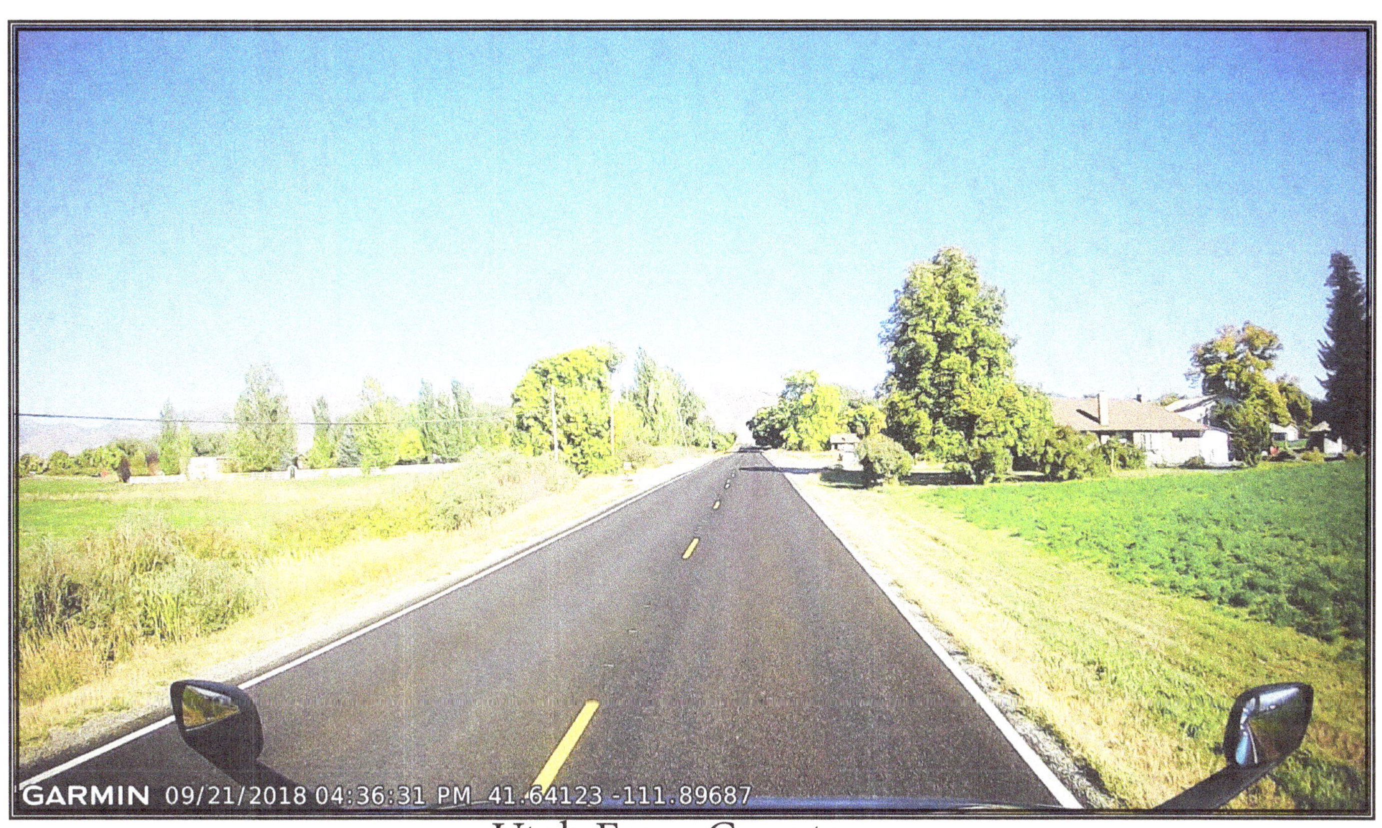

Utah Farm Country
US-101, Wellsville, Utah

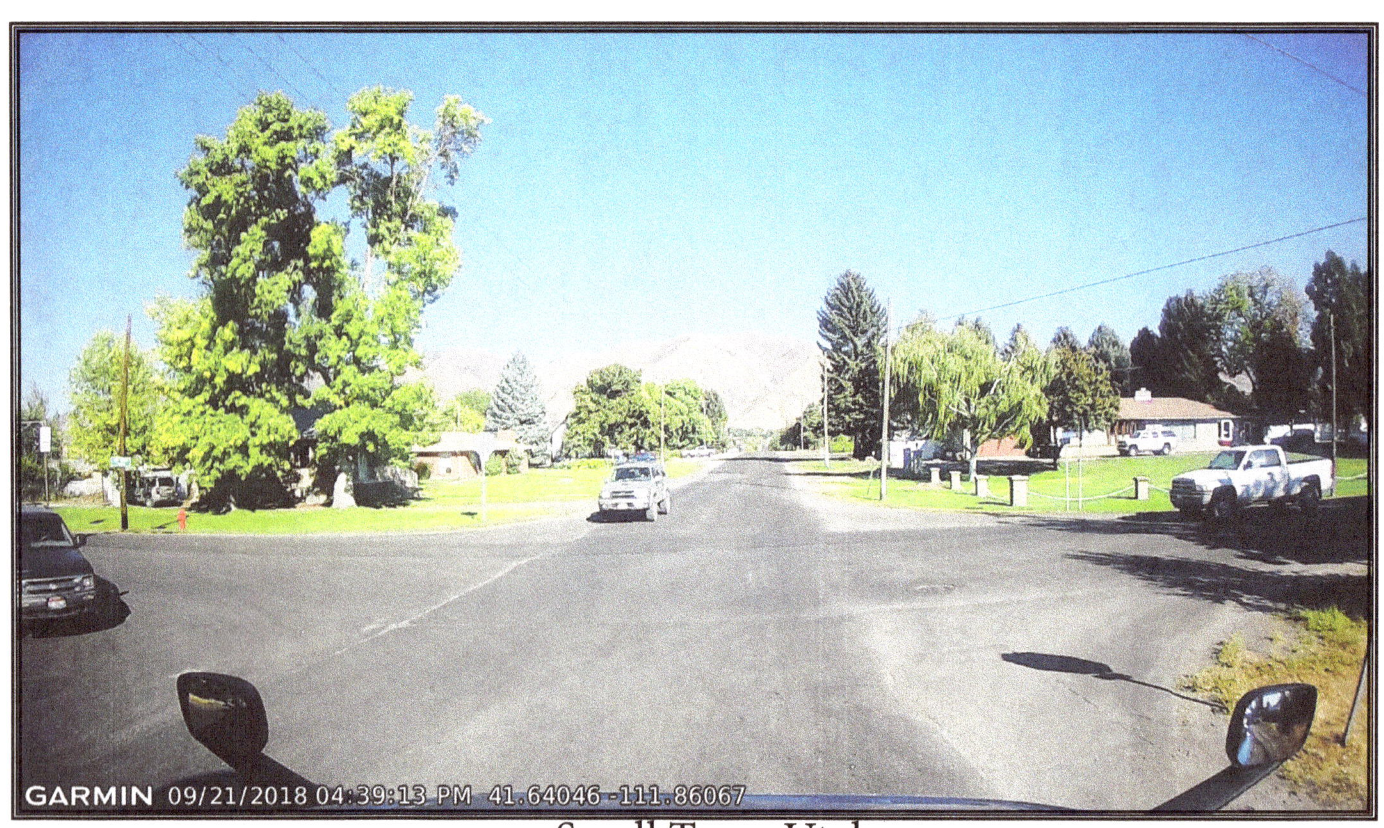

Small Town Utah
Hyrum, Utah

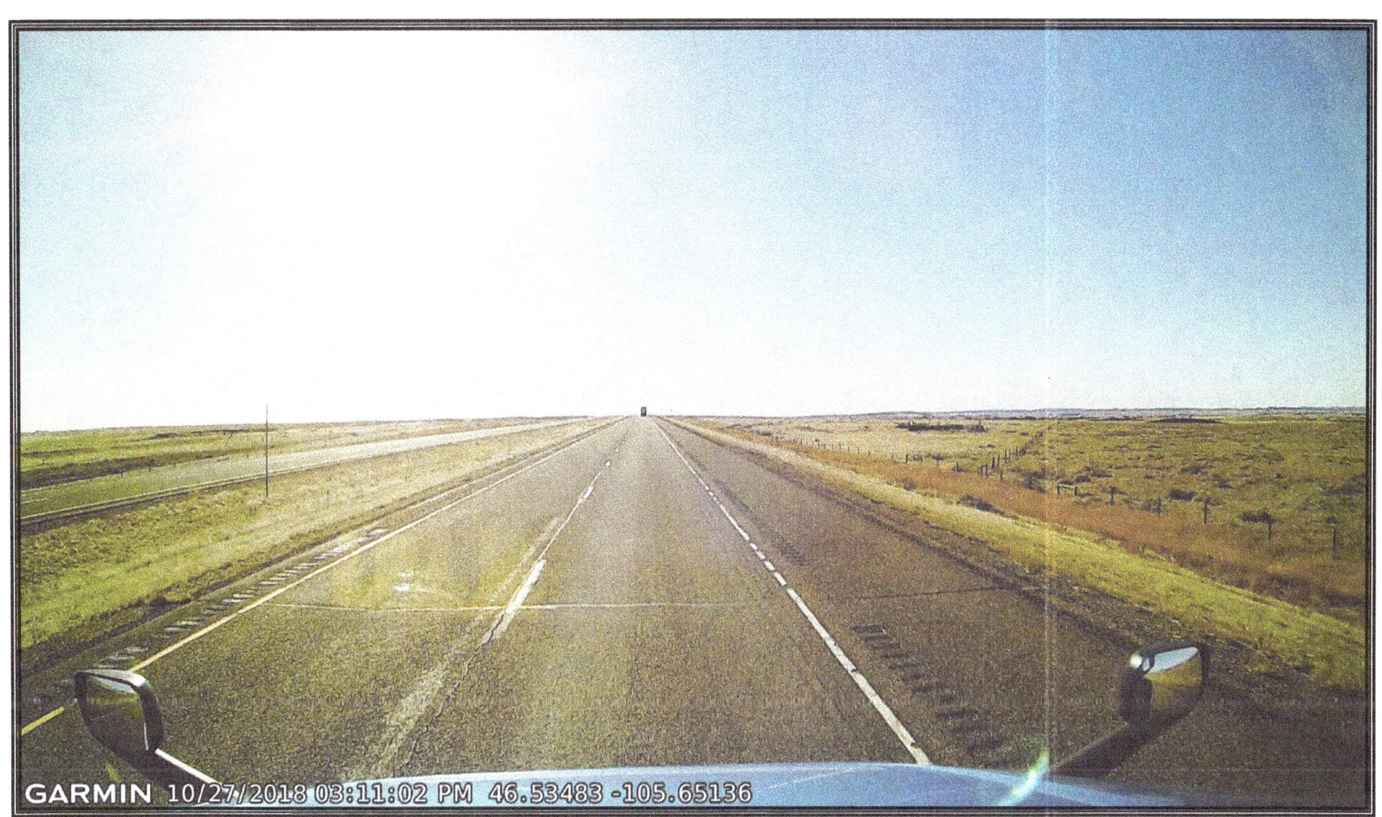

Montana Wilderness
I-94, Miles City, Montana

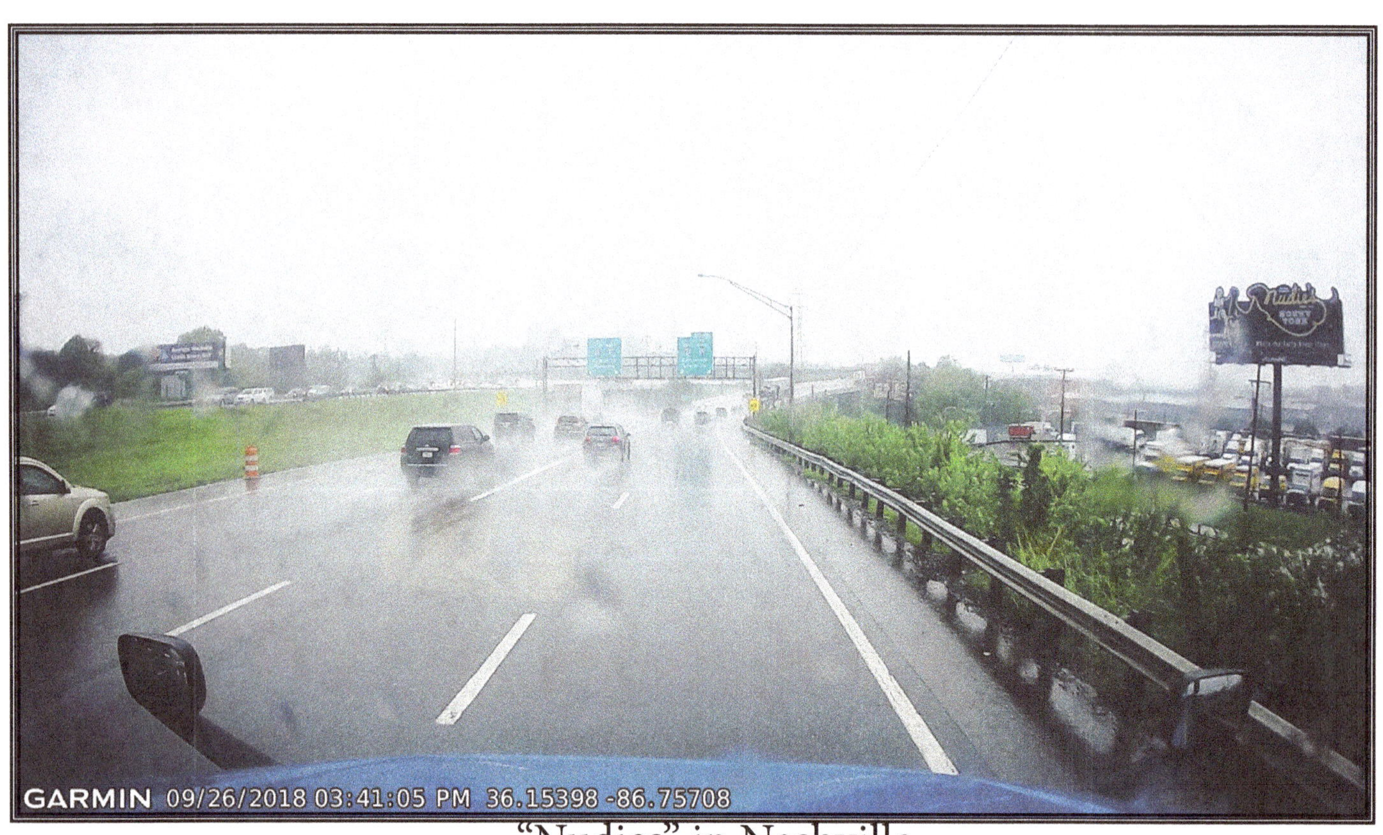

"Nudies" in Nashville
I-24, Nashville, Tennessee

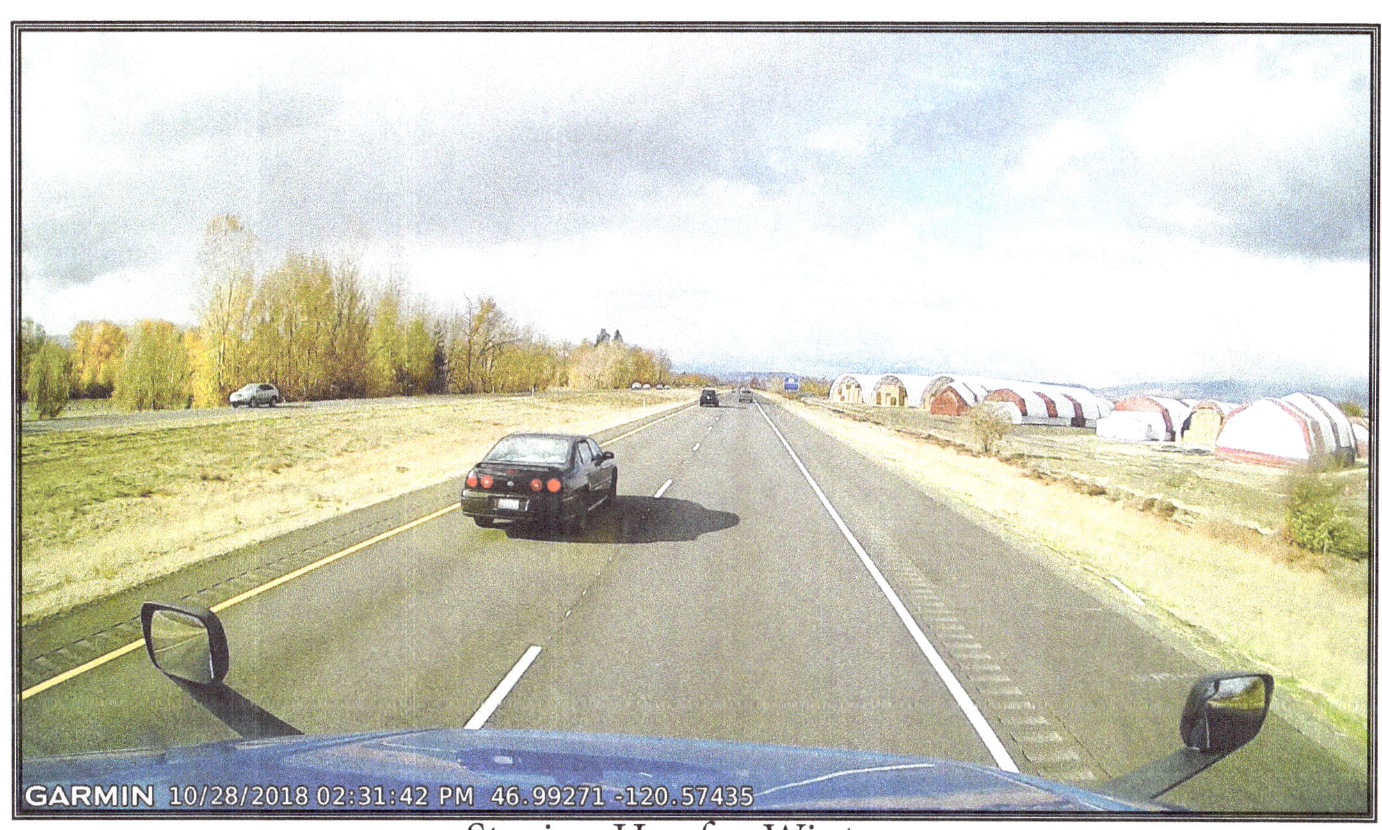

Storing Hay for Winter
I-90, Ellensburg, Washington

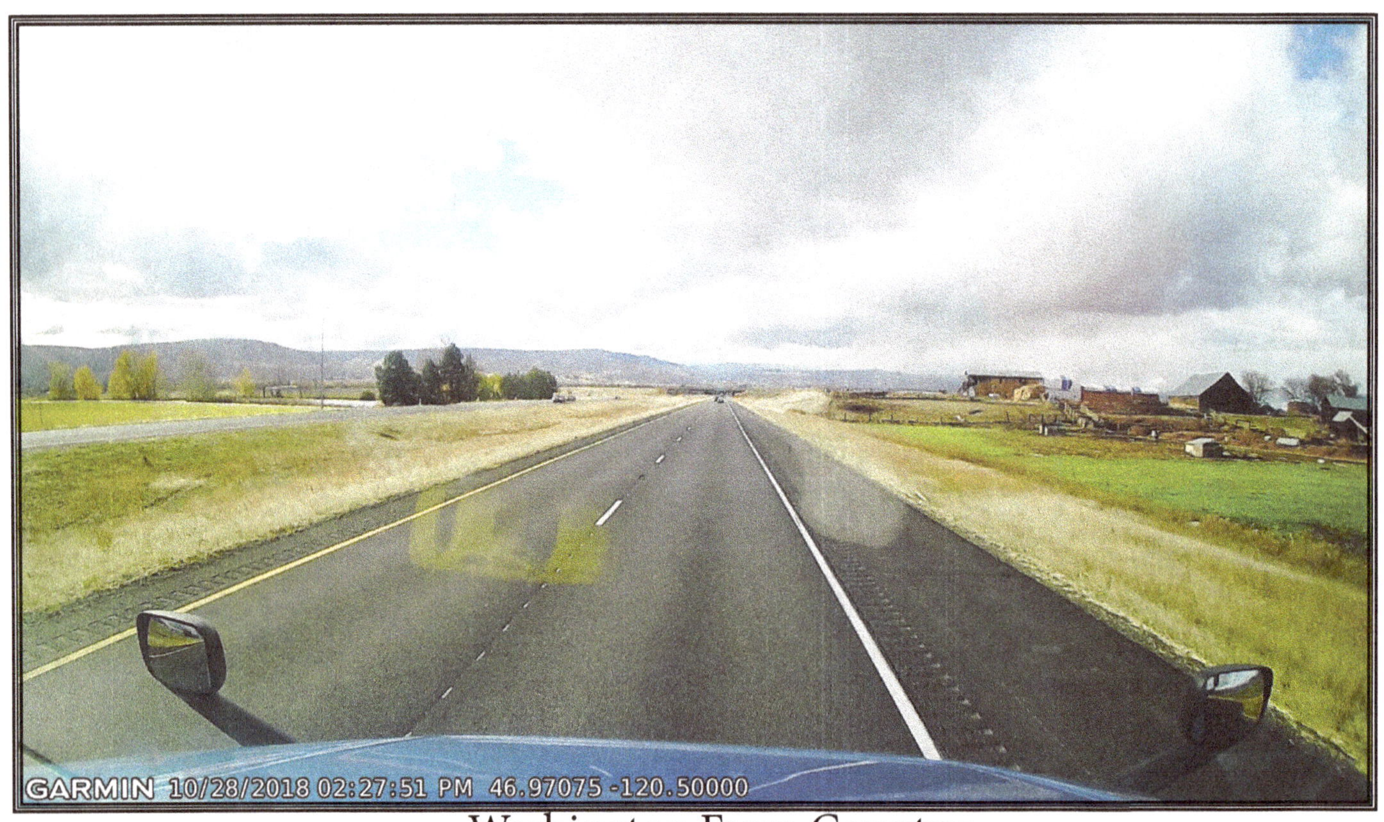

Washington Farm Country
I-90, Ellensburg, Washington

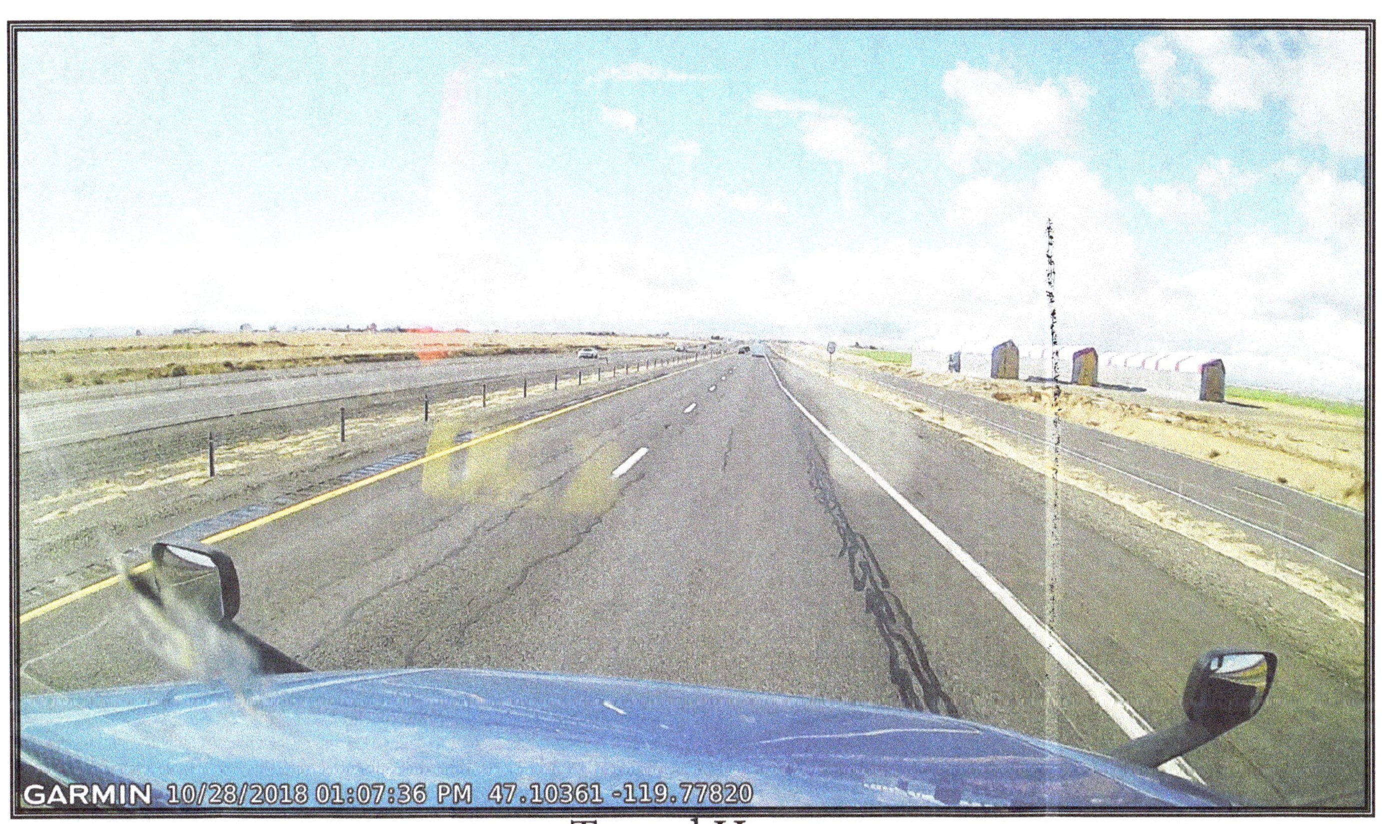

Tarped Hay
I-90, Quincy, Washington

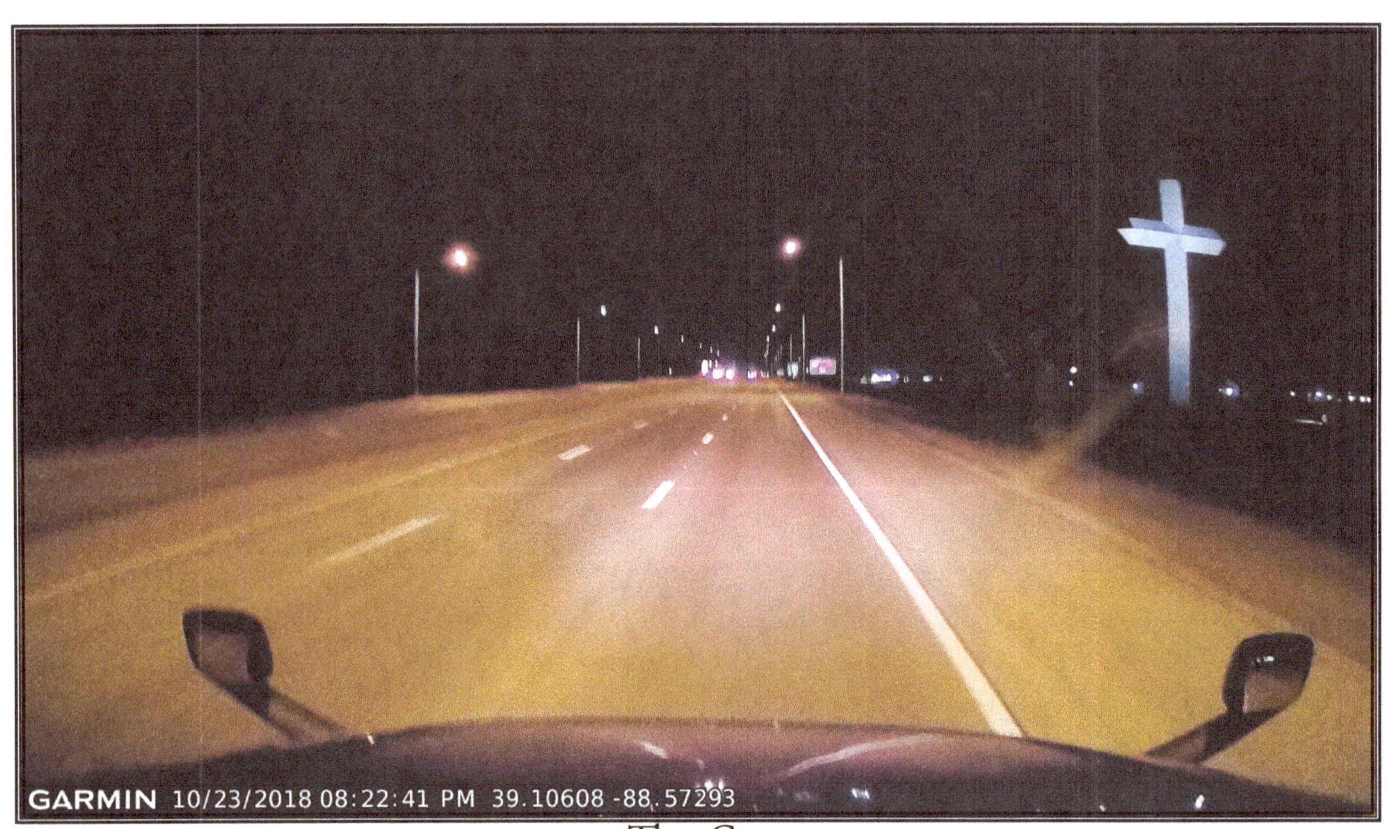

The Cross
I-70, Effingham, Illinois

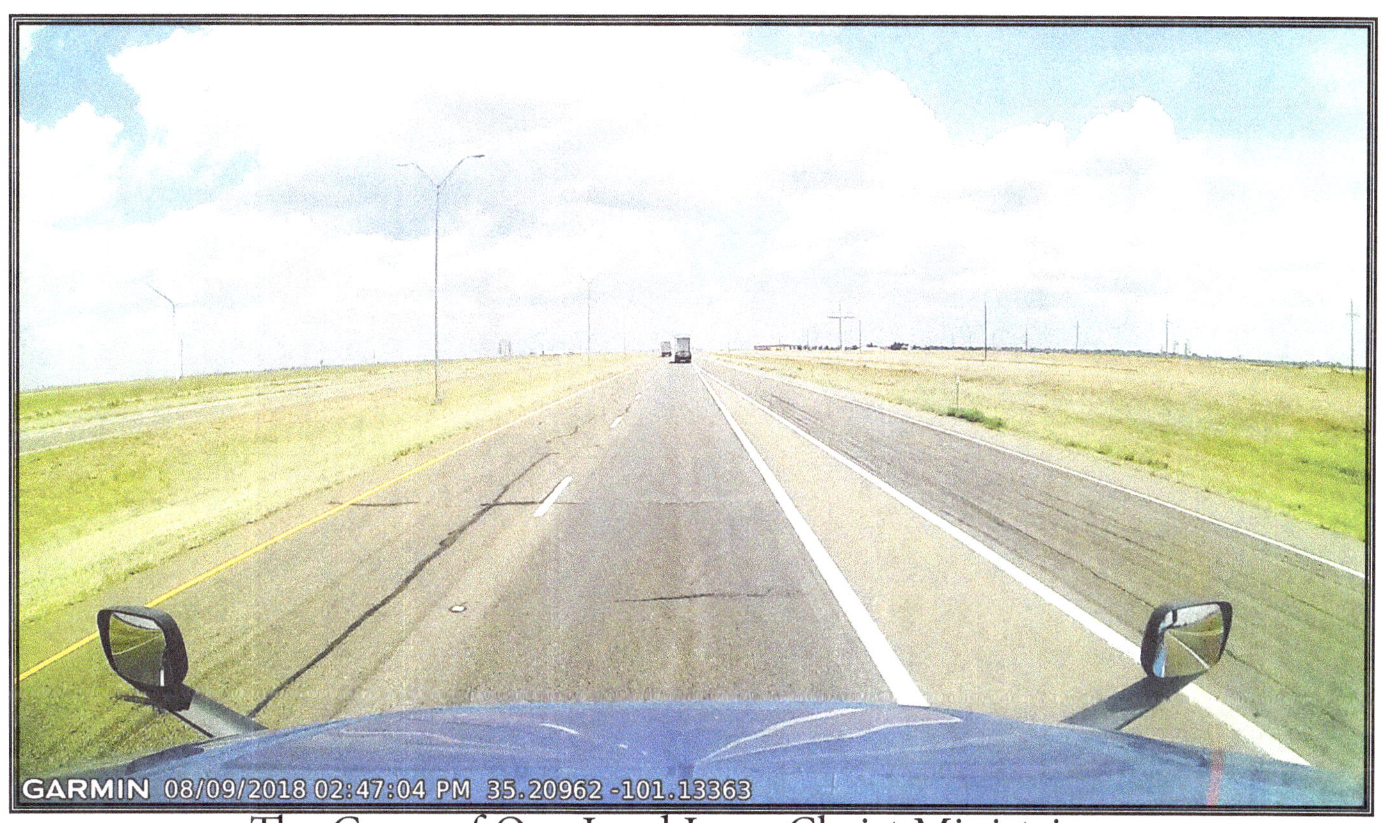

The Cross of Our Lord Jesus Christ Ministries
I-40, Groom, Texas

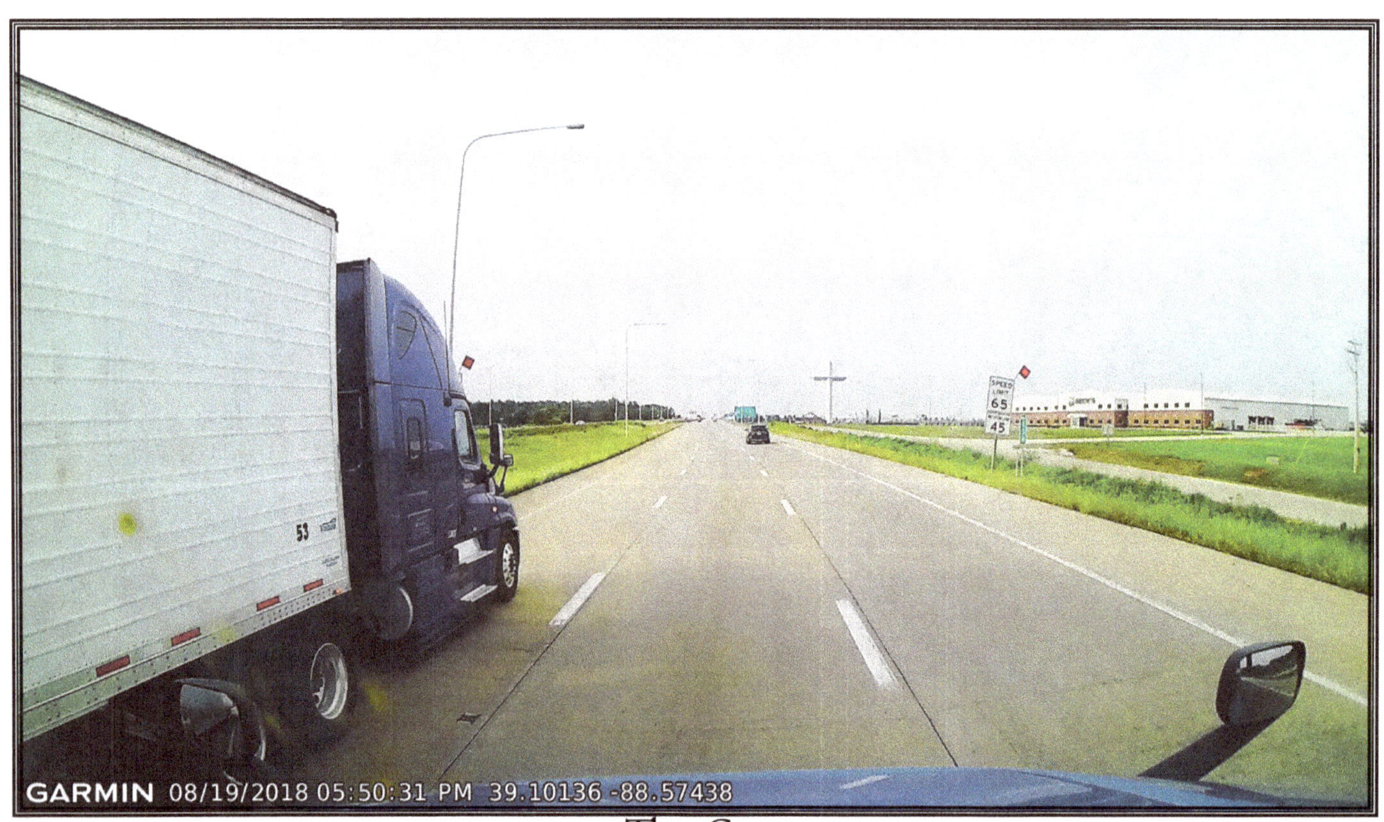

The Cross
I-70, Effingham, Illinois

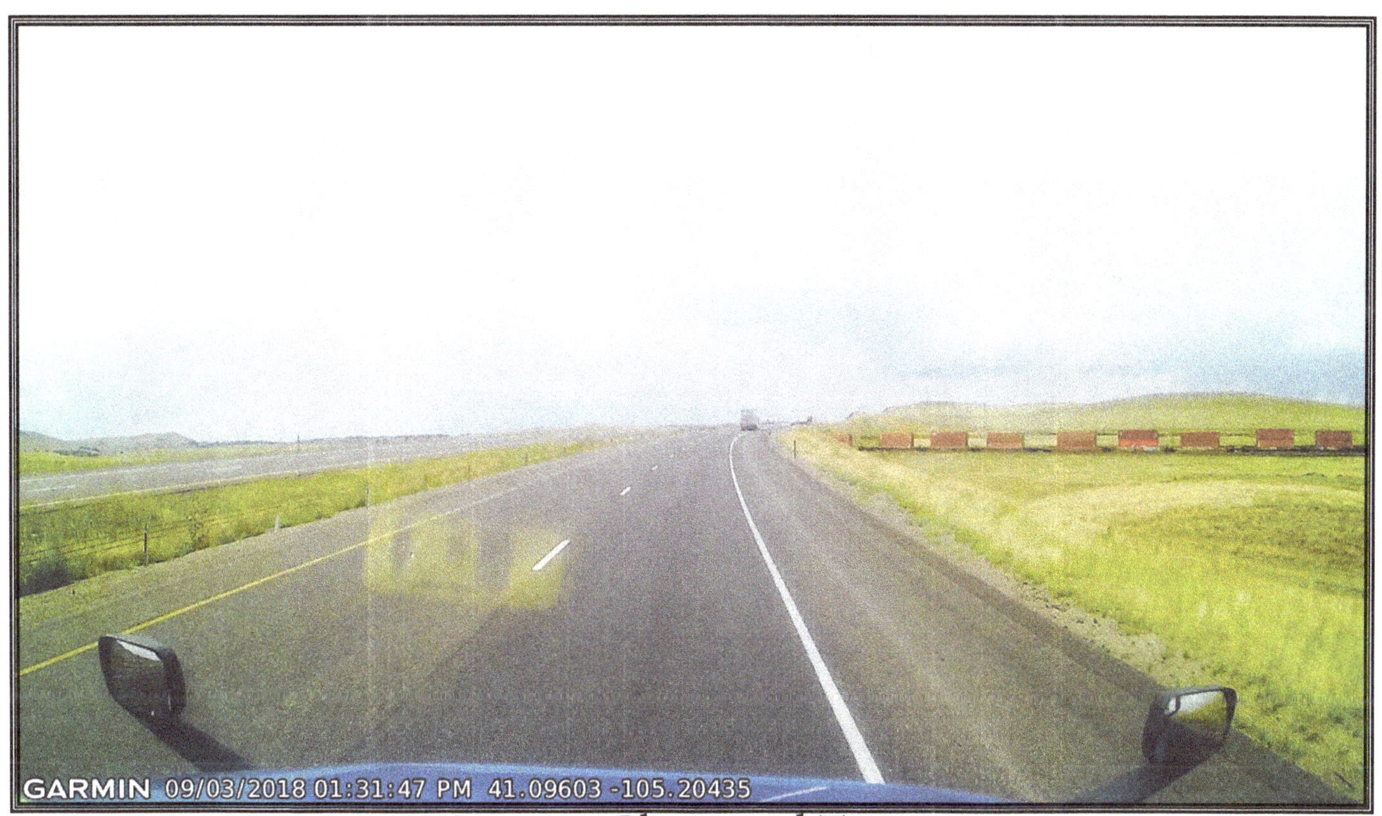

Wyoming Plains and Trains
I-80, Granite, Wyoming

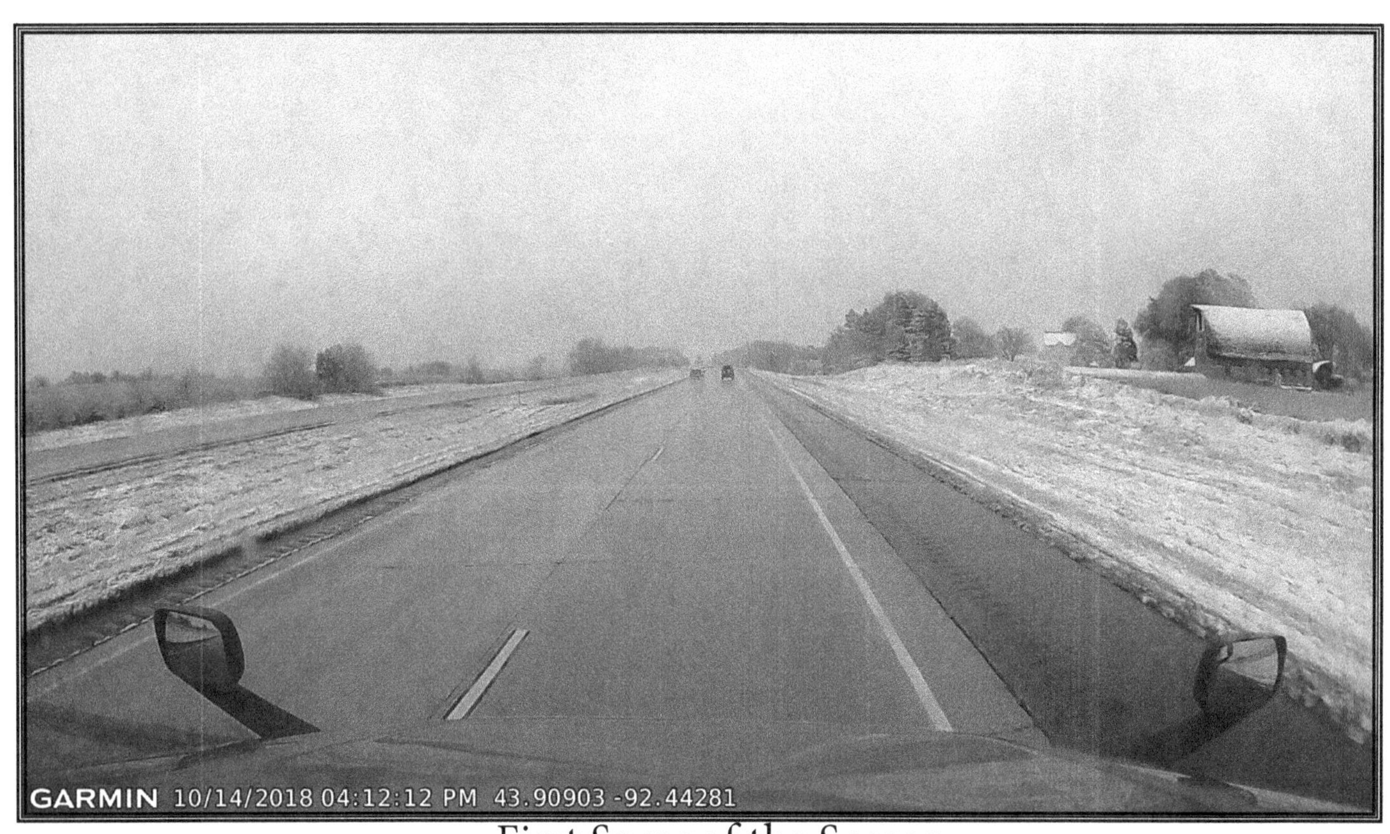

First Snow of the Season
I-90, Rochester, Minnesota

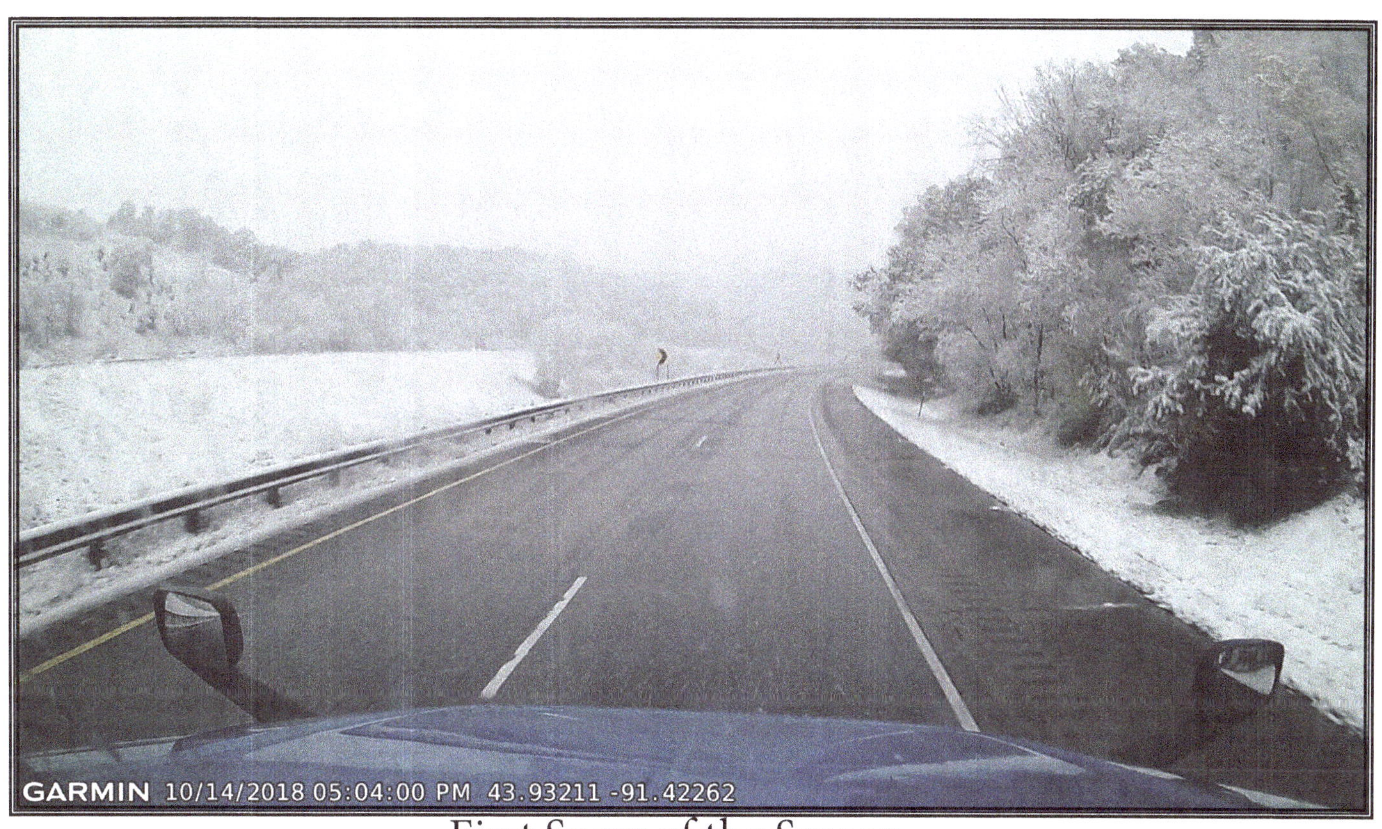

First Snow of the Season
I-90, Dakota, Minnesota

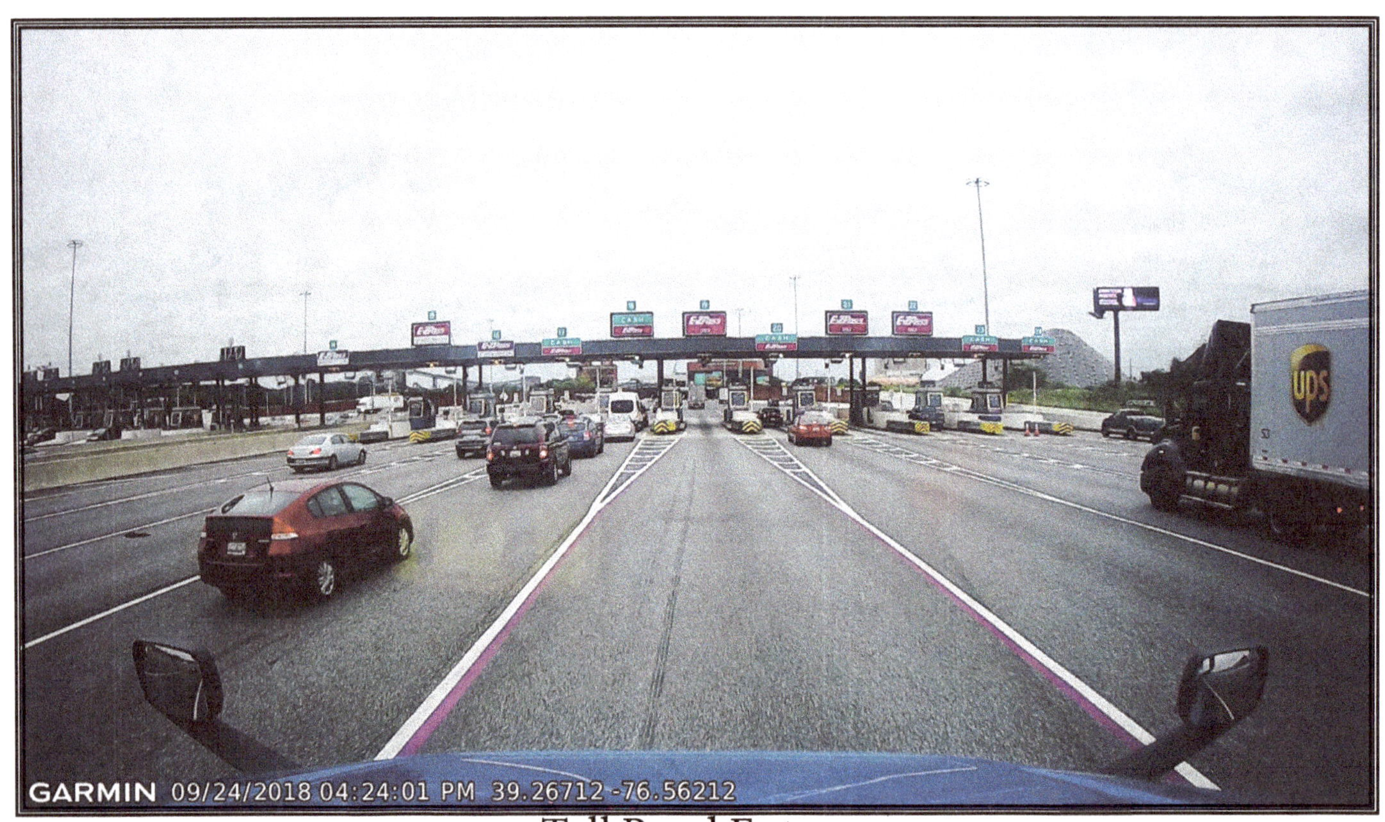

Toll Road Entrance
I-95, Baltimore, Maryland

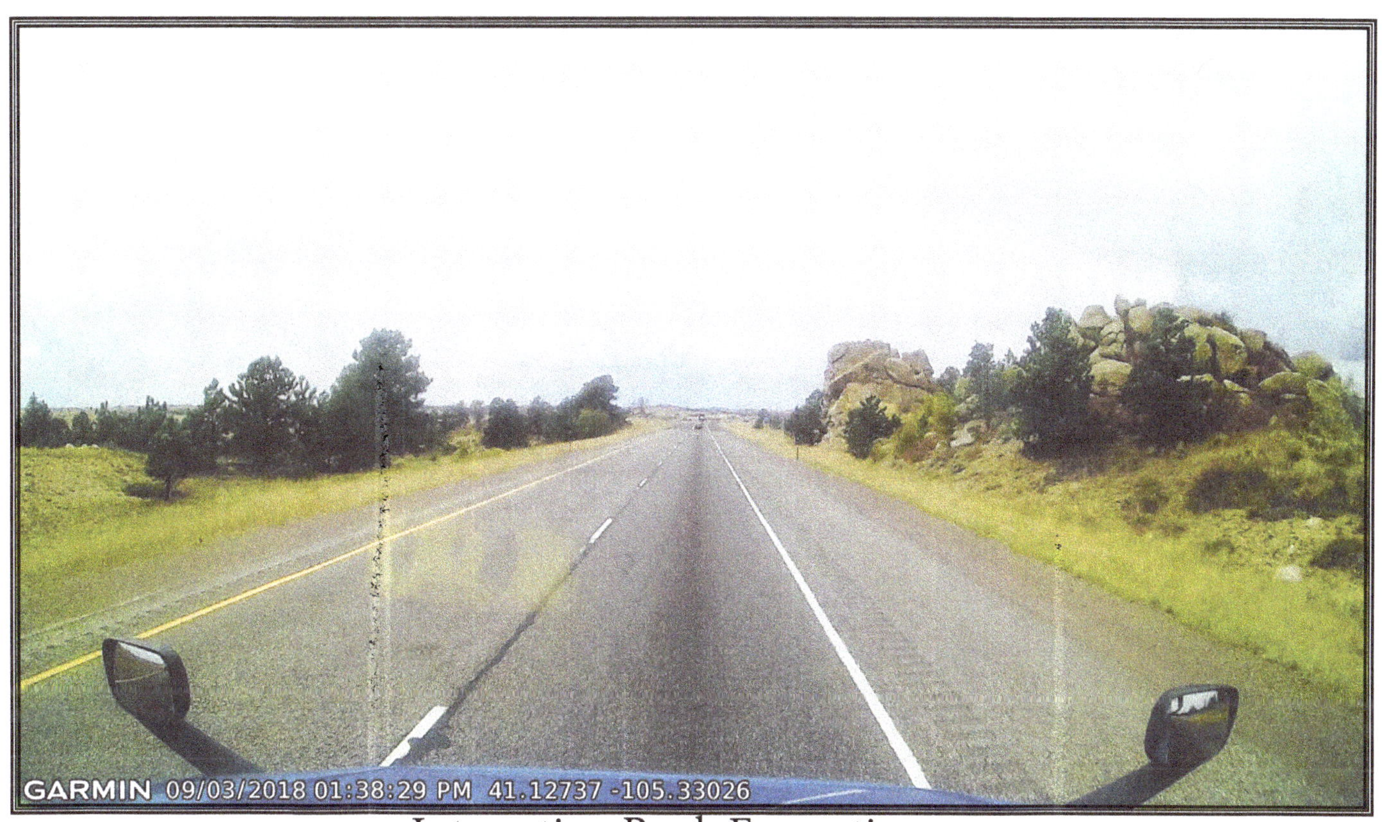

Interesting Rock Formations
I-80, Buford, Wyoming

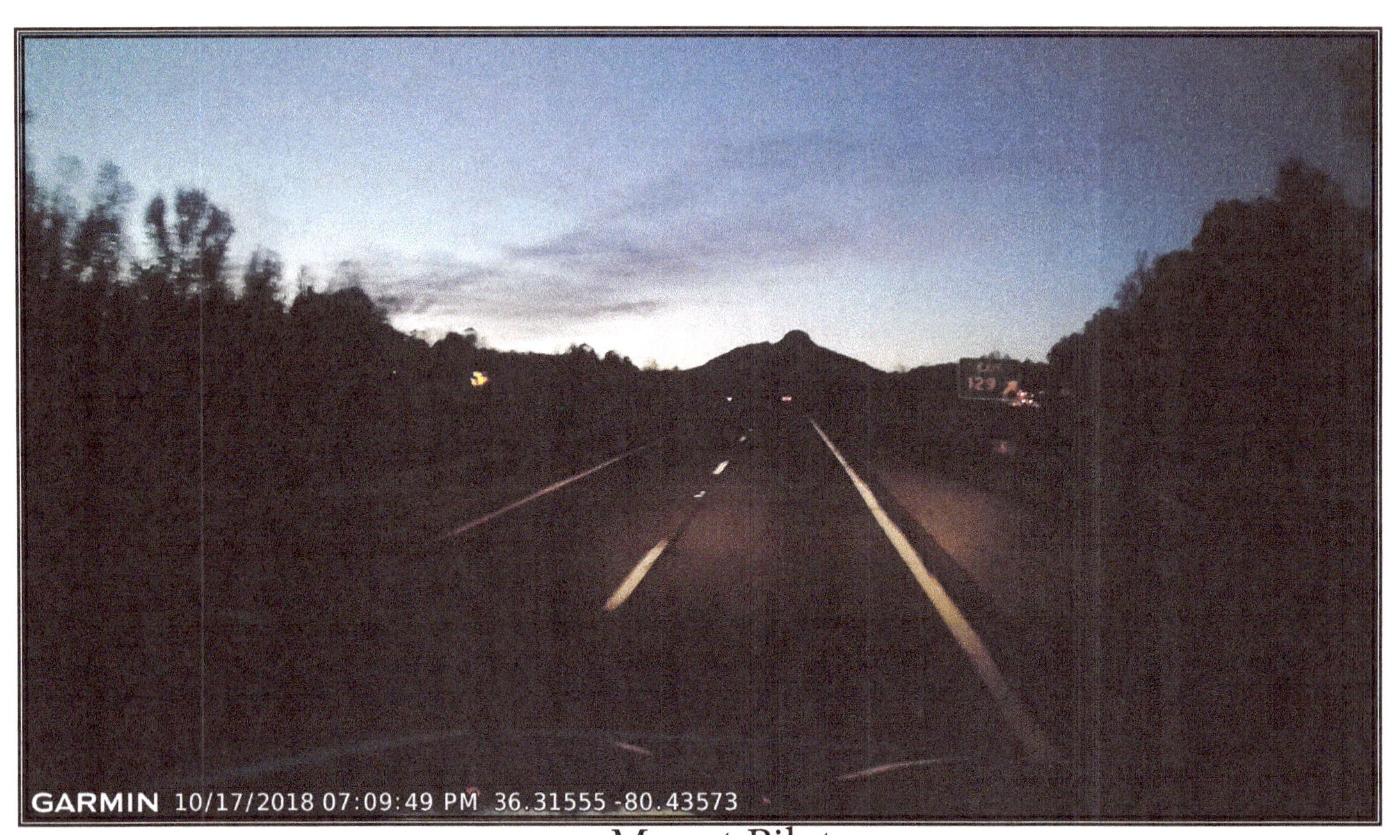

Mount Pilot
US-52, Pinnacle, North Carolina

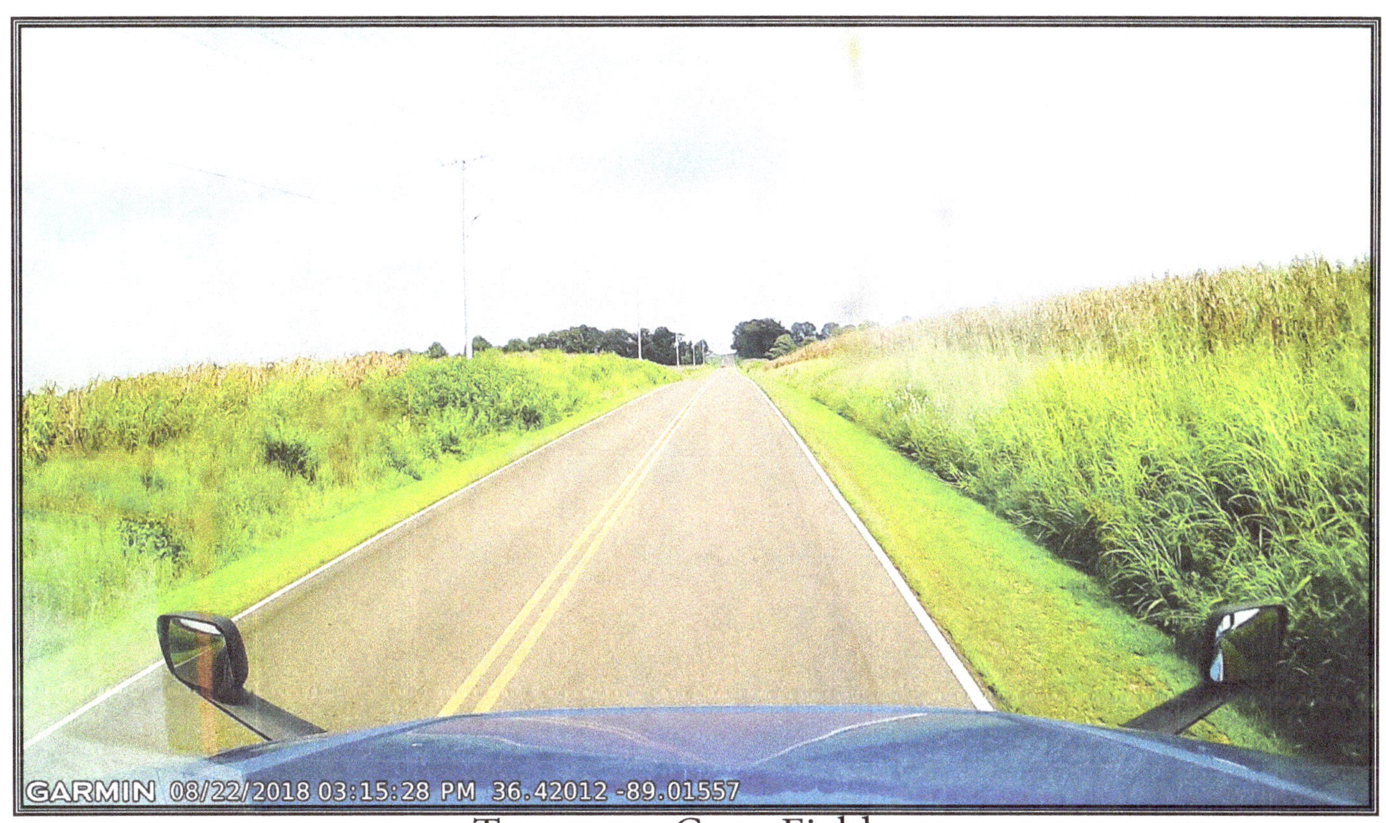

Tennessee Corn Fields
Tyson Drive, Union City, Tennessee

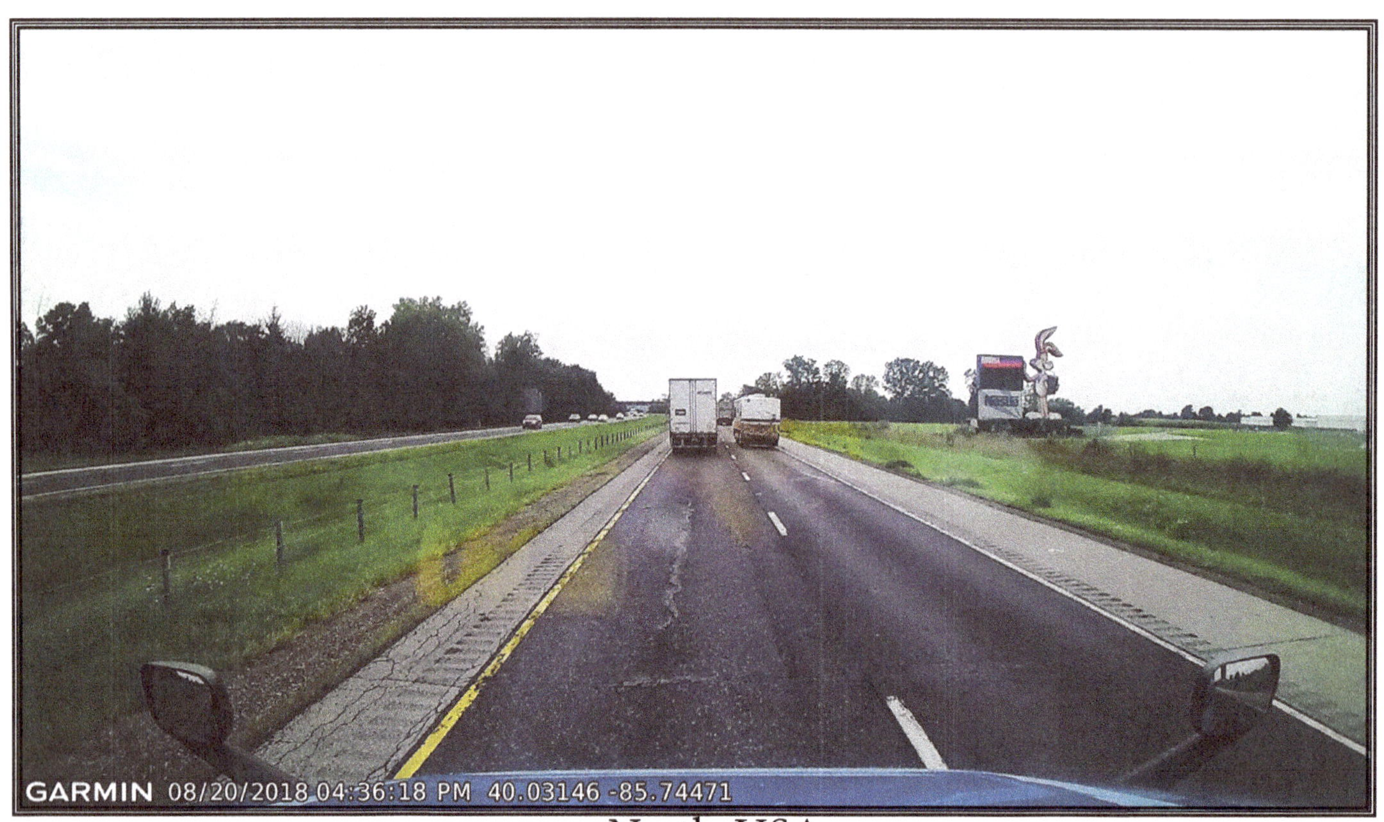

Nestle USA
I-69, Anderson, Indiana

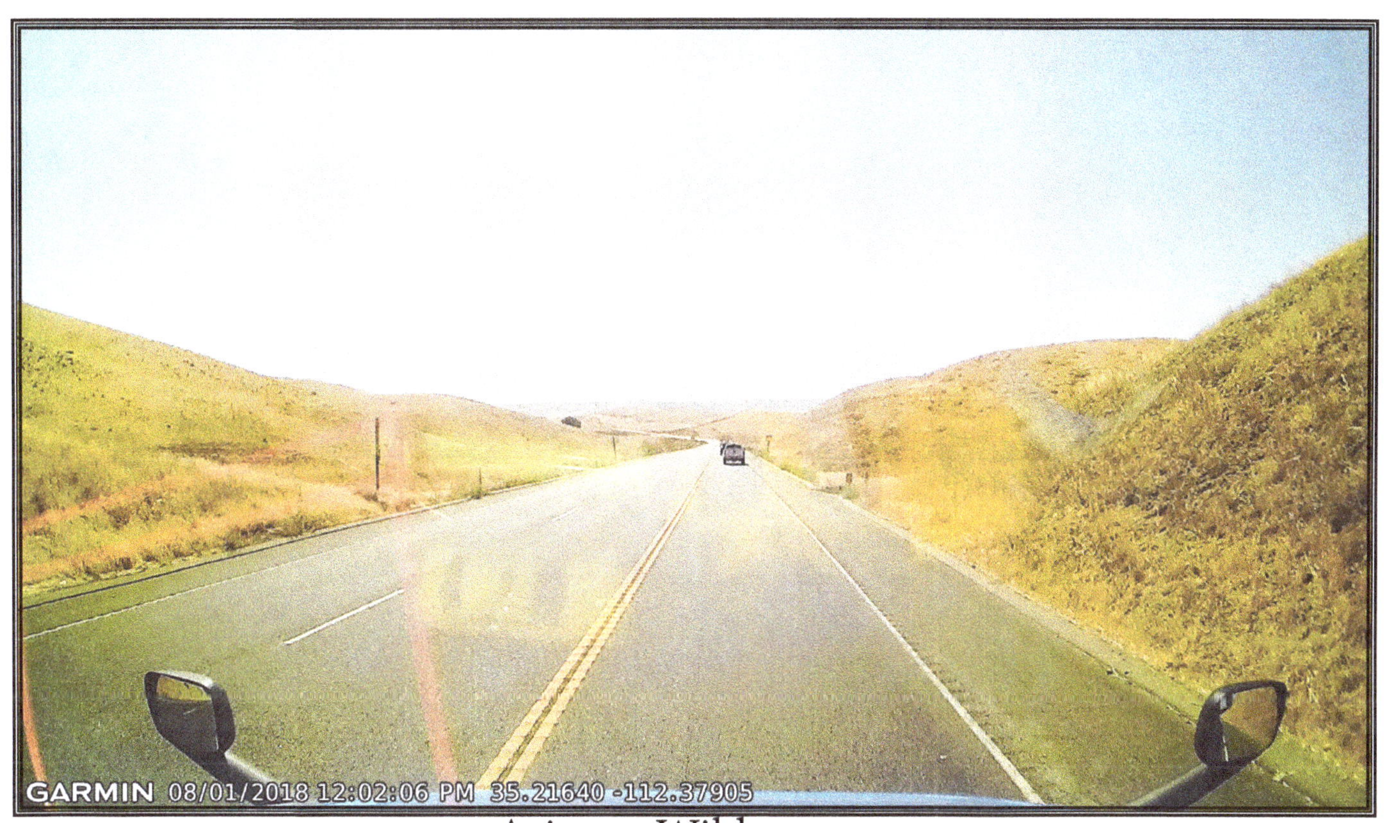

Arizona Wilderness
I-40, Williams, Arizona

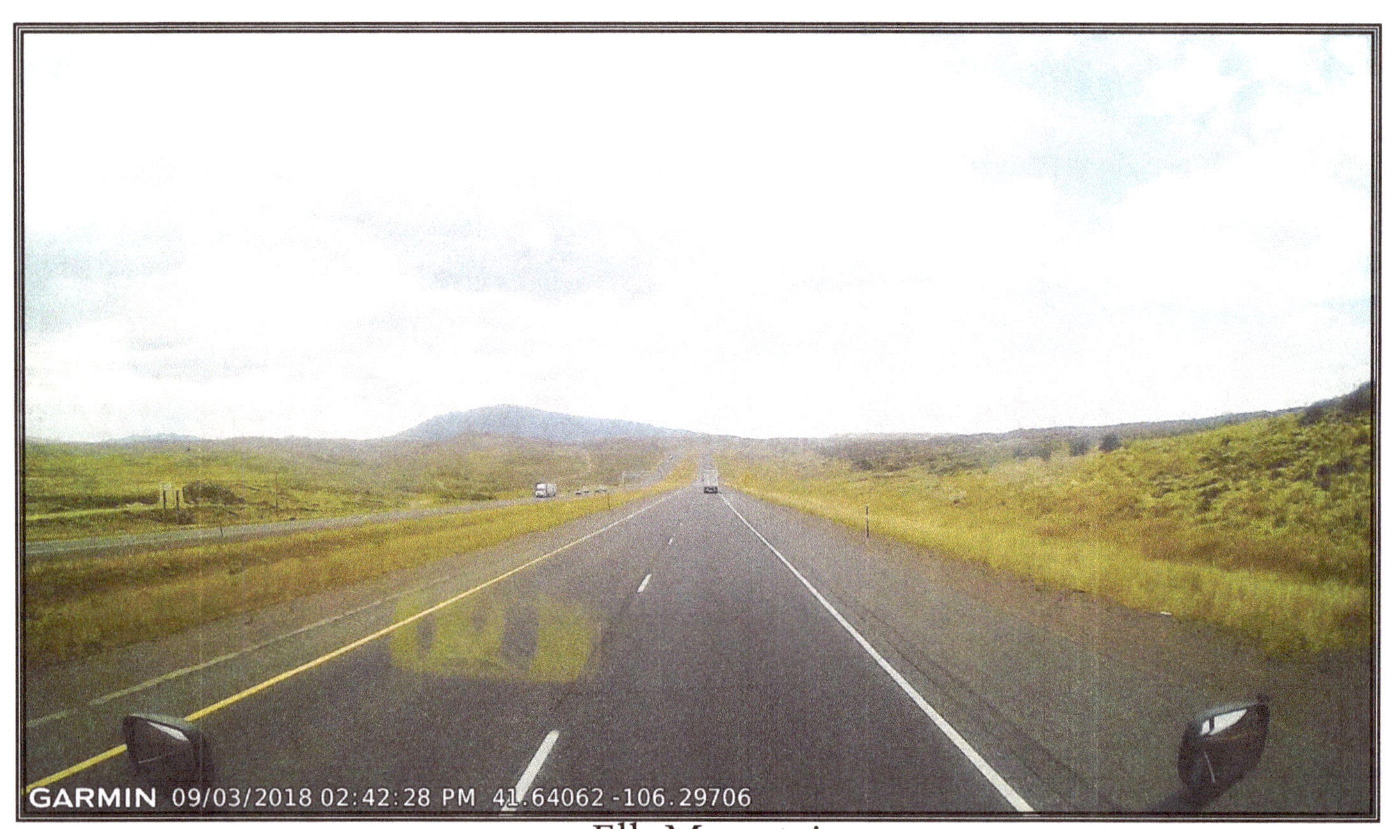

Elk Mountain
I-80, Elk Mountain, Wyoming

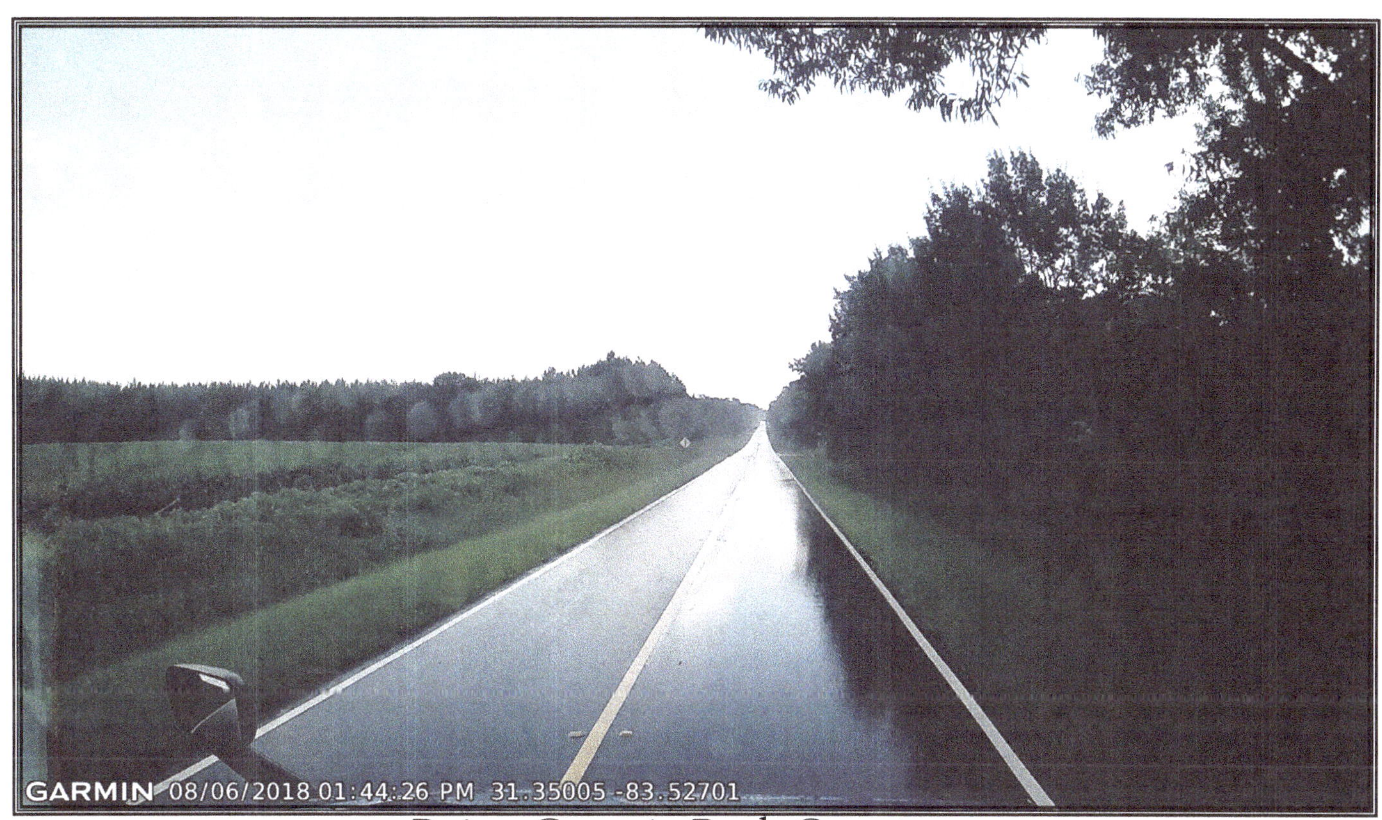

Rainy Georgia Back Country
Tifton, Georgia

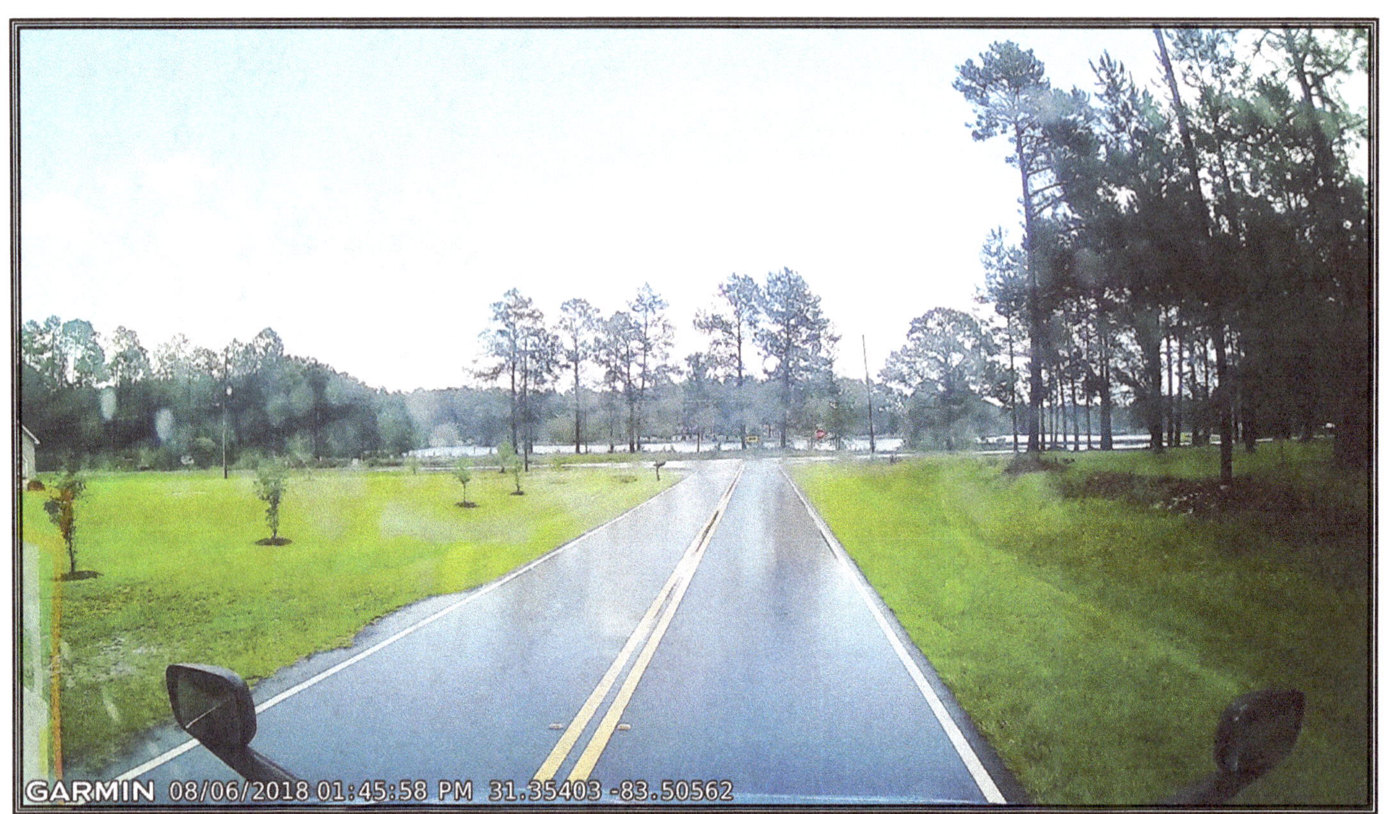

Lake Larry
Tifton, Georgia

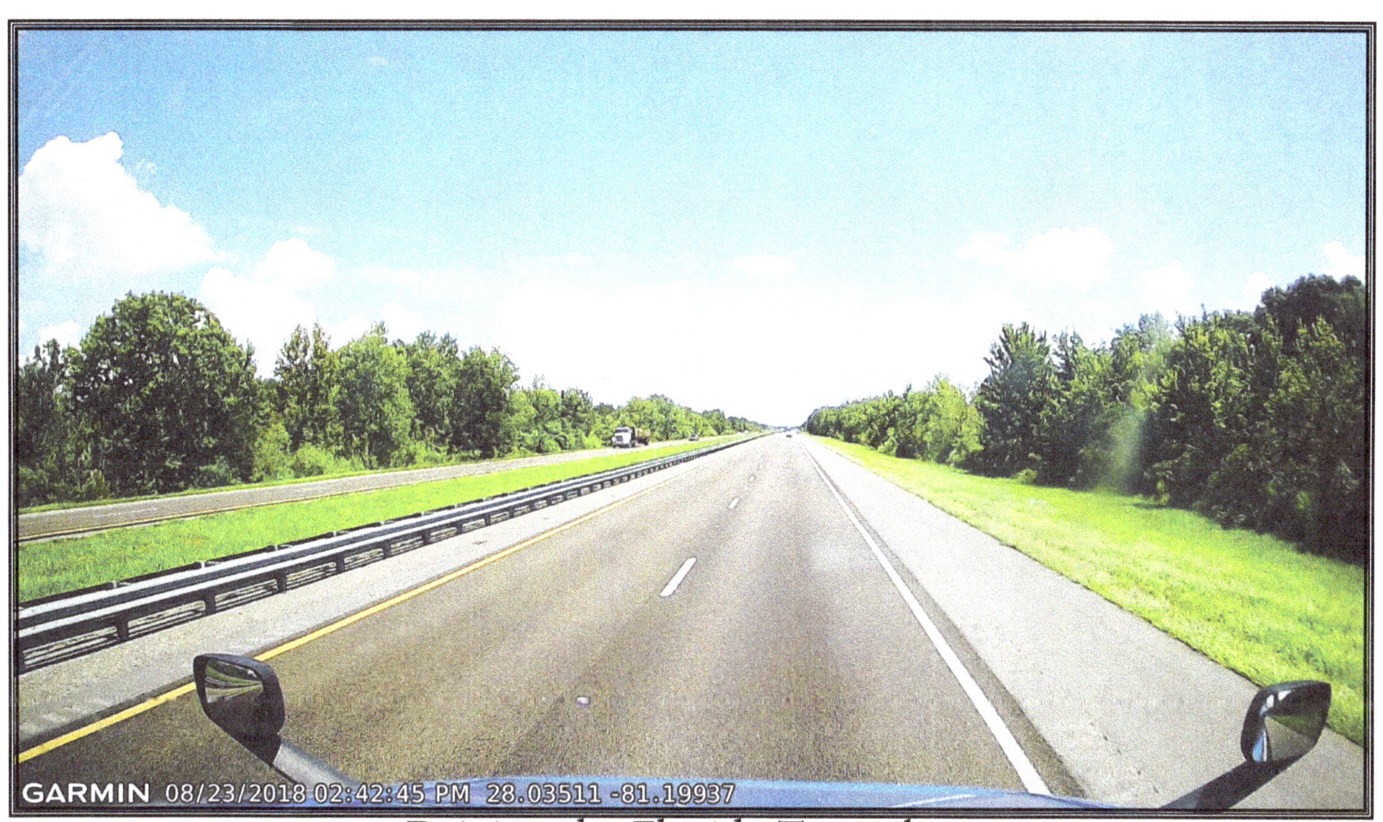

Driving the Florida Turnpike
Florida Turnpike, Kenansville, Florida

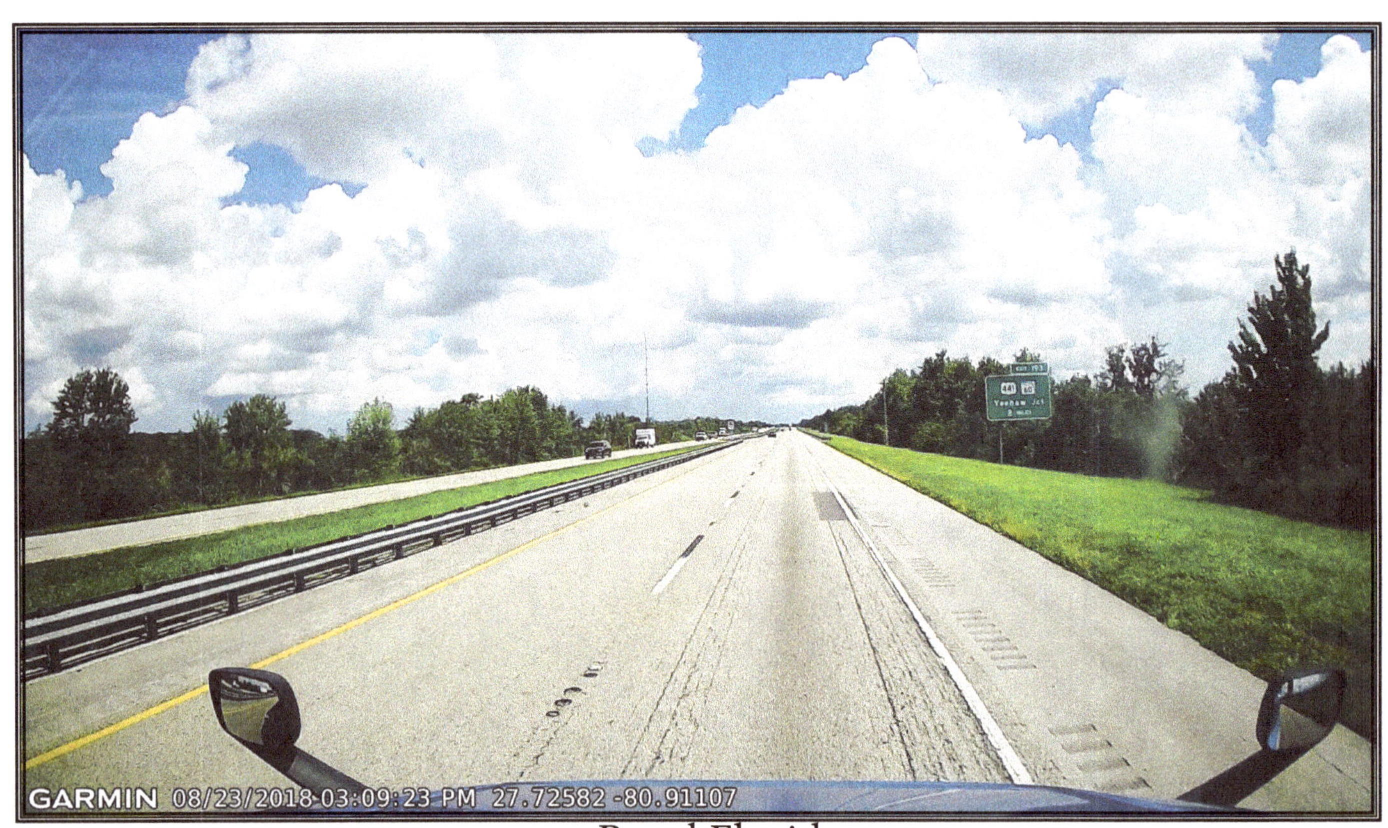

Rural Florida
Florida Turnpike, Okeechobee, Florida

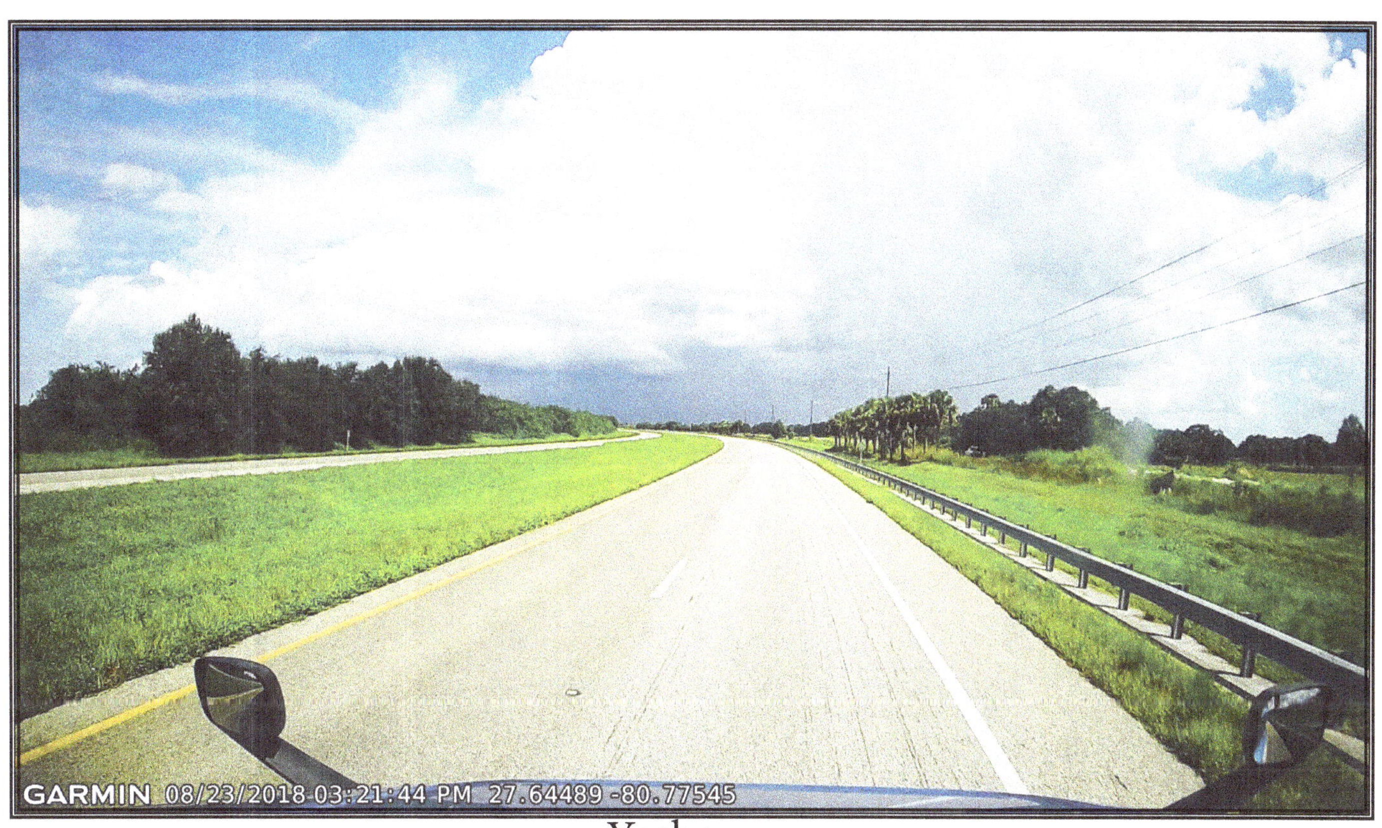

Yeehaw
FL-60, Yeehaw, Florida

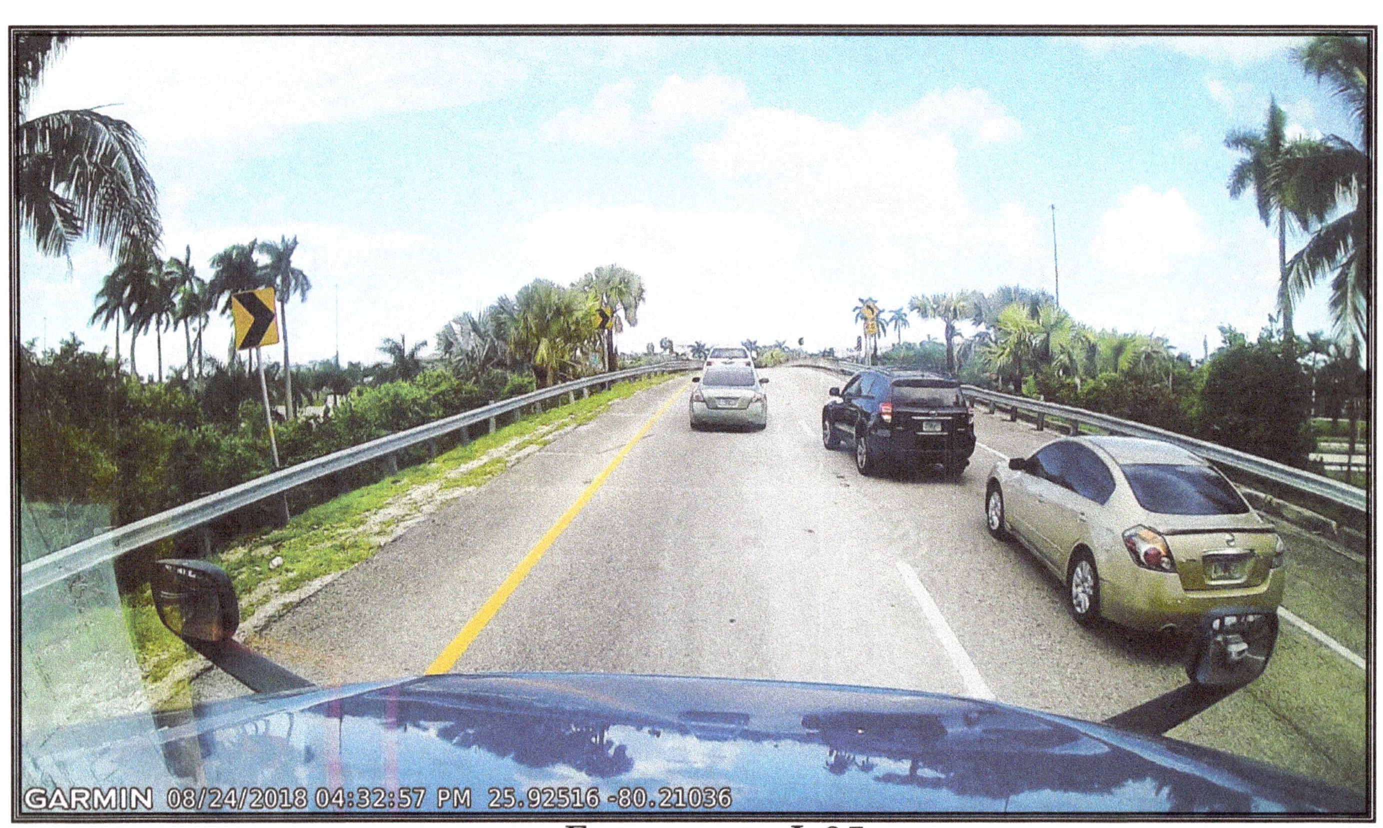

Entrance to I-95
I-95, Miami, Florida

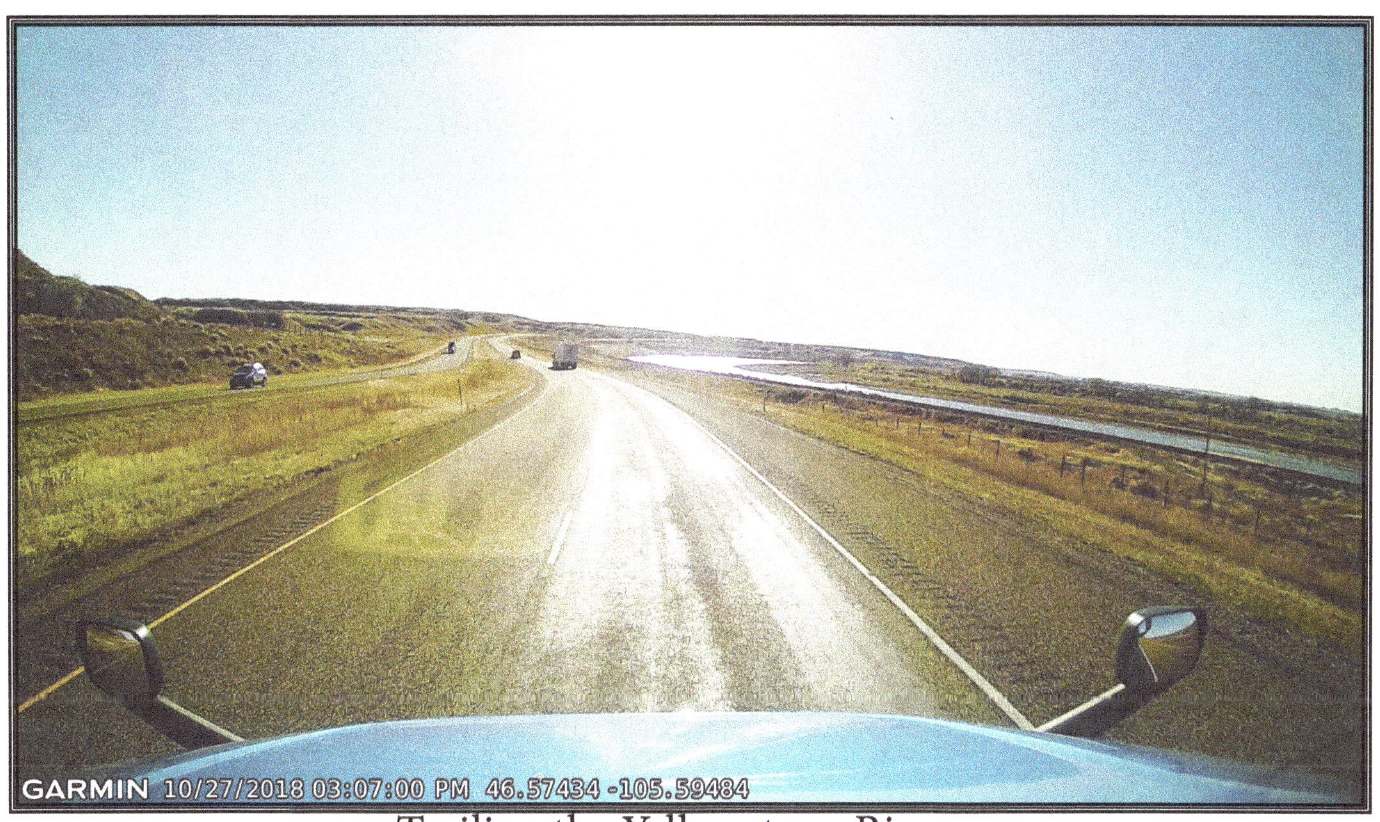

Trailing the Yellowstone River
I-94, Miles City, Wyoming

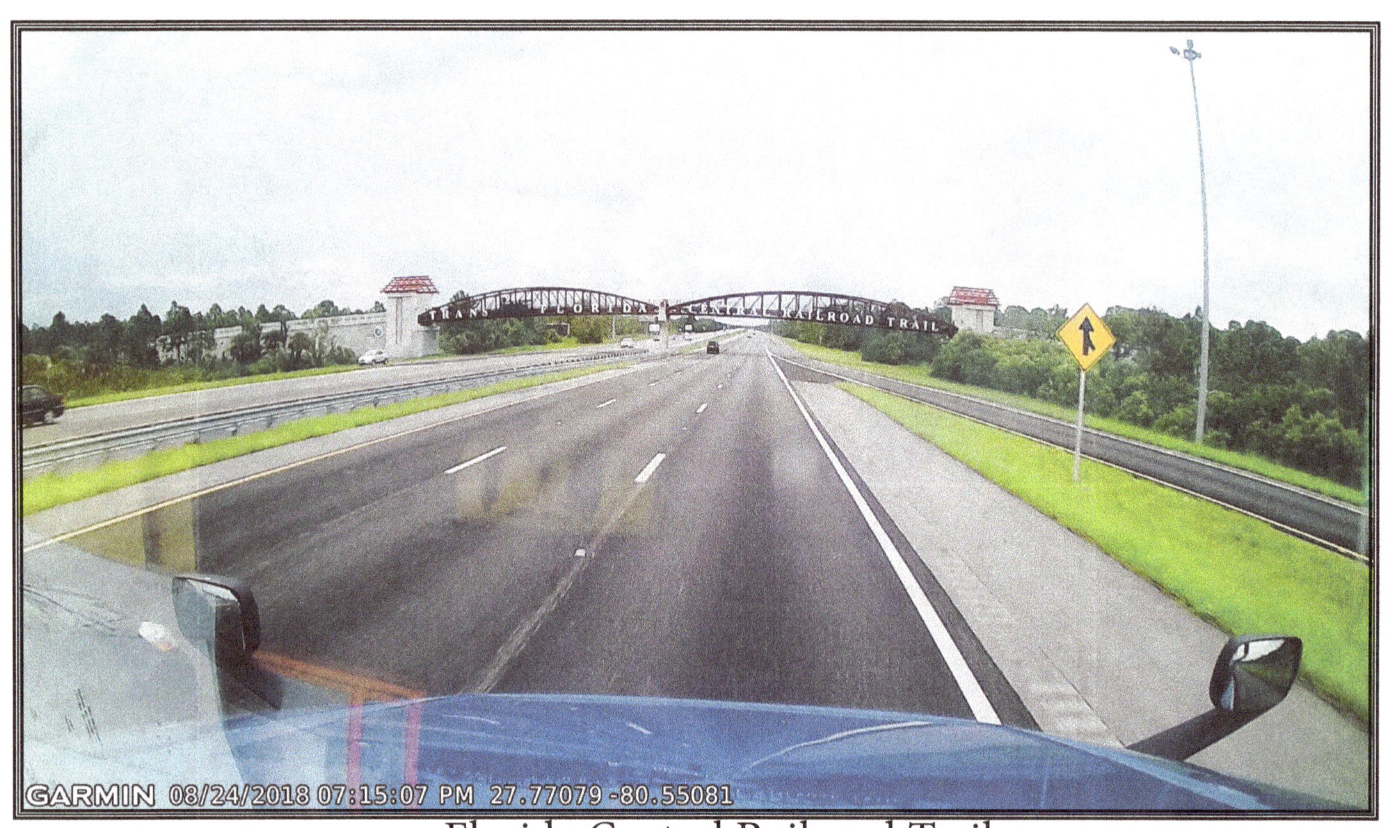

Florida Central Railroad Trail
I-95, Fellsmere, Florida

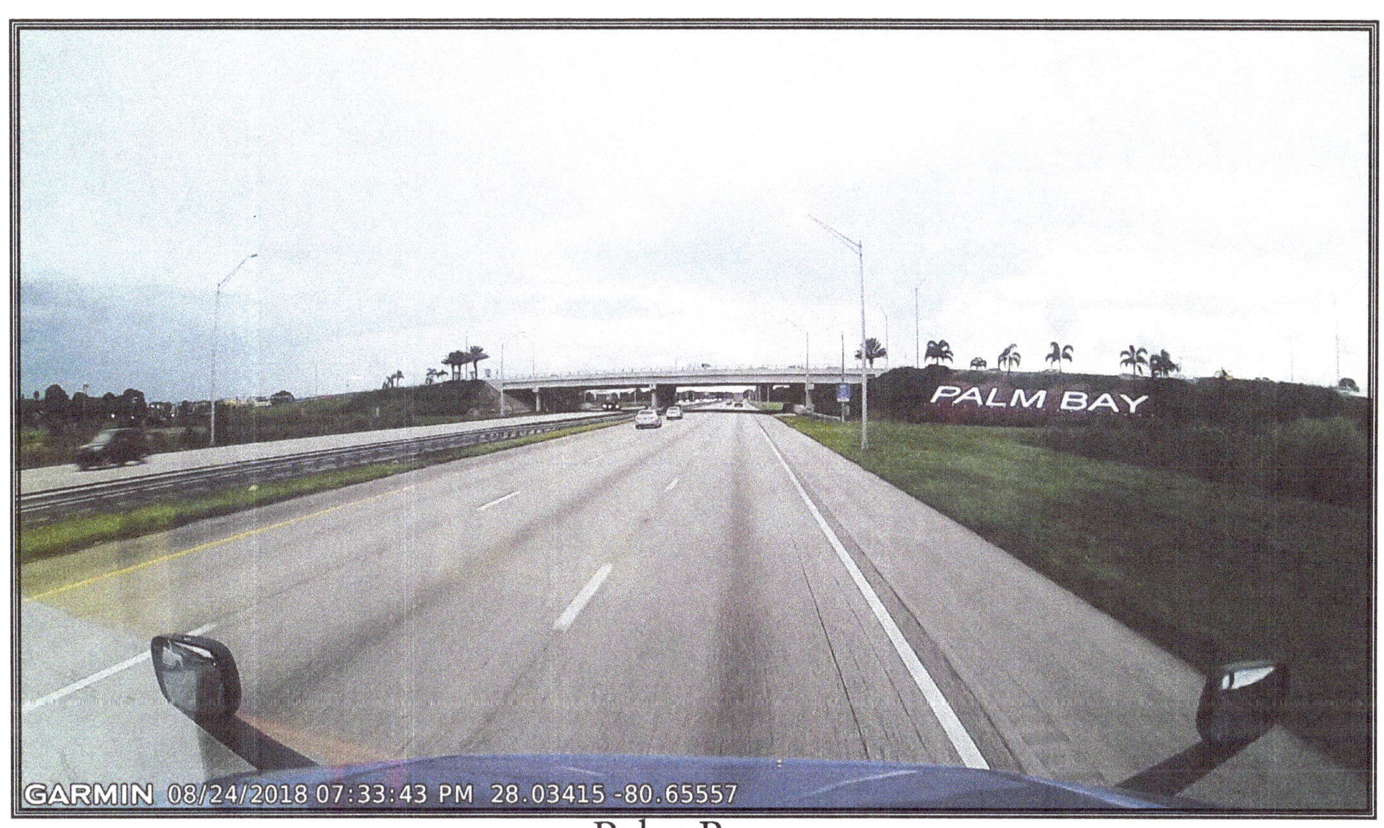

Palm Bay
I-95, Palm Bay, Florida

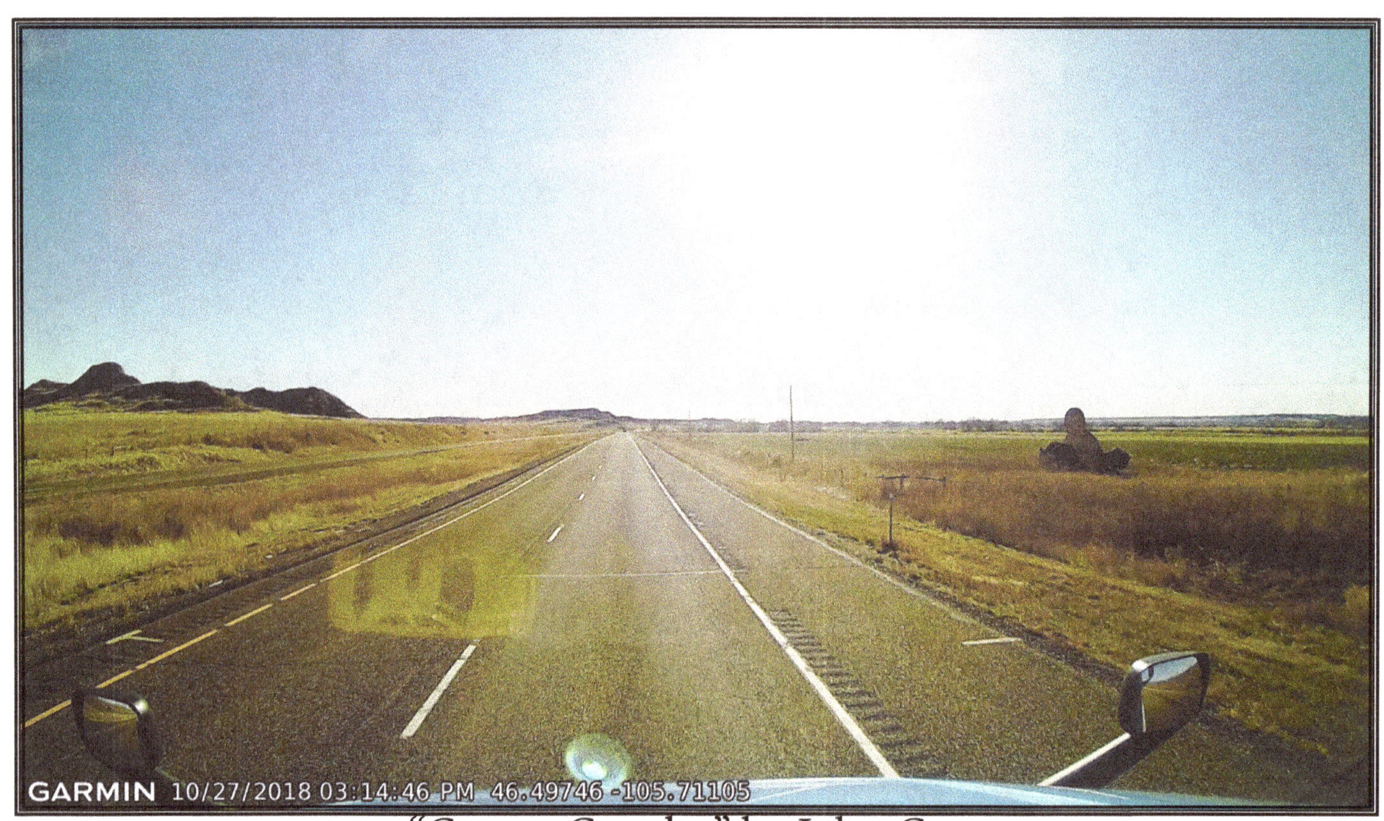

"Creepy Crawler" by John Cerney
I-94, Miles City, Montana

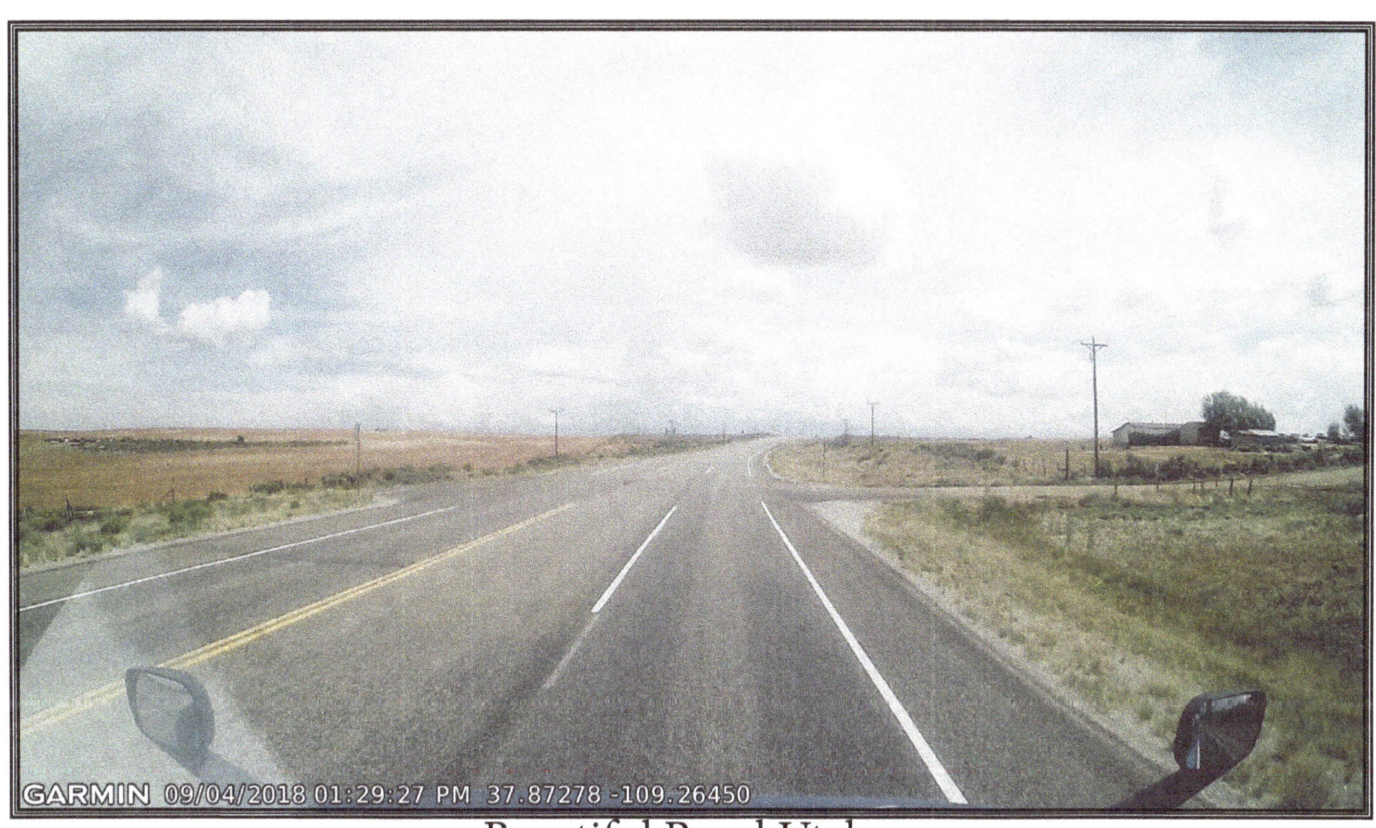

Beautiful Rural Utah
US-491, Monticello, Utah

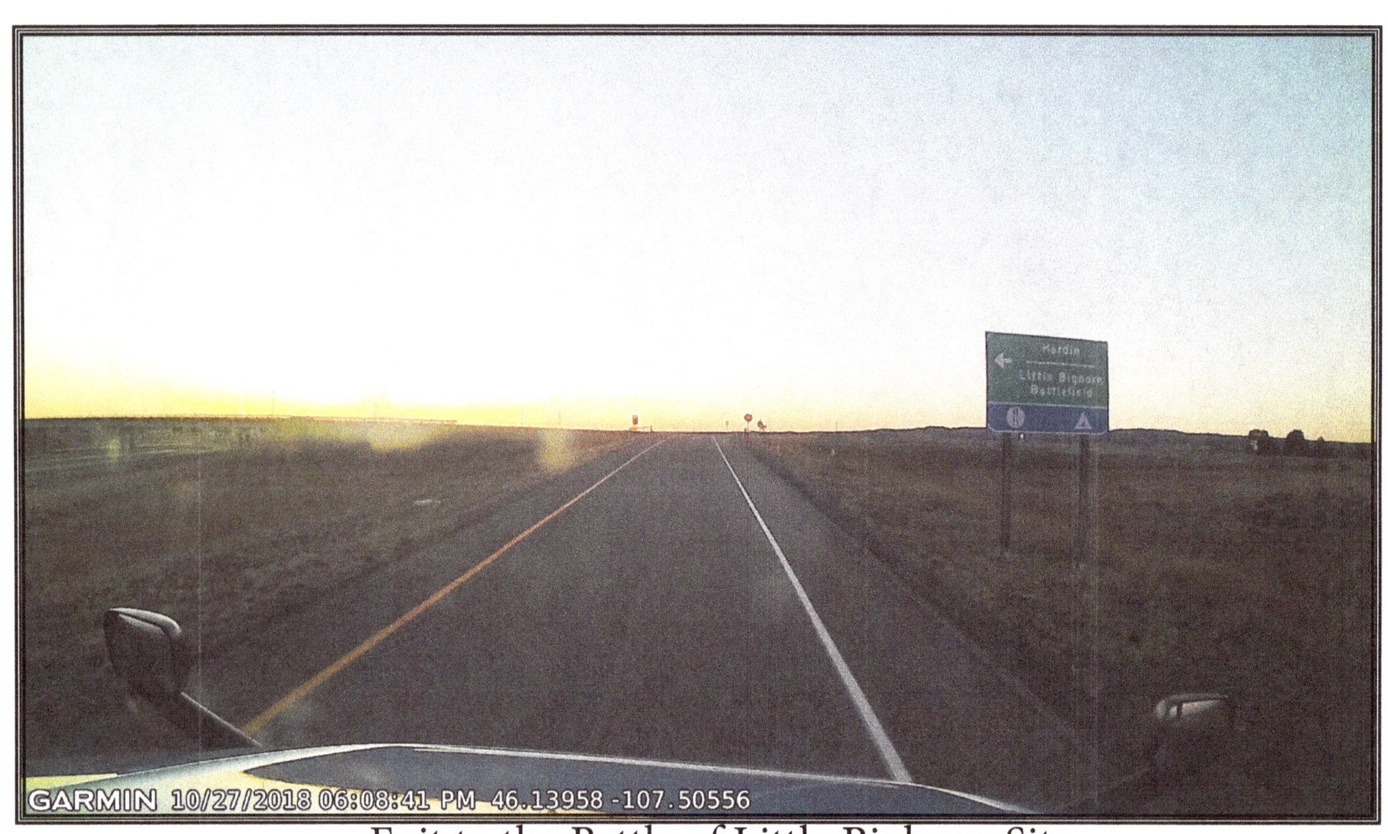

Exit to the Battle of Little Bighorn Site
I-94, Bighorn, Montana

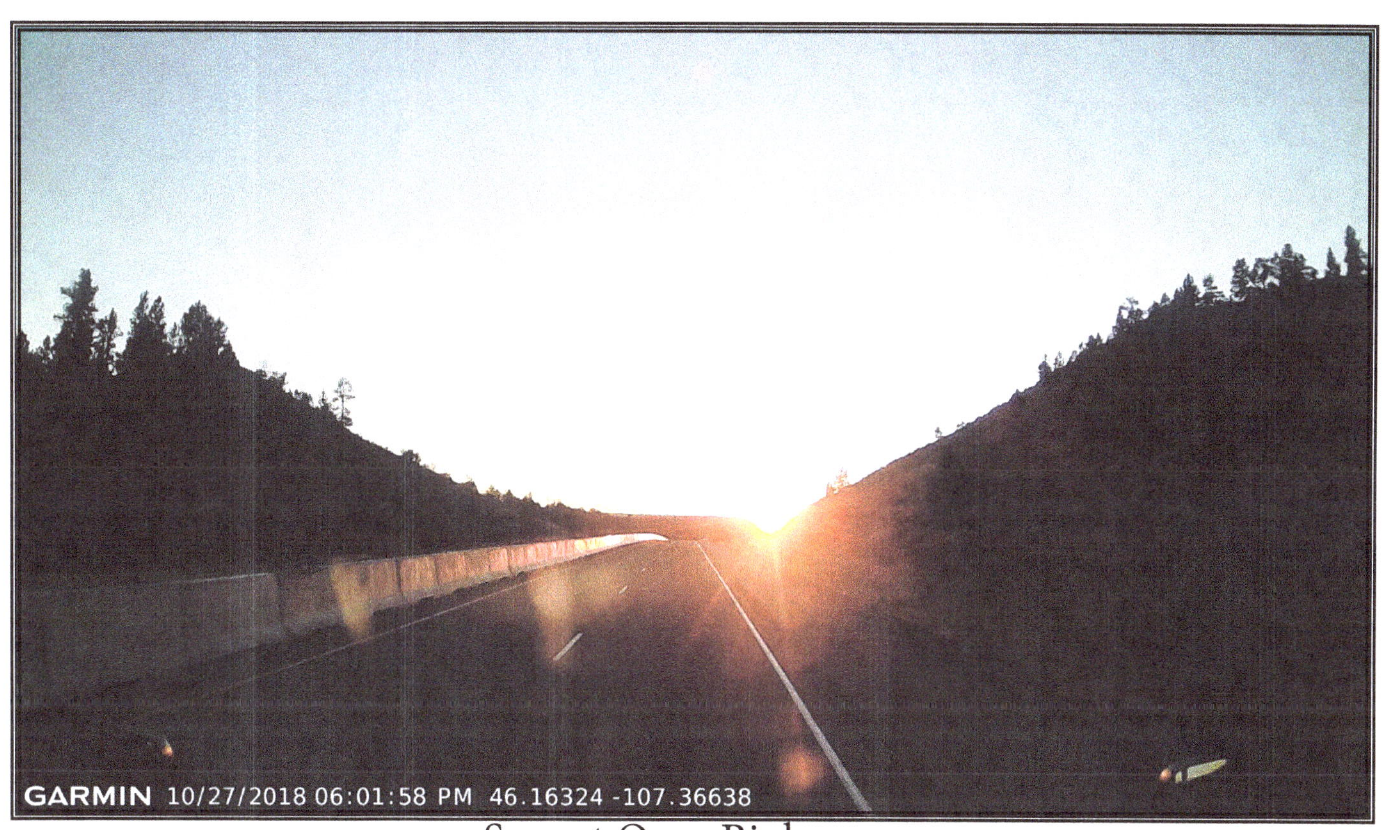

Sunset Over Bighorn
I-94, Bighorn, Montana

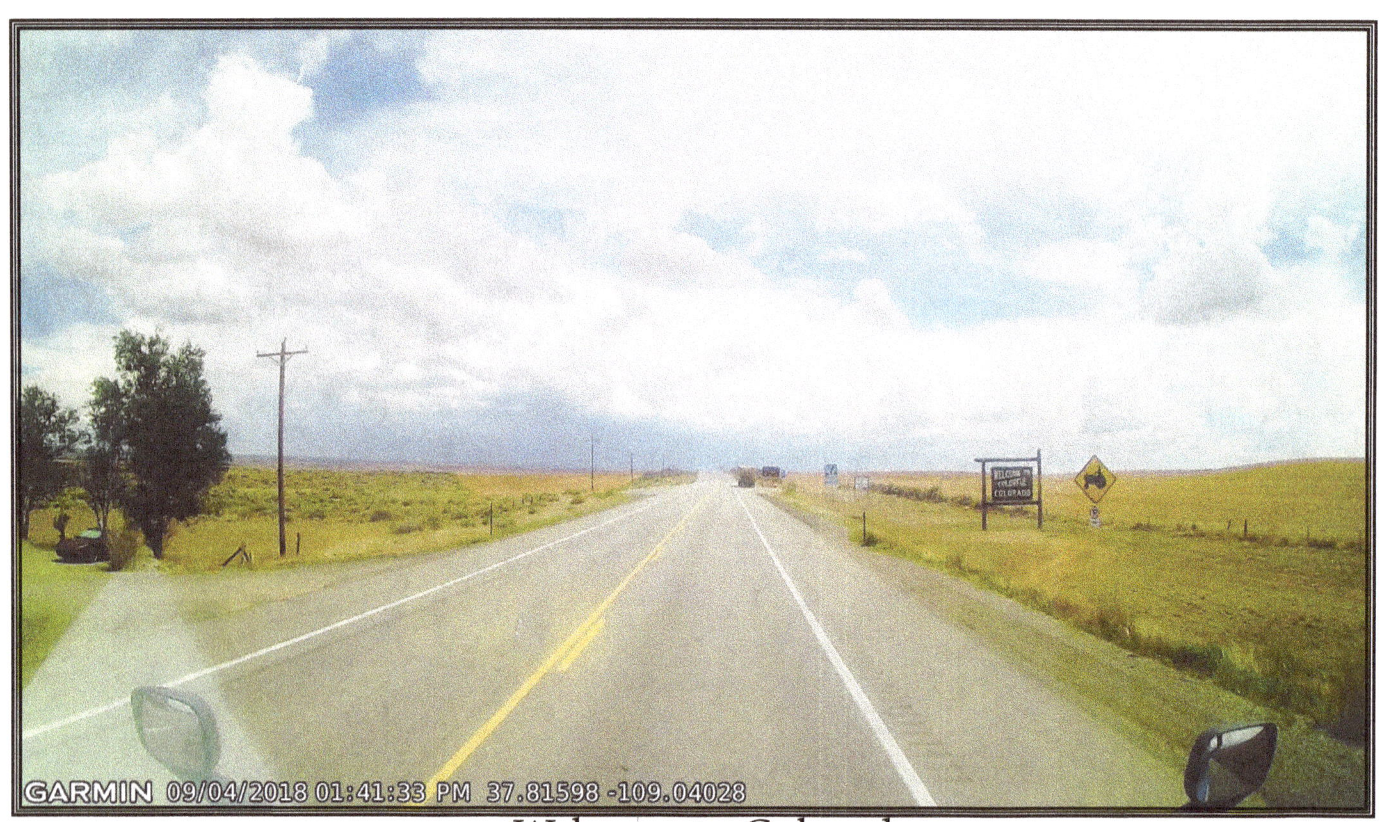

Welcome to Colorado
US-491, Dove Creek, Colorado

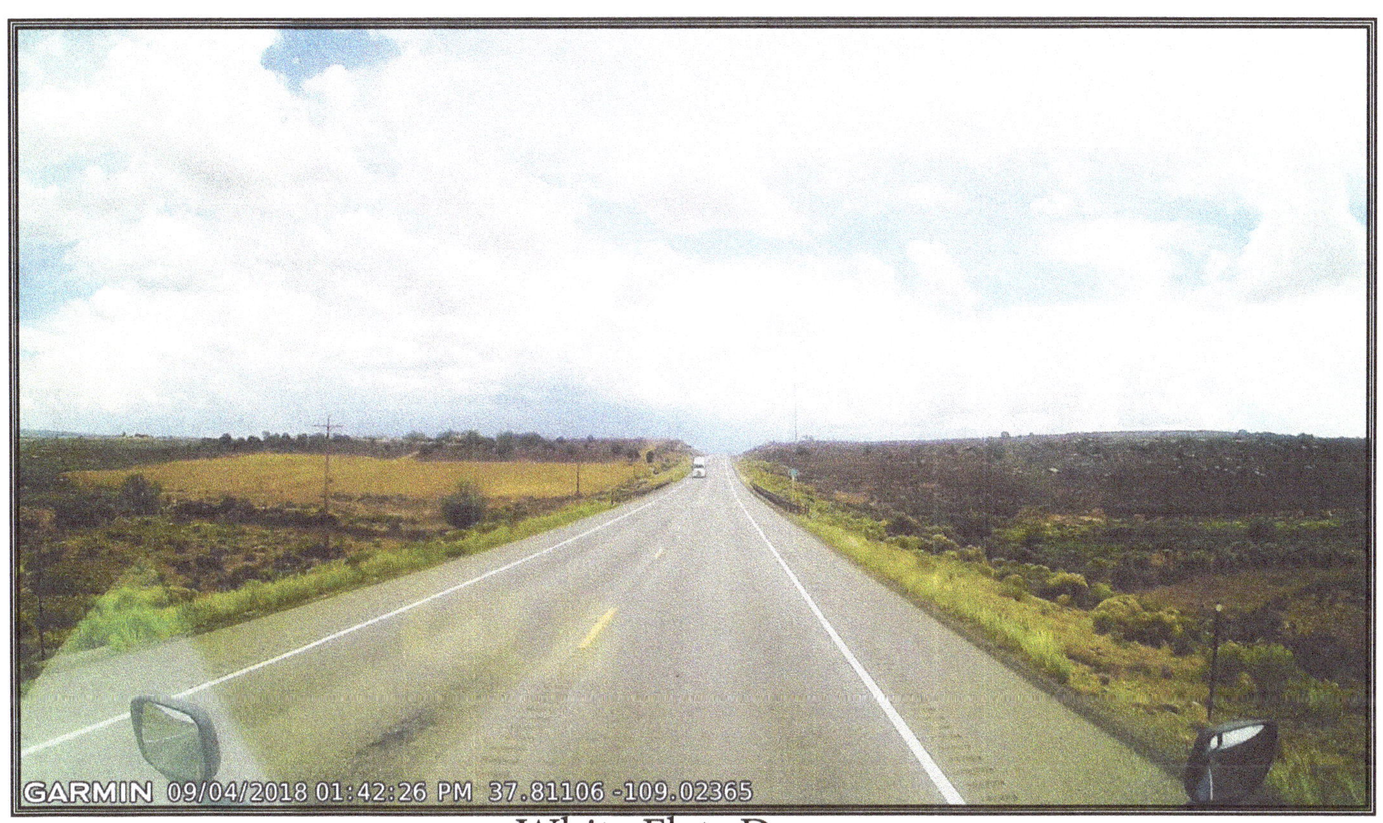

White Flats Draw
US-491, Dove Creek, Colorado

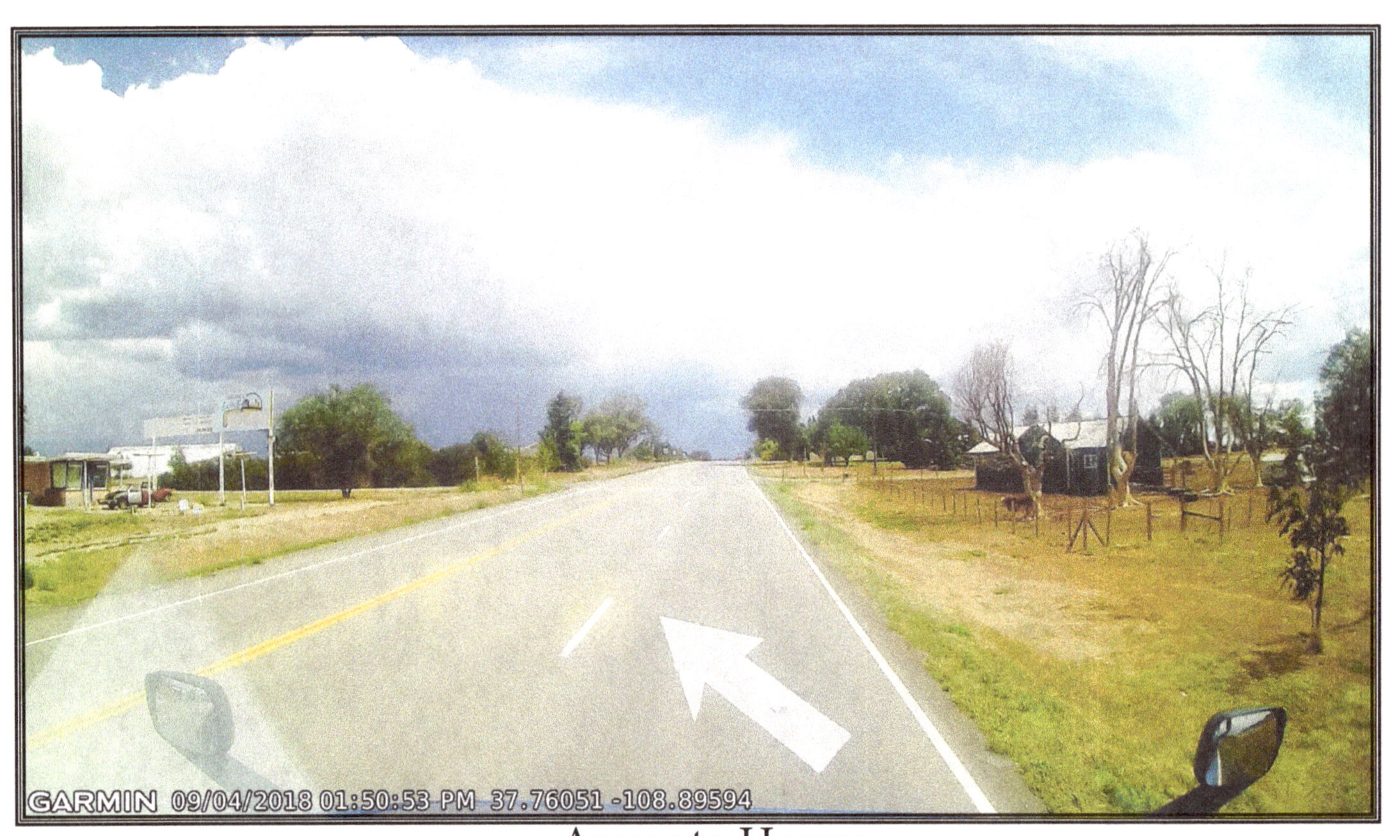

Arrow to Heaven
US-491, Dove Creek, Colorado

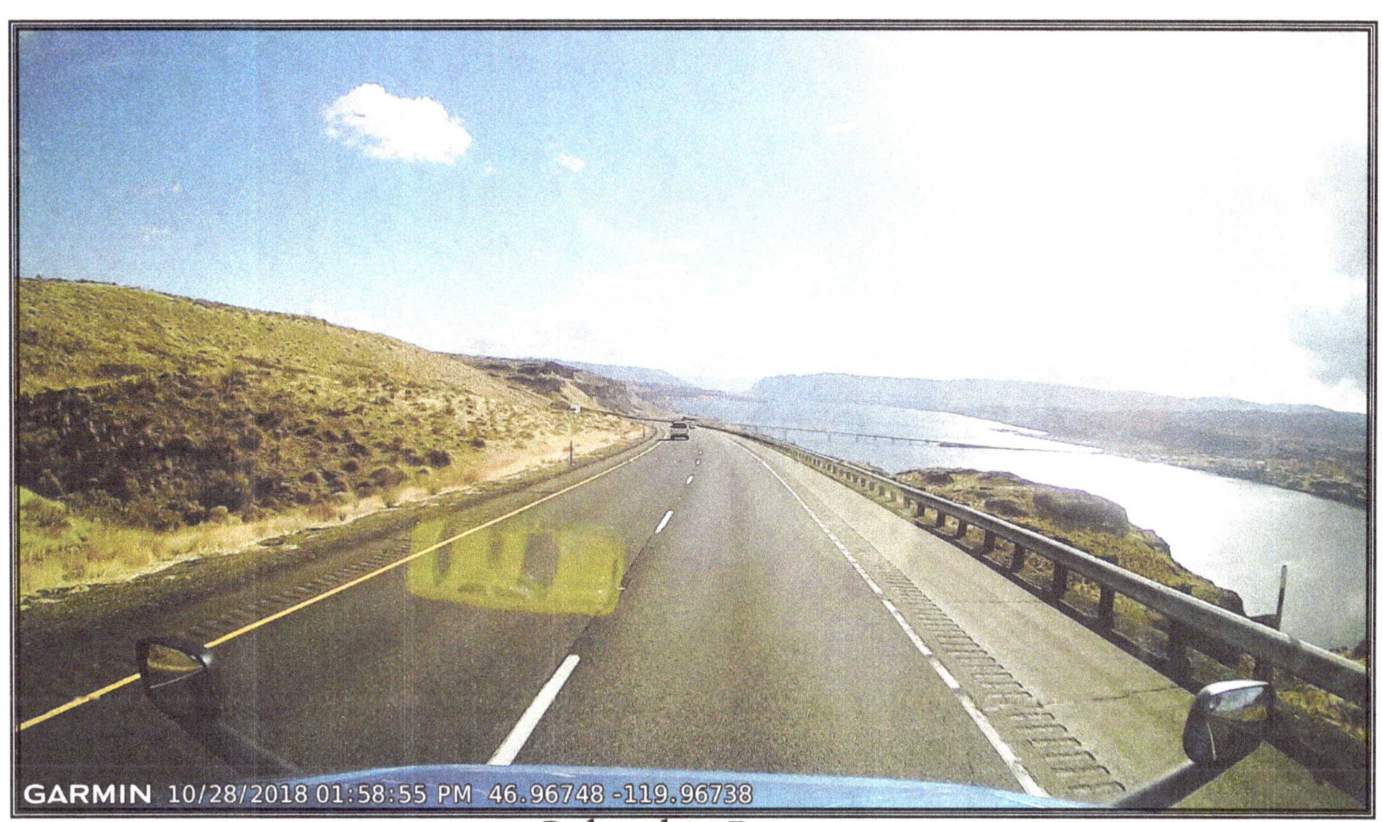

Columbia River
I-90, Vantage, Washington

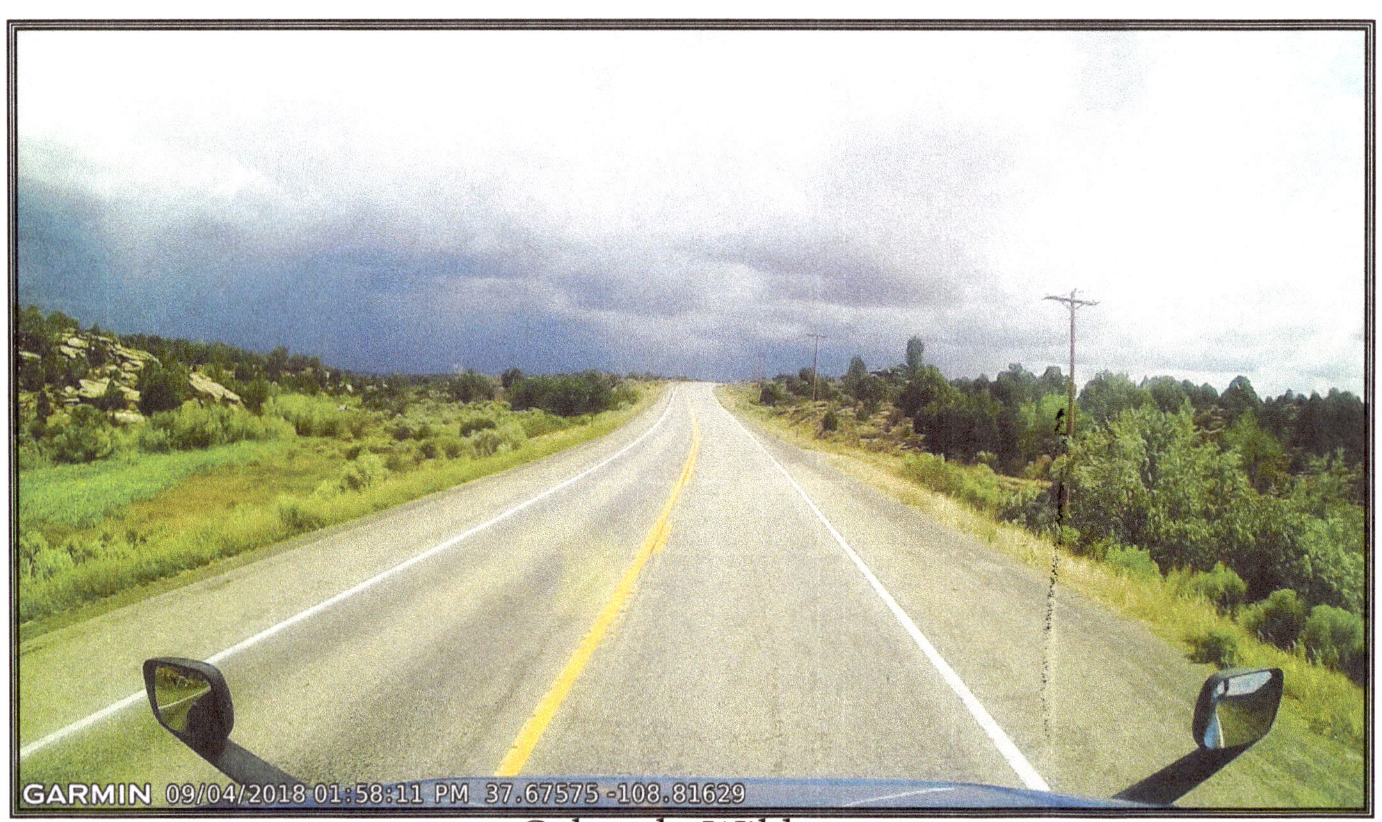

Colorado Wilderness
US-491, Cahone, Colorado

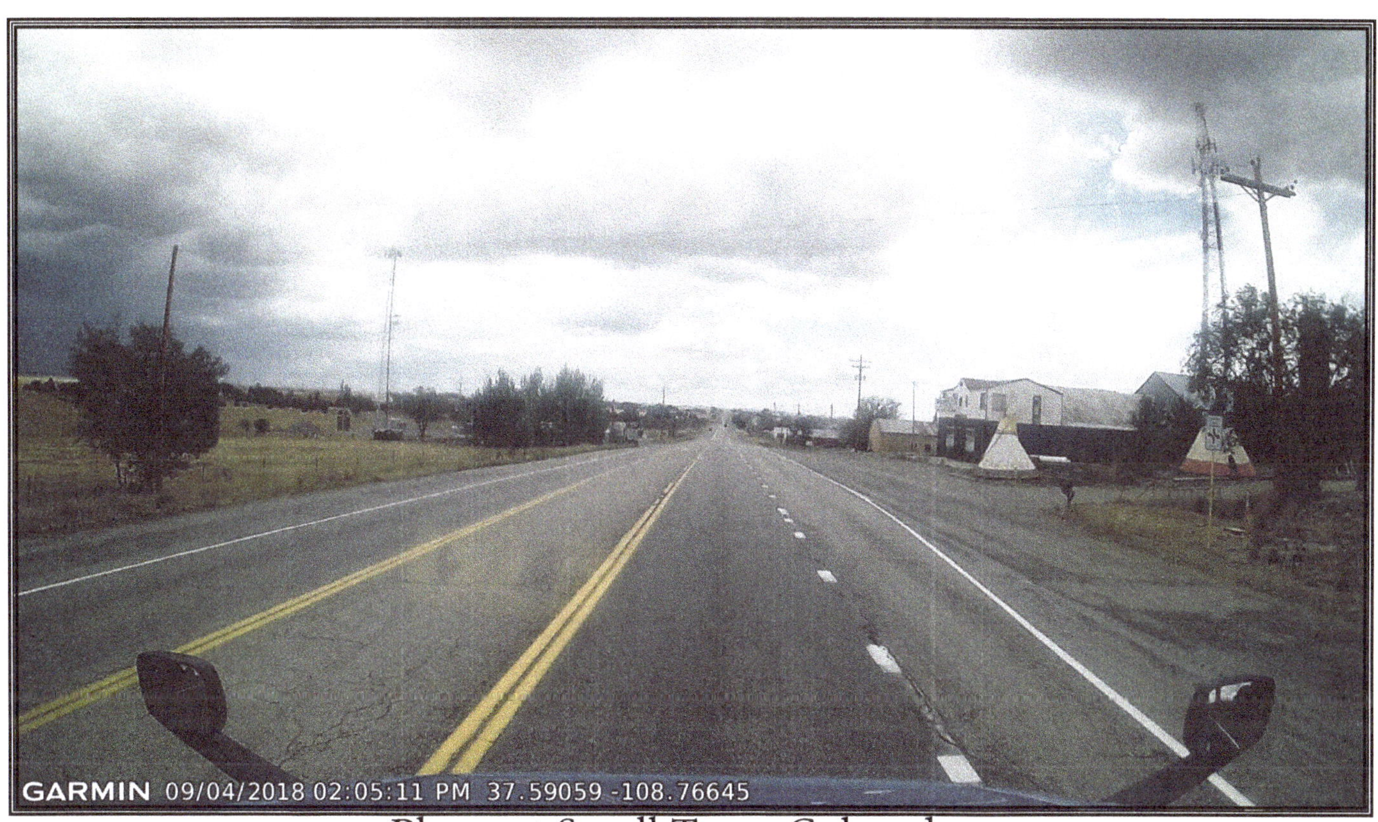

Pleasant Small Town Colorado
US-491, Pleasant View, Colorado

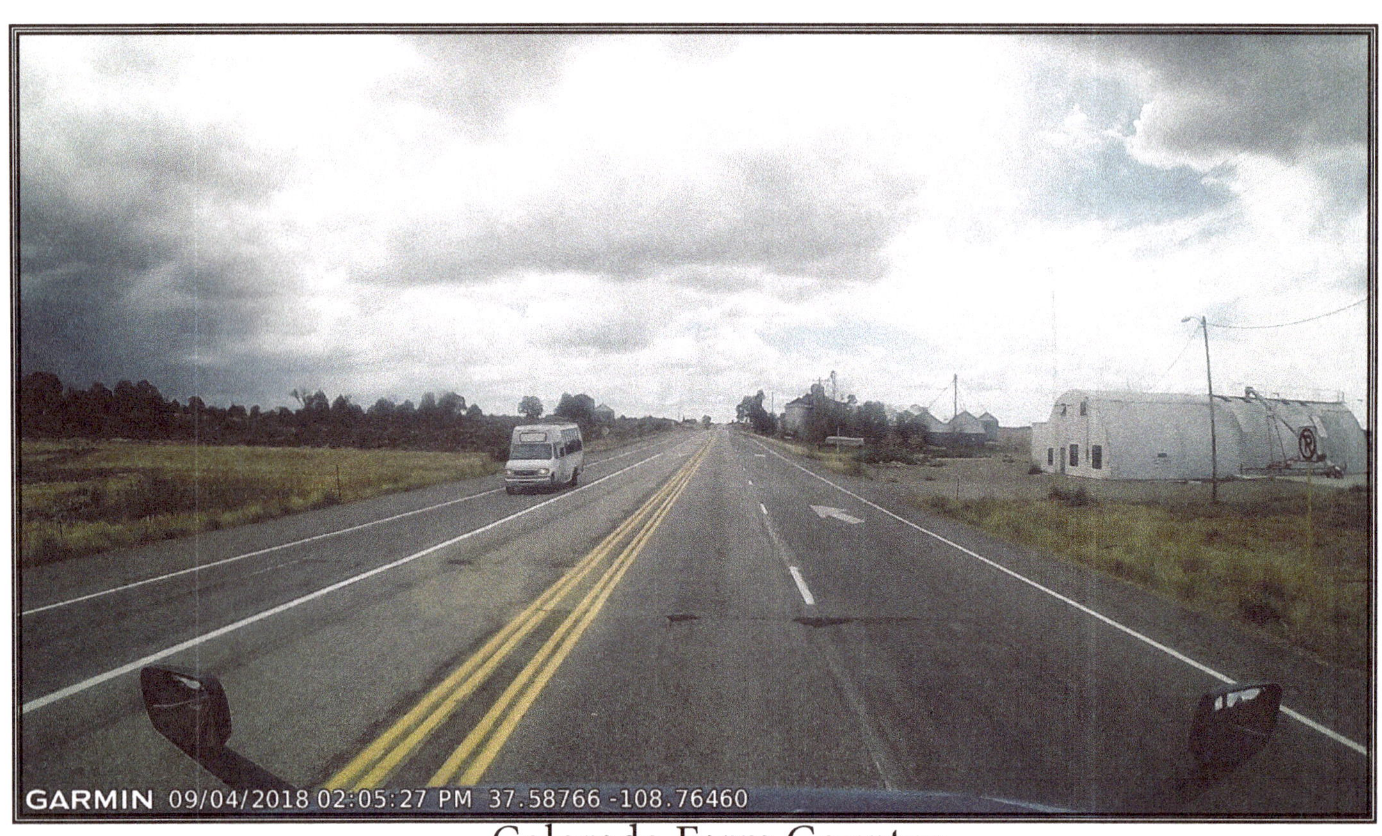

Colorado Farm Country
US-491, Pleasant View, Colorado

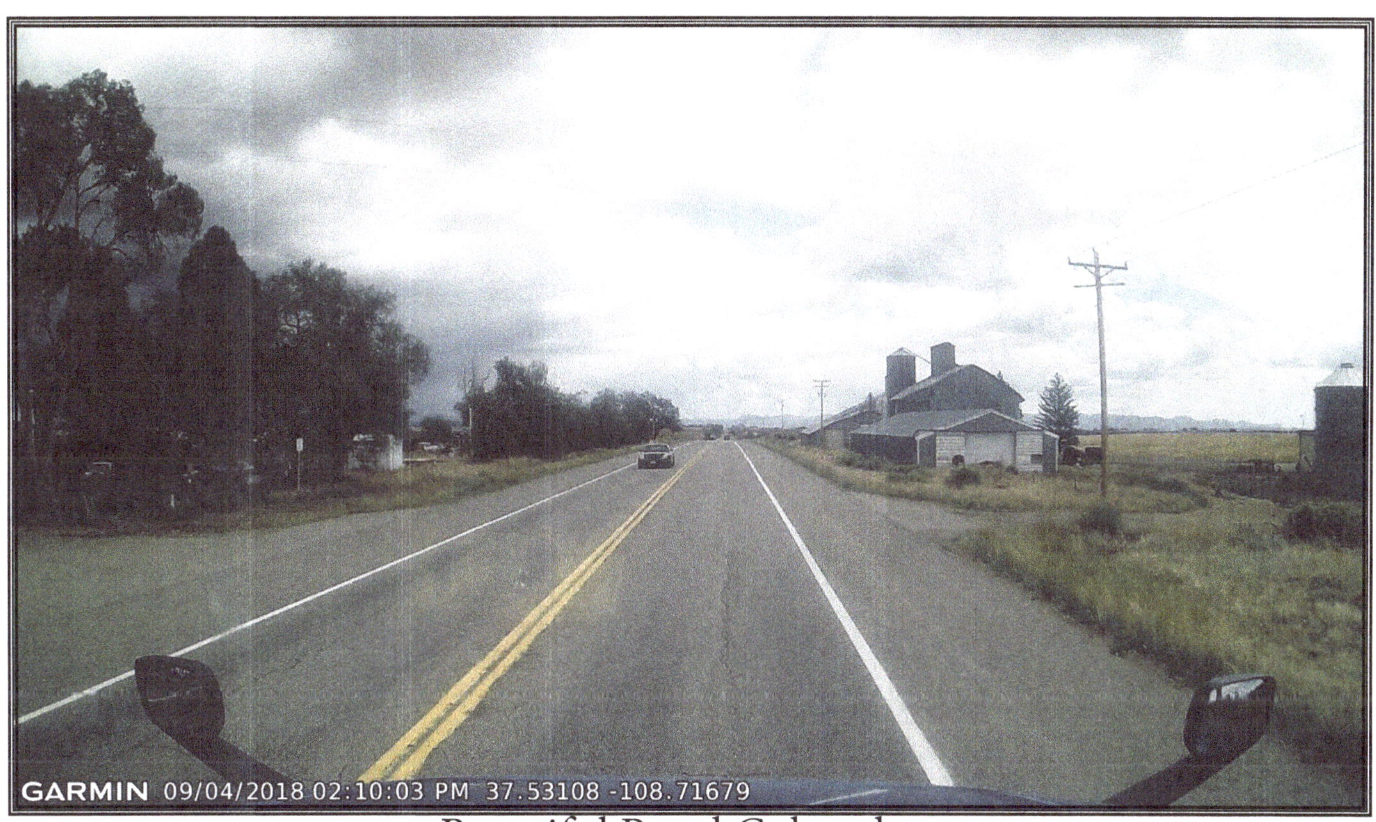

Beautiful Rural Colorado
US-491, Pleasant View, Colorado

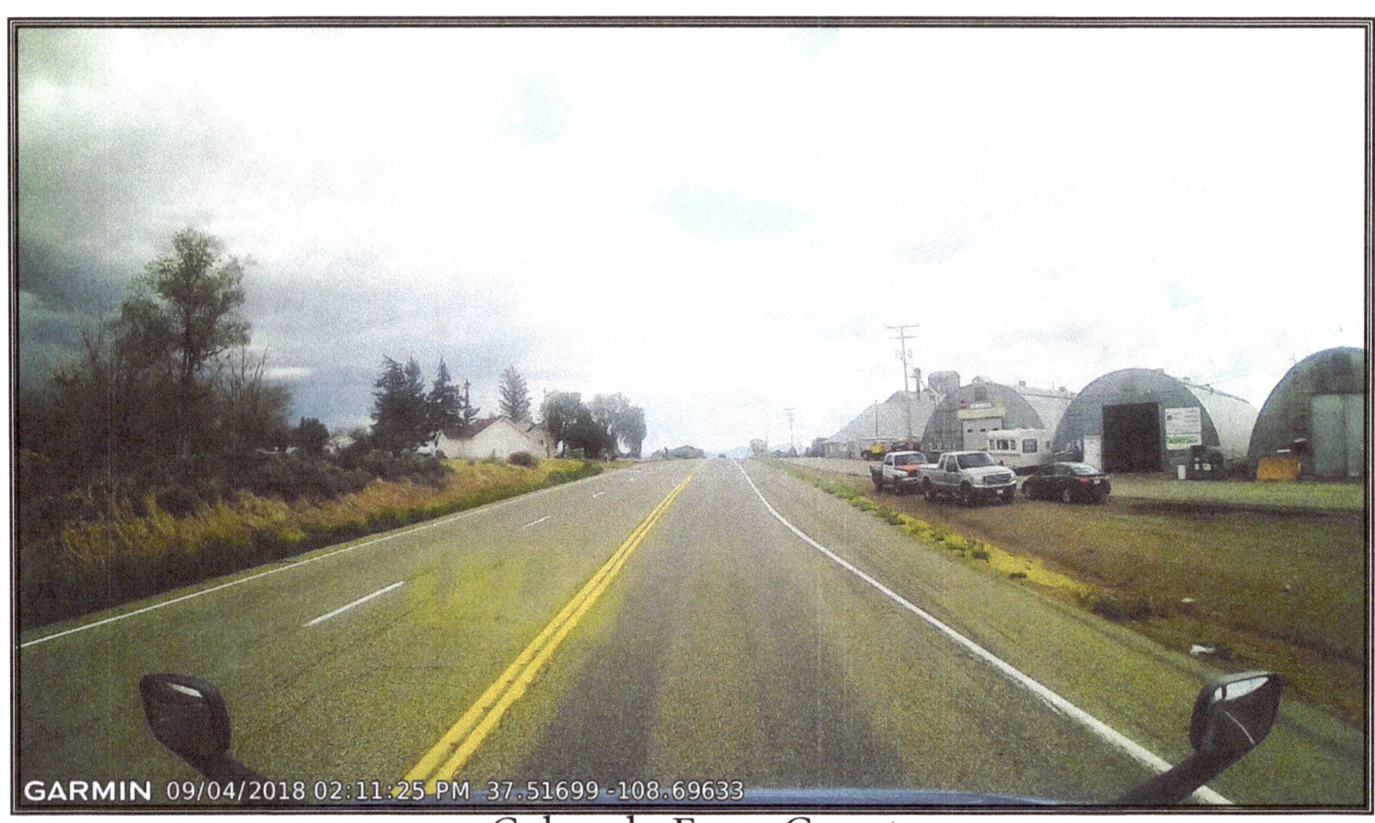

Colorado Farm Country
US-491, Pleasant View, Colorado

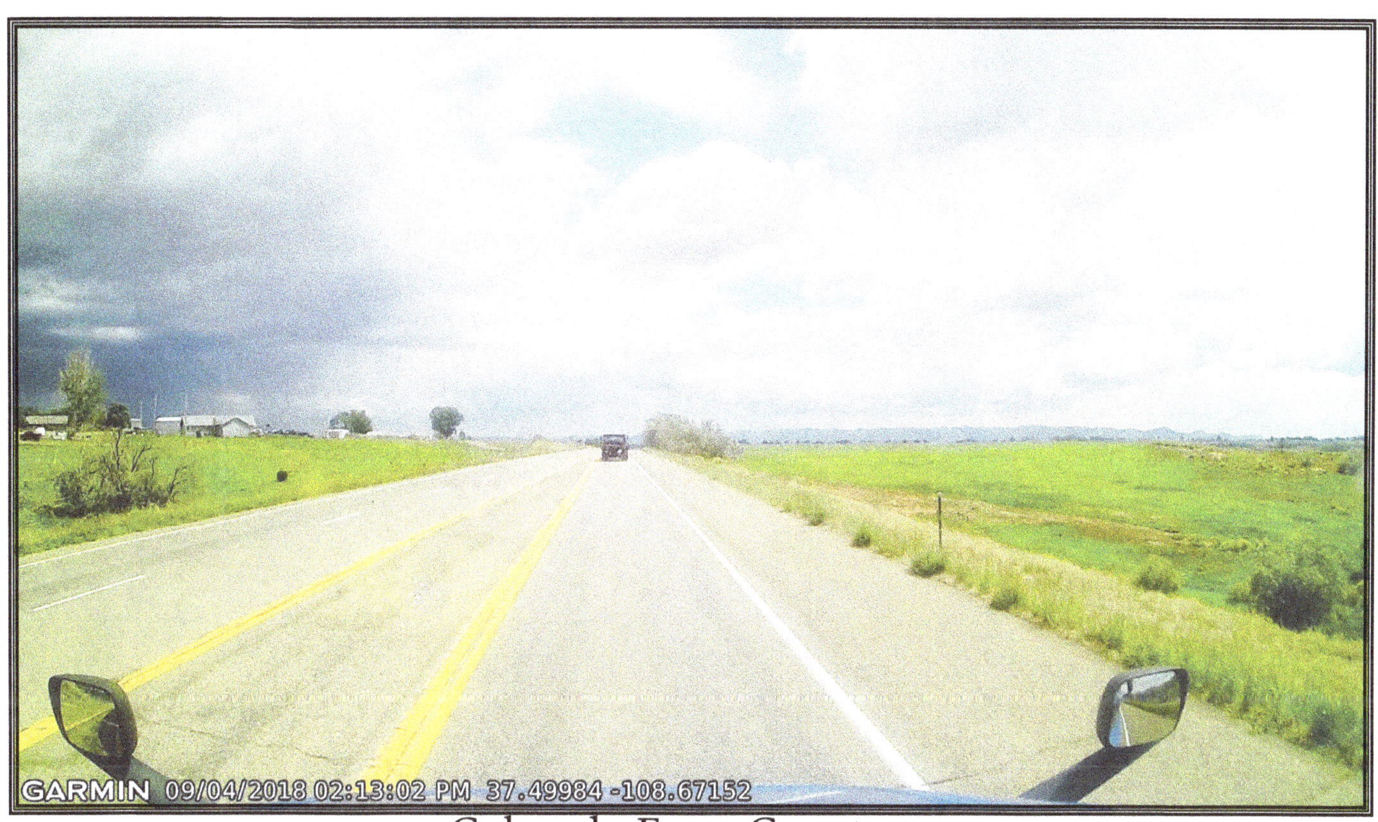

Colorado Farm Country
US-491, Pleasant View, Colorado

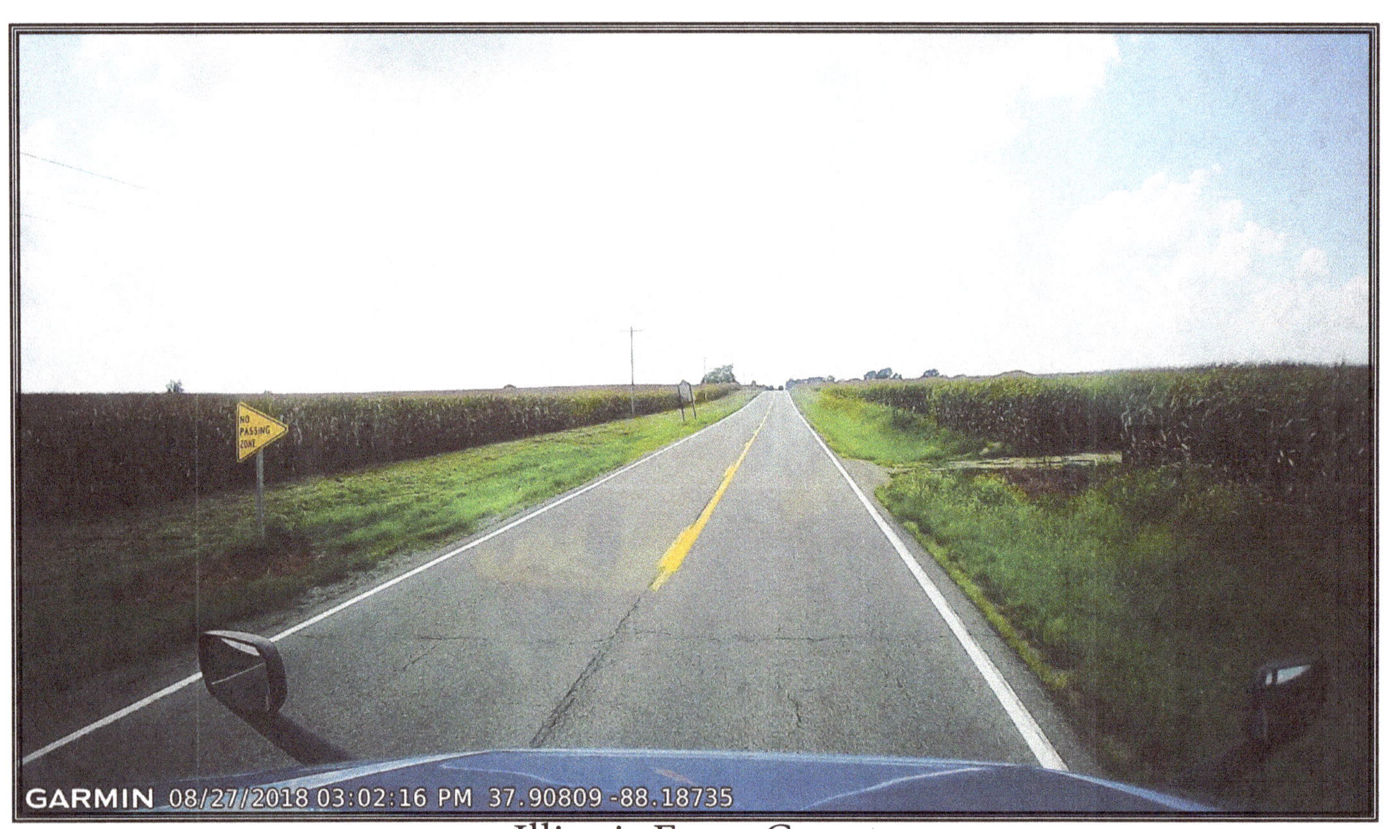

Illinois Farm Country
IL-141, Cottonwood, Illinois

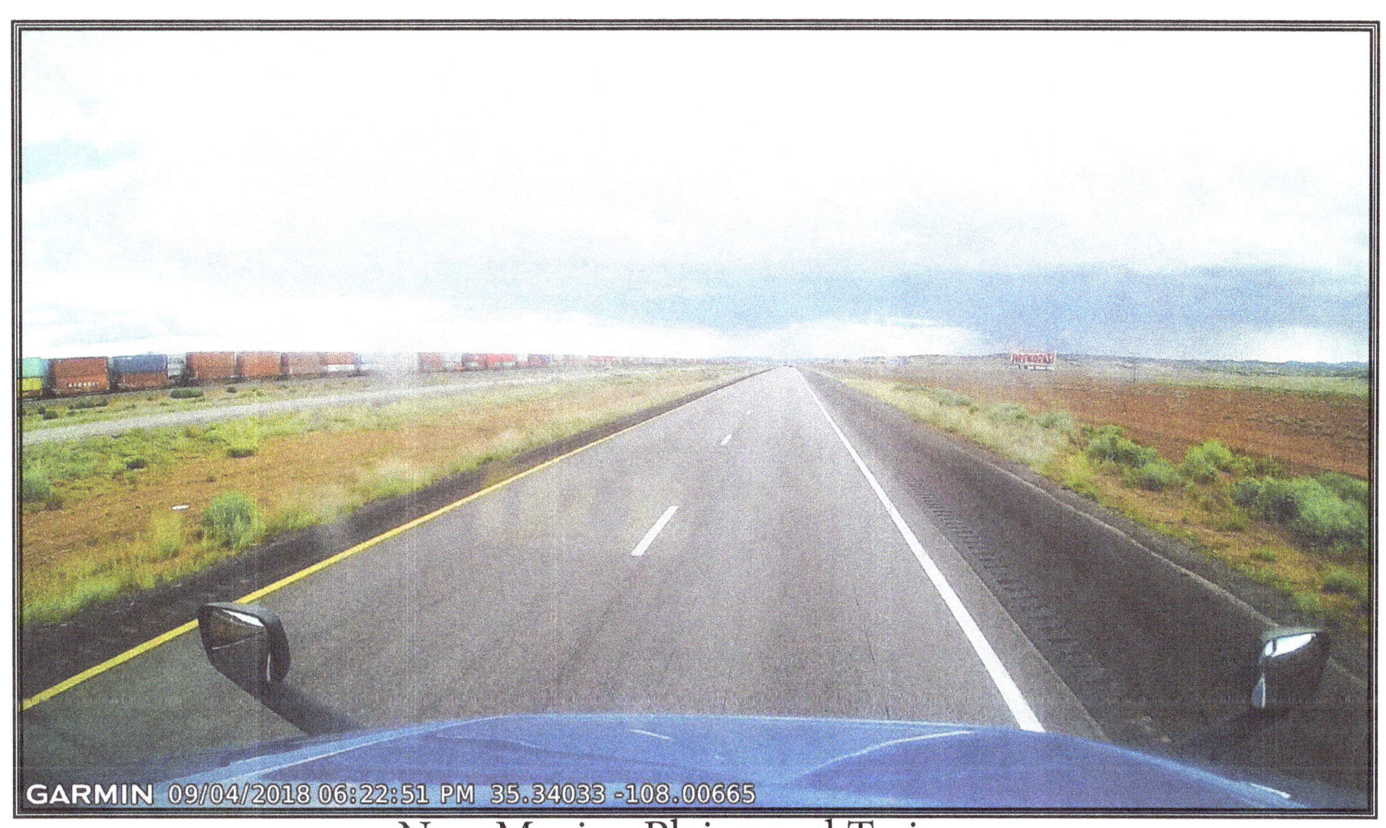

New Mexico Plains and Trains
I-40, Prewitt, New Mexico

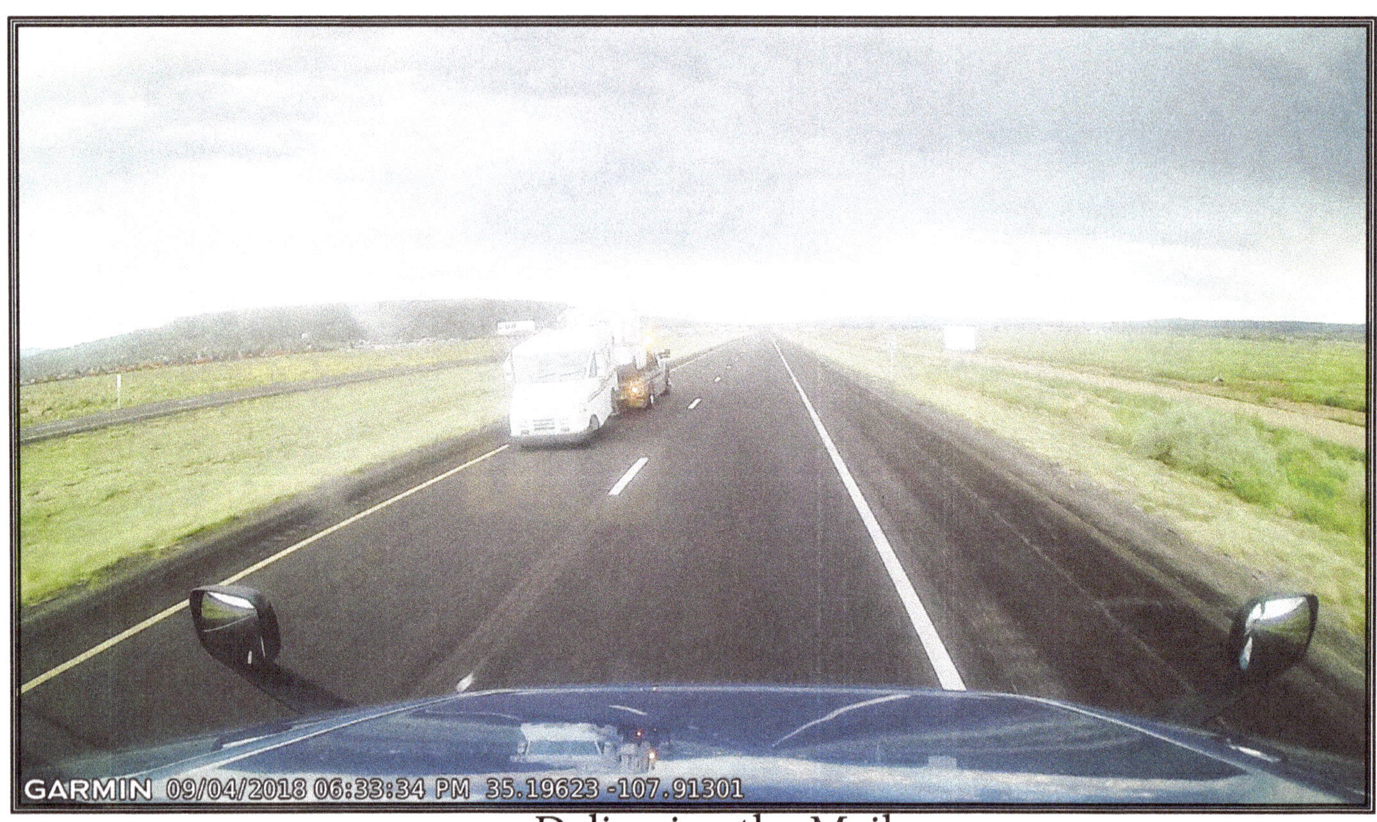

Delivering the Mail
I-40, Milan, New Mexico

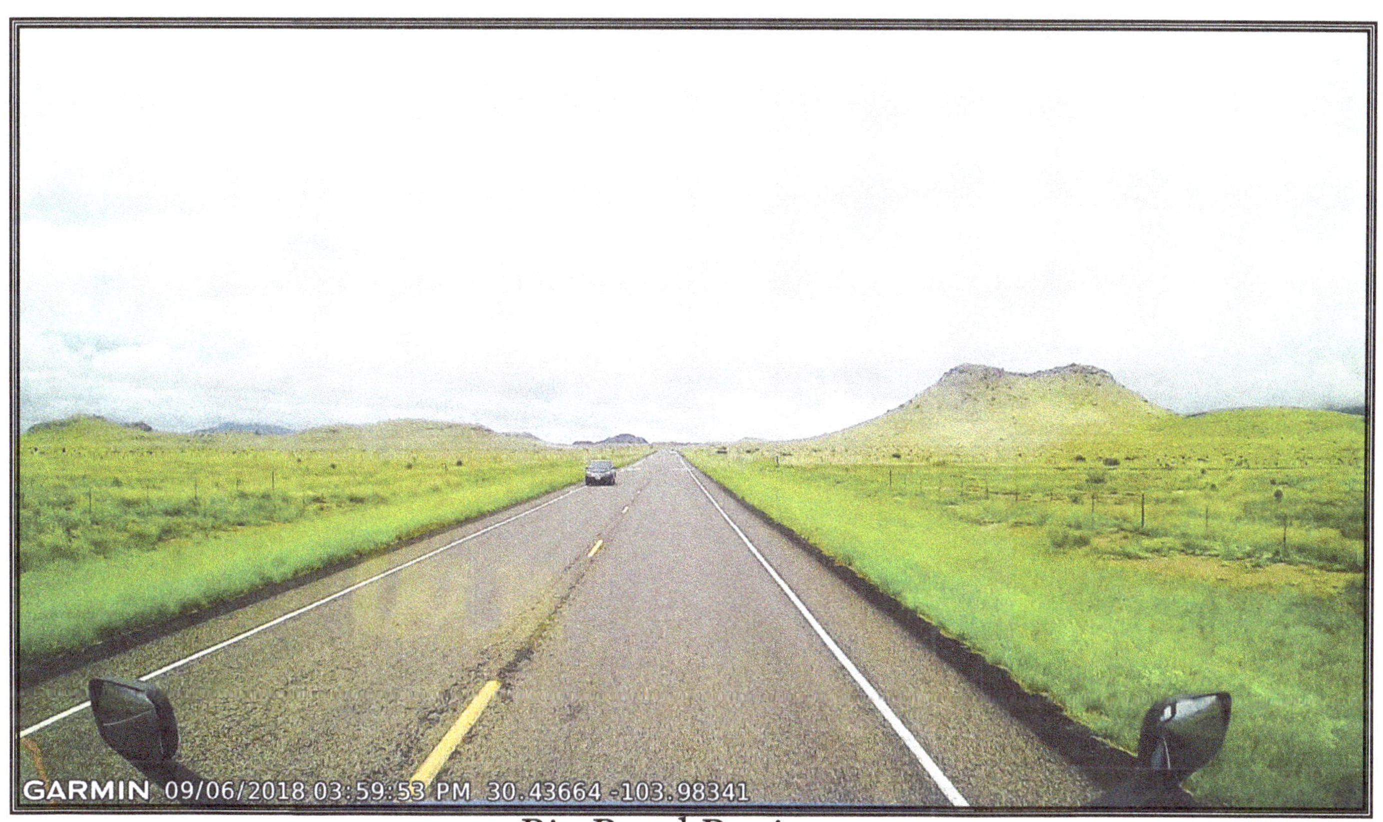

Big Bend Region
TX-17, Marfa, Texas

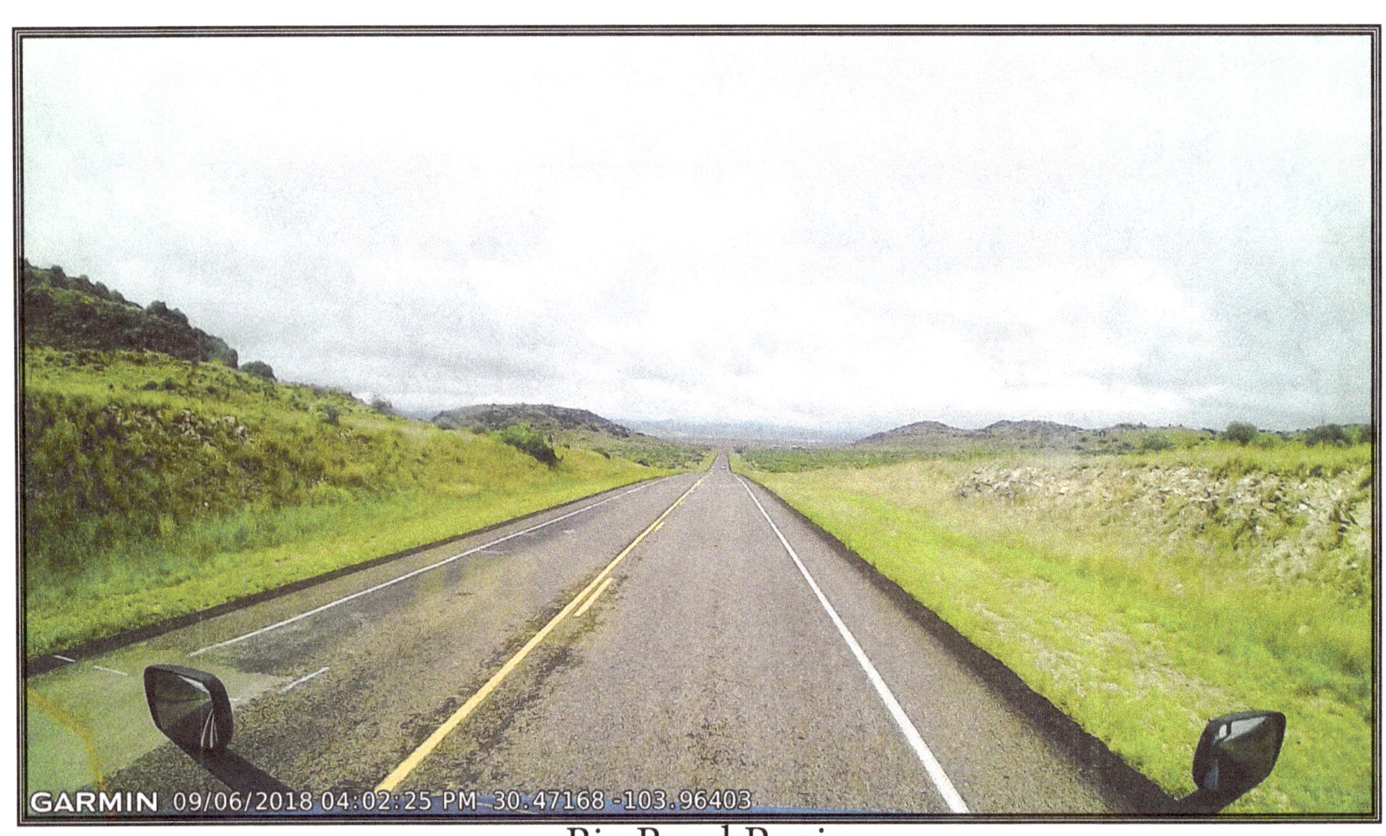

Big Bend Region
TX-17, Marfa, Texas

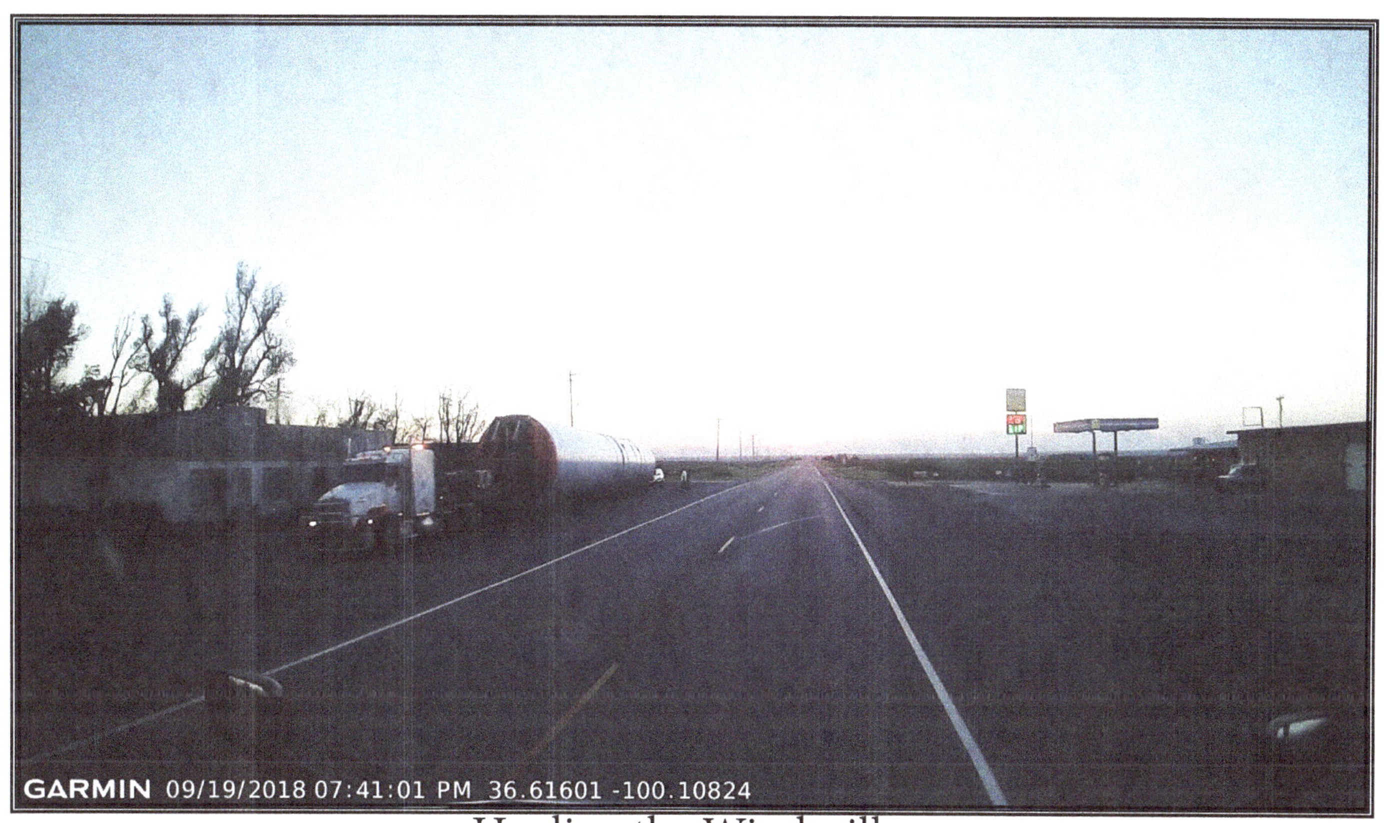

Hauling the Windmill
US-412, Laverne, Oklahoma

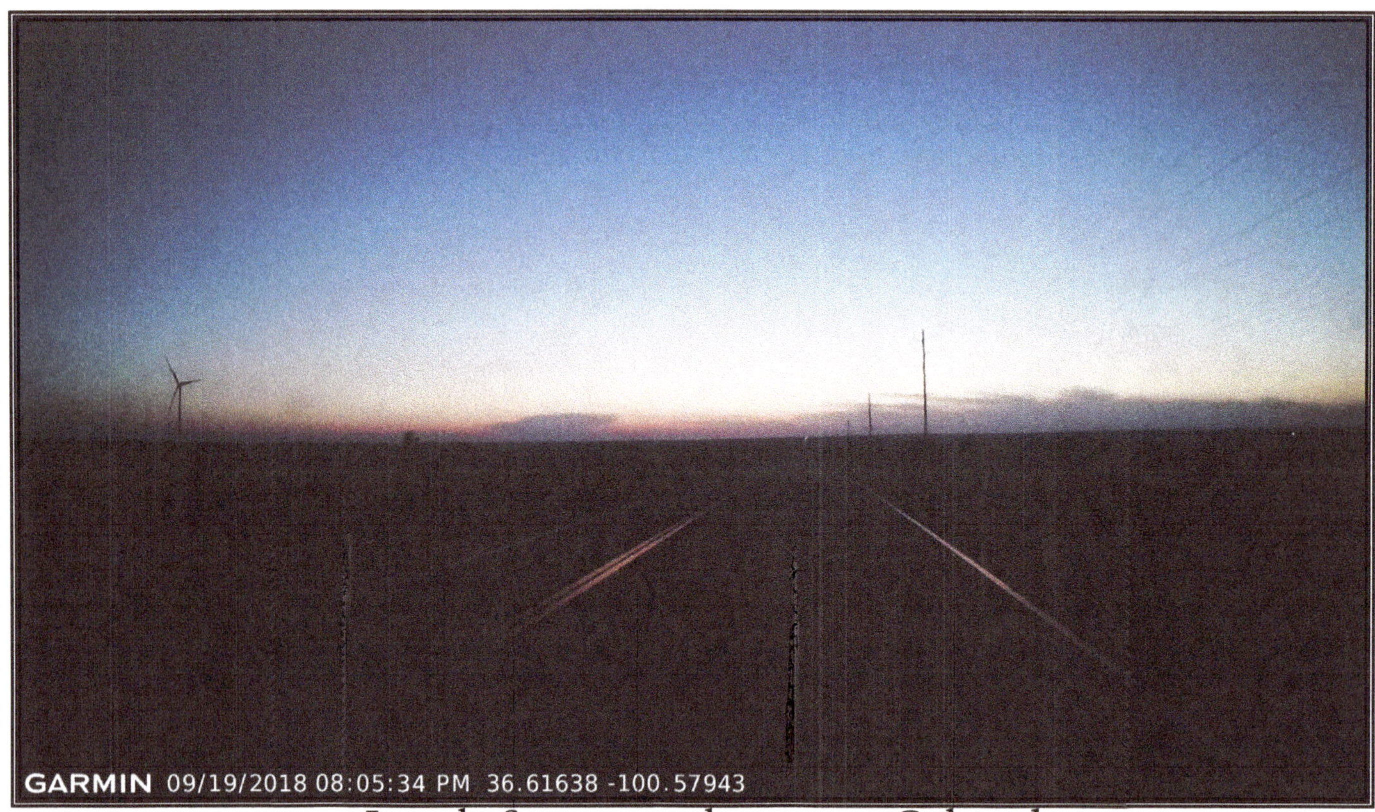

Lonely Sunset on the way to Colorado
US-412, Beaver, Oklahoma

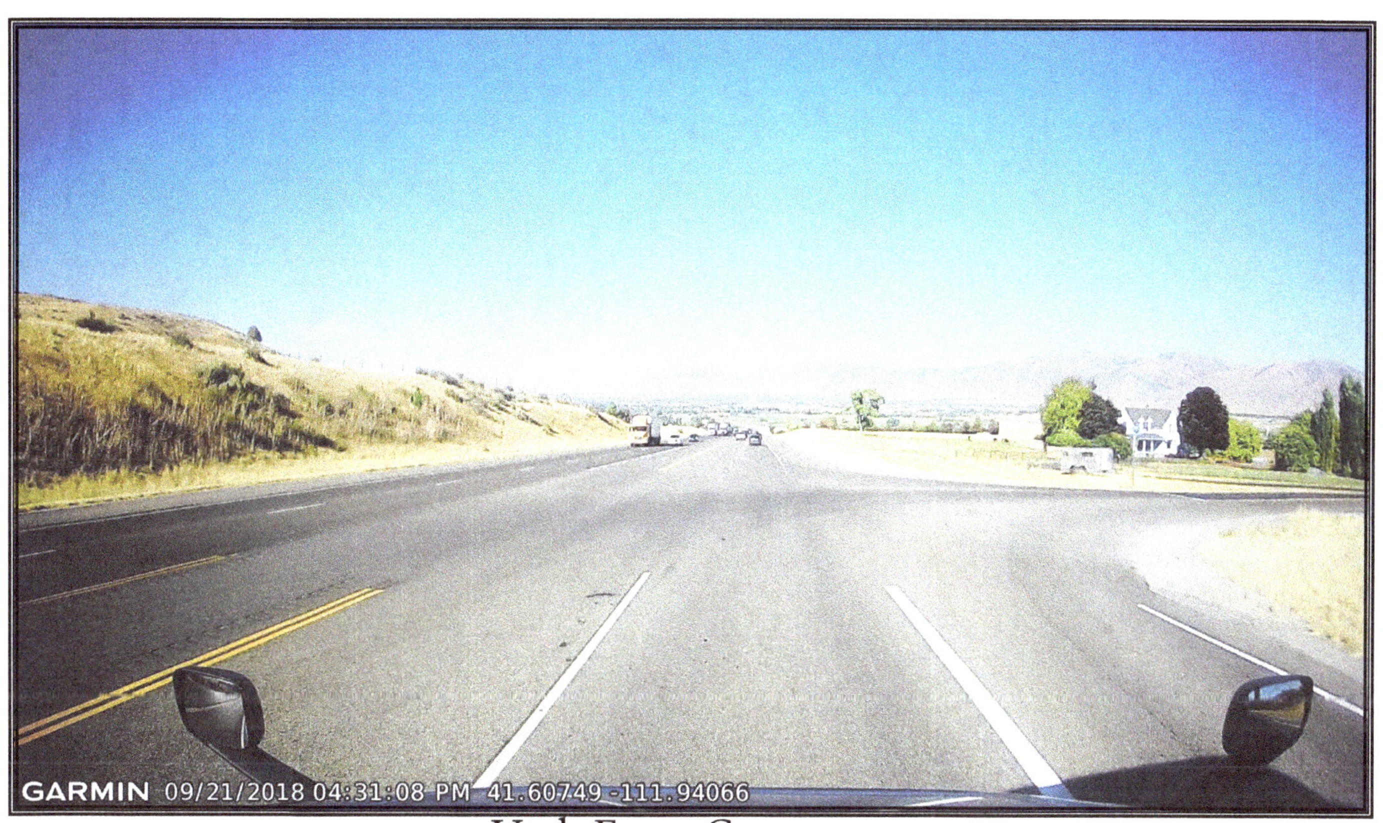

Utah Farm Country
US-91, Wellsville, Utah

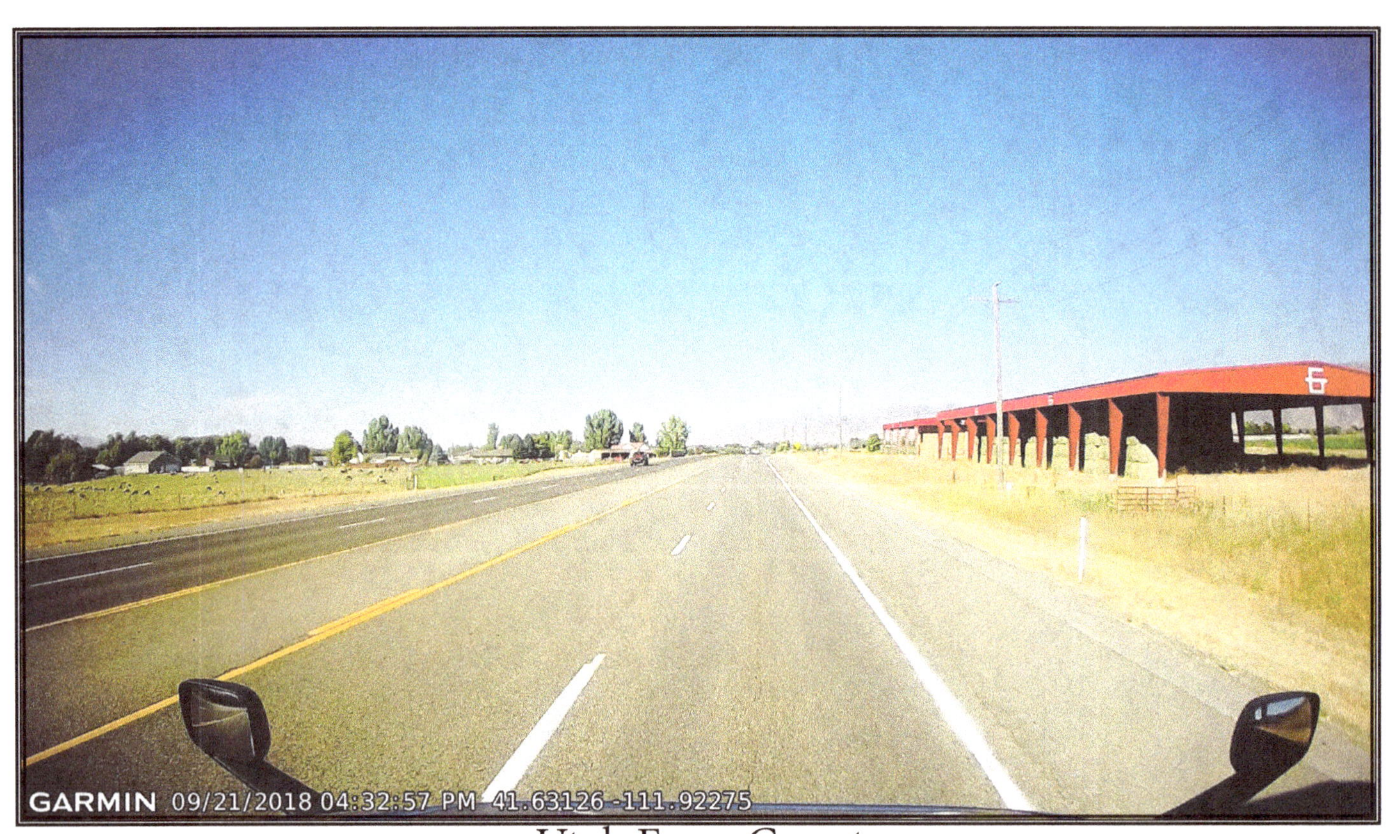

Utah Farm Country
US-91, Wellsville, Utah

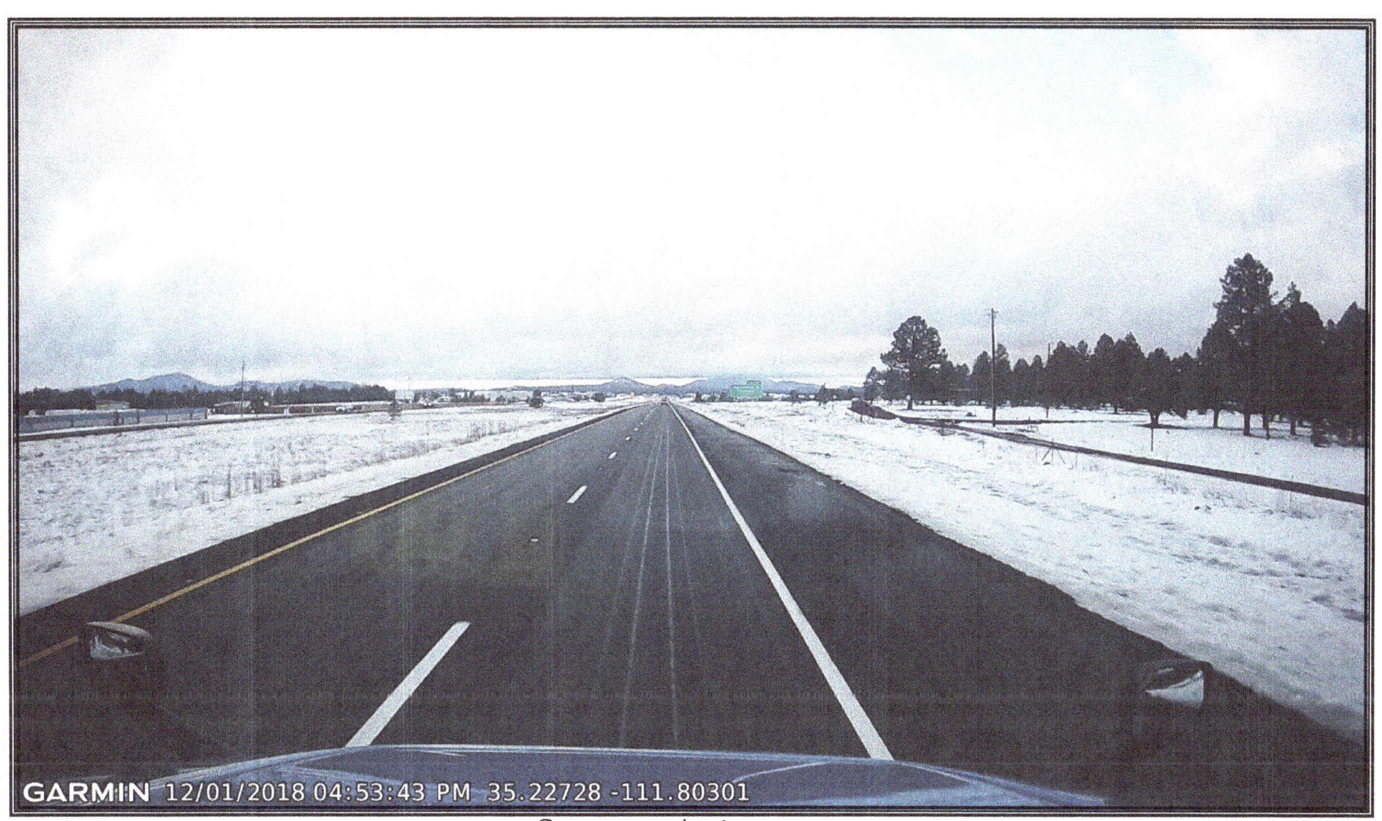

Snowy Arizona
I-40, Bellemont, Arizona

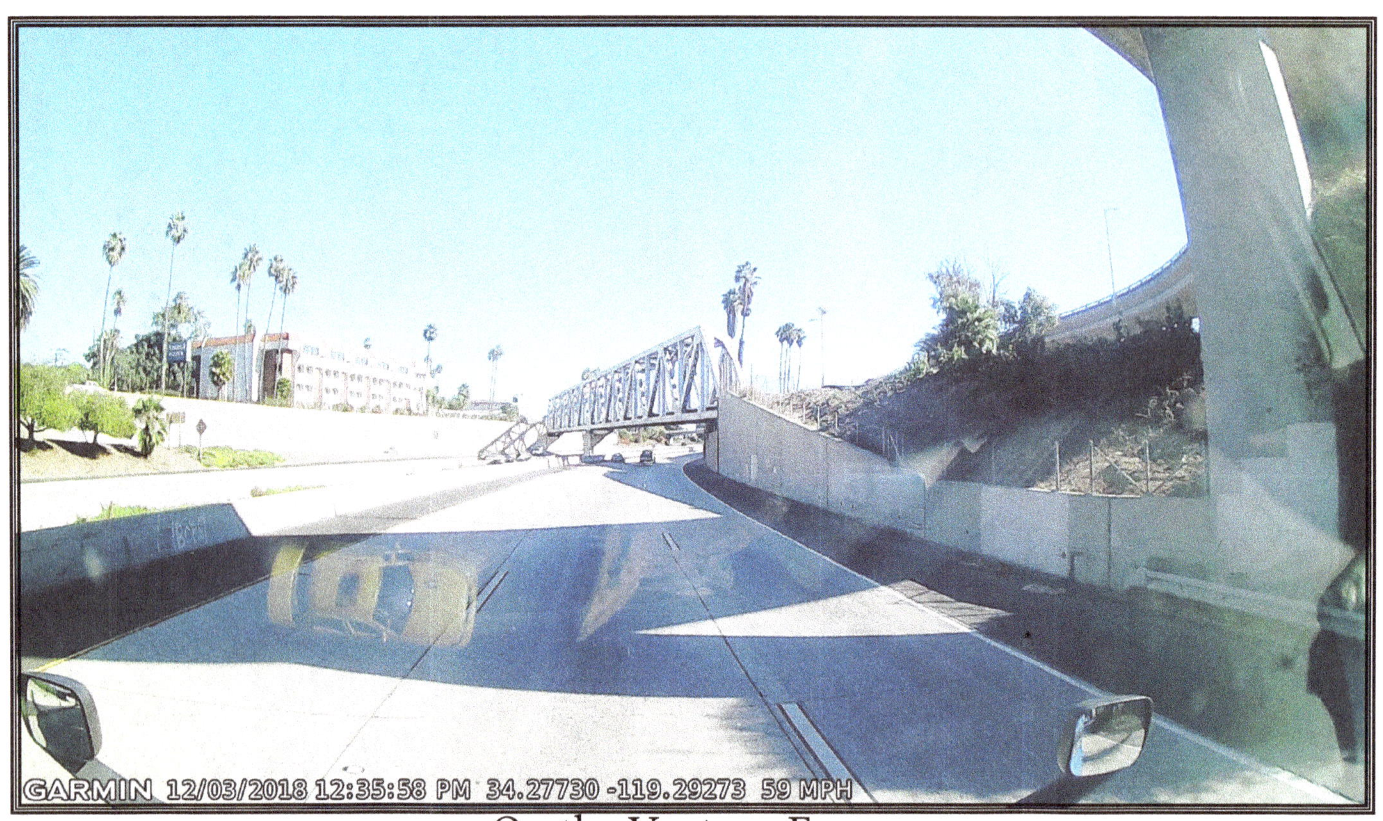

On the Ventura Freeway
US-101, Ventura, California

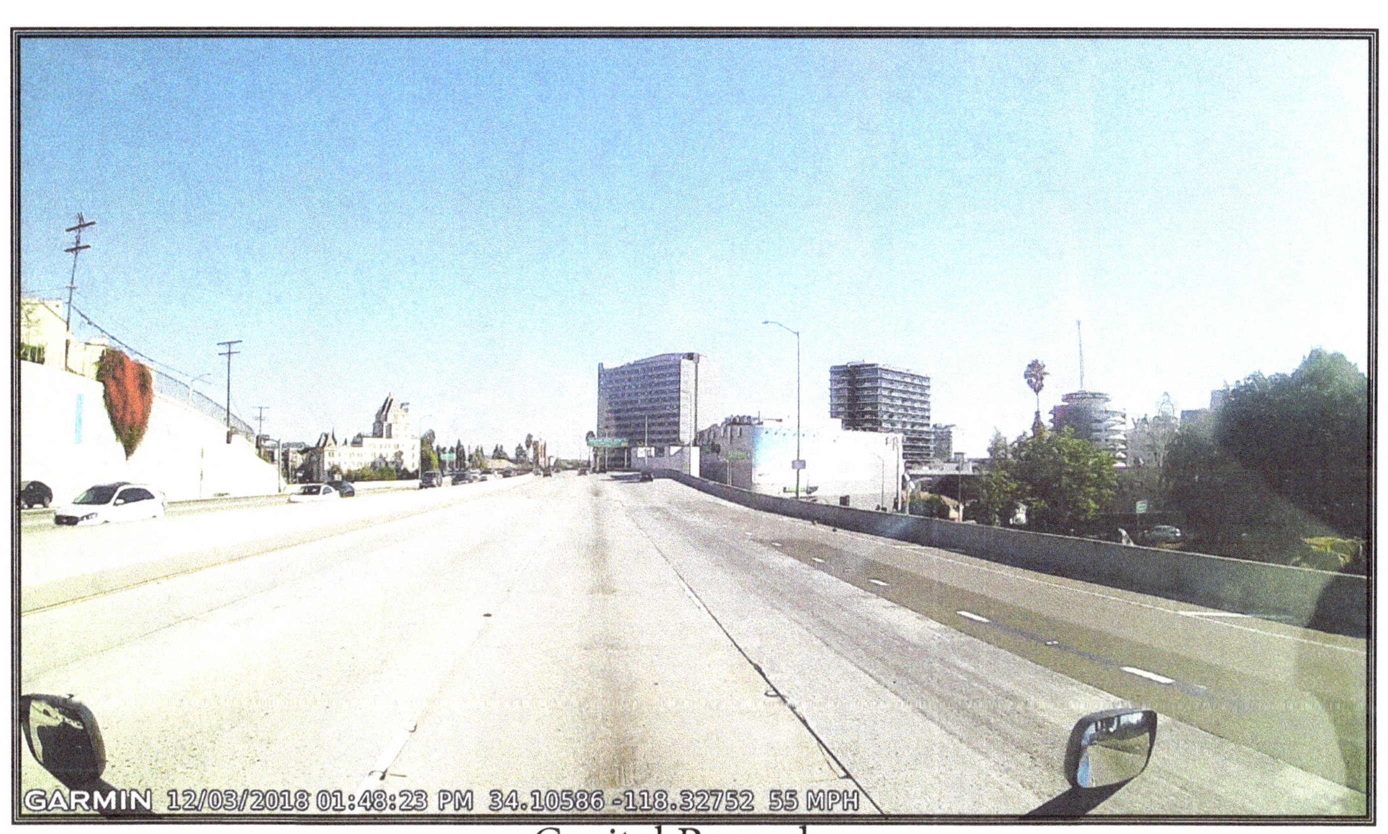

Capital Records
US-101, Los Angeles, California

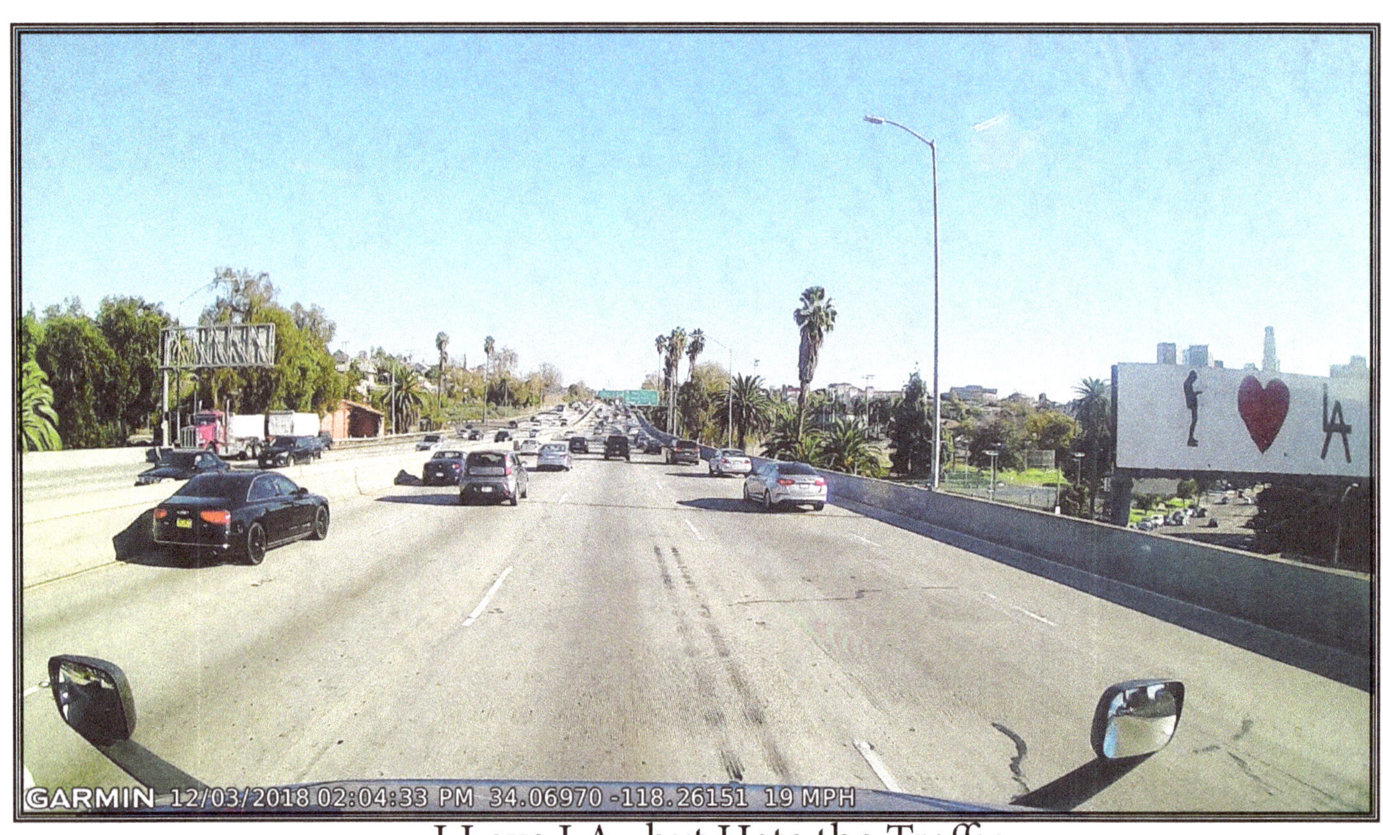

I Love LA...but Hate the Traffic
US-101, Los Angeles, California

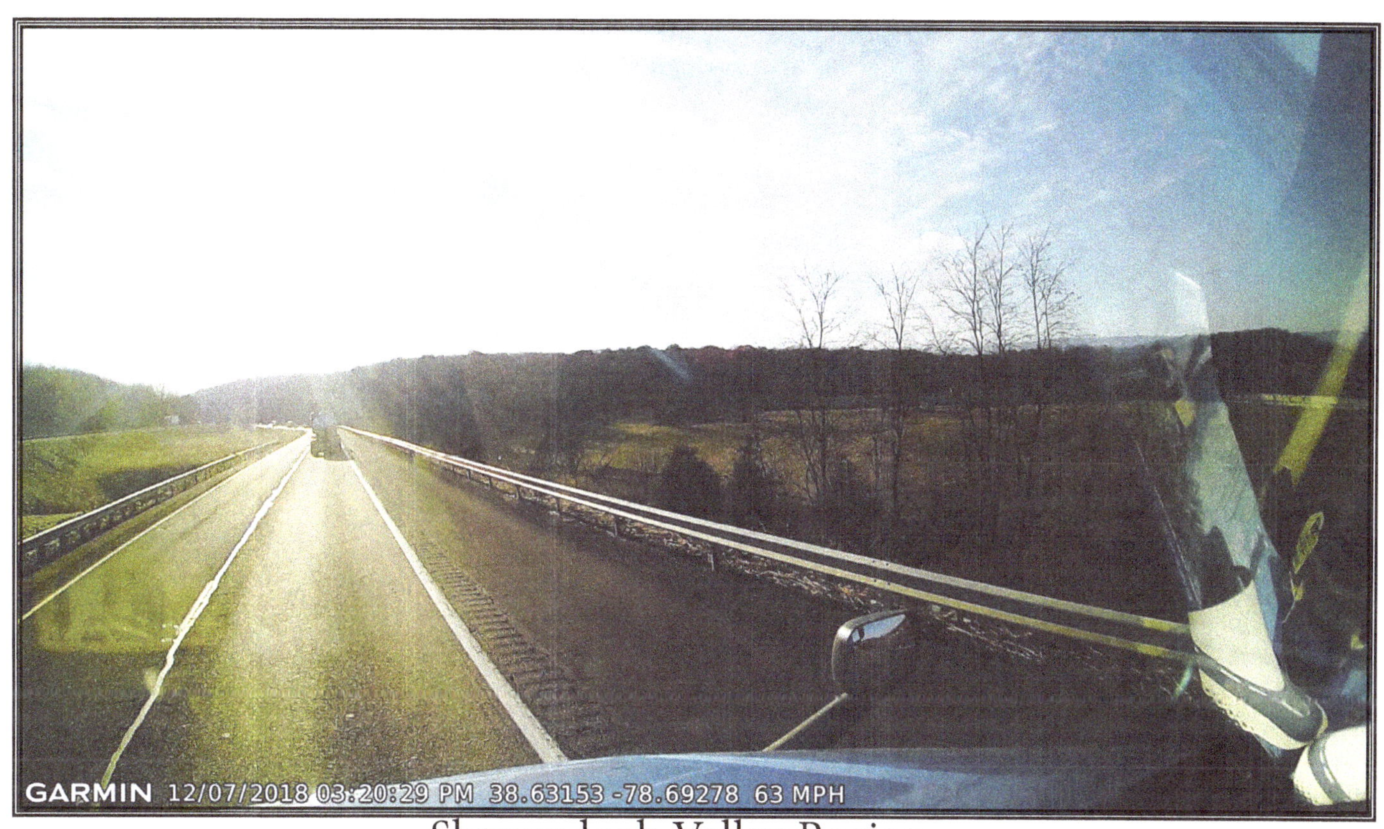

Shenandoah Valley Region
I-81, Timberville, Virginia

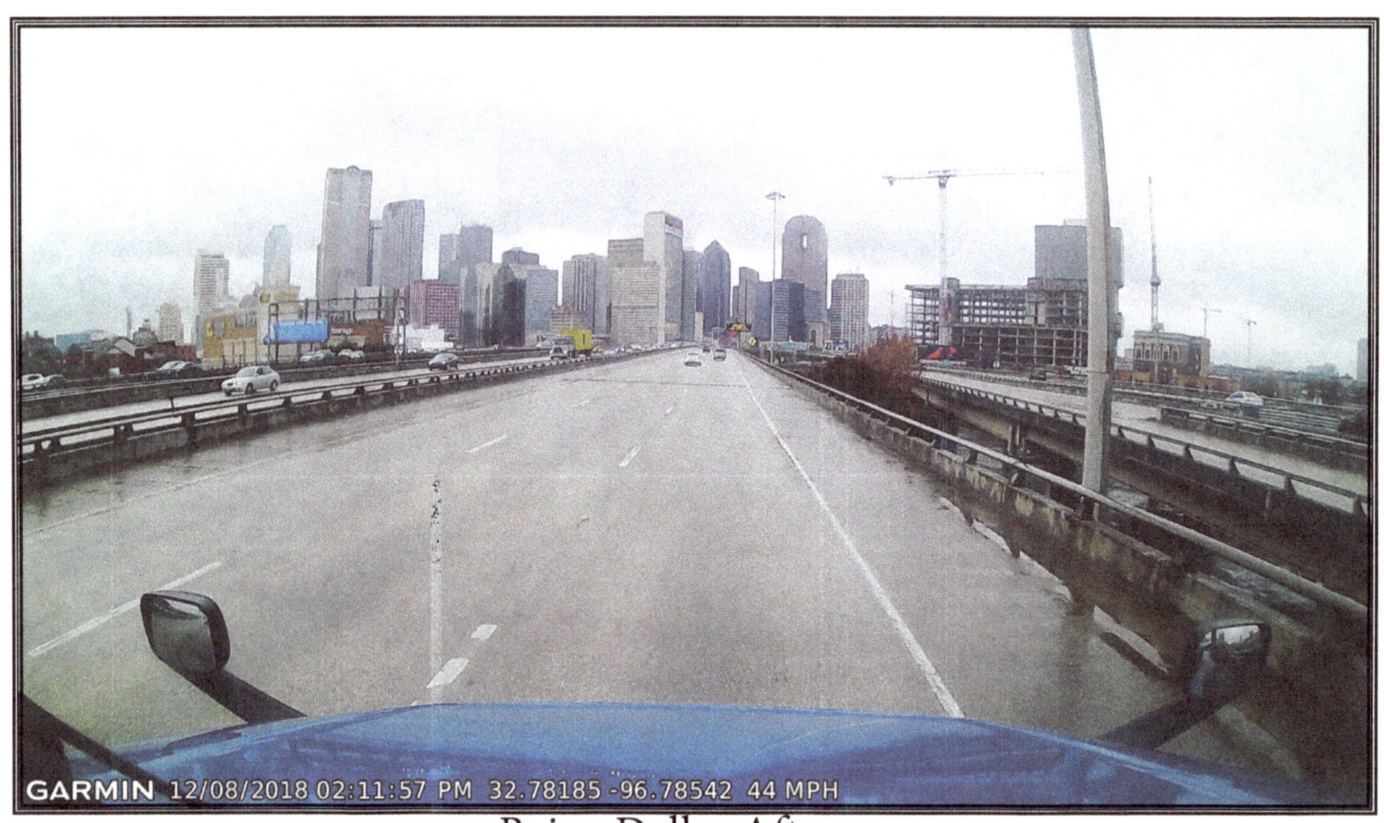

Rainy Dallas Afternoon
US-75, Dallas, Texas

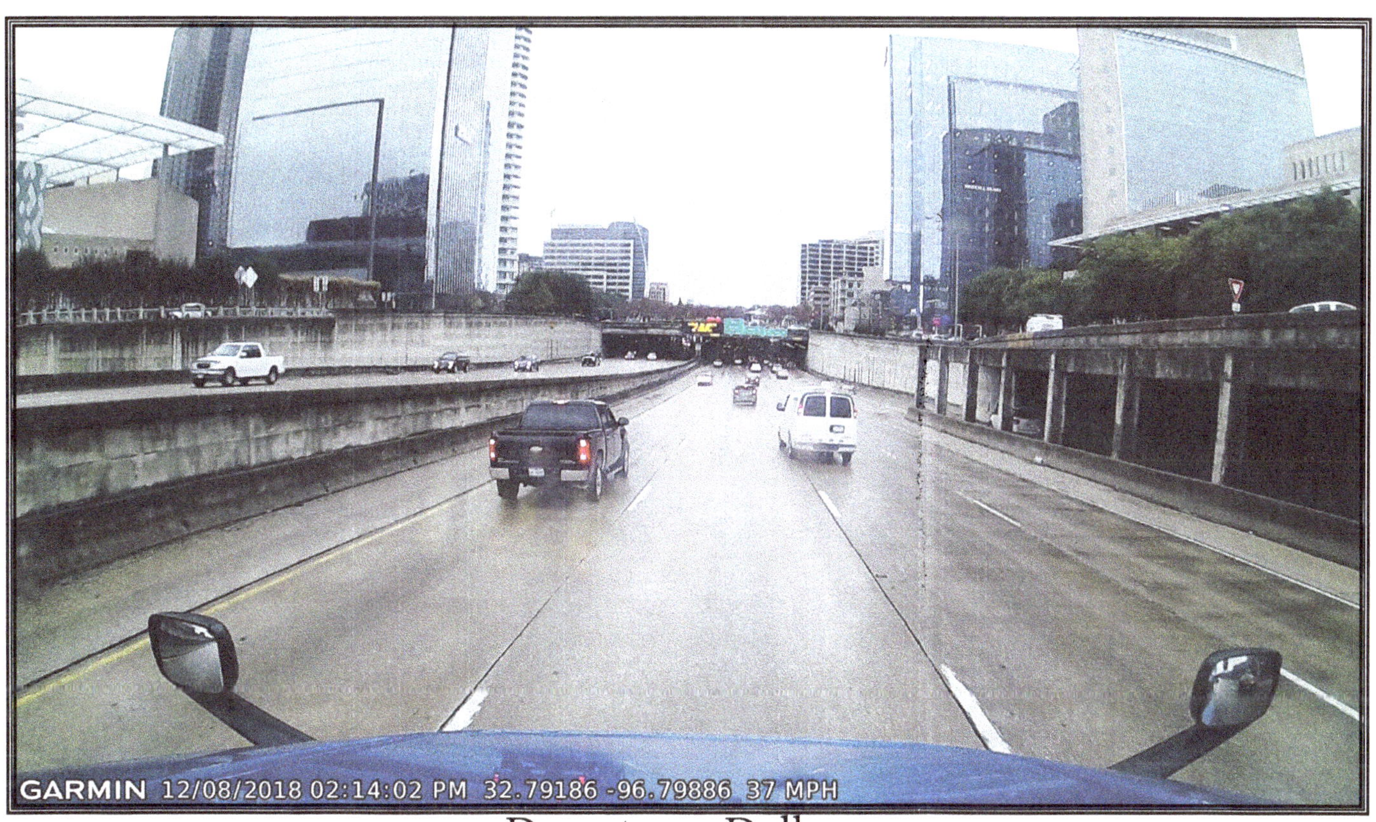

Downtown Dallas
TX-366, Dallas, Texas

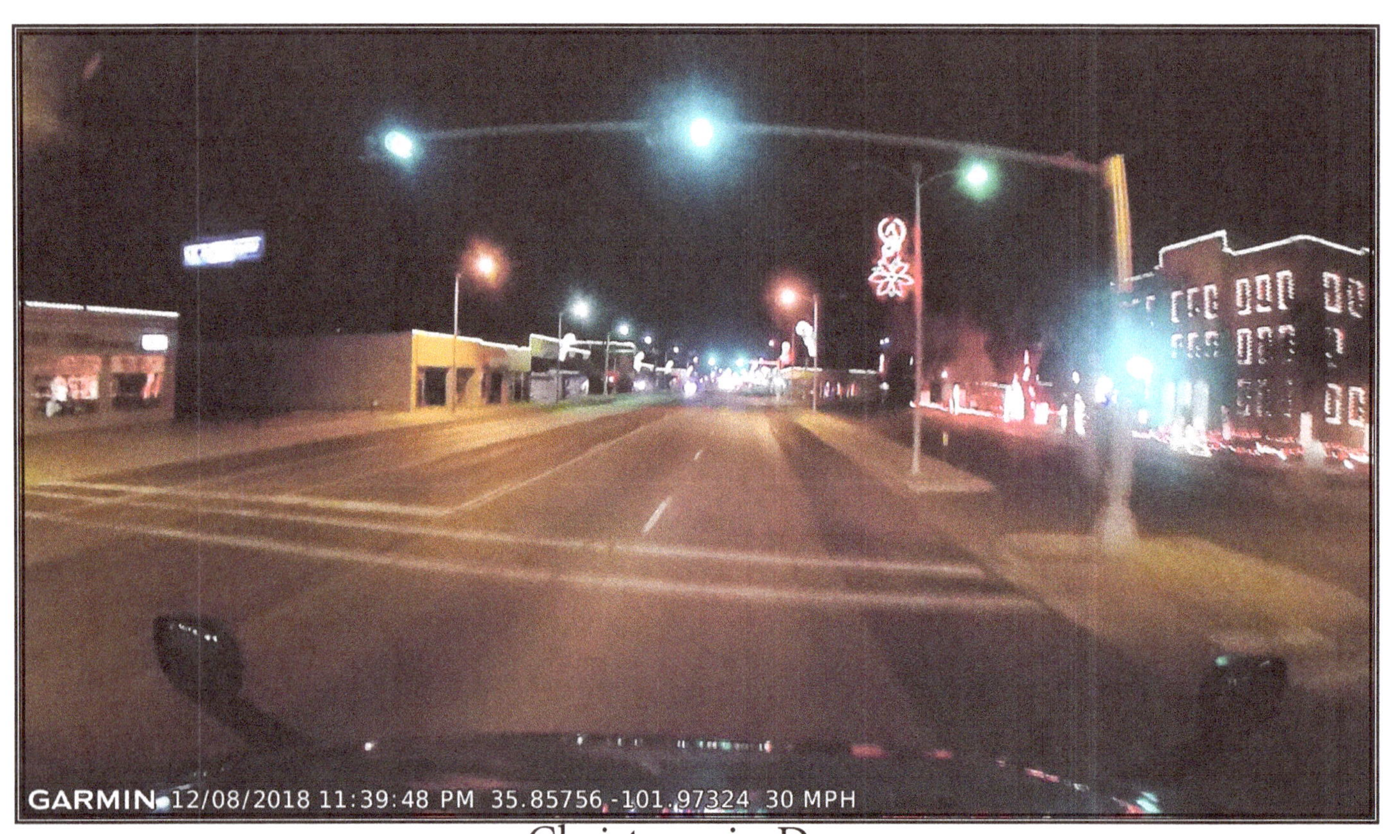

Christmas in Dumas
US-287, Dumas, Texas

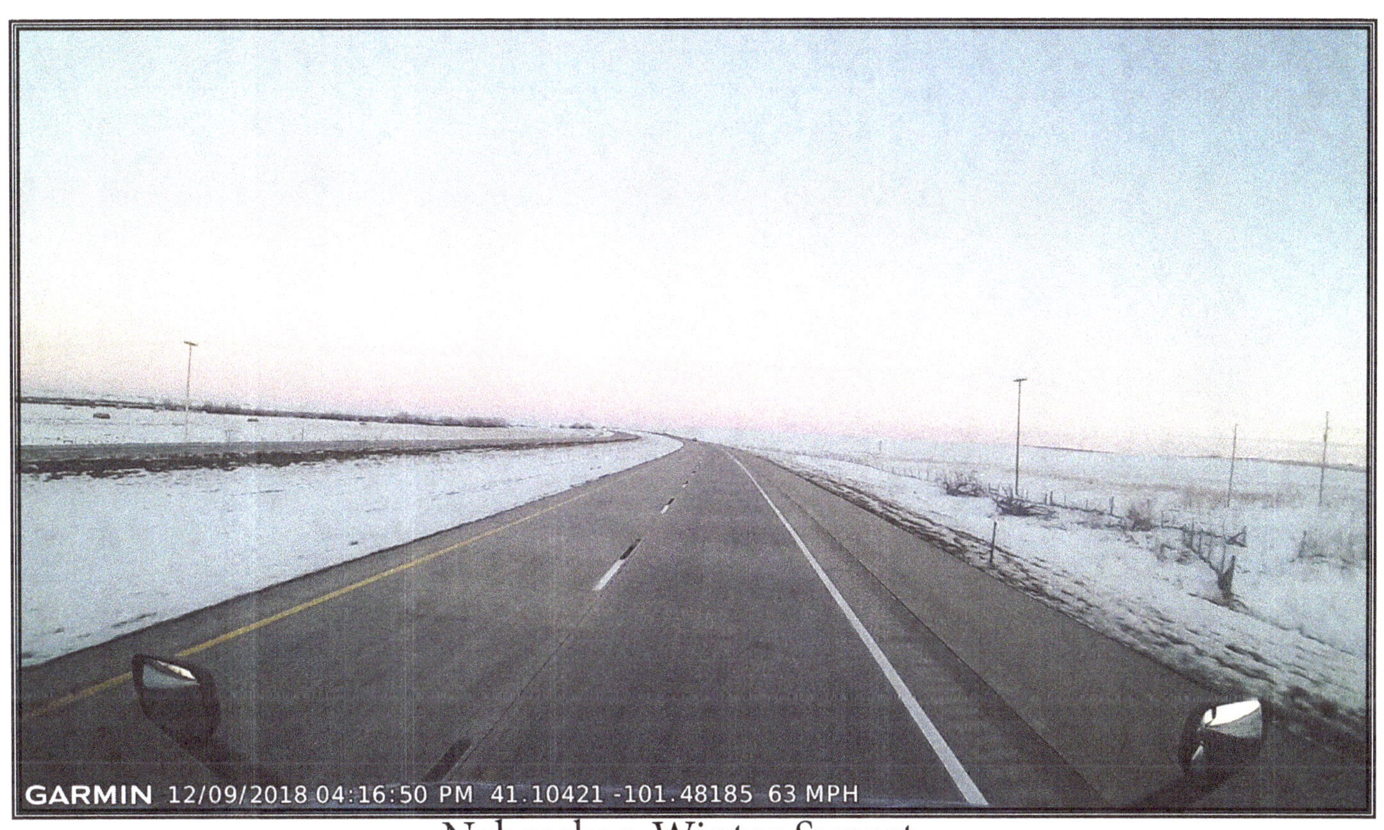

Nebraskan Winter Sunset
I-80, Ogallala, Nebraska

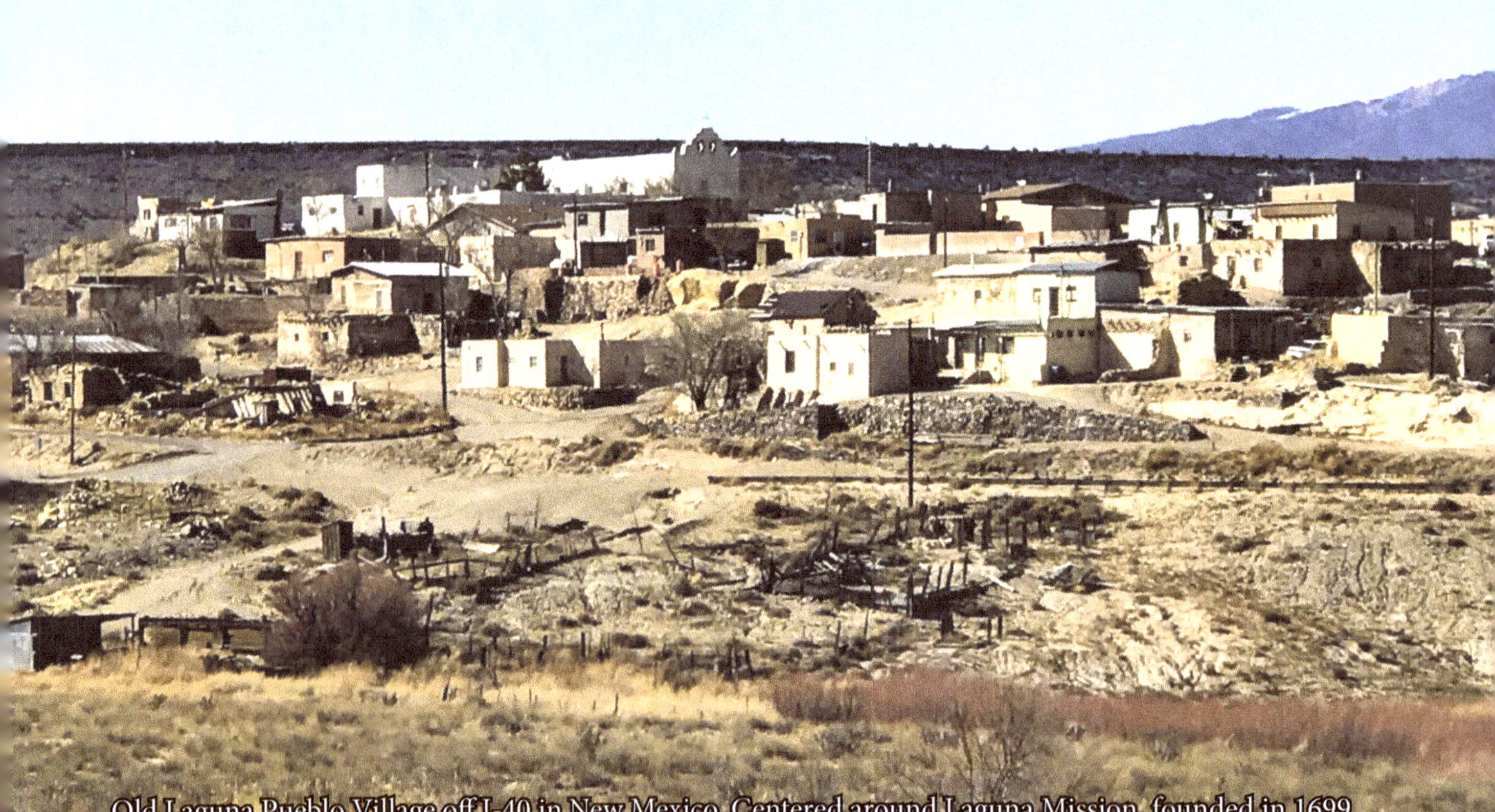

Old Laguna Pueblo Village off I-40 in New Mexico. Centered around Laguna Mission, founded in 1699.

Part Four

Deserts & Mountains

My first real experience with desert-like conditions was the wilderness of West Texas when I was a twenty-three-year-old drug addict hitchhiking his way to sobriety. I found myself outside of Bakersfield, Texas, hiking along a farm road with my best friend in the midst of a drought. We were heading toward the Pecos River to camp for the night and hoping that the river water was potable—and later finding it absolutcly was not—because we had forgotten to fill up our water jugs.

It was not a fun time, but even so I loved the wilderness. It is in the wilderness that we find peace, and I think that is because it is through adversity that we grow stronger, and strength brings peace. Surviving in the deserts and mountains of this world, both very harsh climates and terrains, requires a measure of determination that I think everybody has access to but only special people desire to find within themselves.

Perhaps this is why I will never tire of driving through the Mojave, or pulling a 45,000 pound load up through Deadman's Pass. Beauty is just the beginning. These certainly are beautiful regions, and yet there is so much more. So much history, so many stories of travelers and adventurers who have suffered and even died while making their way through these harsh and unforgiving territories.

I think it wise to get out and experience the mountains and deserts of this world from time to time. Find that adversity that will demand so much from you. And then, perhaps, you will find something within rise to the challenge, and in doing so will find peace.

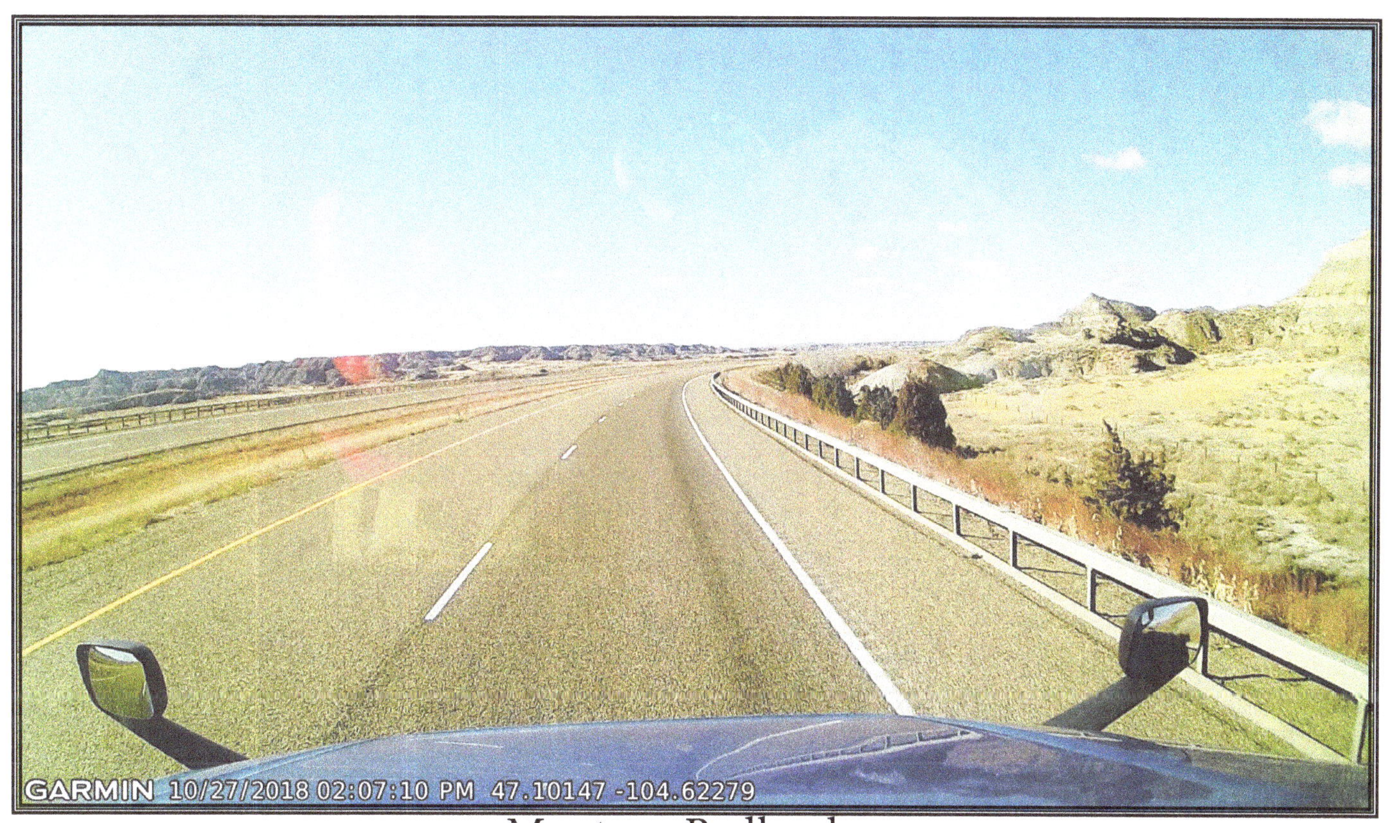

Montana Badlands
I-94, Glendive, Montana

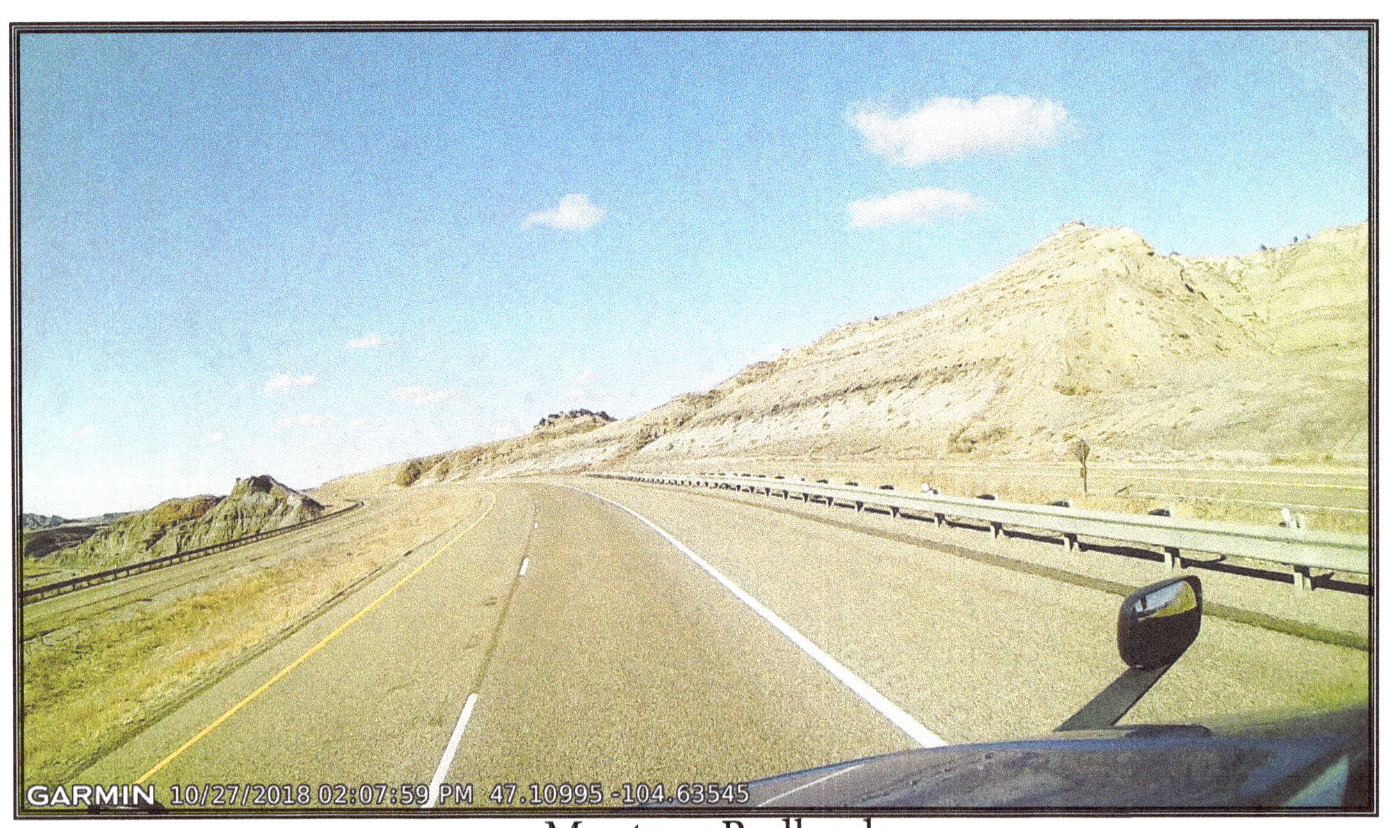

Montana Badlands
I-94, Glendive, Montana

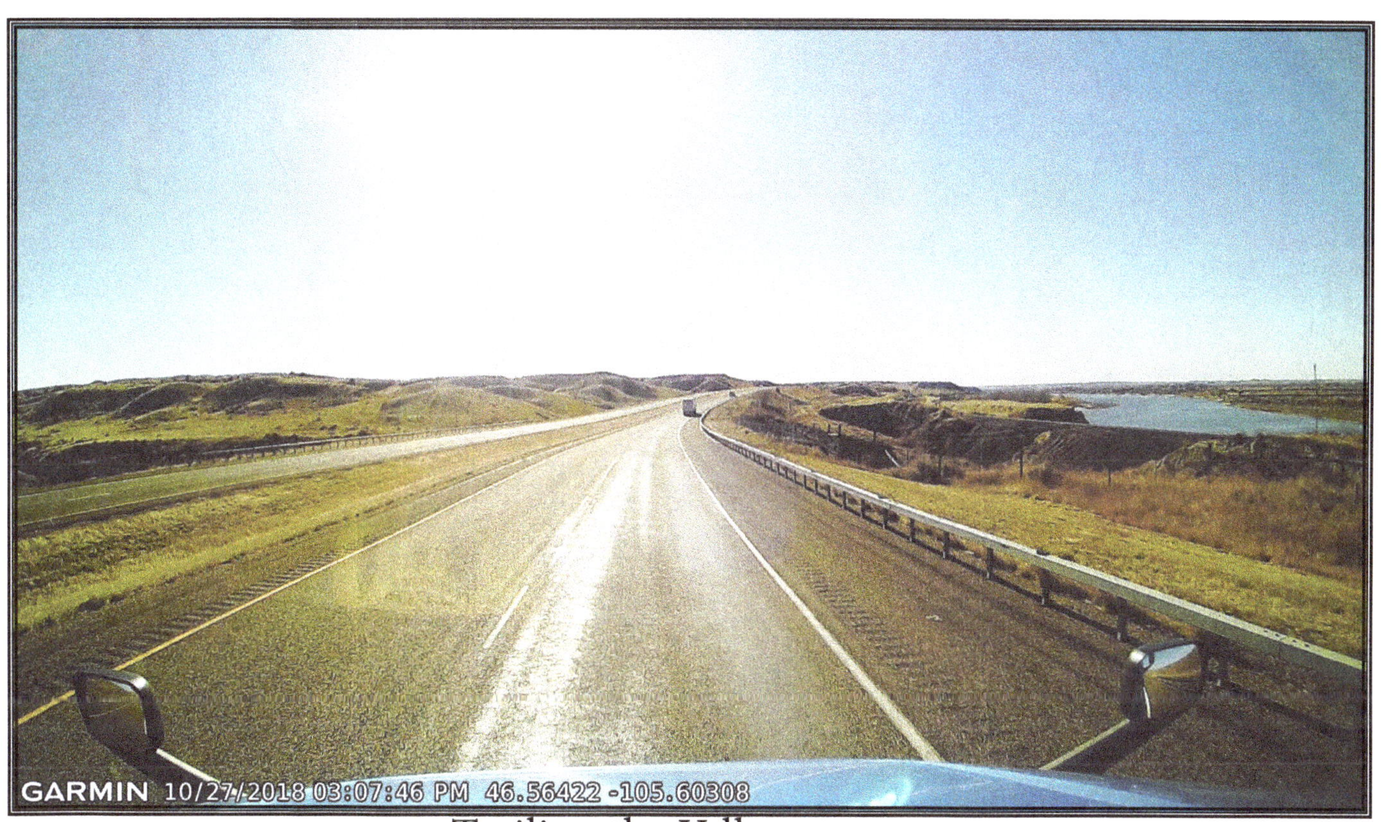

Trailing the Yellowstone
I-94, Miles City, Montana

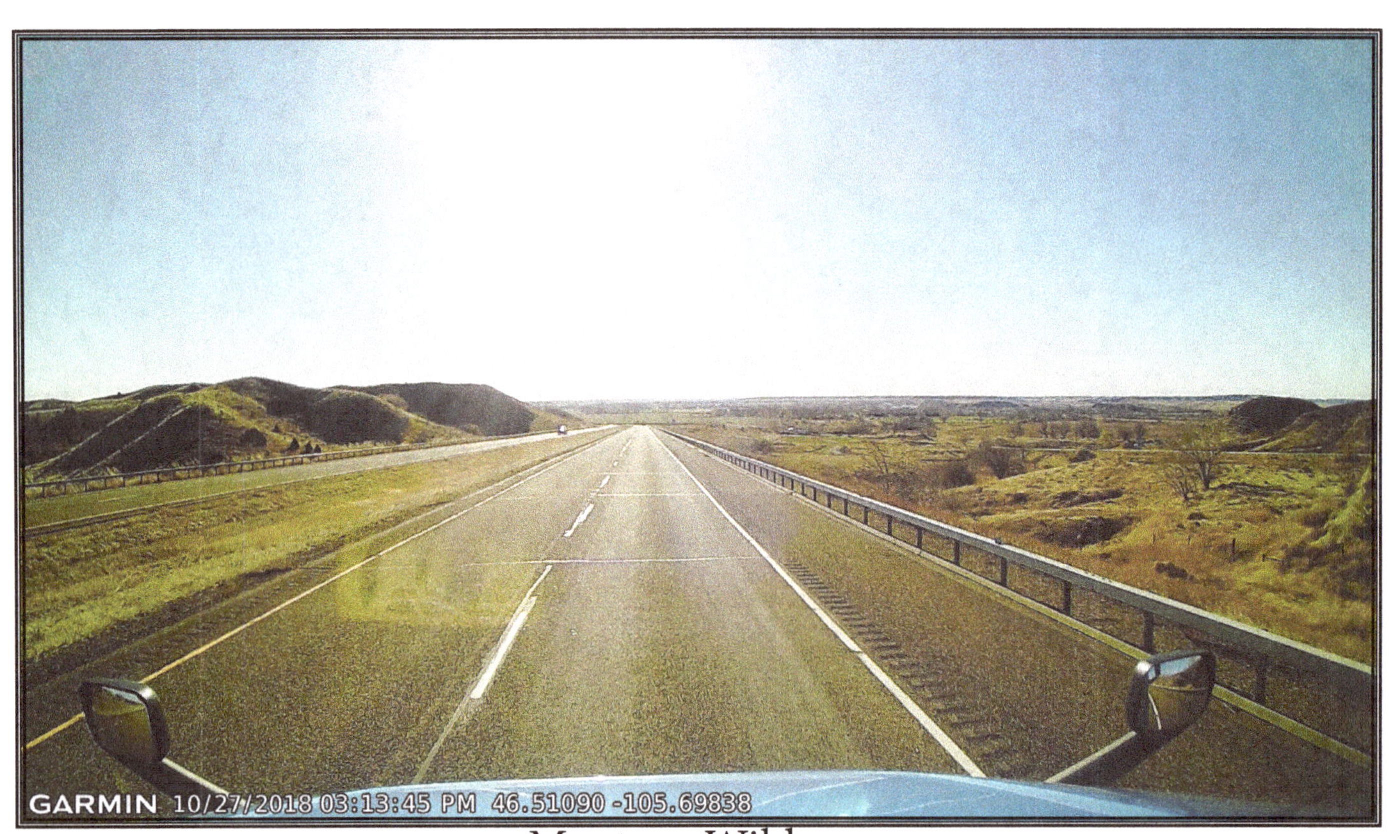

Montana Wilderness
I-94, Miles City, Montana

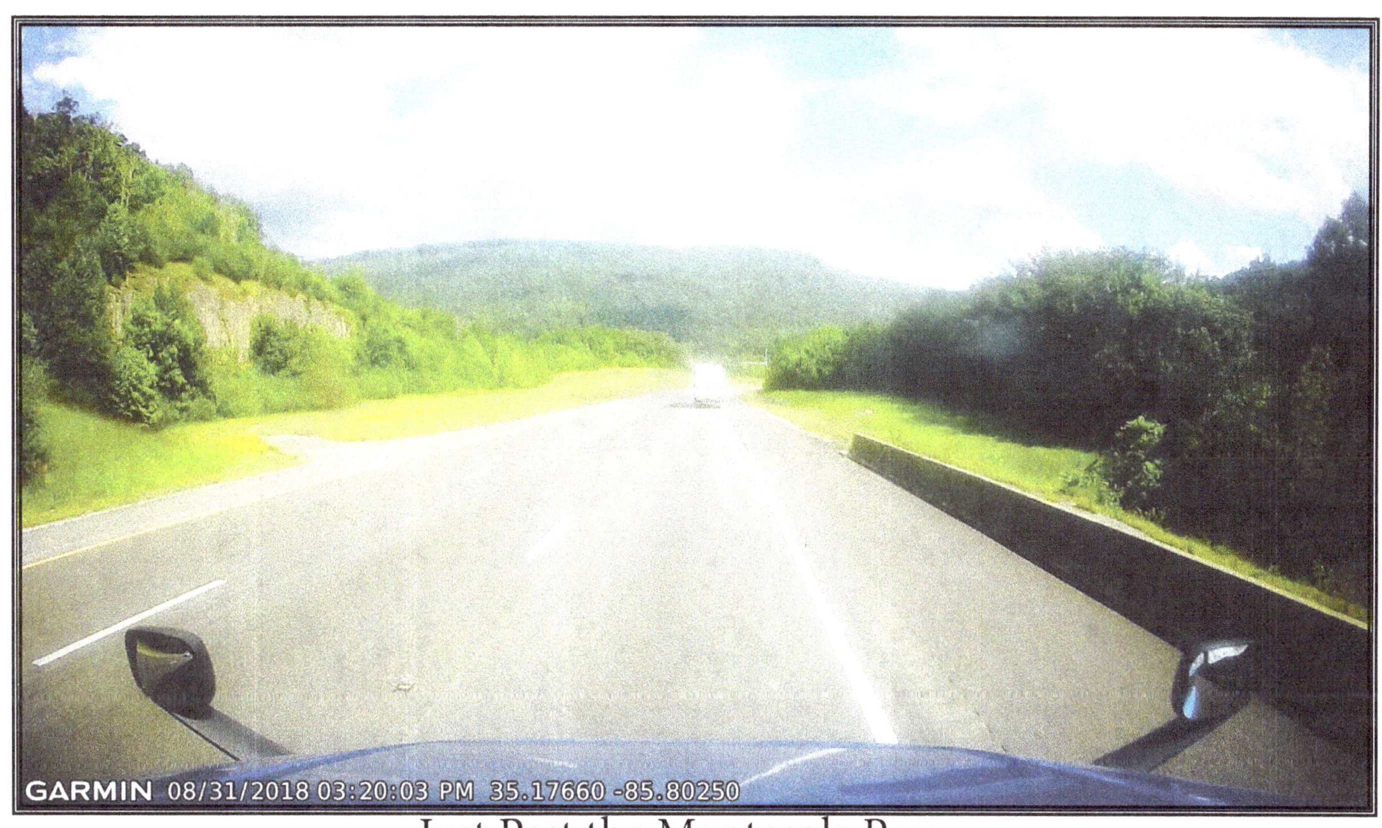

Just Past the Monteagle Pass
I-24, South Pittsburg, Tennessee

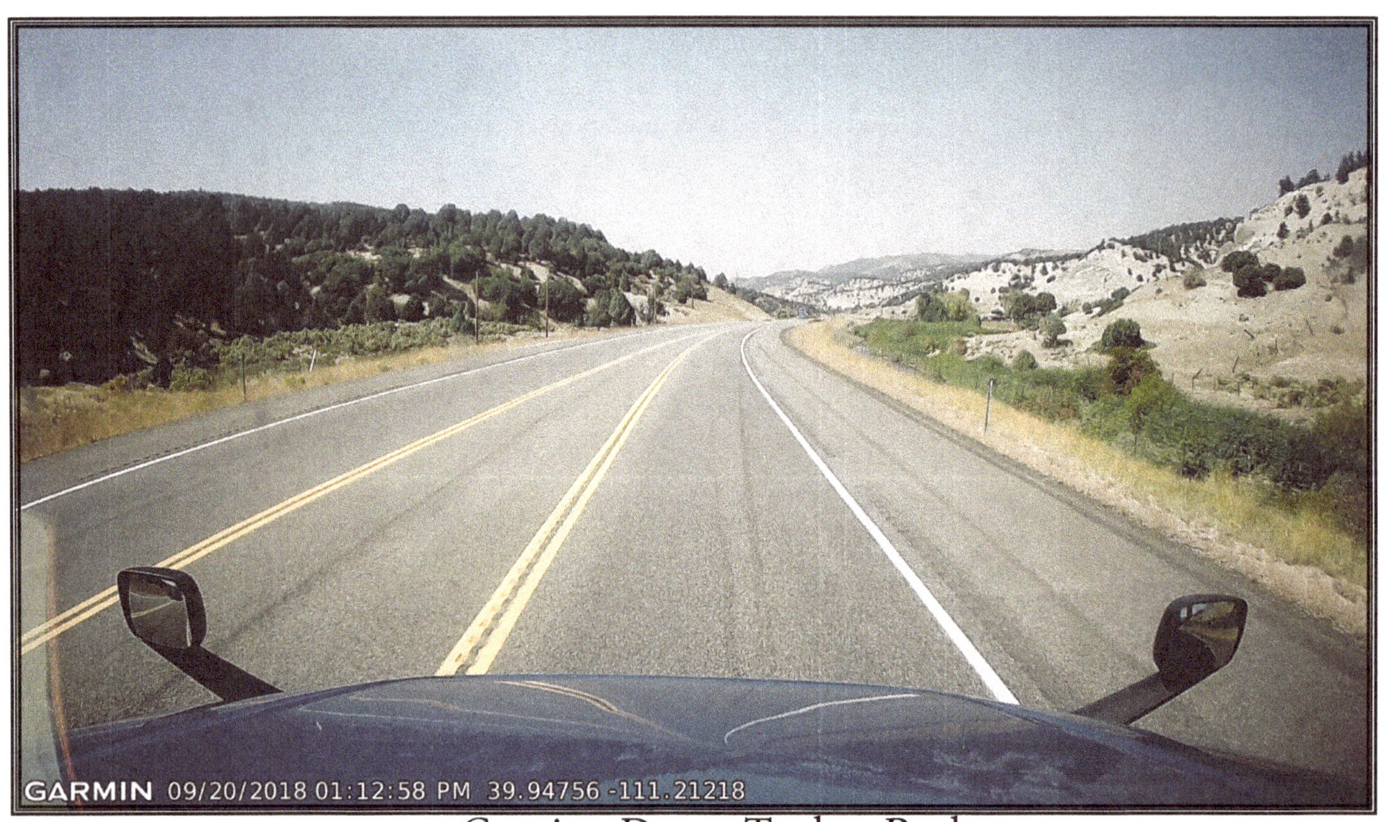

Coming Down Tucker Peak
US-6, Tucker, Utah

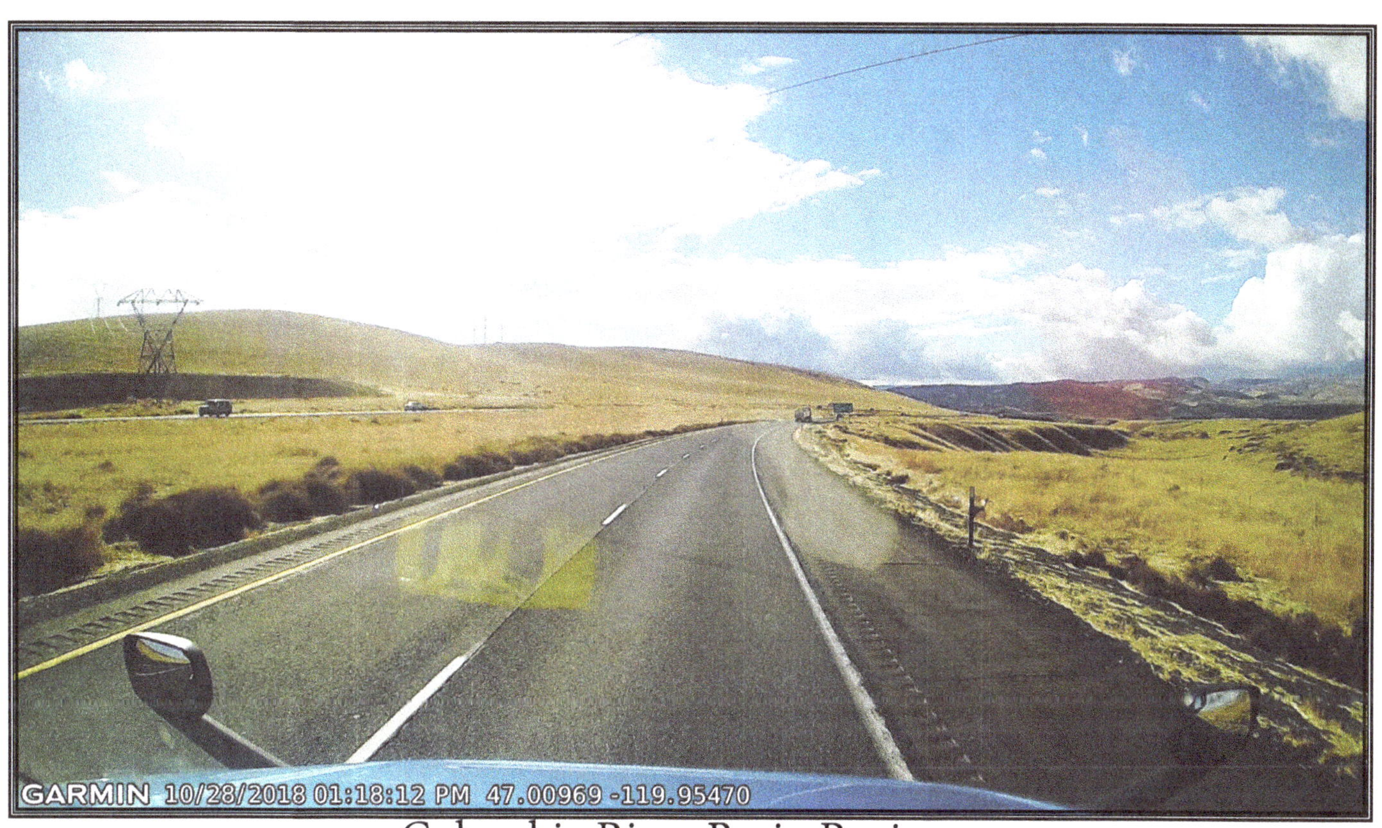

Columbia River Basin Region
I-90, Quincy, Washington

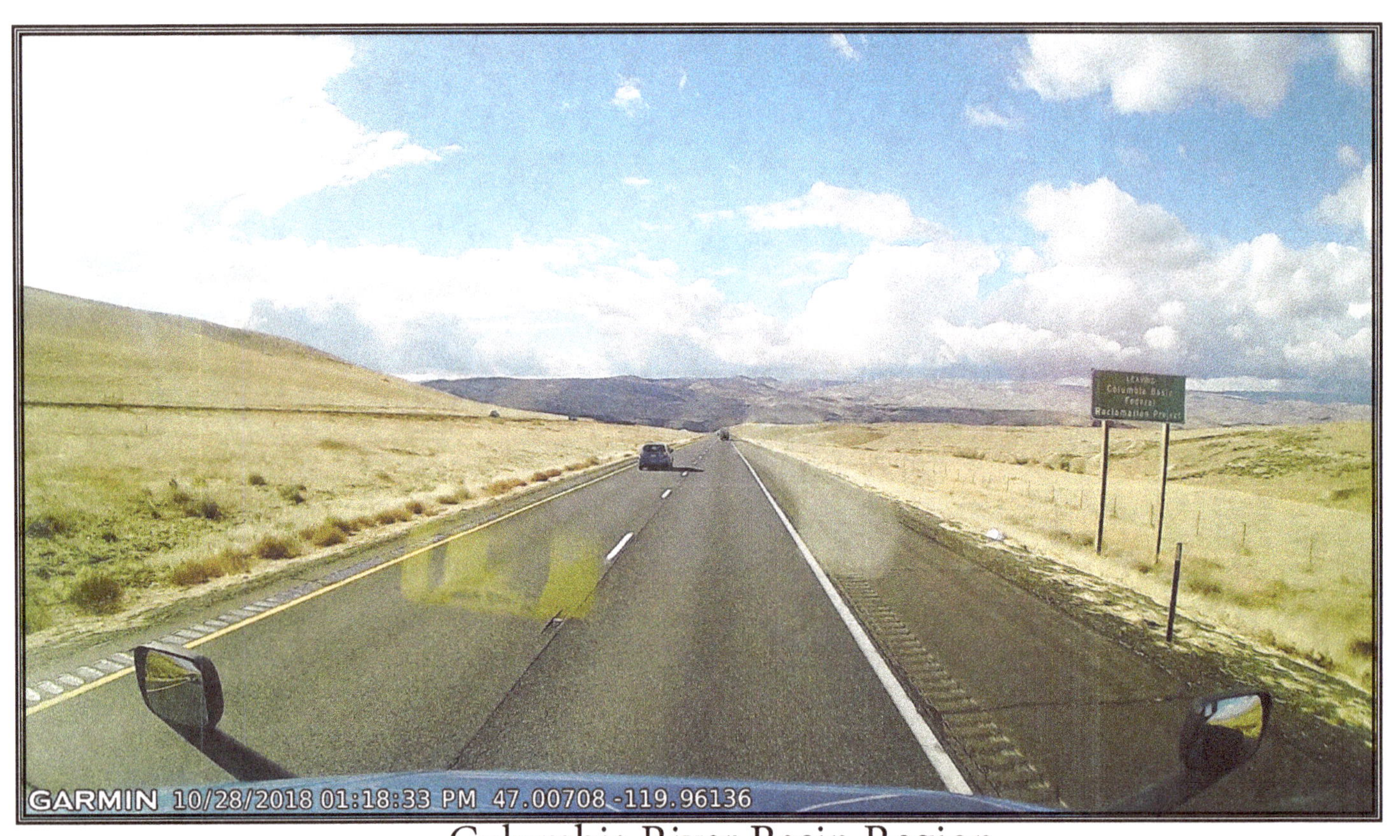

Columbia River Basin Region
I-90, Quincy, Washington

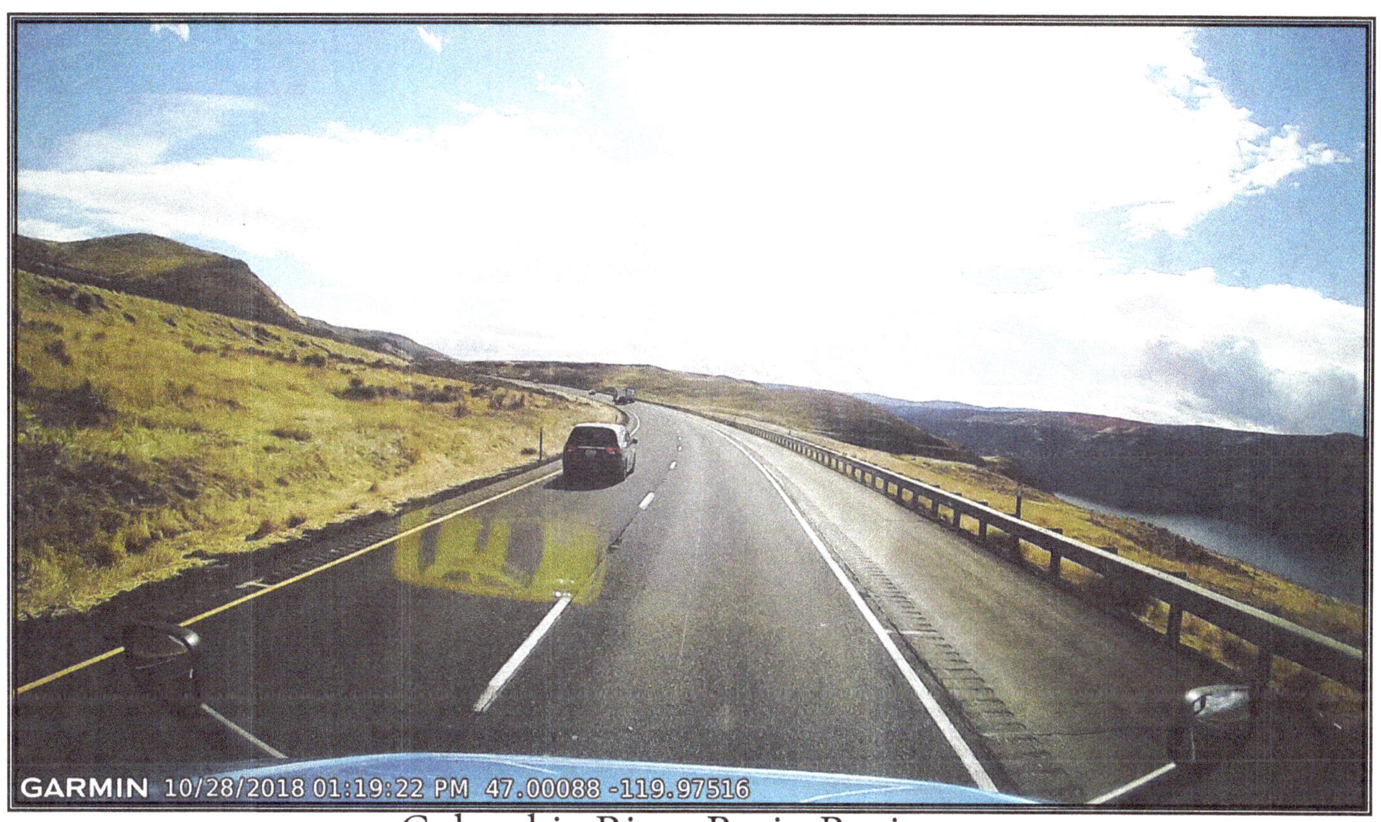

Columbia River Basin Region
I-90, Quincy, Washington

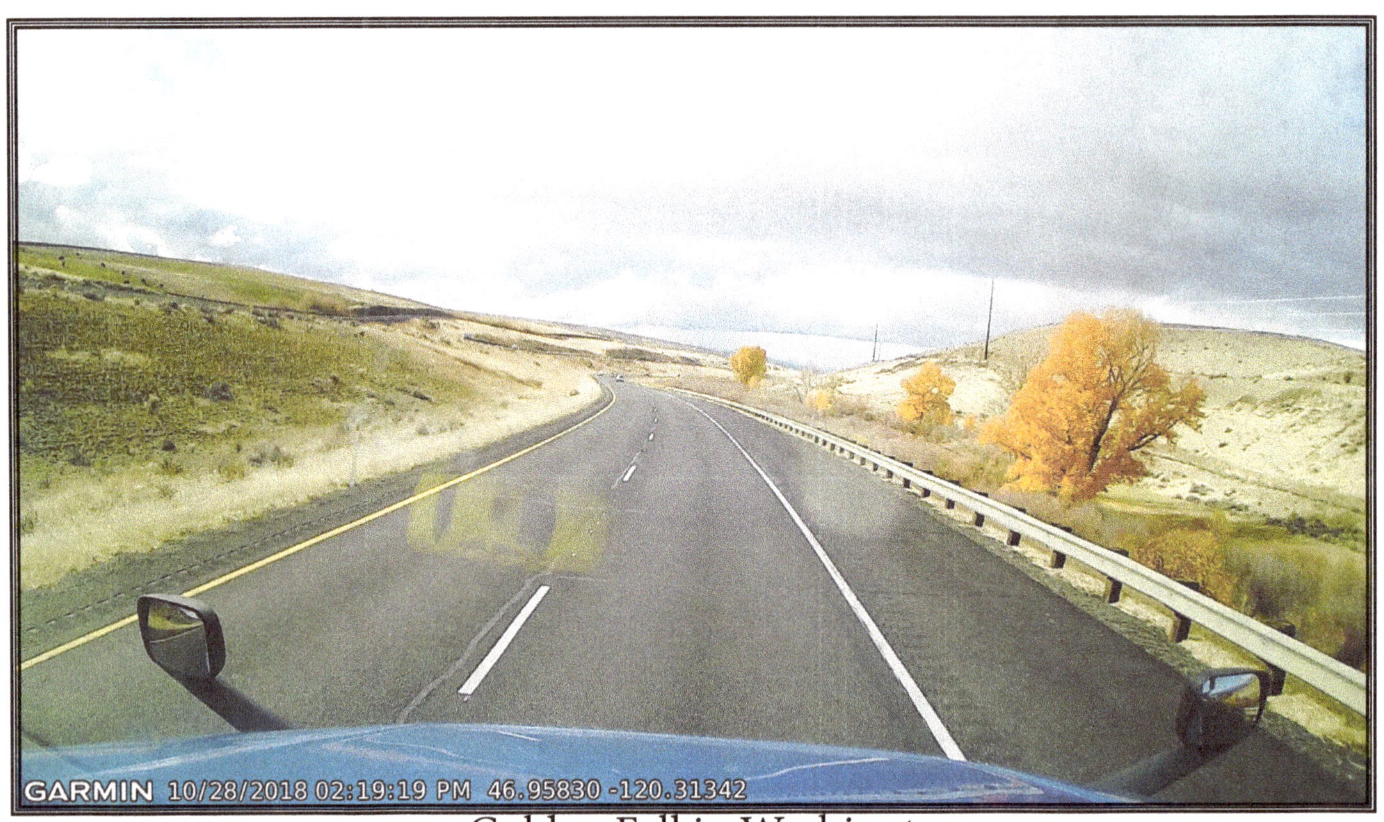

Golden Fall in Washington
I-90, Ellensburg, Washington

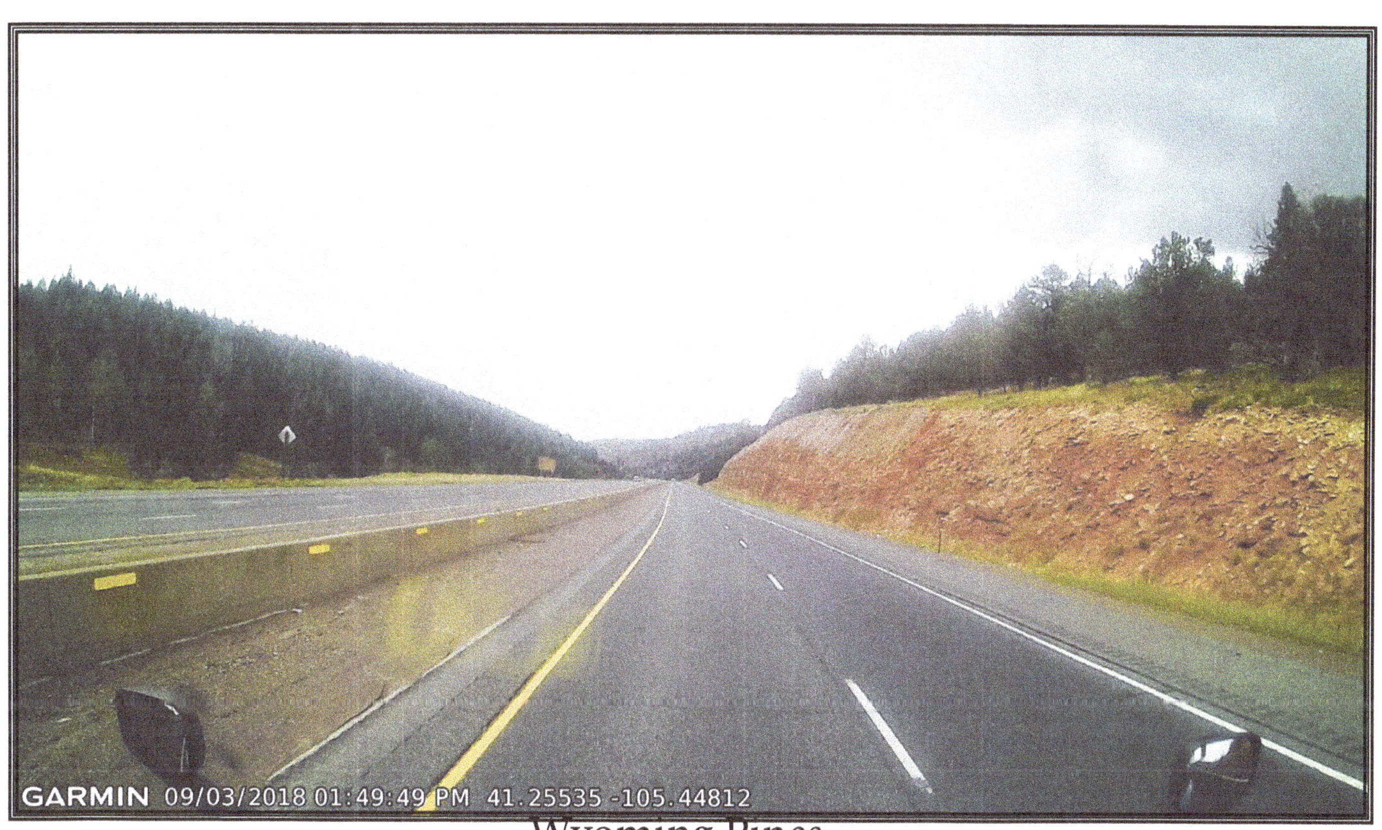

Wyoming Pines
I-80, Laramie, Wyoming

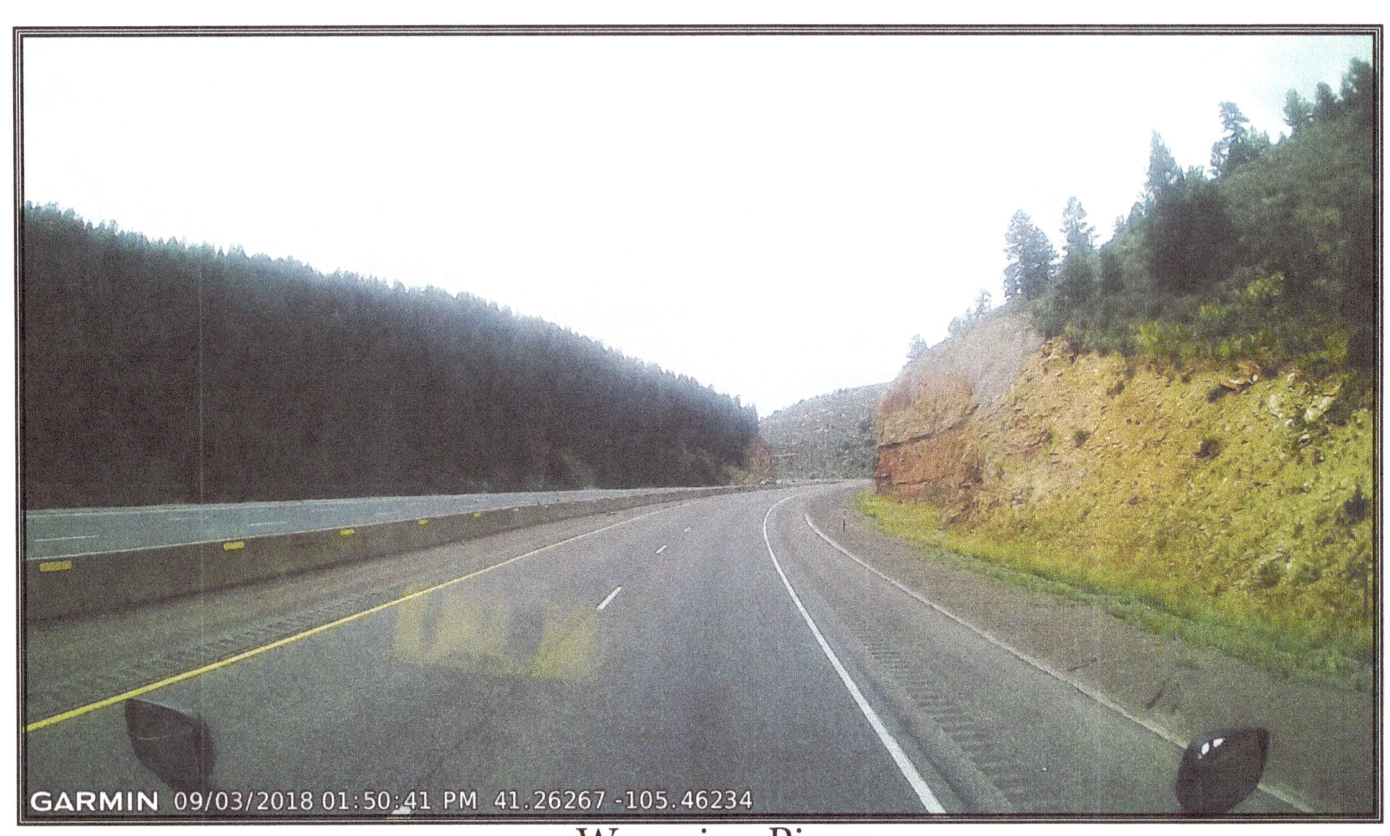

Wyoming Pines
I-70, Laramie, Wyoming

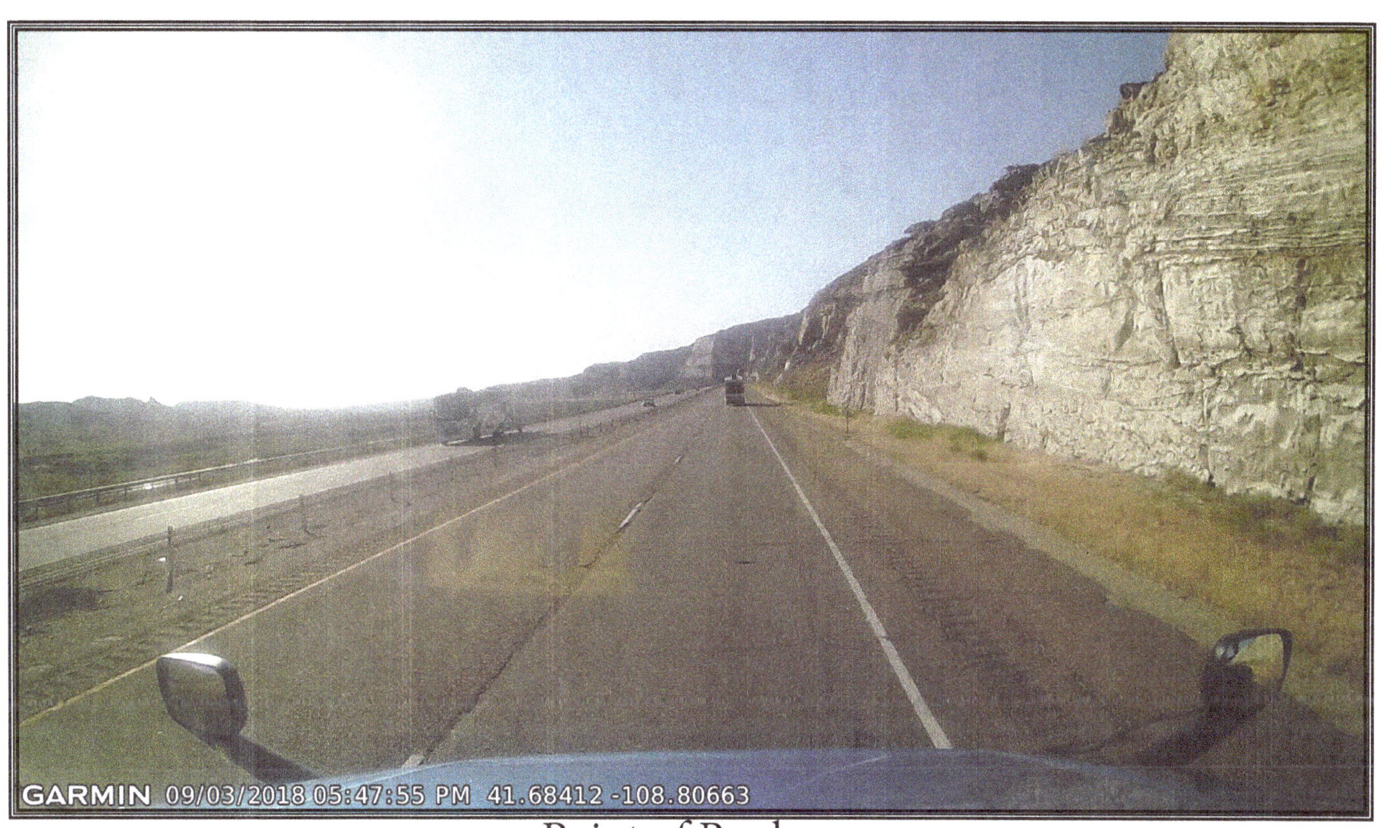

Point of Rocks
I-80, Rock Springs, Wyoming

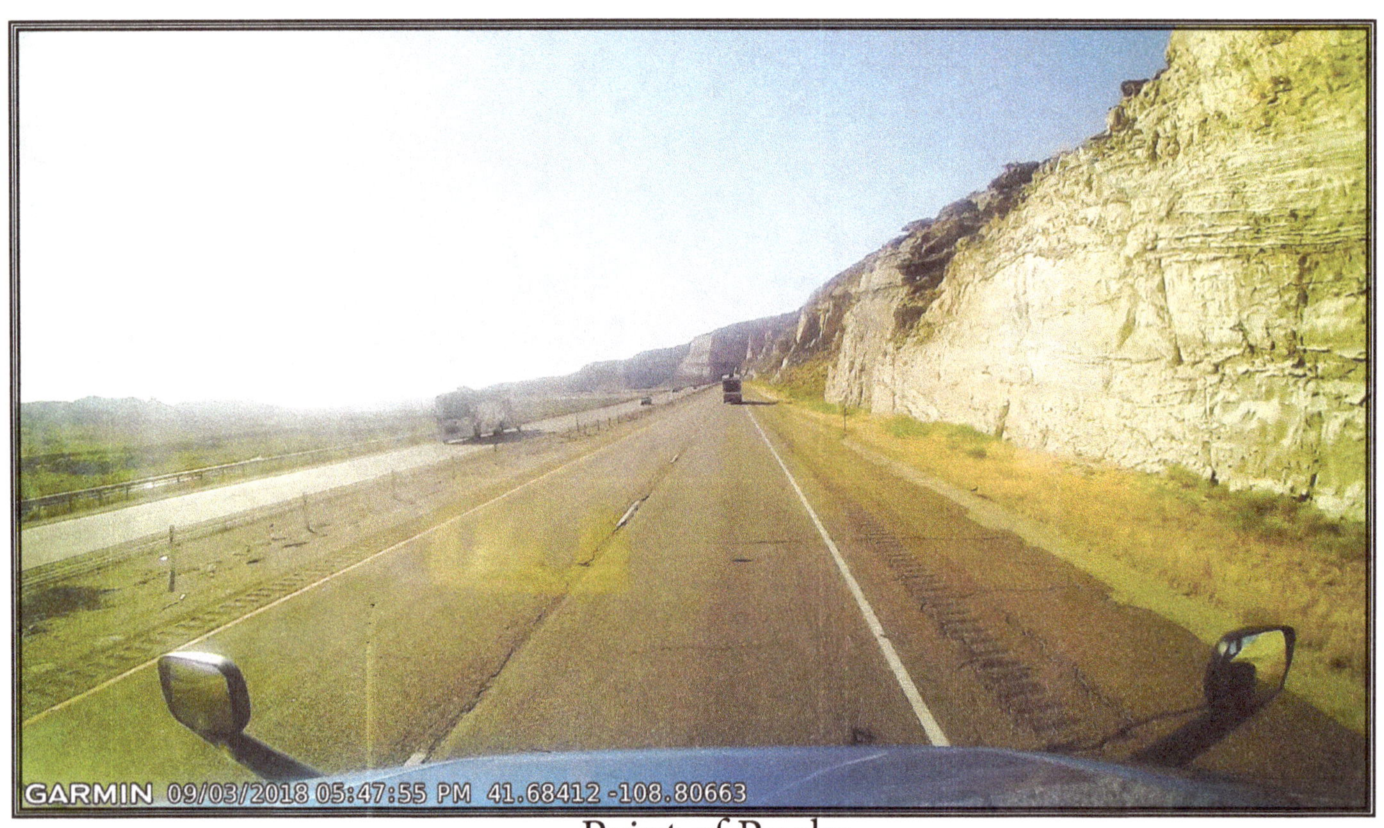

Point of Rocks
I-80, Rock Springs, Wyoming

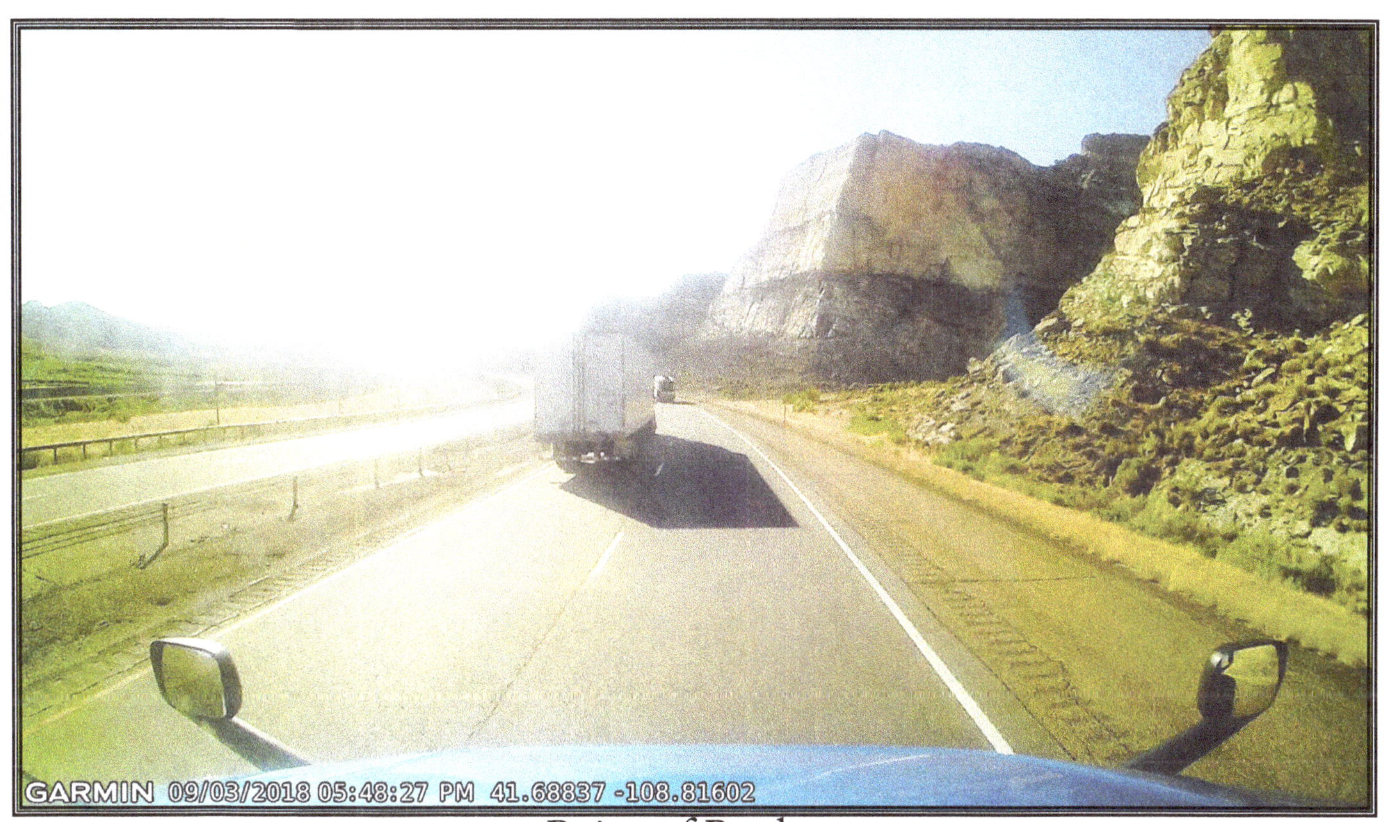

Point of Rocks
I-80, Rock Springs, Wyoming

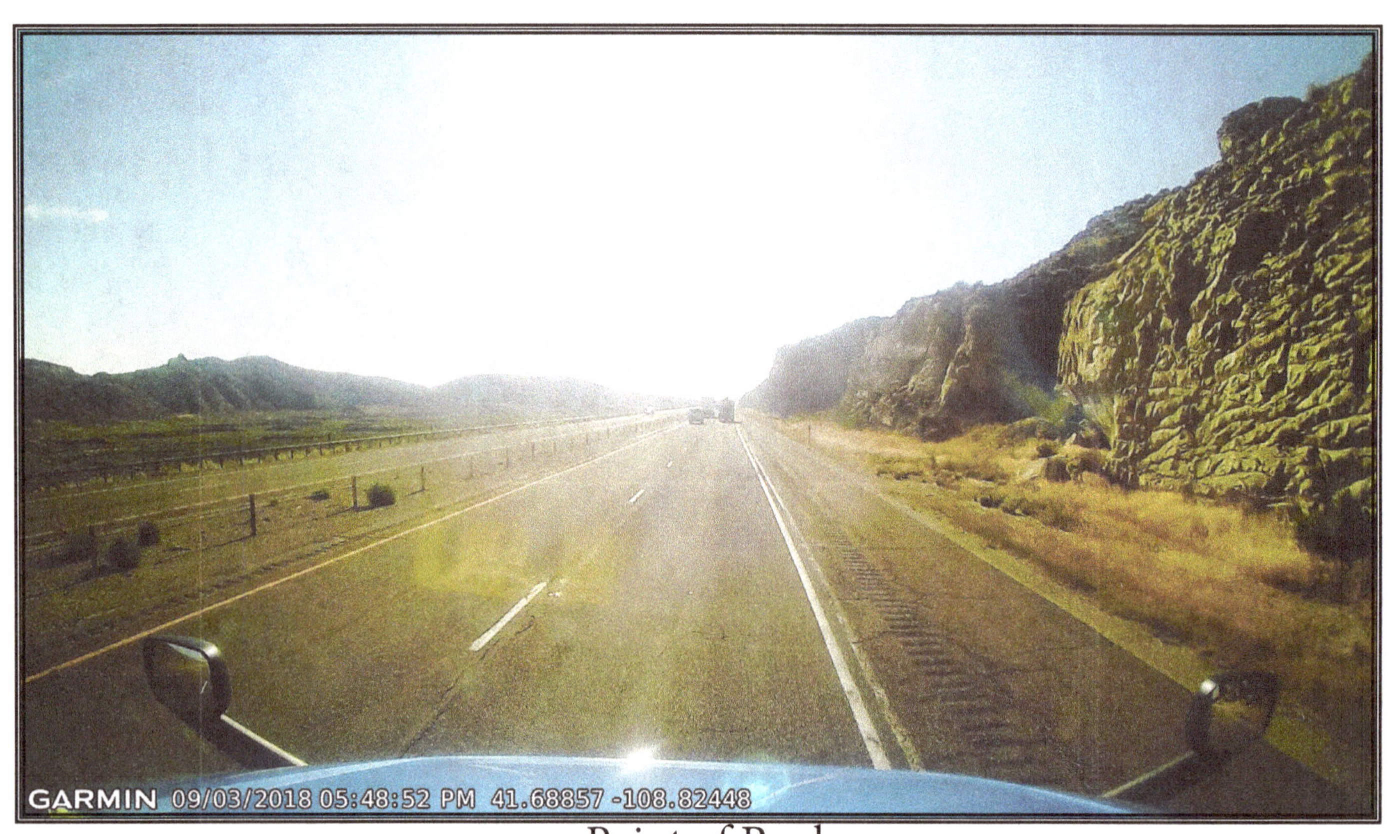

Point of Rocks
I-80, Rock Springs, Wyoming

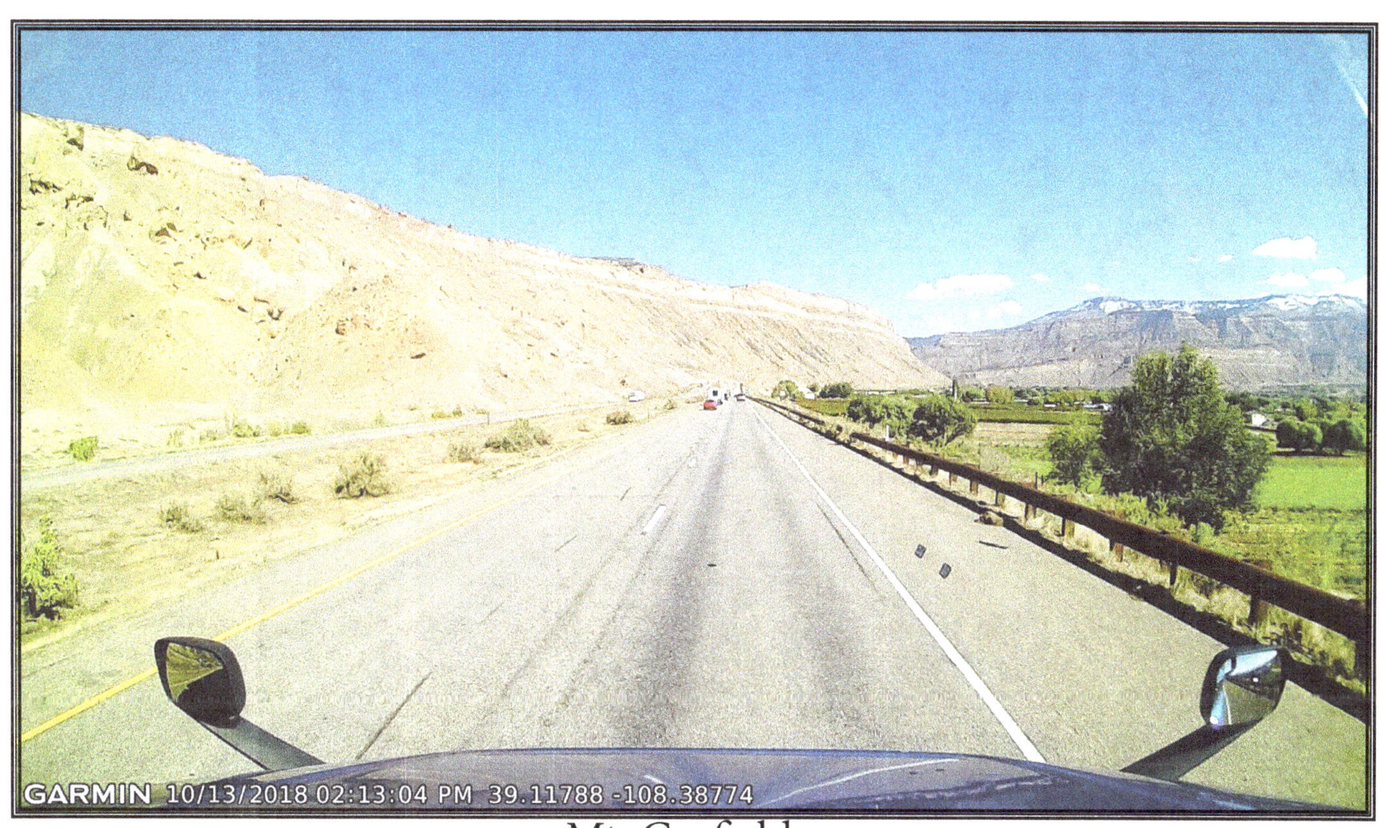

Mt. Garfield
I-70, Pallisade, Colorado

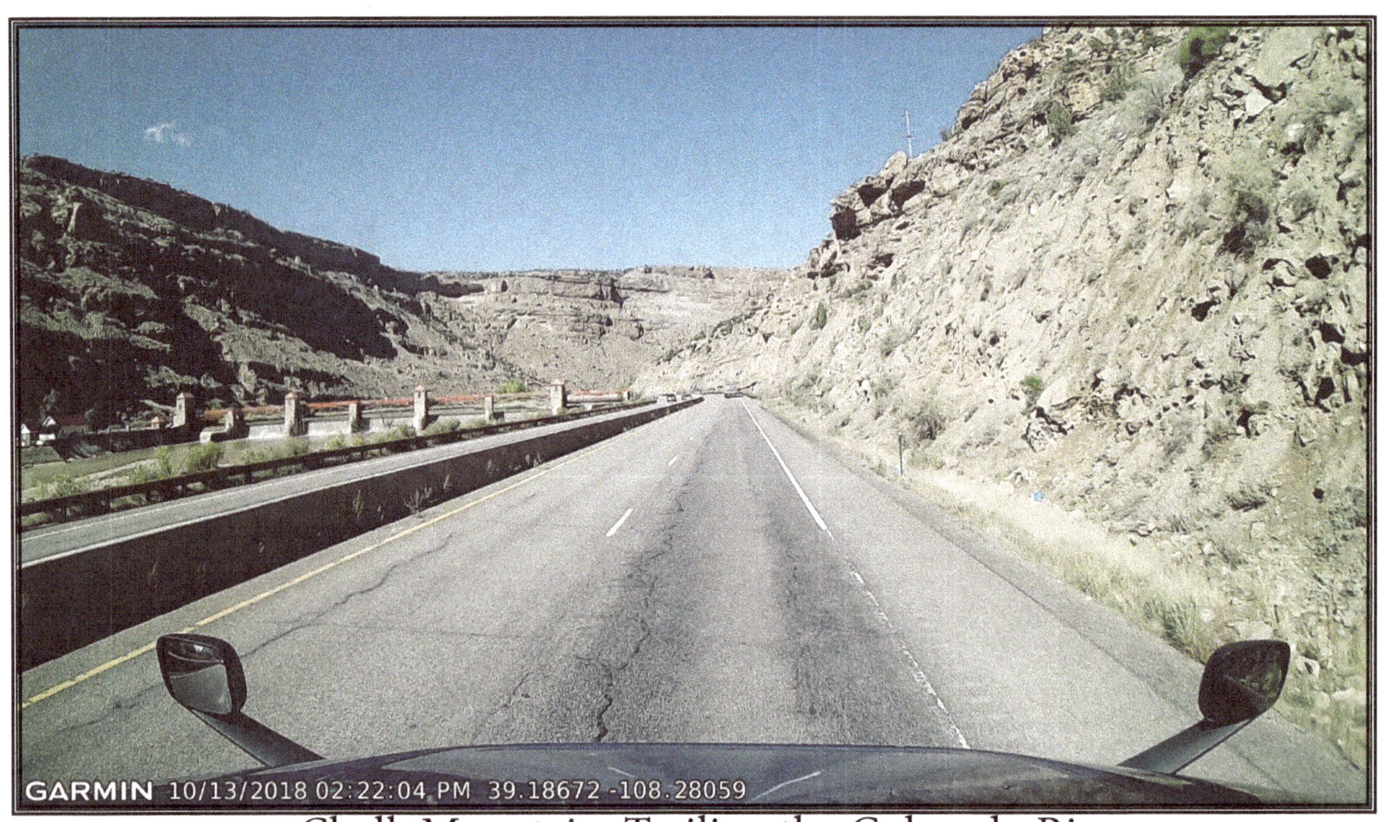

Chalk Mountain, Trailing the Colorado River
I-70, De Beque, Colorado

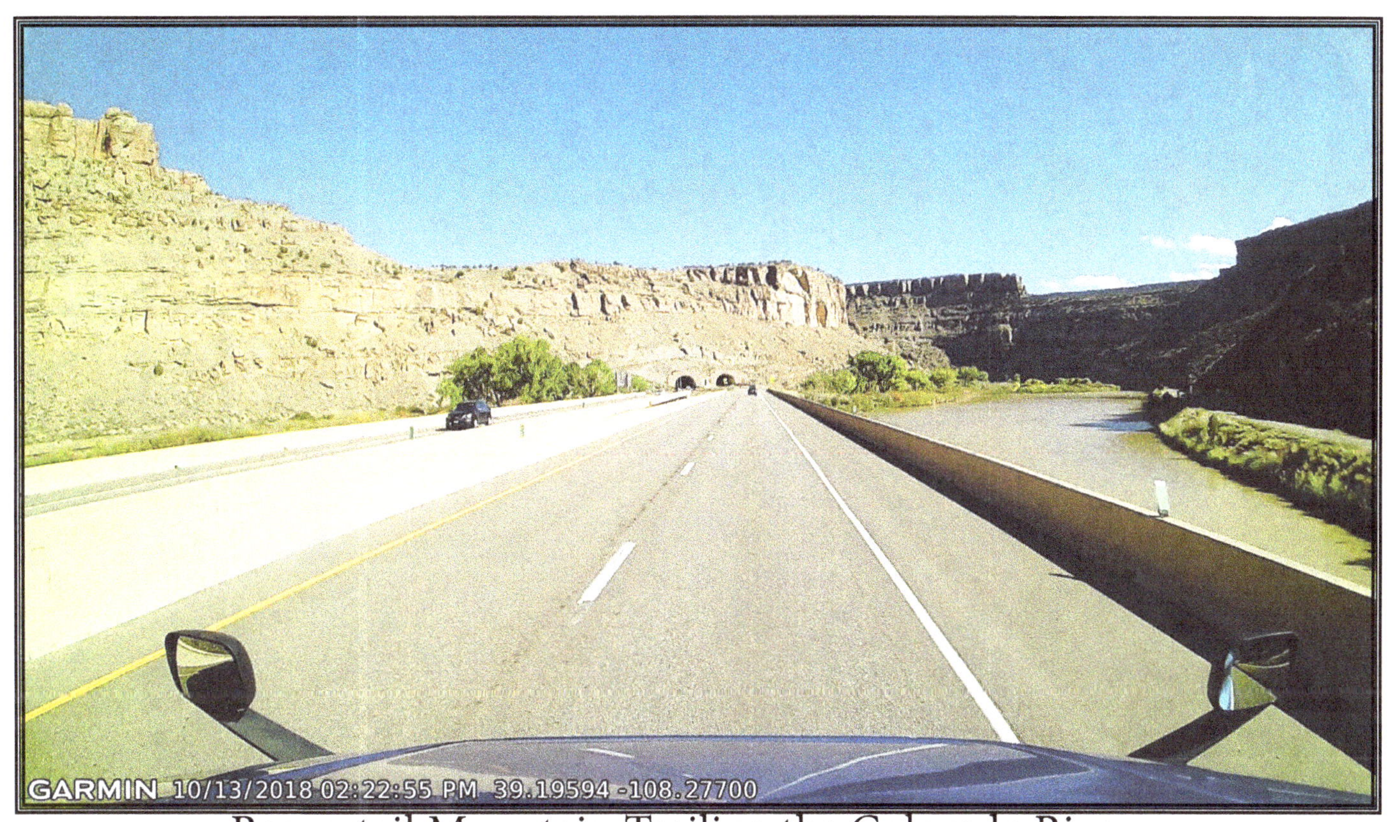

Beavertail Mountain Trailing the Colorado River
I-70, Akin, Colorado

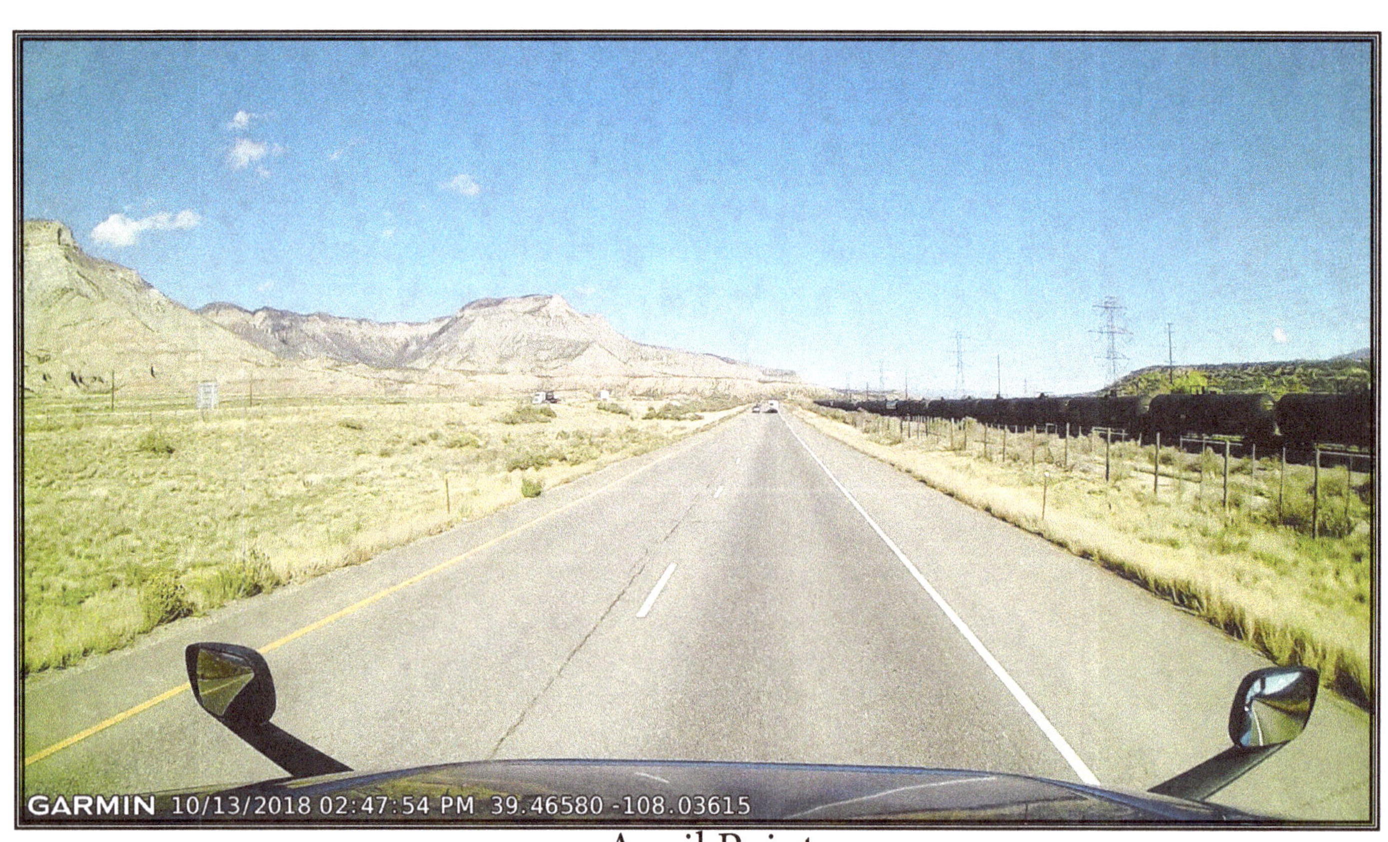

Anvil Points
I-70, Parachute, Colorado

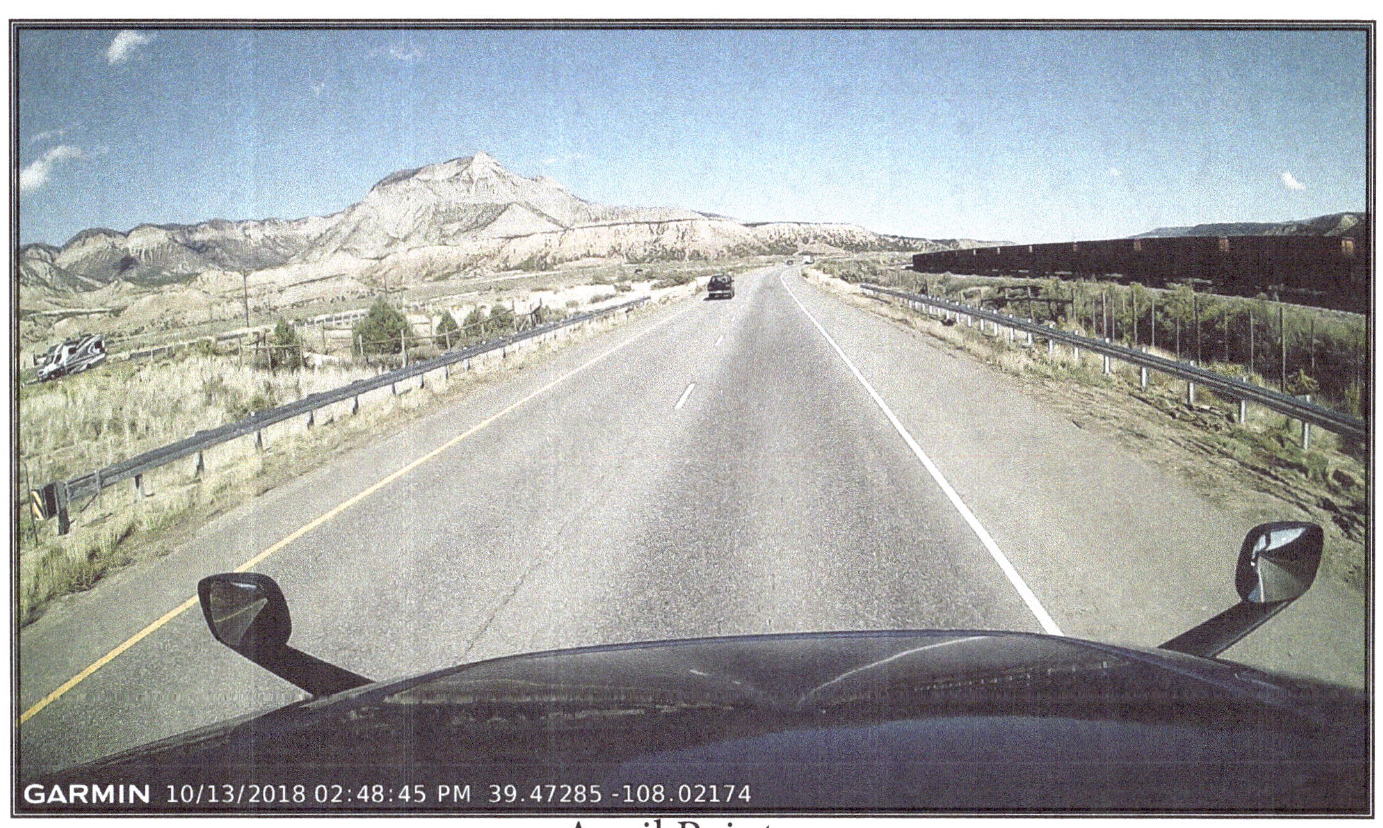

Anvil Points
I-70, Parachute, Colorado

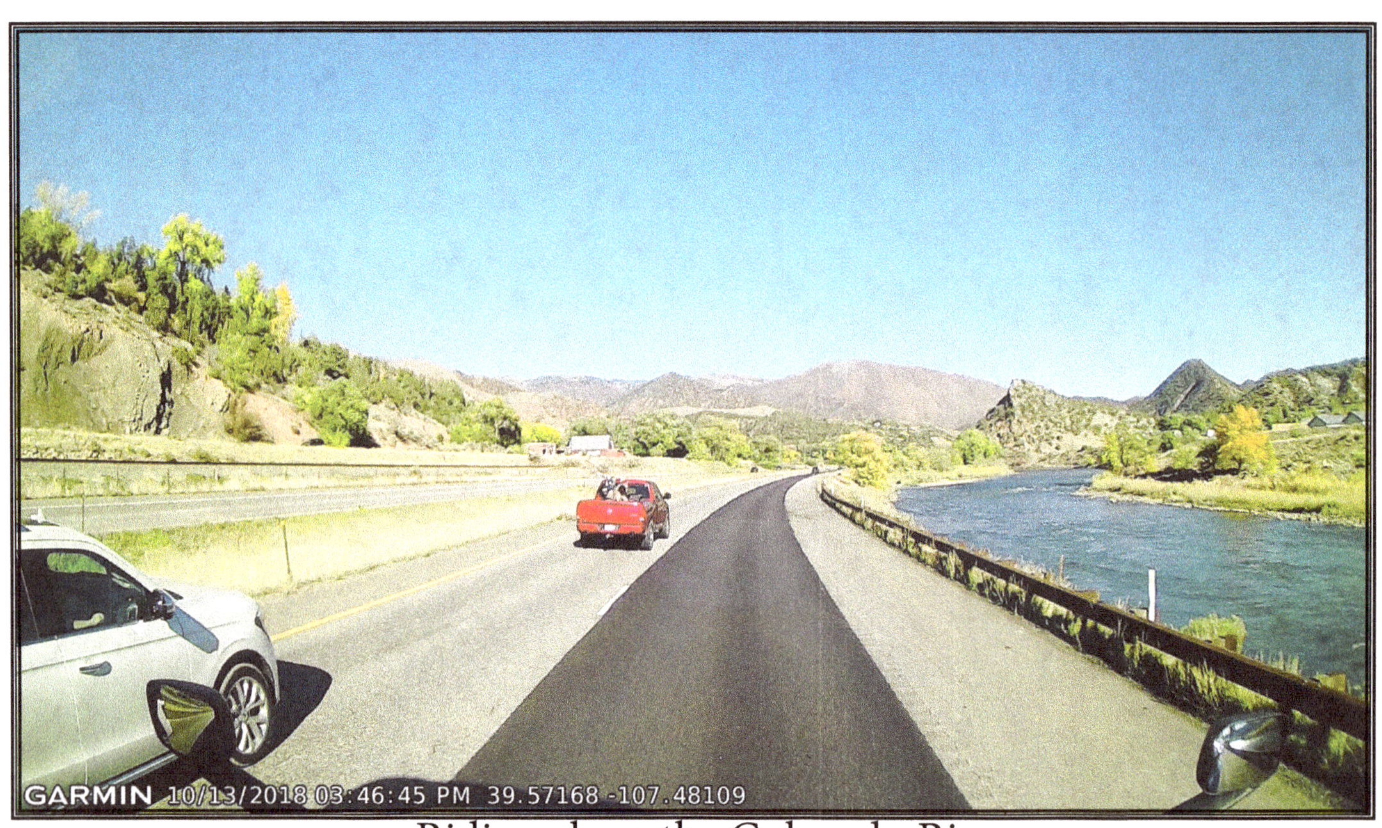

Riding along the Colorado River
I-70, New Castle, Colorado

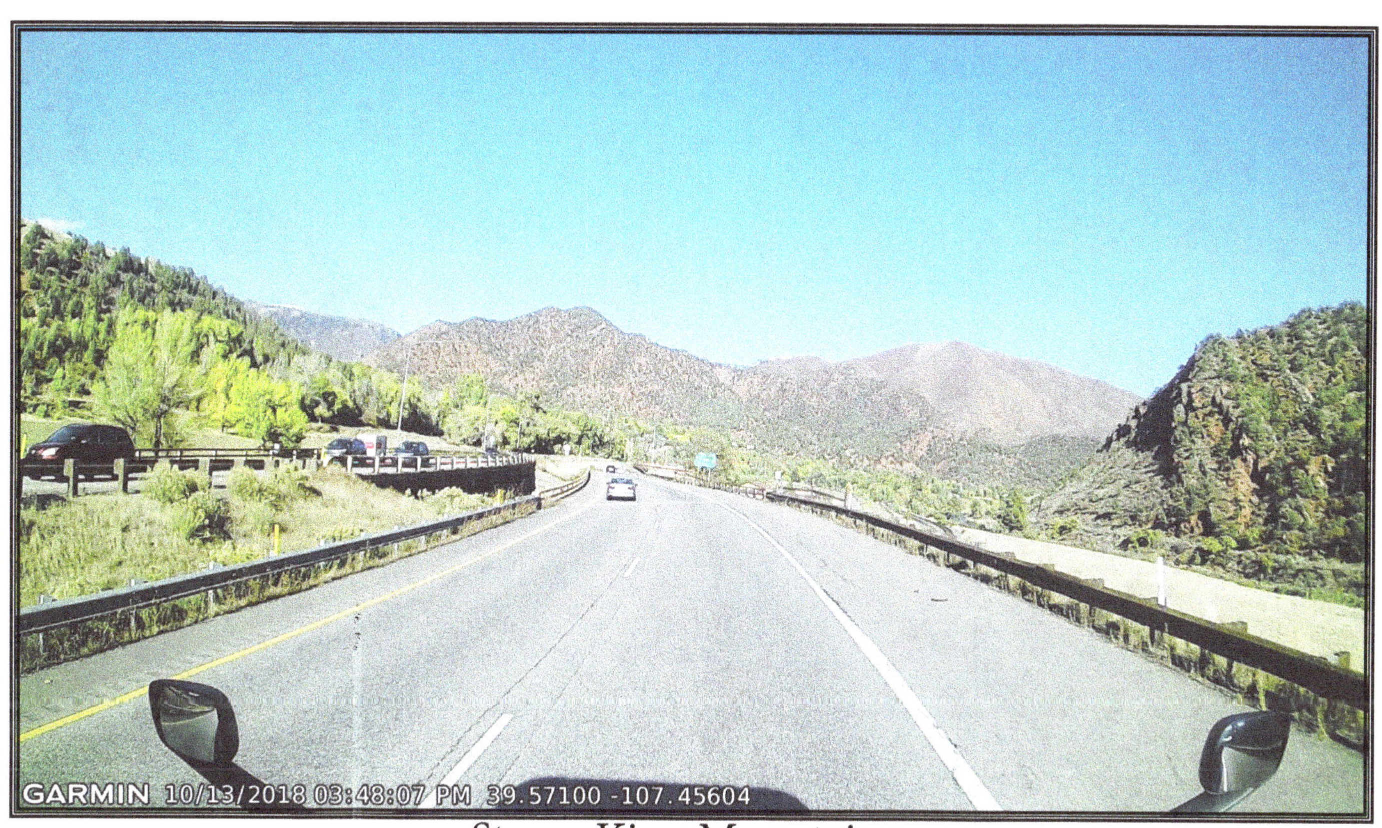

Storm King Mountain
I-70, Glenwood Springs, Colorado

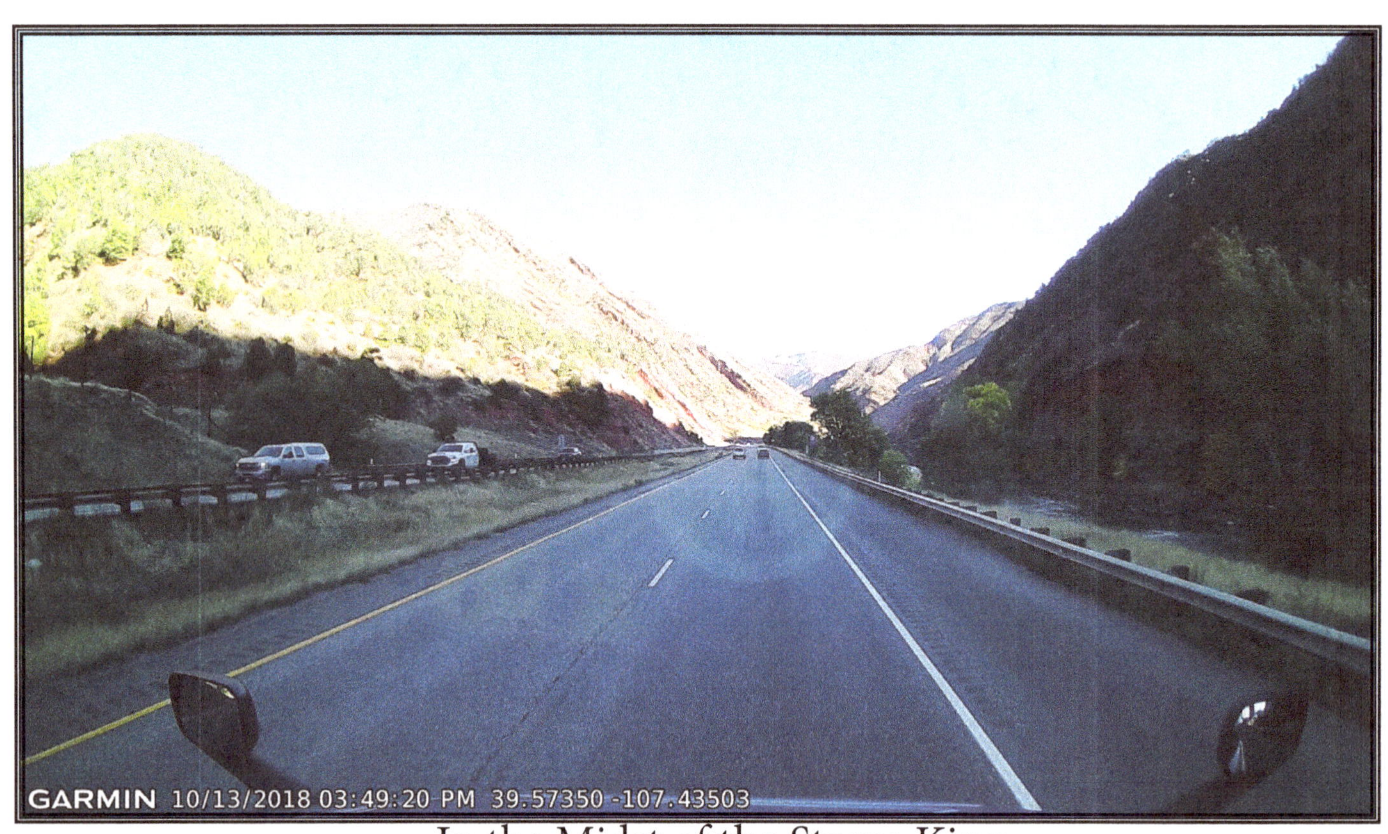

In the Midst of the Storm King
I-70, Glenwood Springs, Colorado

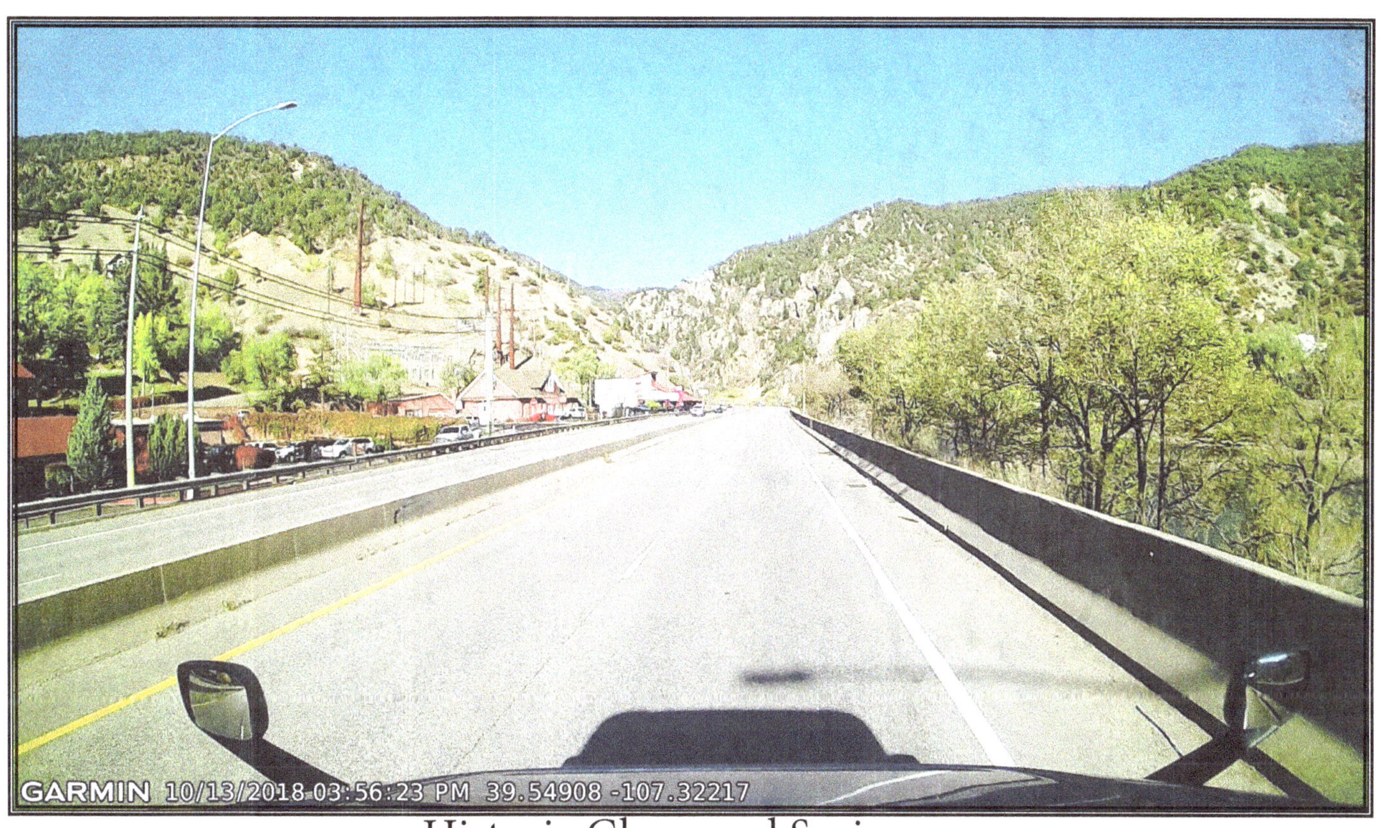

Historic Glenwood Springs
I-70, Glenwood Springs, Colorado

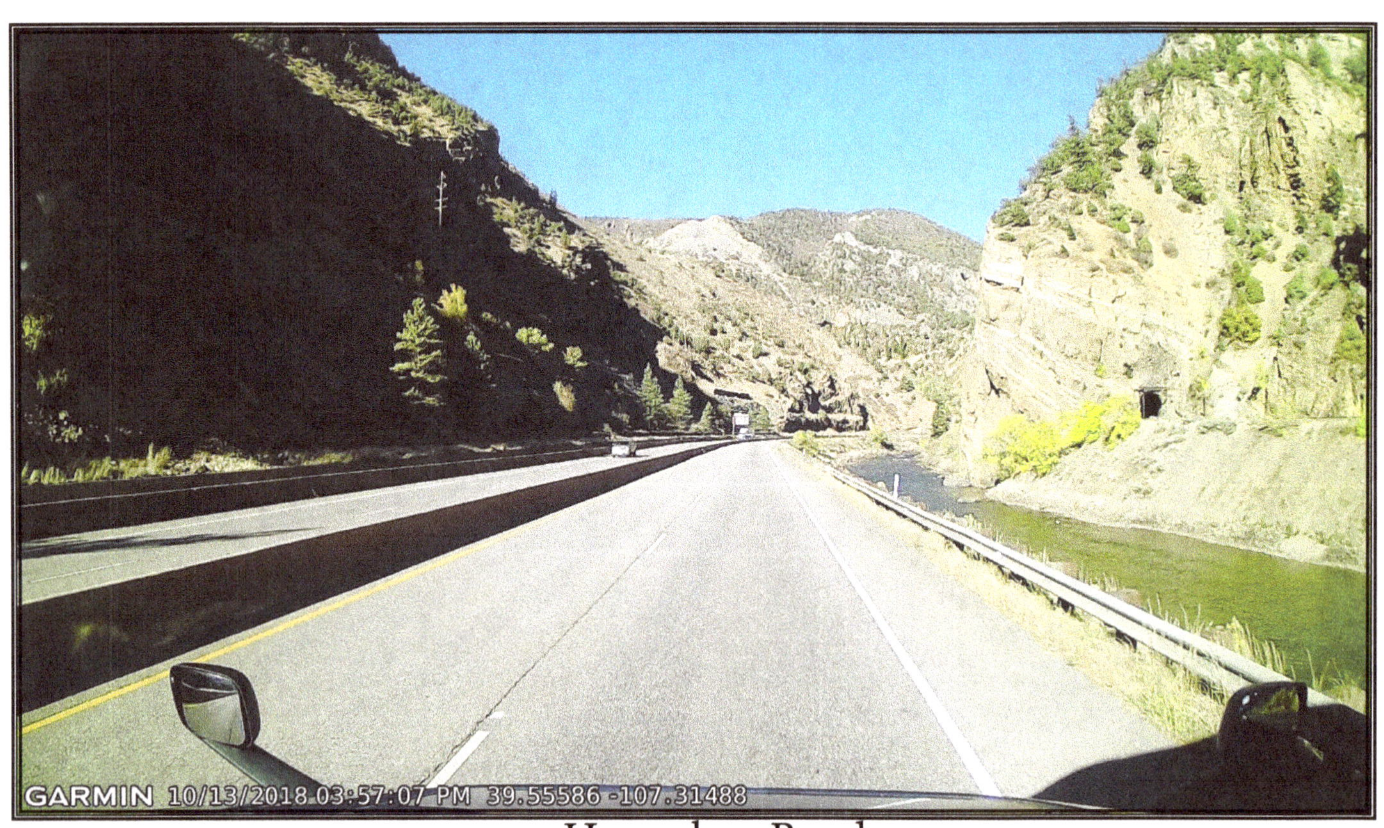

Horseshoe Bend
I-70, Glenwood Springs, Colorado

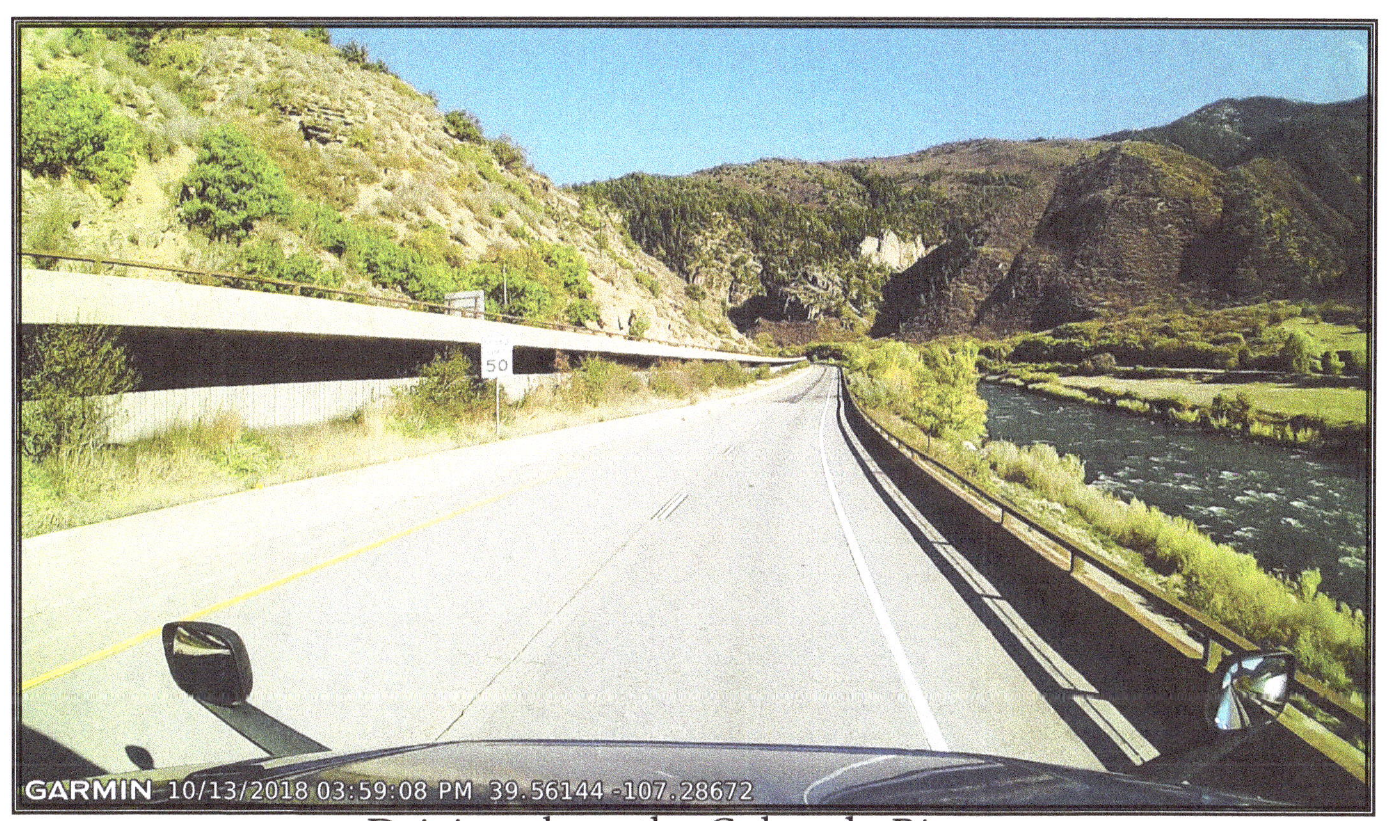

Driving along the Colorado River
I-70, Glenwood Springs, Colorado

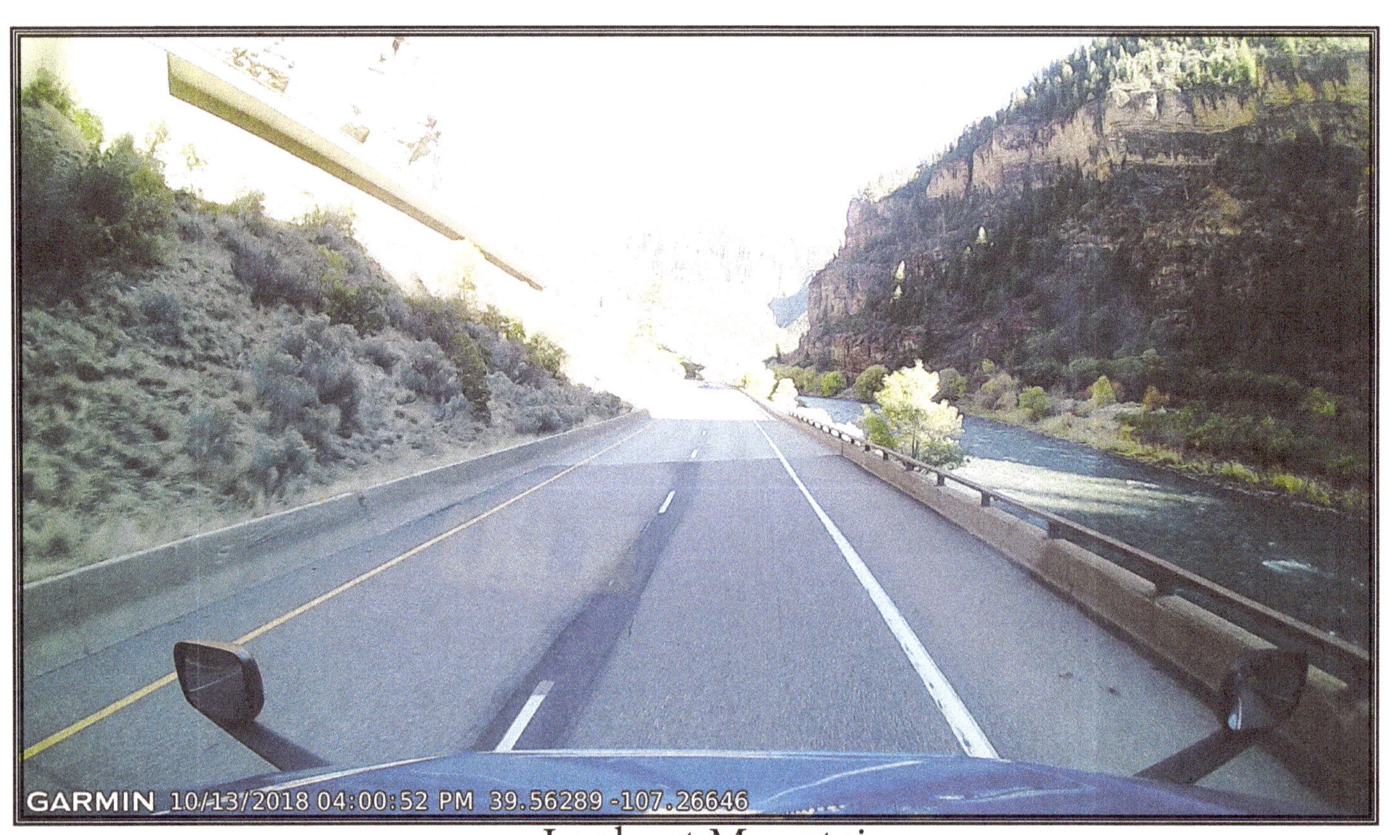

Lookout Mountain
I-70, Glenwood Springs, Colorado

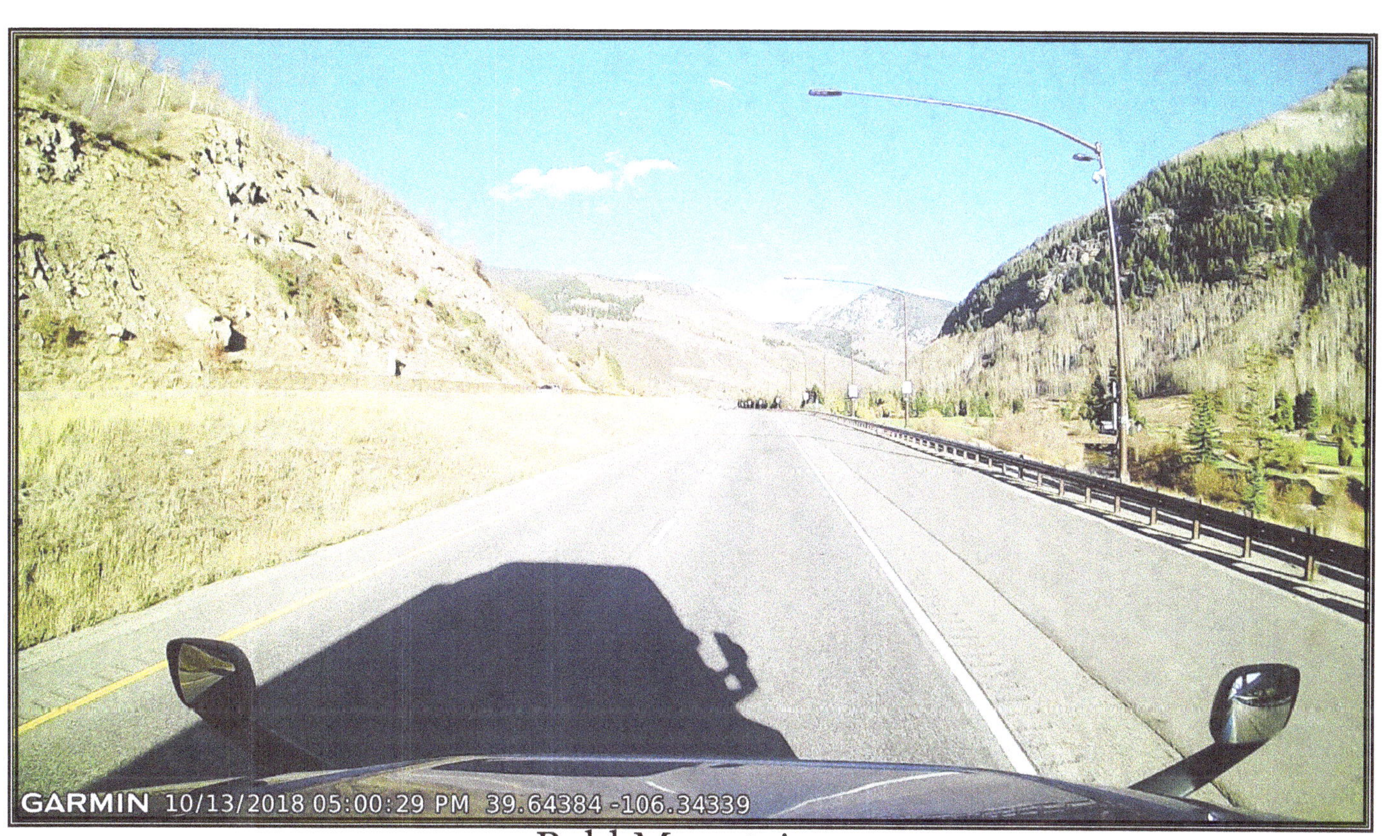

Bald Mountain
I-70, Vail, Colorado

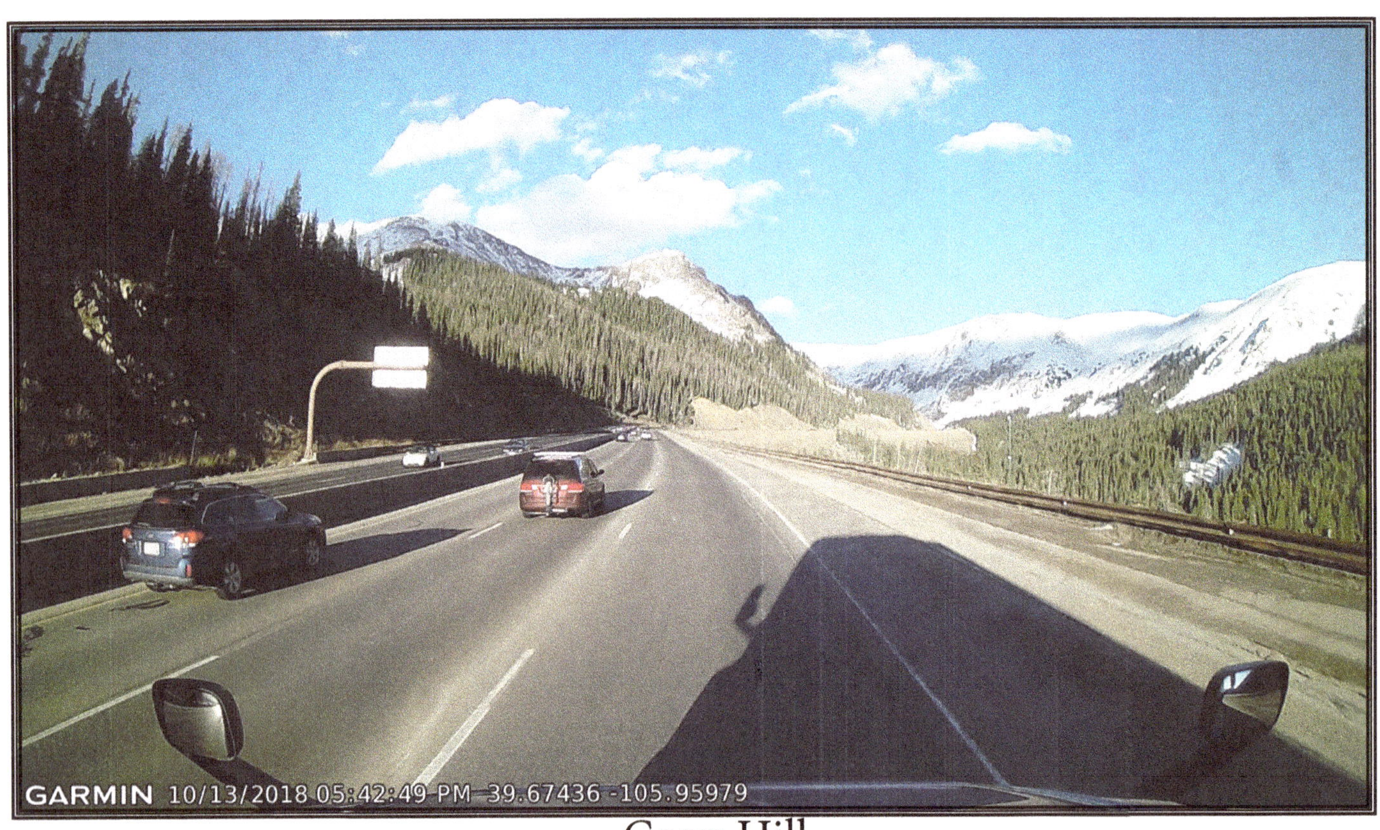

Coon Hill
I-70, Parshall, Colorado

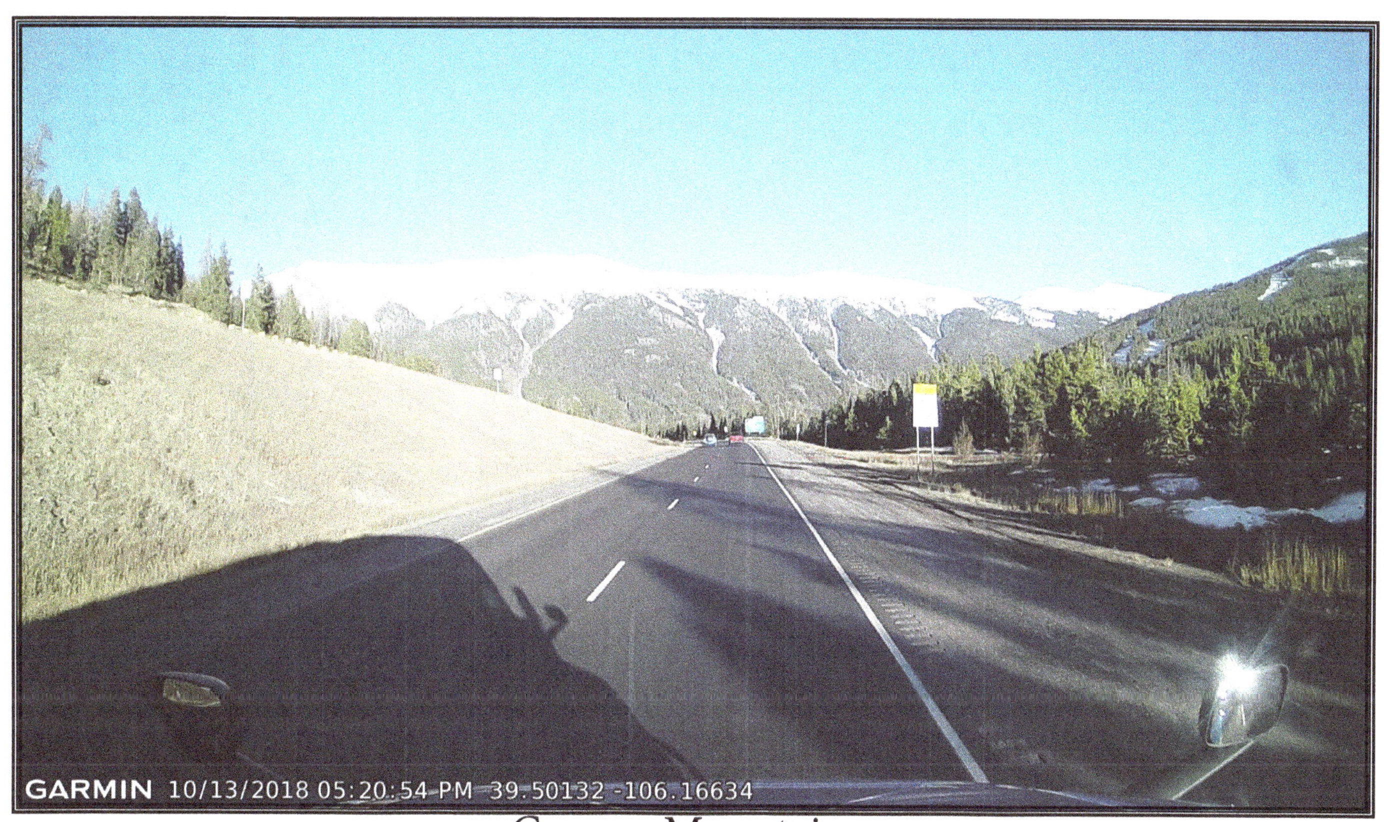

Copper Mountain
I-70, Frisco, Colorado

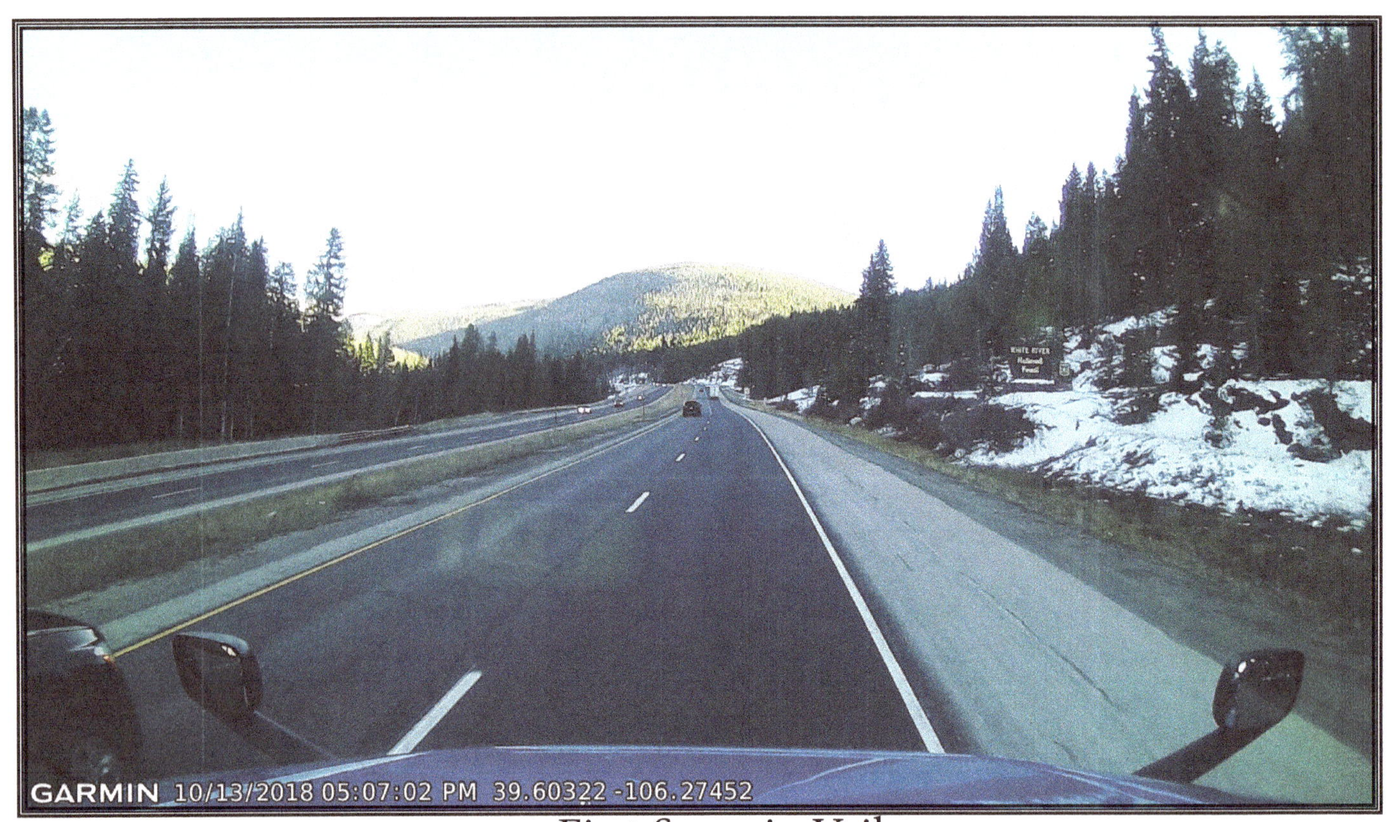

First Snow in Vail
I-70, Vail, Colorado

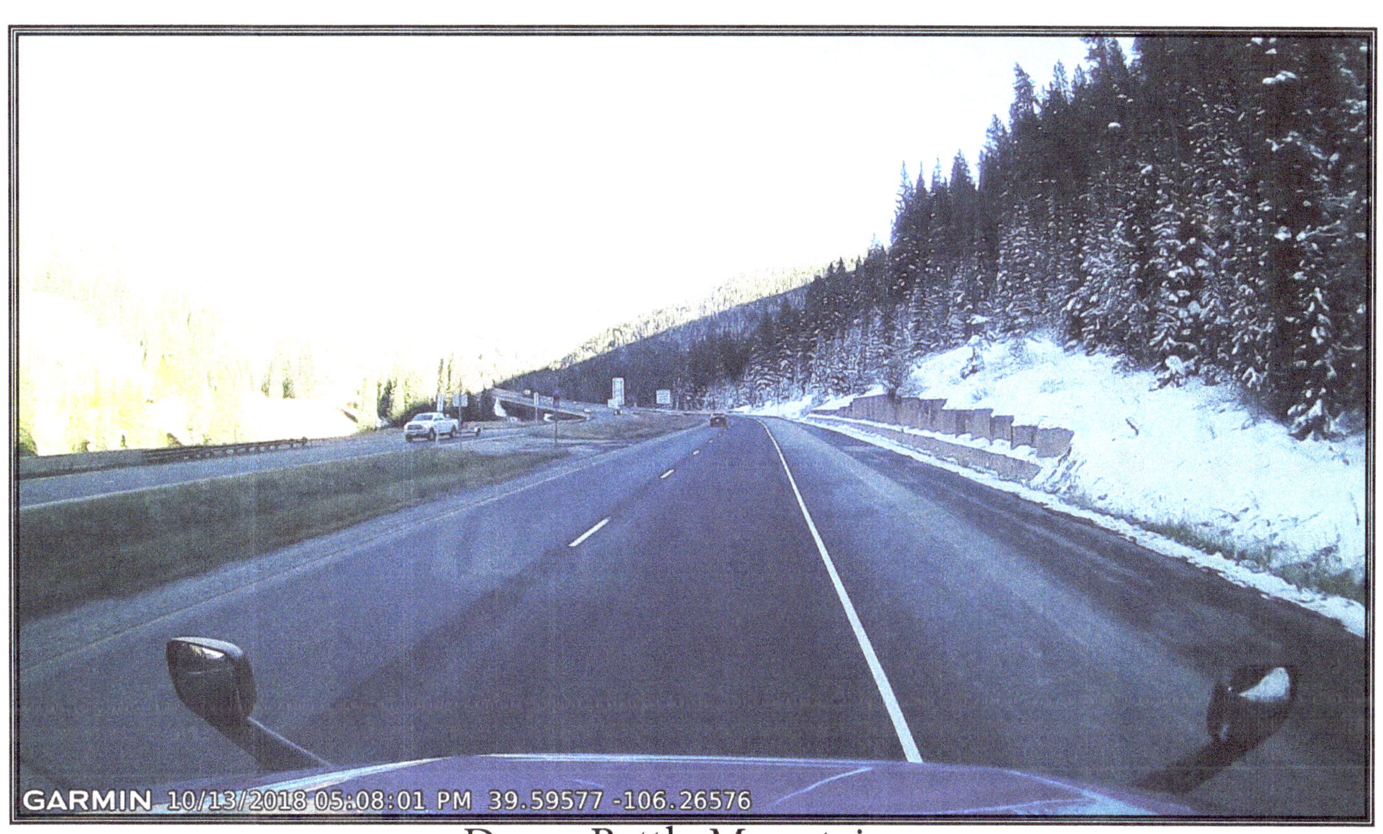

Down Battle Mountain
I-70, Vail, Colorado

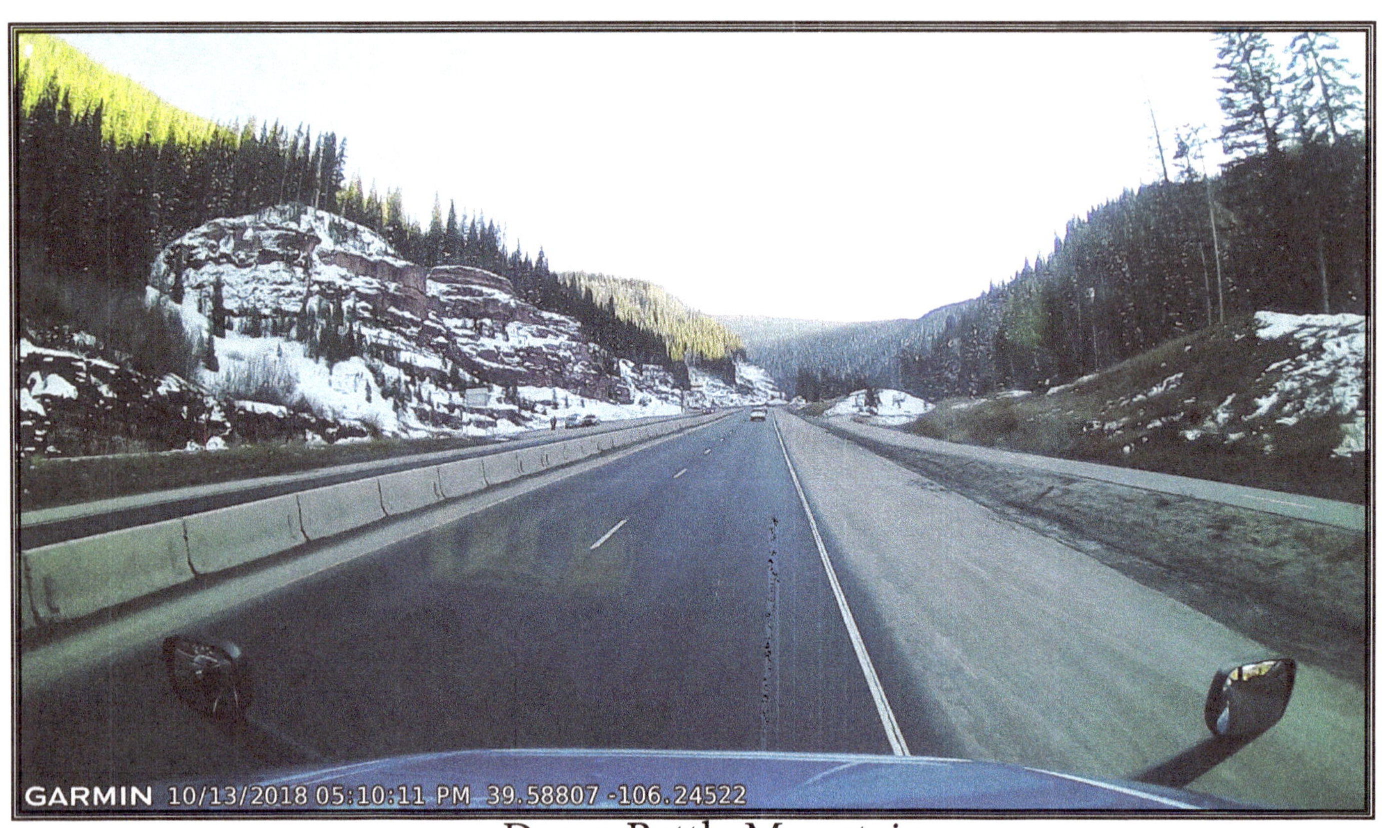

Down Battle Mountain
I-70, Vail, Colorado

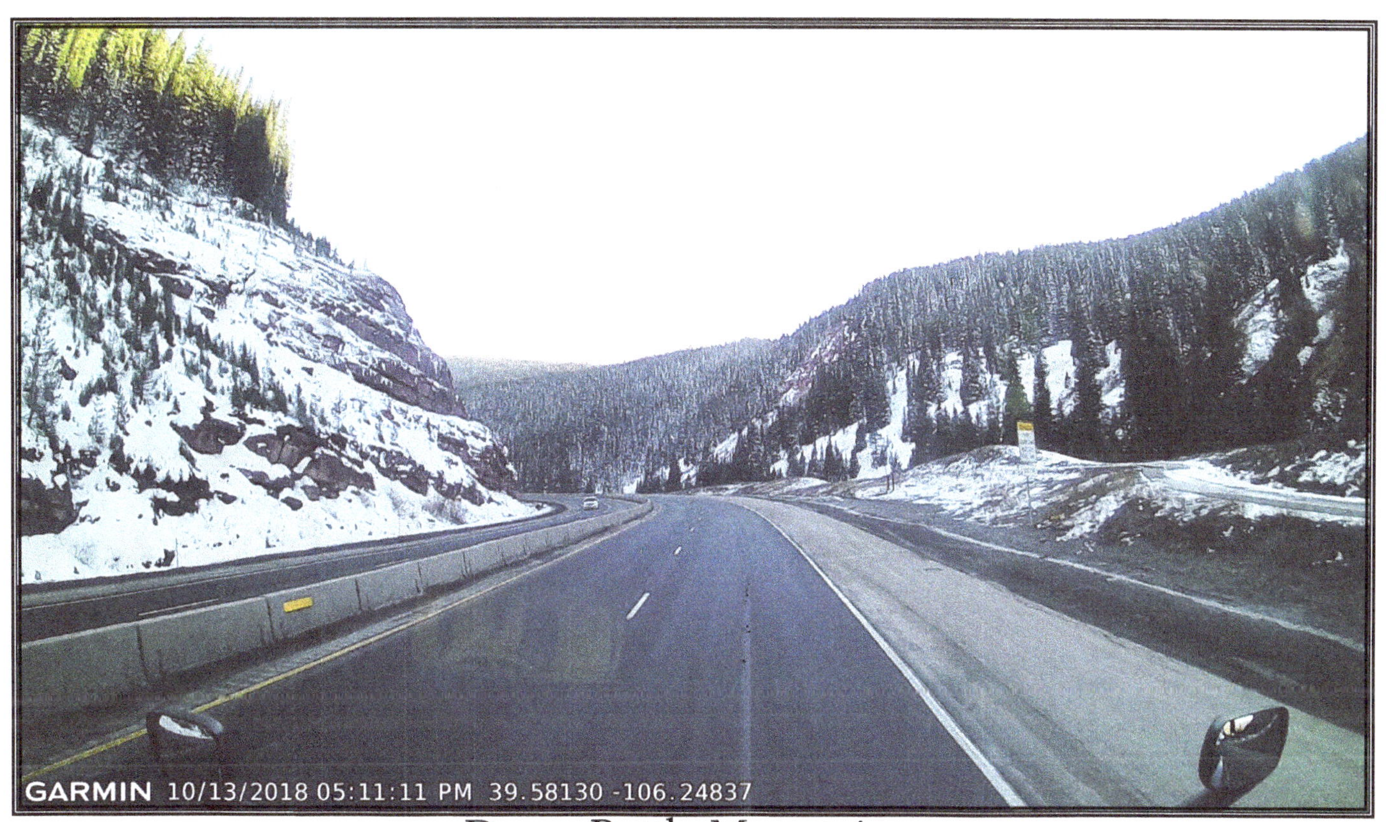

Down Battle Mountain
I-70, Vail, Colorado

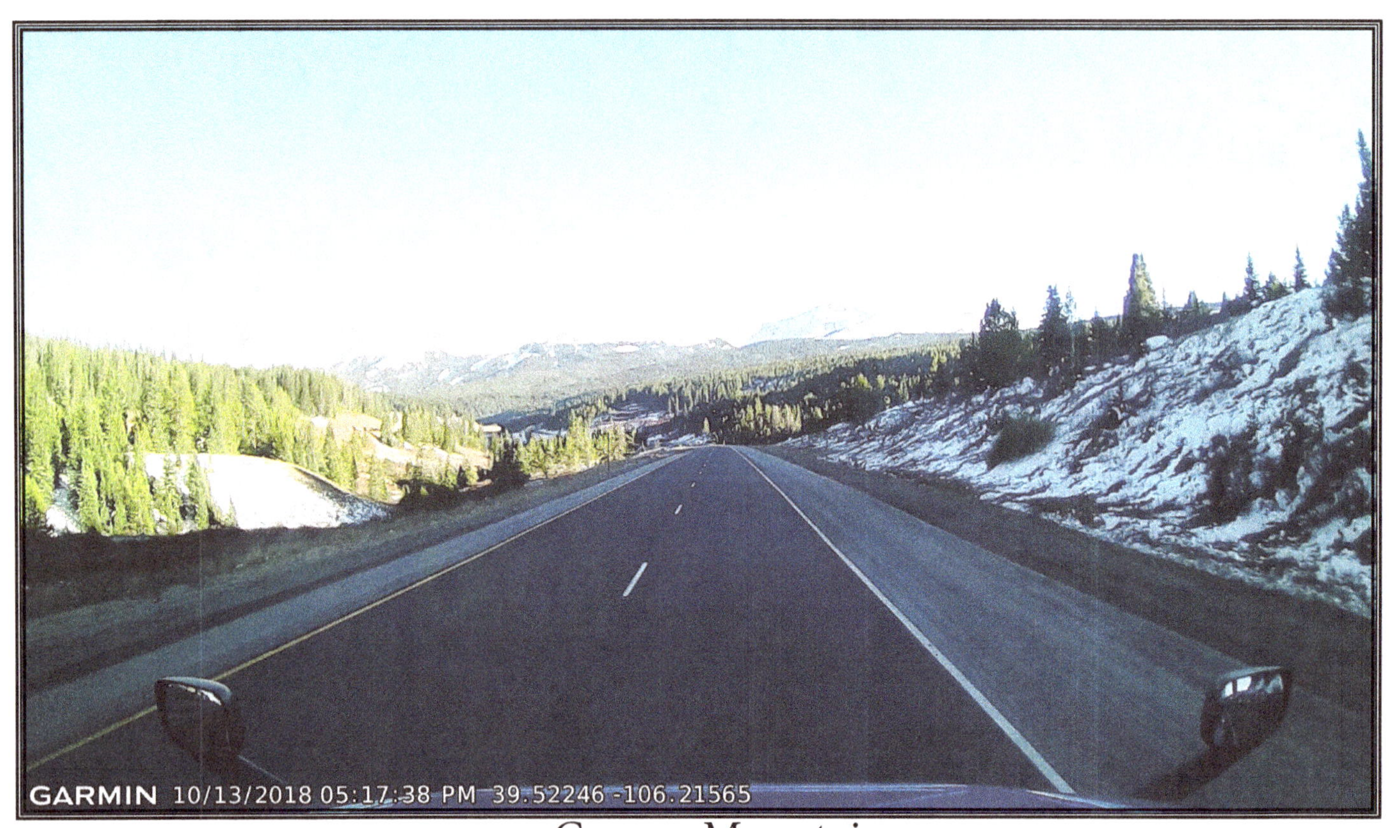

Copper Mountain
I-70, Frisco, Colorado

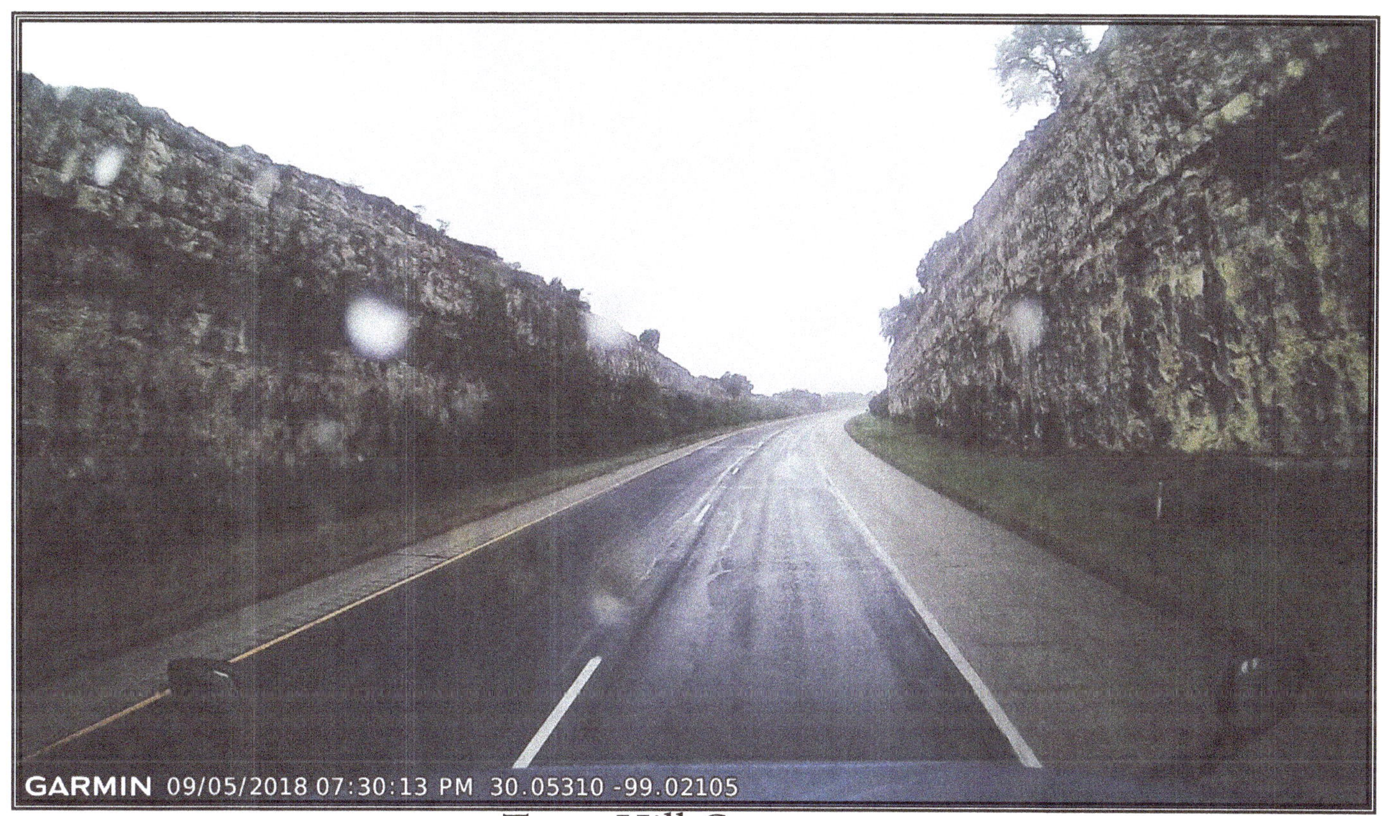

Texas Hill Country
I-10, Kerrville, Texas

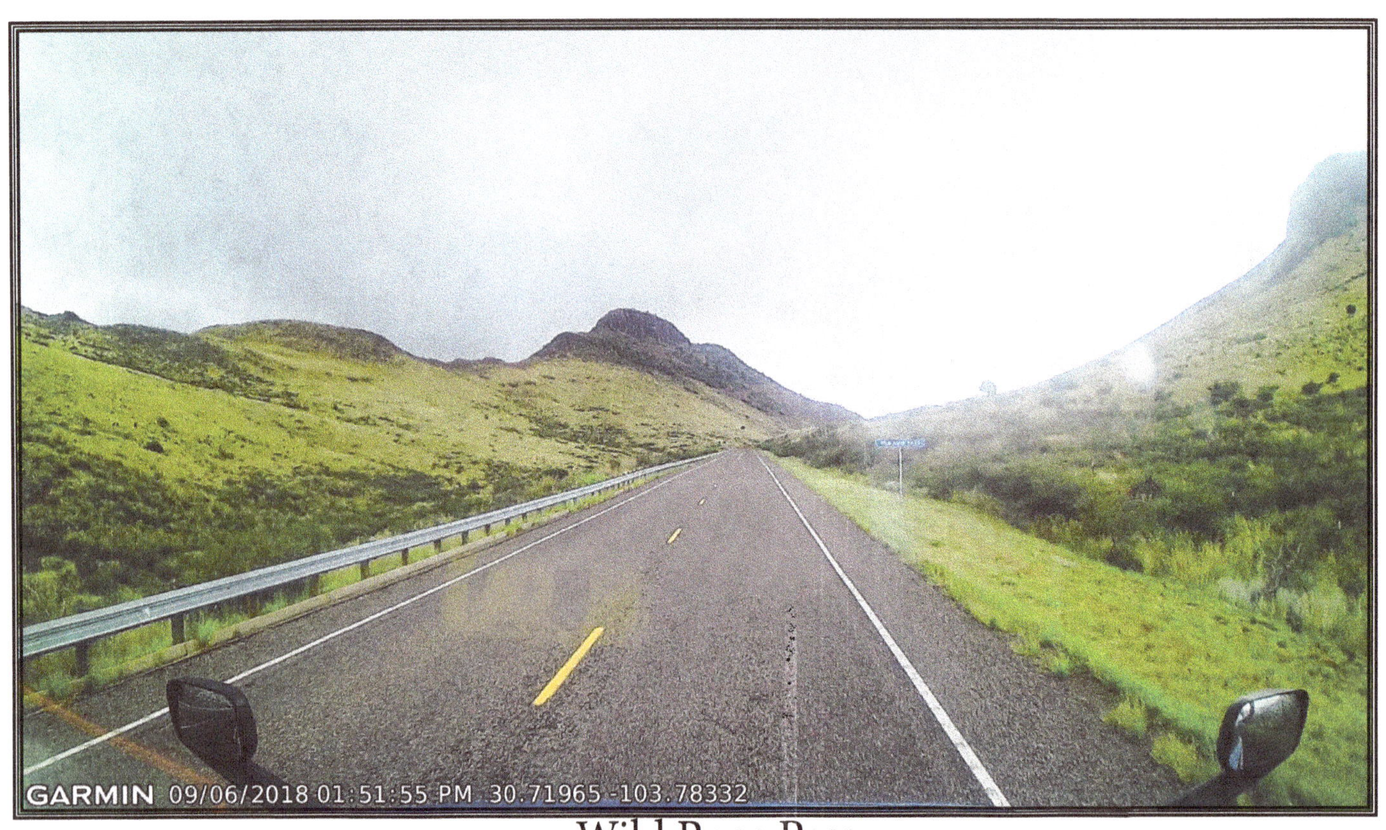

Wild Rose Pass
TX-17, Fort Davis, Texas

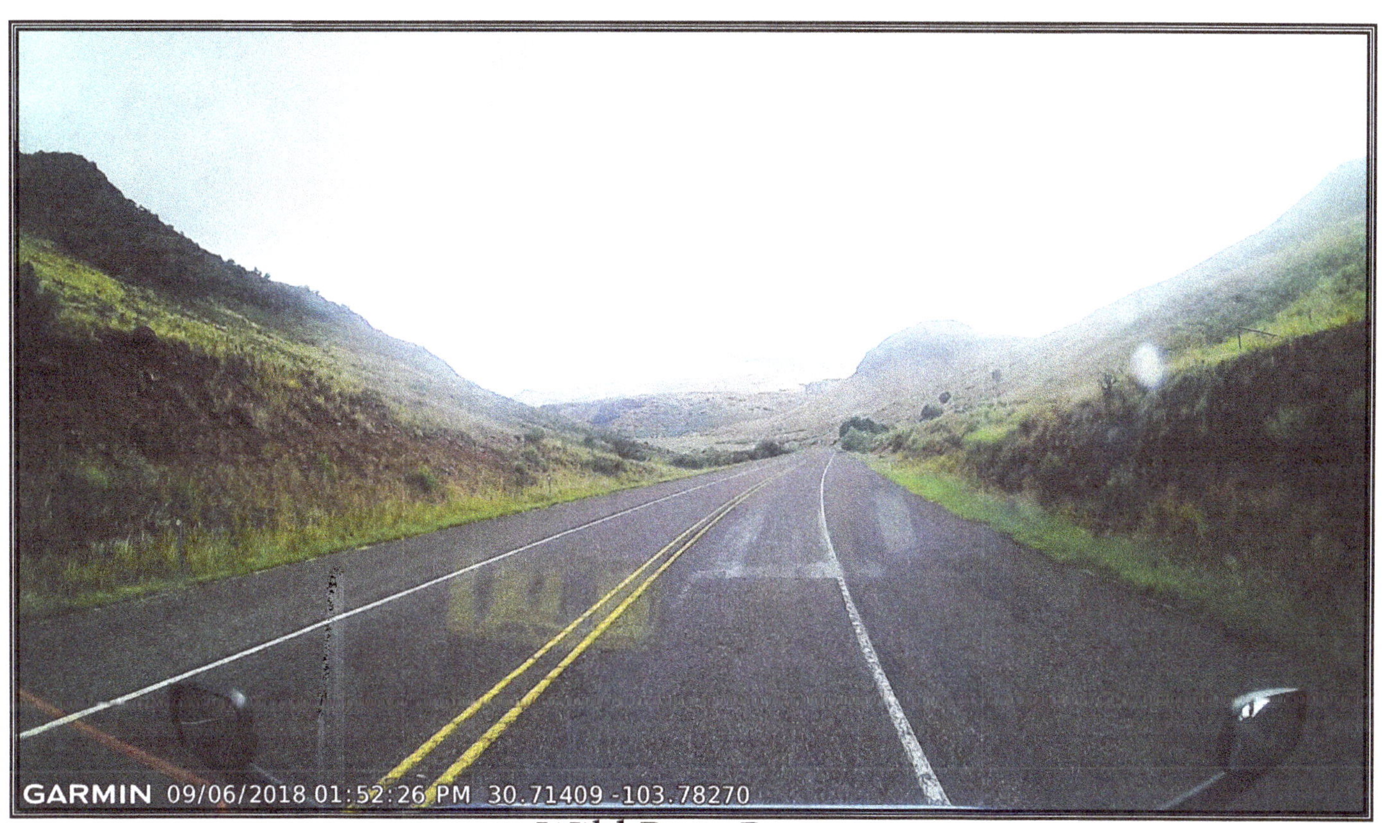

Wild Rose Pass
TX-17, Fort Davis, Texas

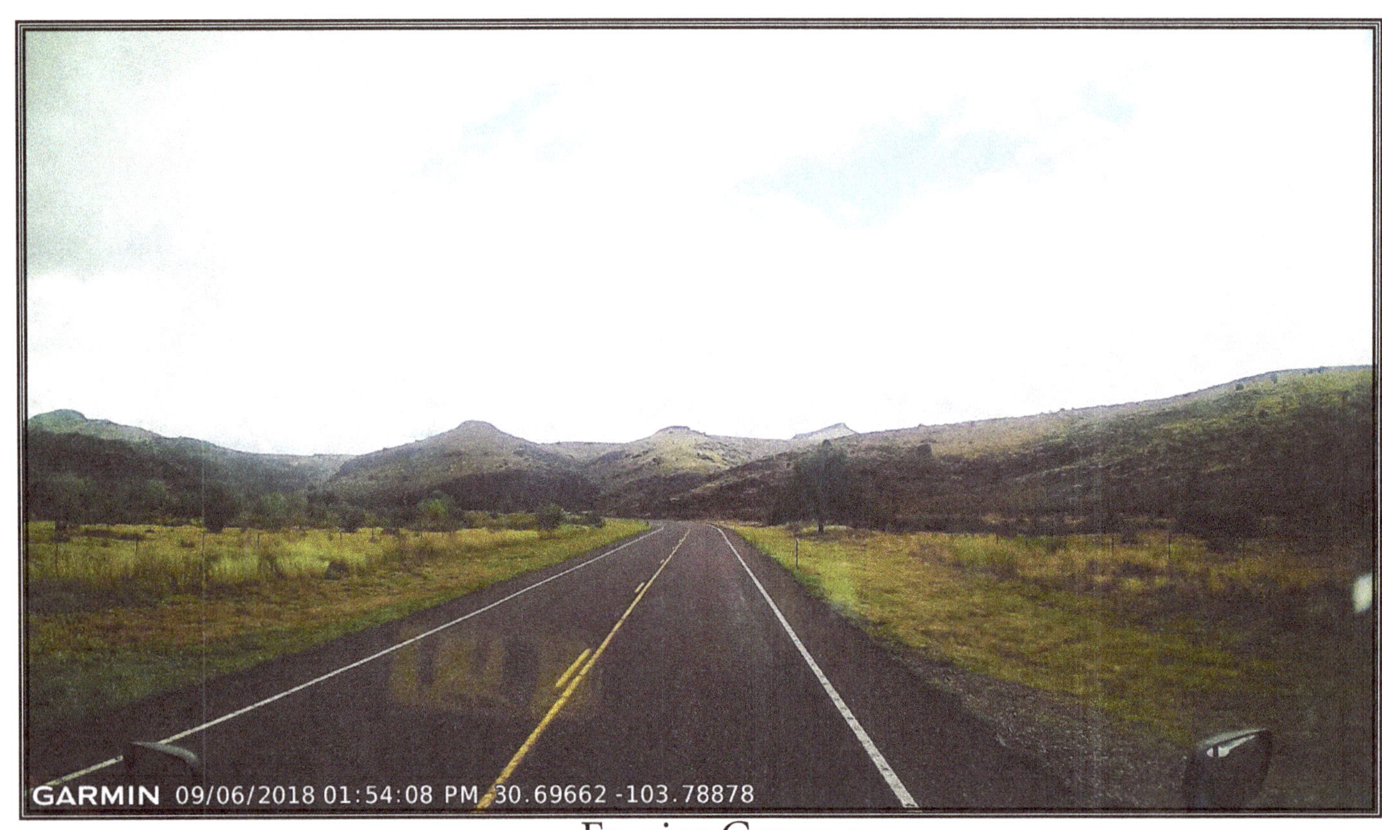

Frazier Canyon
TX-17, Fort Davis, Texas

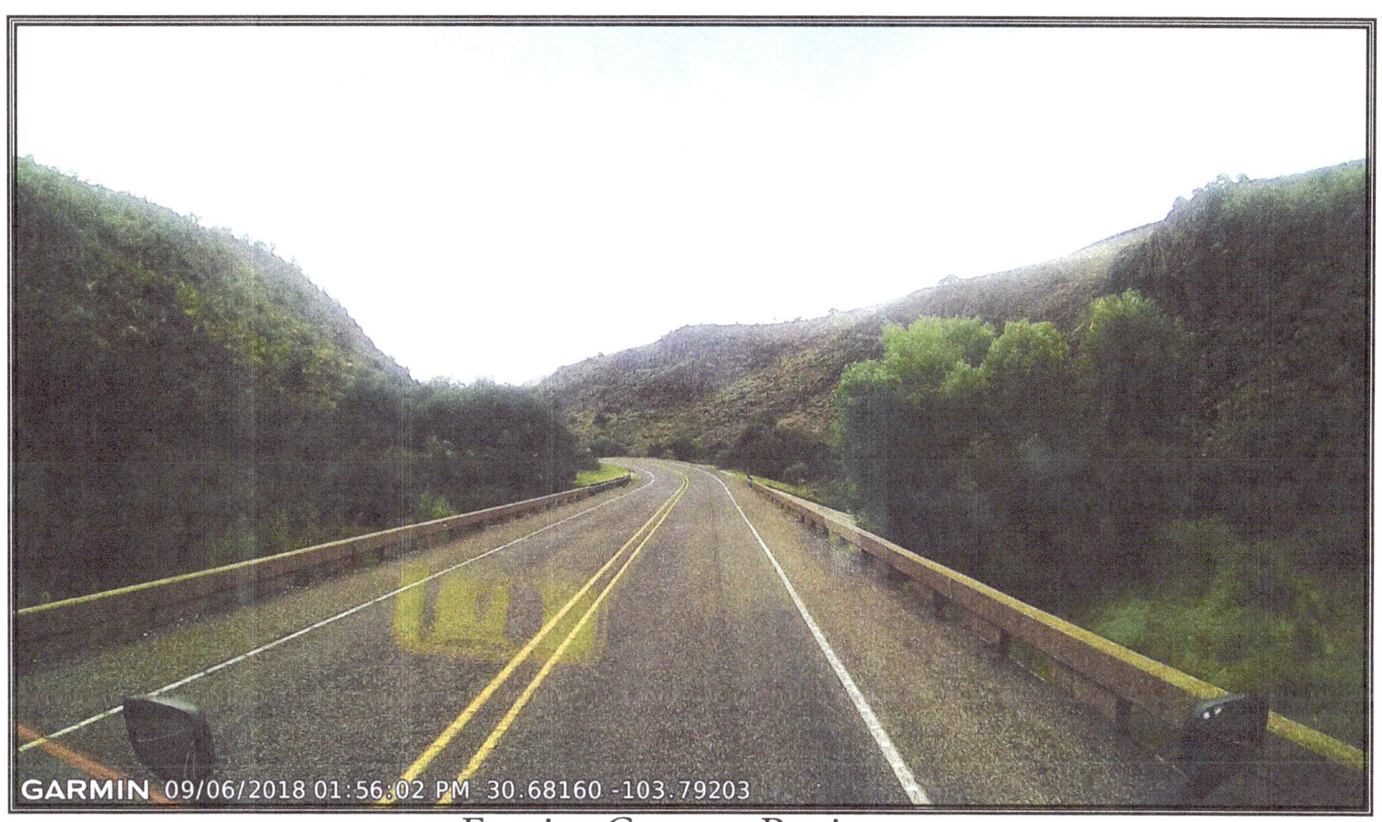

Frazier Canyon Region
TX-17, Fort Davis, Texas

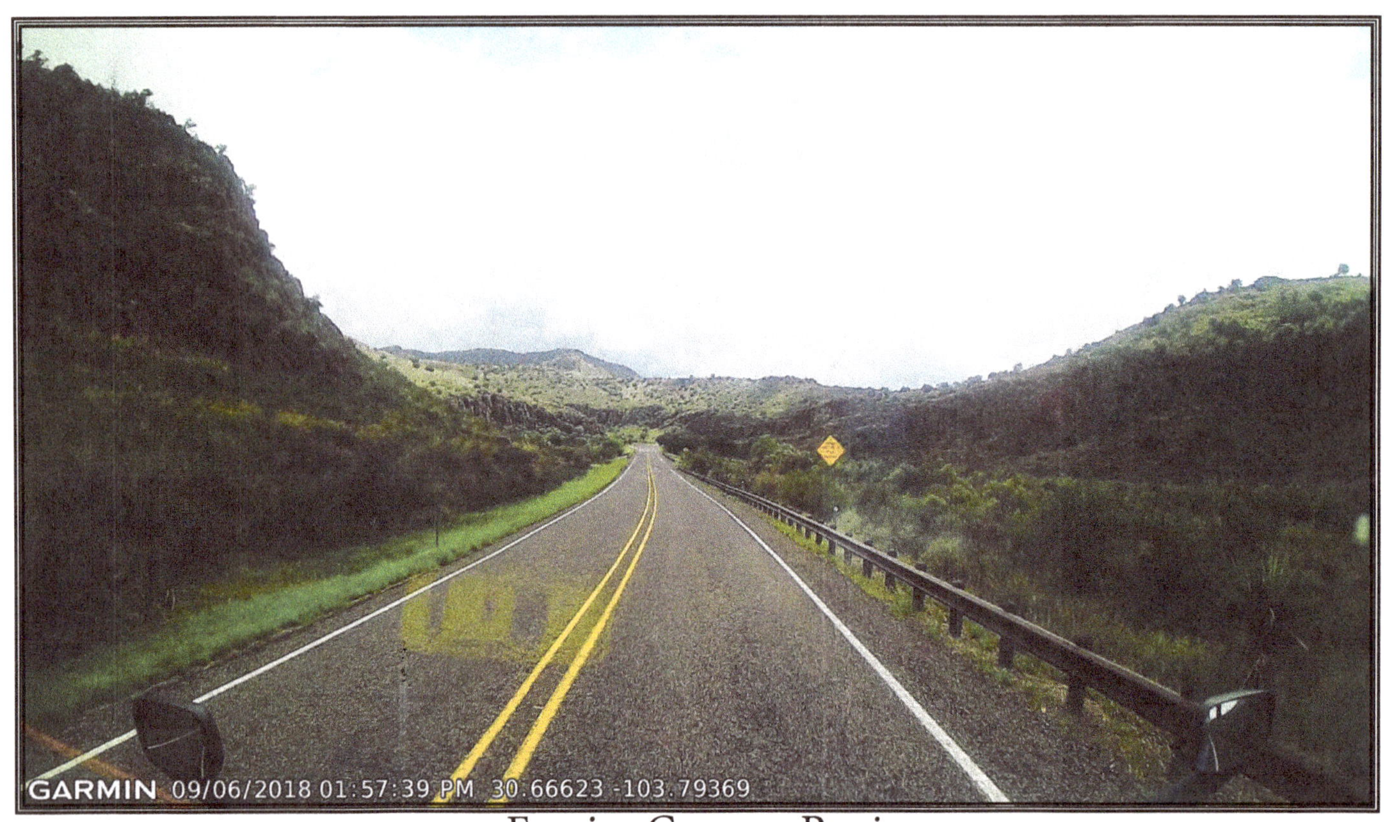

Frazier Canyon Region
TX-17, Fort Davis, Texas

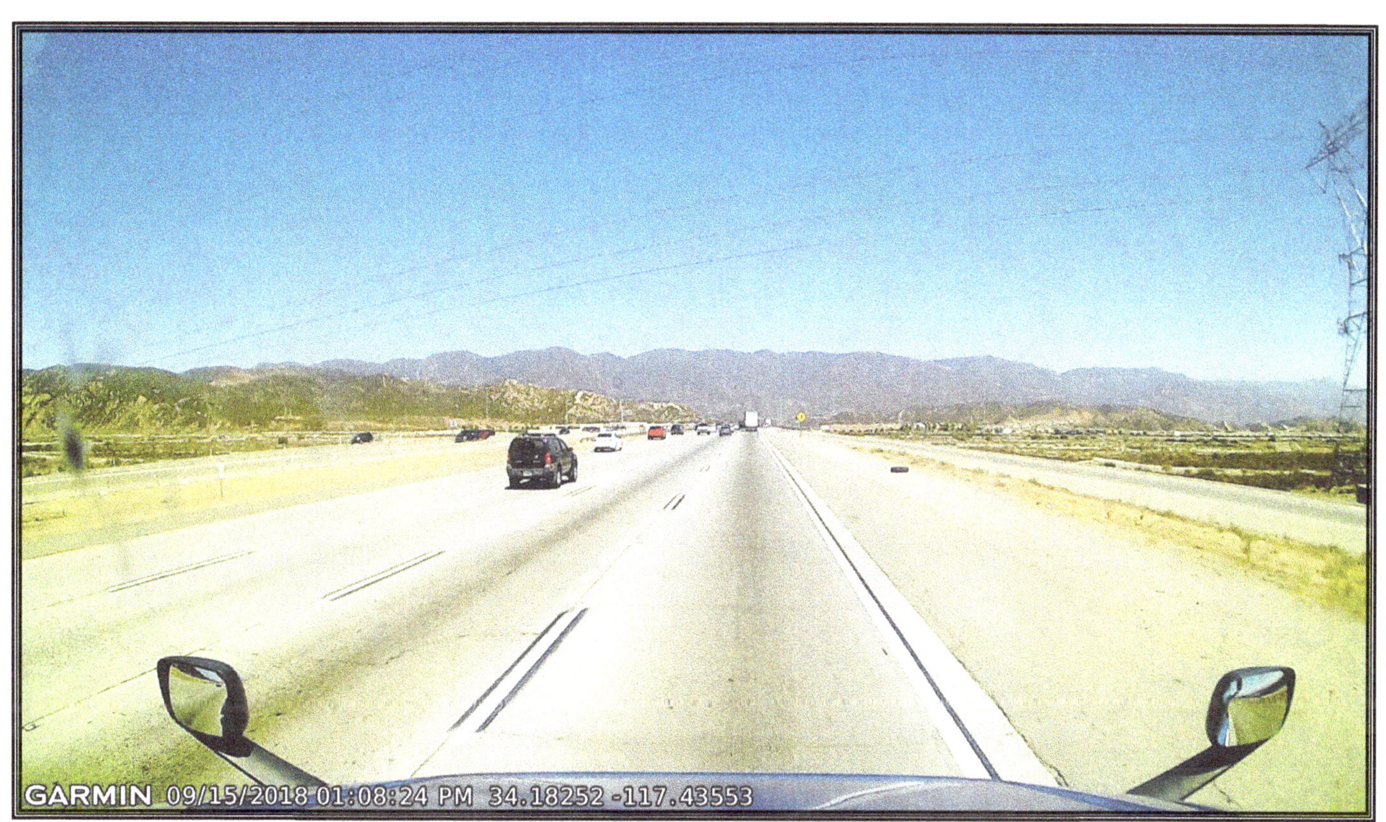

Distant Mount San Antonio
I-15, Fontana, California

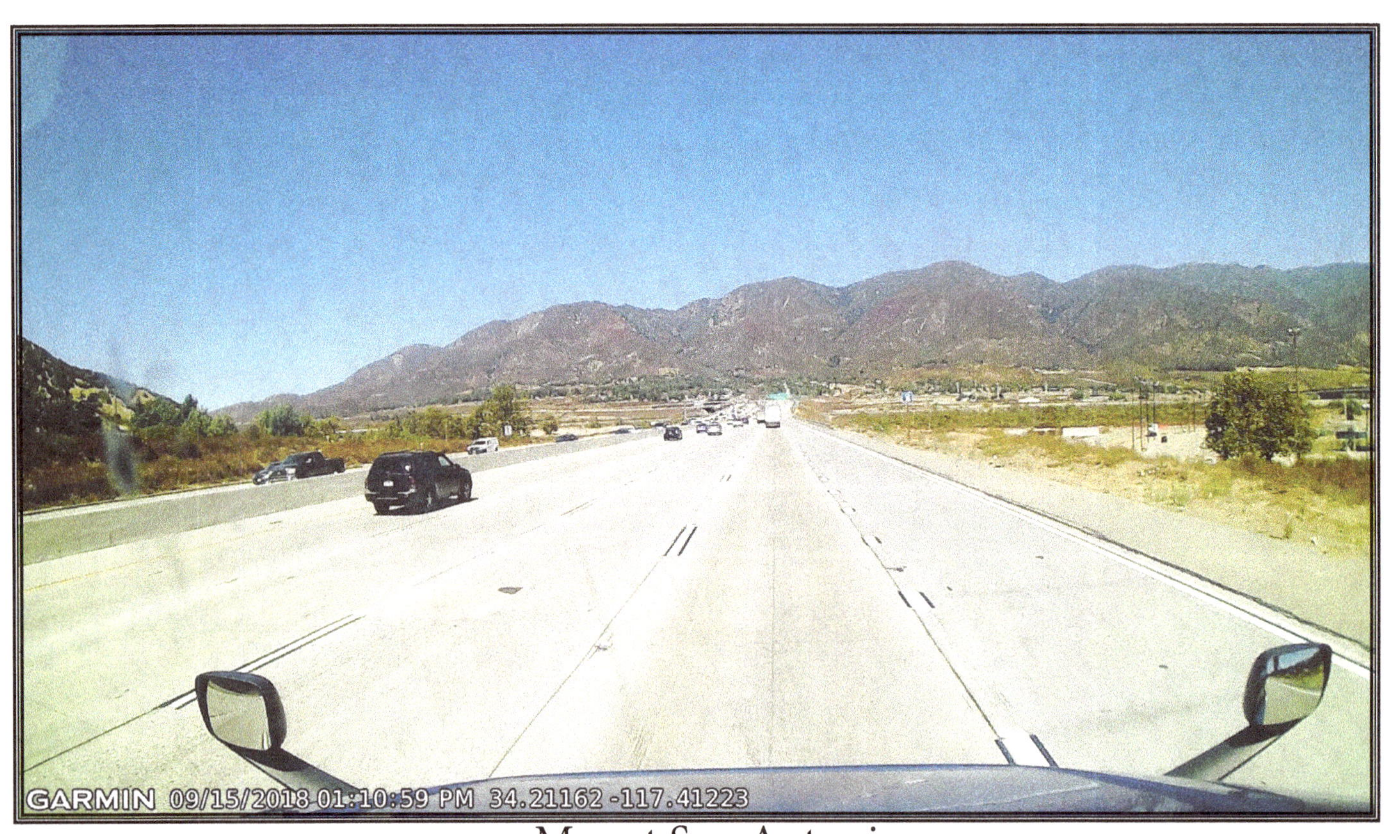

Mount San Antonio
I-15, Fontana, California

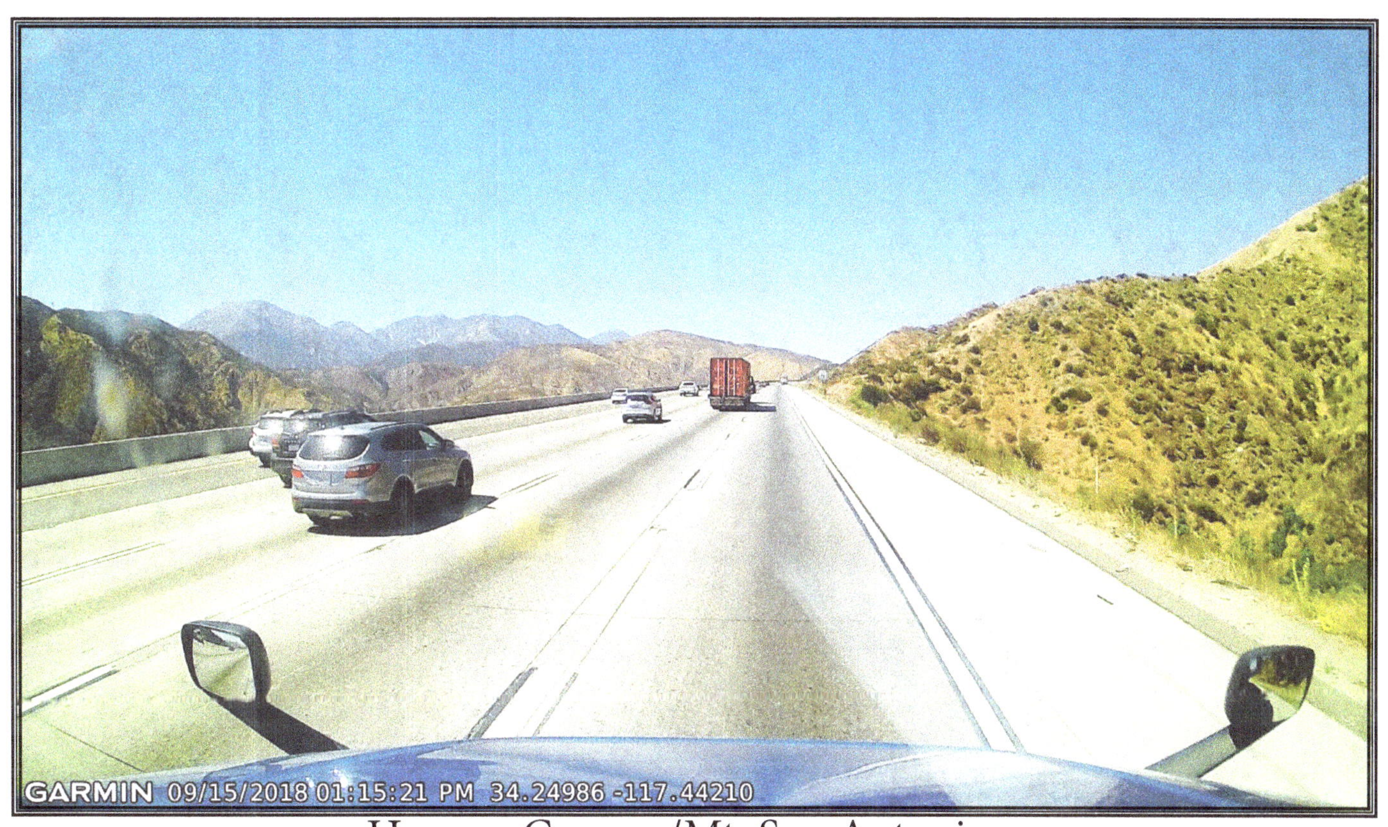

Hopper Canyon/Mt. San Antonio
I-15, San Bernadino, California

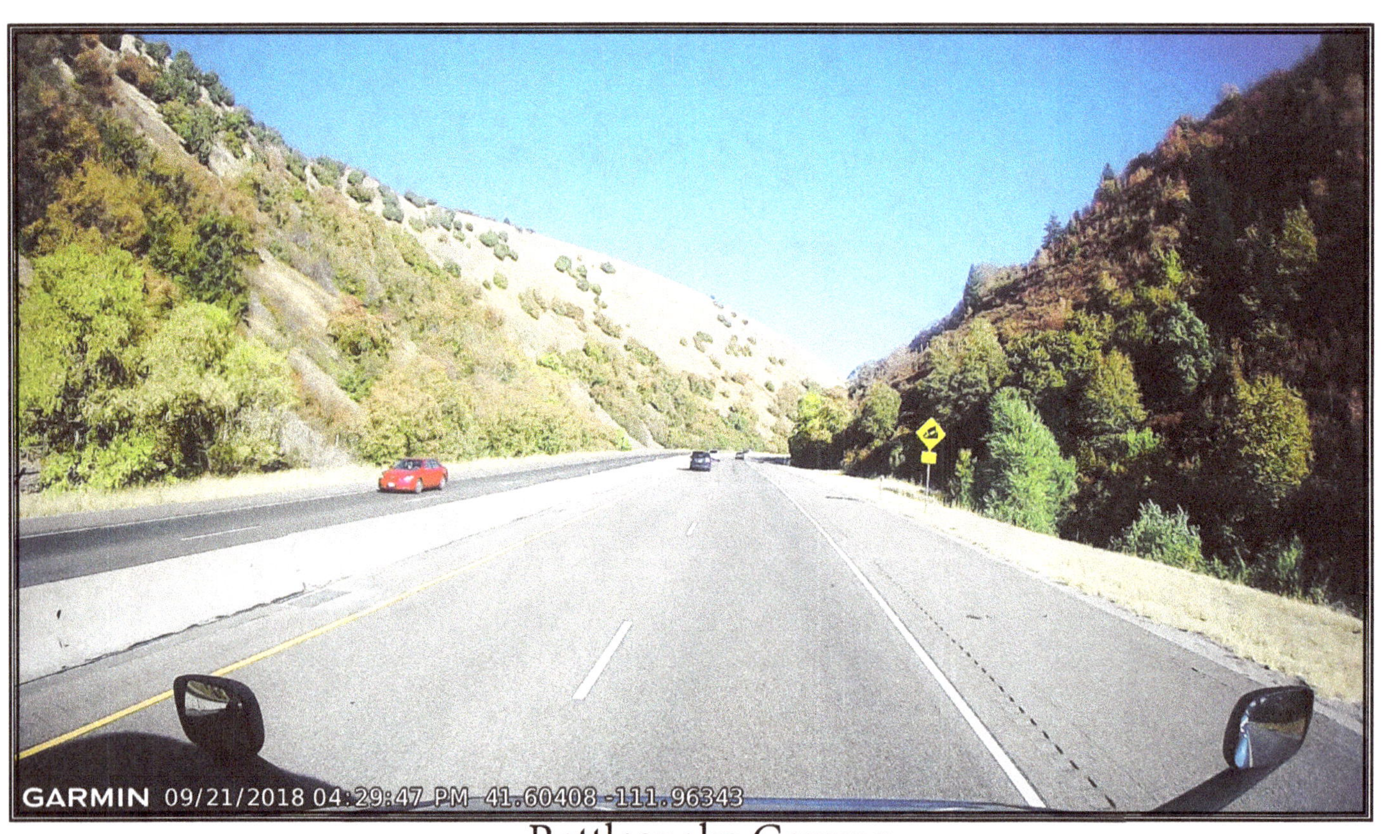

Rattlesnake Canyon
US-89, Wellsville, Utah

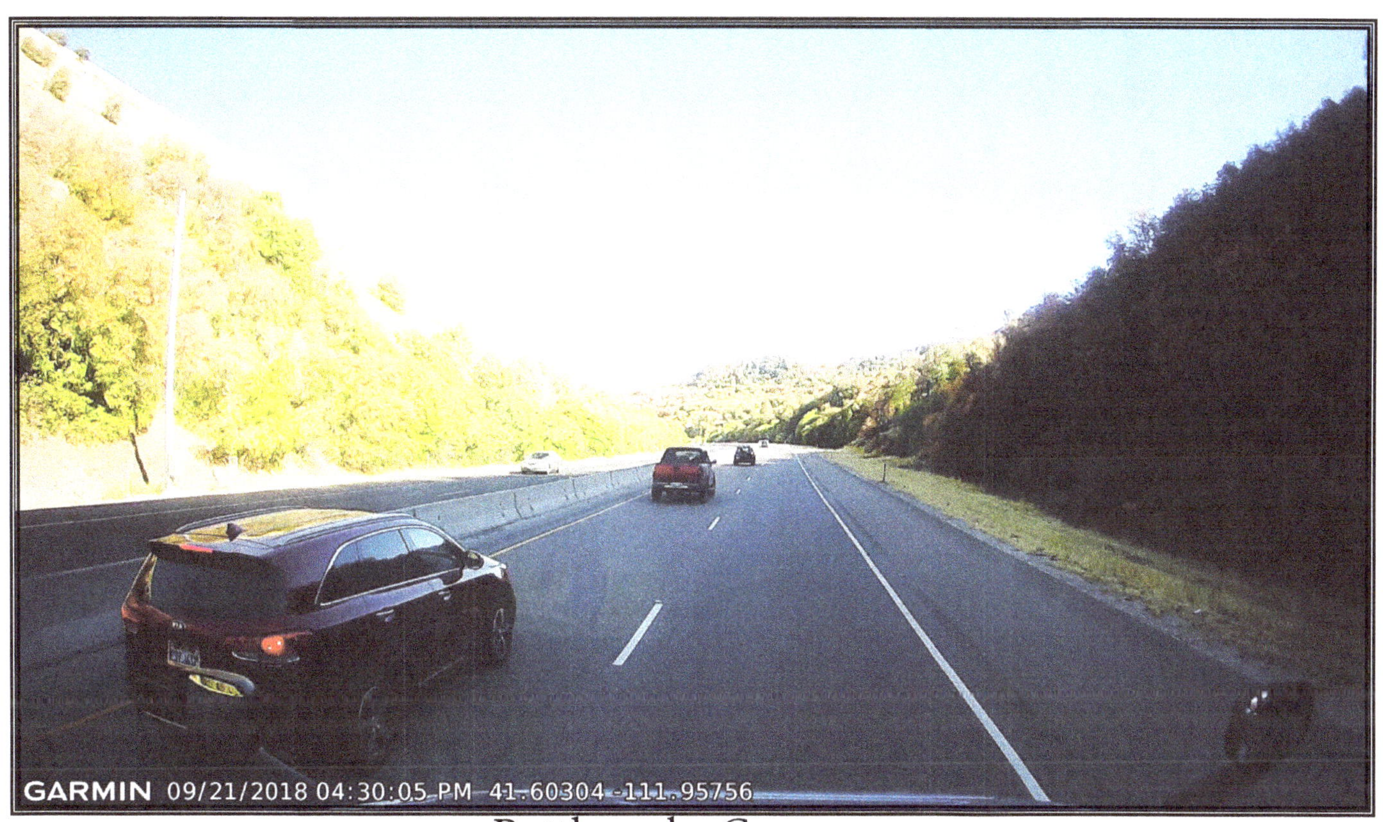

Rattlesnake Canyon
US-89, Wellsville, Utah

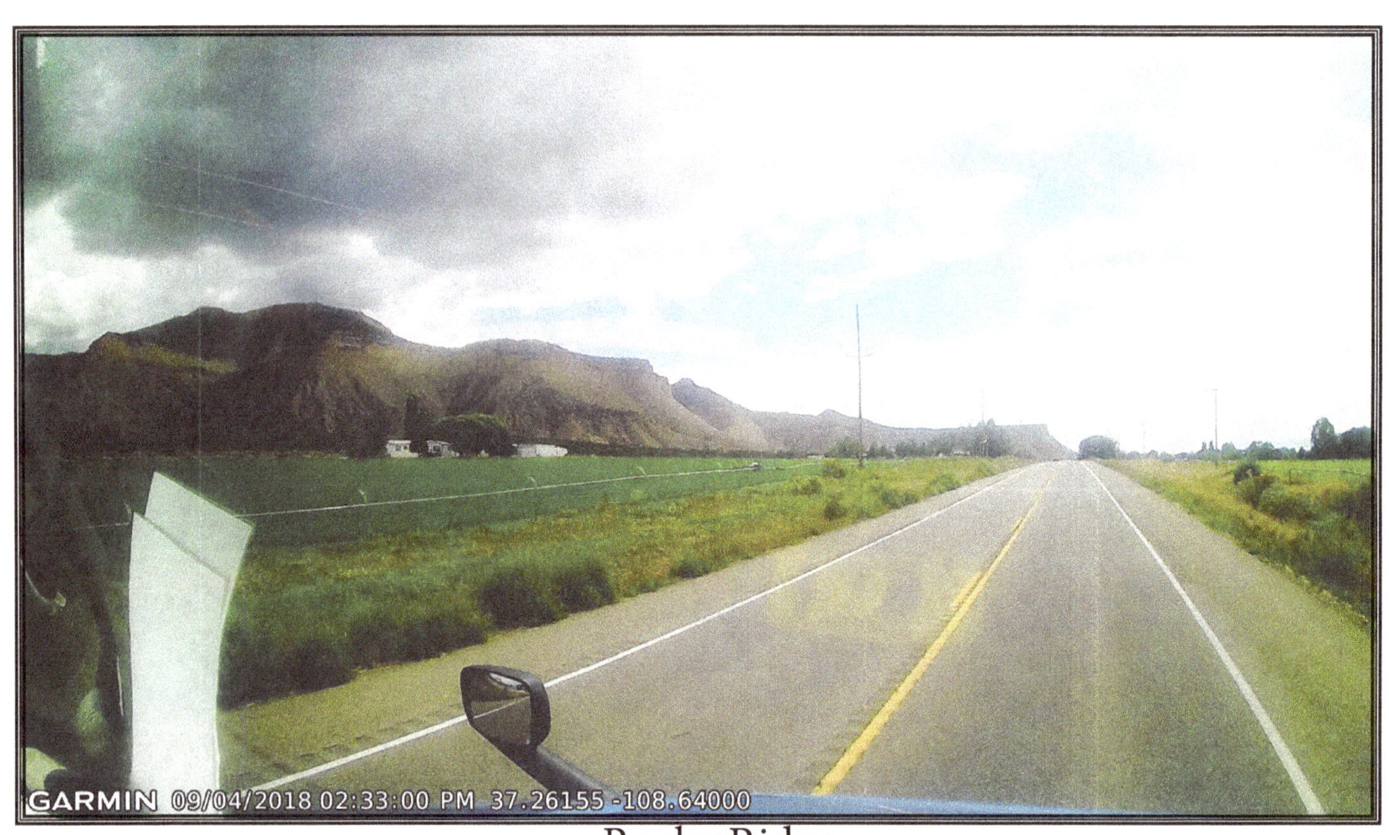

Rocky Ridge
US-491, Cortez, Colorado

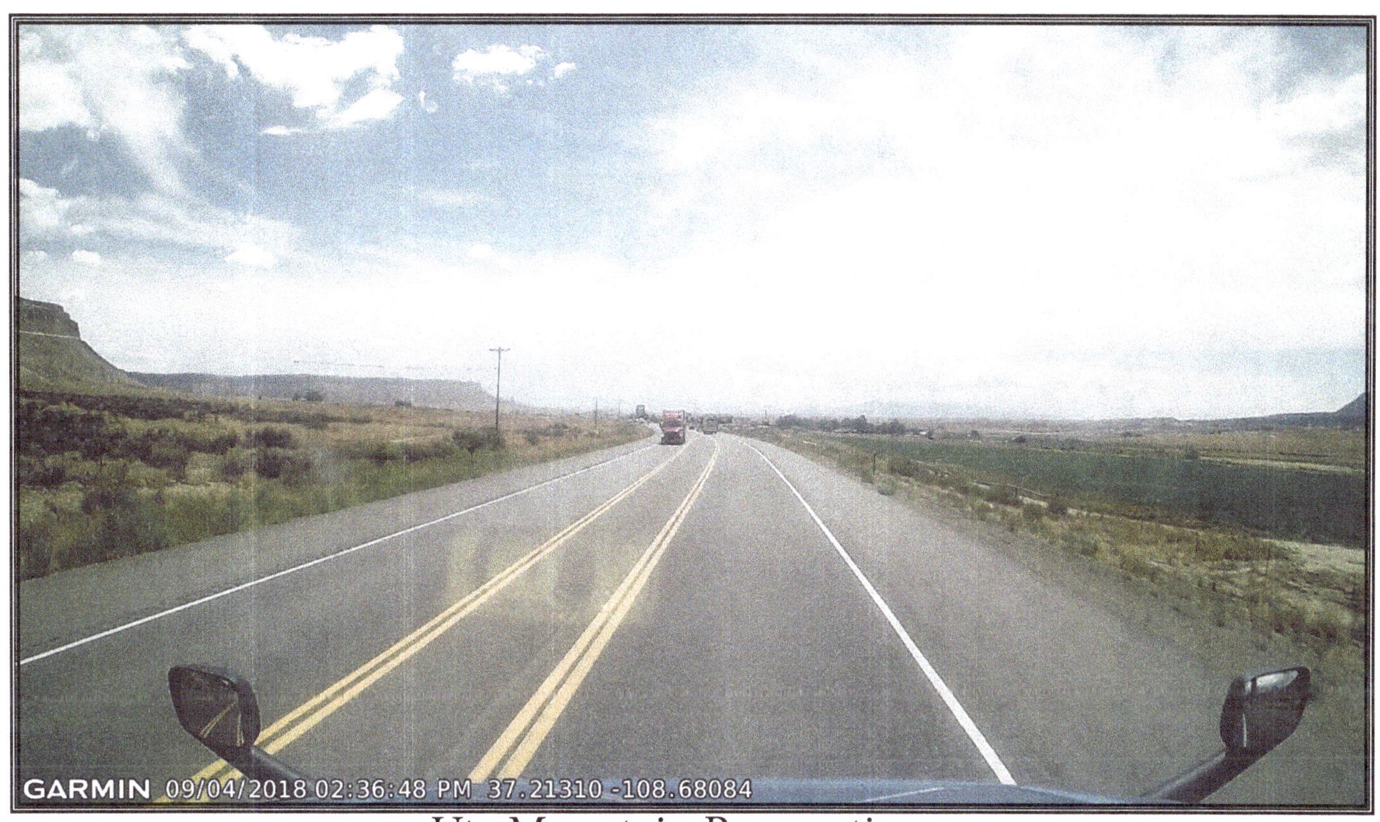

Ute Mountain Reservation
US-491, Cortez, Colorado

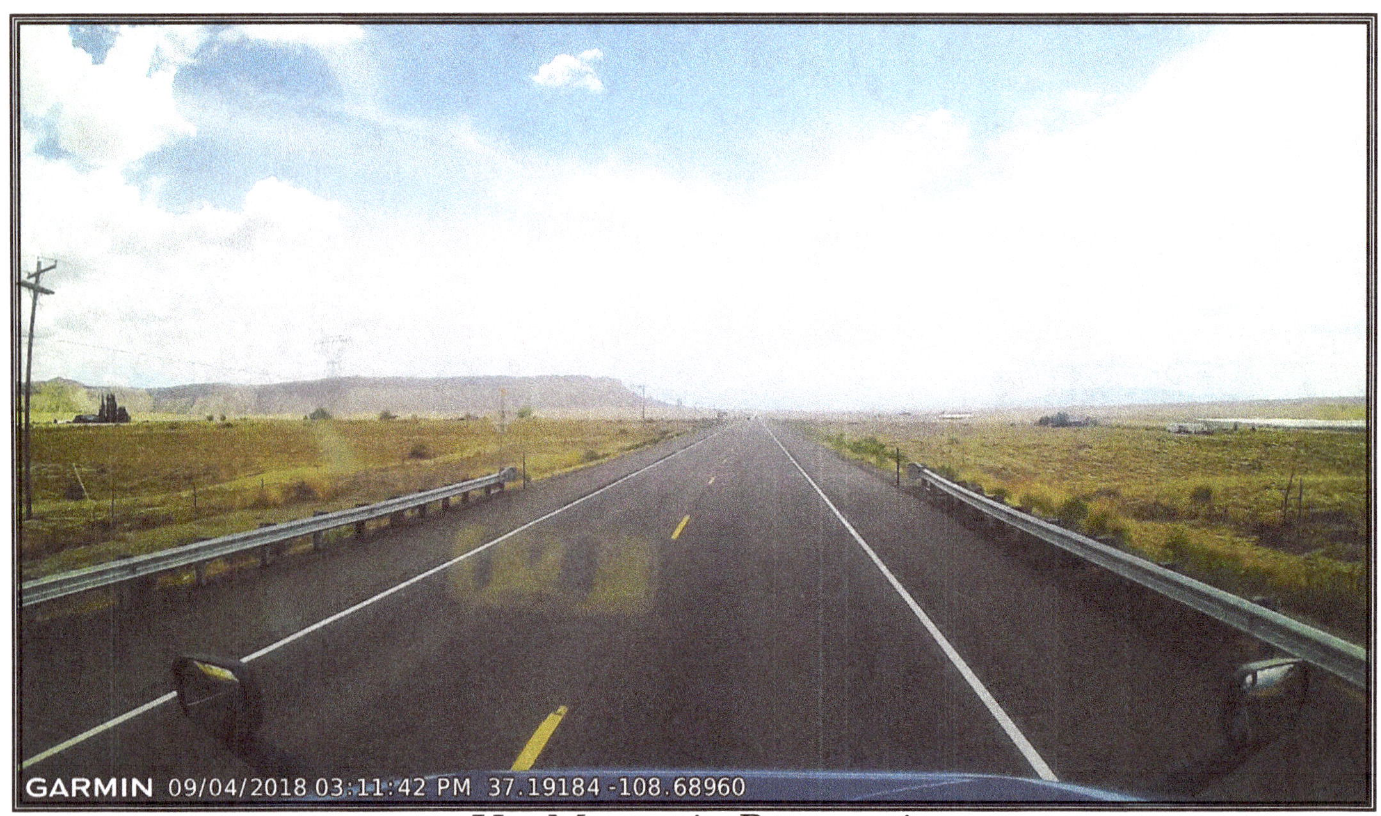

Ute Mountain Reservation
US-491, Cortez, Colorado

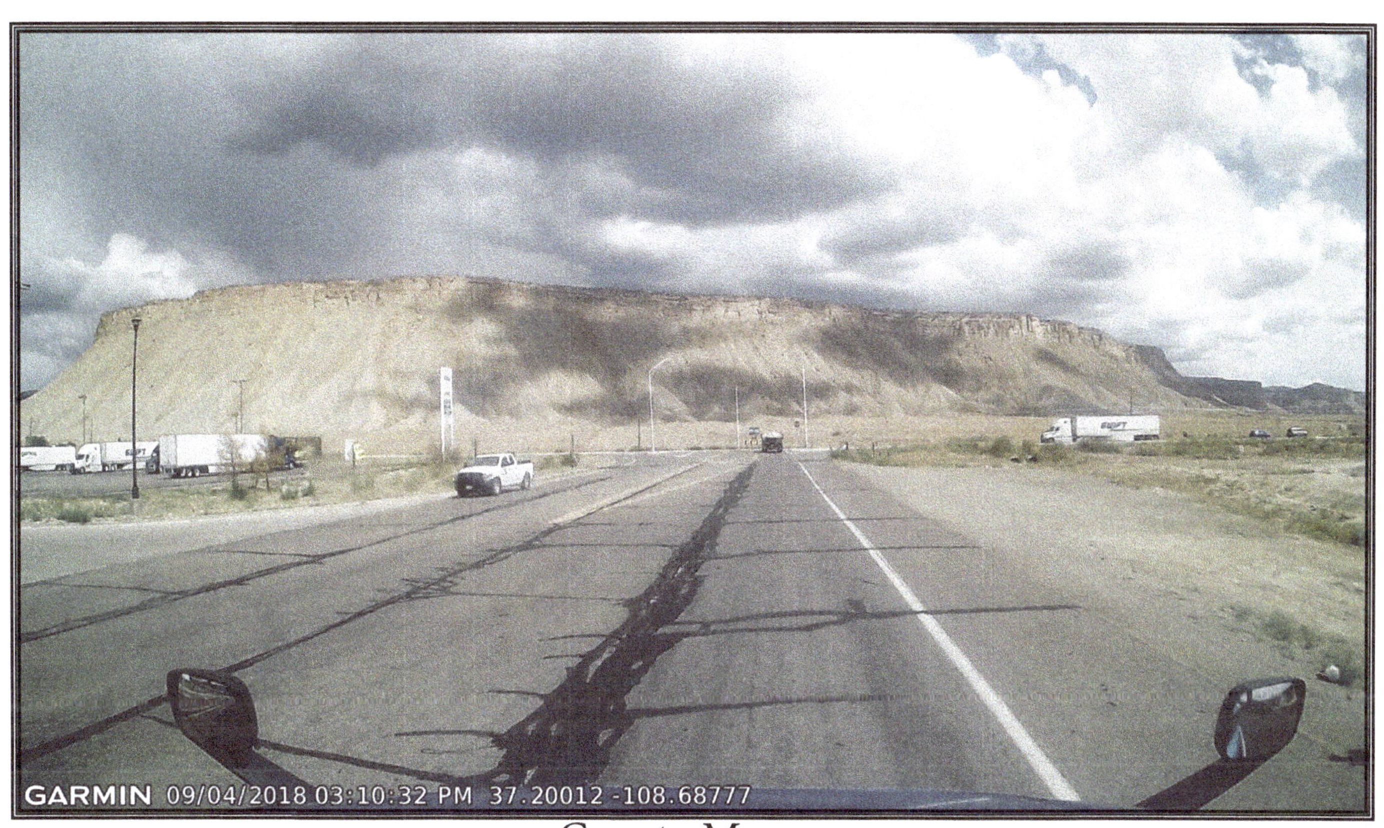

Coyote Mesa
US-491, Cortez, Colorado

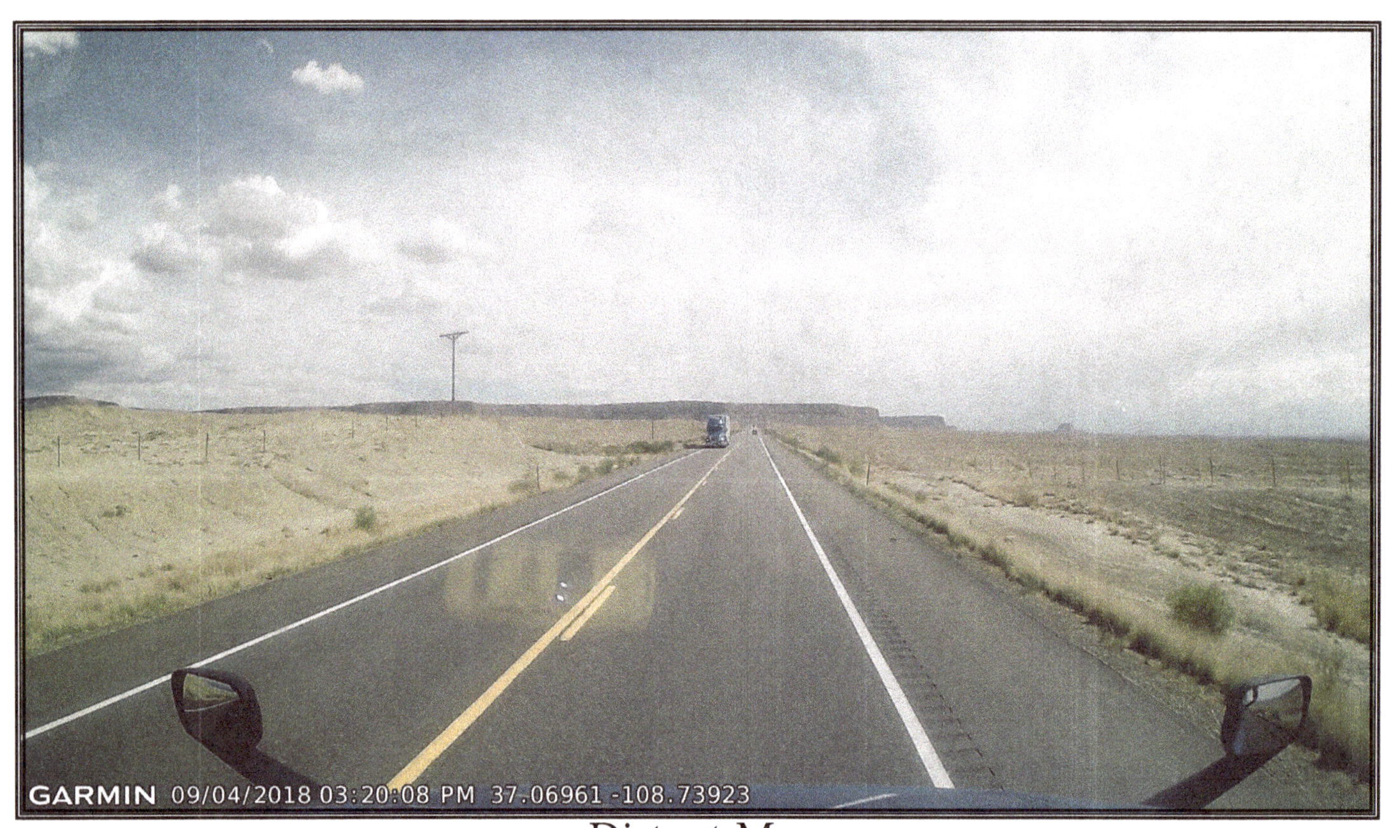

Distant Mesas
US-491, Towaoc, Colorado

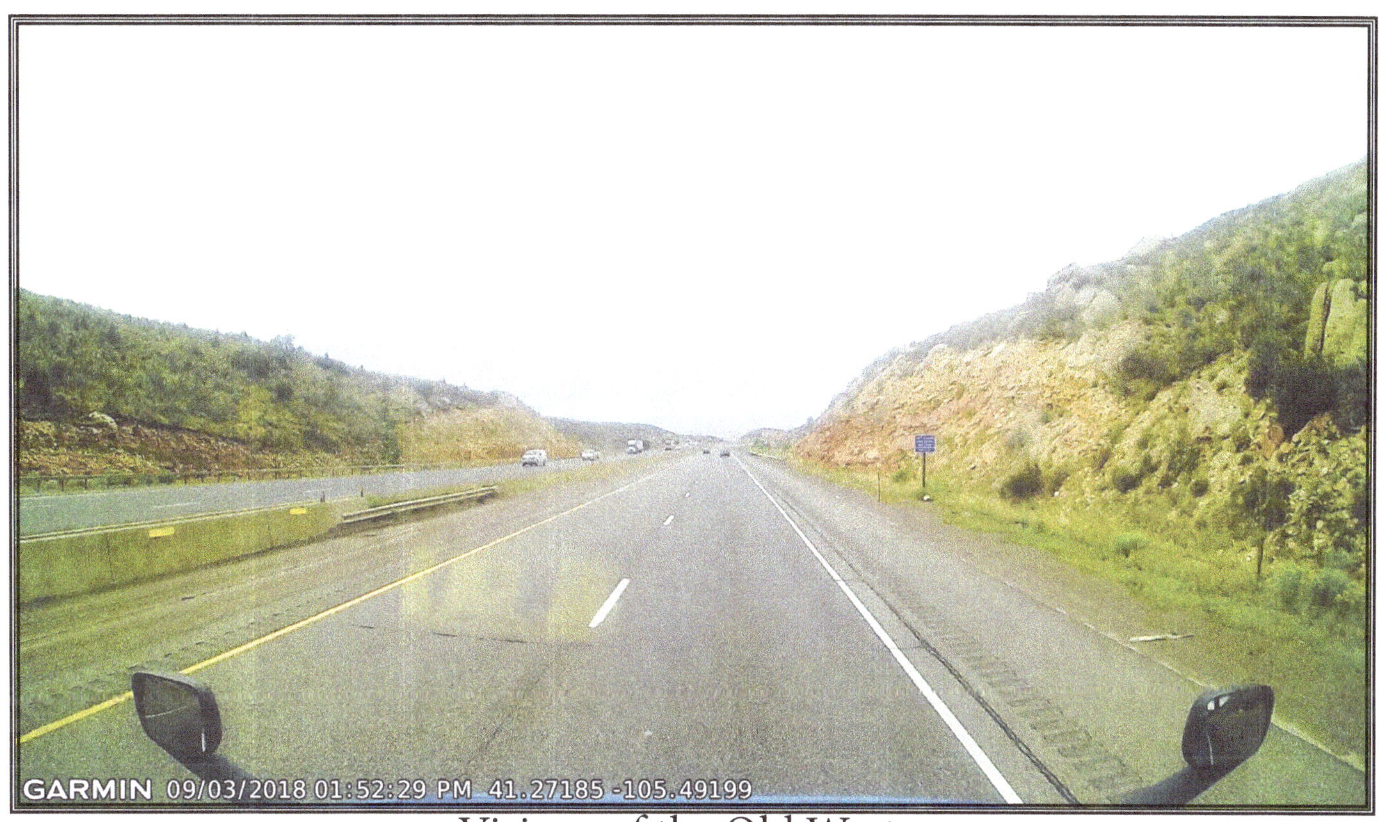

Visions of the Old West
I-80, Laramie, Wyoming

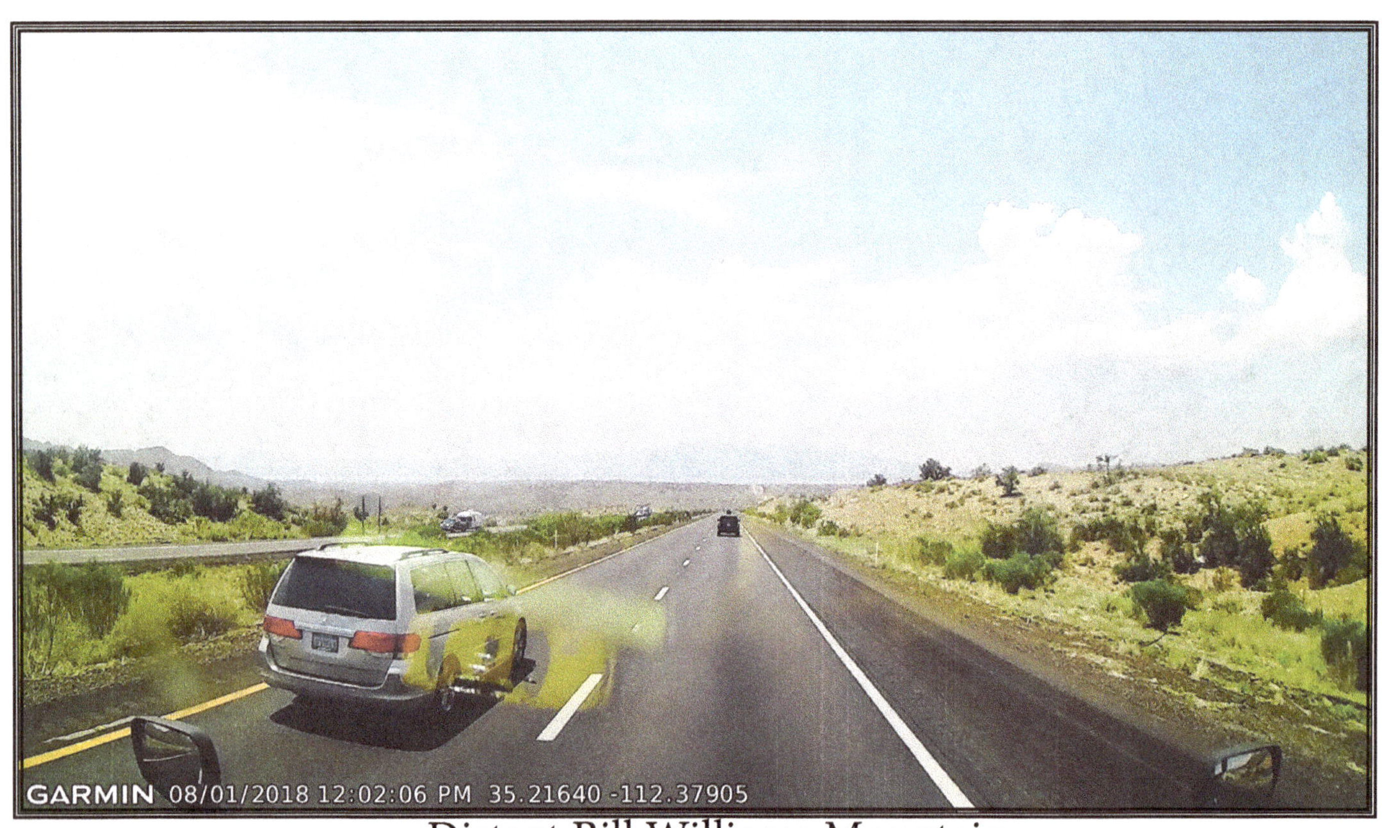

Distant Bill Williams Mountain
I-40, Williams, Arizona

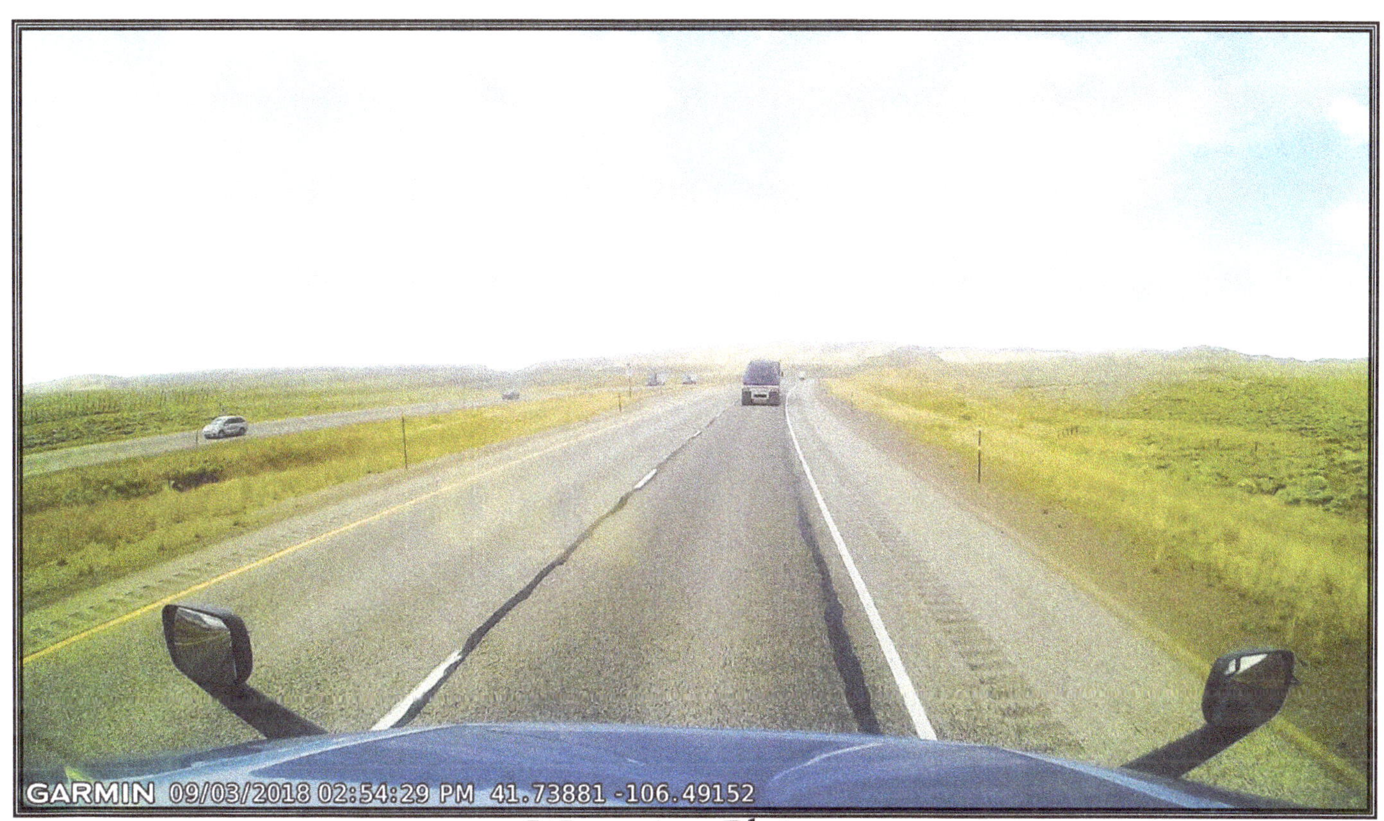

Wyoming Plains
I-80, Elk Mountain, Wyoming

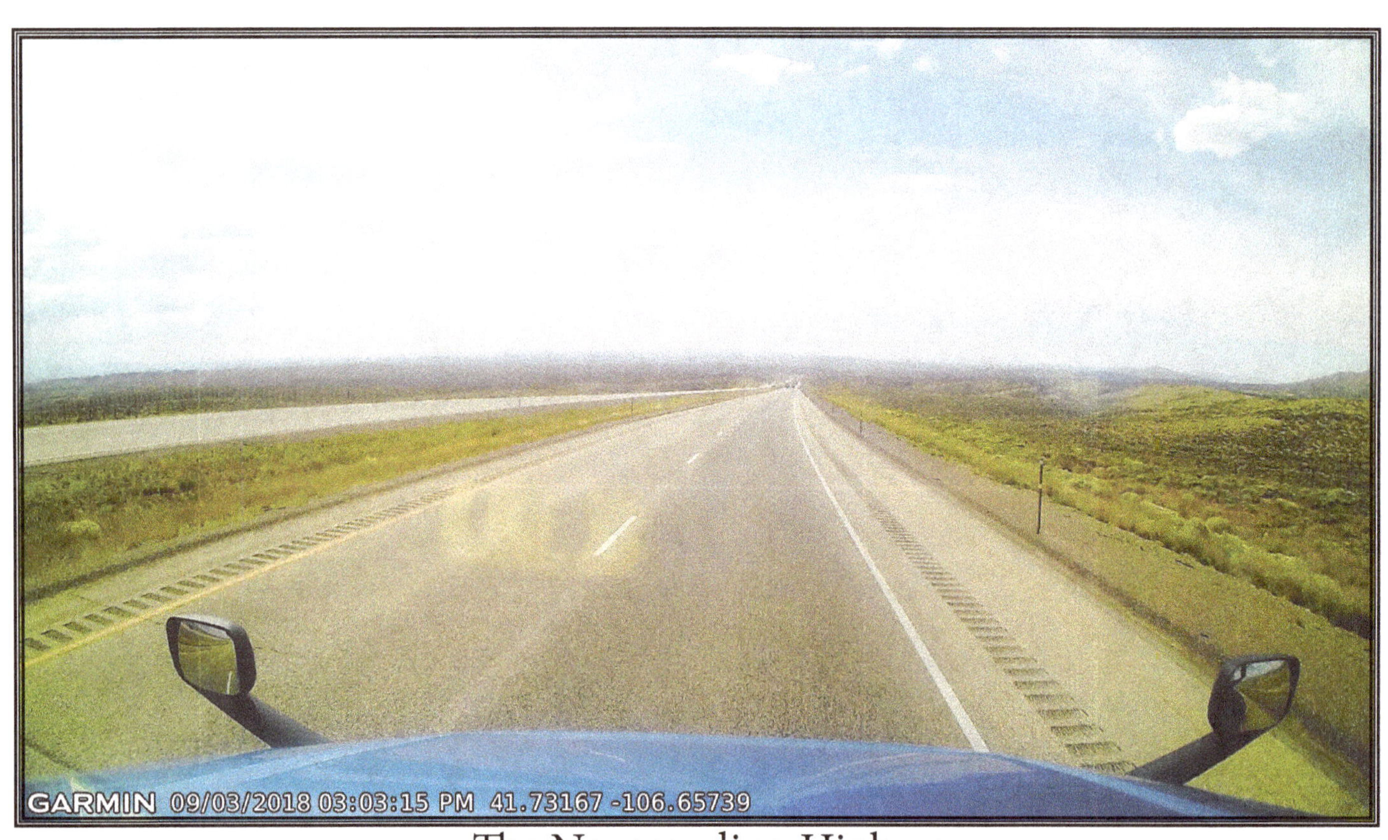

The Neverending Highway
I-80, Walcott, Wyoming

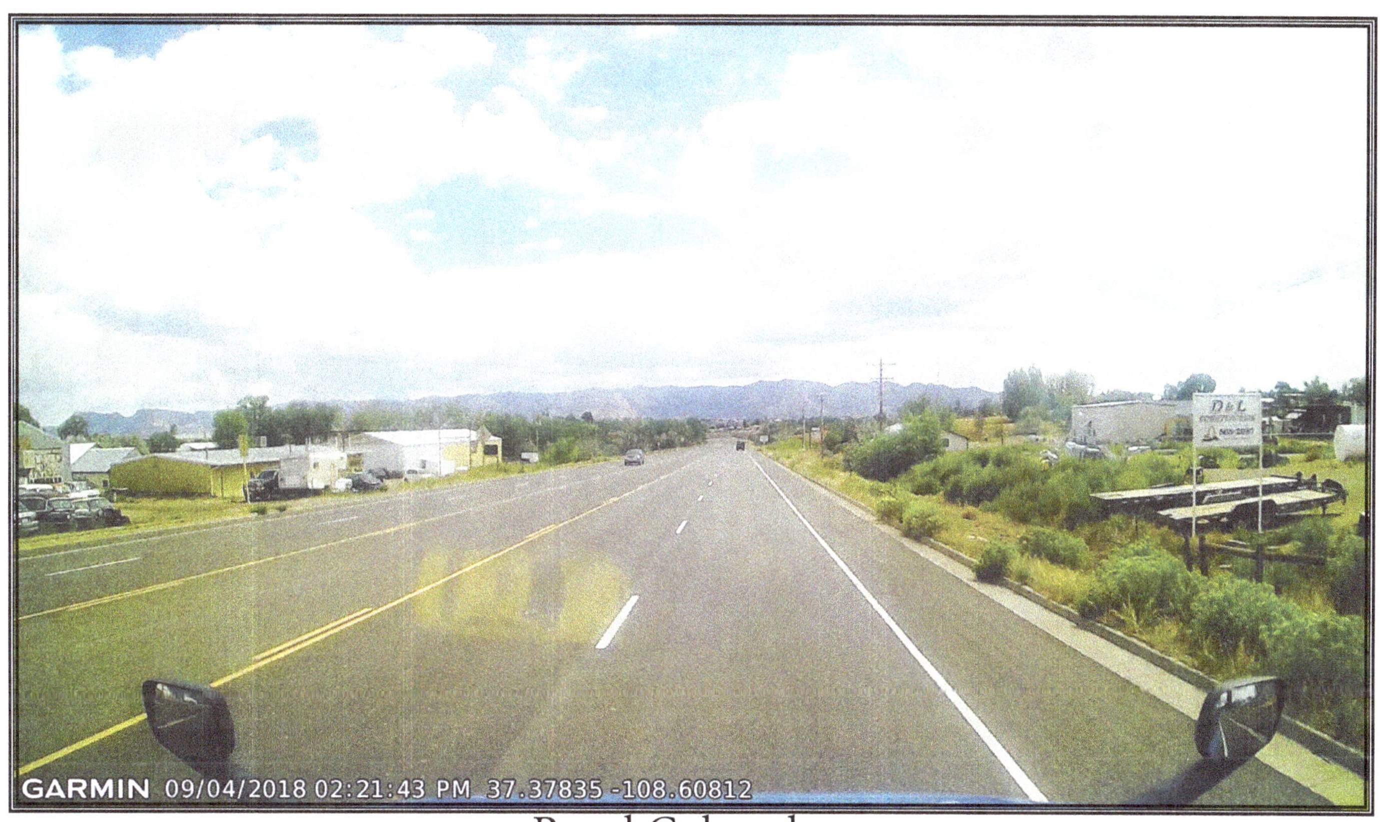

Rural Colorado
US-491, Cortez, Colorado

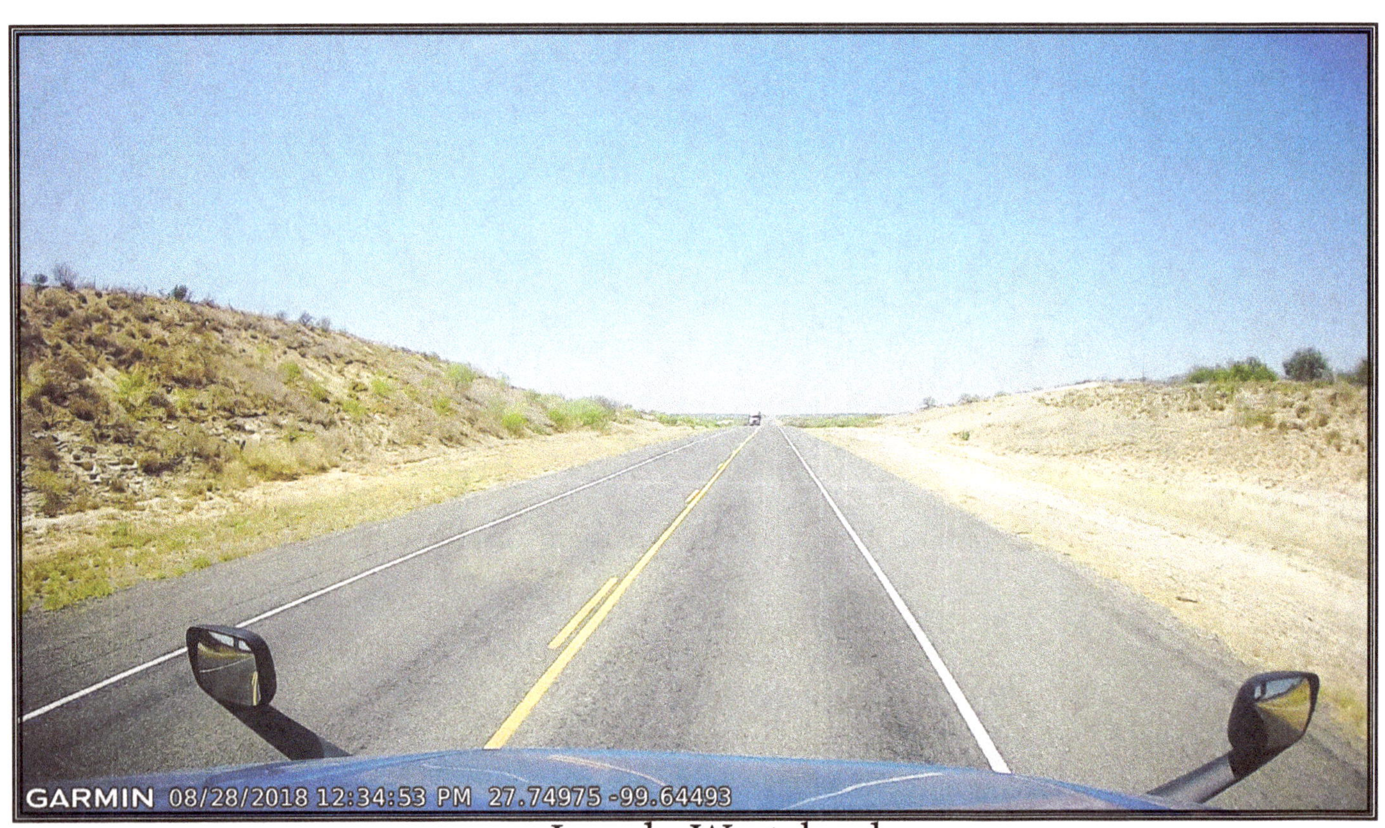

Laredo Wasteland
Laredo, Texas

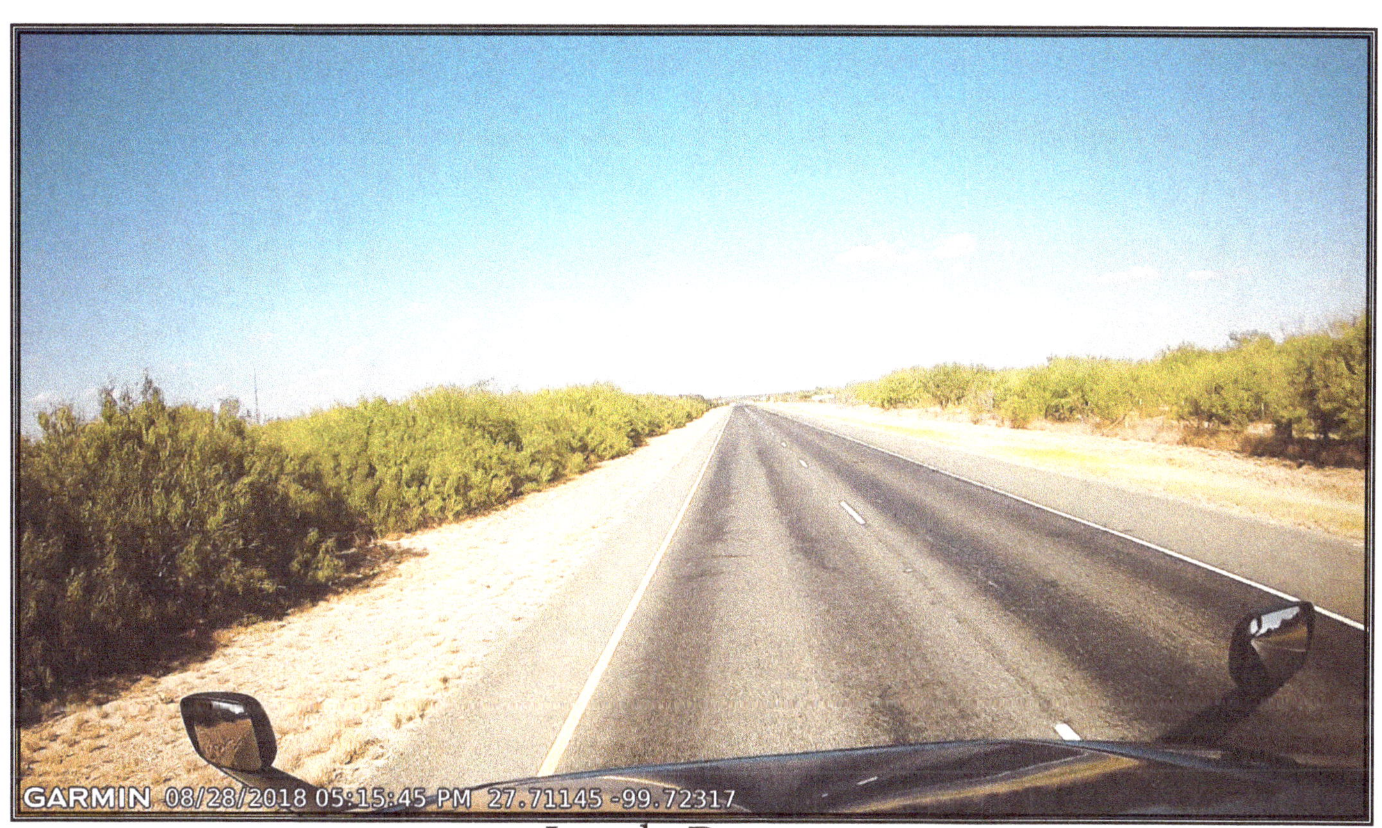

Laredo Desert
Laredo, Texas

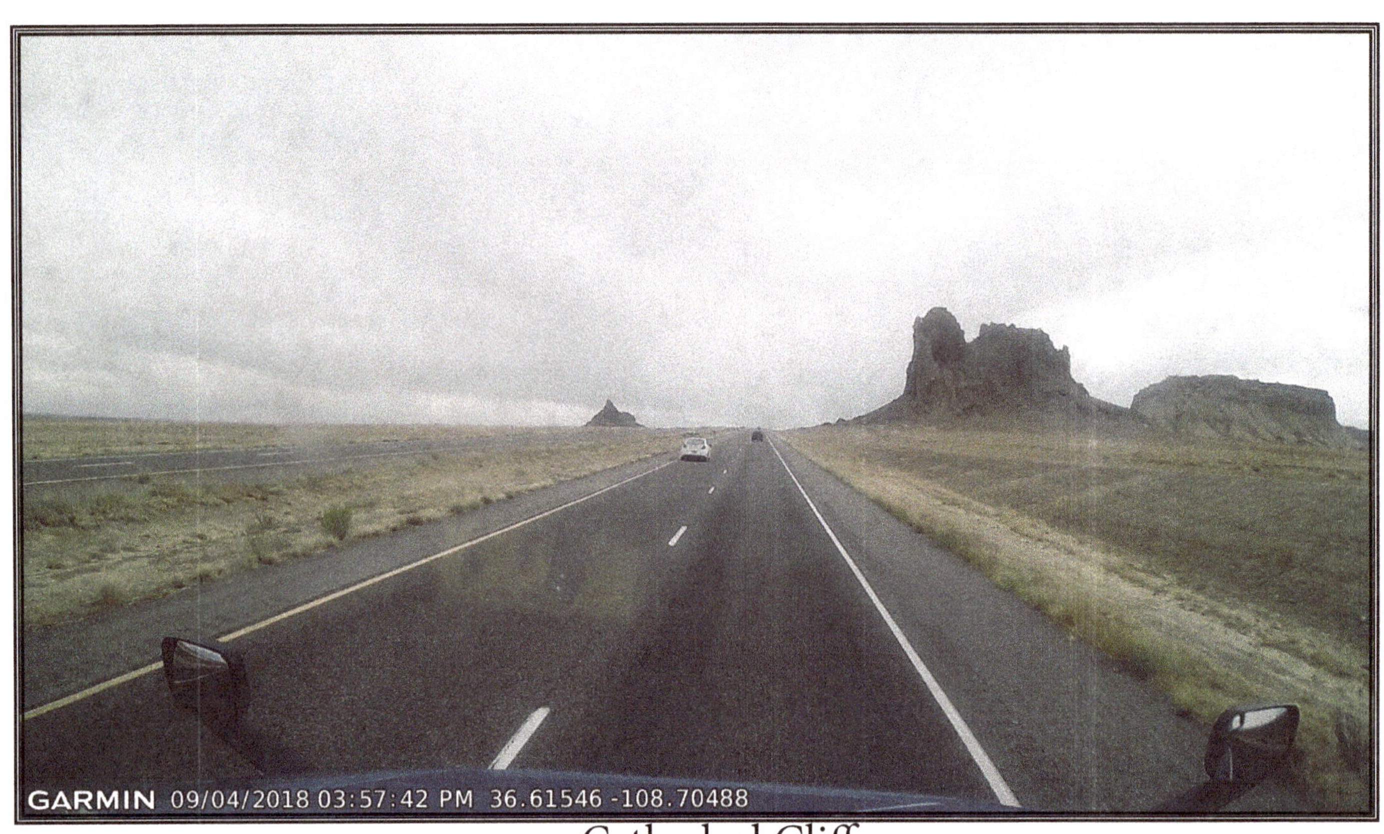

Cathedral Cliff
US-491, Shiprock, New Mexico

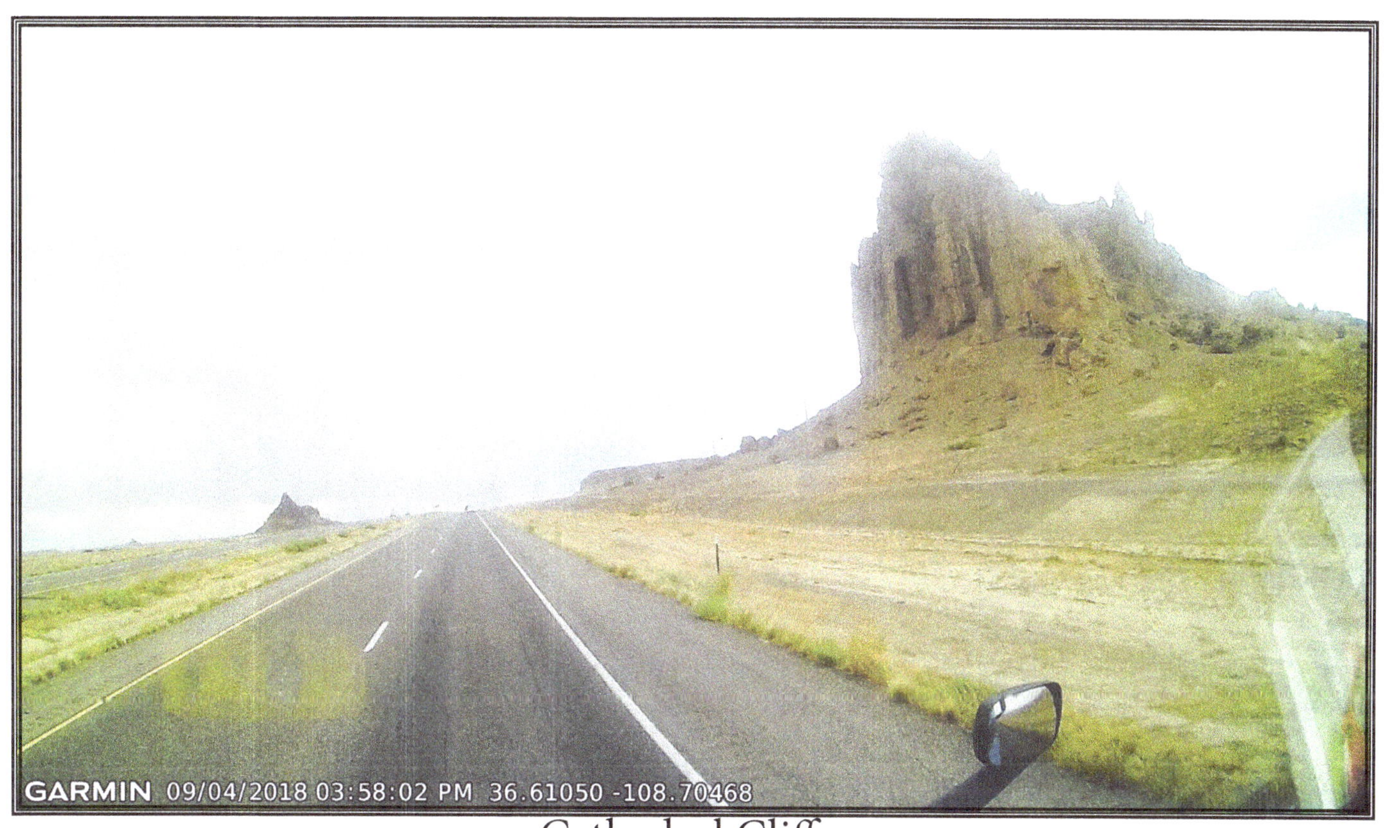

Cathedral Cliff
US-491, Shiprock, New Mexico

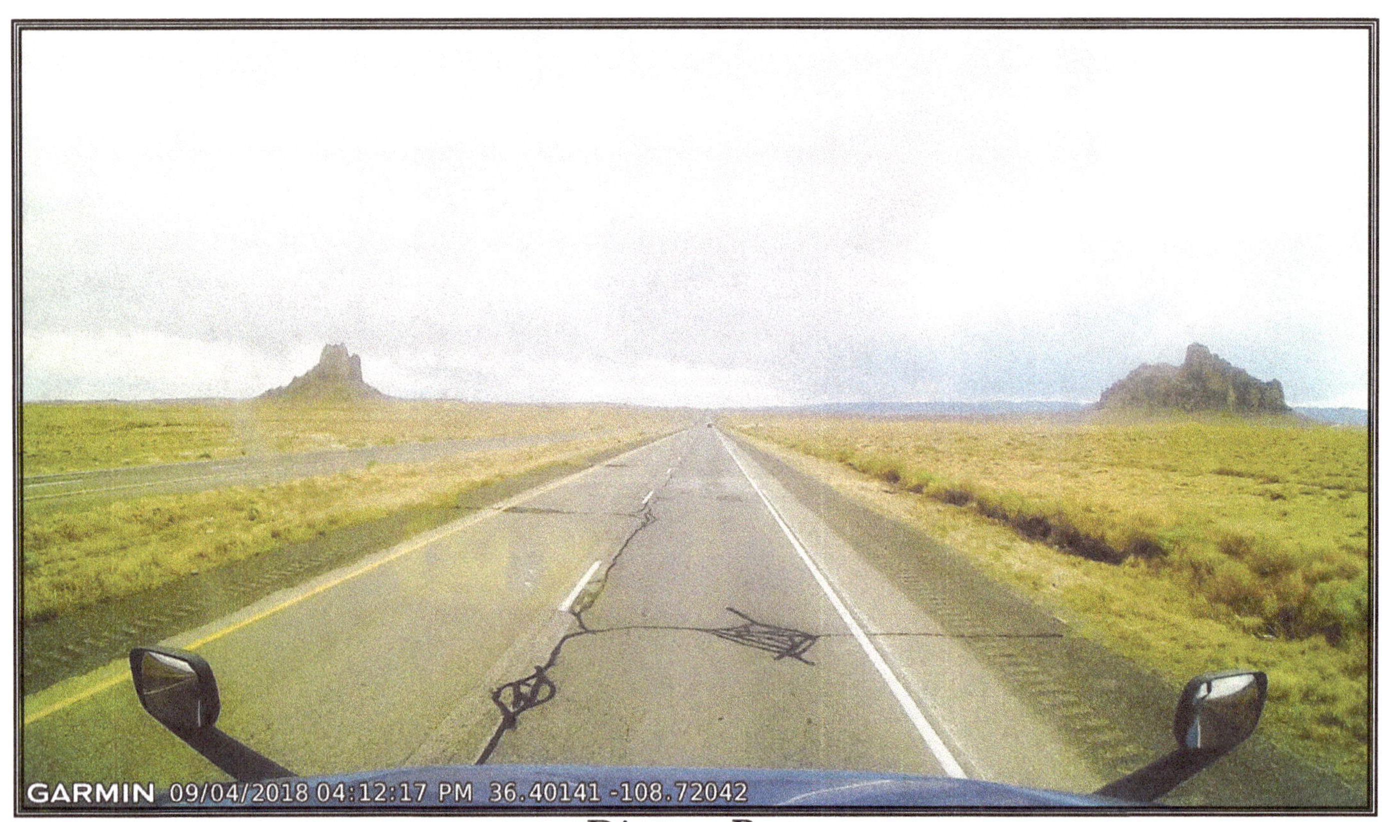

Distant Buttes
US-491, Shiprock, New Mexico

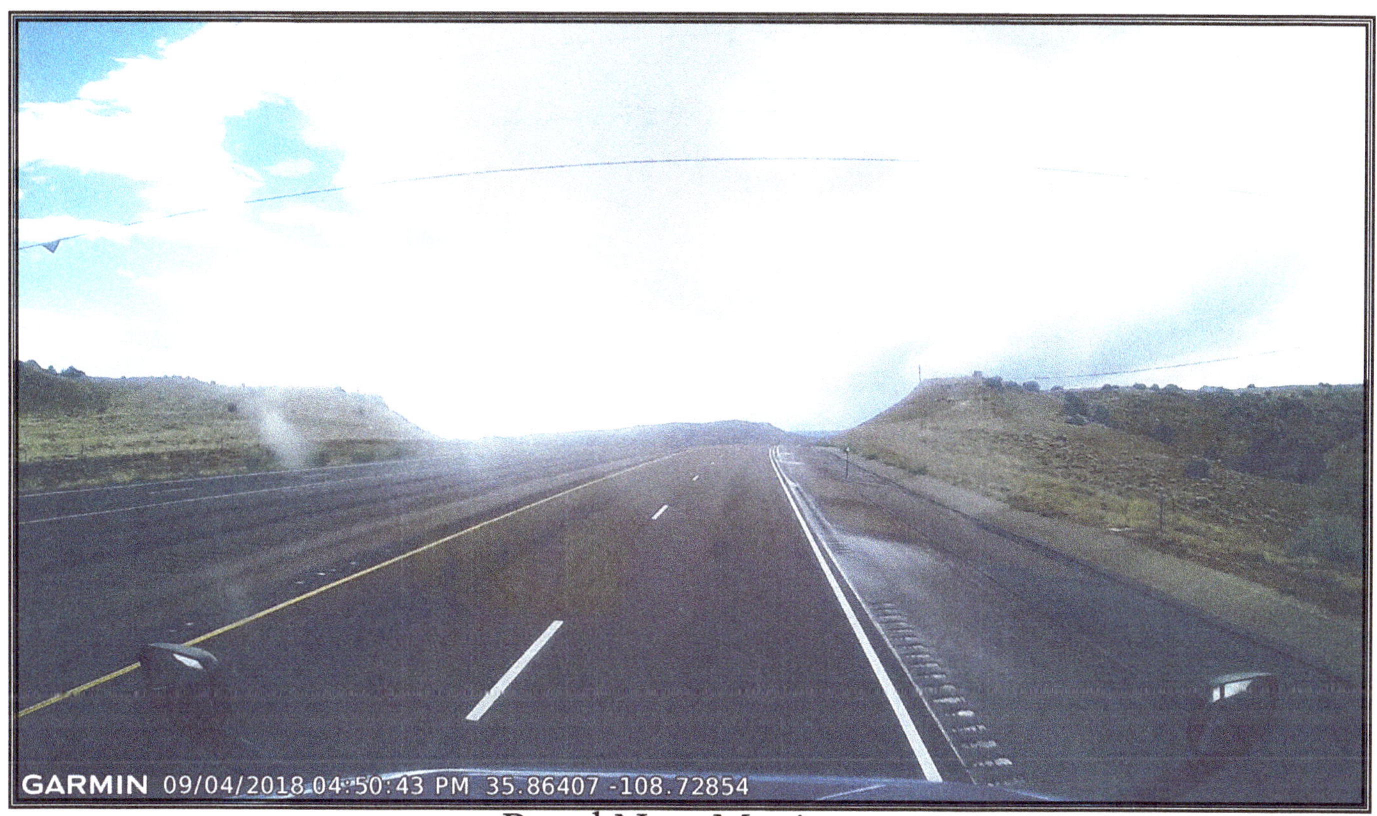

Rural New Mexico
US-491, Tohatchi, New Mexico

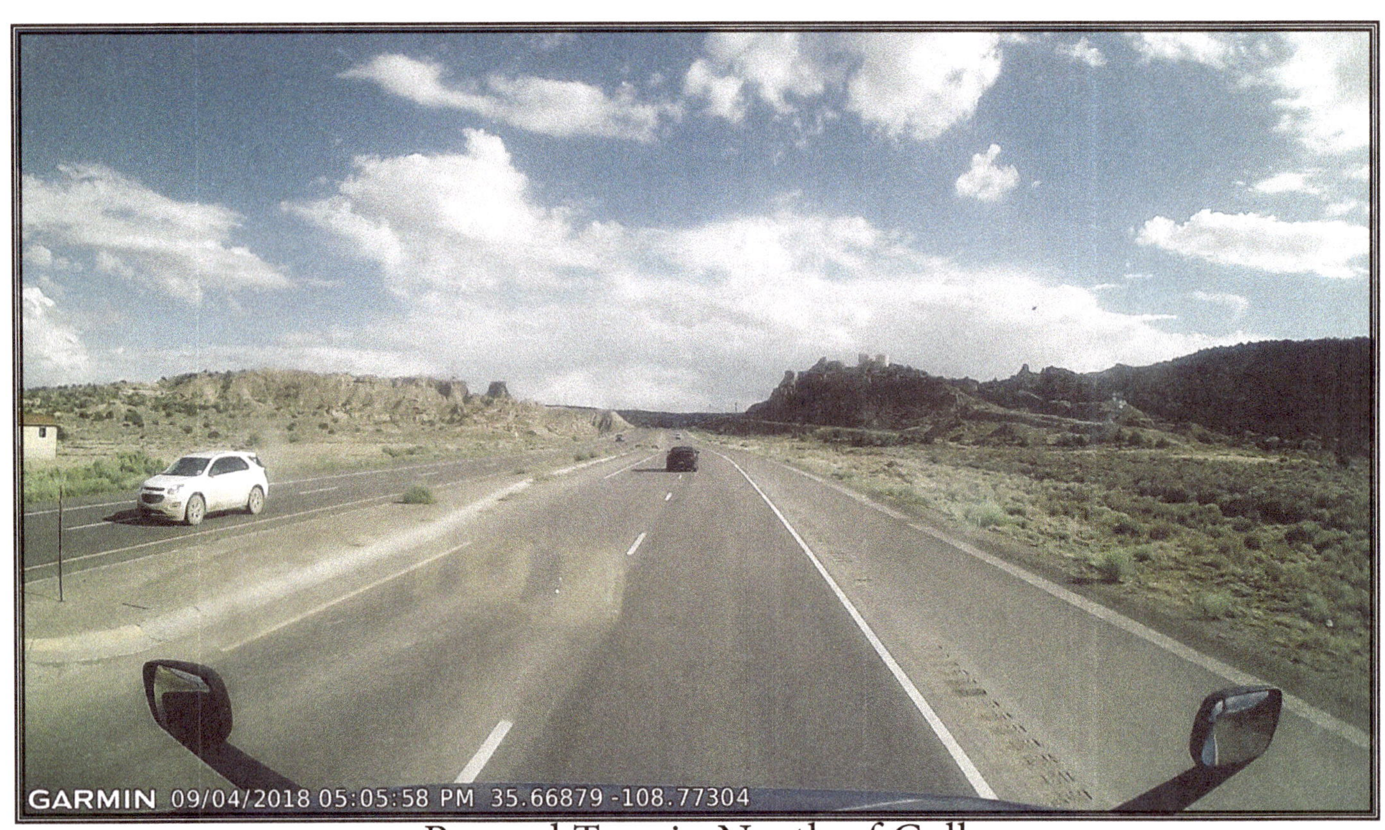

Rugged Terrain North of Gallup
US-491, Gallup, New Mexico

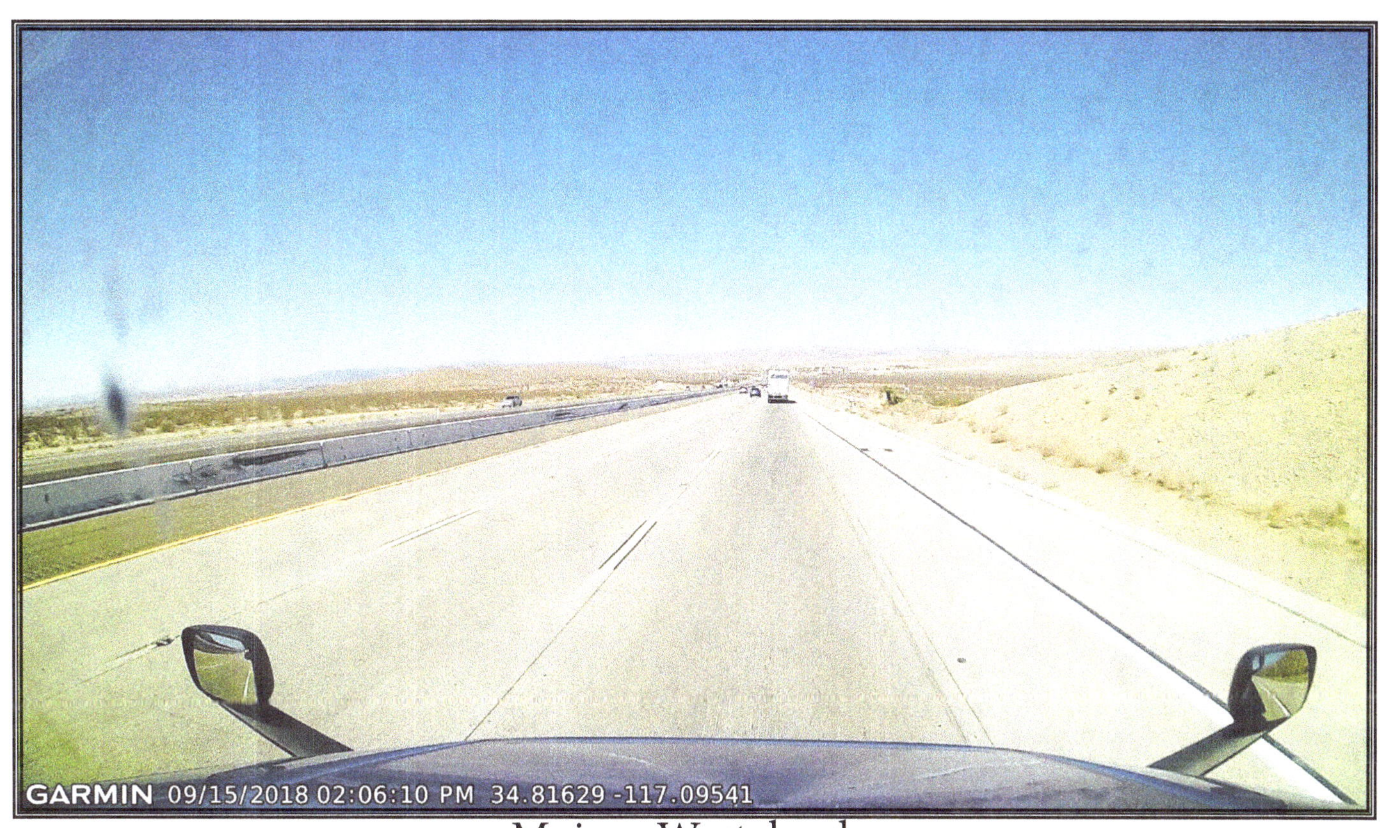

Mojave Wasteland
I-15, Barstow, California

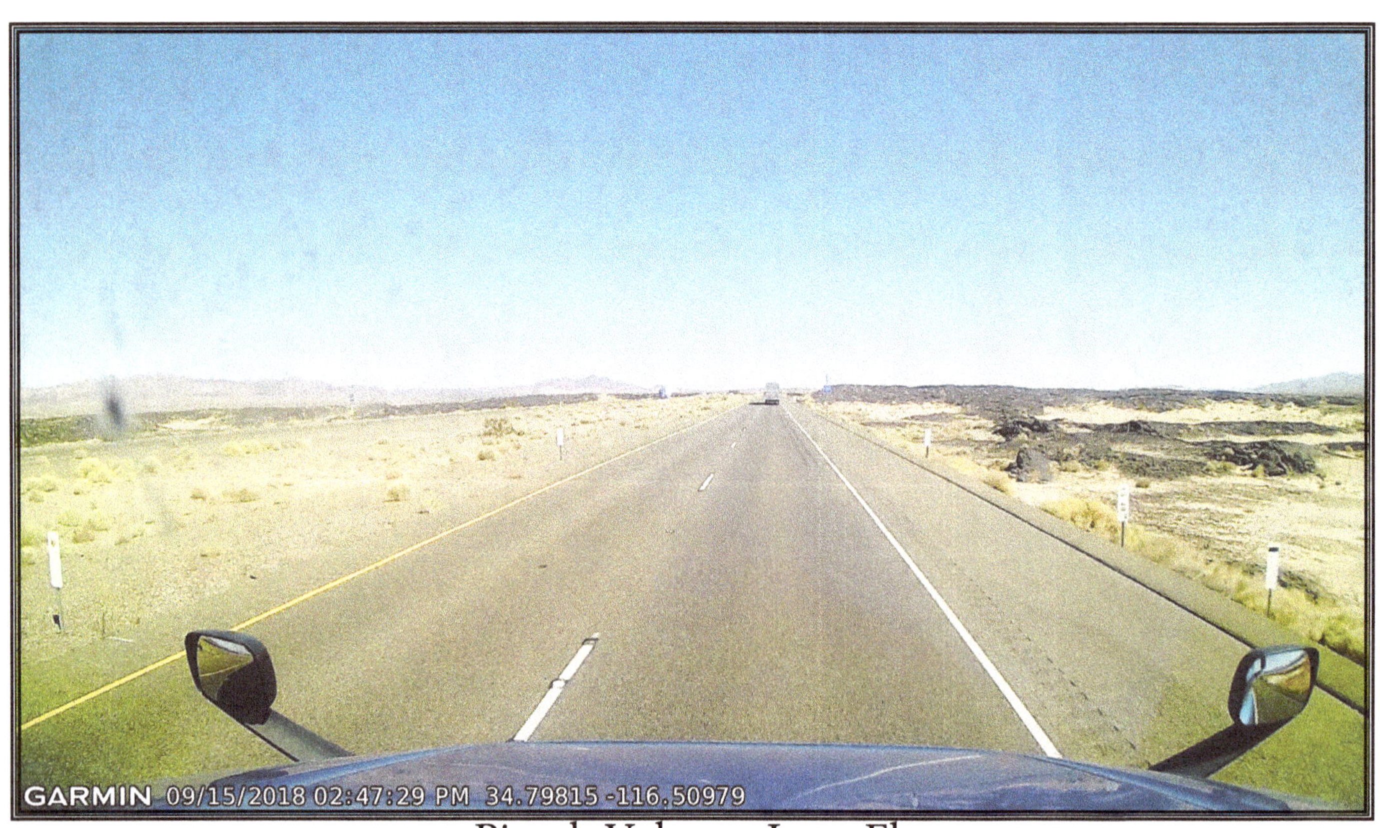

Pisgah Volcano Lava Flow
I-40, Newberry Springs, California

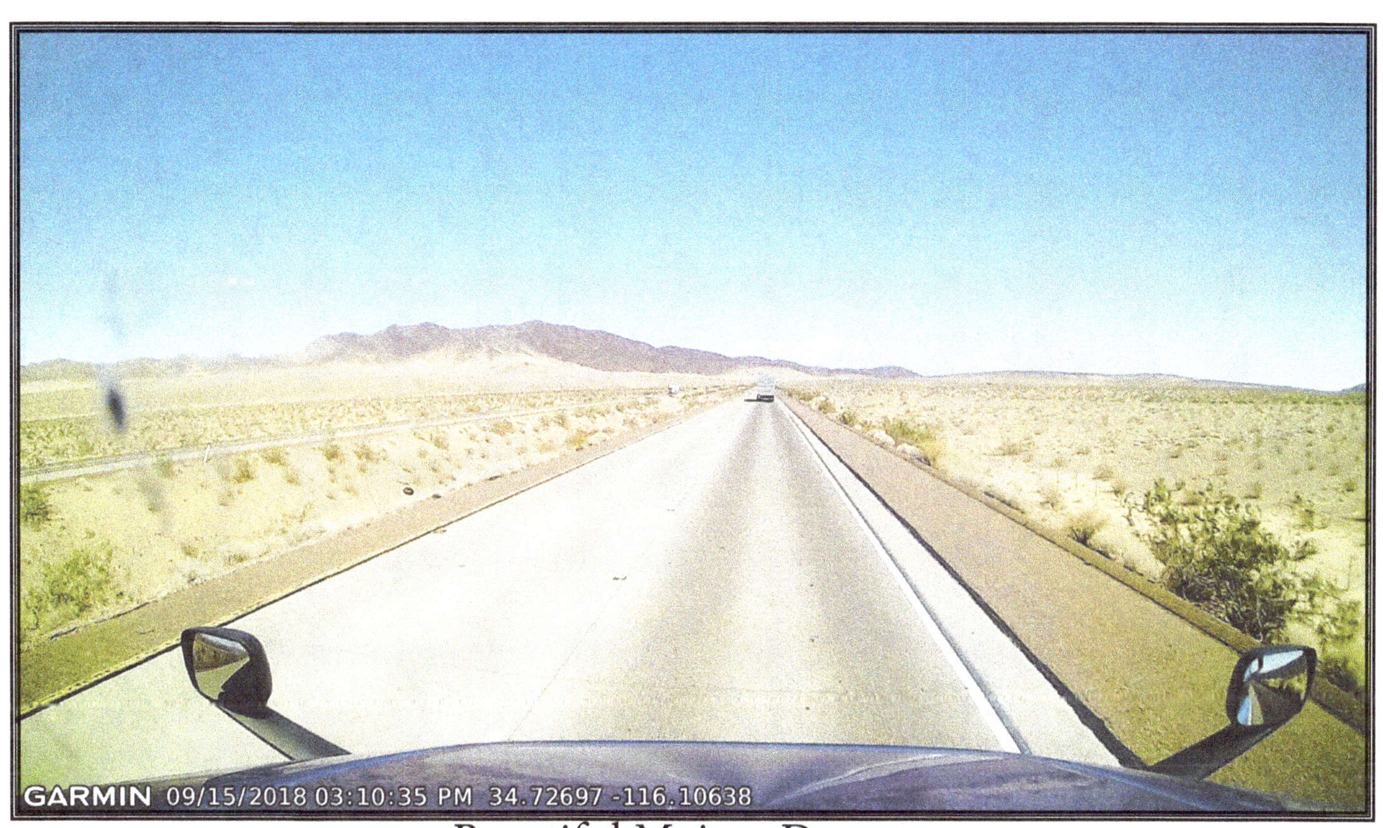

Beautiful Mojave Desert
I-40, Ludlow, California

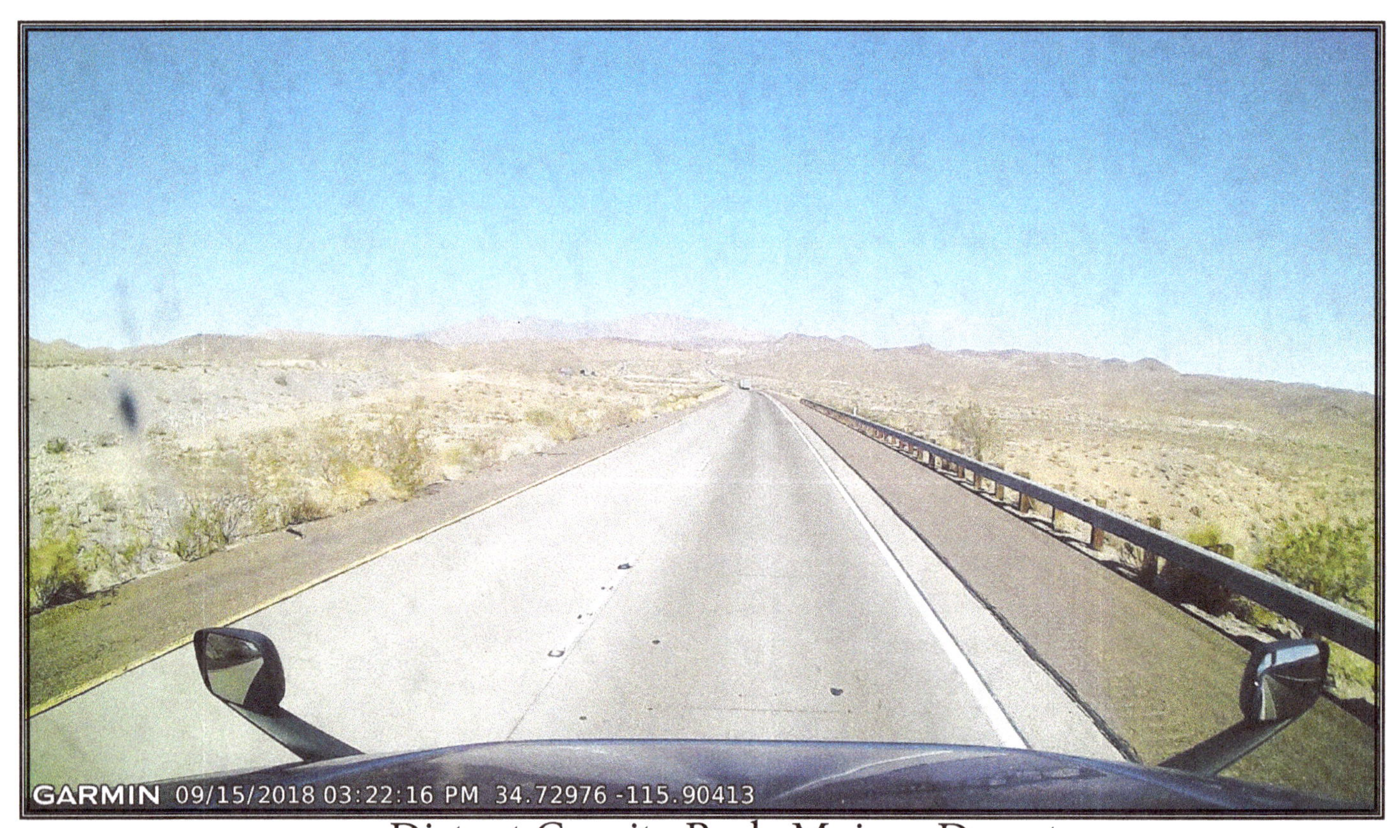

Distant Granite Peak-Mojave Desert
I-40, Klondike, California

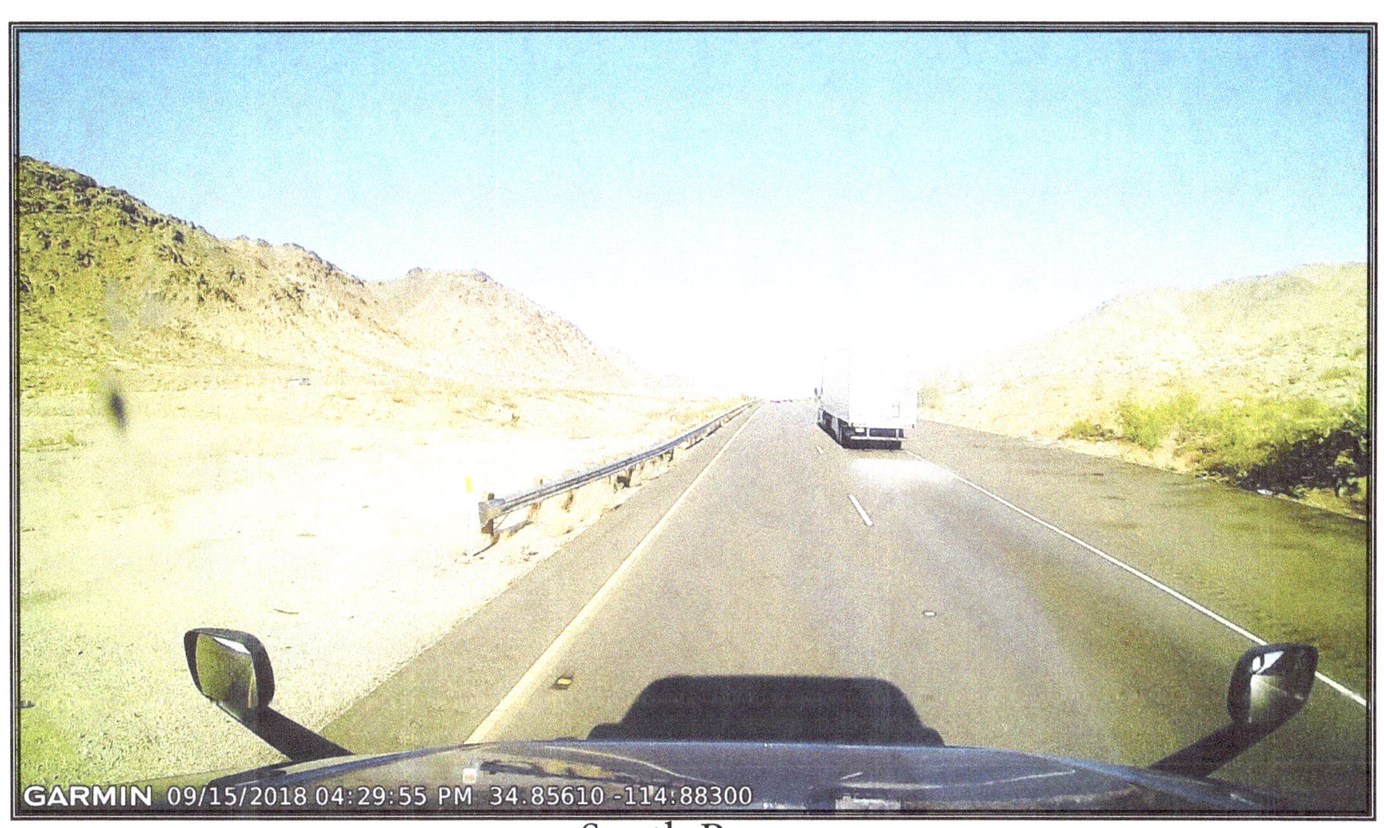

South Pass
I-40, Horner, California

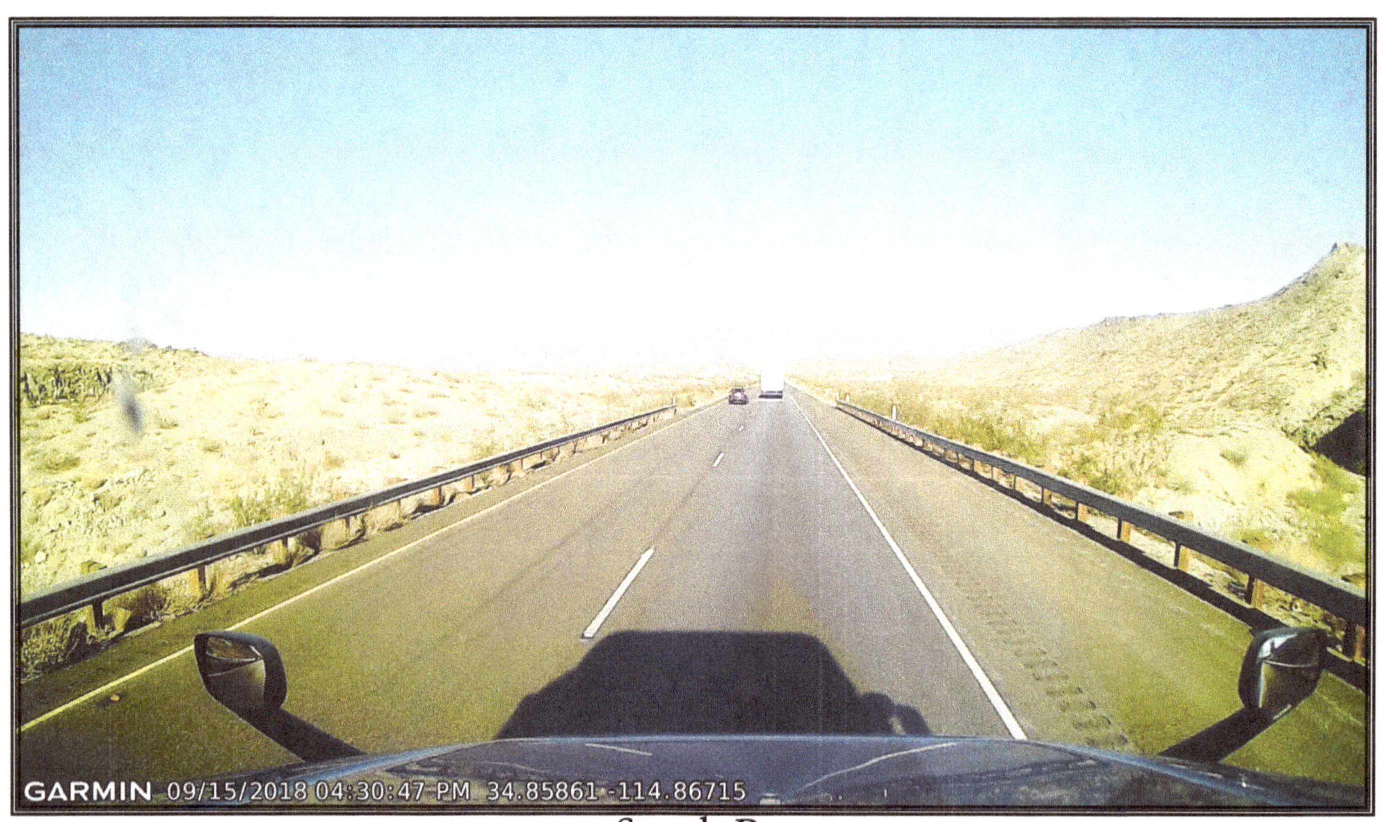

South Pass
I-40, Horner, California

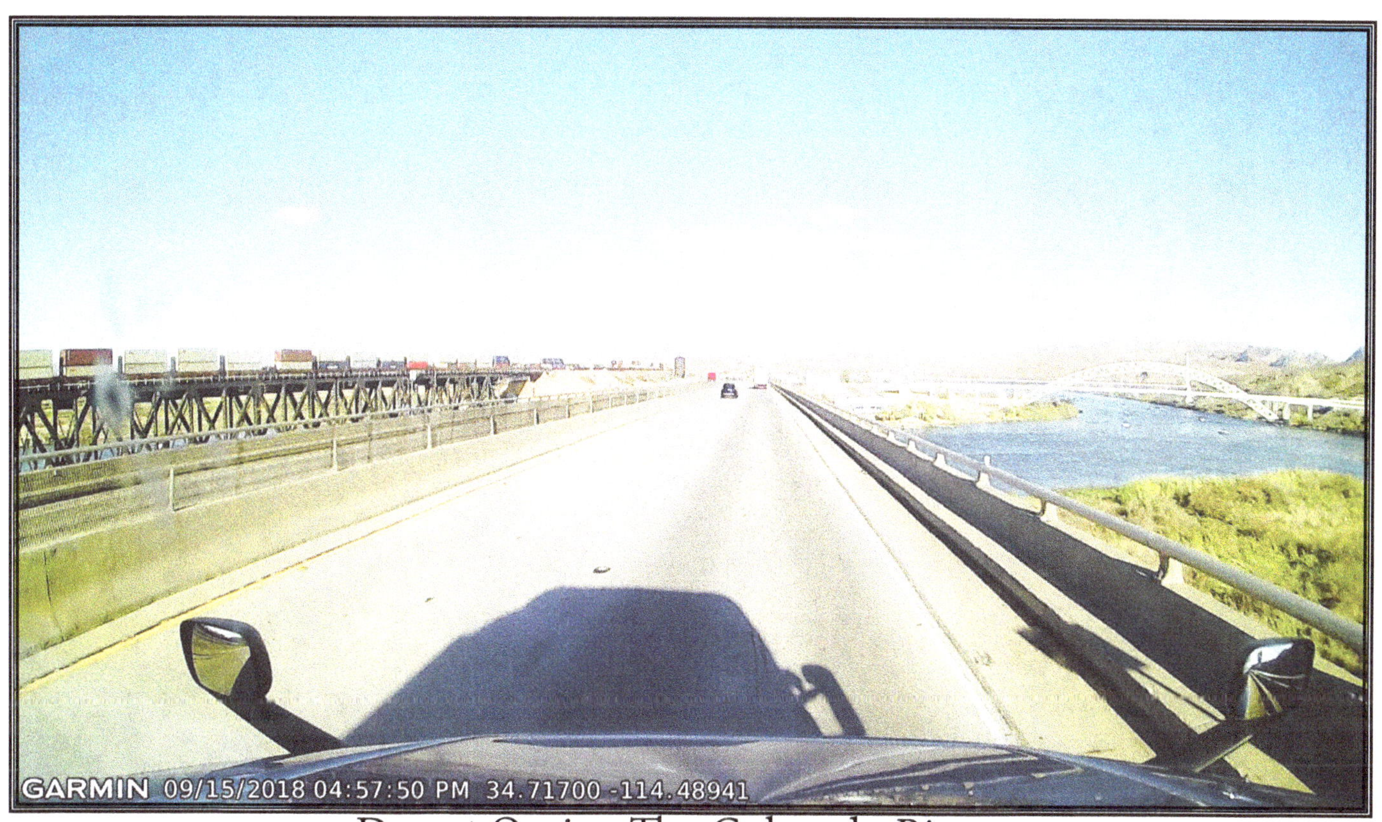

Desert Oasis - The Colorado River
I-40, Needles, California

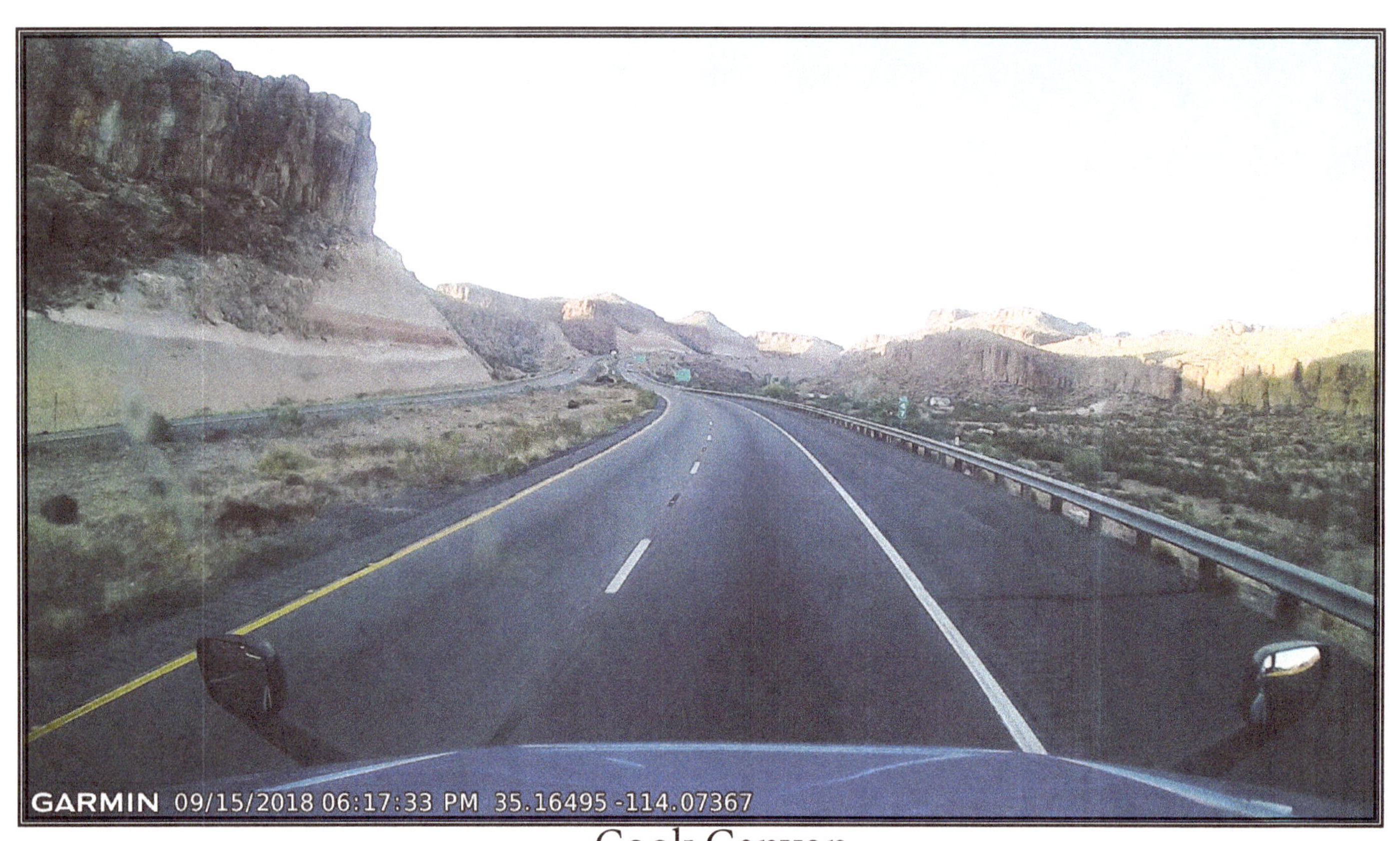

Cook Canyon
I-40, Golden Valley, Arizona

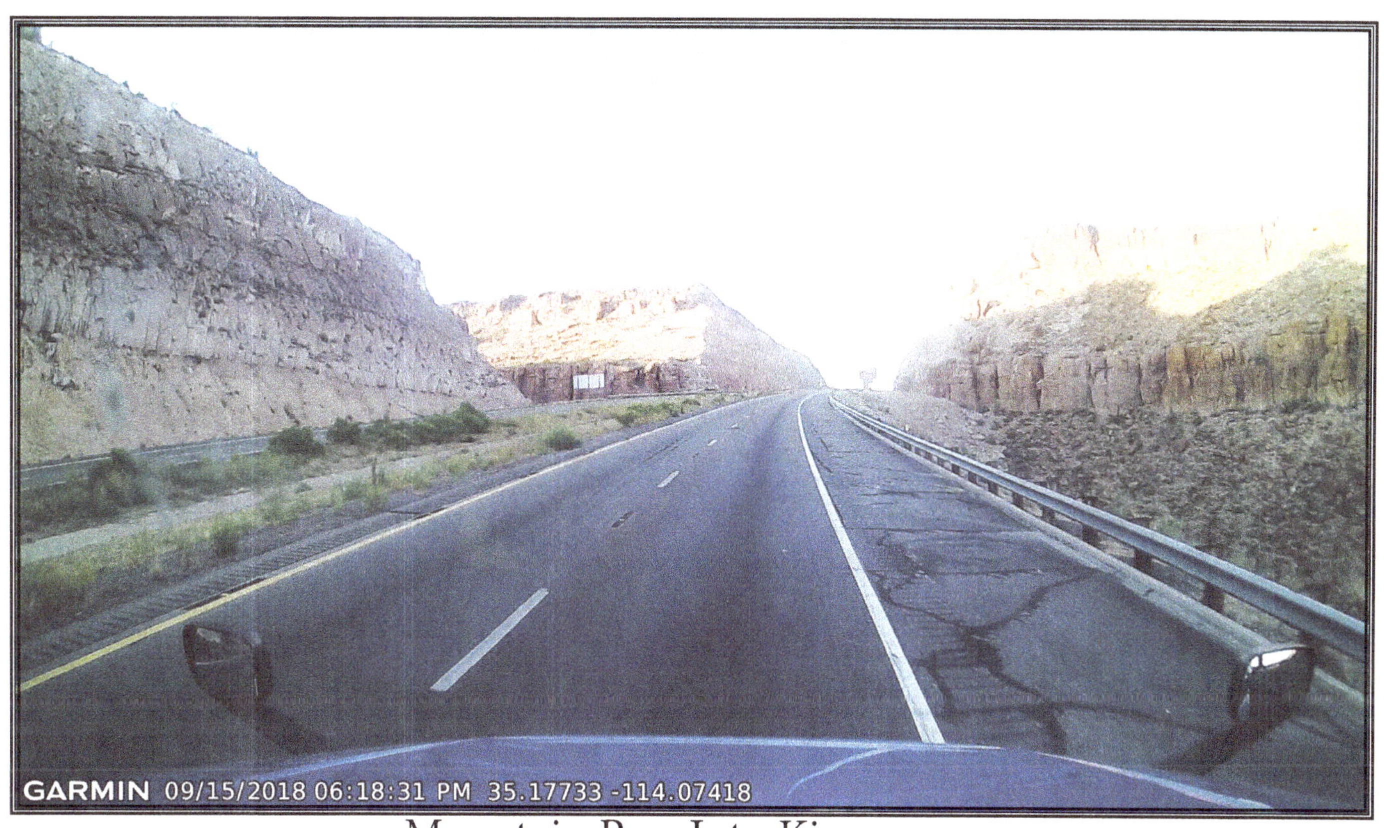

Mountain Pass Into Kingman
I-40, Kingman, Arizona

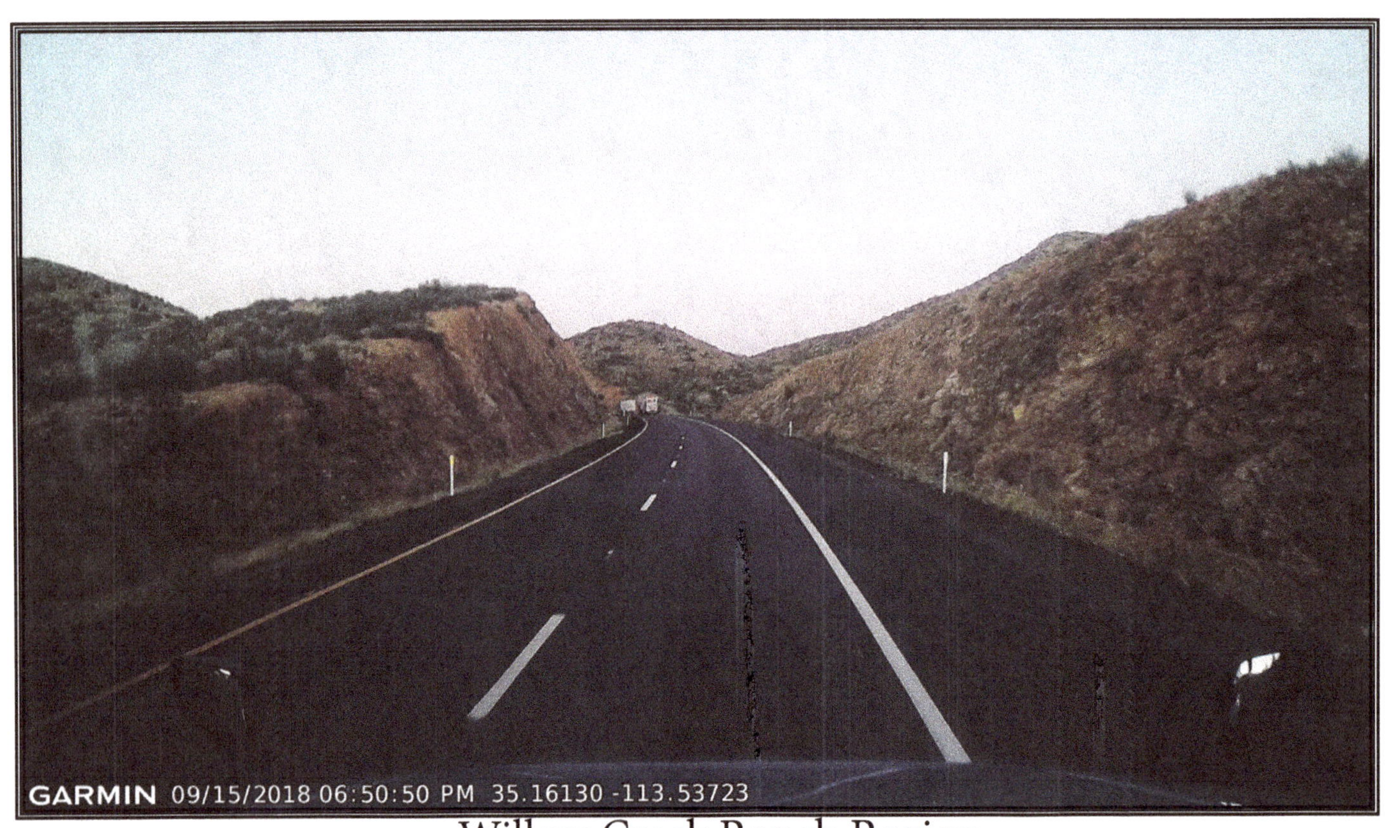

Willow Creek Ranch Region
I-40, Kingman, Arizona

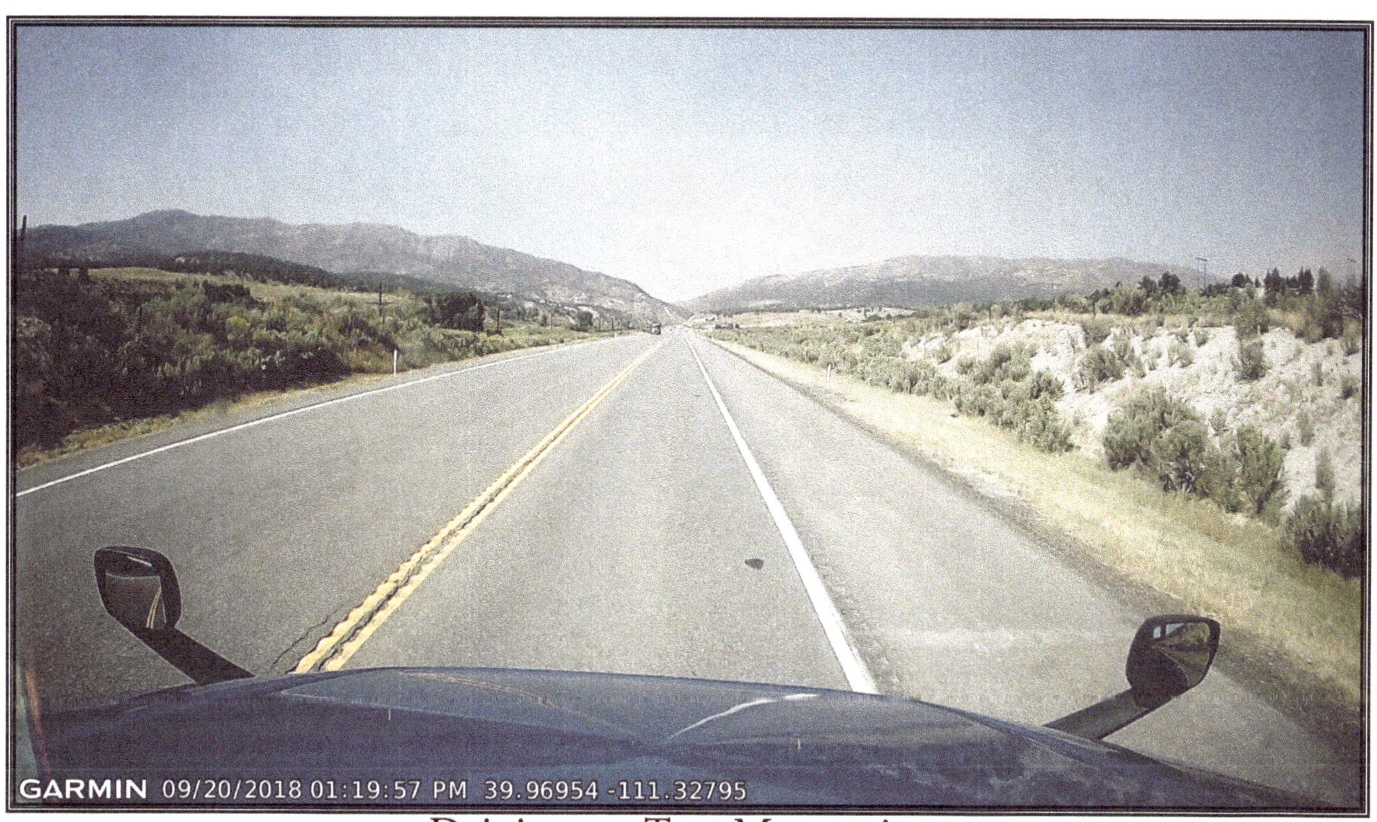

Driving up Teat Mountain
US-6, Spanish Fork, Utah

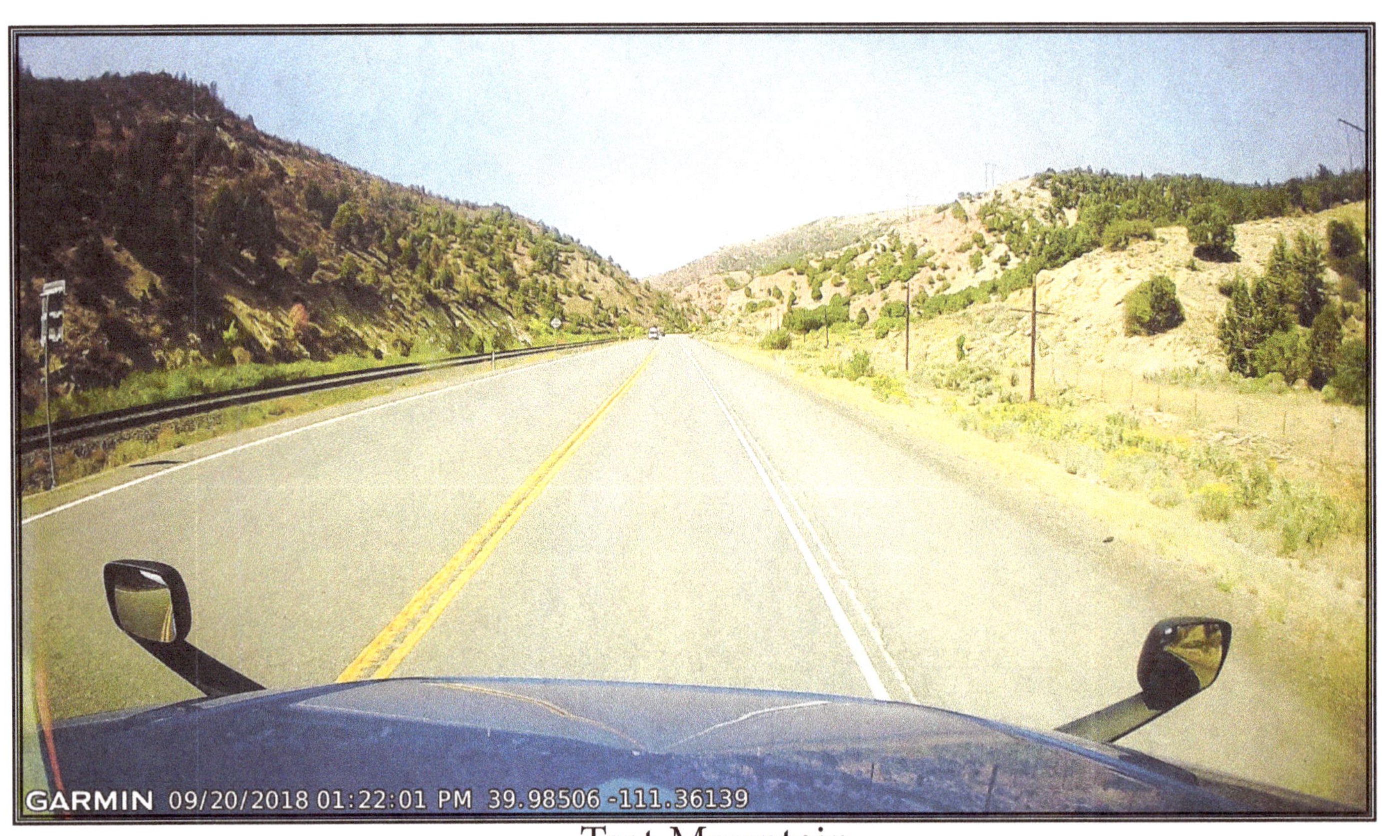

Teat Mountain
US-6, Spanish Fork, Utah

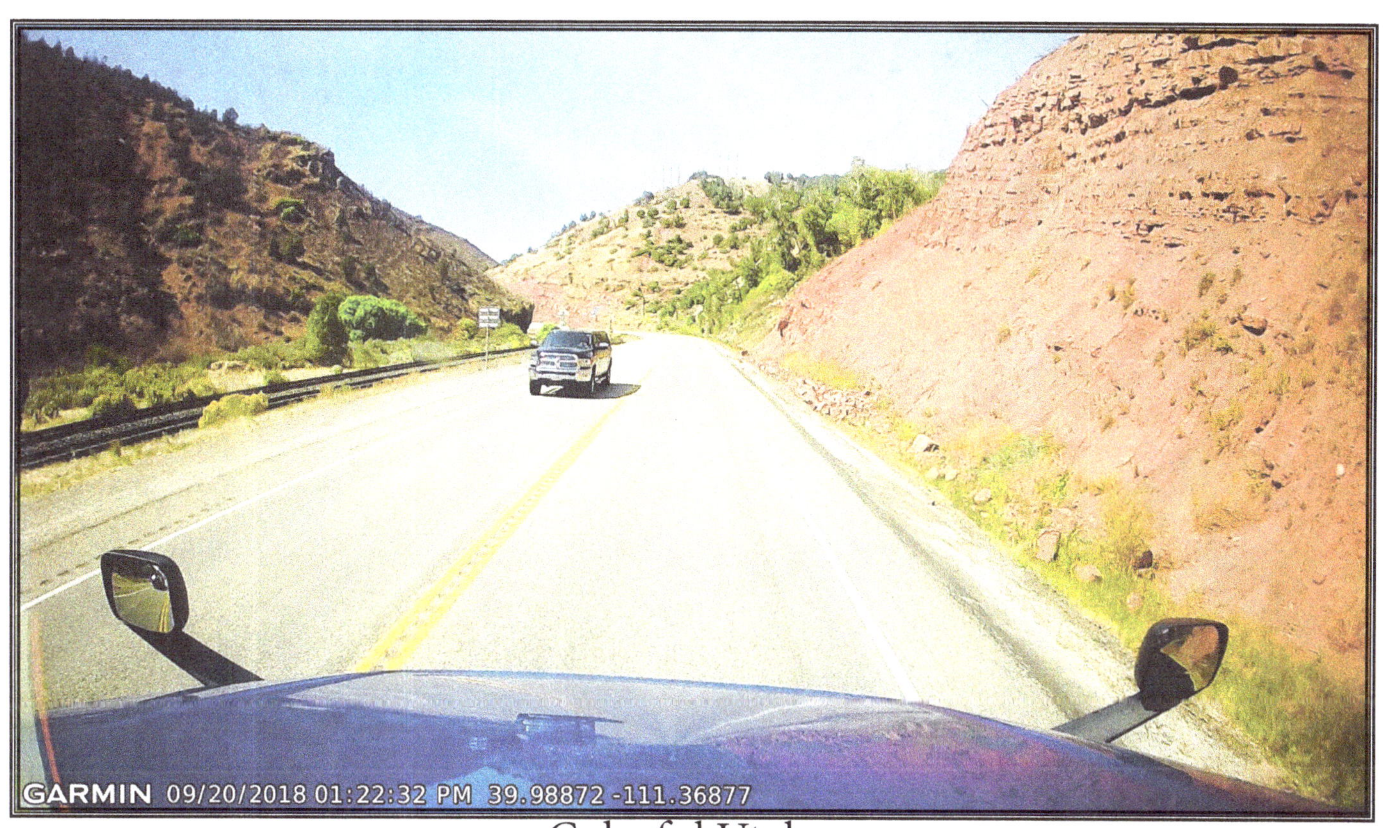

Colorful Utah
US-6, Spanish Fork, Utah

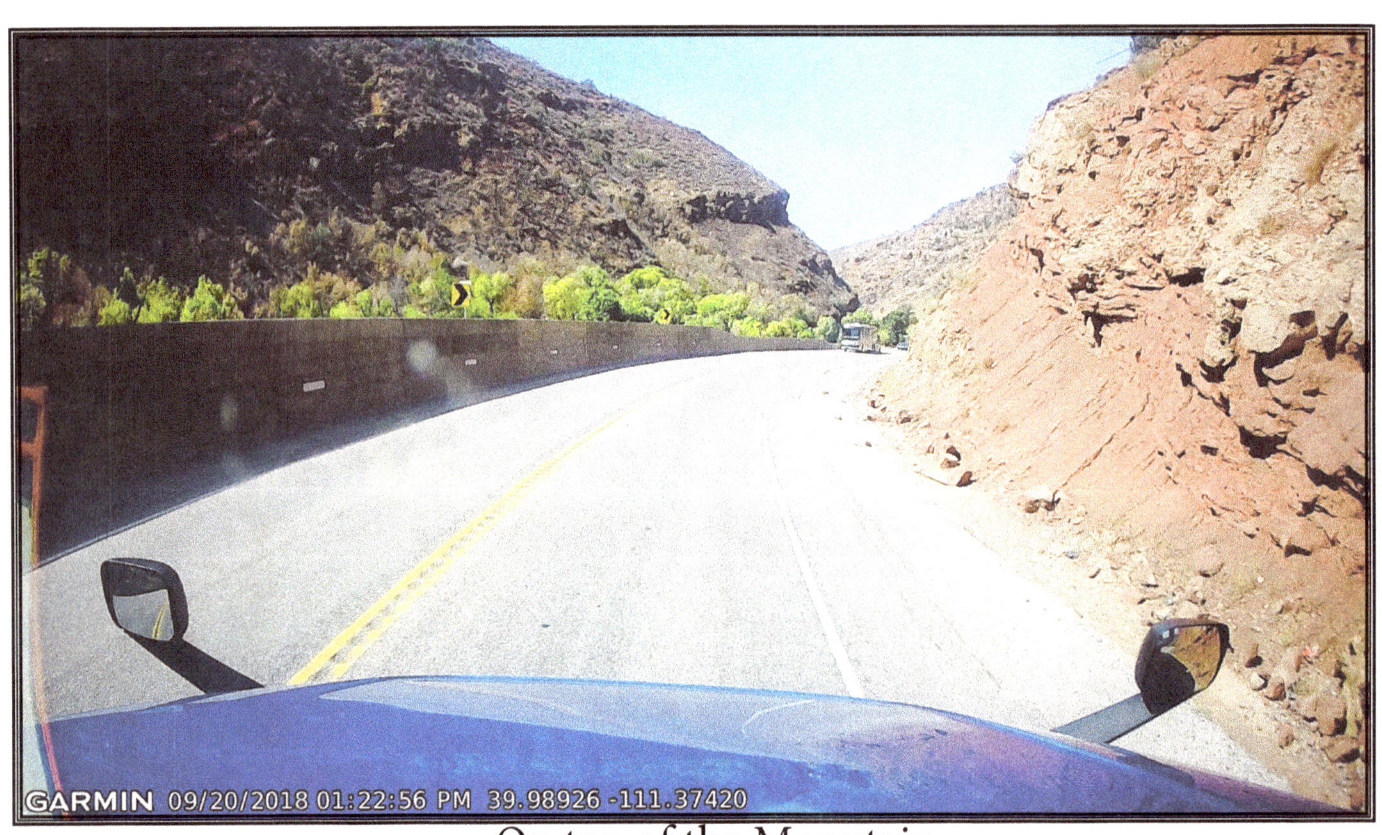

On top of the Mountain
US-6, Spanish Fork, Utah

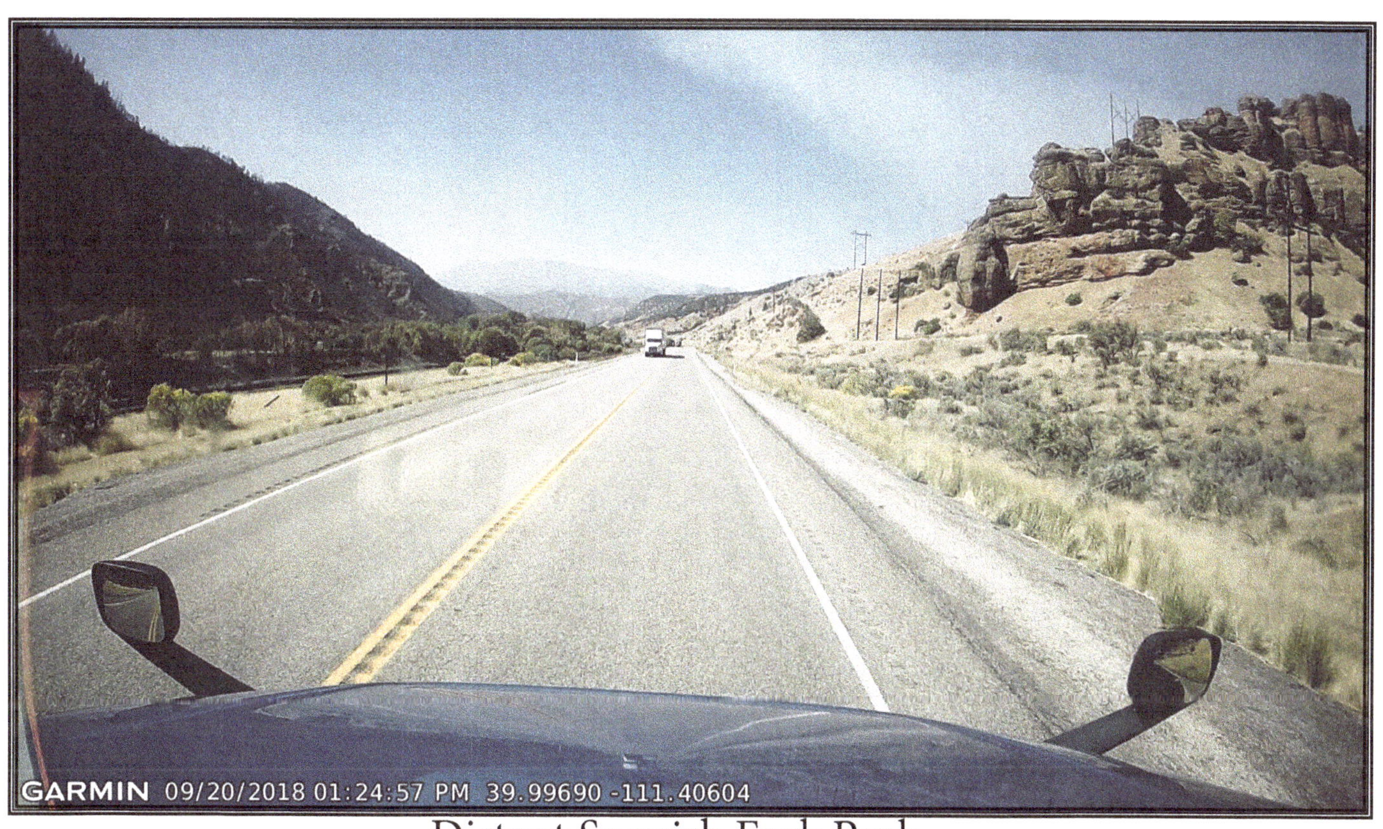

Distant Spanish Fork Peak
US-6, Thistle, Utah

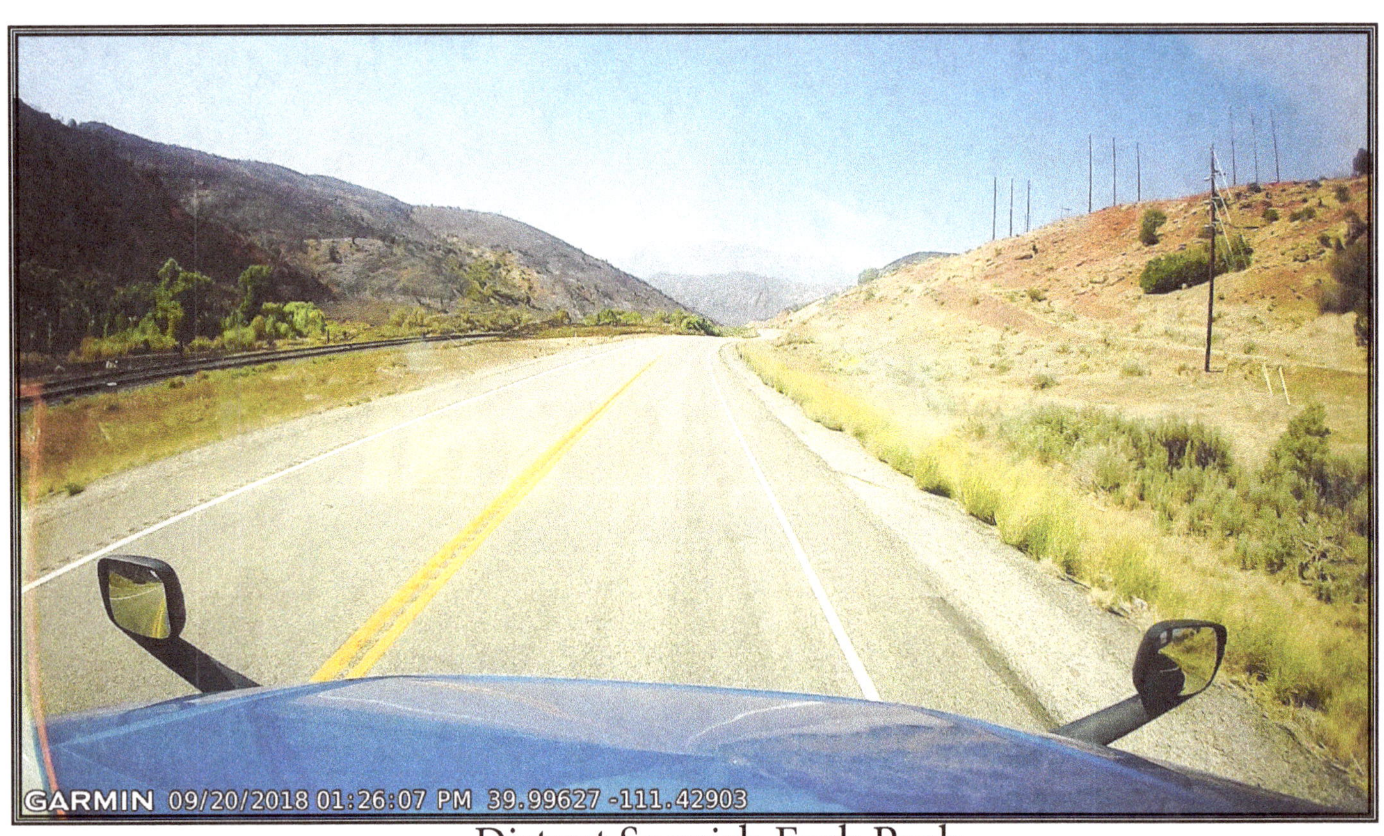

Distant Spanish Fork Peak
US-6, Thistle, Utah

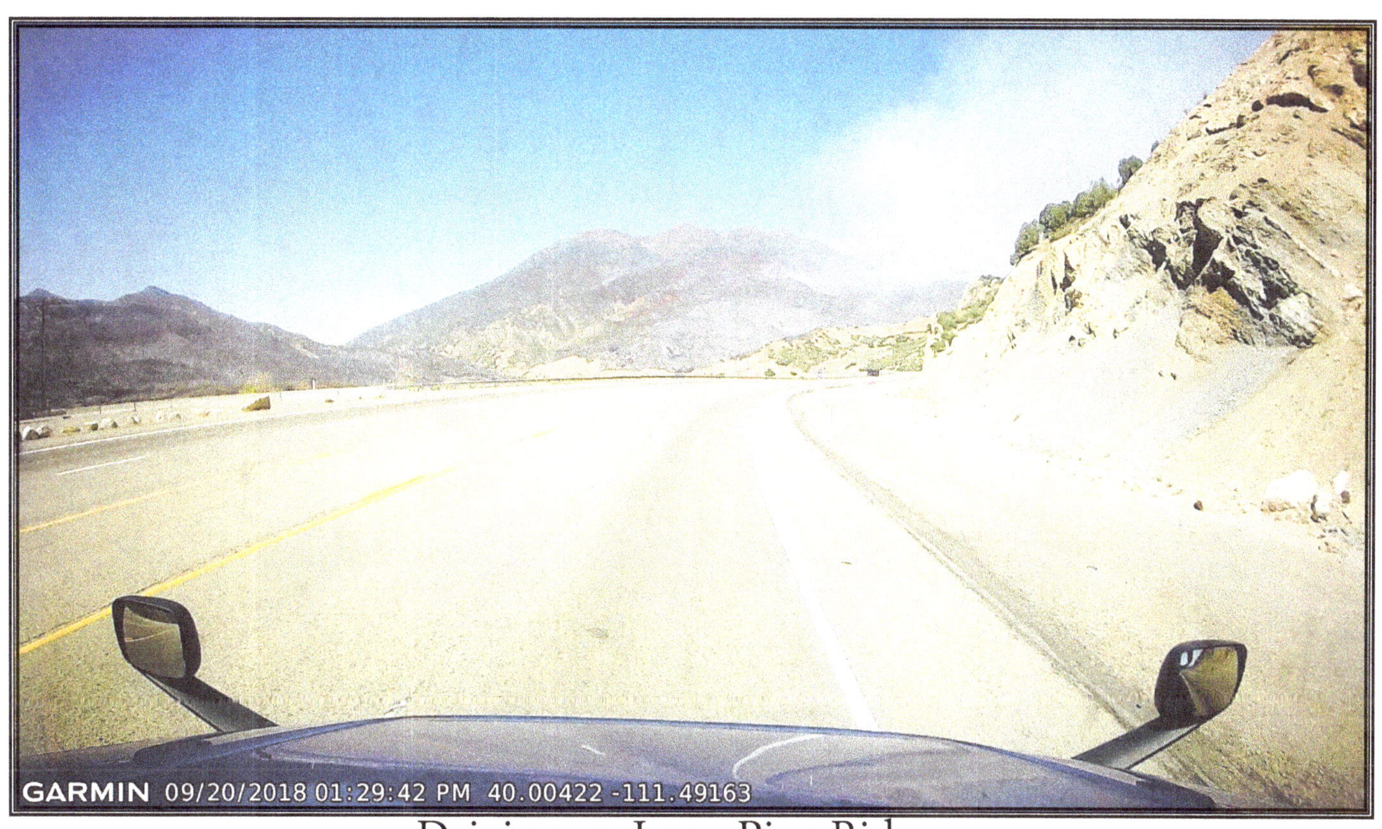

Driving up Lone Pine Ridge
US-6, Thistle, Utah

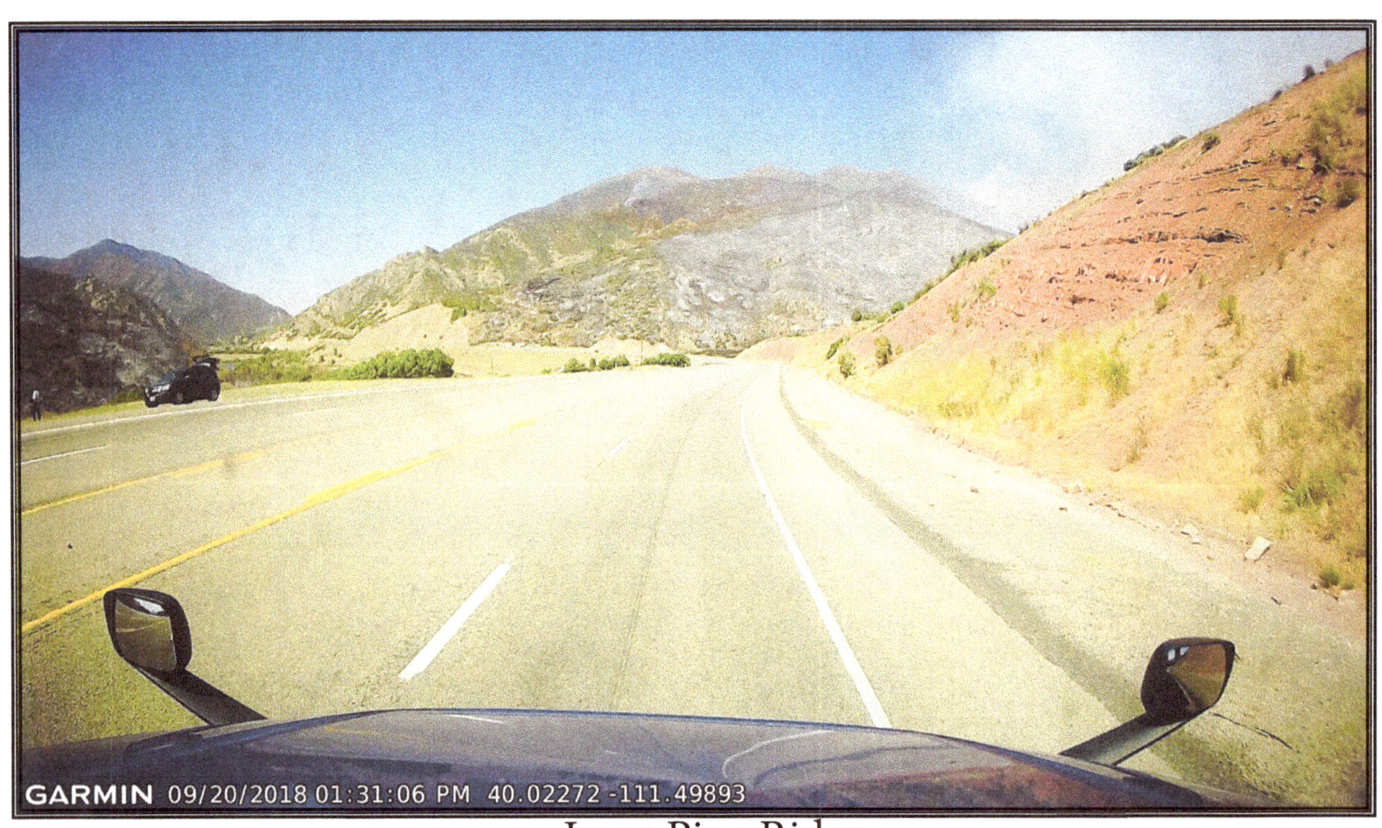

Lone Pine Ridge
US-6, Thistle, Utah

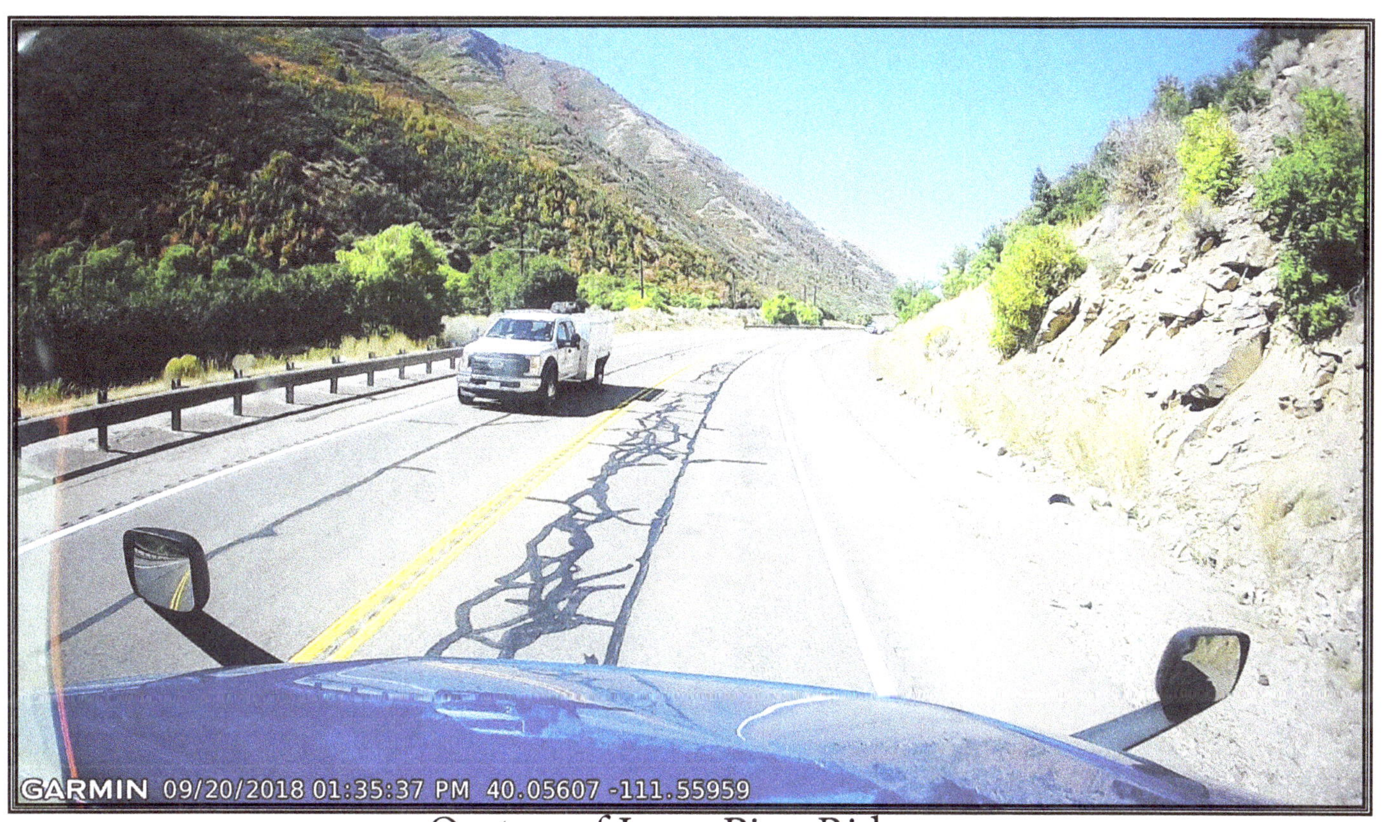

On top of Lone Pine Ridge
US-6, Thistle, Utah

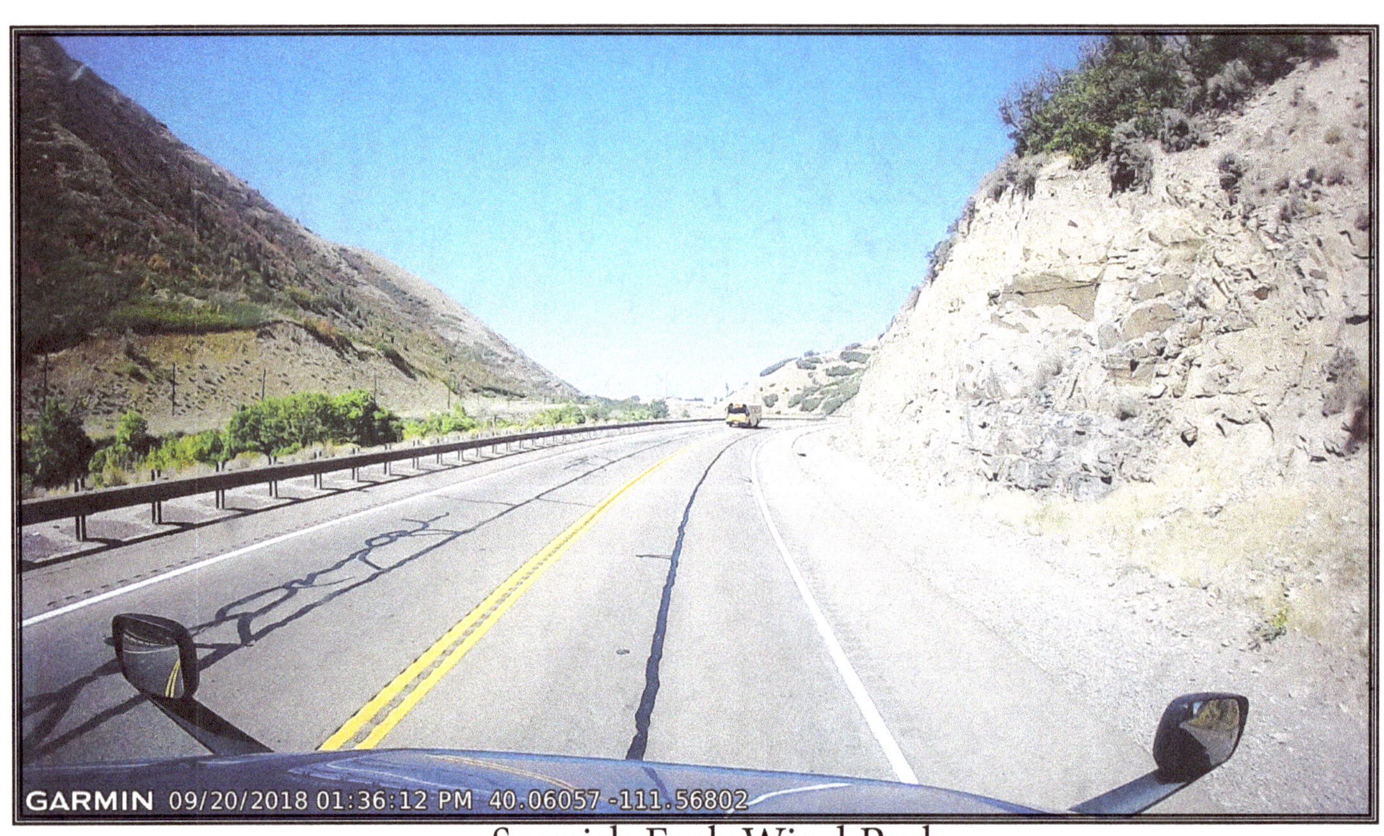

Spanish Fork Wind Park
US-6, Spanish Fork, Utah

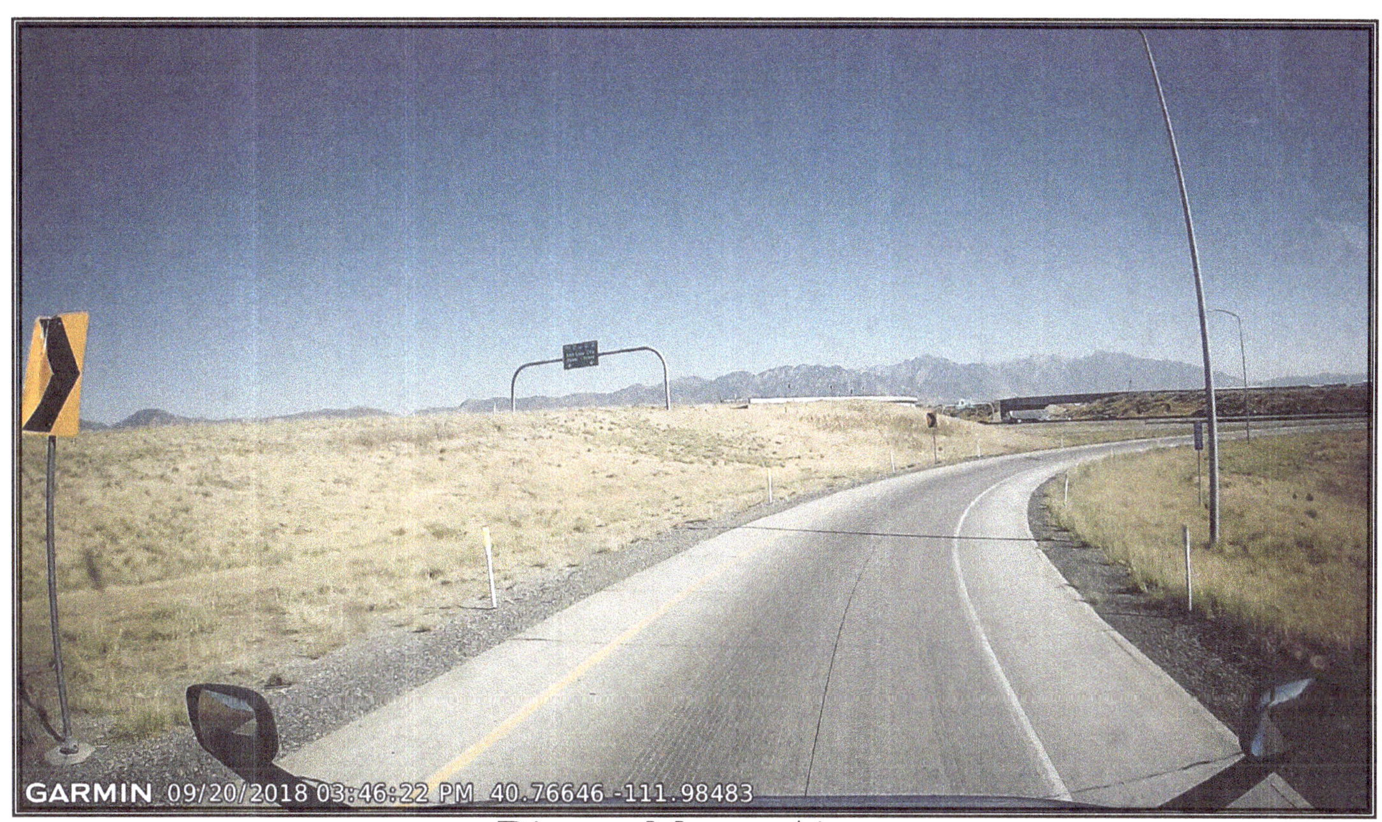

Distant Mount Aire
I-80, Salt Lake City, Utah

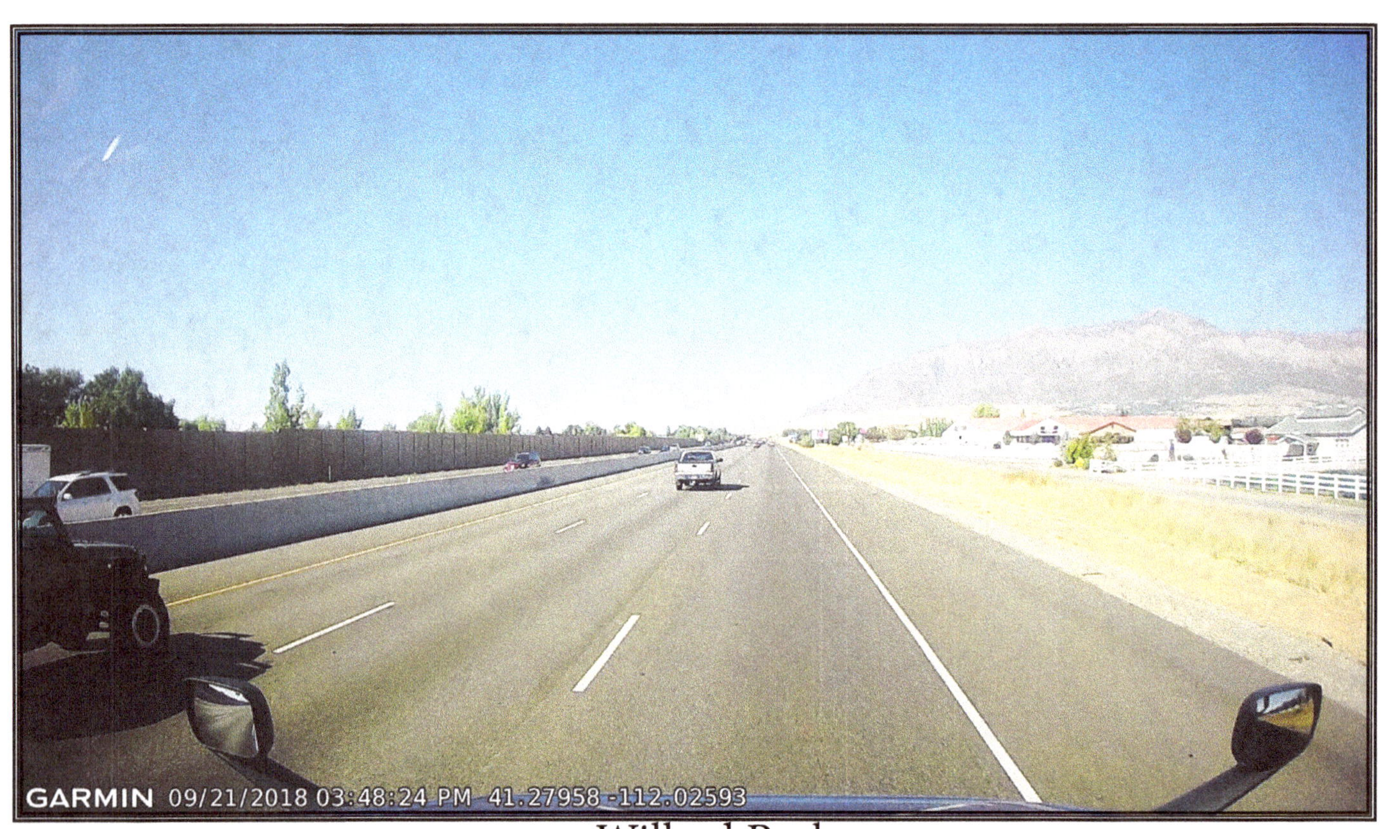

Willard Peak
I-15, Farr West, Utah

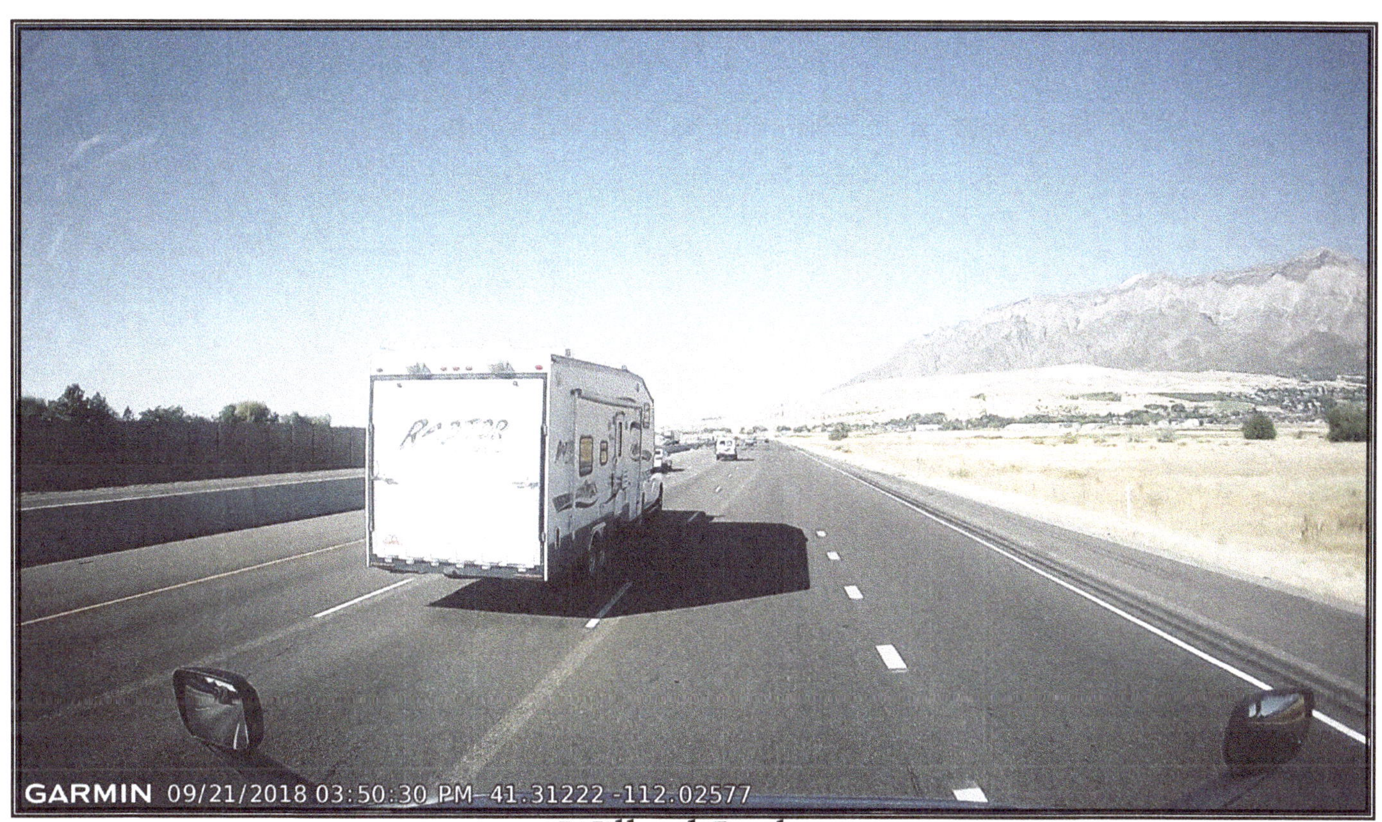

Willard Peak
I-15, Farr West, Utah

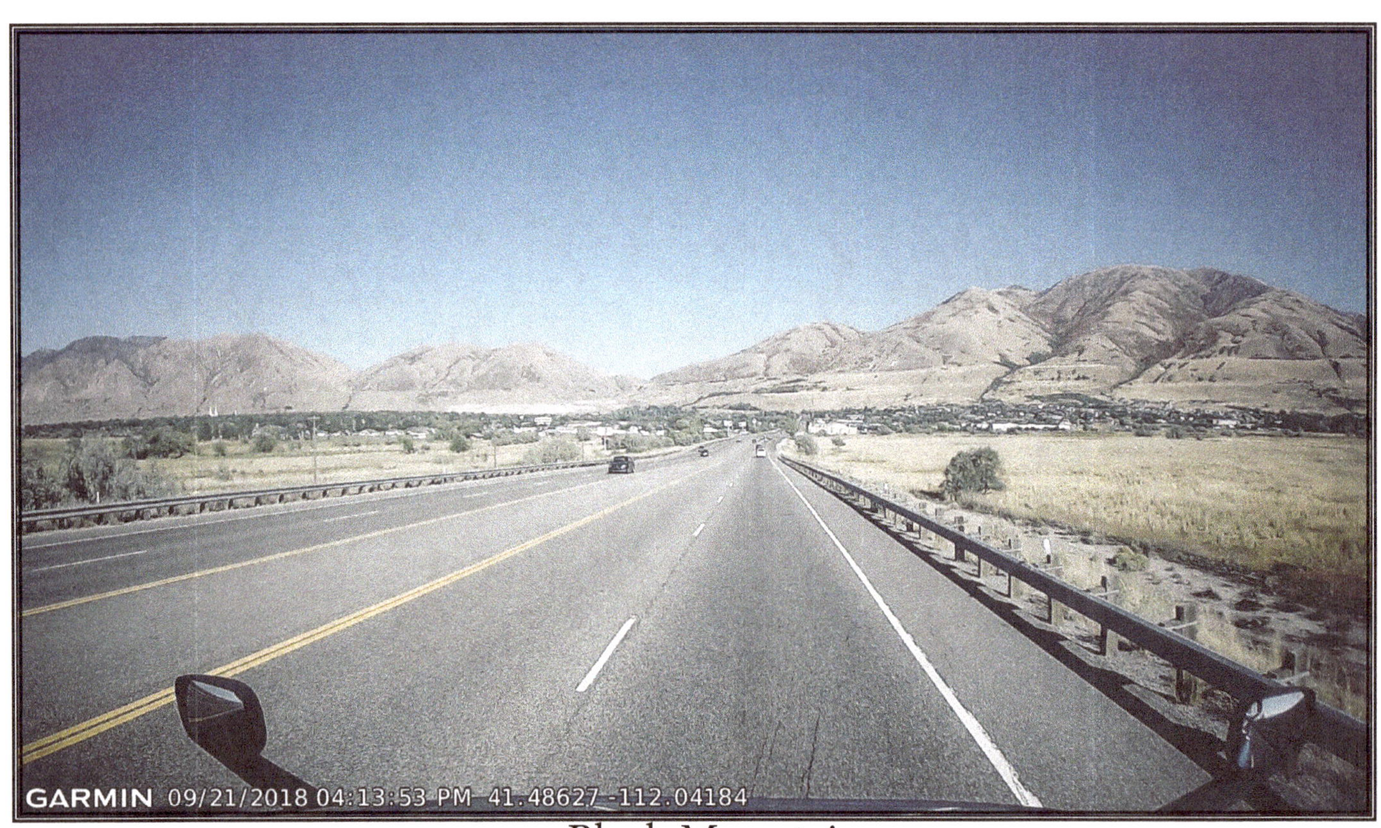

Black Mountain
US-91, Brigham City, Utah

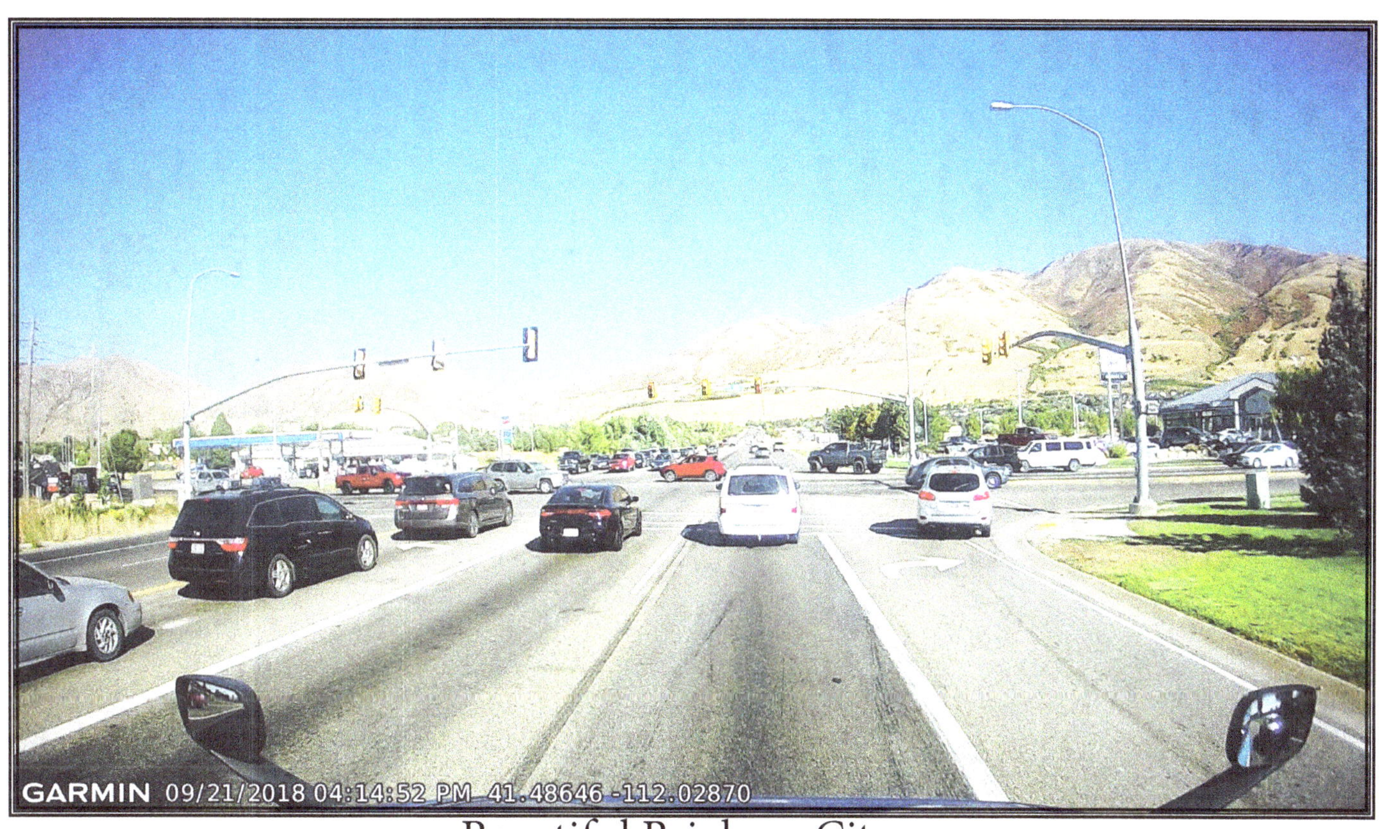

Beautiful Brigham City
US-91, Brigham City, Utah

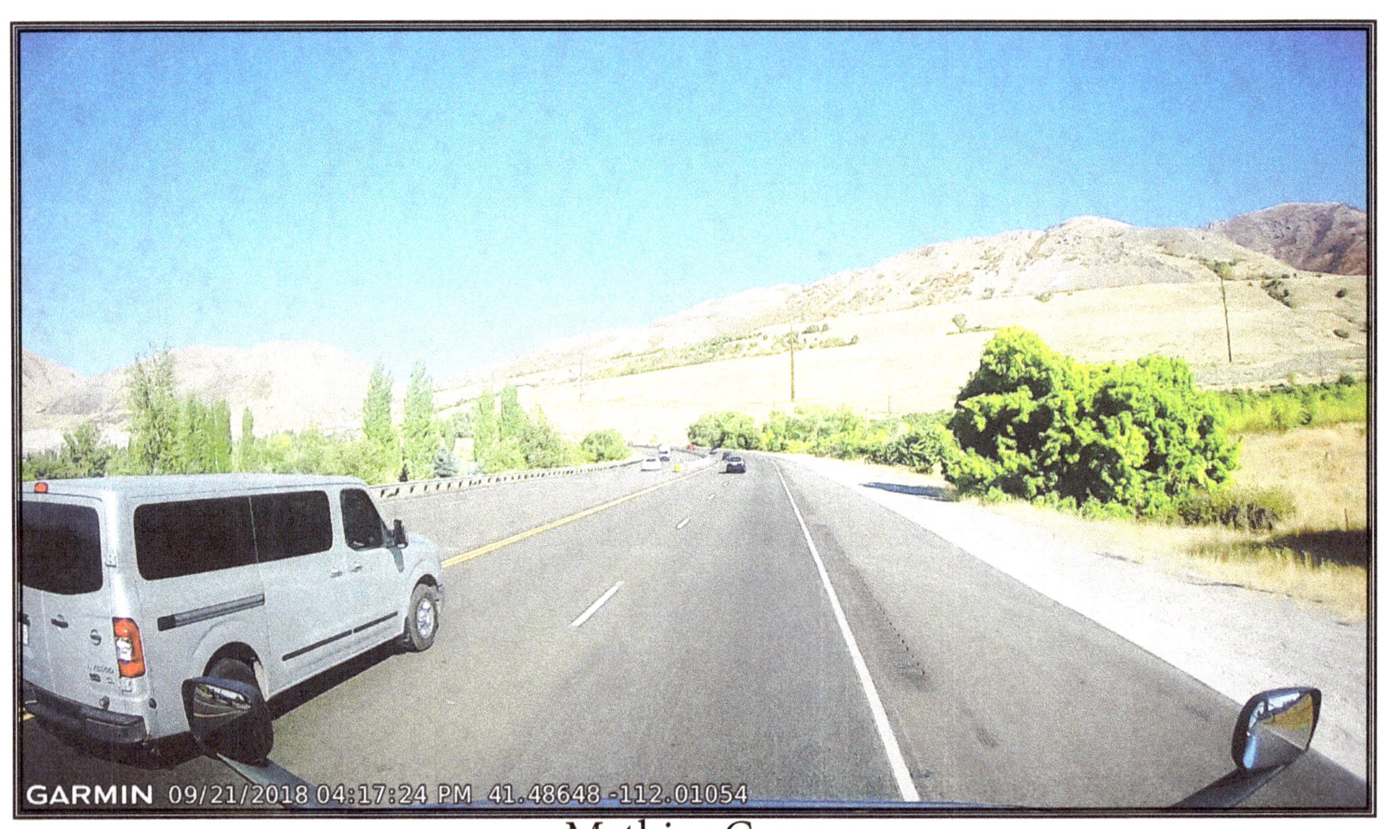

Mathias Canyon
US-91, Brigham City, Utah

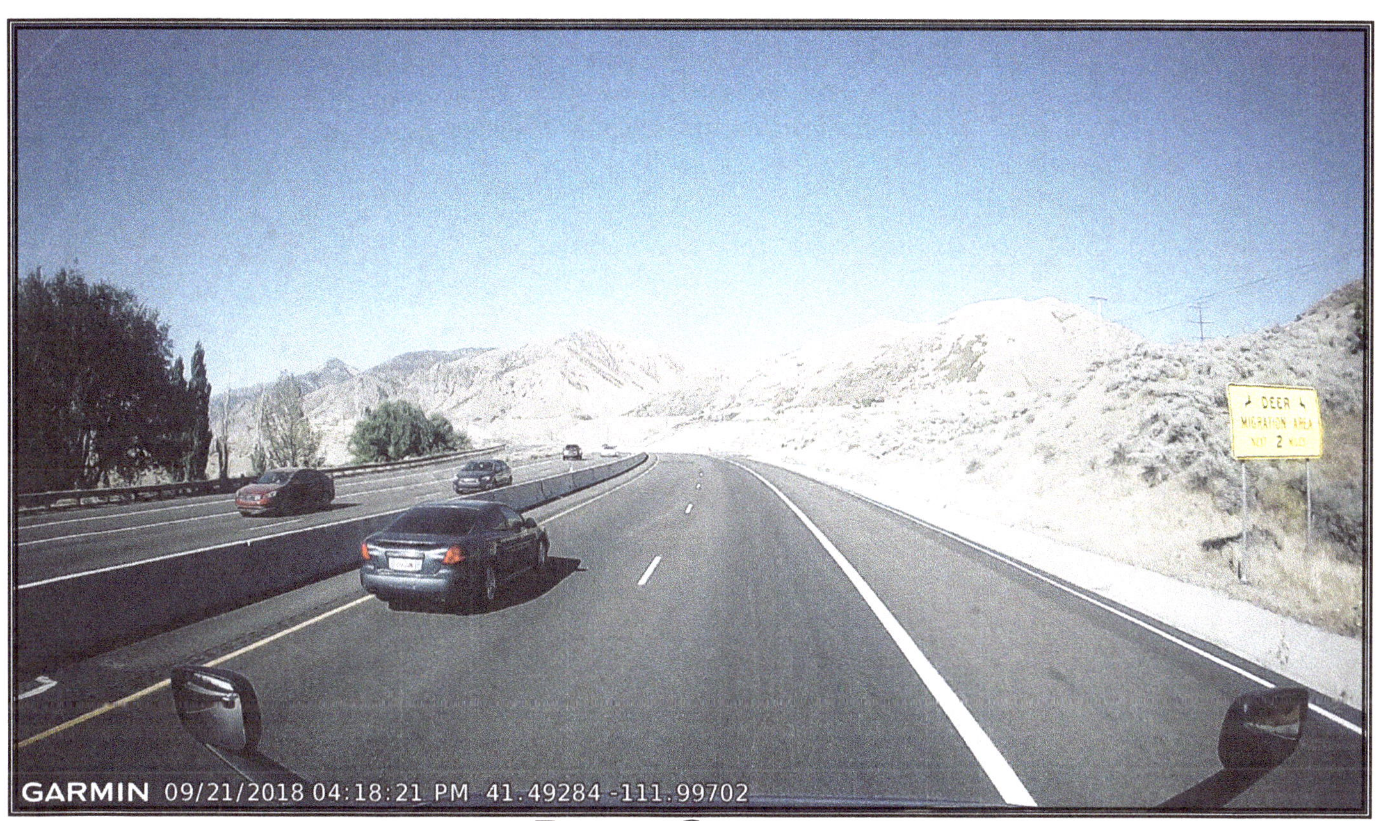

Dunns Canyon
US-91, Brigham City, Utah

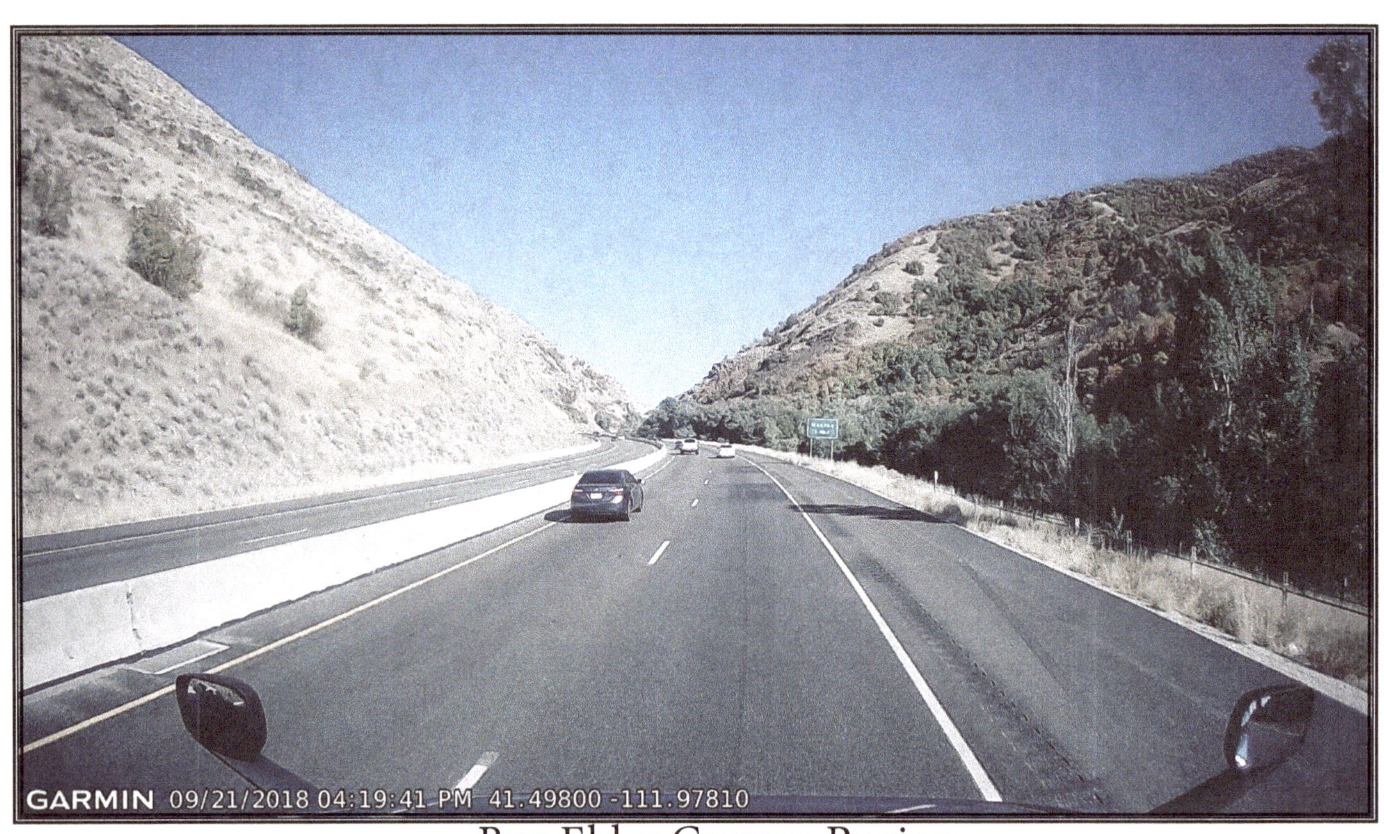

Box Elder Canyon Region
US-89, Brigham City, Utah

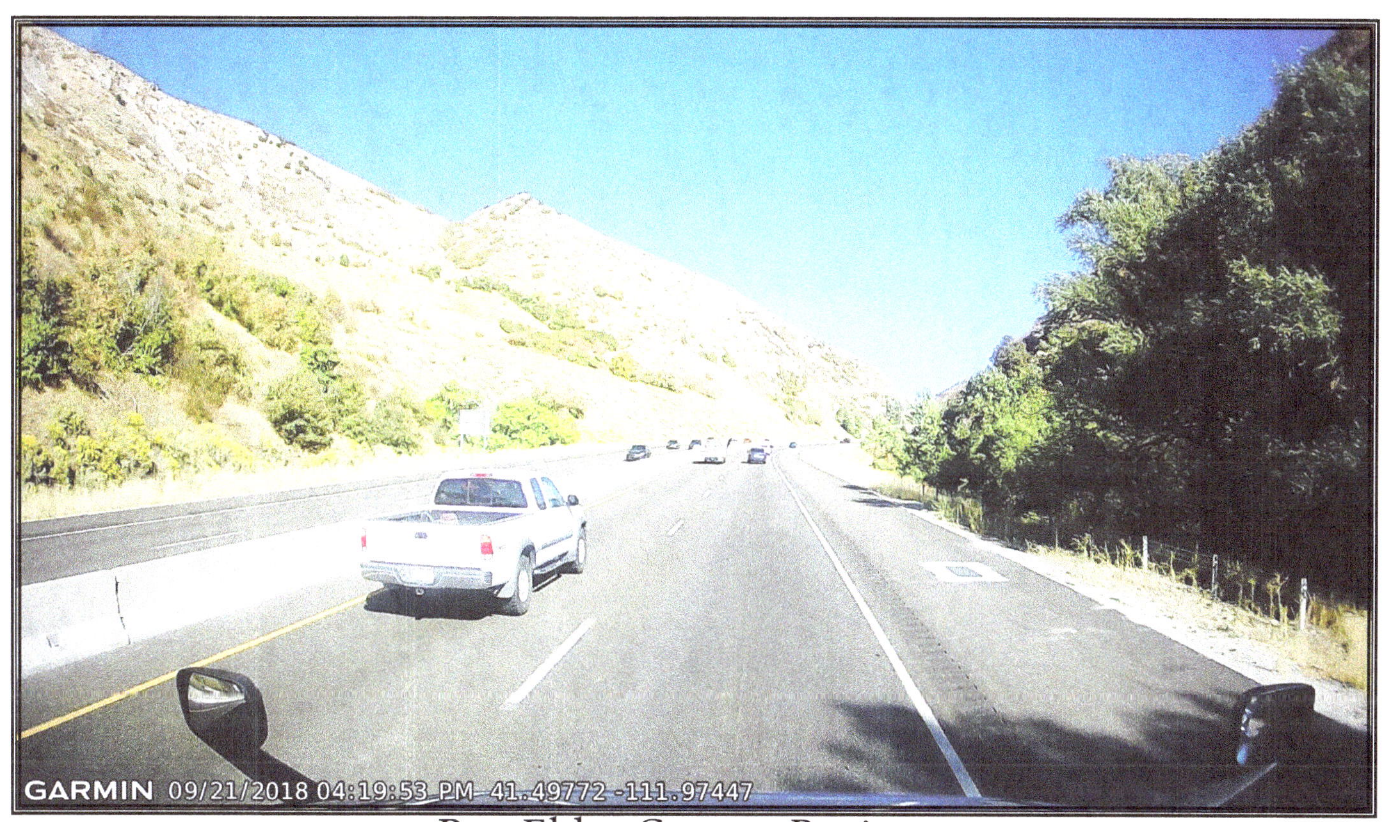

Box Elder Canyon Region
US-89, Brigham City, Utah

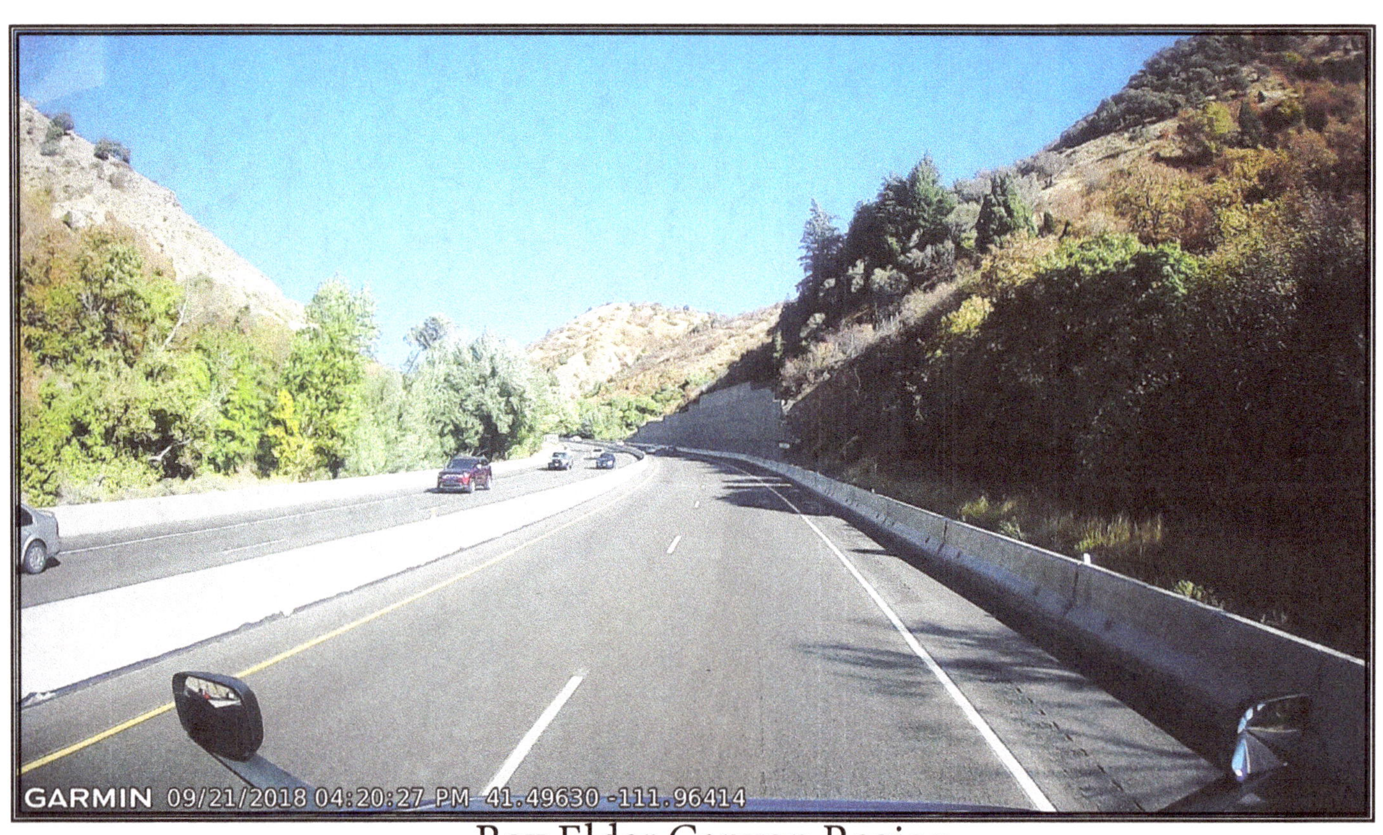

Box Elder Canyon Region
US-89, Brigham City, Utah

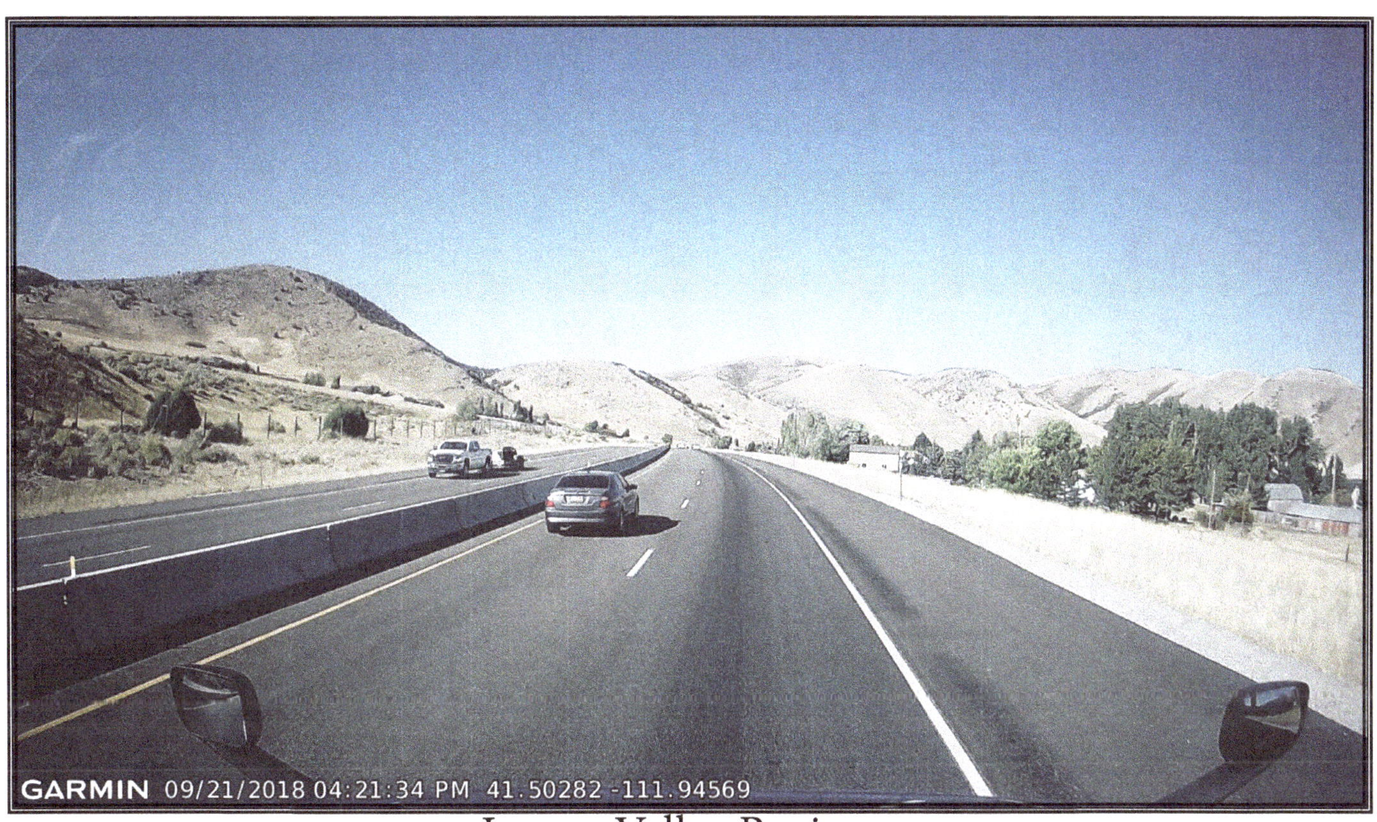

Jepsen Valley Region
US-89, Mantua, Utah

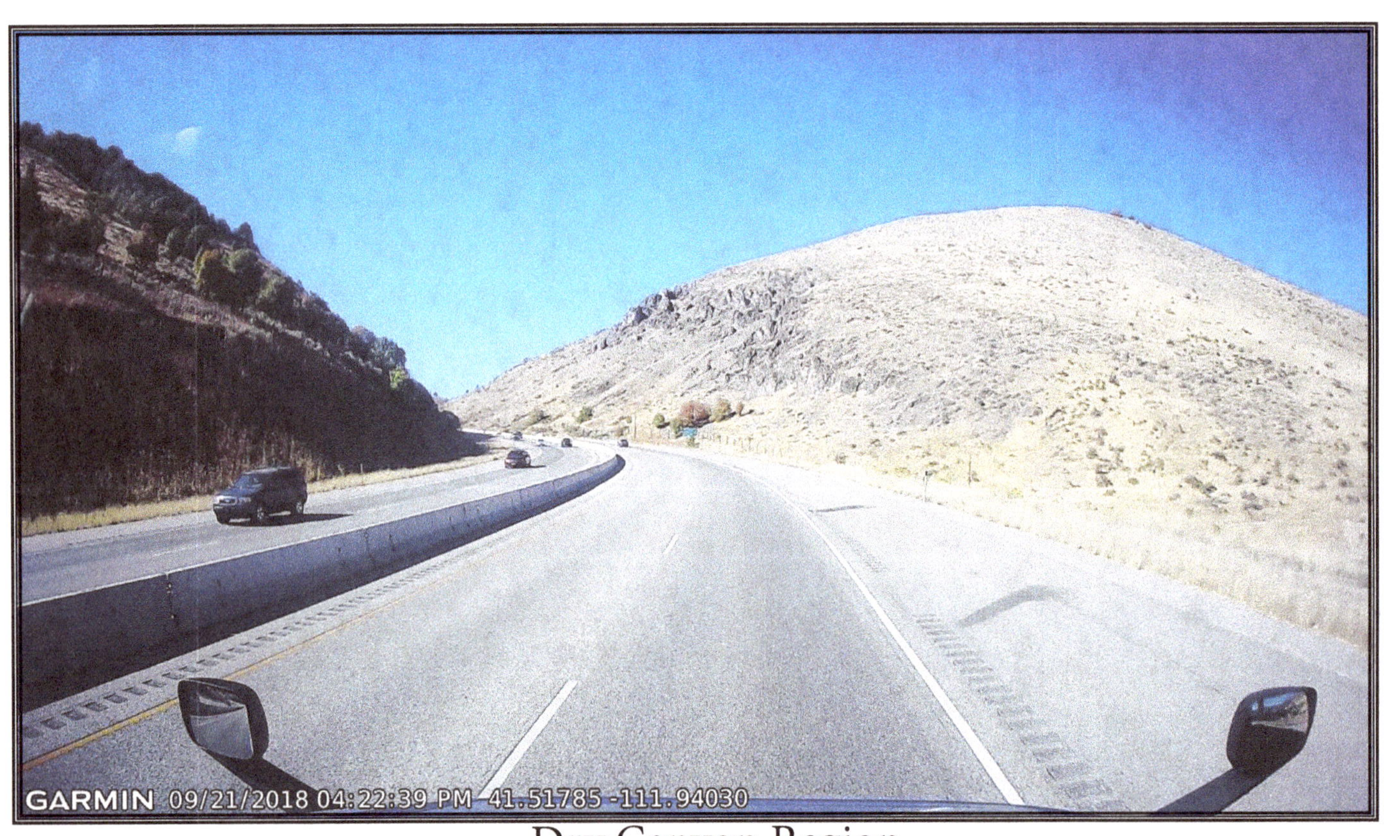

Dry Canyon Region
US-89, Mantua, Utah

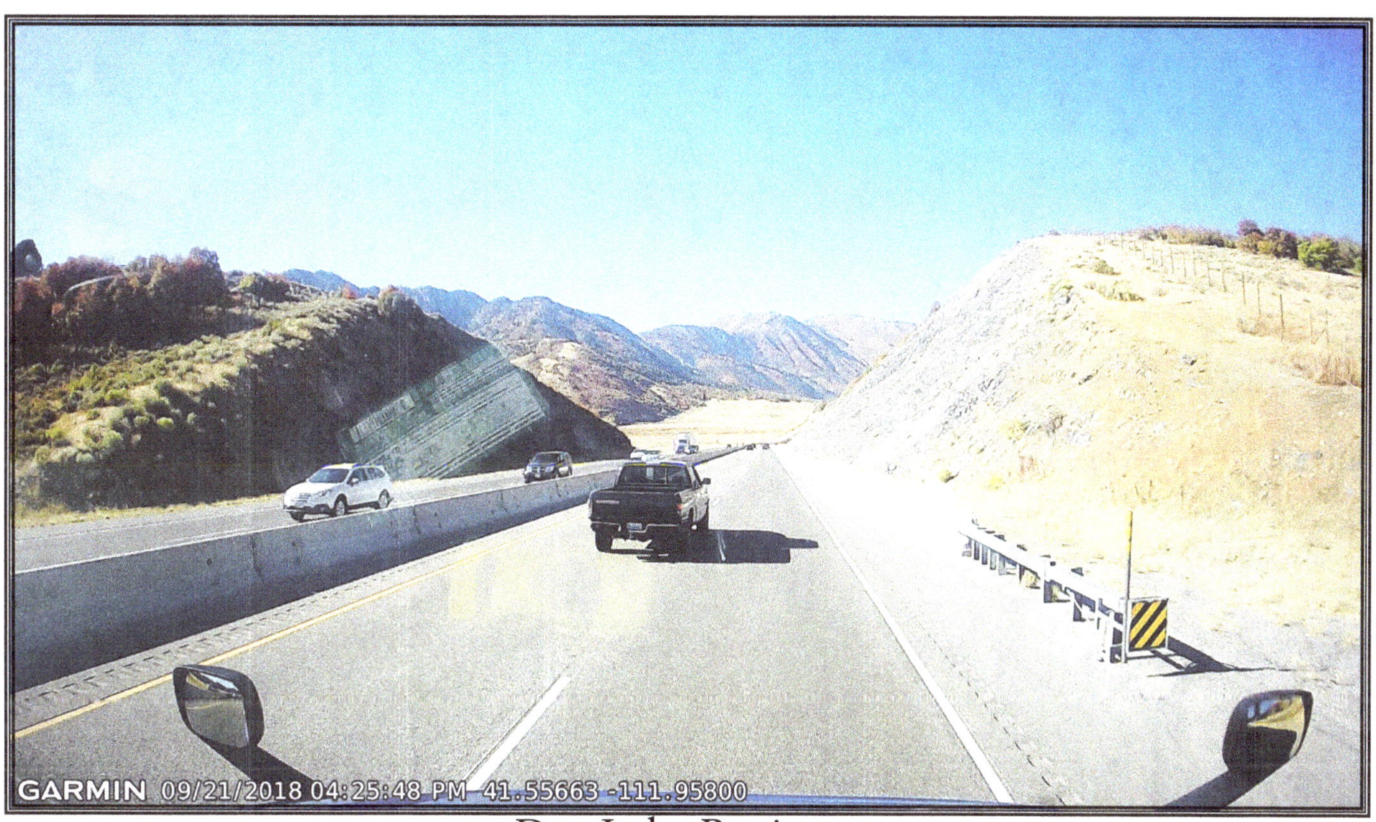

Dry Lake Region
US-89, Wellsville, Utah

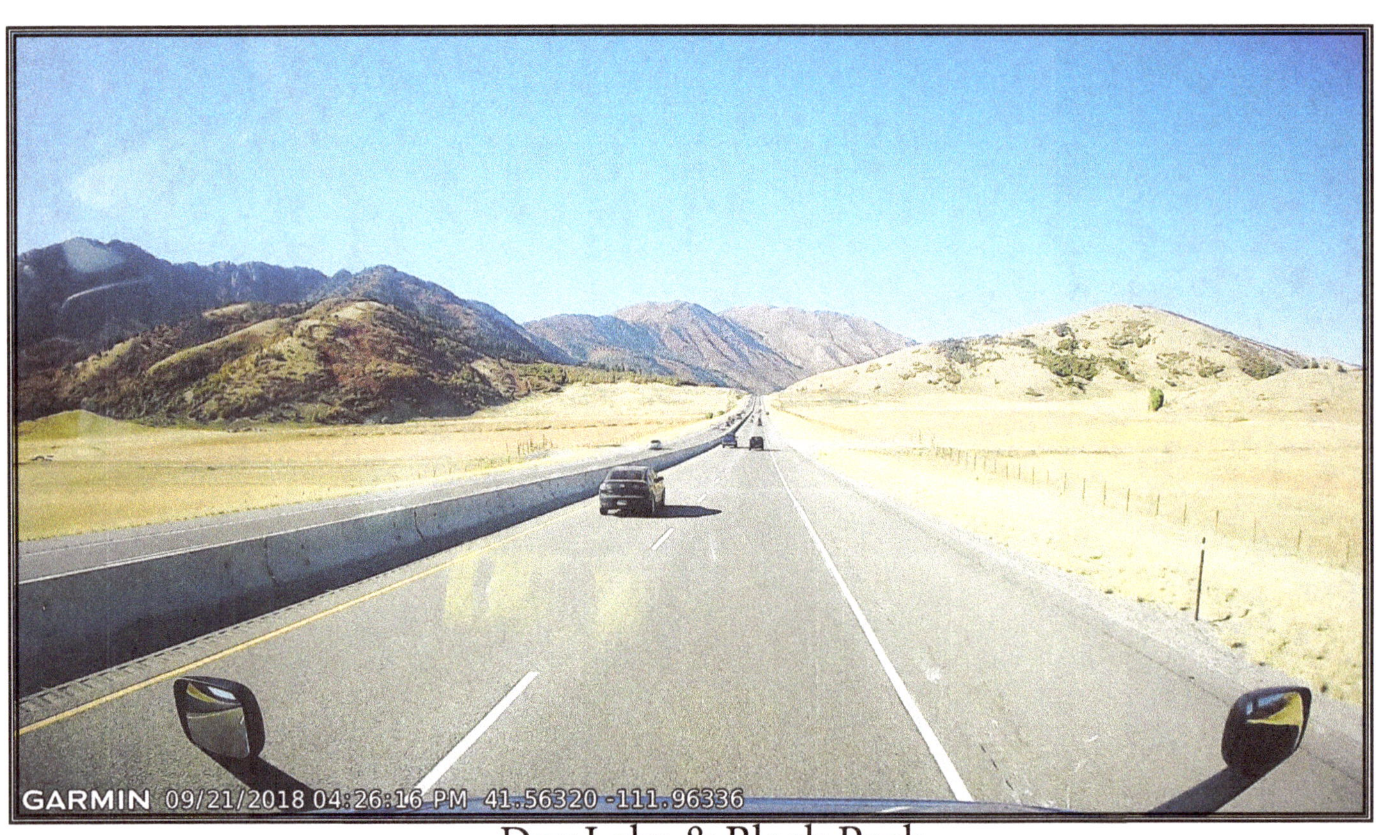

Dry Lake & Black Peak
US-89, Wellsville, Utah

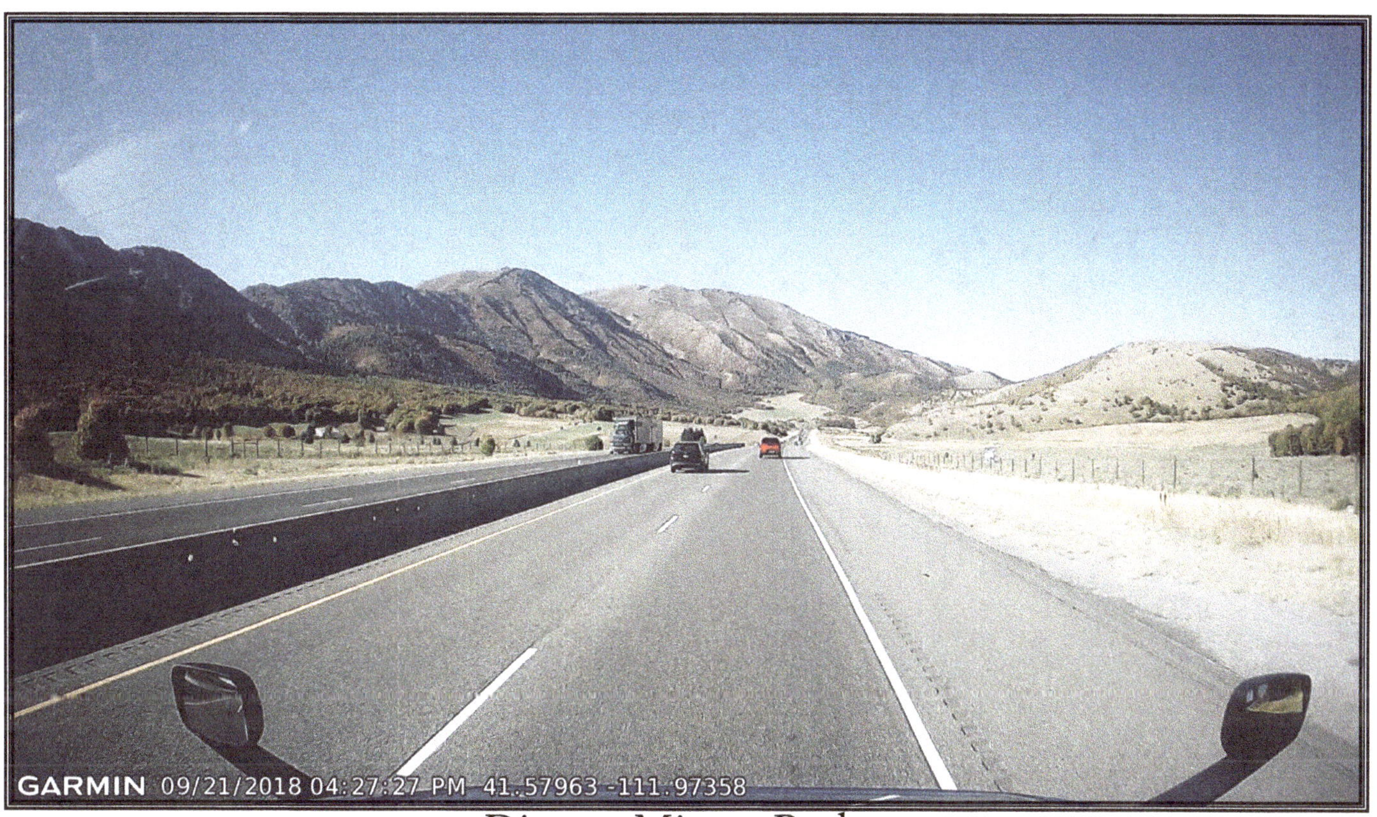

Distant Mitton Peak
US-89, Wellsville, Utah

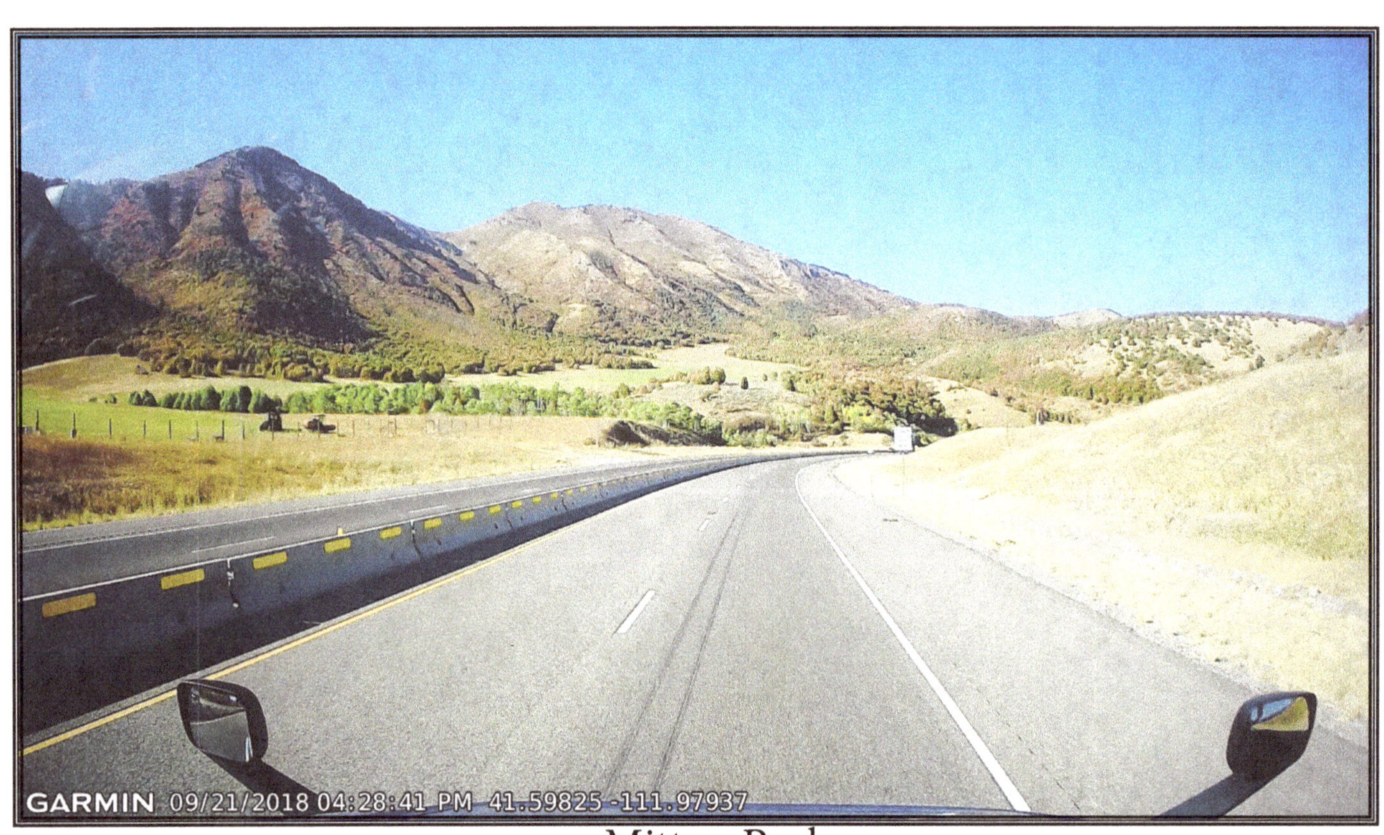

Mitton Peak
US-89, Wellsville, Utah

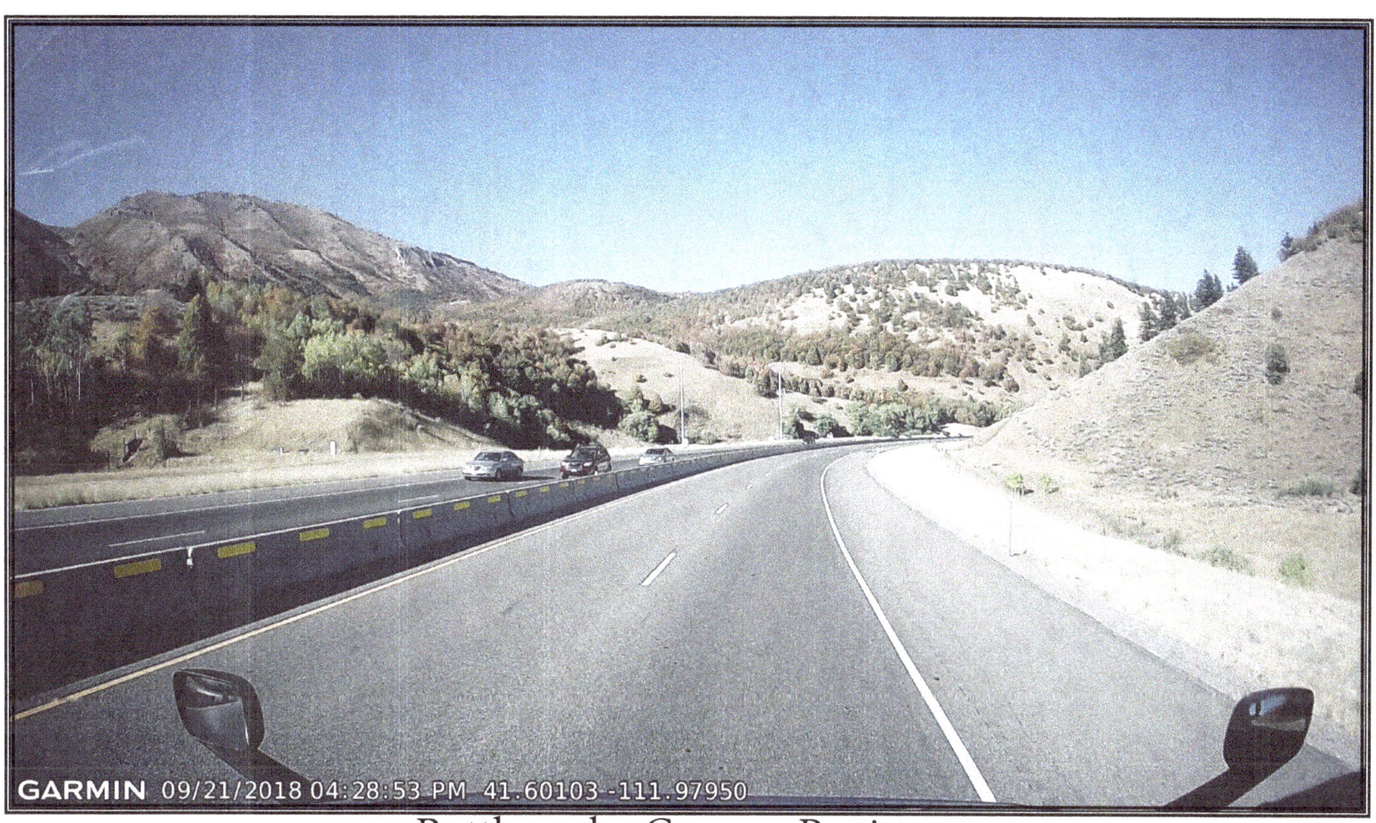

Rattlesnake Canyon Region
US-89, Wellsville, Utah

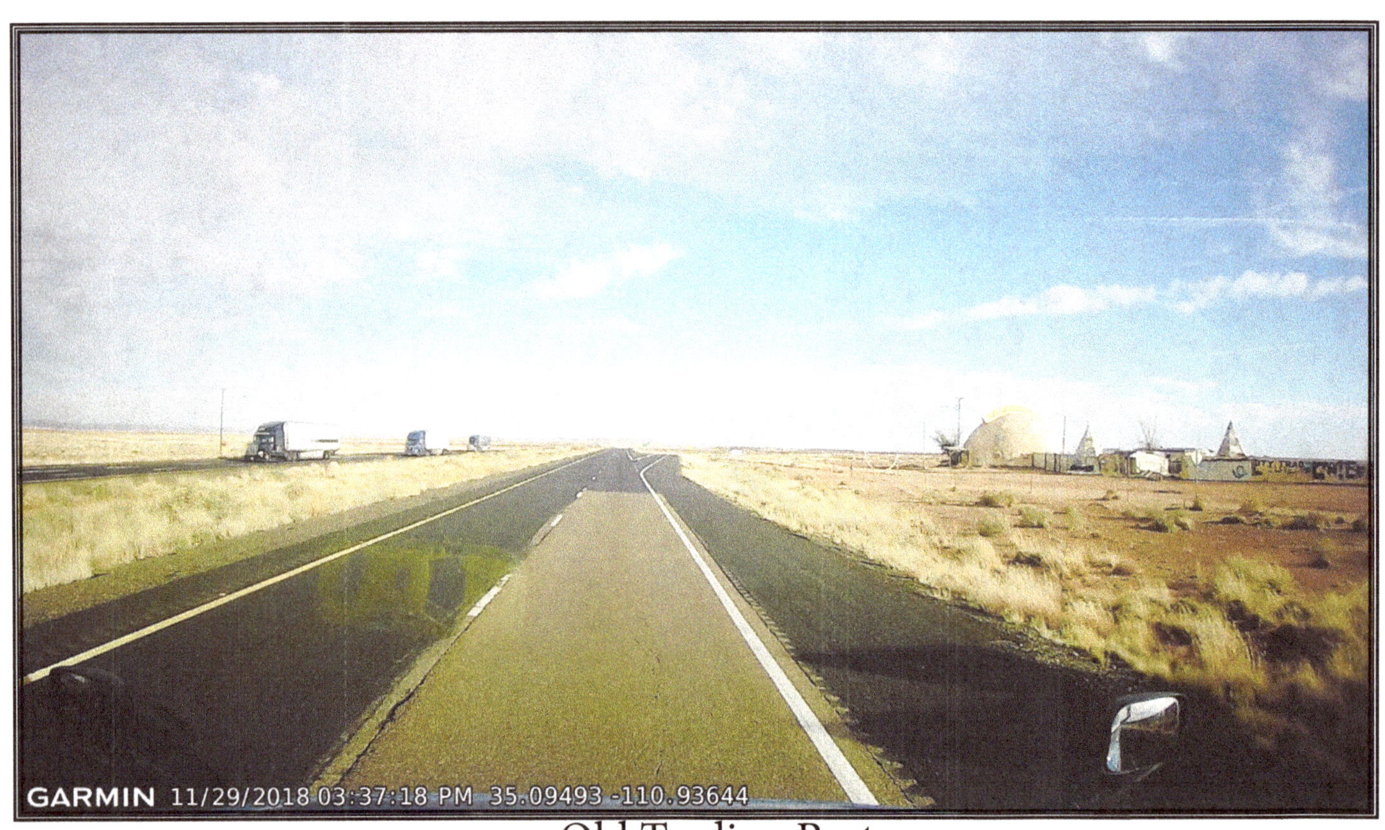

Old Trading Post
I-40, Winslow, Arizona

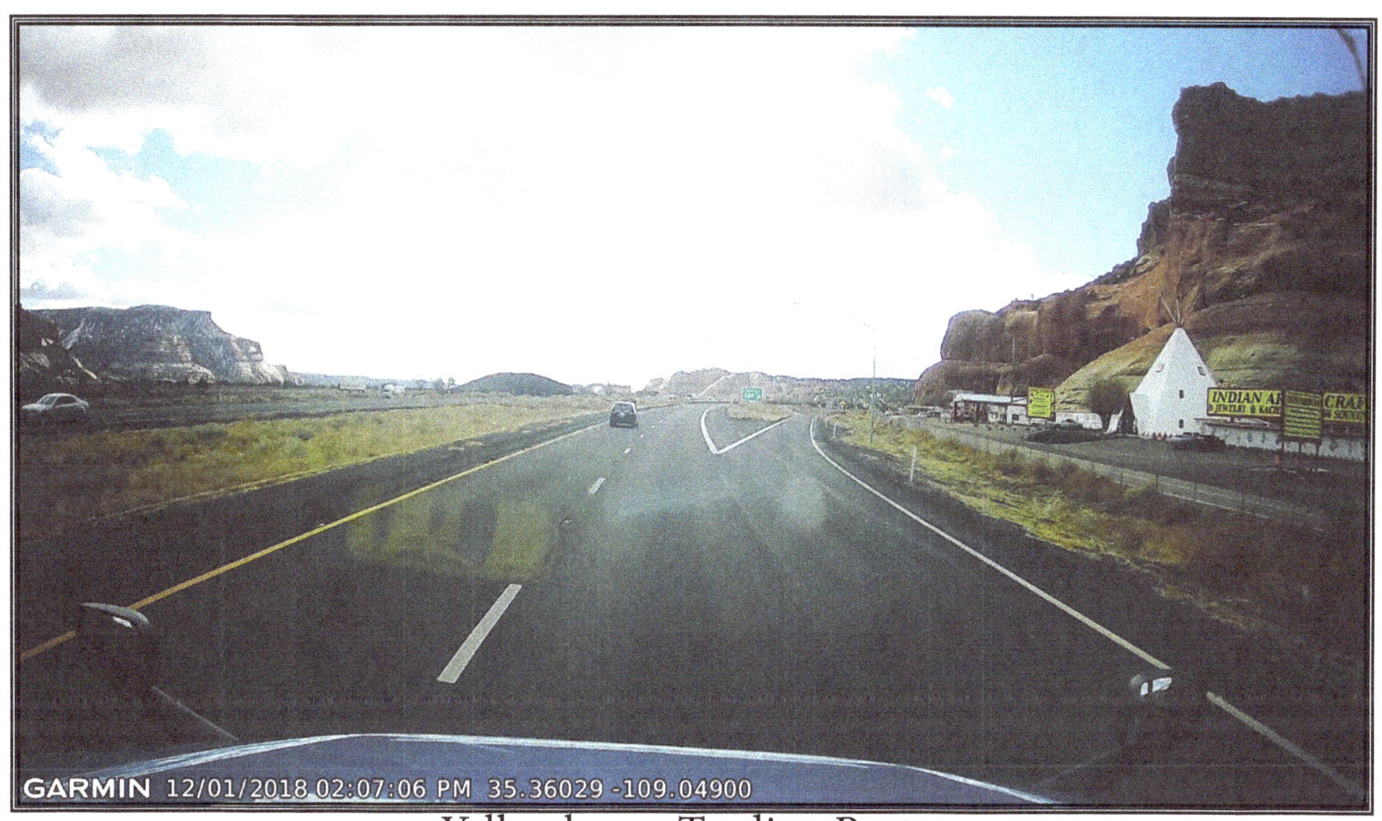

Yellowhorse Trading Post
I-40, Lupton, Arizona

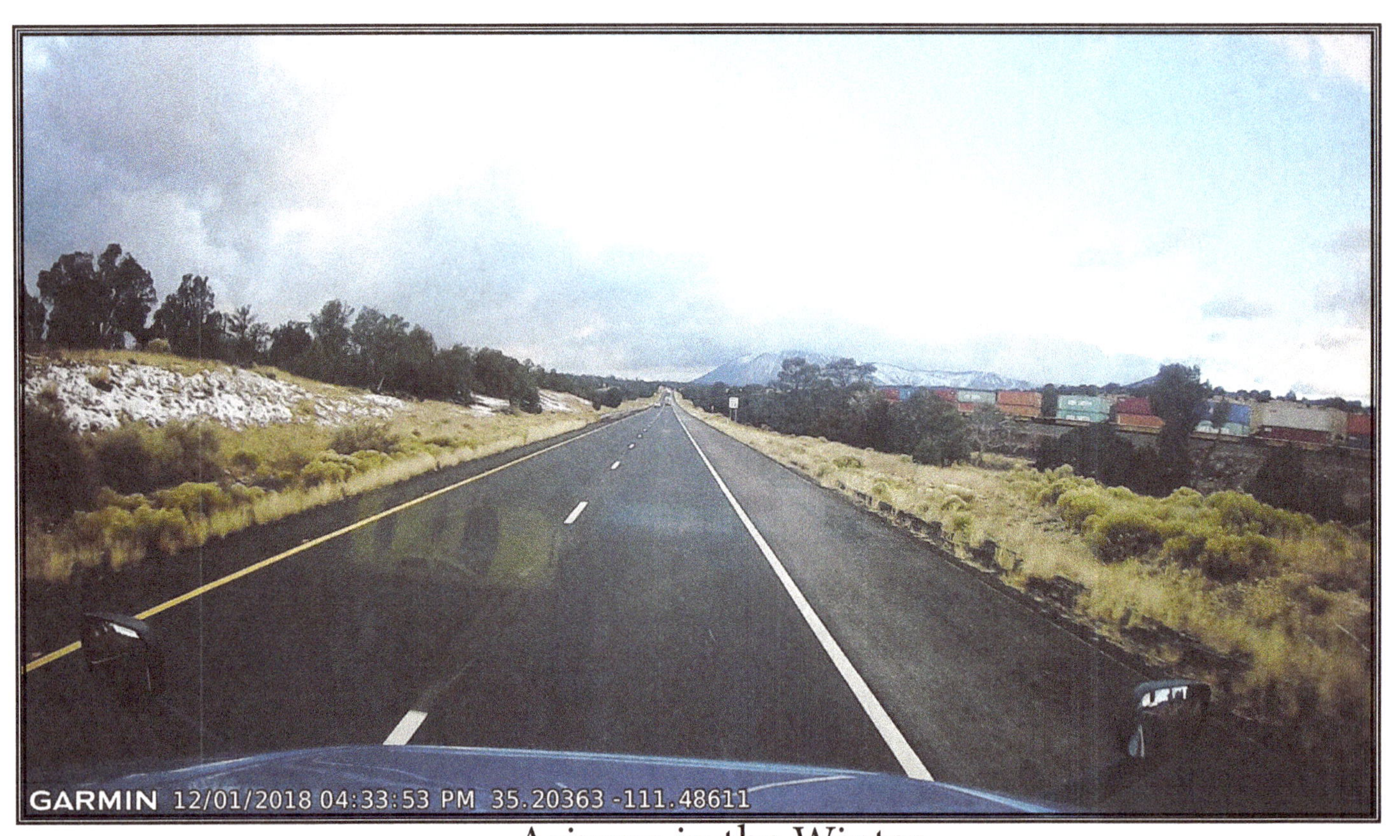

Arizona in the Winter
I-40, Flagstaff, Arizona

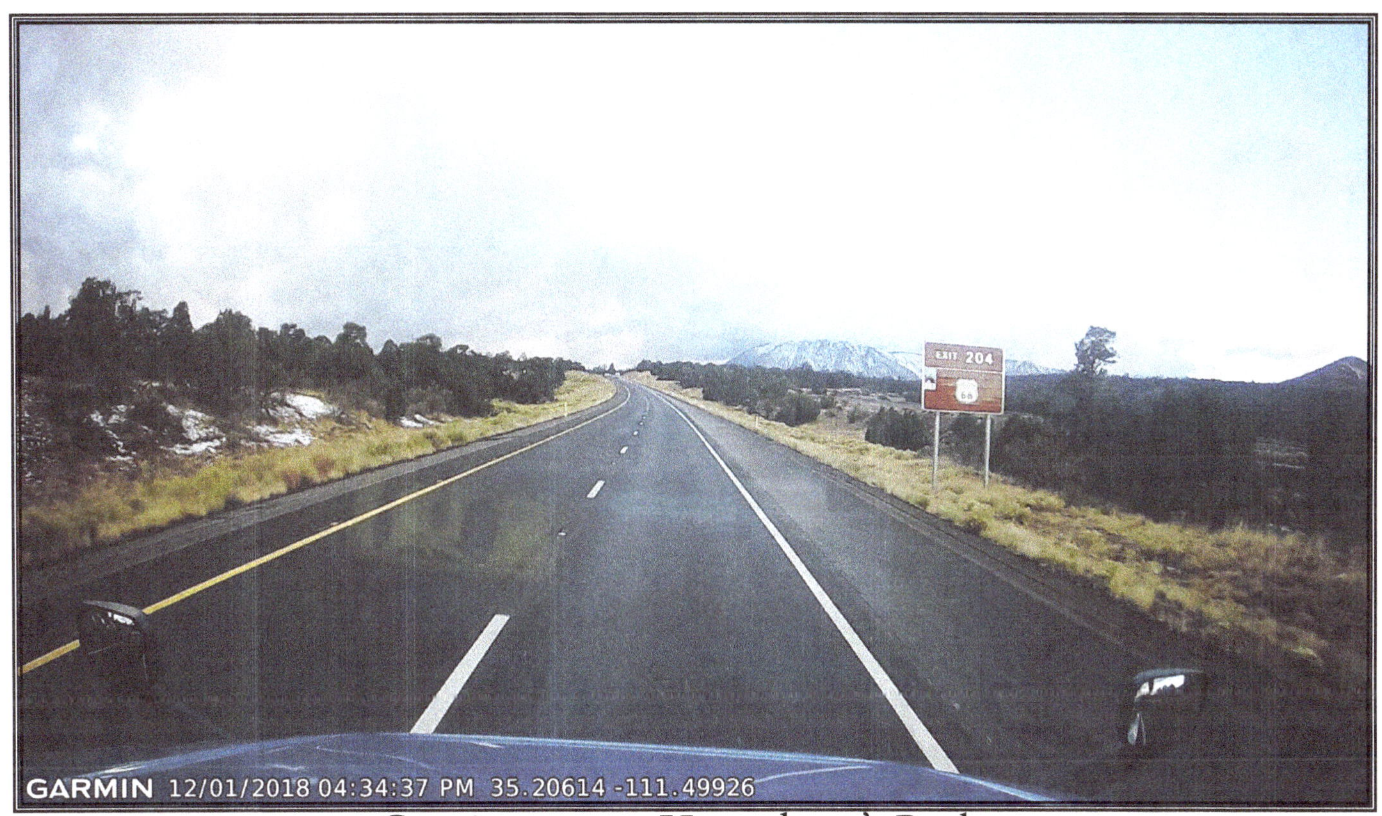

Coming up on Humphrey's Peak
I-40, Flagstaff, Arizona

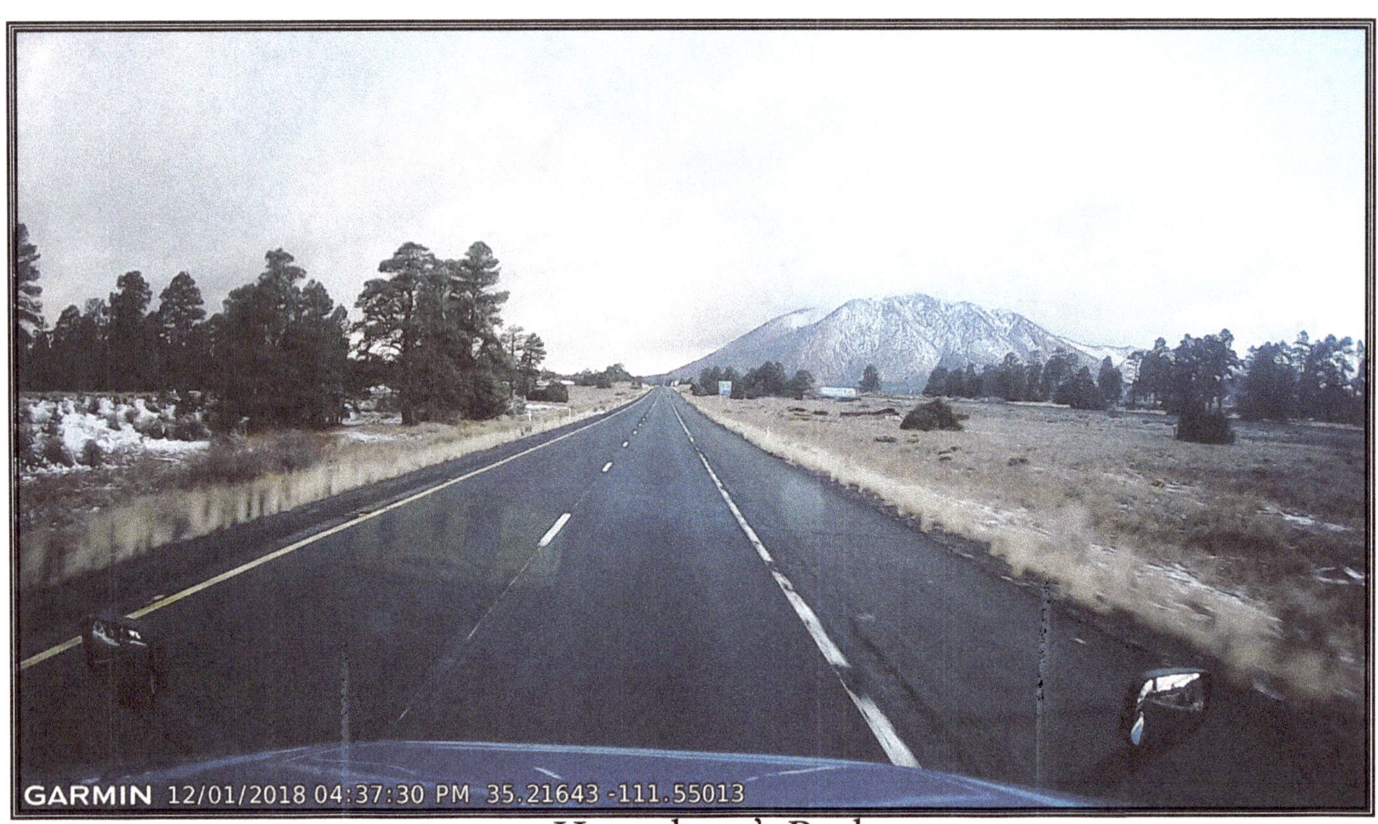

Humphrey's Peak
I-40, Flagstaff, Arizona

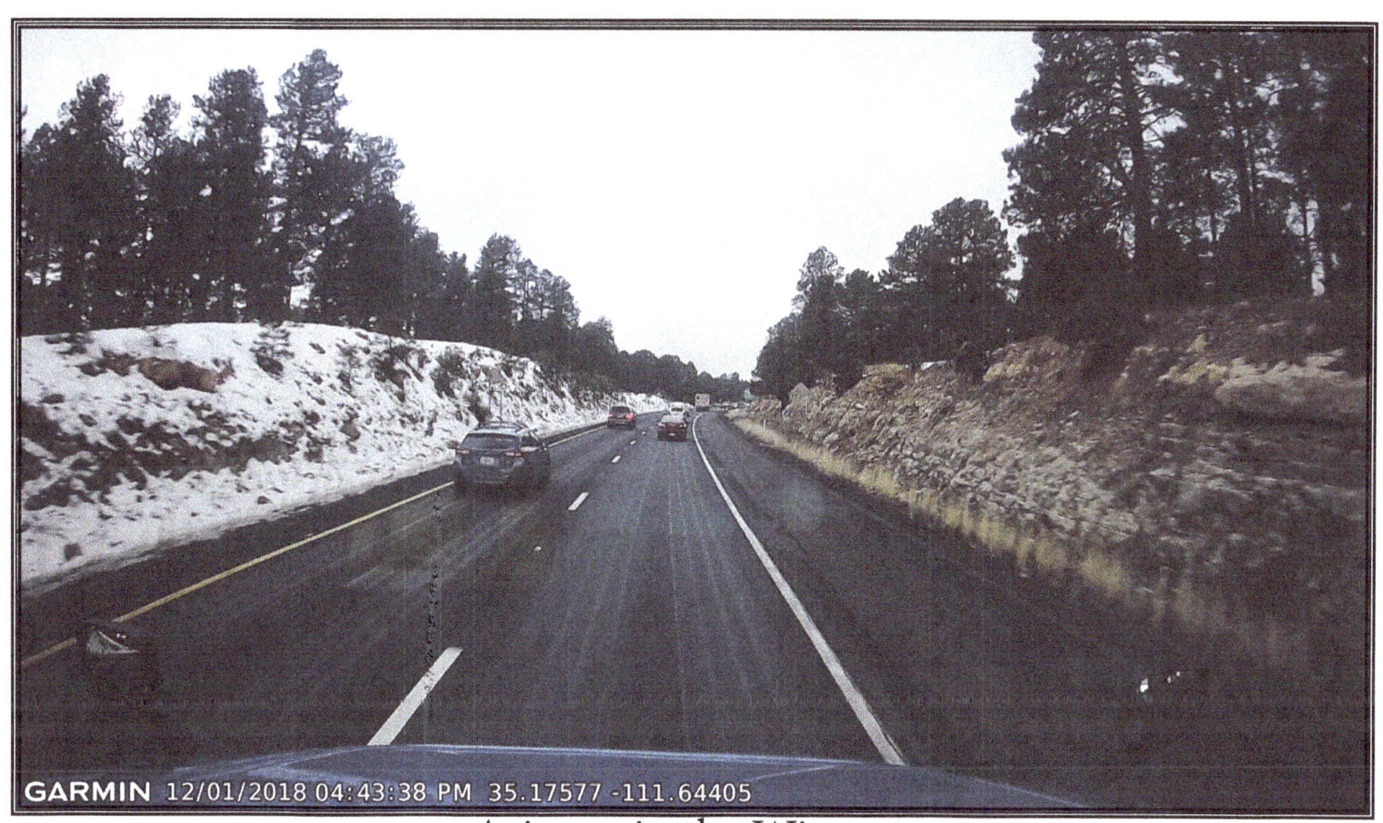

Arizona in the Winter
I-40, Flagstaff, Arizona

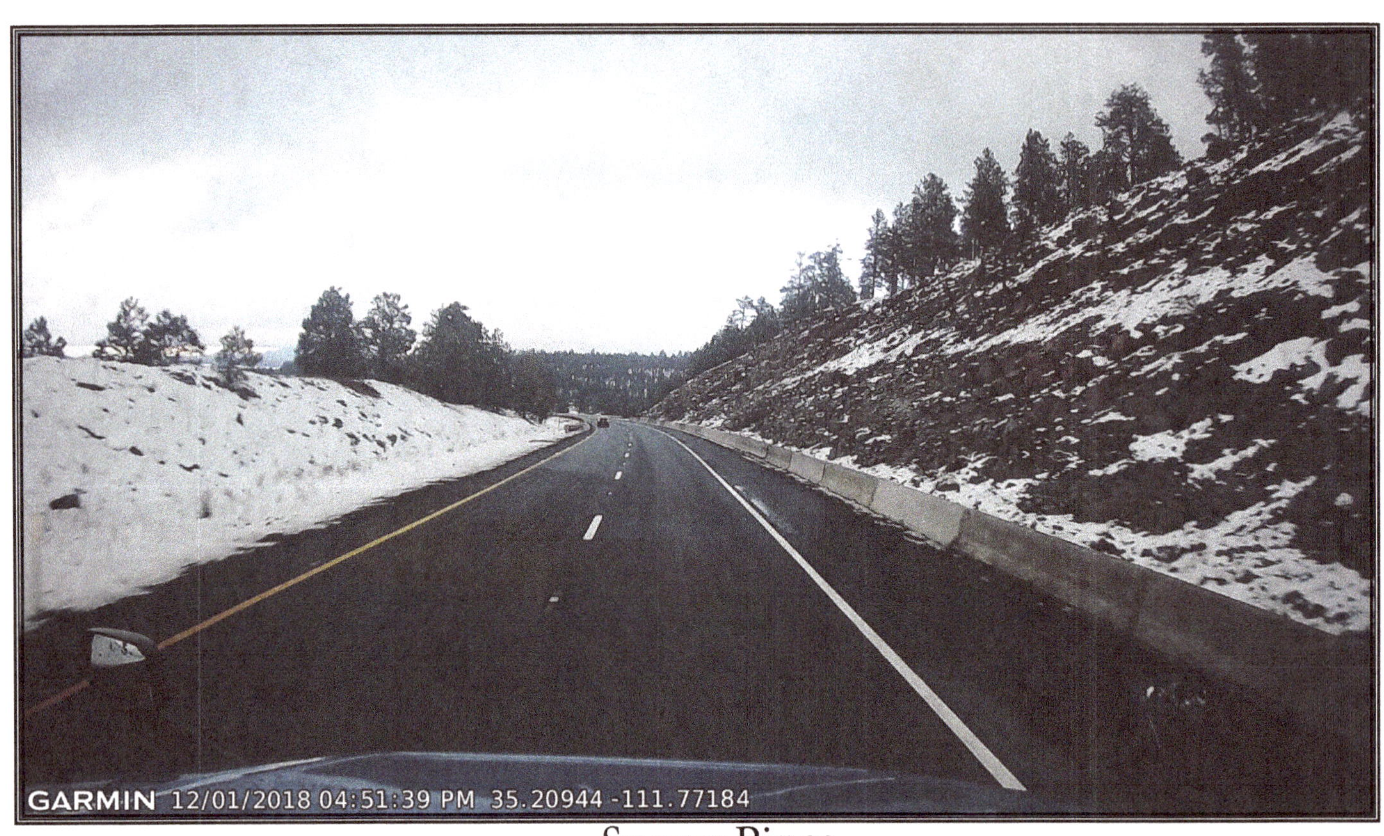

Snowy Pines
I-40, Flagstaff, Arizona

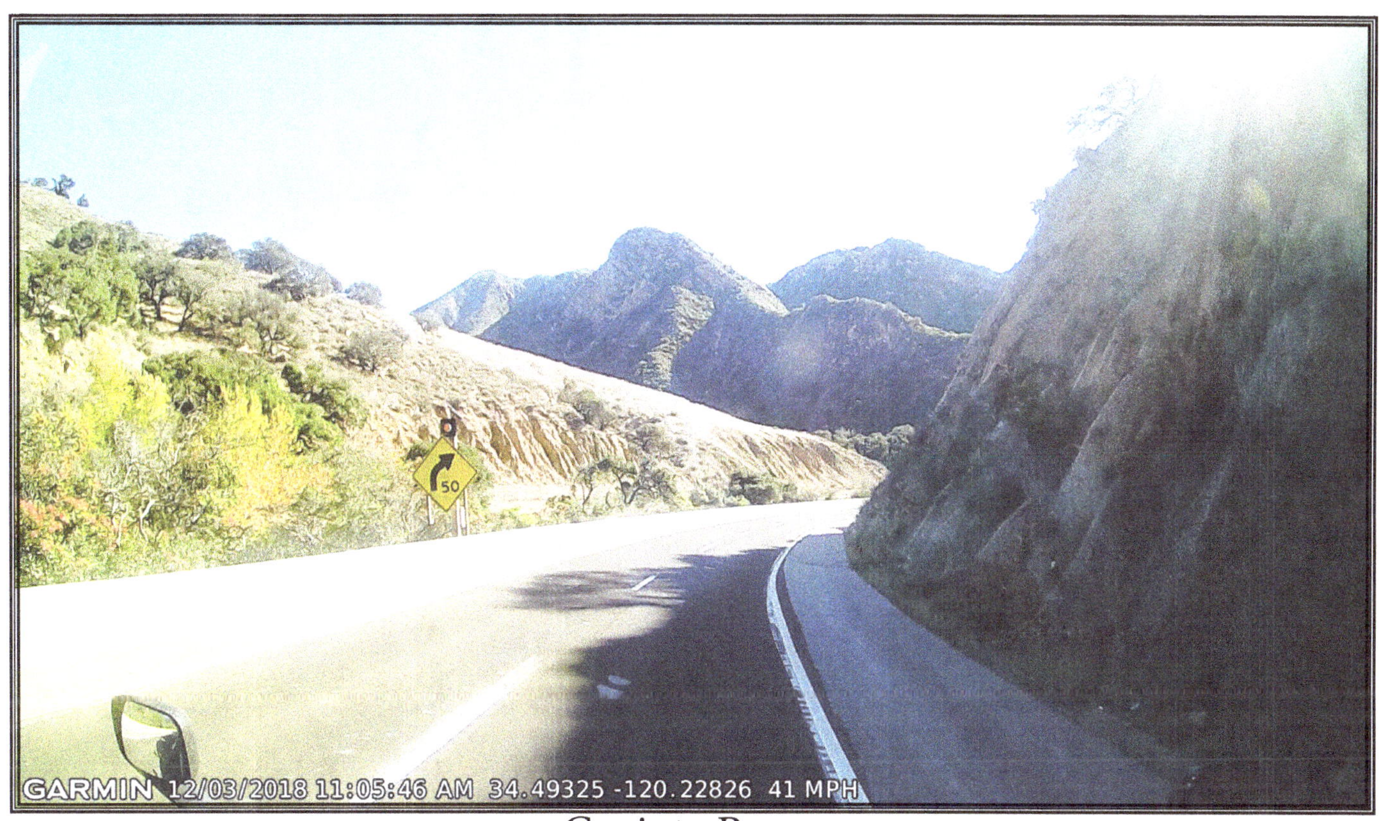

Gaviota Pass
US-101, Las Cruces, California

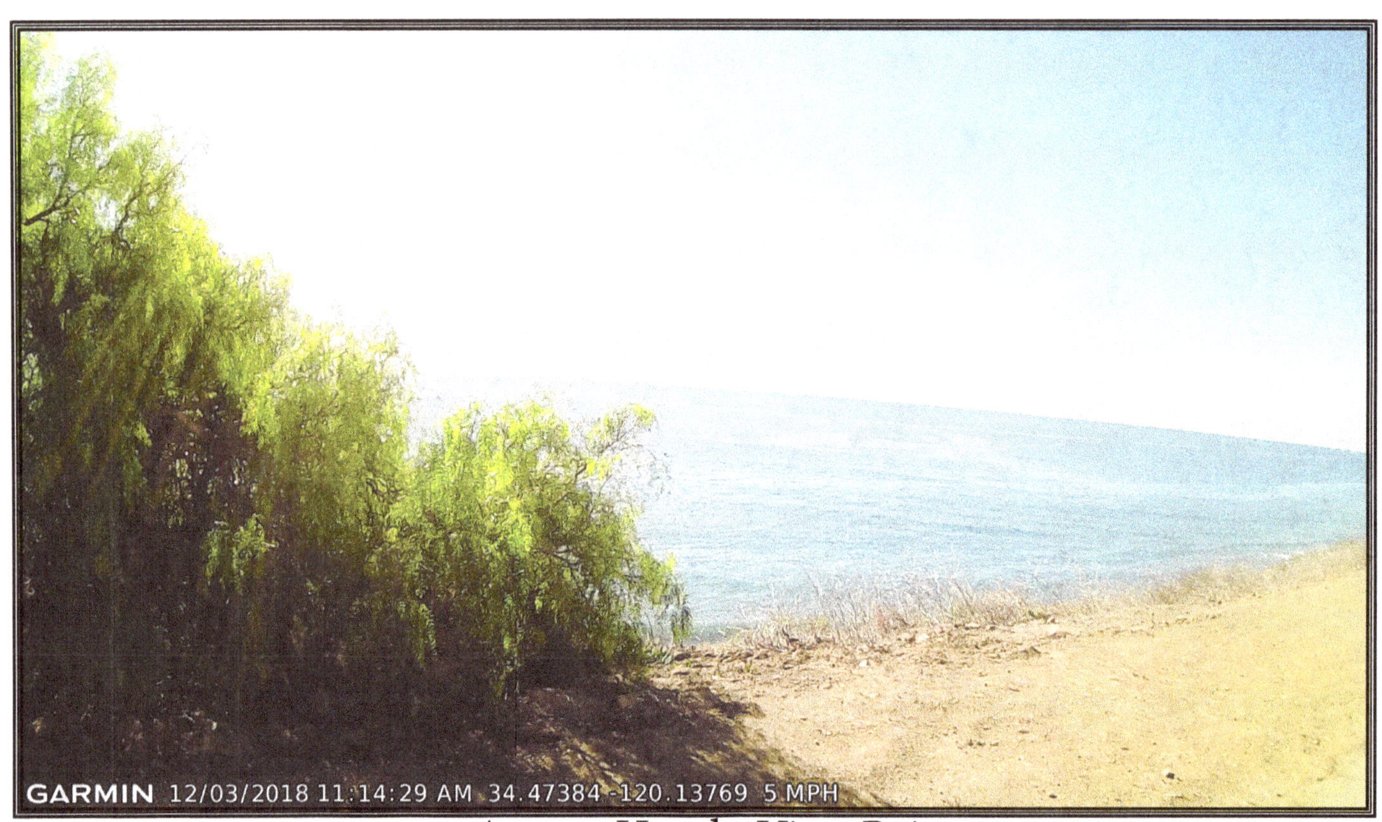

Arroyo Hondo Vista Point
US-101, Solvang, California

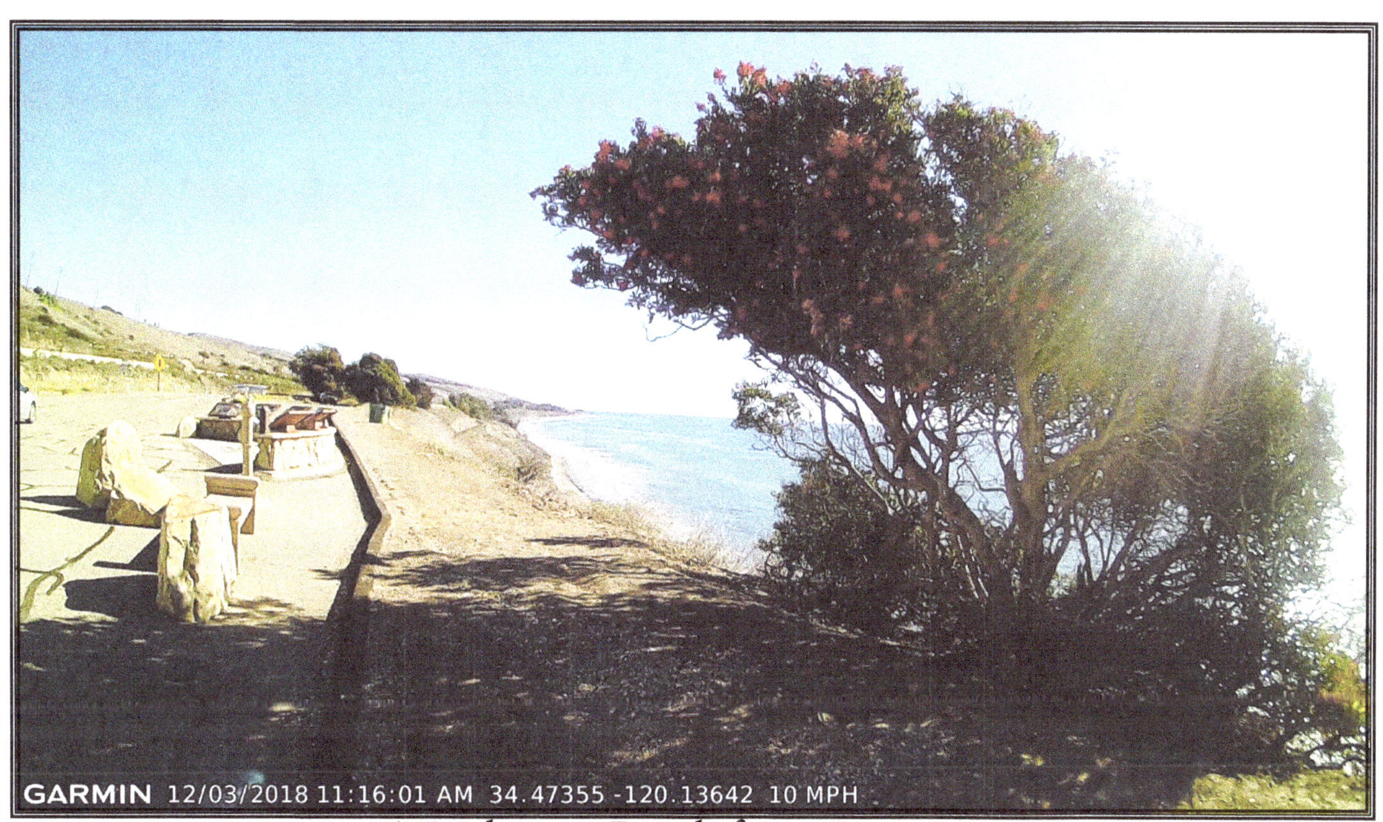

A Welcome Break from Driving
US-101, Solvang, California

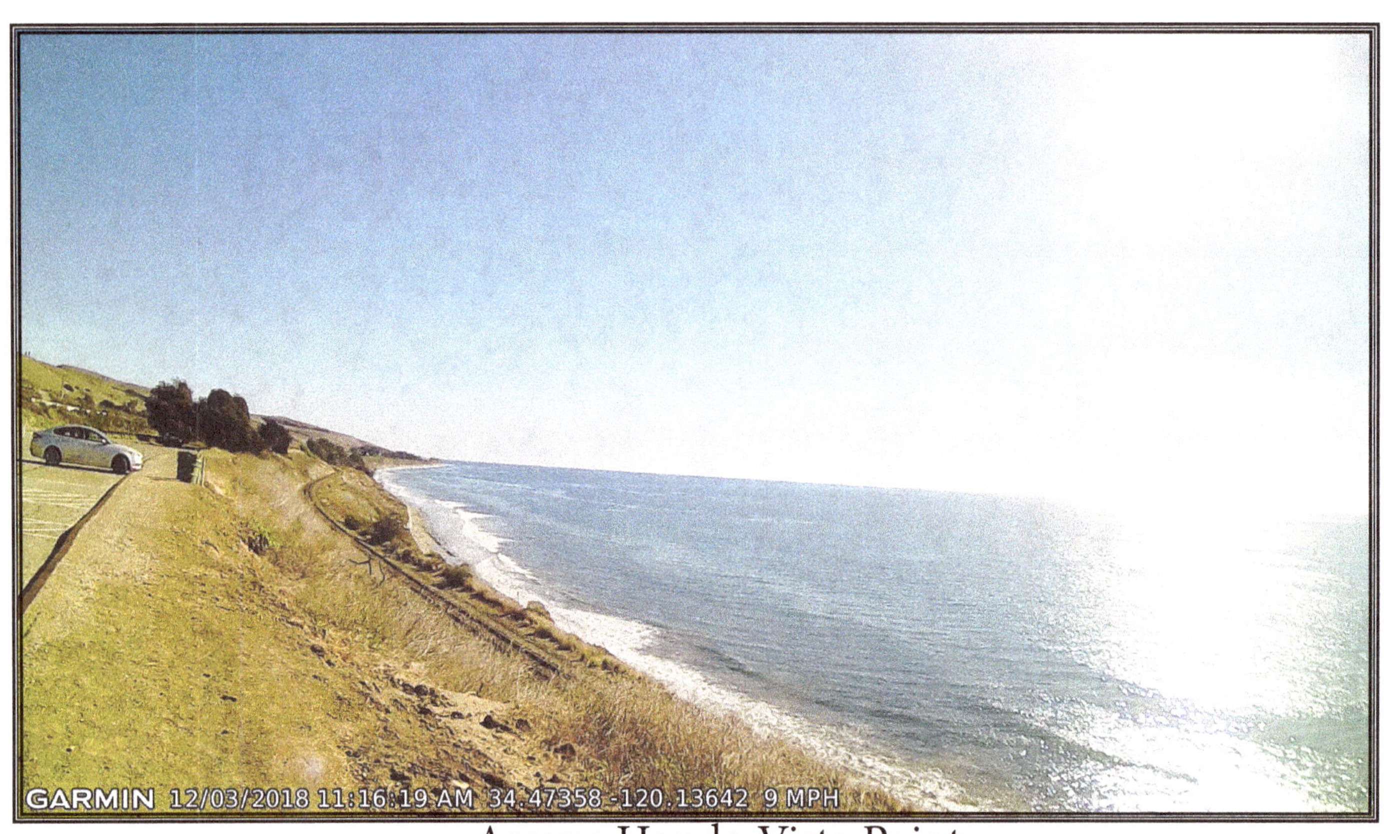

Arroyo Hondo Vista Point
US-101, Solvang, California

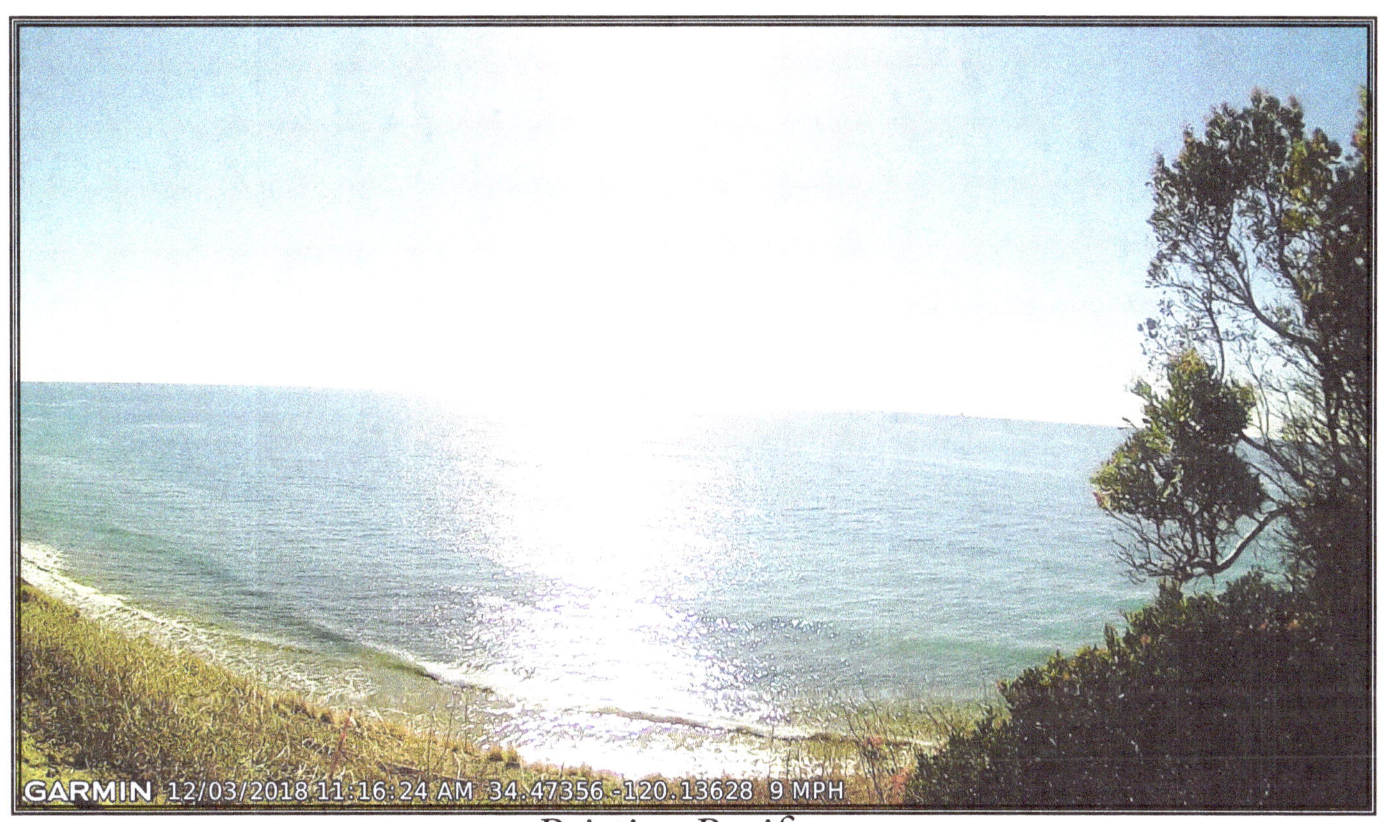

Pristine Pacific
US-101, Solvang, California

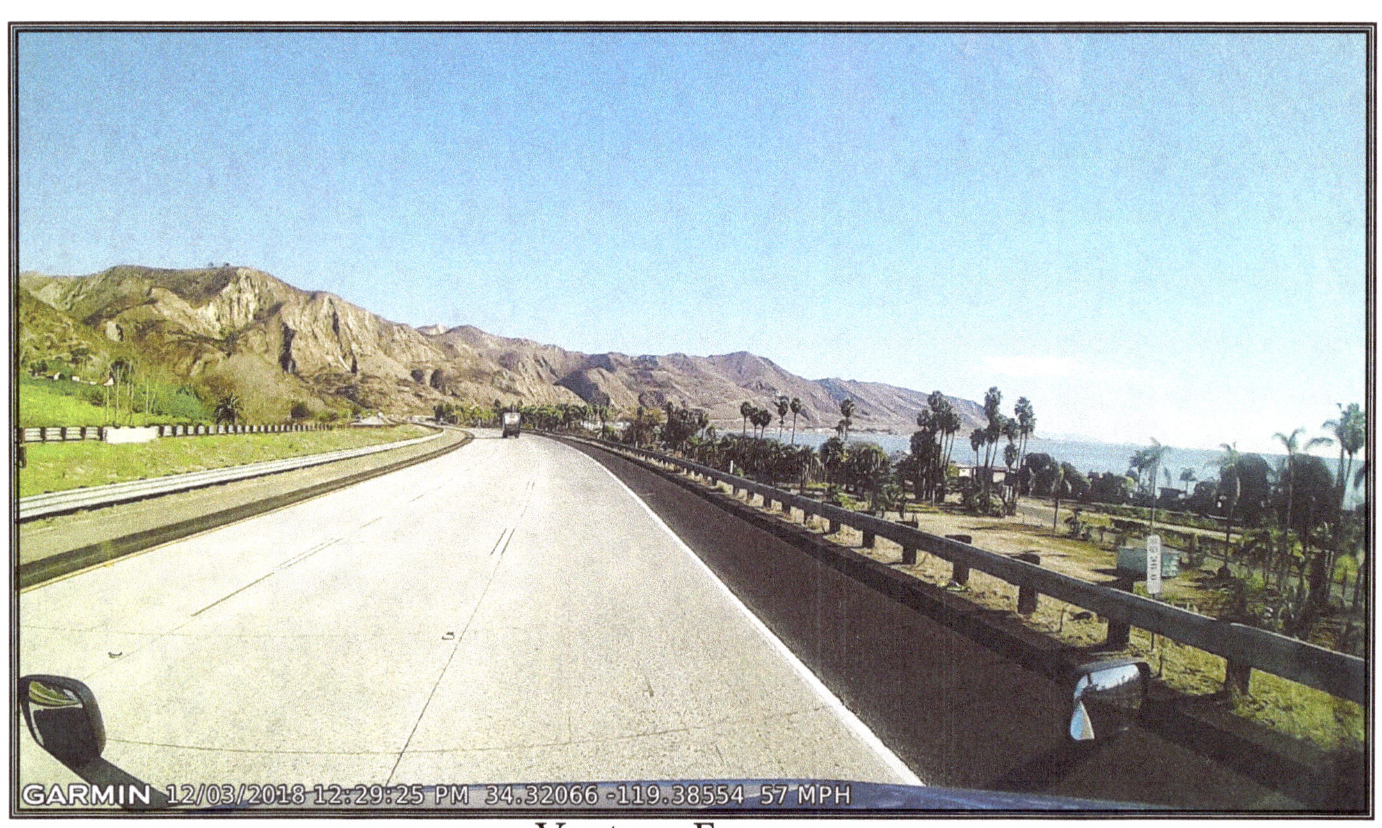

Ventura Freeway
US-101, Ventura, California

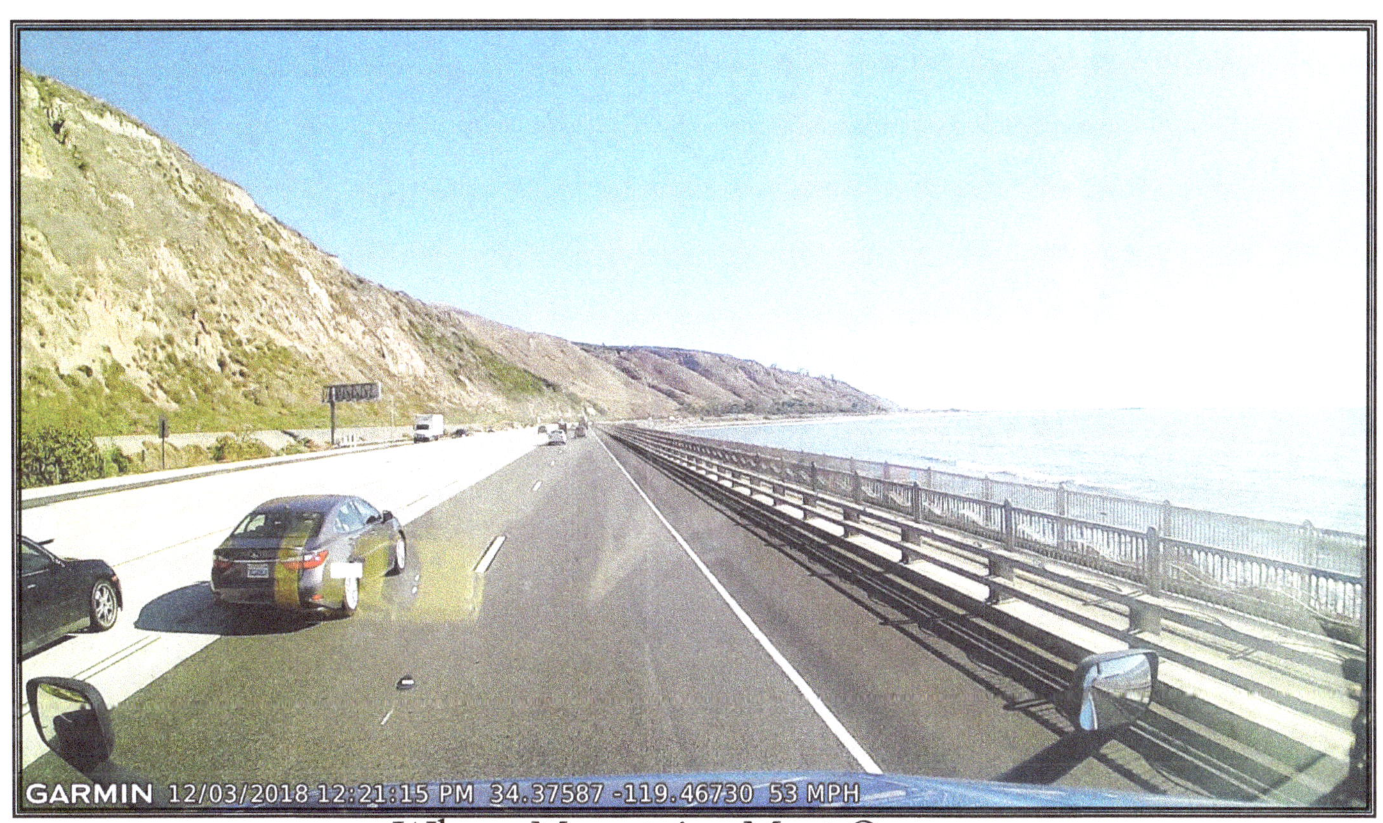

Where Mountains Meet Ocean
US-101, Carpenteria, California

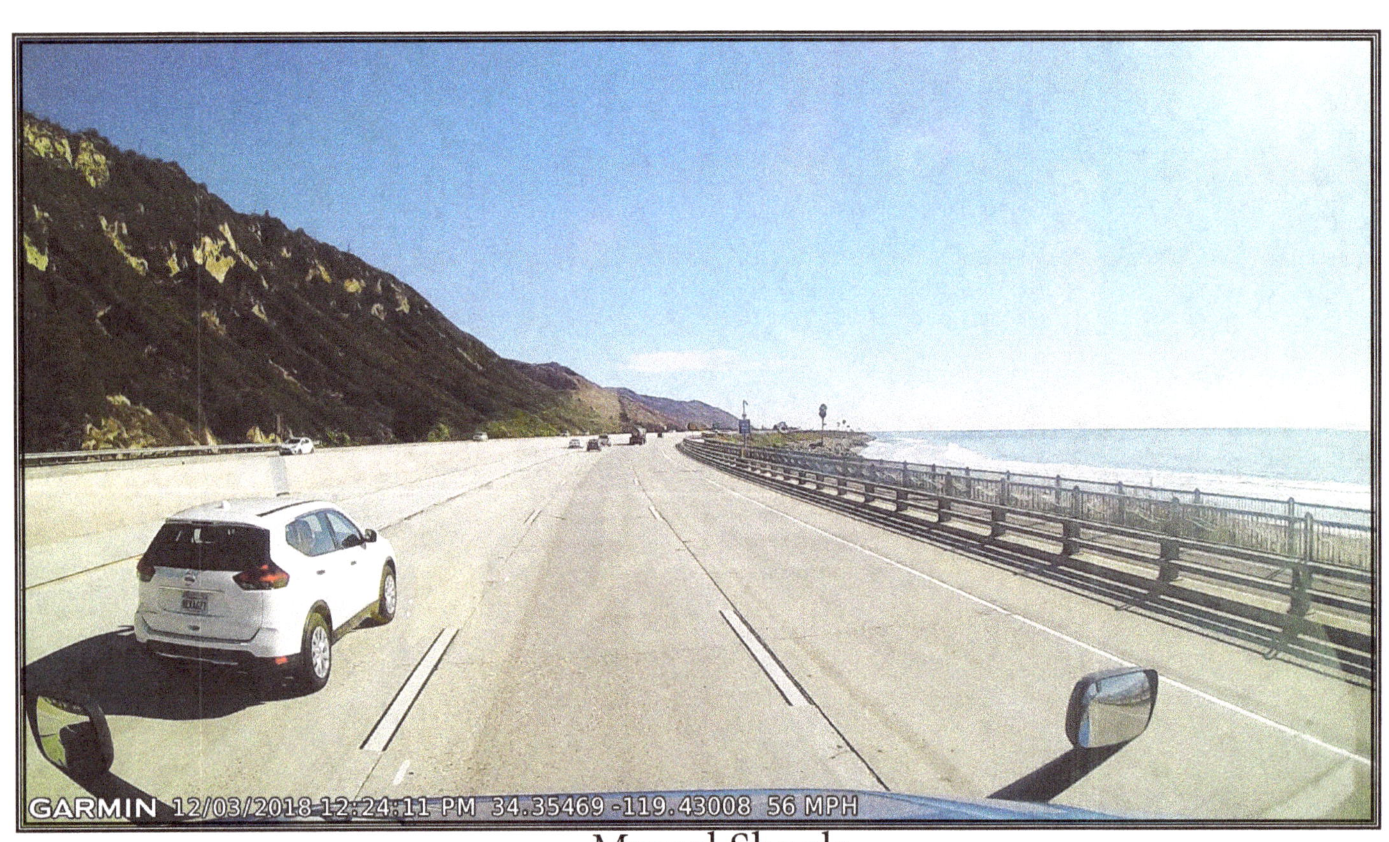

Mussel Shoals
US-101, Ventura, California

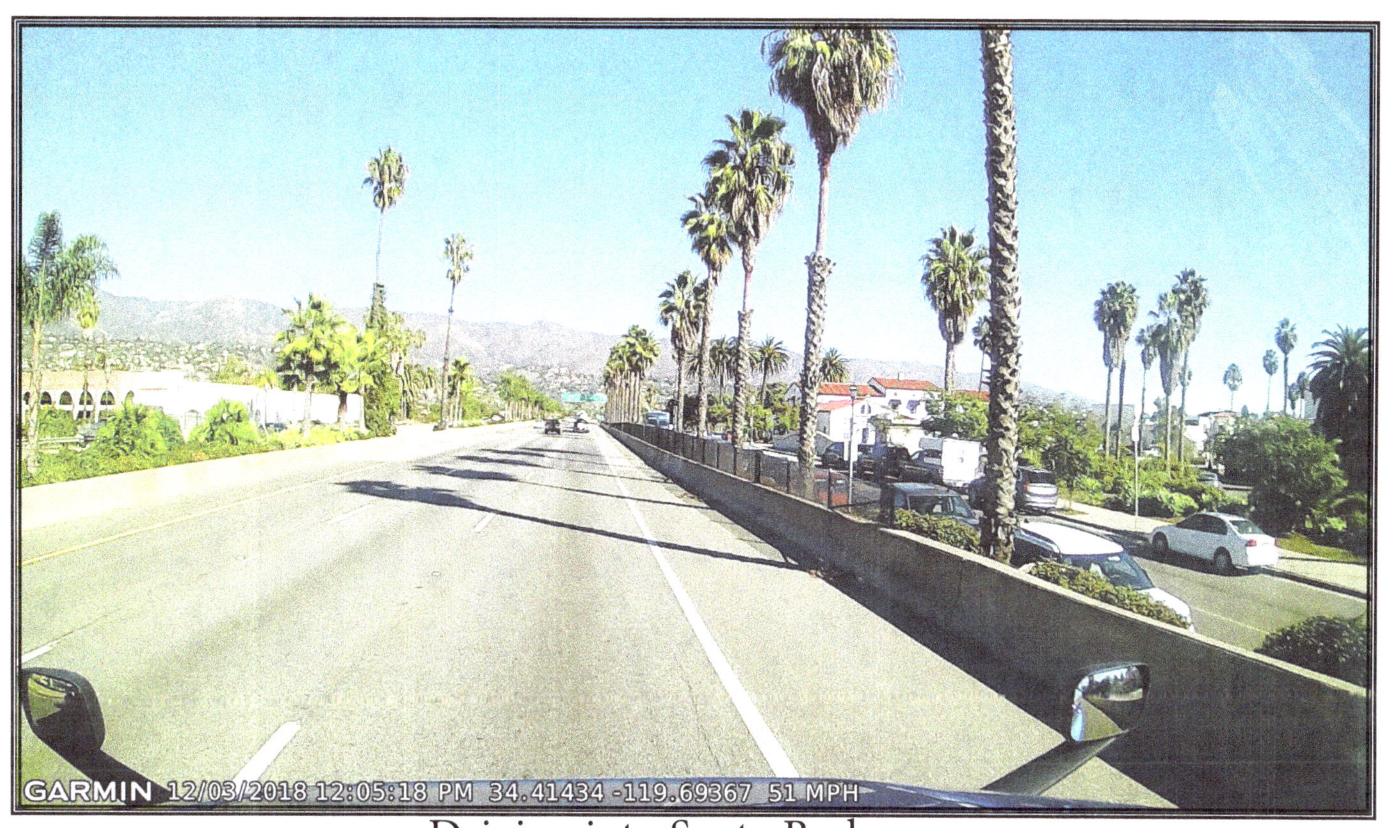

Driving into Santa Barbara
US-101, Santa Barbara, California

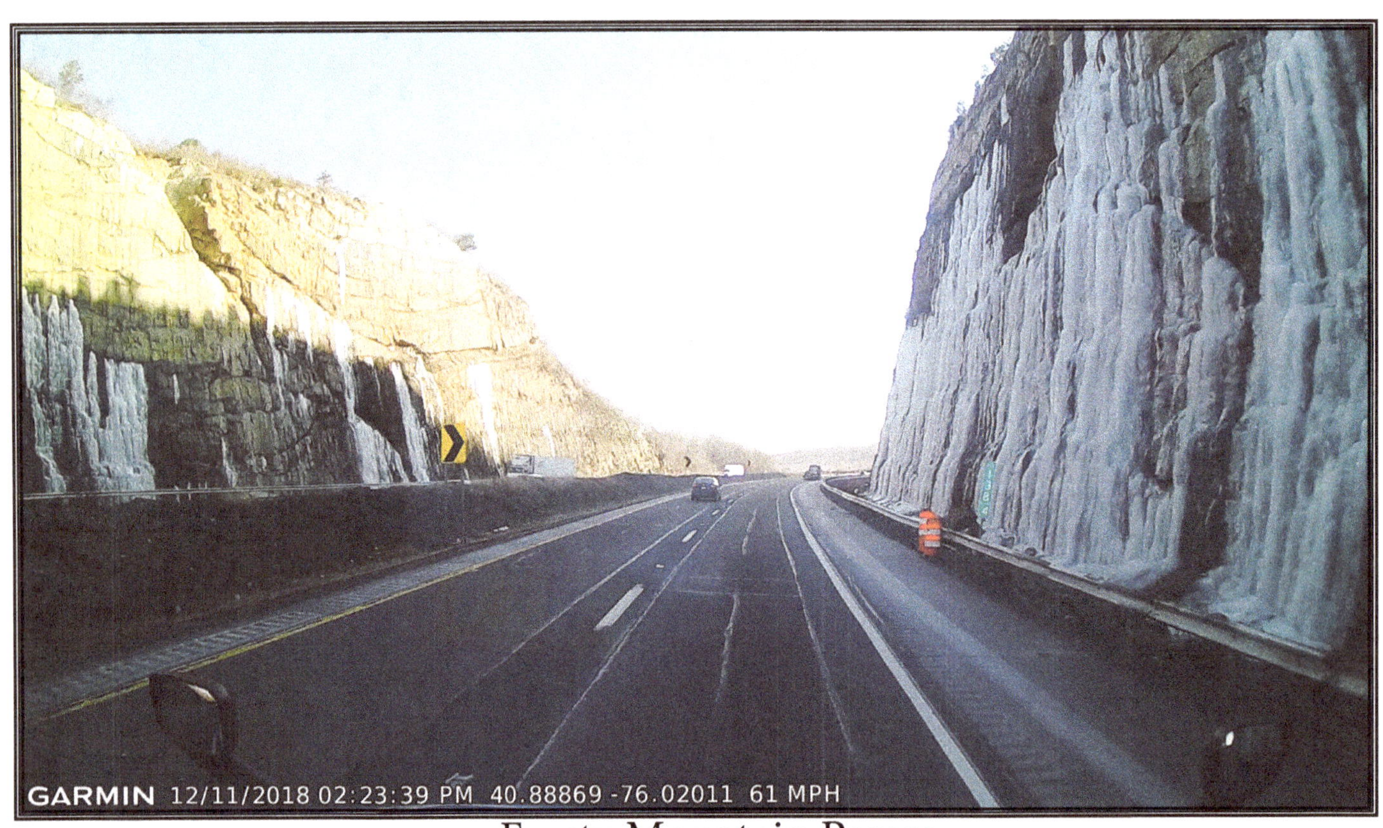

Frosty Mountain Passes
I-81, Ringtown, Pennsylvania

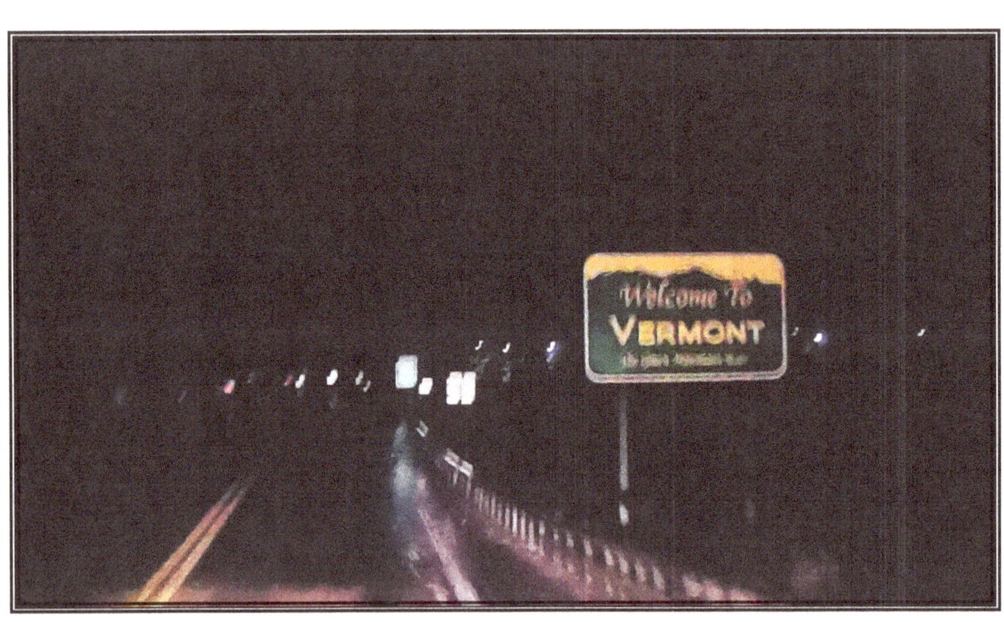

Welcome To
VERMONT
The Green Mountain State

And now you have come to the end of your journey. As for me, I am still traveling across this great nation. I write this from the parking lot of a Petro truck stop in Ontario, California. If you're a trucker, you know the one. If you're not, don't make any great effort to come visit. It's not very nice, but it is one of the only ones we have out here so those of us who traverse such areas are grateful for it. From here I will be heading up to Santa Maria, then over to Bloomington, then way over to Middletown, Connecticut. The truck rarely stops, and that pretty much sums up the life of a trucker.

Below is an important picture to me. Yes, it is blurry and dark and on the whole fairly uninteresting. However, like so many things in life the story behind the thing adds a dimension to it that some, perhaps just me, may find interesting. You see, when I was a young man I had a wanderlust that was insatiable. Yet it, like so many other things in my poverty-stricken youth, was left underfed and malnourished deep inside my heart. When I grew older I did crazy things like hitchhiking and quitting my job to follow my then-barely-girlfriend out of state. Both things worked out extraordinarily well, but they only fueled the wanderlust and did nothing to sate it.

Now, a year into my travels as a truck driver, I have seen Civil War battlefields, volcanoes, beaches, every mountain pass this country has to offer, bridges and tunnels, the greatest cities and the smallest townships, prairies, bluffs, beautiful rivers and dried-out washes in the desert. All told I have traveled a little under 200,000 miles in a bit over twelve months' time, and I have to say my wanderlust was almost wiped out completely. I missed my family more than I could say, was ready to throw in the towel and come home and put this chapter of my life behind me for good. But one thing was missing. I had visited every single state in the lower forty-eight, with one exception: Vermont. Three times I had loads scheduled to pick up there, and three times they were canceled. And then one night in mid-November, I made it to number Forty-Eight.

So my time on the road is almost at an end. I wouldn't trade my adventures for the world, but I am glad they are nearly behind me. Go out and wander a bit if you have the inclination and ability. But never forget to go home.

Paul Speir
December 14th, 2018

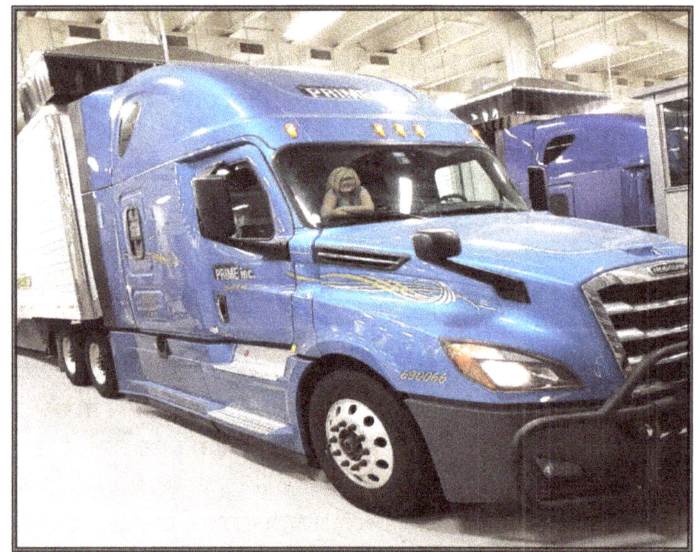

A final farewell to 690066. The last 120,000 miles were a trip.

Acknowledgments

Since writing the closing page to this project I have come off the road, turning in my keys on December 23rd and calling Over the Road driving quits for good. At least, that's the plan—the road beckons to me day and night, and yet my bed is warm and my family quite lovely, and I've grown fond of not living in a closet-sized box that moves constantly. So, we will see, but as for now with that change came the need for a little push to finish up this project, and that came in the form of a GoFundMe campaign, pre-orders, and overall advice.

I would like to thank Tommy for his generous support, my wife Stacy for her tireless work in weeding out the photographs that just did not live up to a standard of excellence that I could not have seen (and making this a *much* smaller book in the process), my good friends Steve and Jennifer for their support throughout my time on the road and beyond, Chris and Kaysha for being such a font of cheer and positivity to myself and my family during my travels, Mark Speir for putting up with me as my co-driver for four tedious months and over 80,000 long miles, BJ Higdon for his tireless work managing my truck throughout my entire time on the road, my trainers Randy and DJ for putting up with me—living with a stranger in a closet-sized box is crazy hard—and finally my three girls who cried every time I left, but held no grudge, and jumped joyfully into my arms every time I came home. All are appreciated beyond words.

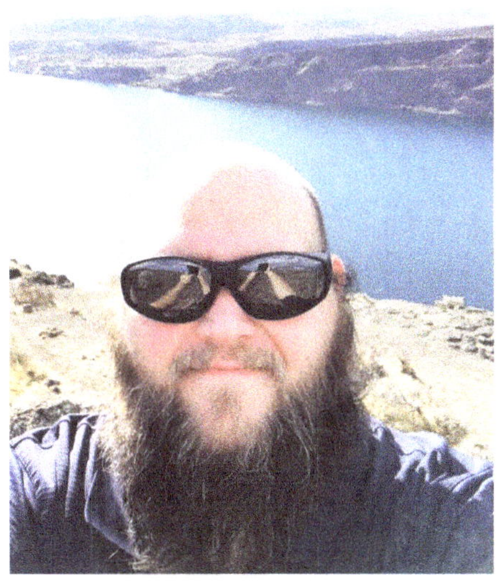

Paul Michael Speir has enjoyed many adventures in his life and anticipates quite a lot more to come. He has been a bag-boy, door-to-door salesman, telemarketer, pizza delivery driver, hitchhiker, musician, executive advocate, writer, publisher, ministry director, thrift store owner, pastor, taxi driver and truck driver. As much as he has enjoyed pursuing his various passions, nothing in his life has been as fulfilling and meaningful as his relationship with his wife Stacy, and three daughters, Willow, River and Aria. A native Texan, he now lives in Oklahoma City.